Sexuality and Identity

The International Library of Essays in Law and Society

Series Editor: Austin Sarat

Titles in the Series:

Law and Religion
Gad Barzilai

Police and Policing Law
Jeannine Bell

Law and Society Approaches to Cyberspace
Paul Schiff Berman

Law and Families
Susan B. Boyd and Helen Rhoades

Rhetoric of Law
Marianne Constable and Felipe Gutterriez

Law in Social Theory
Roger Cotterrell

Ethnography and Law
Eve Darian-Smith

International Law and Society
Laura Dickinson

Legal Lives of Private Organizations
Lauren Edelman and Mark C. Suchman

Courts and Judges
Lee Epstein

Consciousness and Ideology
Patricia Ewick

Prosecutors and Prosecution
Lisa Frohmann

Intellectual Property
William T. Gallagher

Human Rights, Law and Society
Lisa Hajjar

Race, Law and Society
Ian Haney Lopez

The Jury System
Valerie P. Hans

Regulation and Regulatory Processes
Robert Kagan and Cary Coglianese

Crime and Criminal Justice
William T. Lyons, Jr.

Law and Social Movements
Michael McCann

Colonial and Post-Colonial Law
Sally Merry

Social Science in Law
Elizabeth Mertz

Sexuality and Identity
Leslie J. Moran

Law and Poverty
Frank Munger

Rights
Laura Beth Nielsen

Governing Risks
Pat O'Malley

Lawyers and the Legal Profession, Volumes I and II
Tanina Rostain

Capital Punishment, Volumes I and II
Austin Sarat

Legality and Democracy
Stuart A. Scheingold

The Law and Society Canon
Carroll Seron

Popular Culture and Law
Richard K. Sherwin

Law and Science
Susan Silbey

Immigration
Susan Sterett

Gender and Feminist Theory in Law and Society
Madhavi Sunder

Procedural Justice, Volumes I and II
Tom R. Tyler

Trials
Martha Merrill Umphrey

Sexuality and Identity

Edited by

Leslie J. Moran

School of Law, Birkbeck College, University of London, UK

Routledge
Taylor & Francis Group

LONDON AND NEW YORK

First published 2006 by Ashgate Publishing

Reissued 2018 by Routledge
2 Park Square, Milton Park, Abingdon, Oxon OX14 4RN
711 Third Avenue, New York, NY 10017, USA

Routledge is an imprint of the Taylor & Francis Group, an informa business

First issued in paperback 2018

A Library of Congress record exists under LC control number: 2005056779

Notice:
Product or corporate names may be trademarks or registered rademarks, and are used only for identification and explanation without intent to infringe.

Publisher's Note
The publisher has gone to great lengths to ensure the quality of this reprint but points out that some imperfections in the original copies may be apparent.

Disclaimer
The publisher has made every effort to trace copyright holders and welcomes correspondence from those they have been unable to contact.

ISBN 13: 978-0-815-39699-4 (hbk)
ISBN 13: 978-1-138-62052-0 (pbk)
ISBN 13: 978-1-351-12664-9 (ebk)

Contents

Acknowledgements   ix
Series Preface   xi
Introduction   xiii

PART I   TOPICS

Theorizing Sexual Identity
1. Margaret Davies (1999), 'Queer Property, Queer Persons: Self-Ownership and
    Beyond', *Social and Legal Studies*, **8**, pp. 327–52.   5
2. Diana Majury (1994), 'Refashioning the Unfashionable: Claiming Lesbian
    Identities in the Legal Context', *Canadian Journal of Women and the Law*, **7**,
    pp. 286–317.   31
3. Oliver Phillips (1997), 'Zimbabwean Law and the Production of a White Man's
    Disease', *Social and Legal Studies*, **6**, pp. 471–91.   63
4. Andrew Sharpe (2000), 'Transgender Jurisprudence and the Spectre of
    Homosexuality', *Australian Feminist Law Journal*, **14**, pp. 23–37.   85

Histories
5. Gordon Brent Ingram (2003), 'Returning to the Scene of the Crime: Uses of Trial
    Dossiers on Consensual Male Homosexuality for Urban Research, with Examples
    from Twentieth-Century British Columbia', *GLQ: A Journal of Lesbian and Gay
    Studies*, **10**, pp. 77–110.   103
6. Jodie Medd (2002), '"The Cult of the Clitoris": Anatomy of a National Scandal',
    Modernism/Modernity, **9**, pp. 21–49.   137

PART II   LOCATING SEXUAL IDENTITY IN LAW

The State
7. AnnJanette Rosga (1999), 'Policing the State', *Georgetown Journal of Gender
    and the Law*, pp. 145–71.   171
8. Carl F. Stychin (2000), '"A Stranger to its Laws": Sovereign Bodies, Global
    Sexualities, and Transnational Citizens', *Journal of Law and Society*, **27**,
    pp. 601–25.   199

The Criminal Justice System
9. Richard Collier (1997), 'After Dunblane: Crime, Corporeality, and the (Hetero-) Sexing of the Bodies of Men', *Journal of Law and Society*, **24**, pp. 177–98.   227
10. Leslie J. Moran (1995), 'Violence and the Law: The Case of Sado-Masochism', *Social and Legal Studies*, **4**, pp. 225–51.   249
11. Diana Fishbein (2000), 'Sexual Preference, Crime and Punishment', *Women and Criminal Justice*, **11**, pp. 67–84.   277

Public Places
12. Mariana Valverde and Miomir Cirak (2002), 'Governing Bodies, Creating Gay Spaces: Policing and Security Issues in "Gay" Downtown Toronto', *British Journal of Criminology*, **43**, pp. 102–21.   297

The Workplace
13. Paul Skidmore (2004), 'A Legal Perspective on Sexuality and Organization: A Lesbian and Gay Case Study', *Gender, Work and Organization*, **11**, pp. 229–53.   319
14. William B. Rubenstein (1997), 'Some Reflections on the Study of Sexual Orientation Bias in the Legal Profession', *UCLA Women's Law Journal*, **8**, pp. 379–403.   345

Hate
15. Donald P. Green, Dara Z. Strolovitch, Janelle S. Wong and Robert W. Bailey (2001), 'Measuring Gay Populations and Antigay Hate Crime', *Social Science Quarterly*, **82**, pp. 281–96.   373
16. Gail Mason (2001), 'Not Our Kind of Hate Crime', *Law and Critique*, **12**, pp. 253–78.   389
17. Graeme Reid and Teresa Dirsuweit (2002), 'Understanding Systemic Violence: Homophobic Attacks in Johannesburg and its Surrounds', *Urban Forum*, **13**, pp. 99–126.   415

Kinship
18. Susan B. Boyd (1999), 'Family, Law and Sexuality: Feminist Engagements', *Social and Legal Studies*, **8**, pp. 369–90.   445
19. Ruthann Robson (2001), 'Our Children: Kids of Queer Parents and Kids who are Queer: Looking at Sexual Minority Rights from a Different Perspective', *Albany Law Review*, **64**, pp. 915–48.   467
20. Rosemary Auchmuty (2004), 'Same-sex Marriage Revived: Feminist Critique and Legal Strategy', *Feminism and Psychology*, **14**, pp. 101–126.   501

The Cultural Turn

21. Jenni Millbank (1996), 'From Butch to Butcher's Knife: Film, Crime and Lesbian
    Sexuality', *Sydney Law Review*, **18**, pp. 451–73.   529
22. Leslie J. Moran (1998), 'Heros and Brothers in Love: The Male Homosexual as
    Lawyer in Popular Culture', *Studies in Law Politics and Society*, **18**, pp. 3–27.   553

Name Index   579

Acknowledgements

The editor and publishers wish to thank the following for permission to use copyright material.

Blackwell Publishing for the essays: Paul Skidmore (2004), 'A Legal Perspective on Sexuality and Organization: A Lesbian and Gay Case Study', *Gender, Work and Organization*, **11**, pp. 229–53. Copyright © 2004 Blackwell Publishers Ltd; Donald P. Green, Dara Z. Strolovitch, Janelle S. Wong and Robert W. Bailey (2001), 'Measuring Gay Populations and Antigay Hate Crime', *Social Science Quarterly*, **82**, pp. 281–96. Copyright © 2001 Southwestern Social Science Association; Carl F. Stychin (2000), '"A Stranger to its Laws": Sovereign Bodies, Global Sexualities, and Transnational Citizens', *Journal of Law and Society*, **27**, pp. 601–25. Copyright © 2000 Blackwell Publishers Ltd; Richard Collier (1997), 'After Dunblane: Crime, Corporeality, and the (Hetero-) Sexing of the Bodies of Men', *Journal of Law and Society*, **24**, pp. 177–98. Copyright © 1997 Blackwell Publishers Ltd.

Duke University Press for the essay: Gordon Brent Ingram (2003), 'Returning to the Scene of the Crime: Uses of Trial Dossiers on Consensual Male Homosexuality for Urban Research, with Examples From Twentieth-Century British Columbia', *GLQ: A Journal of Lesbian and Gay Studies*, **10**, pp. 77–110. Copyright © 2003 Duke University Press.

Georgetown University of Law Center for the essay: AnnJanette Rosga (1999), 'Policing the State', *Georgetown Journal of Gender and the Law*, pp. 145–71. Copyright © 1999 Georgetown Journal of Gender and the Law.

Haworth Press, Inc. for the essay: Diana Fishbein (2000), 'Sexual Preference, Crime and Punishment', *Women and Criminal Justice*, **11**, pp. 67–84. Copyright © 2000 Haworth Press, Inc.

Johns Hopkins University Press for the essay: Jodie Medd (2002), '"The Cult of the Clitoris": Anatomy of a National Scandal', *Modernism/Modernity*, **9**, pp. 21–49. Copyright © 2002 Johns Hopkins University Press.

Oxford University Press for the essay: Mariana Valverde and Miomir Cirak (2002), 'Governing Bodies, Creating Gay Spaces: Policing and Security Issues in "Gay" Downtown Toronto', *British Journal of Criminology*, **43**, pp. 102–21. Copyright © 2003 Centre for Crime and Justice Studies.

Sage Publications for the essays: Margaret Davies (1999), 'Queer Property, Queer Persons: Self-Ownership and Beyond', *Social and Legal Studies*, **8**, pp. 327–52. Copyright © 1999 Sage Publications; Oliver Phillips (1997), 'Zimbabwean Law and the Production of a White Man's Disease', *Social and Legal Studies*, **6**, pp. 471–91. Copyright © 1997 Sage Publications; Leslie J. Moran (1995), 'Violence and the Law: The Case of Sado-Masochism', *Social and*

Series Preface

The International Library of Essays in Law and Society is designed to provide a broad overview of this important field of interdisciplinary inquiry. Titles in the series will provide access to the best existing scholarship on a wide variety of subjects integral to the understanding of how legal institutions work in and through social arrangements. They collect and synthesize research published in the leading journals of the law and society field. Taken together, these volumes show the richness and complexity of inquiry into law's social life.

Each volume is edited by a recognized expert who has selected a range of scholarship designed to illustrate the most important questions, theoretical approaches, and methods in her/his area of expertise. Each has written an introductory essay which both outlines those questions, approaches, and methods and provides a distinctive analysis of the scholarship presented in the book. Each was asked to identify approximately 20 pieces of work for inclusion in their volume. This has necessitated hard choices since law and society inquiry is vibrant and flourishing.

The International Library of Essays in Law and Society brings together scholars representing different disciplinary traditions and working in different cultural contexts. Since law and society is itself an international field of inquiry it is appropriate that the editors of the volumes in this series come from many different nations and academic contexts. The work of the editors both charts a tradition and opens up new questions. It is my hope that this work will provide a valuable resource for longtime practitioners of law and society scholarship and newcomers to the field.

AUSTIN SARAT
William Nelson Cromwell Professor of Jurisprudence and Political Science
Amherst College

Introduction

Born in the late nineteenth century, sexuality is a relatively new category within the human sciences. Despite its novelty, as Eve Sedgwick (1990) has noted, sexuality is now a central category within Western societies. Furthermore, as some of the essays in this collection demonstrate (see Phillips, Chapter 3), sexuality is also a category that has increasing global significance. It has rapidly become a key concept through which we understand ourselves both as individuals and as members of communities. This volume offers a collection of essays selected to reflect the ever-widening horizons of this area of law and society scholarship, its diverse theoretical and methodological approaches and its complex politics (Weeks, 2000). The essays offer an insight into some of the key themes and developments in this body of work. Each, in its different way, offers an evaluation of the nature, meaning and effects of sexuality thereby providing a critical evaluation of the politics of sexual identity as it appears in and through the law. I want to begin with a few comments on an enigma that is at the core of work on sexuality.

The Enigma of 'Heterosexuality'

Work on sexuality is dominated by work on gay and lesbian sexualities. Heterosexuality, formally the dominant sexuality, appears to occupy a marginal position in work on sexuality in general and law and society work in particular. How are we to make sense of the relative absence of the dominant heterosexuality?

In his study *The Invention of Heterosexuality*, Jonathan Katz notes that '...talk of heterosexuality so often and so easily glides off into talk of homosexuality, leaving heterosexuality, once again, forgotten' (Katz, 1995, p. 12). Here Katz points to the difficulties of making heterosexuality an object of inquiry: it has a tendency to disappear and to turn into a discussion about other sexualities. If one searches various scholarly indexes pertinent to the interdisciplinary and multidisciplinary basis of law and society work, sexuality appears most persistently in association with 'homosexuality', 'lesbian', 'gay', and more recently 'queer'. For example, a search of the *Social Science Citation Index* produced 6273 references for 'gay' and 2893 for 'lesbian'. In contrast, a search by reference to 'heterosexuality' produced just over 3000 references. An examination of the abstracts falling under the category of 'heterosexuality' quickly reveals that the appearance of 'heterosexuality' betrays the fact that the substance of the article is often same-sex, not opposite-sex, relations. A similar search in other domains of scholarship relevant to law and society scholarship produces a similar pattern. How can we explain this state of affairs?

For much of the history of sexuality in Western societies (and now globally), to have a 'sexuality' is to be marked – to be marked as the 'other', the 'outsider' (Butler, 1990, 1993; Fuss, 1991; Foucault, 1980). The norm remains unrepresented and unrepresentable. The term that marks the exception – be it 'homosexual' or, more recently, 'lesbian' or 'gay' – plays a central role in defining the dominant term which formally remains absent (Fuss, 1991). Thus, heterosexual as an erotic/genital relation and, as an identity category, is represented only by way of the exception, such as 'homosexuality' that stands as the 'other', long characterized as the aberration, the abnormal, the perverted, the pathological, the deviation from that which remains unmarked: the norm.

If categories of sexuality emerge by way of the figure of the 'other' or the 'outsider', is the appearance of the term 'heterosexual' a departure from this? Scholarship on heterosexuality suggests not. The term 'heterosexuality' (its invention in the twentieth century – in 1901 – postdates the category 'homosexuality' which is a child of the nineteenth century) makes its first appearance as a mark of the 'other' (Weeks, 1981, 1986). It is used to define 'an abnormal or perverted sexual appetite toward the opposite sex' (quoted in Penelope, 1993). More specifically, heterosexual first names an aberration of opposite-sex relations – as practices of pleasure in contrast to practices of reproduction. This dynamic is still apparent in the recent growth of scholarship on heterosexuality, much of which has emerged in relation to the HIV pandemic.

The problem with heterosexuality that Katz (1995) points to is not so much a problem of the heterosexual as the other, but the problems and difficulties associated with attempts to use 'heterosexuality' to bring the norm into the frame of representation in general and of critical inquiry in particular. Kitzinger and Wilkinson (1993) suggest that the norm of heterosexuality is both always present and that which most resists appearance (see generally Wilkinson and Kitzinger, 1993; Richardson, 1996; Weeks, 1986). As Richard Collier's essay on male heterosexual violence in Chapter 9 of this collection demonstrates, as the unmarked, 'heterosexuality' is not so much absent as the unspoken, the taken-for-granted and the natural – that which is in the background and which remains unquestioned. Collier's essay,[1] focusing on responses to an incident of extreme male violence, offers an excellent example of the operation and constitution of heterosexual masculinity as the norm as absence. In good part, hetero-masculinity remains unquestioned as all attention and effort is focused on making sense of a particular act as the exception, an aberration, and as problematic. But, as Collier skilfully demonstrates, the making of the meaning of the exception is also a process that erases the proximity between that incident and, in this instance, male violence that is an everyday part of hetero-masculinity. Violence in everyday relations between men, in the heterosexual family, in the wider life of the community, all disappear from consideration. His critical engagement with this process seeks to expose the fabrication and maintenance of the silences in order to question and challenge the norm that is being made in this instance. Other essays in this collection such as that by Leslie Moran on litigation criminalizing 'homosexual sado-masochism' (Chapter 10) and that by Andrew Sharpe, focusing on litigation relating to the meaning of the institution of heterosexual marriage explored through the concept of the transsexual (Chapter 4), offer other examples of work in which these issues are explored.

The dominance of work on lesbian and gay sexualities in this collection does not represent a flaw or a weakness in law and society scholarship on sexuality and identity but is, rather,

---

[1]   Another example of work that formally addresses heterosexuality in law and society is the scholarship of Alison Young (see Young, 1990, 1993). For an analysis of the different approaches demonstrated in her work and a more detailed consideration of the absent presence of heterosexuality in early law and society scholarship see Moran (2004).

a reflection of the structures through which the sense and non-sense of sexuality is made. Nor does it represent an absence of consideration of heterosexuality. Work on gay and lesbian sexualities in law and society scholarship offers the most sustained scholarship on heterosexuality to date in that field. A key component of this work is its engagement with the nature, form, effects and institutions of heterosexuality. Terms that point to the relationship between heterosexuality and these other sexualities include 'homophobia', 'heterosexism' and, more recently, 'heteronormativity' (see Warner, 1993). The danger remains that, because of the focus on 'lesbian' or 'gay', 'heterosexuality' may slip out of the frame. The reader and researcher need to be ever vigilant. The challenge, as many essays in this collection demonstrate, is to keep both the norm and the exception in the frame of analysis in order to expose and critique the (re)production of heterosexuality.

From Act to Identity

A key theme in studies of sexuality and identity may be highlighted by reference to the path-breaking and highly influential work of Michel Foucault, *The History of Sexuality Volume 1: An Introduction* (1980). In that study Foucault examines the emergence of the category of sexuality as an identity category in and through new bodies of knowledge such as psychology, psychiatry and sexology (see also Weeks, 1981). He notes a dramatic transformation in the way in which forbidden actions such as sodomy/buggery are understood. In short there has been a shift from thinking about them as forbidden acts to the acts being read as marks or gestures associated with the essence of a person and expressive of a fundamental truth of the one performing the actions – the person's identity. In part, Foucault's study is an attempt to expose the history and politics of identity at work in the emergence of sexuality. His work offers a challenge to the assumption of sexuality as an identity or, more specifically, to some of the characteristics associated with identity in that context, such as the qualities of 'truth', 'nature', 'essence' and fixity. It also challenges the assumption that sexual politics is predominantly a politics of liberation. Liberation appears to work with an idea of sexuality as something pre-given or fixed which is limited, confined or restrained by a force or power external to sexuality and identity, such as law. The object of this liberation politics is the release of that which is confined or limited. Foucault's work exposed this liberation politics' failure to take account of sexuality, with the attributes of 'essence', 'fixity', 'truth', and so on, as categories and experiences that are already informed by power and politics.

Foucault's work has particular significance for work on sexuality, identity and law. Historians of sexuality have noted the importance of sexuality as a form of identity, and associated demands for liberation, in the very earliest political activism and scholarship about sexuality and law. One of the first contexts in which these issues arose was in relation to demands for the decriminalization of specific forbidden acts now associated with sexuality, in particular sodomy and buggery (Lauristen and Thorstad, 1974; Moran, 1996). The very qualities of 'truth', 'nature', 'essence' and fixity associated with sexuality as identity played a key role in making (and limiting) demands for reform. Injustice was associated here with repression, taking the form of the total prohibition and severe punishment of consensual acts that were represented as an expression of a person's nature, the very truth of their being, a manifestation of something at the heart of their being and beyond their control (see Halley, 1993a; Moran, 1996).

As Nicola Lacey (2004) has noted, much work within law and society scholarship that engages with matters of identity is critical of identity politics. More specifically central to that scholarship is a resistance to the model of (sexual) identity as a fixed essence. In turn, much of law and society scholarship offers a critique of identity politics as being nothing more than a politics of liberation. Most law and society scholarship in this field, Lacey suggests, focuses on the role of law as a powerful social discourse that produces, deploys and enforces the category of identity. In this approach 'essence', 'nature', 'fixity' and so on are not so much necessary or pre-given but effects of identity politics in law.

Much of the scholarship that is found in this collection adopts a critical stance with regard to sexual identity with the attributes of 'truth', 'nature', 'essence' and fixity. The essays collected here offer examples of a range of different theoretical approaches and critiques to sexual identity in law drawing upon Queer, feminist, post-colonial, Marxist and post-structuralist scholarship. Here, I want to outline some of the questions and insights raised by the different approaches and critiques of sexual identity found in this collection.

Critiques

Queer Theory foregrounds the materiality of sexuality and challenges the essentializing dimensions of identity politics (Jagose, 1996). At best it offers a multidisciplinary set of tools drawing upon post-structuralist and post-Marxist political theory, and cultural and literary studies. One of the first published essays within law and society scholarship to draw upon Queer theory is Lisa Bowers's, 'Queer Acts and the Politics of "Direct Address": Rethinking Law, Culture, and Community' (1994), which first appeared in *Law and Society Review.* Versions of the essay have subsequently been included in several anthologies such as Shane Phelan's *Playing with Fire,* (1997). Carl Stychin's monograph, *Law's Desire* (1995) is another key text that engages with Queer Theory. Related work includes Moran's monograph, *The Homosexual(ity) of Law* (1996) offering a post-structuralist analysis of sexual identity, this time in the context of English law, and developing a Foucaultian analysis. Janet Halley's (1993a, 1993b,1994) pioneering studies of the US Supreme Court decision of *Bowers* v. *Hardwick* are another excellent example. Her studies of this important moment in US constitutional sexual politics continue to offer some of the best work using techniques of deconstruction to examine the constitution of heterosexuality through homosexuality as 'other'. Andrew Sharpe's essay in this volume (Chapter 4) offers a similar analysis of heterosexuality in the context of transgender jurisprudence (see also his excellent monograph on the subject (Sharpe, 2002)). Also in this collection, Gail Mason's essay 'Not Our Kind of Hate Crime' (Chapter 16) uses an approach that is reminiscent of deconstruction to offer a critique of a key term, 'hate', in the hate crime debate.

Margaret Davis's essay, 'Queer Property, Queer Persons: Self-Ownership and Beyond' (Chapter 1) is a brilliant example of the potential of Queer Theory. In the essay she explores the nature of sexual identity by analysing themes of personality and property. Her work exemplifies Queer Theory's ability to expose the fundamental instability of what appear to be fixed categories of sexuality and to challenge and disrupt the sexual and gender hierarchies through which heterosexuality is given shape and form. Her analysis provides an example of work that challenges identity as the essence, core or foundation of the subject. She reveals not only how deeply embedded these ideas are in Western legal culture, but also how identity is implicated in, and draws upon, other fundamental ideas which might seem to be remote from it, such as property. Another important dimension of this essay is the way in which Davis explores the limits of Queer Theory, particularly how it has rapidly been transformed from a technique of radical and progressive critique into just another (albeit new) identity category (p. 8). For further reading offering a critique of Queer Theory see Backer (1998) and McGhee (2001).

A different, but related, line of critical engagement with identity politics in general and sexual identity in particular is to be found in Susan Boyd's essay (Chapter 18). Here, the critique focuses on the objective of identity politics, which is described as 'a politics of recognition' in contrast to 'a politics of redistribution'. The latter has a more economic focus and is more closely associated with a Marxist and post-Marxist tradition while the former is said to focus more on the social and cultural dimensions of social exclusion. The core of the challenge to sexual politics as a politics of recognition is that social change will fail to deliver social justice as it fails to address the social and economic injustices generated by capitalism. Boyd offers an excellent summary of the debates and also challenges the point of departure that sets recognition and redistribution as two categories that are in a relation of either/or. She explores these issues in relation to debates within feminism and the politics of kinship recognition – more specifically, struggles over the rights and interests of lesbians and gay men in same-sex domestic relations.

Another critique of the politics of recognition found in this collection seeks to question the relationship that is being forged with the state as 'lesbian' and 'gay' become identity markers associated with successful claims for civil and human rights. Drawing upon the work of Wendy Brown (1995), AnnJanette Rosga (Chapter 7) raises some questions about the politics and potential of lesbian and gay engagement with an institution so recently associated with the enforcement of compulsory heterosexuality. She uses her experience as an advocate for hate crime reform, championing the inclusion of 'lesbian' and 'gay' in that reform context, to reflect upon the some of the dangers and limits of turning to the state. For example a state-centred political project may frame a progressive politics by way of conservative parameters. In the context of hate crime reform Rosga highlights a troubling proximity between the progressive demands for access to state services of policing and the contemporary criminal justice agenda that promotes vengeance by way of more severe punishment (for further examples of these concerns see Stanko and Curry, 1997 and Moran and Skeggs, 2004). Another problematic dimension of the state's recognition is the 'lesbian' and 'gay' that is being incorporated into the changing body politic. 'Lesbian' and 'gay' as new subjects/citizens are being defined by way of the constitution of 'new' outsiders (Cf. Phelan, 2001). Respectability is a key theme here. Leslie Moran's essay on 'homosexual sado-masochism' offers one example of criminal litigation in which the terms of the 'good homosexual' have been articulated by reference to a 'new' homosexual outsider. The essays by Susan Boyd, Ruthann Robson and Rosemary Auchmuty (Chapters 18–20), collected in the subsection 'Kinship', provide instances in which the parameters of lesbian and gay respectability are being articulated in another context: the family.

The reification of identity categories is another problematic feature of recognition politics. The totalizing assumptions at work in identity categories, be it in relation to the general category of sexual identity or in more specific identity categories such as 'lesbian' or 'gay', is one of the key concerns addressed in by Diana Majury in Chapter 2. Her analysis pays particular attention to a common feature of sexual politics associated with the terms 'gay' and 'homosexual'. More specifically, she argues that these categories have been generated out of male same-sex experiences and fail to capture either the diversity of same-sex experiences or, more particularly, the experiences of lesbians. Lesbians and lesbian experiences have long been, and remain, marginal in sexual scholarship and sexual politics. Majury's essay draws attention to a key dimension of difference that separates out lesbian experience: gender. The relative exclusion and different histories and experiences of lesbians is a theme that is common to several essays collected here including those by Diana Fishbein (Chapter 11), Gordon Ingram (Chapter 5), Gail Mason (Chapter 16), Jodie Medd (Chapter 6) and Jenni Millbank (Chapter 21).

The problems associated with the essentializing and totalizing dimensions of categories of sexual identity is also a focus of Oliver Phillips's essay (Chapter 3). He brings other dimensions of identity into the frame, in particular racial and ethnic identities and class, and examines their intersection (p. 72) within, and their impact on, the politics of sexuality in Zimbabwe. 'Intersectionality' was a term first coined in the context of feminist politics to challenge the totalizing assumptions associated with the category 'women'. The context in which this emerged was violence against women and feminist responses to it. Kimberley Crenshaw (1995) introduced the term 'intersectionality' in her attempt to bring the different experiences of black and minority ethnic women into the frame of analysis and politics. Phillips's essay draws attention to its significance in the post-colonial context of sexuality (see also Kapur, 1999, 2001). There is now a significant body of work by lesbian and gay scholars on 'intersectionality'. Works that examine the interface between sexuality and gender include Eaton (1994) and Sharpe (2002); the interface between sexuality and race is investigated by Eaton (1995), Hutchinson (1999, 2000), Jefferson (1998) and Kwan (1997); and sexuality and ethnicity is examined by Valdes (1995, 1999). Moran and Sharpe (2004) have explored similar issues in the context of the transgender experience. One theme that remains underdeveloped in this context is work on the role of class, but see Boyd (Chapter 18) and Moran (1999).

Locating Sexuality

Spatial themes have long had importance in work on sexual identity and law. However, as Sedgwick (1990) has noted, the dominant spatial categories have been the 'public' and the 'private'. In Western liberal democracies the binary of public–private does phenomenal work in the cultural arena. Such is its range of meanings, she argues, that it threatens to make it difficult to recognize the importance of other spatial tropes or to imagine other geographies of sexual identity in law. The historians of sexuality reveal the importance of the public–private distinction in early demands for law reform (Lauristen and Thorstad, 1974). The binary also played (and continues to play)[2] a central role in more contemporary reform debates as is illustrated by the dialogue between H.L.A. Hart (1963) and Lord Devlin (1965) that arose out of the proposals of the British government's reform initiative, the Wolfenden Committee, which proposed the decriminalization of certain homosexual acts in private (see Moran, 1996). Various essays in this collection offer a critique of this preoccupation with the public–private

---

[2]   The Hart-Devlin debate played a key role in the decisions of the High Court and Court of Appeal in Botswana in the case of *Kanane* v. *State*. See Bojosi (2004).

distinction, and the collection as a whole challenges the narrow preoccupation with these particular spatial tropes.

Diana Majury's essay (Chapter 2) exposes the way in which the public–private distinction, which offers the private as a sanctuary from state intervention, is a preoccupation that fails to capture lesbian and women's experience of the private sphere more generally. As Majury's (and Auchmuty's) work demonstrates, the domestic sphere and the family, both of which are associated with the private, have long been contexts in which women in general and lesbians in particular have been subjected to the control (and violence) of men and to lawful subordination – hardly the haven promoted by advocates of privacy.

Chapters 13 and 14 by Paul Skidmore and William Rubenstein respectively offer a different location in which sexual identity is formed and battled over: the workplace. Skidmore, in particular, offers a direct engagement with the spatial themes, again dominated by the public–private distinction, that have informed a sexual politics of the workplace. Highlighting the contingency of the public–private division his study explores some of the effects of boundary formation and change. Mariana Valverde's and Miomir Cirak's essay on governance of public space (Chapter 12) offers a somewhat different approach to spatial themes. Their focus is on the formation and governance of sexual identity in and through the fabrication of public places as safer spaces for lesbians and gay men. Like Majury's essay, their work challenges the association of the private as the location of safety and security for lesbians and gay men. Their preoccupation is not so much the exclusion of gays or lesbians from the public but with the management of sexual identity in the constitution of the public.

Carl Stychin's essay (Chapter 8) offers a different spatial focus, being concerned with the interface between ideas of sexual identity and the nation-state and transnationalism (see also Phillips (Chapter 3) and Ingram (Chapter 5) on the nation-state). Stychin's essay also illustrates the importance of insights offered by sexual geographers. His analysis exemplifies the importance of a key spatial trope, the 'boundary' (Cf. Nedelsky, 1991). Gordon Ingham, a geographer, offers an analysis that highlights the complexity of the spatial dimension of sexual identity politics. His historical study reveals the way in which sexuality is made in law by way of the simultaneous operation of several different spatial themes: the urban in contrast to the rural, the colonial and post-colonial, the nation, the cosmopolitan and the public over against the private.

Methodologies

As already indicated, the work collected here is methodologically diverse, reflecting the fact that within scholarship on sexuality in general and like law and society scholarship in particular there is no single methodology. A preoccupation of the essays by Davies (Chapter 1), Phillips (Chapter 3), Sharpe (Chapter 4), Ingram (Chapter 5), Collier (Chapter 9), Moran (Chapters 10 and 22) and Millbank (Chapter 21) is the analysis of texts. The texts studied range from media reports (Collier) to law reports (Phillips, Sharpe, Moran), case files (Phillips, Ingram) to literature and film (Millbank, Moran). In many instances the analysis turns to the insights of post-structuralist theory and deconstruction as a practice. The essays by Ingram and Medd (Chapters 5 and 6) offer a historical analysis. Ingram's work uses contemporary official archives of encounters with the police and prosecutions arising from them. Medd's source is a popular publication that purports to be the transcript of a trial. Ingram, despite his demonstration of the richness of the material, also warns of some of the problems of turning to official reports. In particular, he highlights not only their flawed and partial account of same-sex relations but, more specifically, their limited and partial accounts of the making of sexuality in and through encounters with the agents of the state and law in particular.

Several of the essays have a strong empirical focus, using both quantitative and qualitative methods. Two of the essays found in the subsection 'Hate', by Donald Green *et al.* (Chapter 15) and Graeme Reid and Teresa Dirsuweit (Chapter 17) draw attention to the political importance and methodological challenges of quantitative and qualitative work in the context of homophobic violence. In different ways and in different contexts both examine and explore the challenges of mapping lesbian and gay communities which have been described in the mainstream as 'invisible minorities' and 'invisible communities'. The particular focus of Green *et al.* is urban USA. Reid and Dirsuweit, on the other hand, raise some of the methodological challenges in the context of post-apartheid South Africa. William Rubenstein's essay (Chapter 14) reviews a number of empirical studies of the experience of lesbian and gay lawyers in the USA. Again, this work offers an example of the use of quantitative and qualitative methods in lesbian and gay political initiatives. Rubenstein offers not only an analysis of the knowledge generated but also a critique highlighting some of the limits and exploring future directions for research in that national context. Diana Fishbein's essay on lesbians in prison (Chapter 11) is an example of empirical scholarship that comes from a different disciplinary tradition, criminology. Another different approach is represented in the work of AnnJanette Rosga (Chapter 7). In this instance, her work has a strong ethnographic focus, drawing upon her own experiences as an advocate of lesbian and gay law reform and as a researcher.

Ever-widening Horizons

Finally, I want to acknowledge the diversity of topics represented in this collection. While the essays by Ingram and Medd offer examples of work on the history of sexuality in a legal context most of the essays found here formally engage with contemporary debates about sexuality.[3] Many focus on relations between sexual subjects and the state. Phillips (Chapter 3) and Ingram (Chapter 5) put this within a colonial and post-colonial context. Their essays together with the work of Collier, Fishbein and Rosga, explore this relation in the context of criminal law and criminal justice. Sharpe, Boyd, Robson and Auchmuty (Chapters 4, 18–20) offer insights into the formation of sexual identity in the context of kinship relations and marriage in particular. The essays by Skidmore and Rubenstein (Chapters 13 and 14) focus on employment relations and the workplace whereas those by Rosga and Stychin (Chapters 7 and 8), together with those collected in the subsection 'Hate' might also be categorized as offering an analysis of a nascent and emerging idea of sexual citizenship. As Phelan (2001) has noted, within the tradition of Western liberal democracy safety and security is at the heart of citizenship in general and sexual citizenship in particular. Sharpe's essay (Chapter 4) draws attention to the rise of scholarship informed by transgender activism and analysis. Like Queer Theory, transgender is critical of fixed categories of identity and the disciplines

---

[3]   There is a need for caution here as I am not suggesting that historical studies are exclusively about the past. Historical studies play a key role in explaining the present. Both essays collected here are examples of historical work that engages with issues of sexuality in the present.

and technologies that have generated identity politics in the 'trans' context. The work by Millbank and Moran found in the subsection 'The Cultural Turn' are examples of scholarship that looks at representations of sexuality in law in the context of popular culture. These essays reflect a wider shift in law and society scholarship to incorporate the study of popular culture (Redhead, 1995; Sherwin, 2000, 2004). The turn to popular culture seeks to take account of the importance of popular culture in the formation of experiences of law and legality in both a professional and an everyday context. In Chapter 21 Jenni Millbank examines common themes that inform television, film and popular press representations of lesbians in relation to law and exposes the limits of those representations. The films discussed focus on women (who are represented as being involved in lesbian relationships) and include a New Zealand film, *Heavenly Creatures* (1994) directed by Peter Jackson and the British film, *Butterfly Kiss* (1995) directed by Michael Winterbottom. Leslie Moran's essay (Chapter 22) focuses not so much on sexuality and homosexuality as a mark of the criminal, deviant or pathological, but as the identity of the lawyer, more specifically the lawyer as hero. As a hero the homosexual/ gay lawyer is the one whose voice tells the story of social exclusion in two popular films, *Victim* (1961) a police procedure film by British director Basil Dearden and *Philadelphia* (1993), directed by Jonathan Demme and starring Tom Hanks as a gay lawyer, and Denzel Washington.

Further Reading

In the space available in this volume it is impossible to bring together examples of work that represent the full spectrum of the rich diversity of scholarship on sexuality and identity in law. Equally, it is impossible to reference all key pieces of scholarship from the wide range of different disciplines that inform law and society scholarship on sexuality and identity. The bibliographies and footnotes of the various essays collected here provide one rich source of further reading. I have also offered a selection indicating substantive areas of scholarship not represented here, such as 'Legal Philosophy'. Some key texts from other disciplines have also been included so that readers unfamiliar with this work can gain easy access to exciting and important work on sexuality and identity relevant to the study of law.

References

Bojosi K.N. (2004), 'An Opportunity Missed for Gay rights in Botswana: *Utjiwa Kanane* v. *The State*', *South African Journal of Human Rights*, **20**, pp. 466–81.
Bowers, L. (1994), 'Queer Acts and the Politics of "Direct Address": Rethinking Law, Culture, and Community', *Law and Society Review*, **28**(5), pp. 1009–34.
Brown, W. (1995), *States of Injury: Power and Freedoms in Late Modernity*, Princeton, NJ: Princeton University Press.
Butler, J. (1990), *Gender Trouble: Feminism and the Subversion of Identity*, London: Routledge.
Butler, J. (1993), *Bodies That Matter*, London: Routledge.
Butterfly Kiss (1995), Dir. Michael Winterbottom, GB.
Crenshaw, K. (1995), 'Mapping the Margins: Intersectionality, Identity Politics and Violence', in K. Crenshaw *et al.* (eds), *Critical Race Theory*, New York, The New Press, pp. 357–83.
Devlin, P. (1965), *The Enforcement of Morals*, Oxford: Oxford University Press.

Foucault, M. (1980), *The History of Sexuality, Volume 1: An Introduction*, trans. R. Hurley, New York: Vintage Books.

Fuss, D. (1991), *Inside/Out*, London: Routledge.

Halley, J.E. (1993a), 'Reasoning about Sodomy: Act and Identity in and after *Bowers* v. *Hardwick*,' *Virginia Law Review*, **79**, pp. 1721–80.

Halley, J.E. (1993b), 'The Construction of Heterosexuality', in M. Warner (ed.), *Fear of a Queer Planet: Queer Politics and Social Theory*, Minneapolis: University of Minnesota Press, pp. 82–104.

Halley, J.E. (1994), '*Bowers* v. *Hardwick* in the Renaissance', in J. Goldberg (ed.), *Queering the Renaissance*, Durham, NC: Duke University Press, pp. 145–204.

Hart, H.L.A. (1963), *Law, Liberty and Morality*, Oxford: Oxford University Press.

Heavenly Creatures (1994), Dir. Peter Jackson, NZ.

Jagose, A. (1996), *Queer Theory*, Melbourne: Melbourne University Press.

Kapur, R. (1999), '"A Love Song for our Mongrel Selves": Hybridity, Sexuality and Law', *Social and Legal Studies*, **8**(3), pp. 353–68.

Kapur, R. (2001), 'Postcolonial Erotic Disruptions: Legal Narratives of Culture, Sex and Nation in India', *Columbia Journal of Gender and Law*, pp. 333–84.

Katz, J.N. (1995), *The Invention of Heterosexuality*, New York: Penguin.

Kitzinger, C. and Wilkinson, S. (1993), 'Theorizing Heterosexuality', in S. Wilkinson and C. Kitzinger (eds), *Heterosexuality: A Feminist and Psychology Reader*, London: Sage, pp. 1–32.

Lacey N. (2004), 'The Constitution of Identity: Gender, Feminist Legal Theory and the Law and Society Movement', in A. Sarat (ed.), *The Blackwell Companion to Law and Society*, Malden USA: Blackwell, pp. 471–86.

Lauristen, J. and Thorstad, D. (1974), *The Early Homosexual Rights Movement (1864–1935)*, New York: Times Change Press.

McGhee, D. (2001), *Homosexuality, Law and Resistance*, London: Routledge.

Moran, L.J. (1996), *The Homosexual(ity) of Law*, London: Routledge.

Moran L.J (2004), 'Sexuality in Law and Society Scholarship', in A. Sarat (ed.), *The Blackwell Companion to Law and Society*, Malden USA: Blackwell, pp. 487–506.

Moran, L.J. and Skeggs, B. (2004), *Sexuality and the Politics of Violence and Safety*, London: Routledge.

Nedelsky, J. (1991), 'Law, Boundaries and the Bounded Self', in R. Post (ed.), *Law and the Order of Culture*, Berkeley: University of California Press, pp. 162–90.

Penelope, J. (1993), 'Heterosexual Identity: Out of the Closets', in S. Wilkinson and C. Kitzinger (eds), *Heterosexuality: A Feminist and Psychology Reader*, London: Sage, pp. 261–65.

Phelan, S. (ed.) (1997), *Playing with Fire: Queer Politics, Queer Theories*, New York: Routledge.

Phelan, S. (2001), *Sexual Strangers: Gays, Lesbians and the Dilemmas of Citizenship*, Philadelphia: Temple University Press.

Philadelphia (1993), Dir. Jonathan Demme, USA.

Redhead, S. (1995), *Unpopular Culture: The Birth of Law and Popular Culture*, Manchester: Manchester University Press.

Richardson, D. (ed.) (1996), *Theorizing Heterosexuality*, Buckingham: Open University Press.

Sedgwick, E.K. (1990), *Epistemology of the Closet*, Hemel Hempstead: Harvester Wheatsheaf.

Sharpe, A. (2002), *Transgender Jurisprudence: Dysphoric Bodies of Law*, London: Cavendish.

Sherwin, R. K. (2000), *When Law goes Pop: The Vanishing Line between Law and Popular Culture*, Chicago: Chicago University Press.

Sherwin, R.K. (2004), 'Law in Popular Culture', in A. Sarat (ed.), *The Blackwell Companion to Law and Society*, Malden USA: Blackwell, pp. 95–112.

Stanko, B. and Curry, P. (1997), 'Homophobic Violence and the Self at Risk', *Social and Legal Studies*, **6**(4), pp. 513–32.

Stychin, C. (1995), *Law's Desire*, London: Routledge.

Victim (1961), Dir. Basil Dearden, UK.

Warner, M. (1993), 'Introduction', in M. Warner (ed.), *Fear of a Queer Planet: Queer Politics and Social Theory*, Minneapolis: University of Minnesota Press, pp. vii–xxxi.

Weeks, J. (1981), *Sex, Politics and Society: The Regulation of Sexuality Since 1800*, London: Longmans.

Weeks, J. (1986), *Sexualities*, London: Routledge.

Weeks, J. (2000), 'The Challenge of Lesbian and Gay Studies', in T. Sandfort, J. Schuyf, J.W. Duyvendak and J. Weeks (eds), *Lesbian and Gay Studies: An Introductory, Interdisciplinary Approach*, London: Sage, pp. 1–13.

Wilkinson, S. and Kitzinger, C. (eds) (1993), *Heterosexuality: A Feminist and Psychology Reader*, London: Sage.

Young, A. (1990), *Femininity in Dissent*, London: Routledge.

Young, A. (1993), 'The Authority of the Name', in S. Wilkinson and C. Kitzinger (eds), *Heterosexuality: A Feminist and Psychology Reader*, London: Sage, pp. 37–39.

Further Reading

Heterosexuality

Collier, R. (1992), '"The Art of Living the Married Life": Representations of Male Heterosexuality in Law', *Social and Legal Studies*, **1**(4), pp. 543–63.

Collier, R. (1996), '"Coming Together?": Post-heterosexuality, Masculine Crisis, and the New Men's Movement', *Feminist Legal Studies*, **4**(1), pp. 3–48.

Leonard, L.M. (1990), 'A Missing Voice in Feminist Legal Theory: The Heterosexual Presumption', *Women's Rights Law Reporter*, **12**(1), pp. 39–49.

Queer

Backer, L.K. (1998), 'Queering Theory: An Essay on the Conceit of Revolution in Law', in L. Moran, D. Monk and S. Beresford (eds), *Legal Queeries*, London: Cassell, pp. 185–203.

Herman, D. and Stychin, C. (eds) (1995), *Legal Inversions*, Philadelphia: Temple University Press.

Moran, L.J. (ed.) (1997), 'Legal Perversions', Special edition of *Social and Legal Studies*, **6**(4).

Moran, L.J., Monk, D. and Beresford, S. (eds) (1998), *Legal Queeries*, London: Cassell.

Symposium: Queer Law (2000), *New York University Law Review of Law and Social Change*.

Stychin, C. and Herman, D. (2000), *Sexuality in the Legal Arena*, London: Athlone.

Lesbian

Mason, G. (1997), 'Boundaries of Sexuality: Lesbian Experience and Feminist Discourse on Violence Against Women', *Australian Gay and Lesbian Law Journal*, **7**, pp. 41–56.

Robson, R. (1992), *Lesbian (Out)law*, Ithaca, NY: Firebrand.

Robson, R. (1998), *When Sappho Goes to Law School*, New York: Columbia University Press.

Intersectionality

Eaton, M. (1994), 'At the Intersection of Gender and Sexual Orientation: Towards a Lesbian Jurisprudence', *Southern California Review of Law and Women's Studies*, pp. 183–220.

Eaton, M. (1995), 'Homosexual Unmodified: Speculations on Law's Discourse, Race and the Construction of Sexual Identity', in D. Herman and C. Stychin (eds), *Legal Inversions*, Philadelphia: Temple University Press, pp. 46–76.

Hutchinson, D.L. (1999), 'Ignoring the Sexualisation of Race: Heternormativity, Critical Race Theory and Anti-Racist Politics', *Buffalo Law Review*, 41, Spring/Summer, pp. 1–116.

Hutchinson, D.L. (2000), '"Gay Rights" for "gay whites"? Race, Sexual Identity and Equal Protection Discourse', *Cornell Law Review*, **85**, pp. 1358–91.

Jefferson, T.R. (1998), 'Notes Towards a Black Lesbian Jurisprudence', *Boston College Third World Law Journal*, **18**, Spring, pp. 263–94.

Kwan, P. (1997), 'Jeffrey Dahmer and the Cosynthesis of Categories', *Hastings Law Journal*, **48**, pp. 1257–92.

Moran, L.J. and Sharpe, A. (2004), 'Violence, Identity and Policing: The Case of Violence against Transgender People', *Criminal Justice*, **4**(4), pp. 395–417.

Valdes, F. (1995), 'Sex and Race in Queer Legal Culture', *Review of Law and Women's Studies*, **5**, pp. 25–71.

Valdes, F. (1999), 'Theorizing "Outcrit" Theories: Coalitional Method and Comparative Jurisprudential Experience. Race Crits, Queer Crits, Lat Crits', *University of Miami Law Review*, **53**, pp. 1265–322.

Transgender

Bornstein, K. (1994), *Gender Outlaw: On Men, Women and the Rest of Us*, New York: Routledge.

Califia, P. (1997), *Sex Changes: The Politics of Transgenderism*, San Francisco: Cleis Press.

Feinberg, L. (1992), *Transgender Liberation: A Movement Whose Time has Come*, New York: World View Forum.

Prosser, J. (1998), *Second Skins: The Body Narrative of Transsexuality*, New York: Columbia University Press.

Sharpe, A. (1998), 'Institutionalising Heterosexuality: The Legal Exclusion of "Impossible" (Trans)Sexualities', in L. Moran, D. Monk and S. Beresford (eds), *Legal Queeries*, London: Cassell, pp. 26–43.

Sharpe, A. (1999), 'Transgender Performance and the Discriminating Gaze: A Critique of Anti Discrimination Regulatory Regimes', *Social and Legal Studies*, **8**(1) pp. 5–24.

Whittle, S. (1998) 'Gemeinschaftsfremden – Or How To Be Shafted By Your Friends: Sterilization Requirements and Legal Status Recognition For The Transsexual', in L. Moran, D. Monk and S. Beresford, *Legal Queeries*, London: Cassell, pp. 42-56.

Whittle, S. (2000), *The Transgender Debate*, London: South Street Press.

Legal Philosophical Works

Bamforth, N. (1997), *Sexuality, Morals and Justice*, London: Cassell.

Kaplan, M. (1997), *Sexual Justice*, New York: Routledge.

Mohr, R.D. (1988), *Gays/Justice: A Study of Ethics, Society and Law*, New York: Columbia University Press.

Human and Civil Rights

Heinze, E. (1995), *Sexual Orientation: A Human Right*, Dordrecht: Martiinus Nijhoff.
Herman, D. (1994), *Rights of Passage: Struggles for Lesbian and Gay Legal Equality*, Toronto: University of Toronto Press.
Wintermute, R. (1995), *Sexual Orientation and Human Rights: The United States Constitution, the European Convention, and the Canadian Charter*, Oxford: Clarendon Press.

Histories

Bray, A. (1982), *Homosexuality in Renaissance England*, London: Gay Men's Press.
Chauncey, G. (1994), *Gay New York*, New York: Basic Books.
Cocks, H.G. (2003), *Nameless Offences: Homosexual Desire in the 19th Century*, London, I.B. Tauris.
Cohen, E. (1993), Talk on the Wilde Side: Towards a Genealogy of a Discourse on Male Sexualities, Routledge: New York and London.
Crompton, L. (1980), 'The Myth of Lesbian Impunity', *Journal of Homosexuality*, **6**(1–2), pp. 11–32.
Doan, L. (1997), 'Gross Indecency between Women: Policing Lesbians or Policing Lesbian Police', *Social and Legal Studies*, **6**(4), pp. 533–46.
Doan, L. (2001), *Fashioning Sapphism*, New York: Columbia University Press.
Dugan, L. (2000), *Sapphic Slashers*, Durham, NC: Duke University Press.
Hart, L. (1994), *Fatal Women*, Princeton, NJ: Princeton University Press.
Holland, M. (2003), *Irish Peacock and Scarlet Marquess: The Real Trial of Oscar Wilde*, London: Fourth Estate.
Hyde, H.M. (1973), *The Trials of Oscar Wilde*, London: Dover Books.
Weeks, J. (1977), *Coming Out*, London: Quartet.

The State

Berger, N. (2000), 'Queer Readings of Europe: Gender, Identity, Sexual Orientation and the (Im)potency of Rights Politics at the European Court of Justice', *Social and Legal Studies*, **9**(2), pp. 249–70.
Binnie, J. and Bell. J. (2001), Sexual Citizenship, Cambridge: Polity Press.
Carolan, B. (2001), 'Rights of Sexual Minorities in Ireland and Europe: Rhetoric versus Reality', *Dickinson Journal of International Law*, **19**(3), pp. 387–406.
Cock, J. (2003), 'Engendering Gay and Lesbian Rights: The Equality Clause in the South African Constitution', *Women's Studies International Forum*, **26**, pp. 35–52.
Conway, D. (2004), '"All These Long-haired Fairies Should be Forced to Do Their Military Training, Maybe They Will Become Men", The End Conscription Campaign, Sexuality, Citizenship and Military Conscription in Apartheid South Africa', *South African Journal of Human Rights*, **20**, pp. 207–29.
Cooper, D. (1994), *Sexing the City: Lesbian and Gay Politics within the Activist State*, London: Rivers Oram Press.
Herman, D. (1998), *The Antigay Agenda: Orthodox Vision and the Christian Right*, Chicago: Chicago University Press.
Keen, L. and Goldberg, S.G. (2000), *Strangers to the Law: Gay People on Trial*, Ann Arbor: The University of Michigan Press.
Stein, A. (2001), *The Stranger Next Door: The Story of a Small Community's Battle over Sex, Faith and Civil Rights*, Boston, MA: Beacon Press.
Stychin, C. (1998), *Nation by Rights*, Philadelphia: Temple University Press.

Stychin, C. (2003), *Governing Sexuality: The Changing Politics of Citizenship and Law Reform*, Oxford: Hart.

Waaldijk, K. and Clapham, A. (1993), *Homosexuality: A European Community Issue*, Dordrecht: Martinus Nijhoff.

The Criminal Justice System

Alarid, L.F. (2000), 'Sexual Orientation Perspectives on Incarcerated Bisexual and Gay Men: The County Jail Protective Custody Experience', *Prison Journal*, **80**(1), March, pp. 80–95.

Farr, K.A. (2000), 'Defeminising and Dehumanising Female Murderers: Depictions of Lesbians on Death Row', *Women and Criminal Justice*, **11**(1), pp. 49–66.

Groombridge, N. (1999), 'Perverse Criminologies: The Closet Door of Dr. Lombroso', *Social and Legal Studies*, **8**(4), pp. 531–48.

Leinen, S. (1993), *Gay Cops*, New Brunswick, NJ: Rutgers University Press.

Morgan, W. (1994), 'Identifying Evil for What It Is: Tasmania, Sexual Perversity and the United Nations', *Melbourne University Law Review*, **19**, pp. 740–70.

Morgan, W. (1997), 'A Queer Kind of Law: The Senate Inquiries into Sexuality', *International Journal of Discrimination and Law*, **2**, pp. 317–32.

Rosga, A. (2000), 'Ritual Killings: Anti-gay Violence and Reasonable Justice', in J. James (ed.), *States of Confinement: Policing, Detention and Prisons*, New York: St Martins Press, pp. 172–90.

Tomsen, S. (2002), *Hatred, Murder and Male Honour: Anti-homosexual Homicides in New South Wales, 1980–2000*, Australian Institute of Criminological Research and Policy Series No. 43, Canberra: Australian Institute of Criminology.

Spatial Dimensions

Bell, D. and Valentine, G. (eds) (1995), *Mapping Desire*, London, Routledge.

Brown, M.P. (2000), *Closet Space: Geographies of Metaphor from the Body to the Globe*, London: Routledge.

Humphreys, L. (1970), *The Tearoom Trade*, London: Oxford: Duckworth.

Ingram, G.B., Bouthillette, A-M. and Retter, Y. (eds) (1997), *Queers in Space: Communities/Public Places/Sites of Resistance*, Seattle: Bay Press.

Mason, G. (1995), '(Out)laws: Acts of Proscription in the Sexual Order', in M. Thornton (ed.), *Public and Private: Feminist Legal Debates*, Oxford: Oxford University Press, pp. 66–88.

Moran, L.J. (2002), 'The Poetics of Safety: Lesbians, Gay Men and Home', in A. Crawford (ed.), *Crime, Insecurity, Safety in the New Governance*, Cullompton: Wilans Publishing, pp. 274–99.

Moran, L.J. and McGhee, D. (1980), 'Perverting London: Cartographic Practices of Policing', *Law and Critique*, **IX**(2), pp. 207–24.

Valentine, G. (1993), 'Negotiating and Managing Multiple Sexual Identities: Lesbian Time–Space Strategies', *Transactions of the Institute of British Geographers*, **18**, pp. 237–48.

The Workplace

Pamela D. Bridgewater and Brenda V. Smith (2002) 'Symposium, Homophobia in the Halls of Justice: Sexual Orientation Bias and Its Implications Within the Legal System', *American University Journal of Gender Social Policy and Law*, **11**, pp. 9–12.

Buhrke, R.A. (1997), *A Matter of Justice*, London: Routledge.

Burke, M. (1993), *Coming Out of the Blue*, London: Cassell.

Carolan, B. (1999), 'An Army of Lovers? Queering the Ministry of Defence Report of the Homosexual Policy Assessment Team', *Tulsa Law Journal*, **34**(3), pp. 555–66

Chapman, A. and Mason, G. (1999), 'Women, Sexual Preference and Discrimination Law: A Case Study of the NSW Jurisdiction', *Sydney Law Review*, **21**, pp. 525–66.

Collier, R. (1998), '"Nutty Professors", "Men in Suits" and "New Entrepreneurs": Corporeality, Subjectivity and Change in Law School and Legal Practice', *Social and Legal Studies*, **7**(1), March, pp. 27–53.

Hate

Comstock, G.D. (1991), *Violence against Lesbians and Gay Men*, New York: Columbia University Press.

GenderPAC (1997), *The First National Survey of Transgender Violence* at: http://www.gpac.org/violence/HateCrimeSurvey97/.

Jenness, V. and Broad, K. (1997), *Hate Crimes: New Social Movements and the Politics of Violence*, Hawthorne NY: Aldine deGruyter.

Jenness, V. and Grattet, R. (2001), *Building the Hate Crime Policy Domain: From Social Movement Concept to Law Enforcement Practice*, New York: Russell Sage.Foundation.

Herek, G.M. and Berill, K.T. (1992), *Hate Crimes*, London: Sage.

Howe, A. (1998), '*Green* v. *The Queen*: The Provocation Defence Finally Provoking its own Demise?', *Melbourne University Law Review*, **22**, pp. 466–86.

Janoff, D.V. (2005), *Homophobic Violence in Canada*, Toronto: University of Toronto Press.

Leventhal, B. and Lundy, S.E. (eds) (1999), *Same-Sex Domestic Violence*, Thousand Oaks, CA: Sage.

Loffreda, B. (2000), *Losing Matt Shepard: Life and Politics in the Aftermath of Anti-gay Murder*, New York: Columbia University Press.

Mason, G. (2001), *The Spectacle of Violence*, London: Routledge.

Mason, G. and Tomsen, S. (eds) (1997), *Homophobic Violence*, Sydney: Hawkins Press.

Kinship

Albany Symposium (2001), '"Family" and the Political Landscape for Lesbian, Gay, Bisexual and Transgender People', *Albany Law Review*.

Ball, C.A. (1997), 'Moral Foundations for a Discourse on Same-Sex Marriage: Looking Beyond Political Liberalism', *Georgetown Law Journal*, **85**, pp. 1872–912.

Butler, J. (2002), 'Is Kinship Always Already Heterosexual?', *Differences*, **13**(1) pp. 14–43.

De Vos, P. (2004), 'Same Sex Sexual Desire and the Re-imagining of the South African Family', *South African Journal of Human Rights*, **20**, pp. 179–206.

Goldberg Hiller, J. (2002), The Limits to Union, Ann Arbor: The University of Michigan Press.

Weeks, J., Heaphy, B. and Donovan, C. (2001), *Families of Choice and Other Life Experiments*, London: Routledge.

Wintemute, R. and Andenaes, M. (eds) (2001), *Legal Recognition of Same-sex Partnership: A Study of National, European and International Law*, Oxford: Hart.

The Cultural Turn

Chiu, M.C. (2004), '"Censorship = mission impossible?": A Postcolonial Same Sex Erotic Discourse on Hong Kong Porn Law', *International Journal of Sociology of Law*, **32**, pp. 39–63.

Dalton, D. (2000), 'The Deviant Gaze: Imagining the Homosexual as Criminal through Cinematic and Legal Discourses', in C. Stychin and D. Herman (eds), *Sexuality in the Legal Arena*, London: Athlone, pp. 69–83.

Herman, D. (2004), 'Juliet and Juliet Would Be More My Cup of Tea: Sexuality, Law and Popular Culture', in M. Freeman (ed.), *Law and Popular Culture: Current Legal Issues*, Vol. 7, Oxford: Oxford University Press, pp. 470–90.

Loizidou, E. (1998), 'Intimate Celluloid: Heavenly Creatures and Criminal Law', in L. Moran, D. Monk and S. Beresford (eds), *Legal Queeries,* London: Cassell, pp. 167–84.

Millbank, J. (2004), 'It's about This: Lesbians, Prison and Desire', in M. Freeman (ed.), *Law and Popular Culture: Current Legal Issues*, Vol. 7, Oxford: Oxford University Press, pp. 449–69.

Munt, S. (1994), *Murder by the Book?*, London: Routledge.

Films

Aileen: *Life and Death of a Serial Killer* (1999), Dir. Nick Bloomfield, USA.

Aileen Wuornos: *The Selling of a Serial Killer* (2002), Dir. Nick Bloomfield, USA.

Boys Don't Cry (1999), Dir. Kimberley Pierce, USA.

Monster (2003), Dir. Patty Jenkins, USA.

The Laramie Project (2002), Dir. Moises Kaufmann, USA.

Part I
Topics

Theorizing Sexual Identity

[1]

QUEER PROPERTY, QUEER PERSONS: SELF-OWNERSHIP AND BEYOND

MARGARET DAVIES

Flinders University of South Australia

ABSTRACT

The primary focus of this article is the relationship between property and personality with reference to the specific form of transgression offered by queer theory, that is, transgression of the conventional boundaries of sexual identity and desire. Feminists have strongly challenged the gendered nature of personal relations expressed through property – the association of masculinity with the position of proprietor and femininity with the position of object of property, which in its turn relies upon a fixed opposition between subject and object. It is argued here that attention to certain aspects of queer theory and praxis offers a further ground of critique and the potential for reconfiguration of these fundamental relationships.

The wish for one's own terms and one's proper identity, perhaps the most deeply private property of all, is an impossible desire since both are held in common with others in the community as an effect of the symbolic. (Tyler, 1997: 230)

But if this attribution of property is itself improperly attributed, if it rests on a denial of that property's transferability ... then the repression of that denial will constitute that system internally and, therefore, pose as the promising spectre of its destabilization. (Butler, 1993: 63)

INTRODUCTION

'PROPERTY' AND 'personality' are terms that are heavily theorised and debated in scholarly literature in disciplines as varied as psychology, law, economics, analytical philosophy and cultural studies. Both terms are also part of the everyday language we use to describe our selves, our relationships with others, and our relationships with external objects. Neither term points clearly to a single referent, and both are conceptualised in widely varying ways. It is therefore not possible to deploy either term without making a number of assumptions, and without – whether intentionally or not – raising a whole constellation of social, legal, political and economic associations.

In this article I have chosen to explore the relationship between property and personality through the lens of sexuality and its associated symbolism. My primary focus is upon private property, specifically its *privateness*, but I hope that some of the ideas that I am developing here will suggest new ways of conceptualising property per se, both private and collective. I regard my comments as a selective *reading* of property and personality as it appears in various discourses, which does not even approach a general description or theory: although this is a point I could make in relation to *any* scholarly writing, I wish to emphasise it here because of the obvious need to clear a path through a number of large and often contradictory bodies of literature.

SOME PROPERTIES OF PROPERTY

Technically speaking, property is a crystallisation of a number of legal rights and responsibilities. As such it has an unavoidably intersubjective element, meaning that although it may attach to a concrete or abstract object, 'property' is primarily a relation between legal subjects which has things as its focus.[1] For instance, my property in my piano is the legal *effect* of a system of legal rights and responsibilities (Eleftheriadis, 1996: 39): the quality 'mine' is attributed by law. Emphasis upon the idea that property is a 'bundle of rights' (such as the right to use, enjoy, possess, alienate, exclude, derive income), none of which – except perhaps excludability (Gray, 1991) – is *essential* to the legal construct of property, has led to some debate among legal scholars in the 20th century over whether 'property' is a distinct legal category at all (Penner, 1997).

At the same time, it is frequently observed that property also carries a particular cultural significance: the relational, mediating and dynamic side of property is often repressed in popular language, meaning that it also signifies a much more immediate, personal, sovereign power of a person over objects (Grey, 1980; Macpherson, 1978: 6–9; Waldron, 1988: 26–30). In both legal and popular language the term 'property' is frequently used to refer to the object, rather than to the right. Property is therefore a complex legal relationship, the character of which is highly contestable, and at the same time it is in everyday language a relatively stable reference to things that we own. To say that a legal concept is much more complex than an everyday concept is neither surprising nor usually of much significance. In the case of property, however, I believe it is of great significance: the first purpose of this paper is to indicate some of the ways in which the legal and social meanings of property interact, and why it is important to understand this interaction. I should therefore indicate at the outset that I will be referring to essentially two property concepts: the social and the legal, and hopefully it will be clear by the context which is uppermost at any given moment.

Property is also characterised by an immensely strong symbolic power and is both expressive and constitutive of the person (Nedelsky, 1991), as well as of class, sex and race differences. As I will indicate in more detail later, central social relationships, such as conventional heterosexual ordering, have been symbolised as relationships of ownership (Irigaray, 1985; Pateman, 1988). Moreover, property also obviously holds a central place in the economic order as the legally enforceable mechanism of commodification, enabling capitalist exchange. While it may be true that since the decline of Marxism as a universal explanation of oppression, 'the ownership of economic means of production, that is, property relations, cannot be seen as the source from which all forms of oppression flow' (Edgeworth, 1988: 101), it is also arguable that the metaphorical and symbolic power of property extends well beyond purely legal and state-enforced ownership regimes. The material effects of property are moreover not confined to those flowing from the central categories recognised by legal and economic discourse (see e.g. C. Harris, 1993). The forms of oppression which accumulate around the myth of property do not rest merely in formal legal relationships, but also in the way that property rhetoric is extended and used to structure the realm of the social. I believe the feminist literature already makes this point abundantly clear, but I raise it in a context intended to extend and further explore central feminist insights.

Clearly, therefore, the power of property arises in very complex economic, social and legal ways. Without losing sight of this complexity (but inevitably reducing it in various strategic ways), this article attempts to bring together several further thoughts. As I have indicated, the ways in which certain social hierarchies, in particular those organised around sex and sexuality, are constructed by and reflected in property relationships provide a critical starting point for an analysis of the symbolic power of property. Insofar as it provides a metaphor for personal identity through the notion of self-ownership, for instance, property takes on stereotypically masculine characteristics; but at the same time, the object of property is sometimes said to be structurally female, because the owner/owned, subject/object distinctions all correlate socially and epistemologically to the male/female distinction (Levi-Strauss, 1969; Wittig, 1992). Historical ownership of women by men and the objectification and commodification of women has been the basis of this correlation.

At the same time, arguably, the hierarchy of owner/owned which is expressed in any property relationship translates into other major social divisions, such as those delineated by race and class (Bell, 1988; C. Harris, 1993). The history of slavery, together with its philosophical and scientific justifications, expresses the association of hierarchically constructed race divisions with property relationships.[2] Ongoing processes of colonisation centrally involve constructions of property and racial propriety: this is evidenced in the non-recognition of indigenous custodianship of the land (J. Singer, 1991; Watson, 1997); in the exclusion of racial 'others' from the property of whiteness (C. Harris, 1993); and arguably in the continuing appropriation of the bodies and cultural knowledge of indigenous peoples by the forces of western intellectual property expansionism (Shiva, 1997; cf. Pottage, 1998). In each case appropriation is perpetuated and justified through the exclu-sionary structure of property and its association with a particular type of subject, or a particular type of knowledge. A second intention of this article is therefore to revisit analysis of the way in which the metaphor of property is used to support specific social divisions, and in particular the division male/female. Clearly I do not have space to summarise the whole of this literature or to evaluate it in any detail, but I do rely upon its central insights.

Finally, I have in mind queer attempts to disrupt any form of gendered dichotomies together with their heterosexual imperatives. Queer thinking, which I will outline in the next section, calls into question the myth of the stereotypically masculine liberal self which is based in part on the metaphor of property and which also provides a justification for individualisable private property. At the same time, queer thought aims to challenge what we might term the traditional property, or the exclusive terrain, of sexual categories. Queer offers the promise of subversion of historically entrenched social divisions, while – at least in the hands of theorists who retain a feminist consciousness – refusing to forget or gloss over the violence of existing social relationships, without, that is, undervaluing the fact that power attaches very firmly to certain established social identities (Walters, 1996), and that in order to achieve political recognition, deployment of an identity category is generally essential (Butler, 1993: 229). My third and final intention is therefore to explore queer subversion in relation to concepts of property and personal identity: does queer theory hold any distinct potential for demystifying and undermining both the subject/object distinctions inherent in property and/or the sexualised person figured through the property metaphor? Since gender is so heavily inflected with the thought of property, and since property is so deeply gendered, property is an ideal target for the queer. In its most promising moments, queer thinking may offer not only a critique of the conventional form of property, but also one of many paths towards an altered understanding and practice of property. However, like most social movements, the queer is not immune from the commodifying tendencies of capitalist culture (Hennessey, 1995). It therefore carries a danger that its subversive activities will be confined to a particular terrain, normalised, packaged and reappropriated.

The fascination of property is therefore the ways in which the various dimensions of the property as social myth and legal category interact in a multitude of inexpressibly complex ways. However, because the central social symbolism of property is of something fixed, certain, delimited and absolute, this symbolic and material mobility is forgotten or even repressed in a gesture which reinforces the ideology of centralised power and masks the underlying circulation of meanings.[3]

QUEER THEORY

Having made such a bold beginning, I should preface my comments by making clear that I am not entirely convinced that there is anything *specifically* queer to be said about this particular set of ideas. This is simply because there is not necessarily any distinct content to the notion of 'queer' in the first place. 'Queer' is a term that has been used in a variety of different ways, generally to indicate some deviation or position of marginalisation from whatever is regarded as sexually conventional. For instance, Carl Stychin says that 'Central to a queer identity . . . is the problematisation of categories of sexual identity and sexual propriety, as they have been historically constituted. Queerness in part suggests an unwillingness to fix difference . . .' (Stychin, 1995: 141; see also Jagose, 1996: 72–100). As Stychin points out, 'queer' need not refer to an identity category, but can also be taken to mean an attitude or an approach, the content of which may vary according to context. Queer theory may be antithetical or of little relevance to some types of feminism precisely because of its continuing attempt to destabilise identity categories, including the category 'woman' in its opposition to the category 'man' (cf. Irigaray, 1996: 35–41; Braidotti and Butler, 1997). At the same time, queer theory is continuous with much feminism which has itself challenged the stability of identity categories, foregrounded the social constructedness of both sex and gender, and critiqued the hierarchical nature of conventional relationships between men and women (Dale, 1997; Martin, 1994).

For me, 'queer' is a shorthand way of referring to what is a rather complex heritage of ideas, including (but not limited to) the postmodern critique of identity, feminist insights about the reproduction of hierarchy in (stereo-typical hetero-) sexual relationships, and lesbian and gay theory and practice which aims to call into question both the universality of this hierarchy and also the fact that it gains force as a social and legal presumption – to the ex-clusion of all other sexualities, whether lesbian, gay, bisexual, transgendered or heterosexual, which do not reflect the dominant norms. Whether queer theory is a distinct intellectual enterprise is not an answerable question: it gains distinctness by virtue of claiming a (provisional) space, and by bring-ing together a variety of approaches, but by its very nature queer theory works against proprietorship of ideas as well as identities. Therefore it is only to be expected that the insights generated by any queer analysis may also be said to be consistent with, though not reducible to, strands of postmodern-ism, feminism or lesbian/gay theory.

In fact, if anything may be said with certainty about the 'queer' it is that it owes its existence to a certain position of marginality, or transgression of intellectual frontiers, and that it does not 'own' any particular conceptual terrain (Butler, 1997), any more than it is 'owned' as a discourse by any group of people. The anti-ownership stance of the queer is, indeed, integral to its relationship to property, as I will explain. The difficulty here is that identity as property – that is, identity which is exclusive, separate, categorised and recognised by the state – is generally a desirable prerequisite for access to the social discourses which distribute power through a myriad of social, politi-cal, economic, legal or cultural sources. For instance, the category 'woman' is the basis for oppressive ideas and practices, but it is also the source of strength and visibility for feminist activism. Any attempt – queer or otherwise – to dismantle unilaterally a recognised source of actual or potential social power would appear to be unwise (Robson, 1998). Yet identity categories themselves can be the occasion for mainstream stereotyping: they can be stifling and, in their turn, oppressive to those who are marginalised within the category. At its best, queer thought expresses precisely these dilemmas (Stychin, 1995: 141), attempting to denaturalise sexual identity, while remaining sensitive to current distributions of power. At the same time, 'queer' carries the very real danger that points of resistance to mainstream culture will be disempowered in the name of multiple identities.

A further difficulty concerns the consequences of a queer collision with mainstream culture, in particular what may be termed a reciprocal capitalising on the (cultural and economic) capital of queerness. After only a brief history, the queer already finds itself drawing upon the commodity form as a way of gaining visibility – by relaxing into a queer identity, by participating in the fetishizing of queerness (Hennessey, 1995), or by installing academic icons of queer theory who appear to have some essentialised place in a definable territory. Within and beyond its own contingent borders the queer has become implicated in the commodity culture. Whether these mainstreaming forces provide an opportunity to subvert from a position which is neither outside nor inside, or a slow death by appropriation, or something of both, will depend on the extent to which a self-reflective dynamic can be maintained by queer academics and activists.

To speak of queer property, then, is itself a rather ambiguous and in many respects politically sensitive project which must be undertaken as a contingent, even tentative, exploration. Property – at least in the popular and traditional conceptions I have alluded to – is basically straight, and I mean that it reflects and enforces a conventional heterosexual symbolism which is hierarchical, and also that it relies on the possibility of exclusivity and separation in the objects it seeks to classify (Gray, 1991). In queer theory the relevant opposition is not between heterosexuality and lesbian/gay theory or practice, but rather between what might be called 'the queer mind' and what Wittig called 'the straight mind'. Heterosexual practices may be queer insofar as they do not reflect the dominant cultural norms associated with heterosexuality (Walters, 1996), but queer is not straight in that it is consciously critical of both the presumption of heterosexuality, and of conventional heterosexual symbolism and categories. Queer thought deliberately works against exclusivity and separation in its approach to classification. In contrast to queer thinking which resists the frequently supposed uniformity and singularity of straight laws (cf. Stychin, 1995: 147), the everyday concept of property that I have referred to above establishes a realm of the same, a closed field subject to a unitary law. Queer property is therefore about as odd a juxtaposition as queer law, or queer nation, or even queer theory. But of course as several writers have noted, queer does not destroy boundaries but lives on the edge, parasitical upon the norms it seeks to critique. After all, as Judith Butler says, 'normalising the queer would be . . . its sad finish' (Butler, 1997: 25).

Of course, it is arguable that property in its technical sense is already somewhat queer, because it has lost its distinct identity, meaning that the relationship of the person to the object is no longer hierarchical and direct, but rather is mediated by the complexity of multiple legal relations. Owning is therefore not as straightforward a path to power as it perhaps once was, even though the social meaning of property still reflects and in some ways enables a distinct correlation between property and power. I will come back to this briefly later.

PROPERTY AND IDENTITY: THE LAW OF THE SELF

I would like to proceed by explaining some of the issues which arise out of the relationship between property and personality, and to situate the question of sexuality and self-ownership within this framework. The relationship between property and personality has several dimensions, which I will very briefly summarise.[4] In the first place, Locke's understanding was that a person has property in him-/herself, and he appeared to regard this not only as a symbol for personal autonomy and rights, but as a natural law of self-ownership which could give rise to substantive rights over the world's resources (Locke, 1690/1960: 285–302). The one relatively simple (though often hotly debated) premise thus generated a picture of radical state-of-nature equality, while expressing a justification for unlimited individual appropriation (Macpherson, 1962: 230–1), as well as colonial appropriation of what were regarded as vacant or under-exploited territories (Shiva, 1997: 3; Staves, 1994: 140–2).

At the simplest level, the notion that we may have some natural relationship of ownership to ourselves leads to a bafflingly large range of philosophical issues about, for instance, the status of human tissue, of our public 'identity', of our relationship to our persons (Radin, 1993), and our ability to exclude others from our bodies or our persons broadly conceived. Such philosophical questions have their counterparts in medical law (J. Harris, 1996; Magnusson, 1988), reproductive law (Nedelsky, 1993), intellectual property law (Dangelo, 1989), labour law and criminal law (Naffine, 1997). Whether it is played out on a legal, ethical, cultural or symbolic level, any such conception of actual self-ownership assumes at some point a divided self – that which owns, and that which is owned, which may be the body, the mental capacities, or as in the intellectual property sphere, some more nebulous 'identity' (Davies, 1994: 381–2; Naffine, 1998).

On a symbolic level, this division of the subject-self from the object-self is, for instance, suggested by the famous first line in Catharine MacKinnon's first *Signs* article which states that sexuality for women is most one's own, and most taken away (MacKinnon, 1982: 515). Without going into detail about the various implications of this statement, I would simply comment that if we accept that identity is at least partly an intersubjective, cultural construction and not simply a pre-social attribute,[5] then the 'taking' (perhaps more accurately a giving) of an identity or an aspect of it is in some senses inevitable. There is a sense in which identity is *never* one's own, but a culturally determined aspect of one's person. (I am white, with North European ancestors, born and raised in the mainstream culture of Australia: this is 'my' identity – but in what sense is it 'mine'? How does the general culturally created identity interact with the identities encouraged by the smaller communities through which I have moved during my life?) The implication that there is simply some pre-socially 'owned' sexuality which is 'taken' from women, a sex which becomes a gender, is therefore one I disagree with, but there can still be a very severe disjunction between what one feels as one's identity (whatever its source) and a dominant cultural construction of it. Indeed, the queer subversion of the self-owning person lies partly in the uncovering and exploitation of such disjunctions, for instance in the uncoupling of sex and gender.

These complexities and possibilities are not consistently recognised by the central liberal model of self-ownership, which would have each person as the author and owner of his/her own personality.[6] Even so, without acknowledging the fact that the 'I' who owns and the 'me' who is owned may themselves be an effect of linguistic and cultural messages, the self-ownership paradigm does rely upon a divided, non-self identical, person (Hegel, 1821/1967: section 47): the dichotomising of the self into subject and object which the liberal notion of self-ownership requires, therefore sets up at the very least a possibility that the object side of one's personality may, if not legally, at least symbolically or socially, be object to some subject other than one's self. In other words, the structure of the self-ownership rhetoric inaugurates the very serious possibility of appropriation by another, and the consequential strategic need to draw upon the self-ownership paradigm in order to ensure that any such appropriation does not exceed the bounds of liberal morality (which can be fairly loose, often stopping only at slavery).[7] Paradoxically, the condition for autonomy and individual sovereignty is already a division within the self.

In addition to the liberal concept of *self*-ownership, property in external objects is sometimes said to constitute the human being as a person. In feudal societies a person was legally and socially defined by his/her position in relation to a fixed hierarchy of property and power (Noyes, 1936: 226–7). In post-feudal society, the rigidity of the structure was relaxed: while one of the attributes of legal personality remains the *ability* to own, this is supposedly a *power* of persons – it is not necessary actually to own anything in order to be a legal person. It is no longer the case that only the propertied can enjoy the full potential of legal personality, although it is also undoubtedly true that so-called 'rights' are sometimes meaningless without property. In reality, only the wealthy can protect both their reputation and their interest in free speech, although these benefits of law are formally constructed as available to all.

The counterpoint to the formal legal dissociation of property from recognition of personality, is that proprietorial relationship to the world of external things is still socially, and sometimes philosophically, assumed to define the person. For instance Margaret Radin, drawing upon Hegel, has argued that ownership is important to the way the person is constituted socially, and that therefore the law should pay particular attention to protecting 'property for personhood', as opposed to mere fungible or commodifiable property (Radin, 1993; 35–71). Radin's pragmatic view is based upon an appreciation of the actual social and political importance of property for individuality: given a particular social configuration and political ideology, she asks how it is possible for the law to respond to the needs of persons, and in particular disempowered persons, within this context (Radin, 1993; 6). The main difficulty with this approach is that by taking a particular ideology (property for personhood) as a given, it does not sufficiently reflect upon the ways in which that ideology may also contribute to social division. Having said that, no reform is immune to criticism, and we do need seriously to think about ensuring that encroaching commodification of persons and personal attributes does not result in merely reconfigured oppressions.

Radin is undoubtedly right to emphasise that in addition to owning themselves, the ability to own (conquer, appropriate, control) external things is in western society a constituting feature of the person – sometimes to the extent that the person extends into the physical world of objects associated with her or him, such as cars or houses.[8] The widespread notion that persons have some sort of natural right to own property draws upon the idea that human personhood necessarily contains within it an ability and a need to control external resources. Ideologically, property defines an area of privacy, of personal autonomy and personal sovereignty (Reich, 1991) so that the owner has a much greater sphere of protected rights than the non-owner. This is one of the ways in which the ideology of property is in serious conflict with the ideology of equality (cf. Nedelsky, 1991).

Historically and conceptually, the association of property-ownership with the ideal of self-ownership, enforces and reinforces the alignment of the male owner with the male subject who is autonomous and who owns. Ownership is only justified where the person can be said to own him-/herself and his/her destiny, and of course, this norm culturally applies much more easily to the wealthy male subject. If the subject is not self-owning, then self-ownership as a justification for private property is itself under question. I will return to this matter at the end of the article.

These notions – ownership of the self and ownership of the other as definitive of the self – are therefore not philosophically distinct. Locke's idea was basically that self-ownership provided a *justification* for the ownership of external things, through the mechanism of mixing one's labour with the external world (Locke, 1960: 287–8). In contrast, Hegel argued that a person achieves concrete personality, including self-possession and recognition by others, *as a consequence* of appropriating external things (Hegel, 1821/1967: section 41). In both cases, ownership therefore becomes a necessary element of personhood, and is justified for that reason.

In addition to these two very important aspects of the property/personality problem, I would add a third dimension which arises perhaps as a consequence of the self-ownership ideal. It concerns simply the way in which the person is figured through the metaphor of property and in particular through the notion of excludability and the consequential territorial space attributed to persons. Jennifer Nedelsky has written of the 'bounded self', a concept of the self which draws on the property metaphor, encodes property, if you like, *as* the notion of the self, so that the person, like property, becomes exclusive, territorial and singular, all characteristics of the liberal person which are culturally male (Nedelsky, 1991; cf. Naffine, 1997). I will discuss this masculine side of the self-ownership metaphor in the next section. Traditional and popular notions of property also presuppose a particular version of the person: the sovereign self-empowering and separate subject. The person and the idea of property are therefore conceptually inextricable – property metaphors define the boundaries of the self, and the person determines the shape of property.

On an even more abstract level, we have the metaphysical concept of the proper itself, which is basically a family of ideas, metaphors and assumptions running through western philosophy. As it has been explained by Derrida, the 'metaphysics of the proper' is not an explicit philosophy. It is rather the groundwork, or assumed framework, within which western philosophy operates (Davies, 1998; Derrida, 1974: 26). The proper names the characteristics of the person and property which are pure, exclusive, singular, appropriate, self-defining and legitimate. It is the metaphysics of the proper which makes it so difficult to move beyond the same/other and subject/object distinctions, which are our foundations for the concepts of both self-referential identity and ownership. On the level of social existence, the proper as propriety names a certain socially acceptable behaviour and position. (As such, the proper is precisely the target of the queer, which, whatever else it may or may not be, is certainly not proper.) According to Carol Rose, one of the functions of property as propriety 'is to accord to each person or entity what is "proper" or "appropriate" to him or her . . .' (Rose, 1991: 232). Importantly, therefore, and as one would expect, the notion of the proper person, personality defined through the metaphor of the proper and property, carries class and race connections – the proper is opposed to the common, just as the owner is opposed to the slave – as well as encoding a stereotype of masculinity. I say that these correlations are expected primarily because of the historical relationship of property, masculinity, whiteness and class to legal subjectivity. However, it is also my view that this symbolism has not been lost with attempts to create a formally egalitarian society, and is still influential in the construction of the legal, civic and social person.

Before proceeding, I wish briefly to locate this configuration of ideas in a practical setting. On the level of the legal conceptualisation, there has been historically a separation and hierarchisation of the concepts of the person and property. Basically, the person is not, and cannot be, property (Naffine, 1998). The person is also in theory valued over property. The law has traditionally resisted the notion that a person may legally 'own' her or his body, attributes, identity, because it would debase and potentially commodify the person. This is so even though the metaphor of self-ownership would suggest that we somehow naturally own ourselves (cf. J. Harris, 1996), and even though it has been suggested that a property paradigm may be the most appropriate to express in legal terms the sorts of control one should have over oneself with respect to others (Bray, 1990; Radin, 1993). Since the abolition of slavery, nor can any other legally recognised person be owned: the move which elevates a human being to the status of 'person' is also supposed to ensure that they are not the object of another person's property.

Of course, I should qualify this by stating that whether one has property in one's person or in that of another in the legal context all depends completely on what is recognised as property and, to a lesser extent, on what is regarded as the person in which one potentially has property. While on the one hand the law may officially distinguish between property and persons, so that the two cannot get confused, it may be that in all sorts of legal relationships we can find a property-like dimension with a person as the object, or a set of relationships which are tantamount to property in a person, though not named as such.[9] It is only where property is conceptualised as a formal and legally enforced sovereignty over an object that it is possible to state generally that there is no property in the person, or in the person of another human being.

So whether property in the self or in others is legally recognisable must depend in large part on what is meant by 'property'. It also seems to me that as a result of both technology and the limitless bounds of intellectual property, the lines between the person and property are beginning to blur in the law. The patenting of cell lines from indigenous populations provides an example where one legal person may be said to 'own' an aspect of another (Shiva, 1997). The various ways in which the law protects the celebrity's marketing of his/her image, which is explicitly a property relationship in the United States of America, is an example of self-ownership (Dangelo, 1989; Frow, 1995; B. Singer, 1991).

As a final comment upon this matter, which I will develop further shortly, let me say that where property has the character of sovereignty over an object, self-ownership is primarily sovereignty over the self – individualist and demarcated by conceptually clear frontiers. Where property is a relationship to others, and not simply the ability to exclude them from a protected area, the person will take on a completely different character.

PROPERTY AND SEX

Let me continue by considering the sex of the concept of property, as opposed to the sex of the stereotypical owner. I will state it bluntly – does the concept of property have a sex or a gender? Now this may seem to be a rather odd question, but I raise it as one aspect of the property/personality configuration.

First, there is a long and distinguished feminist tradition which highlights and attacks the literal and figural commodification of women. Women are propertised in the economy of male ownership and property is feminised, as in the boat or car which is referred to as 'she'. Jeanne Schroeder is a feminist Lacanian property analyst, who has been very explicit about the place of property in a heterosexual economy. She argues that:

> ... property serves a function in law parallel to the function of The Woman in the psyche. They are both types of the 'Phallus' in the sense of the psycho-analytic term for the object of desire. Both property, according to Hegelian philosophy, and the Feminine, according to Lacanian psychoanalysis, are fictions we write to serve as the defining external objects enabling us to constitute ourselves as acting subjects. By serving as objects of exchange between subjects, property and the Feminine simultaneously enable subjects to recognise other humans as individual subjects – they enable us to desire and to be desired. (Schroeder, 1995: 816)

According to Schroeder there is not just an *analogy* between women and property. It is rather that they perform the same symbolic function in defining and mediating masculine subjectivity:

> When men speak of possessing a woman in sexual intercourse, they do not make an analogy to the possession of real property as the right to enter and the power to prevent others from entering. The two are not merely similar; they are psychoanalytically identical. (Schroeder, 1994a: 255)

Thus Schroeder's characterisation of the relationship between women and property emphasises their symbolic function. Both are objects of desire to be exclusively possessed in a masculine economy. Although I remain unconvinced of the necessity of the psychoanalytical framework in reaching this understanding, and although I am wary of the potential normalisation of women's lack of subjectivity in psychoanalytical thought, it does represent a descriptive tool which – if not taken literally – may be of some value. I will come back to this briefly in the next section.

Although her analysis is more explicitly psychoanalytical than most, Schroeder is only one of many theorists to notice a parallel between the function of property as a means of exchange and communication between men, and the role of women as objects of mediation. We know of Levi-Strauss, for instance, who described the socio-economic function of women as objects of exchange between men, thereby constituting the means of communication and contract between men (Levi-Strauss, 1969). In very different ways, a number of feminists, such as Pateman, Irigaray and Wittig (who explicitly compares women as a class to the feudal class of serfs), have analysed and critiqued the ownership paradigm of heterosexual relations (Irigaray, 1985; Pateman, 1988; Wittig 1992).[10] It is important to emphasise that the feminist critiques attack not only the symbolic or metaphorical construction of heterosexual relations through the concept of property, but also the material conditions of heterosexual existence, and most importantly the non-reducability of meaning to materiality, and vice-versa.

Feminists have adopted a variety of approaches to combat this structure of male ownership of women. The very successful liberal feminist strategy has been to insist that women too can be subjects and owners, and therefore cannot be the objects of property. Feminists have sometimes rejected the notion of self-ownership because of its potential to commodify (Nedelsky, 1993), and sometimes defended some version of it on the basis that it increases symbolic and actual autonomy (Radin, 1993). As Nedelsky comments, 'property looks to some like the perfect vehicle to power and autonomy and to others like the path to oppression' (Nedelsky, 1993: 350). A somewhat different approach is adopted by Irigaray who suggests a little enigmatically that the commodities might refuse to go to market (Irigaray, 1985: 197), thus rendering it powerless. Whatever else it means, such a suggestion draws on Irigaray's argument that a mimetic engagement with, and reiteration of, gender categories provides a path to rewriting gender and sexual relationships within the framework of dualistic sex difference.

On the other hand, and taking a very different approach to the feminists who have emphasised the centrality of property in the hierarchy of sex, is James Penner, who at the beginning of his recent book entitled The *Idea of Property in Law* presents a somewhat masculinised picture of property:

> Here property, have a drink. Let us light your cigarette for you. Now just start with something simple, something we all understand. What sort of company have you been keeping? Come on, no idea is an island. You say your marriage to Gift has broken down? That's terrible. And been spending all your time with that hustler Contract, hanging around in the market place, have you? Well, well, well, that explains a lot. (Penner, 1997: 1)

In need of some serious therapy, property is suffering an identity crisis, possibly even a sexuality crisis, although this is my own speculation. Property is moreover having some marital problems with its spouse, Gift. Penner does not explicitly sex Gift or Property, and in fact he is careful to use the male pronoun throughout his book, consistently marking all characters – which include a corpse, a doctor, a slave, a prostitute, a trustee, a cashier – as male. Thus the marriage between Gift and Property in Penner's opening metaphor may even be a gay marriage, but I do not think so. (What would property look like if s/he was gay or lesbian?) The purpose of The *Idea of Property in Law* is to restore the confidence of property in its own identity, and to rescue the marital bond from irreconcilable difference by ensuring gift's centrality to property's identity (Penner, 1997: 88–90). Slightly intemperately, and probably reading far too much into a simple metaphor, I am inclined to suggest that an underlying message here is that it is important to ensure property's strongly hetero nature by retaining the feminine complement, and foreclosing the possibility that it does not go queer or degenerate in the manner of Posner's rabid market (cf. Posner, 1992). More moderately, and despite his intentions, the concept of property defended by Penner reflects cultural norms of masculinity, especially insofar as it is regarded as a definable positive object with clear boundaries and an ascertainable and dominant place within the legal context. Interestingly, Penner's metaphor also suggests even more strongly the traditional owning class alignments of property, and what he sees as its currently debased company: no wonder the concept of property is having an identity crisis when he is hanging around in the market place (cf. Rose, 1991: 232–5). The suggestion is that property is made for better, more aristocratic, things. While I am talking about class, I should also mention that the more proprietorial dimensions of the queer also carry particular class alignments – the queer does tend to reflect, if not aristocratic, at least middle class values and concerns (cf. Hennessey, 1995: 33)

The masculinity of property as a metaphor is emphasised in a systematic fashion by Jennifer Nedelsky who draws on the feminist critique of social constructions of masculine separation and self-sufficiency and feminine fluidity and interdependence (Nedelsky, 1991). Not only does property act as a symbol for individual rights (attaching centrally to wealthy white men and only by extension to others) and a method of ordering our social relationships, it also structures our notion of corporeal autonomy, since women's bodies are regarded as essentially penetrable, while the male body is constructed as exclusive and impenetrable. Nedelsky comments that 'When boundary is central and intercourse is violation, women come to be seen and experienced as something less than fully human' (Nedelsky, 1991: 170; see also Naffine, 1997). She argues strongly that the answer is not to 'try to shore up women's boundaries' (Nedelsky, 1991) but rather to develop a relational notion of autonomy for women and men which recognises the value and importance of human co-operation and interdependence.

TRAJECTORIES

We can see some tension, therefore, in the sexual identification of property, which could be explained in several different ways. Insofar as it is an external object against which the self is measured and defined, property is feminised, and insofar as it is a separated, exclusive and autonomous self with proper boundaries, property is masculinised. Equally, the concrete, bodily aspect of property (the thing owned) is female, while the conceptual, abstract, sovereign dimension is male. *Being* property characterises the female condition, while *having* it denotes self-owning masculinity. Sex identity is determined by one's relationship to property, which seems simply to reinstate the sexual hierarchy: whether one is an object of property or a person/proprietor determines one's identity as female or male.

As a feminist I regard the critique of this structure to be of immense importance – on a strategic level so that the current social basis of personal power may be better understood and exploited (or challenged) by women and on a more ideal level so that we can begin to imagine other ways of understanding sexual difference which do not reduce to a subject/male–object/female dichotomy. Even if private property is here to stay – and I must admit that my utopian self would like to imagine its elimination – there is undoubtedly a need to expose the power relations embedded in cultural constructions of property, as well as undertaking the more traditional left-wing project of critiquing the distributional effects of certain policies or ideologies.

To this end, I would like to suggest that there is more sexual ambivalence to be uncovered here. The woman/property and man/proprietor associations rely on relatively stable and self-contained notions of both persons and property, in particular upon a fixed and stereotyped distinction between person and property. It is at this point that the queer emerges as a potential supplement – but as I have said a dangerous one – to feminist approaches to property. As I have briefly indicated above, feminist arguments have had women taking over the role of proprietor equally with men; refusing our object status, or alternatively reconfiguring it; adopting a property metaphor for the body, or rejecting it; and so on. All of these are very important strategies. All involve what might be identified as a 'queer moment' – a transgression of sexual normality in the sense of a crossing of the boundaries of conventional femininity.

However, it is also possible to challenge the theoretical foundations for the system itself, and in particular the fixity of the property/person division. That which I would identify as a 'queer' take on property might involve some crossing over between subject and object, and between the masculine position and the feminine position in property and in the construction of individual personality. Such an approach as I understand it would not be antithetical to any feminism which does not universalise sexual difference, as long as the critique of the power relations within gender is not forgotten. The thoughts outlined in the rest of this article indicate some of the ways in which cracks in the property/person distinction have been identified, and what can be made of these points of ambivalence.

HAVING AND/IS BEING ('I HAVE, THEREFORE I AM/MALE')

The legal concept of property has for some time been going much the same way as its counterpart, identity. For many years now, at least in some areas of philosophy and certainly in feminist thought, we have been speaking of a notion of identity which is relational, contextual, discursively constructed, not underpinned by any essential thing, and which is not entirely stable.[11] The subject is not separable from the social, symbolic and material context within which it is located. The property which is one's personal identity turns out not to be personal at all but rather 'held in common by others in the community as an effect of the symbolic' (Tyler, 1997: 230). Similarly, we could say that private property is held by virtue of communal relations as an effect of the legal. The sovereignty description of property has been superseded, but not entirely replaced, by an appreciation of the way that property is primarily a constructed legal category, not a natural sovereignty over things, and as such has the character of a complex of relationships between persons, not simply a relationship to a thing which confers rights over persons (Eleftheriadis, 1996). There always is an object of property, but this is an effect of the relations between persons, and may be differently constituted in different cases. In other words, the object of property does not exist *as* property but for the legally defined relationships which constitute it as such. There is no essential character of property: it gives rise to a variety of rights, responsibilities and powers but these vary according to the context (Gray, 1991) and are, moreover, in constant flux as the range of potential objects increases to incorporate, for instance, cyberspace (Radin, 1996) and cultural heritage (Herrera, 1994).

Having said that, culturally both property and personality retain a strong connection with the essential, the authentic, the permanent, the territorial and the individual. It is therefore not possible to speak simply of a single discourse of either property or the person: in both cases a decentring, de-essentialising understanding has offered a critique and alternative to the modernist view, which nonetheless remains in certain areas undisturbed and central, and in others retains a certain ideological force. Although some have argued that the modern understanding of property leads to its 'disintegration' (Grey, 1980; Edgeworth, 1988), in fact it is equally plausible to see it as the key which unlocks the potential of universal commodification (Schroeder, 1994a: 243–4). In spite of its legal transformation, property has not yet left behind the symbolism of sovereignty, personal power and masculine control of a feminine other, meaning that instead of disintegration, what we have is arguably an increased realm in which this symbolism can operate.[12] To my mind, there is no simple truth here, but rather a raging conflict: is property dead, or has it taken over the world? Does the process of taking over the world inevitably involve the dilution and ultimate disappearance of property as a central method of structuring our relationships, or will everything become subject to increasingly limited and proprietorial thinking?

As I have indicated above, feminists have adopted a number of important responses to these sexualised subject/object alignments. But I want to ask whether queer theory has the potential to reinvent property itself, just as it reinvents the person and the relationship of the person to sexuality. What does it mean for property and property symbolism if the relation between the subject-self and the objectifiable world is not marked by an absolute frontier? What if the distinction between having and being is a socially enforced illusion which in its more rigid manifestations engenders a sameness and otherness of violent proportions and effect? What if this illusion is shattered? What if the one, same self who provides the justification for ownership is all along an other? Where would this leave the sexual affiliations of property, let alone property itself?

I should make it clear that I do not claim that queer as a theory and practice has in fact managed to create a new understanding of property – clearly, as I have indicated earlier, queer is itself becoming a commodity. Rather, at the risk of sounding prescriptive, my claim is that because having and being are culturally so interwoven, any questioning of 'being' must bring with it – at some level – a questioning of 'having': failure to notice the interdependence of these ideas could simply lead to the re-stereotyping or re-freezing of the identities which are otherwise subject to transgression. Property is potentially a rich target for queer theory, but silent acceptance of established modes of 'having' may undermine the very possibility of reconfiguring 'being'.

In order to begin to elaborate on these matters, I would like to return briefly to Schroeder's psychoanalytic description of the symbolic position of women as the objects mediating the construction of masculine subjectivity. While acknowledging that 'Lacan's theory is virulently misogynist' (Schroeder, 1994a, 318), like Irigaray, Schroeder appears to accept Lacan's fundamental proposition that there is a *necessary* structural difference between the masculine and the feminine written into the symbolic order. Therefore the feminist strategy for Schroeder, as for the European 'sexual difference' feminists, is to *reconfigure* the relationship between masculine and feminine, not to envisage or work towards a queer transgression of the structural dichotomy in sexual symbolism. Schroeder's feminist strategy involves 'the rewriting of the myth of the Feminine as an active mediatrix' which 'requires the creation of feminine subjectivity' (Schroeder, 1994a: 318; cf. 1994b: 165–71). Like Irigaray, Schroeder does not reject the basic sexual dichotomy, but argues instead that *within* our category, it is possible for women to invent a subjectivity, to be active, not passive or invisible, while fulfilling the seemingly necessary function of object-ness or mediation.

Now, psychoanalysis appears to me to be unhelpful in some respects, and especially insofar as it appears to entrench this ontologically stable distinction between the masculine and the feminine. But I do want to ask what may be several naive, but not novel, questions: if the object of property is analogous to the Feminine as a sort of universalised object of desire, what happens when it is women who are doing the desiring? Who is Schroeder's subject who needs the feminine to constitute itself as a subject? Why must the mediating role be characterised as 'feminine', and why is it necessary to adopt such a clearly differentiated gender configuration? There are undoubtedly answers to these questions to be found within psychoanalysis, but the point is also a political one. While I certainly accept the feminist argument that female identity is a politically charged category which makes activism and change possible, I regard this as a strategic necessity, not an ontological one which would lock us into a sexual difference per se.

Judith Butler's 'lesbian phallus' is of some interest here: she has proposed in a rather complex argument that 'having' and 'being' the object of a sexualised property in the heterosexual economy are not necessarily clearly distinguishable (Butler, 1993). This is where the argument starts to become distinctly queer. To simplify rather brutally, in Lacanian theory as Schroeder points out, women are considered to be the phallus, while men have it or own it. Similarly, classical notions of the person demand that a person who is able to own property, is not herself or himself property, whereas the human being who is owned is not a person. The modern resistance to any relationship which would overtly commodify a person owes its force to this logic. One may either *have* property or *be* property. Now, as I have indicated there is already some tension in this distinction when it is applied to the concept of self-ownership, because that implies that one simultaneously is and owns oneself. Having and being oneself defines the person.

Butler argues essentially that the logic of Lacan's system can accommodate a phallus which is 'transferable or plastic property' (Butler, 1993: 62), meaning that it *need not* be attached symbolically to any particular body part, that it does reappear in mutated forms detached from male bodies, and that therefore having it and being it are not necessarily structurally distinct. Therefore, according to Butler, the subversive potential of phallic imagery lies in the fact that, as property, the phallus is subject to appropriation or transfer, and therefore is *capable* of reappearing in places – such as within the structure of lesbian sexuality – where it does not conventionally belong. The reappearance of the signifier of masculinity in an *improper* place emphasises its contingency and the contingency of the power relations it brings. We could even say that the phallus is like intellectual property, which obtains its economic value by a legal fiction restricting its use and therefore creating an artificial scarcity. Intellectual property involves removing a creation from common use in order to give it value, which it does not have 'naturally' since an object of intellectual property is infinitely reproducible (Drahos, 1996: 22). (A loaf of bread runs out, but a computer program can be reproduced over and over, and therefore has no physical limitations to its use. Limitations on use which create the object's value must be artificially created by law: this is done through copyrights, trademarks or patents.) Returning an object of intellectual property to the commons would devalue it, and undermine or even destroy its own status as property. Similarly, the attachment of the phallus as property to masculinity is what gives both masculinity and the phallus their particular status: to argue that the phallus is transferable and plastic suggests not only the devaluation of the imagery as property, but also the subversion of the system which would fix it to a particular group of persons.

Undoubtedly Butler is in part trying to make a point about the psychoanalytic division between masculine and feminine, but in my view the argument can be made without buying into the Lacanian system. On a more simple level, we could generalise first that it is possible to be socially mapped in conflicting ways, according to one's sex, sexuality, personal choices, and so on, and that 'masculine' and 'feminine' are floating signifiers which may become detached from their normalised positions. Second, that the adoption and transformation of heterosexual symbols within lesbian (or gay) culture, while unavoidable, may also pose a challenge to predominant heterosexual symbolism (as well as to the 'purity' of lesbian culture).[13] Butler's intention appears to be to point out the ambivalence in the conventional markers of heterosexuality – not to accept uncritically the psychoanalytical model, but to challenge the assumption of a stable male/female distinction which runs through it. However, what is most interesting about her views is the explicit connection she draws between property and sexed positioning in the symbolic order, and her discussion of having and being, which sets up the property relationship.

For my purposes, such a line of reasoning signals a reconsideration of the dimensions of proprietorship itself – what it involves, and what its dangers are. Some theorists have suggested that a breakdown or subversion of the subject/object distinction will be emancipatory in our ethical relationships (Laclau, 1996: 1), and it seems to me that one aspect of this is a deconstruction of the boundaries between having and being. In particular, the conventional logic which specifies that having (the phallus/a woman/an object of property) is the foundation for being (male) and that being (property/female, etc.) precludes having, is open to reinvention. If property is a complex of relations, and if the person is not simply sovereign, perhaps we may at once have and be property. Patricia Williams has suggested, for example, that rights, including the right to private property ought to be given away freely in an effort to reformulate the individuation of subjects set apart from objects 'so that we may say not that we own gold, but that a luminous golden spirit owns us' (Williams, 1987: 401). The tantalising thought here is that being does not have to be understood as a natural condition or a reflection of our individual efforts at appropriation, but rather may be regarded as a gift in process – connecting the self in perpetuity to the other, and implying a constant effort at reconciliation, rather than domination.

This may all appear to be rather abstract: the central point is that the a queer reading of the relationship between having and being might be seen as posing a challenge to the distinction between person and property – not only to its gendered associations, but also to the structure of property as a grant of personal sovereignty. On the practical level, it is possible to understand the legal relationship between personal rights and property as – in some elementary sense – involving a coming together of self and other, rather than simple domination of the other by the owner. For instance, increasing recognition that property carries both rights and responsibilities (Eleftheriadis, 1996: 40–1) – we own the object, but it also owns us, in that it limits our behaviour – may in fact signal some fundamental movement away from the modern liberal view of the proprietor as sovereign. If my ownership is limited by the interests of others, then the property is a relationship between us, not merely an extension of my personality. (I would like to emphasise that this is not a description of property – which would erase the hierarchical power embedded in current social and legal property configurations – but rather a reading which illustrates a possible reconstruction, far off though it may be.)

QUEER PERSONS AND QUEER PROPERTY

In a more general sense, this ambivalence in the having/being distinction in property may be expressed as the non-reducibility of personal identity to exclusive self-ownership. As I indicated earlier, self-ownership, self-possession, self-identity are all models which attempt to collapse identity into itself, but which inevitably rely upon a fragmented person, and a person who at once is, and has possession of, him-/herself. Current thinking about identity has taken the notion of fragmentation much further: personal identity is not an essence which can in any simple sense own even another aspect of itself, but is rather an effect of cultural and linguistic processes of construction, as well as a metaphysics which sidelines these processes. Finally therefore, I want to ask, if the self is not self-limited or self-possessed, what becomes of ownership of external objects? Does recognition of the queer person provide some potential for a queer property?

In liberal thought it is essentially the *self*-referential nature of the individual which provides the connection between the person and the (private) property.[14] It is because the person is regarded as committed essentially to his/her own identity, and that that identity is primarily self-contained and self-constructing, that these connections can even arise on the different levels in which I have just outlined them (Zucker, 1993: 88). An other-referential self, or, the concept of a person for whom subjectivity including sexuality is a secondary effect of social relationships, cannot sustain in the same way the connection with private property. Where the other is not simply the objectified outside of the self which may be appropriated and reduced, but rather a potentially positive, respected and celebrated element of the context within which a subject is created, the concept of private property as the means of mediation between self-contained persons is no longer sustainable.

Now, queer thinking aims first to expose and challenge 'natural' sex and gender categories. In doing so, one of its central targets is normative heterosexuality and heterosexual assumptions, since this is the institution through which the difference male/female is defined, hierarchised and stabilised culturally. For Judith Butler, for instance, constructed sex difference is based upon performative acts which take place within a system of conventions or laws: gender is not a pre-existing identity but rather the effect of repetition or citation of sexual conventions (Butler, 1990, 140–1). The signs of gender, like all signs, are therefore iterable in the Derridean sense – meaning can only arise through the repetition and repeatability of signs, and any repetition is always predicated both upon a primordial divisibility in any meaningful identity category, as well as the exclusion of an other. Iterability points to the fact that there is always an other in signification, and therefore in any self-identification:

> Iterability supposes a minimal remainder (as well as a minimum of idealization) in order that the identity of the *selfsame* be repeatable and identifiable *in, through,* and even *in view of* its alteration. For the structure of iteration . . . implies *both* identity *and* difference. Iteration in its 'purest' form – and it is always impure – contains *in itself* the discrepancy of a difference that constitutes it as iteration. (Derrida, 1977: 190)

One explanation of the queer is that it draws upon and exploits the instability of the frontier between the other and the same: instead of masking the repetitions and exclusions which go into identity formation, queer thinking aims to highlight not only sexual constructedness, but also the fundamental instability of our gendered identity categories, without forgetting the power of conventional thinking to enforce its codes, often violently (Butler, 1993: 226–7). Drawing on such insights, one of the central goals of queer theory is the subversion of such clear notions of *self*-referential identity, to bring out the otherness of any self, and in particular to emphasise that sexuality is a performance, not an essential object or characteristic which I can own in any simple sense.

Finally, therefore, I would like to suggest that if my relationship to myself is not simply one of self-referentiality, or self-ownership, then I can hardly be said to have a unidirectional, determining, sovereign relationship to anything external which I am said to own. Indeed, one function of private property has been to shore up the ideology of individualism by creating and protecting selves separated along proprietorial lines, but private property itself relies upon this myth of the separate person. If identity is not just personal identity which we each own individually but an identity which is owned and developed in common with others, then it cannot provide a general basis for purely private ownership, because the self always *owes* its own identity to the community. Ordinarily this debt of the person is written off or erased in the name of the individual, and in particular in the name of the self-owning masculine individual: rediscovering it potentially leads to a notion of property which is neither sovereign, limited, nor entirely private.

Envisaging such a conception of property is no easy task, because within this western, Anglo-American legal culture, there is no language that transcends the division of subject and object, of separated self and other, or of male and female. Jennifer Nedelsky captures the problem by saying that we 'will need a new vocabulary, new metaphors to invoke if we are not to be sucked back into the forms we are resisting even as we argue against them' (Nedelsky, 1991: 181). However, as I have tried to show, new forms may be drawn out of the old: by emphasising that which – *within* the complex web of philosophical, legal and social understandings of property – appears to pose a challenge to the traditionally rigid and oppositional rhetoric of property, new approaches will gradually emerge.

Concluding Thoughts

There is not really a thesis or conclusion which can be stated from the above, since it is more of a beginning than an end, and undoubtedly raises more questions than it answers. In particular, the exact dimensions of a 'queer' property as something which exceeds conventional oppositions between private and communal, and self and other, remains in a sense a mysteriously foreign concept. However, there are several comments I would like to make, as a way of summarising some of the central themes which I have suggested.

First, there is a link to be drawn between sexual propriety (that is, the properties conventionally attributed to the sexes which demarcate sexual identity) and the metaphorical deployment of property in constructing sex. Socially, and until this century legally, sexual propriety has meant on the one (male) hand the position of being a self- and other-proprietor, and on the other hand the position of being the object of property. Relationship to property on the metaphorical level therefore remains a powerful indicator of (social) status. Insofar as the queer is concerned to accentuate the *improper* generally, and possibly the improper potential of every person, one important aspect of a queer approach is critique of this propriety, and of property symbolism tied to sex.

Second, the distinction between having and being which has been so important to the person/property distinction and its expression in the subject-male/object-female hierarchy is unsustainable philosophically, and like these other distinctions, is susceptible to deconstruction. This is most immediately evident in the very notion of self-ownership which conflates having and being property, but also flows from recognition of the social nature of the person and of sex and sexuality. Appreciation of the *queer potential* of persons, rather than the fixity and stability of persons as simple self-owners, opens up the concept of property for reconsideration, as well as the positioning of persons in the sexual economy. If persons are never fully private or individuated entities, then the justification for private ownership which relies upon property in the person begins to look decidedly shaky.

Finally, I would not go so far as to say that the future of property is collective or communal, but only that it is not simply private or exclusive. As Kevin Gray has argued, private property is not 'truly private' because it is regulated and protected by the state, and because it confers a very public power over others (Gray, 1991: 304). Nor is the person ever 'truly private': continuing to rethink the question of the relationship between the person and the community with a focus on property must lead to an altered understanding of property as an institution. This, however, is a topic for another article.

NOTES

A short version of this article was presented at the Gender, Sexuality and Law conference, held at Keele University in June 1998. I would like to thank Mary Heath, Ngaire Naffine and the referees for their many useful comments.

1. There is a large and complex debate about the philosophical and legal nature of property. However, I take it as reasonably well established that property does not necessarily signify a specific closed set of rights which are always present whenever property is present. It is a 'bundle' of potential rights which arise between persons in relation to objects (see Edgeworth, 1988; Gray, 1991; Hohfeld, 1913).

2. A recent discussion paper of the Australian Model Criminal Code Officers Committee on slavery deals in part with sex slavery and enforced prostitution of women: clearly here there are questions of race as well as sex, although the report does not specifically talk about race. Through the examples it gives, however, the report does clarify that modern slavery or involuntary servitude is not only about exploitation of women, but also about people with disabilities, those unable to

pay debts, children, exploitation of illegal immigrants and refugees, and overly restrictive labour conditions (Model Criminal Code Officers Committee, 1998).

3. Such a description of the operation of property/power is, of course, derived from Foucault's analysis of power. I sometimes think, however, that in an effort to discredit the sovereignty model of power in favour of the discursive, circulating model of power, Foucault's work has the tendency to undervalue the symbolic force of power as hierarchy and sovereignty. Even if the power of the sovereign/proprietor is nothing more than a crystallisation of an underlying circulation of meanings, it is no less real and effective – in fact it is much more difficult to dispel than mere commodity-power.

4. See Naffine (1998: 198–200) for a fuller account. Naffine distinguishes between 'property for personhood' and 'persons as property'. I have departed slightly from Naffine's taxonomy.

5. Obviously there is an extensive debate about precisely this question, and I am making an assumption which others may not accept.

6. This does not mean that liberal thinkers have not recognised the social nature of the person, but rather that there is nonetheless a high degree of reliance on the pre-social person, or some version of human nature, as opposed to the idea that the individual person is entirely the result of language, culture or metaphysical structures. The liberal person, whether socially constructed or not, is still essentially the intentional and self-conscious person. Moreover, and more importantly, the link between the person and private property assumes an individual autonomous person.

7. Many feminists have defended the self-ownership model, because at the very least it provides some protection for the autonomy of women.

8. Margaret Radin defends this construction of the person through property, arguing that as a basic incident of autonomy an area of 'property for personhood' ought to be market inalienable. See Radin 1987.

9. Calliope Farsides comments that 'The laws of libel and slander could be said to operate on the assumption that I own my good reputation' (Farsides, 1992). Trespass to the person mirrors trespass to goods or land. And arguably 'character merchandising' cases decided on the basis of passing off or 'misleading and deceptive conduct' (s. 52 Trade Practices Act, Australia) come very close to being about appropriation of personality, even though outside Canada and the United States such a cause of action is rarely recognised. See, for example, *Hogan v Koala Dundee* (1989) 87 ALR 14. Similarly, courts do not award specific performance on contracts for personal services, but in cases of breach of such contracts will grant an injunction restricting the defendant's use of his/her own personal capacities. This may be regarded as establishing an exclusive right to an aspect of another person (cf. Owens, 1997).

10. Wittig's concern is, of course, somewhat different from those of Irigaray's and Pateman's, who have each written of a sexual contract between men, which constitutes social and political relationships. Wittig's concern has been to highlight the *heterosexual* nature of the contract: that is, to indicate that it structures the world of sexual relationships *as* heterosexual.

11. The legal fiction of the person, which is not co-extensive with the human being, but is rather a construct based upon the attribution of contextually arising rights and responsibilities also reflects this non-essential notion of personality. However, the law has not been consistent here, also assuming at times a much more essentialised human being.

12. Schroeder makes a similar argument (1994a).

13. Butler makes this point as follows: 'In a sense, the simultaneous acts of privileging the phallus and removing it from the normative heterosexual form of

exchange, and recirculating and reprivileging it between women deploys the phallus to break the signifying chain in which it conventionally operates' (Butler, 1993: 88).

14. See note 6. It has been pointed out to me that queer *theory* can be not only self-referential but also self-reverential: underlining, perhaps, the power of property thinking, and the continuing need for transgression of disciplinary boundaries.

REFERENCES

Bell, Derrick (1988) 'Property Rights in Whiteness – Their Legal Legacy, Their Economic Cost', *Villanova Law Review* 33: 767.

Braidotti, Rosi and Judith Butler (1997) 'Feminism by Any Other Name. Interview' pp. 31–67 in E. Weed and N. Schor (eds) *Feminism Meets Queer Theory*. Bloomington: Indiana University Press.

Bray, Micelle Bourianoff (1990) 'Personalizing Personalty: Toward a Property Right in Human Bodies', *Texas Law Review* 69: 209–44.

Butler, Judith (1990) *Gender Trouble: Feminism and the Subversion of Identity*. New York: Routledge.

Butler, Judith (1993) *Bodies That Matter: On the Discursive Limits of 'Sex'*. New York: Routledge.

Butler, Judith (1997) 'Against Proper Objects', pp. 1–30 in E. Weed and N. Schor (eds) *Feminism Meets Queer Theory*. Bloomington: Indiana University Press.

Dangelo, Kathleen Birkel (1989) 'How Much of You Do You Really Own? A Property Right in Identity', *Cleveland State Law Review* 37: 499–524.

Dale, Catherine (1997) 'A Debate Between Queer and Feminism', *Critical InQueeries* 1: 145–57.

Davies, Margaret (1994) 'Feminist Appropriations: Law, Property, and Personality', *Social and Legal Studies* 3: 365–91.

Davies, Margaret (1998) 'The Proper: Discourses of Purity', *Law and Critique* 9: 1–28.

Derrida, Jacques (1974) *Of Grammatology*. Baltimore: Johns Hopkins University Press.

Derrida, Jacques (1977) 'Limited Inc. a b c . . .' *Glyph* 2: 162.

Drahos, Peter (1996) *A Philosophy of Intellectual Property*. Aldershot: Dartmouth.

Edgeworth, Brendan (1988) 'Post-Property? A Postmodern Conception of Private Property', *University of New South Wales Law Journal* 11: 87–116.

Eleftheriadis, Pavlos (1996) 'The Analysis of Property Rights', *Oxford Journal of Legal Studies* 16: 31–53.

Farsides, Calliope (1992) 'Body Ownership', pp. 35–51 in S. McVeigh and S. Wheeler (eds) *Law, Health, and Medical Regulation*. Aldershot: Dartmouth.

Frow, John (1995) 'Elvis' Fame: The Commodity Form and the Form of the Person', *Cardozo Studies in Law and Literature* 7: 131–71.

Gray, Kevin (1991) 'Property in Thin Air', *Cambridge Law Journal* 252–307.

Grey, Thomas (1980) 'The Disintegration of Property', *Nomos XXII*: 69–85.

Harris, Cheryl (1993) 'Whiteness as Property', *Harvard Law Review* 106: 1707–91.

Harris, J. W. (1996) 'Who Owns My Body?', *Oxford Journal Of Legal Studies* 16: 55–84.

Hegel, G. W. F. (1821/1967) *Philosophy of Right*, T. M. Knox (trans.). Oxford: Oxford University Press.

Hennessy, Rosemary (1995) 'Queer Visibility in Commodity Culture', *Cultural Critique* 1994–95: 31–76.

Herrera, Jessica (1994) 'Not Even His Name: Is the Denigration of Crazy Horse Custer's Final Revenge?', *Harvard Civil Rights-Civil Liberties Law Review* 29: 175–95.

Hohfeld, Wesley Newcomb (1913) 'Some Fundamental Legal Conceptions as Applied in Judicial Reasoning', *Yale Law Journal* 23: 16–59.

Hohfeld, Wesley Newcomb (1917) 'Fundamental Legal Conceptions as Applied in Judicial Reasoning', *Yale Law Journal* 26: 710–70.

Irigaray, Luce (1985) 'Commodities Among Themselves', pp. 192–197 in *This Sex Which is Not One*. Ithaca: Cornell University Press.

Irigaray, Luce (1996) *i love to you: Sketch of a Possible Felicity in History*. London: Routledge.

Jagose, Annamarie (1996) *Queer Theory*. Melbourne: Melbourne University Press.

Laclau, Ernesto (1996) *Emancipation(s)*. London: Verso.

Levi-Strauss, Claude (1969) *Elementary Structures of Kinship*. London: Eyre and Spottiswoode.

Locke, John (1690/1960) *Two Treatises of Government*, Peter Laslett (ed.). Cambridge: Cambridge University Press.

MacKinnon, Catharine (1982) 'Feminism, Marxism, Method and the State: An Agenda for Theory', *Signs* 7: 515–44.

Macpherson, C. B. (1962) *The Political Theory of Possessive Individualism*. Oxford: Clarendon Press.

Macpherson, C. B. (1978) 'The Meaning of Property', pp. 1–13 in C. B. Macpherson (ed.) *Property: Mainstream and Critical Positions*. Toronto: University of Toronto Press.

Magnusson, Roger (1988) 'The Recognition of Proprietary Rights in Human Tissue in Common Law Jurisdictions', *Melbourne University Law Review* 18: 601–29.

Martin, Biddy (1994) 'Sexualities Without Genders and Other Queer Utopias', *Diacritics* 24: 104–21.

Model Criminal Code Officers Committee (1998) *Offences Against Humanity – Slavery: Discussion Paper*.

Naffine, Ngaire (1997) 'The Body Bag', pp. 79–93 in N. Naffine and R. Owens (eds) *Sexing the Subject of Law*. Sydney: Law Book Company.

Naffine, Ngaire (1998) 'The Legal Structure of Self-Ownership: Or the Self-Possessed Man and the Woman Possessed', *Journal of Law and Society* 25: 193–212.

Nedelsky, Jennifer (1991) 'Law, Boundaries, and the Bounded Self', pp. 162–89 in Robert Post (ed.) *Law and the Order of Culture*. Berkeley: University of California Press.

Nedelsky, Jennifer (1993) 'Property in Potential Life: A Relational Approach to Choosing Legal Categories', *Canadian Journal of Law and Jurisprudence* 6: 343–65.

Noyes, C. Reinold (1936) *The Institution of Property: A Study of the Development, Substance, and Arrangement of the System of Property in Modern Anglo-American Law*. London: Longman, Green and Co.

Owens, Rosemary (1997) 'Working in the Sex Market', pp. 119–46 in N. Naffine and R. Owens (eds) *Sexing the Subject of Law*. Sydney: Law Book Company.

Pateman, Carol (1988) *The Sexual Contract*. Cambridge: Polity Press.

Penner, J. E. (1997) *The Idea of Property in Law*. Oxford: Oxford University Press.

Posner, Richard (1992) *Sex and Reason*. Cambridge, Mass.: Harvard University Press.

Pottage, Alain (1998) 'The Inscription of Life in Law: Genes, Patents, and Biopolitics', *Modern Law Review* 61: 740–65.

Radin, Margaret (1987) 'Market-Inalienability', *Harvard Law Review* 100: 1849–1937.

Radin, Margaret (1993) *Reinterpreting Property*. Chicago: Chicago University Press.

352   SOCIAL & LEGAL STUDIES 8(3)

Radin, Margaret (1996) 'Property Evolving in Cyberspace', *Journal of Law and Commerce* 15: 509–26.

Reich, Charles A. (1991) 'The Individual Sector', *Yale Law Journal* 100: 1409–48.

Robson, Ruthann (1998) *Sappho Goes to Law School: Fragments in Lesbian Legal Theory*. New York: Columbia University Press.

Rose, Carol (1991) 'Property as Wealth, Property as Propriety', *Nomos* 33: 223–47.

Schroeder, Jeanne (1994a) 'Chix Nix Bundle-O-Stix: A Feminist Critique of the Disaggregation of Property', *Michigan Law Review* 93: 239–319.

Schroeder, Jeanne (1994b) 'Virgin Territory: Margaret Radin's Imagery of Personal Property as the Inviolate Feminine Body', *Minnesota Law Review* 79: 55–171.

Schroeder, Jeanne (1995) 'The Vestal and the Fasces: Property and the Feminine in Law and Psychoanalysis', *Cardozo Law Review* 16: 805–924.

Shiva, Vandana (1997) *Biopiracy: The Plunder of Nature and Knowledge*. Boston: South End Press.

Singer, Barbara (1991) 'The Right of Publicity: Star Vehicle or Shooting Star?', *Cardozo Arts and Entertainment Law Journal* 1–49.

Singer, Joseph William (1991) 'Property and Sovereignty', *Northwestern University Law Review* 86: 1–56.

Staves, Susan (1994) 'Chattel Property Rules and the Construction of Englishness, 1660–1800', *Law and History Review* 12: 123–53.

Stychin, Carl (1995) *Law's Desire: Sexuality and the Limits of Justice*. London: Routledge.

Tyler, Carole-Anne (1997) 'Passing: Narcissism, Identity, and Difference', pp. 227–65 in Elizabeth Weed and Naomi Schor (eds) *Feminism Meets Queer Theory*. Bloomington: Indiana University Press.

Waldron, Jeremy (1988) *The Right to Private Property*. Oxford: Clarendon Press.

Walters, Suzanne Danuta (1996) 'From Here to Queer: Radical Feminism, Postmodernism, and the Lesbian Menace (Or, Why Can't a Woman Be More Like a Fag?)', *Signs* 21: 830–69.

Watson, Irene (1997) 'Indigenous Peoples' Law-Ways: Survival Against the Colonial State', *Australian Feminist Law Journal* 8: 39–58.

Weed, Elizabeth and Schor, Naomi (eds) (1997) *Feminism Meets Queer Theory*. Bloomington: Indiana University Press.

Williams, Patricia (1987) 'Alchemical Notes: Reconstructing Ideals from Deconstructed Rights', *Harvard Civil Rights – Civil Liberties Law Review* 22: 401.

Wittig (1992) 'On the Social Contract', pp. 33–45 in *The Straight Mind and Other Essays*. London: Harvester Wheatsheaf.

Zucker, Ross (1993) 'Unequal Property and Subjective Personality in Liberal Theories', *Ratio Juris* 6: 86.

[2]

Refashioning the Unfashionable: Claiming Lesbian Identities in the Legal Context

Diana Majury

Dans cet article, Diana Majury est à la recherche de la meilleure façon de caractériser l'oppression vécue par les lesbiennes aux fins d'une intervention juridique. Elle examine de façon critique la terminologie actuelle relative à la discrimination fondée sur l'orientation sexuelle et elle constate que cette terminologie est inadéquate pour plusieurs raisons. Son analyse, fondée en partie sur une reformulation de la politique de l'identité lesbienne, l'amène à conclure que l'oppression vécue par les lesbiennes est mieux comprise lorsque vue sous l'angle de la discrimination sexuelle, et souvent concurremment avec d'autres formes d'oppression qui ont également un impact sur elle, que sous l'angle de tout autre forme de discrimination reconnue par la loi. Elle estime que, sur les plans politique et stratégique, l'analyse de l'oppression des lesbiennes fondée sur la discrimination sexuelle est celle qui est la plus susceptible de faire comprendre la profondeur et la signification de la peur et de la haine largement répandues des lesbiennes.

In this article, Diana Majury explores the question of how most appropriately to characterize the oppression lesbians experience for the purposes of legal intervention. She critically examines the prevailing terminology of sexual

I wish to thank Alison Dewar for the title, literally, and also figuratively in terms of teaching me and challenging me to claim what I believe even when it is unfashionable; and I thank her for her encouragement and all of the discussions we have that are so central to my thinking, as well as my being. Connie Backhouse provided inspiration, support and helpful comments on an early draft of this paper. Lynne Pearlman's comments and suggestions were, as always, incredibly thoughtful and thought provoking, pushing me to examine the issues more fully and more radically; much of the analysis and many of the ideas in this paper come from and through conversations with Lynne. Ruthann Robson's comments helped me to focus and clarify my thinking and were wonderfully supportive despite her disagreement with some of what I say. Lisa Clement provided me with excellent research assistance with her usual grace and diligence. Sharing the experience of the human rights consultations with Carol Allen and Mary Eaton was critically important in directing my thinking on these issues and I thank both of them. I further thank Mary for the ground-breaking work she has done and continues to do in developing lesbian legal theory in Canada. And finally, I thank Claire Young for her patience and gentleness in her painstaking edit of this article.

orientation discrimination and finds it inadequate on a number of grounds. Her analysis, based in part on what she describes as a refashioned lesbian identity politics, leads her to conclude that lesbian oppression is more accurately understood as sex discrimination, frequently in conjunction with and transformed by other forms of oppression, than as any other form of legally recognized discrimination. She argues that, politically and strategically, the sex discrimination analysis of lesbian oppression offers the most promise for understanding the full depth and meaning of the widespread fear and hatred of lesbians.

Introduction

In this article, I explore the question of how to conceptualize lesbian inequality within a legal context; that is how lesbian inequality might be characterized for legal purposes. There are major differences among lesbians, as well as between lesbians and non-lesbians, in terms of identifying and responding to lesbian oppression through law.[1] The questions which these differences raise are important, both practically and in terms of the development of lesbian legal theory. Here, I trace some of my own thinking on issues of language and strategy that has led me to my currently, if somewhat tentatively, held belief that lesbian oppression is more accurately understood as sex discrimination than as any other form of legally recognized discrimination. My reliance on lesbian identity politics in my analysis, as well as the conclusion that I draw from that analysis, that lesbian discrimination is sex discrimination, both seem to me highly unfashionable positions at present; hence the title of this piece. I hope that in (re)claiming lesbian identity, and understanding it as a powerful form of sex resistance,[2] I am contributing to a refashioning of both lesbian identity politics and sex discrimination theory.

In Canada, it is only recently that lesbians have been given any legal protection from discrimination.[3] In a number of ways, this "protection" is inadequate or flawed. In the first place, the protections are jurisdictionally limited. Only eight out of 13 jurisdictions in Canada have included some form of

---

[1]   One of the most fundamental of these differences is the issue of whether or not lesbians "should" try to use law to challenge their oppression. Despite the merits of arguments against lesbians engaging with law in this way, a number of lesbians have chosen or been forced to try to assert or defend themselves as lesbians in legal contexts. Given this, it seems to me that as a lesbian legal academic. I might do better trying to help frame these arguments in lesbian positive ways than to decry lesbian co-optation through law.

[2]   By this, I mean resistance to the social construct, woman.

[3]   In 1977, Quebec was the first province in Canada to include a prohibition against sexual orientation discrimination in its human rights legislation. *Charter of Human Rights and Freedoms*, S.Q. 1977, c. 6, s 1.

protection for lesbians in their human rights legislation.[4] While discrimination against lesbians is not presently thought to be included under a prohibited ground of discrimination listed in either the *Canadian Charter of Rights and Freedoms*[5] or the *Canadian Human Rights Act*,[6] sexual orientation has consistently, and now probably unequivocally, been included as an analogous ground under the *Charter*[7] and, via the *Charter* has been read in as a prohibited ground of discrimination under the *Canadian Human Rights Act*.[8]

Second, even where human rights legislation does include a prohibition against sexual orientation discrimination, the protection has been held to be limited by other "inconsistent" provisions. Most notable of these "inconsistencies" is the inclusion of heterosexual terms such as "marital status" and "spouse"[9] that have been interpreted, albeit not consistently, to restrict family and/or sexual partner

4. See in British Columbia, *Human Rights Act*, S.B.C. 1992, c. 42; in Manitoba, *Human Rights Code*, S.M. 1987-88, c. 45, s. 9(2)(h); in New Brunswick, *An Act to Amend the Human Rights Act*, S.N.B. 1992, c. 30; in Nova Scotia, *Human Rights Act* R.S.N.S. 1989, c. 214, as amended by S.N.S. 1991, c. 12, s. 5(1)(n); in Ontario, *Human Rights Code*, 1981, S.O. 1981, c. 53, as amended by S.O.1986, c. 64, s. 18(1); in Quebec, *Charter of Human Rights and Freedoms*, R.S.Q. 1977, c. C-12; in Saskatchewan, *Saskatchewan Human Rights Code*, S.S. 1979, c. S-24.1, as amended by S.S. 1993, c. 61; and in the Yukon, *Human Rights Act*, R.S.Y. 1986, c. 11, as amended by S.Y. 1987, c. 3, s. 6(g). See Brenda Cossman and Bruce Ryder, *Gay, Lesbian and Unmarried Heterosexual Couples and the "Family Law Act": Accommodating a Diversity of Family Forms*, 1993, research paper available from the Ontario Law Reform Commission, at 108, n255.
5. Part I of the *Constitution Act, 1982*, being Schedule B of the *Canada Act 1982* (U.K.), 1982, c. 11 [hereinafter referred to as the *Charter*].
6. R.S.C. 1985 c. H-6, as amended. In January 1992, the Minister of Justice for Canada, Kim Campbell, announced her intention to introduce a series of amendments to the *Canadian Human Rights Act*. The Minister sponsored a three-day consultation session in March 1992 to discuss possible amendments. I participated in the working group on lesbian and gay issues at this consultation. Much of my sense, as articulated in this article, of the current issues and conflicts facing lesbians and gays in terms of how the law has constructed us as "homosexuals" and where and how we might try to challenge or re-direct those legal constructs, comes from that meeting. In December 1992, the Minister of Justice introduced Bill C-108, *An Act to Amend the Canadian Human Rights Act*. It provided that sexual orientation would be a prohibited ground of discrimination. However, "marital status" in the *Canadian Human Rights Act* would continue to be defined as "partners of the opposite sex", suggesting that relationship-based benefits would be denied lesbian and gay couples. Lesbian and gay organizations, among others, mounted an active lobbying campaign against the Bill and the Bill died on the order paper when Parliament was prorogued on September 8, 1993. All of this took place against the back drop of *Haig* v. *Canada (Minister of Justice)* (1992), 9 O.R. (3d) 495 (Ont. C.A.) in which the Court read "sexual orientation" into the *Canadian Human Rights Act* as a prohibited ground of discrimination.
7. According to Cossman and Ryder, "There is a clear consensus that sexual orientation is an analogous ground of discrimination for the purposes of s. 15 of the *Charter* in the academic commentary, in government reports and in judicial decisions". *Supra* note 4 at 108-109.
8. See *Haig* v. *Canada (Minister of Justice)*, *supra* note 6.
9. See *e.g.*, Ontario *Human Rights Code*, R.S.O. 1990, s. 10(1).

Vol. 7   *1994*   289

benefits to heterosexual couples.[10]

The third, and probably most entrenched, flaw in the legislative prohibitions against discrimination is that they are framed in terms of "sexual orientation", a label that is seen to include lesbians and gays and possibly "other sexual minorities". The term sexual orientation is, from my perspective, problematic for a number of reasons. It has been narrowly interpreted by tribunals and courts and, in its gender neutrality, it promotes a gay male standard to which lesbians are assumed or expected to conform. The meaning of being a lesbian and the inequalities we[11] experience as lesbians are not represented in the label sexual orientation. My discomfort with the term is one of the major pieces, coupled with, and related to, my feminist analysis of gender, that leads me to reject the categorization of discrimination against lesbians as sexual orientation discrimination. I explore that discomfort in this article looking both at the historical invisibility of lesbians in law and the limits inherent in a gender neutral umbrella term. Having problematized the term sexual orientation, I conclude with the beginnings of an analysis of lesbian discrimination as sex discrimination.

The Historical Omission of Lesbians

Lesbians and lesbian issues receive little attention in current legal literature. Until recently, the limited work in this area focused largely on lesbian mothers and lesbian custody cases.[12] While this is not surprising because custody has

---

10. See Cossman and Ryder, *supra* note 4 at 112-133.

11. I switch back and forth between "we" and "they" in my references to lesbians. At one level, this is about "me" and "we" and, at another level, it is not. And while "they" seems unduly distancing, it sometimes feels more appropriate than the constant self-reference of "we". I do not want to generalize lesbian experience based on my white, middle class, non-disabled, christian experiences as a lesbian; nor do I wish to deny our social and political differences. (I used to use the term christian-raised because I wanted to signal my rejection of "christianity". However, it has been pointed out to me that I cannot so easily divest myself of the privilege, values, and internalized dominance of my christian rearing.) At the same time, I do not wish to "other" those who are not the same as me. I want to participate in the development of a Canadian-based lesbian political legal analysis that responds to differentiated experiences of lesbian oppression, an analysis that stands somewhere between "we" and "they" and which challenges that dichotomy.

12. The following list was largely drawn from the bibliography compiled by Mary Eaton in *Theorizing Sexual Orientation*. (LL.M. Thesis. Queen's University, 1991) and then updated by me While the list is no doubt incomplete, its length attests to the significance that has been accorded to lesbian custody and related issues. In Canada, see Katherine Arnup, "Finding Fathers: Artificial Insemination. Lesbians and the Law" (1994) 7 Canadian Journal of Women and the Law 97; and "Mothers Just Like Others: Lesbians, Divorce and Child Custody in Canada" (1987) 3 Canadian Journal of Women and the Law 18; Christine Boyle, "Custody, Adoption and the Homosexual Parent" (1976) 23 Report of Family Law 129; Harvey Brownstone, "The Homosexual Parent in Custody Disputes" (1980) 5 Queen's Law Journal 199; Mary Anne Coffey. "Of Father Born: A Lesbian Feminist Critique of the Ontario Law Reform Commission Recommendation on Artificial Insemination" (1986) 1 Canadian Journal of Women and the Law 424; Wendy Gross, "Judging the Best Interests of the Child: Child Custody and the Homosexual

been a pressing legal concern for many lesbians, this limited focus has produced a circumscribed picture of lesbians and lesbian legal issues.[13] Larger questions of lesbian legal theory, the relationship between lesbians and law, and the construction of lesbians in and by law are issues which have just started to emerge in legal scholarship.[14]

Parent" (1986) 1 Canadian Journal of Women and the Law 505. In the United States, see Courtney Bagett, "Sexual Orientation: Should It Affect Child Custody Rulings" (1991) 16 Law and Psychology Review 189; Margaret Clemens, "In the Best Interests of the Child' and the Lesbian Mother: A Proposal for Legislative Change in New York" (1984) 48 Albany Law Review 1021; Matt Coles, "The Right Forum, The Right Issue: Initiatives and Family Values" (1993) 8 Berkeley Women's Law Journal 180; Carole Cullum, "Co-Parent Adoptions: Lesbian and Gay Parenting" (1993) 29 Trial 28; Paula Ettelbrick, "Who is a Parent? The Need to Develop Lesbian Conscious Family Law" (1993) New York Law School Journal of Human Rights 513; Marie Gil de Lamadrid, "Expanding the Definition of Family: A Universal Issue" (1993) 8 Berkeley Women's Law Journal 170; Lynne Harne, "Lesbian Mothers and the Courts" (1985) 9 Legal Action 9; Deborah Hensen, "A Lesbian Feminist Critique of Susan Okin's *Justice, Gender, and the Family*: Lesbian Families with Children as a Non-Heterosexist Model for the Development of Morality and Justice" (1993) 4 Hastings Women's Law Journal 249; Phillip Kraft, "Lesbian Child Custody" (1983) Harvard Women's Law Journal 183; D.G. Malloy, "Another Mother? The Courts' Denial of Legal Status to the Non-Biological Parent upon Dissolution of Lesbian Families" (1992/1993) 31 Louisville Journal of Family Law 981; Nancy Polikoff, "Lesbian Mothers, Lesbian Families: Legal Obstacles, Legal Challenges" (1986) 14 New York University Review of Law and Social Change 907, and "The Child Does Have Two Mothers: Redefining Parenthood to Meet the Needs of Children in Lesbian-Mother and other Nontraditional Families" (1990) 78 Georgetown Law Journal; Lisa Pooley, "Heterosexism and Children's Best Interests" (1993) 27 University of San Francisco Law Review 477; Marilyn Riley, "The Lesbian Mother", (1975) 12 San Diego Law Review 821; David Rosenblum, "Custody Rights of Gay and Lesbian Parents" (1991) 36 Villanova Law Review; Annamay Sheppard, "Lesbian Mothers II: Long Night's Journey into Day" (1985) 8 Women's Rights Law Reporter 219; Steve Susoeff, "Assessing Children's Best Interests When A Parent Is Gay or Lesbian: Toward A Rational Custody Standard" (1985) 32 University of California Law Review 852; Stuart Sutton, "The Lesbian Family: Rights in Conflict under the California Uniform Parentage Act" (1980) 10 Golden Gate Law Review 1007; Elizabeth Zuckerman, "Second Parent Adoption for Lesbian-Parented Families: Legal Recognition of the Other Mother" (1986) 19 University of California Davis Law Review 729.

13. Other pressing legal concerns for lesbians relating, for example, to job (in)security, access to housing, and psychiatric interventions have been largely ignored, possibly because of the very different risks and challenges they involve.

14. Ruthannn Robson and Mary Eaton are the only lesbians in North America of whom I am aware who are publishing extensively on lesbian legal theory and lesbian legal issues. This is why this special issue of the Canadian Journal of Women and the Law is of such significance. See Ruthann Robson, "Resisting the Family: Repositioning Lesbians in Legal Theory" (1994) 19 Signs: Journal of Women in Culture and Society 975; "Posner's Lesbians: Neither Sexy Nor Reasonable" (1993) 25 Connecticut 491; "The Specter of a Lesbian Supreme Court Justice: Problems of Identity in Lesbian Legal Theorizing" (1993) 5 Saint Thomas Law Review 433; *Lesbian (Out)Law* (New York: Firebrand, 1992); "Looking for Lesbian Legal Theory: A Surprising Journey" (1990) 42 Sinister Wisdom 32; "Lesbianism in Anglo and European Legal History" (1990) 5 Wisconsin Women's Law Journal 1; "Lesbian Jurisprudence?" (1989-90) 8 Law and Inequality 443; "Lavender Bruises: Intra-Lesbian Violence, Law and Lesbian Legal

Legal history is no exception to the general absence of discussion of lesbians in legal scholarship. Lesbians have also been largely ignored as a subject of legal historical inquiry.[15] It is, at this time, impossible to say whether lesbians were not recognized as legal actors in their own time or whether the current lack of acknowledgment of lesbian existence serves also to conceal lesbian legal history. Furthermore, historians may not know what to look for and where to look for lesbian legal stories; what might have been obvious and recognized as indicators of women in primary relationships with other women in the 1890s, may not be recognized so easily, or characterized as lesbian by a scholar in the 1990s.[16] Gay

Theory" (1990) 20 Golden Gate University Law Review 567; " Lifting Belly: Privacy, Sexuality and Lesbianism" (1990) 12 Women's Rights Law Reporter 177; and Ruthann Robson and Sarah Valentine, "Lov(h)ers: Lesbians as Intimate Partners" (1990) 63 Temple Law Quarterly 511. See Mary Eaton, "Lesbians and the Law" in Sharon Dale Stone, ed., *Lesbians in Canada* (Toronto: Between the Lines, 1990); "Theorizing Sexual Orientation", *supra* note 12; and Mary Eaton and Cynthia Petersen, "Andrews v. Ontario (Ministry of Health)" (1987-88) 2 Canadian Journal of Women and the Law 416. For additional Canadian lesbian legal theory, see also Didi Herman "Are We Family?: Lesbian Rights and Women's Liberation" (1989) 28 Osgoode Hall Law Journal 789; Margaret Leopold and Wendy King, "Compulsory Heterosexuality, Lesbians and the Law: The Case for Constitutional Protection" (1985) 1 Canadian Journal of Women and the Law 163, and Lynne Pearlman, "Rethinking Clara Brett Martin: A Jewish Lesbian Perspective" (retitled by author) (1992) 5 Canadian Journal of Women and the Law 317.

15. See Robson, "Lesbianism in Anglo and European Legal History", *ibid.*

16. This raises the thorny question of who is a lesbian. I adopt the strategy of Sarah Hoagland in *Lesbian Ethics: Toward New Value* (Palo Alto, CA: Institute of Lesbian Studies, 1988) and refuse to define lesbian. She states at 8:

> In naming the word "lesbian", I invoke a lesbian context. And for this reason I choose not to define the term. To define "lesbian" is, in my opinion, to succumb to a context of heterosexualism.

While there are clearly women who fall within any definition of lesbian, and probably women who fall outside any definition of lesbian, I am not clear exactly where to draw the line or even if line drawing is the most appropriate way to assess the meaning of lesbian and of who is and who is not a lesbian. This becomes even more problematic when one looks back in time and tries to find and claim a lesbian history for periods when the concept "lesbian" did not exist. However, lesbian practice and lesbian consciousness did exist and it is based on these that we can claim a lesbian history. See *e.g.*, Lillian Faderman, *Surpassing the Love of Men* (New York: William Morrow and Company, 1981) and *Odd Girls and Twilight Lovers* (New York: Columbia University Press, 1991); Elizabeth Lapovsky Kennedy and Madeline Davis, *Boots of Leather, Slippers of Gold* (New York: Routledge, 1993)

In refusing to define lesbian. I do not want to be understood as subscribing to Adrienne Rich's notion of a lesbian continuum, described in "Compulsory Heterosexuality and Lesbian Existence" in, among many other publications, Ann Snitow, Christine Stansell and Sharon Thompson, eds., *Powers of Desire: The Politics of Sexuality* (New York: Monthly Review Press, 1983). I refer to the multiple re-publications of this article because they attest to the significance of this particular work to lesbians and within feminist theory. I find Rich's concept of compulsory heterosexuality as powerful today as I did when I first read this article over 10 years ago. However, the idea of the lesbian continuum which I initially found very appealing, now seems to me to dilute the meaning and politic of lesbianism. My adoption of the notion of lesbian context may appear consistent with a lesbian continuum, but I do not think that all women can

men are much more present in historical legal records as a result of their criminal prosecution for offences directed against gay male sexual practices.[17]

While it may be premature to speculate, preliminary indications are that lesbians were, until fairly recently, little known to, or acknowledged in, law as lesbians.[18] In the introduction to her magnificent study of women and law in nineteenth century Canada, Constance Backhouse makes the following comment on the apparent absence of lesbians in the context of her own work:

> The most glaring omission is the absence of lesbian women from the stories that follow. Some of the women I discuss may have been lesbian, but the historical record treats them all as heterosexual. Undoubtedly lesbians found themselves intertwined with law in nineteenth-century Canada. But the discipline of history has tended to ignore lesbianism and male homosexuality, claiming that sources that reveal sexual non-conformity have been destroyed, hidden, and generally restricted from use. The stigmatization that still attaches to same-sex sexual orientation prevented many men and women from disclosing their sexual preferences historically and intimidates some researchers even today.[19]

or should be supported in claiming some lesbian identity. I think that the lesbian continuum enables heterosexual and bisexual women to downplay their heterosexual privilege, to feel comfortable with and unthreatened by lesbians and lesbianism, and to feel good about the woman identification they have, instead of questioning why they have chosen to draw the limits they have drawn. While I think it is to some extent undefinable, I believe that there is something definitive about being a lesbian that the lesbian continuum denies.

17. See discussion *infra* and Barry Adam, *The Rise of a Gay and Lesbian Movement* (Boston: Twayne Publications, 1987); Gary Kinsman, *The Regulation of Desire: Sexuality in Canada* (Montreal: Black Rose Books, 1987). See also Robson, *Lesbian (Out)Law*, *supra* note 14.

18. There are a few well known trials involving lesbians. Perhaps the most famous is the trial described in Lillian Faderman, *Scotch Verdict: Miss Pirie and Miss Woods v. Dame Cumming Gordon* (New York: William Morrow and Company, 1983). Eaton's research, *supra* note 12 at 106-109, discloses in Canada one conviction against lesbians for engaging in sex that was upheld on appeal, and two convictions that were overturned on appeal.

19. Constance Backhouse, *Petticoats and Prejudice: Women and Law in Nineteenth Century Canada* (Toronto: The Osgoode Society, 1991) at 7. It must be both interesting and difficult to grapple with the decision of what to do with historical documents that indicate the likelihood that the subject of one's study was a lesbian when she publicly did not and would not have acknowledged that fact. I have had some thought provoking discussions on this topic with a woman who is writing a biography of a friend of my parents who died a number of years ago. Despite the fact that I have acknowledged myself as a lesbian for at least 12 years, it only occurred to me fairly recently – with a shock of dyke antenna recognition as I went through old photos of my parents – that this woman might have been a lesbian. I am confident that my parents had no inkling of this, although they are also both dead and I am unable to have that conversation with them. The biographer has confirmed that she thinks that this woman was a lesbian, based on personal correspondence and other such documents. The ethics and politics of what to do with this information are fascinating and troubling. Is it outing when the person is dead? Dead for how long? Is it disrespectful, or a kind of breach of faith, to disclose this

Mary Eaton reviewed Canadian case law for explicit references to lesbians and/or gay men.[20] Of the 229 "homosexual" cases she found, only 29 dealt with lesbians alone. These relatively few lesbian cases dealt almost exclusively with either child custody and/or divorce, or obscenity charges involving pornography depicting male creations of "lesbian sex" for male consumption.[21] Almost 78 per cent of the "homosexual" cases Eaton found dealt with gay men; the vast majority of these, 90 per cent, were criminal prosecutions for sexual offences.[22]

This case history of criminal prosecutions of gay men for sexual offences provides a basis for, and an indication of, how the law perceives gay men. Eaton demonstrates that the law has constructed gays as aggressive sexual predators. The law's preoccupation with, and attempts to eradicate, gay sex through sexual offence prosecutions against gay men is rationalized, through circular logic, as a legitimate "response to the threat that gay men are perceived to pose to heterosexual men. That threat is of uncontrollable and indiscriminately aggressive and/or predatory sexuality".[23] This stereotype of gays as sexually dangerous has led courts, most overtly in the United States, but also in Canada, to develop, in the context of human rights litigation, what Eaton describes as the conduct/orientation distinction.[24] Human rights protection, where it has been granted at all, has been

---

information: is it misleading, or dishonest, or disrespectful not to?

20. Eaton, *supra* note 12.
21. *Ibid.* at 85-148.
22. *Ibid.* at 32.
23. *Ibid.* at 70.
24. *Ibid.* at 179-184. Kinsman, *supra* note 17 at 212 talks about a similar distinction in his historically-grounded exploration of Canadian gay (and lesbian – see discussion following) liberation:

> While on an abstract and formal level, the federal government recognizes that we should enjoy equal rights with heterosexuals, they are still not willing to endorse the actual sexual activities in which we engage. Our rights as private individuals are recognized, while our real social and material differences – our erotic pleasures and the gender of those we love, are still not recognized as valid and equal.

While Kinsman acknowledges and discusses the impact of the stereotype of gays as sexual aggressors, the private/public distinction is a much more prominent theme in his inquiry and analysis. I have problematized Kinsman's description of his work as including a history of lesbian, as well as gay, liberation because I think that description is inaccurate. While he explains that as a gay man his focus is on "erotic activity among men" and acknowledges "that lesbianism cannot be lumped uncritically with male homosexuality for purposes of analysis" (at 17), it seems to me that he proceeds to do precisely that. At different points throughout his text, Kinsman refers to ways in which lesbians are different from gay men. The differences that he refers to, and that I consider of major significance, stem from male domination and female subordination within the gay and lesbian "community", as well as in the larger society. But Kinsman never really explores these differences, nor their ramifications in terms of the possibility of a gay and lesbian movement. He appears to think that the presence of lesbians, or of some lesbians, in organizations that initially described themselves as gay and were forced to change their names to include lesbians, means that those organizations proceeded to represent lesbians' interests and concerns, despite the acknowledged male domination of those organizations. Contrary to his

limited, according to Eaton, through judicial interpretation, to "homosexual" orientation, that is the status of being lesbian or gay.

The practice of "homosexuality", that is lesbian or gay sexual conduct, has not been given human rights protection. While tribunals and courts have extended their legal tolerance to "homosexual existence in the abstract",[25] they have been unwilling to grant "legal recognition/acceptance of homosexual sexuality".[26] Eaton argues that it is the legal construction of gays as sexual aggressors that underlies these decisions and provides the justification for the courts' unwillingness to be seen in any way to condone gay sexual conduct.[27] According to Eaton, the conduct/orientation distinction, derived from a negative stereotype of gay male sexuality, has been transposed in a gender neutral fashion to lesbians. Lesbians have been caught within the legal construct of gays as sexual aggressors, without any apparent thought being given to gender differences between lesbians and gay men. However inappropriate this legal construct may be for gay men, Eaton argues that its application to lesbians is completely without foundation. Gay male sexuality has been constructed as criminal and prosecuted as such; lesbian sexuality has not. It may well be that lesbian sexuality and sex practices have historically been subject to state sanction, for example, under vagrancy and prostitution laws, through police harassment, and through incarceration in psychiatric institutions.[28] However, in terms of public record, the case reports do not disclose a pattern of criminal prosecutions explicitly against lesbians for engaging in lesbian sex, as they do for gay men.[29] Eaton's analysis demonstrates that lesbians have been denied human rights protection, except for their right to be lesbian in the abstract, based on a legal construction of gay men and gay male sexuality that has absolutely no connection with lesbian sex or sexuality. Lesbians have been included under this legal construct because they are seen as gay, not as

stated purpose, "in a broader sense to account for both lesbian and gay oppression and resistance in a historical perspective" (at 14), Kinsman's book confirms for me the need for the separation of lesbian struggles from the gay male liberation movement.

25. Eaton, *supra* note 12 at 199.

26. *Ibid.*

27. A number of legal analysts in the United States have reached similar conclusions about the U.S. experience. See for example, Andrew Jacobs, "The Rhetorical Construction of Rights: The Case of the Gay Rights Movement, 1969-1991" (1993) 72 Nebraska Law Review 723; Andrew Koppelman, "Miscegenation Analogy: Sodomy Law as Sex Discrimination" (1988) 98 Yale Law Journal 145; Sylvia Law, "Homosexuality and the Social Meaning of Gender" [1988] Wisconsin Law Review 187; Carl Stychin, "Identities, Sexualities, and the Postmodern Subject: An Analysis of Artistic Funding by National Endowment for the Arts" (1993) 12 Cardozo Arts and Entertainment Law Journal 79.

28. Eaton, *supra* note 12 at 87-91. See also Robson, "Lesbianism in Anglo and European Legal History", *supra* note 14 and Robson, "*Lesbian (Out)Law, supra* note 14.

29. Part of the reason for this may be that what lesbians do sexually is generally not considered "sex" because in a heterosexist culture sex is defined in terms of penile penetration. See Marilyn Frye, *The Politics of Reality: Essays in Feminist Theory* (Freedom, CA: The Crossing Press, 1983).

lesbian. Based on her analysis of the reported "homosexual" cases, Eaton reaches the conclusion that lesbians need to assert their specificity and disassociate from the male-defined, gender neutral terms, "gay" and "sexual orientation". She says:

> Because courts apply gay equality law to lesbians in a gender-blind [sic] fashion, as if it were gender neutral in origin and effect, this thesis concludes that the pursuit of "sexual orientation" rights will not only be of little benefit, but may ultimately prove to be harmful to lesbian interests. Separation from gay male equality litigation emerges as a viable and perhaps necessary choice for lesbians in the legal fight against discrimination.[30]

I appreciate Eaton's analysis immensely and regard it as a major contribution to the study of lesbian and gay legal issues. Her work demonstrates that the stereotype of gay men as sexual aggressors is an important and extremely problematic piece in the legal construction of gays and, more recently, in the legal construction of "sexual orientation". But this is not the full story. Other readings of the cases and other legal history sources and readings will provide new pieces in the legal construction of lesbians, gays, and sexual orientation. These new pieces will not necessarily, or even probably, render the legal construct any more accurate in terms of the lives of lesbians or gay men, but they will reveal the construct in greater detail and complexity. I look forward to the further work of Eaton and of others in producing new stories that will add to the fullness of our understanding of this issue.

While I have trouble accepting that the legal construction of gays is as one dimensional as Eaton depicts, I have no trouble accepting her conclusion in terms of the need to assert lesbian specificity and, possibly, the need to reject the legal grouping of lesbians with gay men, whether that be under the rubric of sexual orientation or some other umbrella term.[31] This conclusion is consistent with other critiques of the use of gender neutral terms in a male dominated society[32]

---

30. Eaton, *supra* note 12 at 1.
31. Eaton, *ibid.*, points out that the legal construction of gays as sexual aggressors is inaccurate for the vast majority of gay men. Her conclusion that lesbians perhaps should separate from gay male equality litigation raises the question as to whether it might be more politically appropriate for lesbians to stand beside gay men to challenge the inaccurate legal construction rather than desert gay men in the name of lesbian specificity. However, I think there are other reasons, relating to male dominance and the gendered experiences of "sexual orientation" oppression, that do support a lesbian separatist strategy (see discussion, *infra*).
32. See *e.g.*, Gillian Walker's critique of the historical shift from gender specific terms such as "battered wives" to the gender neutral terms such as "spouse abuse", "interspousal violence episodes" and "family violence" *Family Violence and the Women's Movement* (Toronto: University of Toronto Press, 1990) at 95-110; and the critique of the gender neutral media coverage of the murder of 14 female engineering students in Montreal in Louise Malette and Marie Challouh, eds., *Montreal Massacre* (Charlottetown: Gynergy Books, 1991).

and with the criticisms that have been raised by some lesbians since the beginning of the gay movement.[33] The apparently gender neutral terms "gay"[34] and "sexual orientation" are male defined and fail to take into account the specific experiences of lesbian inequality. It is the separatist analysis in Eaton's work that I find most interesting and challenging, and that I think is at the heart of her thesis. It is this analysis that opened the door for me to consider the possibility of rejecting the sexual orientation label altogether,[35] and to explore the question of how better to characterize and articulate lesbian inequality in law. I am in search of the most effective legal tools for addressing/redressing the inequalities experienced by us as lesbians and through which we will be able to express those experiences with integrity.[36]

33. See *e.g.*, Jill Johnston, who suggests that "considering the centrality of lesbianism to the Women's Movement it should now seem absurd to persist in associating lesbian women with the male homosexual movement. Lesbians are feminists, not homosexuals"; and Mary Daly who defines lesbians as "women who are woman-identified, having rejected false loyalties to men on all levels" and gay women as "women who, although they relate genitally to women, give their allegiance to men and male myths, ideologies, styles, practices, institutions and professions". *Contra*, see Chris Bearchell, "[e]very time a lesbian is a feminist to the world and a lesbian only to her feminist friends she is behaving with the same 'closetry' that characterized much of ghetto life, with the additional betrayal that she is doing so in the name of freedom for women". The foregoing are all cited by Adam, *supra* note 17 at 94-95.

34. It is now generally accepted that gay refers to gay men and those women who self identify as gay rather than lesbian. At this time, most, if not all, organizations that once described themselves as gay now describe themselves as lesbian and gay.

35. Eaton's work made me realize that I had uncritically, if also unenthusiastically, accepted that there is a basis of inequality, usually described as sexual orientation, and that despite the differences between lesbians and gay men in terms of their experiences of that inequality, there is enough commonality to warrant a single label, at least for the purposes of anti-discrimination law. It is this assumption and its concomitant strategy implications that Eaton challenges. Her challenge strikes a familiar and positive chord with me.

36. Some lesbians argue that lesbians should not resort to the malestream legal system. "The law" is seen as irredeemably male dominated and heterosexist, and as purely an instrument of lesbian oppression. This echoes the argument of many non-dominant groups that law should be rejected. While I have some gut level and abstract sympathy, even admiration for this position, I think that it is misguided, both practically and theoretically. Many lesbians have little or no choice about their involvement with the law in, for example, child custody cases, divorce situations and criminal prosecutions. In addition, the "choice" of whether or not to invoke the law is circumscribed by other factors that may make the rejection of possible legal remedies a luxury many lesbians cannot afford. For many what is described as "choice" in a liberal democracy is not experienced as such by members of subordinated groups. For example, a working class lesbian single mother faced with the prospect of losing her job does not have the same range of choices as a middle class lesbian who has either a job or some other form of financial security. From a theoretical perspective, an unqualified rejection of law seems to posit law as a unidimensional, ahistorical monolith separate from, and ruling over, society. I see law much more in terms of its being a creation of and reflection of society, in a dialectical relationship of change and changing within society. The male dominance and heterosexism, as well as the racism, classism, ageism, and ablism, that permeate law also permeate society. Law is one among a multitude of potential forums in which to try to effect change in these patterns and practices of

Vol. 7   *1994*   297

The Limits of "Sexual Orientation"

For approximately the last 10 years in Canada, gays, and to a lesser extent lesbians, have been lobbying for the inclusion of sexual orientation among the prohibited grounds of discrimination in human rights legislation. While the gay lobby has not been successful throughout the country, they have managed to get sexual orientation protection in the human rights legislation of seven provinces and one territory.[37] And they continue to advocate for sexual orientation to be added to the remaining human rights codes and the *Charter*. Despite widespread support within the gay community for the inclusion of sexual orientation protection, I believe that the umbrella term "sexual orientation" is problematic. The conduct/orientation distinction, derived from the stereotype of "homosexuals" as sexual predators which, as Eaton's research demonstrates, the courts have read into the term sexual orientation, may require us to search for a new term. In addition, the problems to which I now turn are significant enough, in my mind, for both lesbians and gays, but in particular for lesbians, to warrant reconsideration of the continued usage of the term.

"Sexual orientation" is the most commonly used term in Canada at the present, both in popular and statutory language. Sexual orientation suffers from similar problems to the term "sexual preference" which was in common usage in the 1960s and 1970s but which has now largely fallen out of favour with lesbians and gays. Both terms are outward directed, defined in terms of with whom one has sex rather than in terms of who one is. Orientation denotes a leaning in a specific direction and, like preference, seems to downplay the significance of

dominance.

Robson's discussion of the need for lesbians to resort to "either a lesbian jurisprudential construct or a patriarchal one, depending on the circumstances", "Lesbian Jurisprudence?", *supra* note 14 at 466, reflects, I think, a similar understanding that total rejection of "law" is impossible and unrealistic. In the context of this discussion, she raises the question of whether legally trained lesbians have a vested interest in "the law" that precludes us from being able fully to de-centre law in our own thinking and analysis. I continue to struggle with this important question. Eaton, *supra* note 12 at 6 briefly discusses lesbian separatism as a continuously evolving, politically-based practice and methodology. This evolution has, in some contexts, meant moving on from initial responses of total disengagement from men and male institutions to confrontational interaction with men and male institutions, recognizing such actions as sometimes necessary in order "to establish our rights, to obtain resources and support other women" (quoting from Joyce Trebilcot "Letter" (1986) 4:2 Women's Review of Books 4). The movement from total rejection of law to critical and confrontational engagement with law, and the creation of lesbian legal alternatives, is, I think, part of the same evolutionary redefining of lesbian separatism as a political practice.

37. *Supra* note 4.

sexuality as part of self identity.[38] In my reading of them, the terms "orientation" and "preference" lack depth and commitment, as if one can easily and without serious consequence re-orient oneself, or switch one's preference.[39]

There have been, over time, a number of different terms used to denote the basis for the discrimination assumed to be experienced jointly by lesbians and gays. Of all these terms, I prefer "sexual identity" to "sexual orientation".[40] Sexual identity is, to me, a stronger term that more accurately reflects the full import of what it means to be a lesbian, or a heterosexual woman, or... . Being

38. See Bev Jo, Linda Strega and Rushton, eds., *Dykes-Loving-Dykes: Dyke Separatist Politics for Lesbians Only* (Oakland CA: Battleaxe, 1990) at 7:

> Lesbianism is far more than a "sexual preference" or "sexual orientation". Everything we do and feel in our lives we do *as Lesbians*. Our political and creative work is *Lesbian*. *Our friendships are* Lesbian *relationships*. [Emphasis in original]

I refer to the analysis of *Dykes-Loving-Dykes* a few times in this paper. But I do so with a great deal of hesitation. This is very clearly and explicitly a separatist lesbian book; it is a book for lesbians only. In quoting from this book, I am giving non-lesbians access to, and knowledge of, this work and I fear that, in doing so, I am breaching the trust and intention of the authors. And yet, I think that, perhaps, part of that trust is that other lesbians will use their work and their thinking with circumspection and respect, to challenge oneself and others without violating the authors. I hope that I have done so.

39. This is not to endorse a biologically based or essentialist view of sexual identity. I know that people can and do change sexual identity, but I think that this is a change, whatever the change is, of fundamental significance and major consequences; a change not made lightly and not to be taken lightly.

40. In stating my preference for the term sexual identity, it is no doubt clear that I am claiming, rather than rejecting, the now somewhat unpopular notion of identity politics. I hope that my invocation of identity politics is not done in a simplistic way that focuses on a single identity and draws false generalizations or even universalization from it. Part of identity politics has to be the recognition and integration of the intersections of multiple oppressions, as well as the intersections of subordination and domination, that are in each of us and in all of the groups of which we are members; that is the recognition of our identities as complex and multiple. This recognition of the complexity and multiplicity of our identities does not lead me to reject identity categories – that is a simplistic approach – but instead to struggle to integrate the complexity into the discussion and analysis of every category.
Neither does identity politics necessarily rely upon essentialism, i.e., a static, biologically based understanding of what one's identity is and where it comes from. There is in my mind nothing contradictory between identity politics and theories of social construction. I certainly believe that identities, as I refer to them, are social constructs. But being social constructs does not negate those identities, does not make them unreal or insignificant. The social construction of our identities takes place in and through a heterosexist, lesbian- and gay-hating, misogynist, racist, anti-disability, anti-semitic, classist, ageist society. It is a society in which dominance and subordination are manifested in relation to these categories on every level, in economic, political, social, cultural and ideological terms. It is this social context which makes identity politics so meaningful and so urgent.

Vol. 7   *1994*   299

a lesbian is more than a sexual orientation toward women; it is who I am[41] – emotionally, psychologically, politically, physically. Being a lesbian is not only, or even primarily, about having sexual relations with another woman. Most lesbians do have sexual relationships with other women, but this is a component of being a lesbian, not the defining feature. Similarly, while most heterosexuals engage in heterosexual sexual relations, heterosexual sexual practice *per se* is not all there is to heterosexuality.[42] Sexual identity is not a complete or exclusive identity. One also has a race identity, a class identity, an abled identity, and a gender identity, among others. As pieces of one's identity, these are aspects of the person that can be used to judge, stereotype, discriminate against or to privilege one. It is sexual identity, not sexual orientation, that constitutes the basis upon which people discriminate. The discrimination is because of who one is seen to be and what one is seen to do, which includes, but is not limited to, with whom one has sex.

Despite my preference for sexual identity over sexual orientation, the former term is not problem free. It shares the same inadequacies in describing lesbian oppression as any other umbrella term. A major problem for an umbrella term used to denote a basis of discrimination is that it does not identify the group that is discriminated against. This is not a problem unique to sexual orientation/identity as a ground of discrimination; all of the listed grounds, with the exception of disability,[43] fail to distinguish the dominant from the subordinate within the category. Thus, for example, because the category is "sex" not "women", men have felt that they are as entitled as women to bring sex discrimination complaints.[44] Heterosexuals may, at least initially, be similarly considered

---

41. Being a lesbian is not all of who I am, but each component of my identity is in itself a whole rather than simply a piece of my identity. I first learnt this notion of the wholeness of parts from listening to and reading the work of Chrystos. See Chrystos, *Not Vanishing* (Vancouver: Press Gang, 1988).

42. See *infra* note 45 for a discussion of the meaning of heterosexuality.

43. It seems to me that this exception is a reflection of the overwhelming ableism of our society in which it is inconceivable that absence of disability might possibly be a basis for "discrimination" and in which non-discrimination is described as "accommodation".

44. In the early days of the *Charter*, the majority of the sex discrimination arguments were put forward by men, as has been the case with the equal protection clause under the U.S. Constitution. This is how formal equality works. See Gwen Brodsky and Shelagh Day, *Canadian Charter Equality Rights for Women. One Step Forward or Two Steps Back?* (Ottawa: Canadian Advisory Council on the Status of Women, 1989). However, the decision in *Law Society of British Columbia* v. *Andrews*, [1989] 1 S.C.R. 143 [hereinafter *Andrews*] and the movement away from formal equality that it represents should make men's complaints of sex discrimination much more difficult, if not impossible, to make. See, for example, *R.* v. *M. (H.L.)* [1989] S.J. No. 604 (Sask. C.A.) in which Bayda C.J.S applied *Andrews* with respect to a criminal charge involving sex with a female under 14 years of age and stated the following:

When one examines the "larger social, political and legal context" one quickly concludes that to characterize adult males generally or more specifically adult males who are potential accused under s. 146(1), (whichever is the applicable group in those

entitled to complain of discrimination on the basis of sexual orientation.[45] This is a formal equality, rather than an inequality-based,[46] model of anti-discrimination legislation. The formal equality model assumes that discrimination and inequality cut both ways; it ignores the impact of power and the histories of discrimination and inequality that frame current practices. Difficult as it may be

circumstances) as a "discrete and insular minority", a disadvantaged group in need of society's protection or nurture, borders on the alarming if not the preposterous.... To hold in favour of the appellant on this point would not only "overshoot the actual purpose of the right or freedom in question" (see *R.* v. *Big M. Drug Mart* at 344), but it would fly in the face of and mock the underlying purpose of s. 15.

For a further example, see *Keyes* v. *Pandora Press Publishing Association (No. 2)* (1992) 16 C.H.R.R. D/148 (N.S. Bd. of Inquiry) in which the Board held that Pandora's policy of publishing only letters from women did not constitute discrimination against men.

45. *Green* v. *Howard* (DC Super. Ct. No. 91- CAO4194, 12/4/92, as summarized in *Daily Labour Report*, January 6, 1993, The Bureau of National Affairs Inc., Washington, D.C.) is the only case of which I am aware in which a heterosexual has successfully argued sexual orientation discrimination based on her heterosexuality. Green was successful in her complaint that her employment "lay off" was in retaliation for her complaints of her supervisor's favouritism toward lesbian nurses. This "pattern of conduct manifesting sexual orientation discrimination" was found to have resulted in a "hostile work environment" for Green. The supervisor and other nurses involved denied that they were lesbians. Green was awarded $140,000 and reinstatement. However, I understand that there is a human rights case in Australia that has been decided the other way. The dearth of sexual orientation discrimination cases being brought by heterosexuals may be a testament to the hegemony of heterosexualism (see below) which has not yet been seriously challenged through the legal system. As soon as we start to see successful sexual orientation complaints being brought by lesbians and gays, heterosexuals will be sure to follow suit to claim their equal rights. And, it may be, as has been the case with other dominant groups, that, at least initially, heterosexuals and bisexuals will win their claims more easily and in larger numbers than lesbians and gays. *Green* v. *Howard* may be a portent of future sexual orientation litigation. On the other hand, it is possible that our courts will recognize the inappropriateness of heterosexual claims to sexual orientation discrimination and apply a contextualized, inequality-based analysis similar to that demonstrated by the Saskatchewan Court of Appeal in *R.* v. *M.*, *ibid.*

I borrow the term heterosexualism from Sarah Hoagland, *supra* note 16 at 7, who describes the term in the following manner:

What I am talking about when I talk about heterosexualism is not simply a matter of men having procreative sex with women. I am talking about an entire way of life promoted and enforced by every formal and informal institution of the fathers' society, from religion to pornography to unpaid housework to medicine. Heterosexualism is a way of living that normalizes the dominance of one person and the subordination of another.

46. For a discussion of an inequality-based approach, see Diana Majury, "Strategizing In Equality" (1987) 3 Wisconsin Women's Law Journal 169 and "Inequality and Discrimination According to the Supreme Court of Canada" (1991) 4 Canadian Journal of Women and the Law 407.

with respect to some forms of discrimination,[47] an inequality-based model would require that inequalities giving rise to legal remedies be conceptualized exclusively in terms of the subordinated groups within a particular category.

This analysis, which requires the identification of the subordinated groups within a particular category, raises another problem with umbrella terms like sexual orientation; that is, who falls under the umbrella?[48] To a large extent the gay movement has rallied under the sexual liberation banner, in support of the goal of opening up the "world of sexual possibilities".[49] From this vantage point, all "sexual minorities", including bisexuals, transsexuals, transvestites, and transgendered persons as well, arguably, as paedophiles,[50] would be covered under the anti-discrimination protection being sought. However, I would not characterize the issue for lesbians as one of being a sexual minority. Such a characterization focuses on sexual practices in a narrow and de-politicized way. The sexual minority argument is really about sexual pluralism and is not a position that I support.[51] A pluralist approach lumps together disparate groups with no acknowledgement of power and other significant differences between

---

47　It may be difficult, for example, to list, comprehensively and accurately, the subordinated groups that are subjected to race discrimination in Canada. This would be true for a number of the listed grounds, including religion, creed colour and nationality. It may be that there are more appropriate ways to achieve the goal of excluding dominant groups than simply listing the subordinated groups. Lynne Pearlman, in her comments on this article suggested "Perhaps one practical way of dealing with this problem is to leave enumerations as they are, and add an express legislative statement directing that the purpose of the protections is for (historically) disempowered groups, so that proof of disempowerment of one's group becomes a threshold test for bringing an equality claim." Much of the post-*Andrews* case law would certainly support such an approach *supra* note 44.

48.　This question was a particularly contentious one at the gay and lesbian consultation on the *Canadian Human Rights Act supra* note 6.

49.　Adam, *supra* note 17 at 78. See also Gayle Rubin, "Thinking Sex: Notes for a Radical Theory of the Politics of Sexuality" in Carol Vance, ed., *Pleasure and Danger: Exploring Female Sexuality* (Boston: Routledge & Kegan Paul, 1984) 267.

50.　The issue of whether paedophiles should be supported as a sexual minority or rejected as sexual abusers, has caused a great deal of debate and dissention among lesbians and between gays and lesbians See Adam, *ibid.* and Rubin, *ibid*

51.　Put in these terms, sexual orientation becomes a piece in the feminist "sexuality debates" that have focused primarily on the issue of pornography. For discussions of the pornography issue, see Susan Cole, *Pornography and the Sex Crisis* (Toronto: Amanita Publications, 1989); Andrea Dworkin, "Against the Male Flood: Censorship, Pornography and Equality" (1985) 8 Harvard Women's Law Journal 1; and Catharine MacKinnon, "Not A Moral Issue" (1984) 2 Yale Law and Policy Review 321. See also Varda Burstyn, ed., *Women Against Censorship* (Vancouver: Douglas and McIntyre, 1985); and Vance, *supra* note 49. My problem is that I do not think that the issue of lesbian oppression properly falls within this debate. Lesbian oppression is not about sexual practices but about heterosexualism, about sex and sexism and women's resistance. See Pearlman, *supra* note 14 at 318 for a powerful description of a lesbian's experience of how resistance begets backlash, which then can lead to more insightful and more radical forms of resistance and then more overt and brutal forms of backlash in a "continuous cycle of deepened learning"

best, the sexual minorities argument promotes a liberal formal equality model; at worst, it promotes sexual abuse.

The argument is that these other sexual minorities need human rights protection and should be included beside lesbians and gays. I do not think that adults who want to have sex with children should have the right to engage in their "sexual practice"; I would therefore not support extending human rights protection to paedophiles. The extent that bisexuals suffer inequalities as members of a non-dominant group is the extent to which they are perceived to be lesbian or gay; they would therefore be covered in terms of experienced inequalities that derive from their subordinated position by any protection accorded to lesbians and gays.[52] While I would support the inclusion of transsexuals, transvestites and transgendered persons under human rights protection, I am not sure that the discrimination they experience is sufficiently similar to that experienced by lesbians to warrant inclusion under the same term.[53] For some, an umbrella term that includes lesbians and gays, but is not limited to lesbians and gays, is important because it would arguably provide protection for any sexual practice; it would be a sexual minority umbrella. For me, this is an argument for rejecting an umbrella term. Human rights protection is not, to me, about protecting sexual practices but about protecting oppressed people.

While all of the preceding concerns with the term sexual orientation may have

52. In addition to those lesbians who will critique this approach from a sexual minorities perspective, there are no doubt other lesbians who will critique it from the other end of the spectrum. For example, Marilyn Murphy *Are You Girls Travelling Alone? Adventures in Lesbianic Logic* (Los Angeles: Clothespin Fever Press, 1991) at 53 rejects "the premise that bisexual women are penalized in straight society". She argues that bisexual women are seen by straight society, not as rejecting heterosexuality, but as simply in a phase. If they do engage in sex with other women, this is considered sexy and a potential source of titillating "lesbian stories" to be taken back to their heterosexual world. She concludes at 56:

> Women who call themselves bisexual – not because they are in transition or are afraid of their lesbianism – but because they choose to relate sexually to both women and men, are the only women who are really heterosexual. They are the only women who choose to relate to men after having known and experienced our non-compulsory alternative.

I am sympathetic to Murphy's views on bisexuality. I think there is a lot right in what she says and I love the directness with which she puts it forward. However, I am not convinced that bisexual women do not suffer any negative treatment from the heterosexual world and so I continue to argue that they do need to be granted protection against discrimination.

53. To my knowledge, very little has been written by transsexuals, transvestites or transgendered people describing their understanding of their own oppression. However, this would be the place to start in terms of trying to figure out how best to conceptualize their discrimination for purposes of inclusion in human rights protections. For one of the few pieces that I am aware of, see C. Cailin Thompson, "She walks, she talks, she crawls on her belly like a reptile" (1993) 38 *Fireweed* 24. Leslie Feinberg's book, *Stone Butch Blues* (Ithaca, New York: Firebrand, 1993) has given me a lot to think about on these and related issues. The story that Feinberg tells in this book is, in my reading of it, a story of the oppression of gender constructs, a story that is consistent with my analysis of lesbian discrimination as sex discrimination.

particular meanings for lesbians, there is a concern that has primary significance for lesbians. The problem, raised by Eaton's research discussed in the context of the omission of lesbians in law, is that the term sexual orientation as applied to lesbians and gays has been largely defined in terms of gay men. Lesbians are being drawn into and judged by a standard that may have very little to do with the realities of their lives, their self definition, the inequalities they experience and the priorities they would set for change.[54] Eaton's research demonstrates that the

54. I am faced here with the recurring problem of discussing a group, in this case lesbians, as if we were a single homogeneous group when we are, of course, a diverse group in terms of class, race, age, and disability. These differences lead to different experiences of being a lesbian which make it difficult, if not impossible, to talk about lesbian experience generally or in the abstract. At the same time, I do think that it is necessary, because we are a subordinated group, oppressed because we are lesbians (for many on other interconnected bases as well) to theorize and strategize as lesbians In addition, there are differences, at least in part related to the differences referred to above, in terms of what it means to each of us to be a lesbian and how we define ourselves. Some women choose to describe themselves as gay and not as lesbian. According to a gay analysis, sexual orientation is the source of oppression. Gender is not primary or possibly even relevant in this context, and the characterization of sexual orientation as male defined and male dominated is seen as misplaced.

In focusing on the issue of gender, I do not wish to establish a hierarchy of oppressions. In the context of the present discussion, it is not clear which is the dominant group or, more appropriately, whether women or gay men are the more subordinated in our society. My assertion is only that when lesbians and gay men are in a group together, men are in a position of dominance vis-a-vis women of the same race, class and disability status. All that I can say about those women who self define as gay instead of lesbian is that we disagree in the analysis of our oppression and in group identification and as well, I think, in terms of our self identity. The differences are, I think, deeply political and fundamentally important, not only in terms of means but in terms of ends as well. In thinking about this, I found helpful the work of Celia Kitzinger, *The Social Construction of Lesbianism* (London: Sage Publications, 1987). In her response to the range of lesbian identities she found in her interviews with lesbians, Kitzinger critiques liberal humanistic accounts of lesbianism. While this criticism is different than the one I would make of gay women, our critiques come from a similar place. Kitzinger acknowledges the political basis of that critique at 93:

> I have strong beliefs about which of the identities presented here is "best". Unlike them [other researchers self-defined as objective], I do not glorify this identity account by designating it as the most "well-adjusted", or placing it at the apex of some developmental hierarchy, with all other identity accounts trailing behind, indicative of psychological immaturity, but instead argue for my value claims from an overtly political perspective. I illustrate which of the identity accounts conform to liberal humanistic ideology, and argue that they thereby function to privatize lesbianism, removing it from the political domain. When women use these accounts, they are undermining radical feminist claims for lesbianism as a major political force, and for those of us who share those aims, such accounts are a tactical error. Liberal humanistic accounts of lesbianism are neither "inaccurate" nor "developmentally immature": they are politically inexpedient from a radical feminist perspective.

I would describe liberal humanistic accounts of lesbianism, or, in the context of the present discussion, gay identification by lesbians, as more than "politically inexpedient" or "tactical errors" The differences are more than strategic, they reflect different fundamental values. While

legal construction of gays and lesbians, and more recently of sexual orientation, is premised, at least in part, on heterosexual male fears and stereotypes of gay male sexuality. This example is only one of a number of ways in which these terms have been and are male defined, and uncritically assumed to apply to lesbians. Although he fails to explore their significance,[55] Gary Kinsman, in his historical study of sexuality in Canada, refers to a number of the manifestations of male dominance and lesbian omission or lesbian mis(male)characterization. He recognizes this in general terms in his introduction to his book:

> Given differences in the social organization of gender as it affects our sexual lives, any use of a unitary homosexual category for both male and female experiences necessarily distorts lesbian experience to fit the male category. Lesbians are thereby transformed into female homosexual "men". Differences in the social organization of gender – of forms of masculinity, femininity, and sexuality – tend to become obscured and the effect of patriarchal organization overlooked.[56]

In the course of his book, he provides a number of specific examples.[57] Given Kinsman's recognition of the differences between lesbians and gay men and the gendered power imbalance that functions to disempower lesbians vis-a-vis gay men, it is surprising, and perhaps somewhat self-serving, that he continues to talk in terms of a lesbian and gay movement, as if such a thing exists and exists unproblematically.[58]

Marilyn Frye questions the assumption that there is a natural alliance between lesbians and gay men.[59] According to Frye, there is some common ground in that the abuse and oppression that lesbians and gays experience flow from a common source in the "social and political structures of sex and gender"[60] and that both lesbians and gays are punished for their deviation from "sexuality organized

---

no doubt there are points of commonality, there are also points of departure that may be irreconcilable. My rejection of gay identity for myself and my critique of it as perpetuating a male standard come from my lesbian feminist values and political perspective. The analysis that I put forward is rooted in that politic and is certainly not shared by all lesbians or by all feminists.

55. *Supra* note 17.

56. *Ibid.* at 17.

57. See *e.g.*, *ibid.* at 180, 181, 182, 184, 186, 187, 189.

58. While I direct this critique specifically to Kinsman's work, it also applies to the analysis of many gay men who talk about lesbian and gay issues. I refer to Kinsman's work because I know him and I know his work, and I respect both, and thus I would hope that he will take my criticisms seriously and thoughtfully and understand where they come from.

59. Marilyn Frye, "Lesbian Feminism and the Gay Rights Movement: Another View of Male Supremacy, Another Separatism" in *The Politics of Reality: Essays in Feminist Theory, supra* note 29 at 128.

60. *Ibid.* at 129.

around male-dominant, female-subordinate genital intercourse."[61] But the social reality of male supremacy situates the women who deviate from this norm very differently from the men who do so. Frye argues that gay male culture and the gay rights movement in many ways share the values and principles of the male supremacist culture.[62] In this context, gay men have much more connection with, and investment in, heterosexual men, than they do with women, whether lesbian or heterosexual. Frye sees the gay movement as trying to strengthen this connection, and render it unthreatening:

> [M]ale homosexuality is congruent with and a logical extension of straight male-supremacist culture. It seems that straight men just don't understand the congruency and are frightened by the "logical extension." In response, the male gay rights movement attempts to educate and encourage straight men to an appreciation of the normalcy and harmlessness of gay men. It does not challenge the principles of male-supremacist culture.[63]

Such a position is antithetical to the interests of women, particularly of lesbian-identified out lesbians, who are arguably the most noticeable and marginalized resisters of male supremacy.

Frye's analysis does not apply to all gay men, or even all gay organizations.[64] The values and principles of the gay movement are undoubtedly more complex and self-contradictory than unmitigated male supremacy. However, Frye's analysis does raise, in clear and unequivocal terms, the fundamental question of lesbian alliance with gay men. Until the gay movement recognizes and challenges its own participation in, and allegiance to, male supremacy, there would seem little reason for lesbians to be involved in the movement. In fact, in

---

61. *Ibid.*
62. See *ibid.* at 130 where Frye lists the following as among the fundamental principles and values of male supremacist culture:
    1. The presumption of male citizenship;
    2. Worship of the penis;
    3. Male homoeroticism, or man-loving;
    4. Contempt for women, or woman-hating;
    5. Compulsory male heterosexuality;
    6. The presumption of general phallic access.
    John Stoltenberg, in "A Coupla Things I've Been Meaning To Say About Really Confronting Male Power" (Key Note Speech to the 15th National Men and Masculinity Conference, Atlanta, Georgia, 1990) [unpublished] acknowledges and challenges the male supremacist values of gay liberation. Paper available from Diana Majury; Department of Law, Carleton University.
63. Frye, *ibid.* at 144.
64. Some gay men and gay organizations have explicitly tried to undermine their own male privilege and to challenge male supremacy. See, for example, Adam's discussion of the "radical faeries" *supra* note 17 at 96 and Stoltenberg, *supra* note 62.

promoting gay rights, lesbians may be further entrenching their own disempowerment as "deviant" women in a male dominated society.

Lesbians have been subject to the sexism and male dominance of gay men within joint organizations. Lesbian specificity is ignored both in gay organizations[65] and society at large. As a result, lesbians have been assumed to be the same as gay men; they have been subjected to, and judged by, the stereotypes of gay men; they have been assumed to have the same interests, goals and needs as gay men; they have been assumed to suffer from the same forms of discrimination, and in the same ways, as gay men.

As a female in this society, a lesbian's experience of inequality is very different from that of a gay man.[66] She is likely to be in a worse economic situation than a gay man, in terms of current finances and economic opportunities; she is likely to have more limited and less remunerative job prospects than he; she

65. A prime example of this kind of failure to acknowledge lesbian specificity which leads to the unproblematized assertion of lesbian and gay shared interests is the organization "equality for gays and lesbians everywhere" (EGALE). Founded in 1986, to lobby for the inclusion of sexual orientation in federal human rights legislation, EGALE has been the almost exclusive preserve of a small Ottawa-based group of white, non-disabled gay men. A number of lesbians have been actively involved in EGALE, but only for relatively short periods of time and with little or no effect in terms of making the organization responsive and accountable to lesbians. Despite its lack of representativeness, EGALE has attained some degree of public visibility with respect to both media and funding, possibly because it describes itself as "the only group in Canada to concentrate on federal issues" (letter to the editor from Denis LeBlanc, president EGALE, (1993) 6 *GO INFO* at 4 (Ottawa: Association of Gays and Lesbians of Ottawa)). At the request of two lesbians who had resigned from EGALE in frustration, I attended a public meeting held by EGALE in October of 1992. EGALE had decided to formalize its existence and structures and the meeting was to respond to and ratify a proposed constitution. There were only about 30 people at the meeting, of whom six were lesbians. Most, if not all of the lesbians in attendance were there, as was I, to voice concerns. Our questions about the lack of representativeness of the organization in terms of race, disability, and gender were met with a mixture of hostility, resentment, and concern. This meeting had been advertised in the local lesbian and gay newspaper; this was the extent of the outreach to the lesbian and gay communities not already involved in EGALE. The overriding message was that all lesbians and gays were welcome to join the existing organization and that given this openness, the organization would continue to lobby and advocate on behalf of "gays and lesbians everywhere". The lesbians at the meeting, in conjunction with a few of the gay men present, managed to forestall the adoption of the constitution and obtain a commitment that those involved in EGALE would reconsider their name and focus, so that they more accurately represented who and what the organization is. The lesbians demanded that, at the very least, the "L" from EGALE be removed to eliminate the misleading inclusion of lesbians, which was in name only. I was disheartened, but not surprised, to pick up a copy of Ottawa's gay and lesbian newspaper, 6 *GO INFO*, and find that EGALE had proceeded after that October meeting to organize a general membership meeting in January at which the proposed constitution was approved. It seems to be business as usual at EGALE, unrepresentative as it may be.

66. The negative comparison that follows only holds true when gender is the only difference between the lesbian and the gay man. Race, disability, age, and class differences will either mitigate or exacerbate the gender differences.

Vol. 7   *1994*   307

is more likely to be trying to support children, with all of the attendant problems and expenses that child care presents in the context of the paid work force. Reproduction and child custody are issues of central concern to some lesbians,[67] while, at best, they have been seen as peripheral to gay issues. While the use of psychiatry against lesbians and the pathologization of lesbians as mentally ill have been common practices historically, they have received little attention as gay concerns. The physical and sexual violence inflicted upon lesbians is different, in terms of where it takes place, the forms it takes, and its overall impact, from the violence to which gay men are subjected. The focus and import of issues of sex, sexuality, and sexual practice are different for lesbians than they are for gay men. Lesbians, particularly outspoken lesbian-identified lesbians, are being subjected to a vicious and virulent anti-lesbian, anti-woman backlash.

The term sexual orientation seems inappropriate and inadequate to ground the specific inequalities experienced by lesbians. There is no doubt that lesbians should support gay men as an oppressed group, as we should support any oppressed group. But the question is, given all of the differences between lesbians and gay men, played out as they are in the context of the power imbalance of gender, is there enough in common to warrant a single group for anti-discrimination purposes? Are the discriminations experienced by lesbians and gays sufficiently similar to be lumped together under a single ground of discrimination? Are we looking for a new gender neutral term such as, for example, "sexual identity" that might more accurately capture the meaning of being a lesbian and that is capable of being defined in law and society as including lesbians in their realities, as well as gay men in theirs? Or is the hegemony of male dominance so overpowering, are the experiences and issues for lesbians and gays so different, as to necessitate that lesbians resist the identification of lesbian inequality with gay inequality and insist on the recognition of lesbians as a distinct group, experiencing discrimination, not under some umbrella term that includes gay men, but specific to lesbians? Or is lesbian discrimination an extreme form of discrimination against women; is sex discrimination the more appropriate umbrella under which to challenge lesbian discrimination?

Lesbian Inequality as Sex Inequality

My focus on the appropriate naming of the "ground" of discrimination avoids the larger question of whether or not "grounds" of discrimination are an effective way to address the inequalities. Given that a lesbian identity is only one piece of that person's identity, it may be misleading and inaccurate to ground a discrimination complaint on that lesbian identity. Our complex and interwoven

---

67. There is some debate about whether or not reproduction and custody are lesbian issues. Some lesbians include the rejection of male sperm as part of their definition of lesbianism and characterize reproduction and custody issues as a function of heterosexual privilege.

identities are not so easily severable. This is particularly true for people who belong to more than one oppressed group and who cannot usually single out one of their oppressed identities as the sole target of the discrimination. Relying on multiple grounds of discrimination becomes a critical strategy in resisting this isolated factor approach to discrimination, and in making clear the simultaneity and indivisibility of oppressions.[68] However, the approach remains one of picking out factors, be they single or multiple, and as such the larger concern of fragmentation and distortion remains. Despite this concern, I continue my focus on lesbian discrimination, to be named alone or in conjunction with other grounds of discrimination, because even though this naming may not be the end point, it is, to me, an important part of a process of assertion.

The argument that discrimination against lesbians and gays is sex discrimination has generally been articulated, where it has been argued at all, as a formal equality argument. The argument, under the formal equality model, is that it is sex discrimination to deny women the rights that men have, or to restrict women in ways that men are not restricted in the exercise of their rights, including the right to have full and committed sexual relationships with women. The argument applies, in the converse,[69] to support gay male rights. Thus, for example, the argument in support of the right to gay marriage is that "to permit a man to marry a woman but at the same time to deny him the right to marry another man is to construct an unconstitutional classification "on account of sex."[70] This is the classic formal equality, "but for sex" argument in which sex

68. See Kim Crenshaw, "Demarginalizing the Intersection of Race and Sex: A Black Feminist Critique of Antidiscrimination Doctrine, Feminist Theory and Antiracist Politics" (1989) University of Chicago Legal Forum 139 and Nitya Duclos (now Nitya Iyer), "Disappearing Women: Racial Minority Women in Human Rights Cases" (1993) 6 Canadian Journal of Women and the Law 25. Emily Carasco, "A Case of Double Jeopardy: Race and Gender" (1993) 6 Canadian Journal of Women and the Law 142, discusses the difficulty of choosing or even "knowing" the bases upon which one has been discriminated. On a related point, as one means of rejecting the isolated factor approach, those of us who organize conferences should stop scheduling all of the group-based caucuses at the same time, and thereby stop requiring women who belong to more than one of the caucus groups to choose their most pressing identity for that moment.

69. It is the fact that the argument does work in the converse, that it applies equally to both lesbians and gays, women and men, that has enabled courts to reject this articulation of the sex discrimination argument. See, for example, Donnelly J. in *State* v. *Walsh* (1986), 713 S.W.2d 508 (Mo.) at 509:
    The State concedes that the statute prohibits men from doing what women do, namely engage in sexual activity with men. However, the State argues that it likewise prohibits women from doing something which men do: engage in sexual activity with women. We believe that it applies equally to men and women because it prohibits both classes from engaging in sexual activity with members of their own sex.

70. *Singer* v. *Hara* (1974), 11 Wash. App. 247 at 251. See also *DeSantis* v. *Pacific Tel. & Tel. Co. Inc.* (1979), 608 F.2d 327 (9th Cir.) in which the defendant's refusal to hire or retain homosexuals was held not to constitute sex discrimination; and *State* v. *Walsh, ibid.*

Vol. 7   *1994*   309

is put forward as the sole impediment to the right, privilege or benefit being sought.[71] In the lesbian or gay context, the argument is that "but for" my gender, or alternatively "but for" the gender of my chosen partner, I would have access to the right being denied me. While the simplicity of this "but for sex" version of a sex equality argument may make it appear attractive, it is an argument that undermines, if not contradicts, an inequality-based approach. As with all formal equality arguments, the "but for sex" argument is premised on an assertion of compliance with the dominant standard. Lesbians and gays are put forward as the same as heterosexuals, gender being cast as an insignificant difference. To the extent that lesbians and gays are able and willing to "heterosexualize" themselves, they argue that they should have access to the privileges of heterosexuality. Thus lesbian mothers have been granted custody of their children as long as they appear to be heterosexual, that is that they are not politically or sexually active as lesbians.[72] A successful formal equality analysis in this context would mean that the least oppressed lesbians and gays, that is those most like the dominant group, would be granted heterosexual status. As a corollary, the most oppressed lesbians and gays[73] would be further marginalized and subject to more extreme forms of discrimination and subordination.

The fact that gays have by and large not been successful even under the formal equality model of sex discrimination[74] is a reflection of the depth and

---

71. Dickson, C.J., applied this "but for sex" analysis to the issue of sexual harassment in *Janzen* v. *Platy Enterprises Ltd*, [1989] 1 S.C.R. 1252. He found that, but for their sex, the complainants would not have been harassed and that this fact is what makes the harassment constitute sex discrimination. This analysis is as problematic in this context as it is with respect to discrimination against lesbians. It is not the fact of gender, but the meaning of gender in a male dominant society, that makes sexual harassment an act of sex discrimination, regardless of whether the harasser also sexually harasses men.

72. See *e.g.*, *Barkley* v. *Barkley* (1980), 28 O.R. (3d) 141 (Prov. Ct.) and *Bezaire* v. *Bezaire* (1980), 20 R.F.L. (2d) 361 (Ont. C.A.). For a full discussion of this issue, see Arnup, *supra* note 12.

73. Pearlman, *supra* note 14 at 342 discusses what she describes as "a continuum of outness" whereby the more one deviates from, or otherwise challenges their gender stereotype, the more extreme are the forms of discrimination and hatred to which one is subjected. This is not simply a linear uni-dimensional continuum: class, race, and (dis)ability are also significant factors in terms of one's location on the continuum.

74. See *supra* note 70. *Contra*. see *Baehr* v. *Lewin* (1993), 852 P. 2d 44 (Hawaii S.C.). For examples of Canadian cases, see *Vogel* v. *Government of Manitoba* (1983), 4 C.H.R.R. (Board of Adjudication) in which sex was one of the grounds of discrimination argued and *Bd of Governors of the U of Sask.* v. *Sask H.R.C.*, [1976] 3 W.W.R. 385 (Sask. Q.B.) in which sex discrimination was the only ground argued. In the Canadian cases, as in the U.S. cases referred to above, the complainants were gay men. I am only aware of two Canadian cases, *Nielsen* v. *Canada H.R.C.* and *OPSEU (Pearlman)* v. *Metro Tenants Legal Services*, (presently the subject of a labour arbitration), in which a lesbian is basing her claim, in part, on the ground of sex discrimination. Given that almost all of the cases relating to discrimination against lesbians and gays have been brought by gay men, it is not surprising that so few lesbians have brought sex discrimination complaints, even though the lesbian sex discrimination claim is probably stronger than the gay male claim of sex discrimination.

resistance of the hatred and fear of lesbians and gays.[75] Even when lesbians and gays present themselves as the same as heterosexuals, they are not accepted. If lesbians and gays were "just like" heterosexuals, then the only threat that we would pose would be to the strict gender differentiation imposed by heterosexuality. The rejection of even assimilated lesbians and gays is strong testament to the commitment to retain gender difference, that is to the preservation of gender inequality. This recognition that gender and sex inequality are the underpinnings of "sexual orientation" discrimination gives rise to the more complex, inequality-based analysis of lesbian discrimination[76] as sex

While the sex discrimination ground has yet to be fully argued in *Nielsen*, it was rejected as a potential ground in the context of a mandamus application seeking to bring the complaint forward for a hearing:

> It is quite apparent, or observable, without formally deciding, that the applicant's claim for dental services rendered to her partner was not declined because of sex. After all the dental care plan is, it seems, available to both women and men equally, so the fact of the applicant's being a woman is not the basis for the alleged discrimination.

Nielsen v. *Canada H.R.C.*, F.T.D., March 18, 1992, [unreported] at 6.

While the preliminary outline of this ground, as set out in Nielsen's mandamus application, disclosed a complex sex discrimination analysis, the judge apparently read and heard it only as a "but for sex" argument. I am aware of the *Nielsen* and *Pearlman* cases because of my work in the lesbian legal community. There may be many more lesbian discrimination cases and sex discrimination arguments being put forward by lesbians or gays that have not yet been reported or otherwise come to my attention.

75. I choose not to use the term "homophobia" for a number of reasons. In its gender neutrality, it masks the specific ways in which lesbian hatred is manifested. Male dominance and gay male notoriety are such that homophobia tends to be seen primarily as the ways in which gay hatred is acted out; lesbians, if thought about at all in this context, are assumed to have the same experiences of oppression as gay men. It is for these reasons that many lesbians have adopted the term "lesbophobia" or "lesbianphobia". However, the use of "phobia" is also problematic. Phobia denotes an irrational fear and is based in pathology, indicating that the phobic person has no control over their fear. Lesbians do represent a threat to the foundations of heterosexualism, and those who fear that lesbian threat may be fully rational in their fear. Neither are the so-called "phobic" ones victims, as the epitaph phobia might imply; they are the perpetrators of hatred and oppression and should be held responsible and accountable as such. The preceding argument is derived from Celia Kitzinger, "Heteropatriarchal Language, The Case Against 'Homophobia'" (1983) 5 Gossip 15. See also *Dykes-Loving-Dykes, supra* note 38 at 15, in which the editors retain the term lesbophobia to refer to "many het women's reactions as well as some Lesbians' revulsion at and terror of their own and others' Lesbianism, because Lesbians and het women don't have a reasonable reason to fear Lesbianism." Unreasonable reasons that heterosexual women may fear lesbians might include the challenge to heterosexual women in terms of their choices and the possibilities for change and the stereotyped fear of lesbians as female sexual predators out to seduce or coerce all heterosexual women.

76. I refer mostly to lesbian discrimination rather than lesbian and gay discrimination because, while there is a parallel analysis of gay discrimination as sex discrimination, the differences are more important than the similarities. One of the major reasons for doing the sex discrimination analysis is to understand the gendered nature and impact of the discrimination and make known the specificities of discrimination against lesbians.

Vol. 7   *1994*   311

discrimination.[77] Judicial rejection of the formal sex equality analysis of discrimination against lesbians and gays is premised on an asserted difference between lesbians and gays and their relationships on the one hand and heterosexuals and heterosexual relationships on the other. This "difference" is all about gender; it is described primarily in terms of sexual intercourse and reproduction,[78] but also in terms of gender roles and ascribed gender qualities.[79]

Lesbians are discriminated against because they challenge dominant understandings and meanings of gender in our society. And the more, and the more overtly, we challenge gender, the more, and the more overtly, we are discriminated against. Gender differentiation, premised on the subordination of women, is as essential to heterosexualism as it is to sexism. Lesbian inequalities are sex inequalities because they are rooted in a highly circumscribed definition of gender and gender roles, according to which women are seen only in relation to men. Women who define themselves, and who, in so doing, define themselves without any reference to men, are de-sexed; either they are seen as not women or their "sex", that is their lesbianism, is denied. Either way, this is sex discrimination at its most extreme.

Sexuality is one of the defining features of gender, in terms of both reproduction and presumed male sexual access to females. Gender stereotypes and the gender hierarchy[80] are premised on heterosexuality. Heterosexuality and the gender stereotypes and hierarchy to which it gives rise have, in the past, been assumed to be biologically based, that is seen as essential components of one's biological sex. In this heterosexual sexual context, the male is seen as aggressive, independent, dominant; the female is seen as passive, dependent, submissive. Male sexual violence against women is a reflection of, as well as a function of, the deeply rooted connections between gender inequality, sex and sexuality.

---

77. See Law, *supra* note 27. It is interesting that Law relies explicitly on feminist theory in making what is a gender neutral analysis of discrimination against lesbians and gays as sex discrimination.

78. See *e.g.*, *Andrews* v *Ontario (Minister of Health)* (1988), 64 O.R. (2d) 258 (Ont C.J.) at 263 where McRae J said:

> Homosexual couples are *not* similarly situated to heterosexual couples. Heterosexual couples procreate and raise children. They marry or are potential marriage partners and most importantly they have legal obligations to support for their children whether born in wedlock or out and for their spouses ... A same-sex partner does not and cannot have these obligations. [Emphasis in original]

79. See, for example, *Anderson* v. *Luoma* (1986), 50 R.F.L. (2d) 126 (B.C.S.C.) at 141 where Dohm J. said:

> The phrase "living together as man and wife" ... can only mean what it says, namely a man and woman living together and not married. Two persons of the same gender living together misses the mark by 50 per cent. The defendant in my view can never be a "parent" and it is highly unlikely she could ever become a "stepparent" to the children.

80. Even the image here is a (hetero)sexual one, with the male on the top and the female on the bottom.

Heterosexuality becomes one of the demarcations and reinforcers of gender "difference" and of women's inequality. Heterosexuality is prescribed and promoted through law as through other social institutions:

> History suggests that a primary purpose and effect of state enforcement of heterosexuality is to preserve gender differentiation and the relationships premised upon it. Thus, constitutional restraints against gender discrimination must also be applied to laws censuring homosexuality.[81]

Lesbian oppression functions to reinforce and perpetuate strict notions of gender differentiation. Lesbian inequality is the warning to girls and women not to challenge the prescribed meaning of being female in this society. Those girls and women who do start to assert their autonomy and to challenge their sexual subordination and the centrality/necessity of men in women's lives are often quickly and powerfully reminded that it could get worse. They are called "lesbian" or "dyke", not because they do, or are even thought to, have "sex" with women, but because the ostracism and increased inequality that the label "lesbian" represents are used to try to bring women back into gender line.[82] Women and girls who do not focus their attention on men are called "man-haters", a term stereotypically understood as synonymous with lesbian, a term that is explicitly designed to re-focus attention back on men.[83]

Discrimination against lesbians is sex discrimination, perhaps in its starkest and most overt form. It is important to argue lesbian discrimination as sex discrimination in legal fora as elsewhere, because this analysis challenges sex inequality in fundamental and radical ways. However, strategically, it is probably not advisable to leave lesbian inequalities to be addressed exclusively through the prohibition of sex discrimination. The lesbian discrimination as sex discrimination analysis requires a fairly sophisticated understanding of sex equality/inequality.[84] As with any other uncharted equality territory, rejection of a sex equality analysis, at the first instance, is indicative neither of its validity as equality theory nor of its

81. Law, *supra* note 27 at 230.
82. There is a significant difference in impact when the label "dyke" is used to attack a heterosexual woman as compared to a lesbian. For the heterosexual woman, it is a warning of the potential for increased hostility and danger; for the lesbian, it is a reminder of these as the realities with which she lives.
83. It is interesting to me that while man-hating is one of the prevailing stereotypes of lesbians, gay men are not accused of women-hating. The problem with gay men is not that their focus is men, only that their focus on men is overtly sexualized. In making this point, I am not intending to invoke a formal equality comparison of man-hating and woman-hating. While the former is for some a position of resistance to male dominance, the latter is a form of woman abuse.
84. Lynne Pearlman's suggestions in her comments on this paper helped me a great deal in the wording of what follows.

potential eventually to be integrated into our jurisprudence. It may take time for the lesbian sex discrimination analysis to be heard and understood in the court room[85] which is precisely why it is important to continue to speak it, develop it, argue its appropriateness and insist that it be heard and understood on our terms. Some of the equality arguments which now seem commonplace in our jurisprudence at first instance seemed incredibly risky and impossible to expect courts to understand.

It seems to me that there might, in most cases, be a substantial difference between arguing lesbian inequality as sex discrimination rather than as sexual orientation discrimination or even lesbian discrimination. Take, for instance, the "spousal" benefit cases. These cases have generally been presented in terms of heterosexual couples being given something that has not been given to so called "same-sex" couples. Lesbian and gay couples are seen as being denied these benefits because of their sexual orientation. A sex equality analysis of spousal benefits would more readily and clearly expose the gendered assumptions of dependence, need, and obligation upon which most of these benefits are premised. Spousal benefits then perpetuate the gendered conditions which lend credence to these gendered assumptions. It is a self-perpetuating system of sexual inequality. A sex equality analysis would question the fundamental premise that benefits should necessarily or logically be disseminated through sexual relationships. A sex equality analysis would open up the larger question of why we as a society endorse such benefits and to whom, in the interests of fairness and equity, they should be allocated. If the issues are dependence, need, and obligation, why then are these not the criteria for distribution? Such an approach may provide the grounding for arguments for universalized benefits. It may be that not only the analysis, but the result, might be quite different from a sex equality perspective.

However, in the interim as lesbian sex equality analysis is being developed, lesbians need to be named specifically as a protected group in order to avoid lesbian claims being dismissed summarily, leaving lesbians without any legal protection against discrimination. While the sexual orientation umbrella, as it has been legally and socially constructed in the context of male supremacy, may be inappropriate, the sex umbrella, as it has been legally constructed, may, at least for the moment, be inadequate. The legal recognition of discrimination against lesbians as a prohibited ground of discrimination will provide the foot in the door that will enable the sex discrimination arguments to be made. Sex discrimination can be claimed and argued as a separate ground, in conjunction with the lesbian discrimination ground, as well as in conjunction with any other ground that may

85. New legal argument and analysis are frequently met by incomprehension, scepticism, and resistance in the court room. The quote from *Nielsen, supra* note 74, is an example of at least one if not all three of these ways of refusing to engage with the sex discrimination analysis. On the other hand, this same judge could see that the refusal to extend dental benefits to Carol Nielsen's partner and their child *might* constitute sexual orientation discrimination.

apply.[86] While lesbian discrimination may be the ground which the court feels required to hear and consider in full, they will have to sit through, and at least give some thought to, the sex discrimination argument as well. In addition, the lesbian discrimination ground would be argued in terms of sex discrimination, that discrimination against lesbians is discrimination against women who are challenging the circumscribed meanings of gender. In Canada, sexual harassment had first to be included as a separate ground of discrimination before it was definitively recognized as a form of sex discrimination;[87] lesbian discrimination may have to follow this same path.

Conclusion

I am left at the end of this analysis with the conclusion that, strategically, it is in lesbians' interests to pursue the explicit inclusion of discrimination against lesbians as a prohibited ground of discrimination in human rights codes and in the *Charter*.[88] As a political strategy, this might best be done in coalition with gay groups, as well as independently. However, coalition is only possible if consensus can be reached on both goals and strategy, and lesbians are confident that the hegemony of male dominance will not once again leave them out of the process.[89] The recognition of lesbian specificity is of fundamental importance.

86. *Supra* note 68.
87. Initially sexual harassment claims were rejected by human rights commissions as outside their jurisdiction, that is as not being covered under the prohibition against sex discrimination (See Constance Backhouse and Leah Cohen, *The Secret Oppression: Sexual Harassment of Working Women* (Toronto: MacMillan, 1978). This led to the successful lobbying for the express inclusion of a claim for sexual harassment in most Canadian human rights codes. Simultaneously, as the lobbying efforts got underway, some human rights boards of inquiry held that sexual harassment was covered under sex discrimination (See Constance Backhouse, "Bell v. Flaming Steer Steak House Tavern: Canada's First Sexual Harassment Decision" (1981) 19 University of Western Ontario Law Review 141). The Supreme Court of Canada decision in *Janzen*, *supra* note 71, in which the Court unanimously held that sexual harassment is a form of sex discrimination was handed down in 1990. Up to that time, Canadian tribunals and courts had been generally, but not unanimously, moving in that direction. For a contrary ruling, see *Janzen* v. *Platy Enterprises Ltd* (1986), 33 D.L.R. (4th) 32 (Man. C.A.).
88. I am not, in the context of this paper, dealing with the important question as to whether human rights legislation offers lesbians, or any other oppressed group, any meaningful protection. This question warrants much greater attention than I can give it here. But, at present it is my view that limited, and to a large extent illusory as they are, the protections offered oppressed groups under human rights laws are not worthless and are not counter productive. I therefore think that they are worth fighting for as a piece – a mobilizing piece, an educational piece, a theory-building piece, as well as a rights piece – in the struggle for equality.
89. Gay groups have, to date, been very resistant to the suggestion of replacing the term "sexual orientation", the label they have adopted and been fighting for 10 years. They feel that lesbians who are raising issues of lesbian specificity are dividing the "movement" and undermining the chances of getting any further legal protections. This resistance to re-considering a ten-year-old position does not auger well for the possibilities for coalition building between lesbians and gays.

But that specificity is grounded in socially constructed (and desperately and tenaciously hung onto by society) gender differences. Hence, the need to present and analyze lesbian discrimination as sex discrimination.

This being my conclusion strategically, I am left with two theoretical questions that continue to make me pause to think. The first is whether by arguing that discrimination against lesbians is sex discrimination, and a particularly entrenched and protected form, I have inappropriately collapsed lesbian discrimination into sex discrimination. The second related question, is whether, as a white, middle class, christian lesbian who is not at present disabled, I have privileged gender over other forms of oppression in my analysis of lesbian oppression.

While I feel myself on the verge of saying that discrimination against lesbians is fully understood and conceptualized as sex discrimination, I always seem to pull back just short of that assertion. Is there something more that is discrimination against lesbians that is not captured by a sex discrimination analysis? While I have some persisting sense that there is something more and that I am missing a piece that makes lesbian inequality something separate from sex inequality, I do not know what that piece is.

Ruthann Robson argues that lesbian jurisprudence is not the same as feminist jurisprudence:

> Feminist jurisprudence is most often concerned with women *vis-a-vis* men; the difference/sameness debates on equality issues evince this preoccupation. The essential exercise is comparing women with men; the essential goal is equality with men.
>
> As I conceptualize lesbian jurisprudence, it has a different focus. If lesbians are women-identified women, then measurements are not relative to men; men's measurements are in some sense irrelevant.[90]

While I think (hope) that feminist jurisprudence is becoming less focused on women in relation to men and more on women in their own right, I would agree with Robson that lesbian jurisprudence cannot be collapsed into feminist jurisprudence. However, I do not think that the same argument applies to lesbian inequality as sex inequality. The sex inequality analysis is very much focused on lesbians as women, not in comparison to men, but in terms of challenging notions of gender. An inequality-based approach is directed toward redressing the inequalities experienced by lesbians, not to making the treatment of lesbians

90. Robson, "Lesbian Jurisprudence?" *supra* note 14 at 449.

accord with the treatment of non-lesbians.[91] However, Robson's rejection of attempts to collapse lesbianism into gender[92] reinforces my concern that I am missing something unique about lesbian inequality.

Then I go on to wonder if, in my analysis of the limitations of sexual orientation, I am privileging gender and down playing other forms of oppression that give rise to differences and power imbalances among lesbians and gays. I certainly know that those "differences" mean that we experience our oppressions differently and that we oppress each other, even as we fight our own oppression. Are race and (dis)ability as essential in sexual identity discrimination as gender, or is even thinking in these terms an inherently hierarchal approach? This takes me back to my first question. I am not arguing that gender is an oppression that we experience simultaneously with sexual identity oppression and that thereby transforms the experience of both oppressions, but rather, at least for lesbians, sexual identity oppression is gender oppression. If my doubts about collapsing lesbian inequality into gender inequality have grounding, then my fear that I am privileging gender has grounding too. However, if lesbian oppression is a form of *gender oppression, then I am only privileging gender to the extent that focusing* on one form of oppression means that one is, to some extent, downplaying other forms of oppression.[93]

This brings me back to the more fundamental question of whether all of these categories are irredeemably problematic because they are apparently mutually exclusive and negate the complexity and specificity of compound forms of discrimination.[94] Perhaps this whole "boxed" human rights approach is so rigid and narrowly focused as to be incapable of expansion or flexibility. These same

91. The example that Robson uses, *ibid.* at 450, of funding for a university lesbian bowling team, and the assessment of the team's needs on its own terms, not in comparison to male bowling teams or other male sports teams, accords with the inequality-based approach that I am pursuing. Robson uses this example to demonstrate the distinction between lesbian jurisprudence and feminist jurisprudence, but I do not think that it works for this purpose. The distinction she demonstrates is between different approaches to equality; there is nothing definitively feminist or lesbian about either of these approaches. I think more and more feminists, lesbian and not, are adopting what Robson describes as the woman-centred lesbian approach. Such a woman-centred lesbian approach would be consistent with equality jurisprudence in Canada flowing from *Andrews, supra* note 44.

92. Robson, "Looking for Lesbian Legal Theory" *supra* note 14 at 33 says: "Either the *real* problem was gender or the *real* problem was sexual orientation, but lesbianism definitely did not qualify as real within the realm of legal theory." I am arguing in this paper that the *real* problem for lesbians is gender. But in doing so, do I necessarily diffuse the lesbian focus?

93. While such a single oppression focus has the problem of downplaying other forms of oppression, such an intense focus, as long as it is applied with self-consciousness as to its limitations, can lead to fuller and more complex understandings of the oppression under scrutiny.

94. For a fuller discussion of these issues, see Kim Crenshaw and Nitya Iyer, *supra* note 68 and also see Nitya Iyer, "Categorical Denials: Equality Rights and the Shaping of Social Identity" (1993) 1 Queen's Law Journal 179 and Martha Minnow, *Making All the Difference: Inclusion, Exclusion and American Law* (Ithaca: Cornell University Press, 1990).

questions apply to the category lesbian itself. But, in the face of the current very real oppression of lesbians, I think it politically unwise for lesbians and their supporters to abandon the category. To me this is tantamount to abandoning each other. Instead I claim with pride, joy, and fear – my lesbian identity.

[3]

ZIMBABWEAN LAW AND THE PRODUCTION OF A WHITE MAN'S DISEASE

OLIVER PHILLIPS

Institute of Criminology, University of Cambridge, UK

... to support the presence of these people (gays and lesbians) in this country is to be an accomplice in promoting lechery. . . . It means, if we support them, we want our nation to be vile. We want our nation to be unchaste. We want our people to be animal-like and immoral in behaviour. In cultural terms, what it amounts to is that the homosexuals are like a witch weed in Zimbabwe, which in Shona we call 'bise'. It is therefore supposed to be eradicated. The moment you see it you eradicate it. . . .

The whole body is far more important than any single dispensable part. When your finger starts festering and becomes a danger to the body you cut it off. The moment you come to the conclusion that you cannot cure the finger, you cut it off. The purpose for cutting it off is to preserve the body. . . . The homosexuals are the festering finger endangering the body and we chop them off. (Anias Chigwedere, MP, *Zimbabwe Parliamentary Debate* on motion of 'The Evil and Iniquitous Practice of Homosexualism and Lesbianism', *Hansard*, 28 September 1995: 2779–81)

IN AUGUST 1995, the usually uncontentious Zimbabwe International Book Fair (ZIBF) erupted into controversy as the organizers obediently carried out a government order to expel the Gays and Lesbians of Zimbabwe (GALZ) from the fair, despite the dedication of that year's fair to the theme of 'Human Rights and Justice' (Dunton and Palmberg, 1996). In defending the expulsion of GALZ from this event, President Mugabe asserted that it was 'outrageous' and 'repugnant' that homosexual rights should have any advocates whatsoever, adding 'I don't believe they should have any rights at all' (ZIBF Opening Speech and Press Conference, 1 August 1995). This saw the start of a deluge of homophobic outbursts by the President and other senior Zimbabwean politicians, the content of which invariably 'white-washed' homosexuality as a 'sickness' imported by white settlers. President Mugabe denounced 'sodomists and sexual perverts' (*Herald*, 2/8/95: 1) as 'behaving worse than dogs and pigs' (*The Herald*, 12/8/95: 1); he referred to homosexuality as a threat to the moral fibre of society and proclaimed a return to 'traditional' culture saying: 'We have our own culture, and we must rededicate ourselves to our traditional values that make us human beings' (*The Citizen*, 12/8/95).

This vituperation is evidence of attempts to reject homosexual behaviour as extrinsic to Zimbabwean culture, relying on the notion that it 'is mainly done by whites and is alien to the Zimbabwean society in general' (President Mugabe GALZ *Newsletter*, Issue 11, 1/94: 13). This was amplified through repeated use of the metaphor of homosexuality as a white man's disease infecting the African nation's virtuous heterosexual inclination. In this way, homosexuality has not only been treated as something *un*Zimbabwean and *un*African, but as something specifically *anti*Zimbabwean and *anti*African. This portrayal of such a confluence of racial and sexual degeneration was intended to carry the twin implications that, first, white western European 'culture' is depraved as it corrupts other cultures with the 'evil' practice of homosexuality; and that, second, homosexuals must be white, as they are, by definition, 'depraved'. Thus, the signifier of homosexuality is used to denounce 'white culture', and the colouring of homosexuals as 'white' is used to denounce them as non-Zimbabwean.

This article sets out to explore the manner in which the law and the social context of its enforcement contributes to a 'racially contoured . . . mono-chromatic image of homosexuality' (Eaton, 1995: 47) of the kind articulated by President Mugabe. Through an analysis of court records and socio-economic context, it can be seen that the law is heavily implicated in the pro-duction of such a discourse through rendering visible the 'unnatural offences' of men who are predominantly white. This is a small fragment of a wider analysis currently in progress and is not intended to be definitive, but should rather be seen as a contribution to an ongoing debate. I must however preface my engagement with the qualification that most of my attention has been focused on the experiences of men. This is because the analysis is centered not only on a law which is preoccupied with men and is blind to the possi-bilities presented by lesbians but on account of my own sexual orientation, gender identity and biological maleness, which have variously facilitated and prioritized my research with men.

It must also be emphasized that this work is done by a white queer[1] working from Cambridge – an irony that could in itself be construed as evi-dence supporting Mugabe's claims. But the inflammatory and sinister content of his remarks demands a riposte as it so contradicts the experience and understanding of the situation that I discovered growing up in the country and subsequently living there as an adult. Indeed, while President Mugabe's statements attempt to render black homosexuality and bisexuality invisible, the effect of his remarks has in fact been the opposite. Since August 1995, there has been a considerable and deliberate increase in the visibility of black men and women actively identifying themselves as 'gay' or 'lesbian'. Further, to shy away from speaking out on account of my position as a white homosexual with colonialist roots, would be to permit a denial of the possibility for white people to assume a Zimbabwean identity, and to impose a silence on the denial of the rights of people of any colour who have same-sex partners in Zimbabwe. Most pertinently, the experience of living as a queer white man in a black country where sexual identity is presented as racially contoured, is one which leads to an acute consciousness of the discursive intersections of race, class, gender and sexuality. To be so obliged to scrutinize, challenge and defend multiple ingredients of one's identity, is to occupy a position replete with the potential for recognizing the dynamics jostling between, across and through each social marker and around each breach of different categorical boundaries. In personifying a number of locally marginal and targeted social identities as a white queer intellectual, one is obliged to negotiate the transformation and reinvention of a wide variety of cultural signifiers. Homi Bhabha explains the issue thus:

> The move away from the singularities of 'class' or 'gender' as primary conceptual and organizational categories, has resulted in an awareness of the subject positions – of race, gender, generation, institutional location, geopolitical locale, sexual orientation – that inhabit any claim to identity in the modern world. What is theoretically innovative, and politically crucial, is the need to think beyond narratives of originary and initial subjectivities and to focus on those moments or processes that are produced in the articulation of cultural differences. These 'in-between' spaces provide the terrain for elaborating strategies of selfhood – singular or communal – that initiate new signs of identity, and innovative sites of collaboration, and contestation, in the act of defining the idea of society itself. (1994: 1–2)

Occupying this interstitial space therefore provides the opportunity to develop new pathways through the maze of conflicting claims attempting to assert their proper notions of what constitutes 'Zimbabwean' society. The reflexivity of articulating this social location does not so much reinforce the sex/race conjunction used by Mugabe to assert a heterosexist national identity, as it does emphasize the significance of subjectivity in analysing the trajectories of identity, the demarcations of marginality, and the landscape of the 'in-between' spaces. In this case specifically, it is used to consider how the law has impacted on these interstitial spaces to bring sexuality into such a prominent position in the process of 'collaboration and contestation' which delivers notions of Zimbabwean society and a national identity.

474   OLIVER PHILLIPS

'ALIEN TO ZIMBABWEAN CULTURE'

I just want to warn our heroic people that if we allow or condone such bas-
tardly acts under the so-called human rights banners, if we are not careful, we
shall also have rapists, murderers, criminals and those sodomists who are mili-
tating to have sex with four year olds claiming to have human rights. . . . In our
African cultural inheritance, there is no room for such devients [sic] in culture,
this abominable practice of homosexualism and lesbianism is totally foreign to
the African culture, it encourages devilish acts and in my view, it should be
thoroughly punished. (Mr Mudariki, MP, *Zimbabwe Parliamentary Debate* on
'Homosexualism and Lesbianism', *Hansard*, 6 September 1995: 2513)

Claims that homosexuality is 'alien to Zimbabwean culture' suggest a confusion between an identity which might not have existed traditionally, with
a practice which certainly did. Identity is formed through a series of actions
and social reactions, and is differently constructed according to different
local histories and contexts. Just as the notion of a singular 'African' culture
dangerously misrepresents the wide variety of a multiplicity of African cultures, so it is misguided to assume that the same behaviour will be construed
as 'sexual' within different locales. Before the arrival of white settlers in the
area now known as Zimbabwe, the social reaction to (what are now more
commonly understood to be) homosexual acts is difficult to state with any
degree of clarity, but it would be wrong to suggest that they did not take
place at all. Across the continent of Africa, homosexual acts took place in
various social contexts with differing reactions. While some groups paid it
no attention, others, like the Azande, whose warriors had boy-wives, institutionalized it (Evans-Pritchard, 1970: 1428; Seligman and Seligman, 1932:
506–7). Similarly the Ekkpahians, the Abuan and the Western Ikwerri
devoted considerable resources to the construction of lavish buildings
specifically for the purposes of male homosexual sex as it was believed to
increase crop and human fertility by magical means (Talbot, 1967: 35–6).
Indeed, De Rachewiltz suggests that 'Homosexuality is obligatory in the
Siwa Oasis where persons of social distinction exchange their sons. A man
who is not a dedicated homosexual is considered odd . . .' (1964: 280).
Others, like the Mandari (Buxton, 1973: 22) were said to severely punish
homosexuality as non-procreative and destructive (De Rachewiltz, 1964;
Pittin, 1983; Greenberg, 1988).
   What is clear is that to suggest that homosexual acts are against 'African
Culture' is to misrepresent Africa as statically monocultural, to ignore the
richness of differing cultural constructions of desire, and in suggesting such
a totalized notion of African culture, one simply replicates much of the colonial discourse on African sexuality. More specifically, while attitudes
towards homosexual sex among Shona or Ndebele people could have been
prohibitory or permissive, to claim that they never experienced any homosexual sex prior to the arrival of white settlers, is to deprive them of a corporeal imagination enjoyed by the rest of the continent.

COLONIALISM AND THE 'CIVILIZING MISSION'

Rather than new activities or behaviours, what is more likely to have been imported by Victorian colonials taught to feel guilty after the most solitary masturbation, is the eroticization of repression. Through the notion that 'innocence' was a 'natural' state ignorant of the 'dangers' of lust and the pleasures of the flesh, and the concomitant creation of a cognitive concept of a sexuality in need of policing as an object in itself, ideas and practices around sexual morality were considerably changed. Prior to colonialism, the emphasis had been on the reproduction of the patrilineal order through the regulation of reproductive relationships; procreation and social alliances directed men's selection of heterosexual partners for themselves or their daughters/wards, and sexual behaviour was regulated at the level of the body with the primary purpose of protecting a man's exclusive access to his wife/wives. What was important was consequential physical activity rather than projected cognitive desire.

But with the arrival of European settlers, came a whole new concept of 'sex' which, in the nineteenth century, was being formulated into a 'sexuality' – and this was a sexuality regulated not just through the structure of reproductive relationships but through fantasy and denial, giving it the capacity alternatively to create or censure identities. It is this western conjuring of sexuality and power, conducted through a discourse of repression, which reached its apotheosis in the nineteenth century, and was central to the whole notion of a 'civilizing mission' – repression and discipline being two definitive ingredients constituting Victorian ideals of 'civilization'. Add to this the proselytizing of the Christian notion of sin and the introduction of a capitalist economy, and it suggests the development of a consciousness based on the commodification of sex and the erotic regulation of individual desire rather than the prioritizing of procreation and the making of social alliances.

The arrival of Christian 'civilization' and colonial authority also brought with it the imposition of an 'anatamo-politics' (health and hygiene [Burke, 1996], work, efficiency, morality, production) of the individual body as well as a demographic regulation (land apportionment, pass laws, curfews, compounds, etc.) of the social body, in an attempt to produce self-disciplined 'obedient subjects' (Foucault, 1978: 139–41). Rather than being perceived as just symbolic of life and causative of procreation, sex slowly began to be reconceptualized as the location of truth; a treasure trove of dangerous but vital secrets in need of investigation, monitoring and correction through techniques which would render truth rational, engender discipline of the self and carry through the sexual erethism of the nineteenth century. Thus, while the possibilities of different sexual activities remained the same, they were excitedly 'discovered' to be imbued with new associated labels of perversion:

> The growth of perversions is not a moralizing theme that obsessed the scrupulous minds of the Victorians. It is the real product of the encroachment of a type of power on bodies and their pleasures. It is possible that the West has not been

capable of inventing any new pleasures, and it has doubtless not discovered any
original vices. But it has defined new rules for the game of powers and pleasures. The frozen countenance of the perversions is a fixture of this game.
(Foucault, 1978: 48)

For instance, in Zimbabwe oral historians have suggested that sexual activity
between children of the same sex was expected as 'normal' behaviour, particularly around the age of puberty, but that thereafter 'it was frowned upon'
(Chavanduka *Interview*, 1993; see also Colson, 1958: 272, 274; Wilson, 1951:
87, 196–7). The extent of this disapproval remains obscure, on account of the
intervention of Christian missionaries from the mid-nineteenth century
onwards who were actively involved in remoulding tradition and altering
conceptions of morality. They appear to have been especially zealous when
genitalia or sex were involved. For it is clear that rituals of circumcision and
ceremonies of initiation were substantially changed and in some cases became
extinct, on account of missionaries' objections to what they saw as 'lascivi-
ous songs' and 'immoral acts' which accompanied the celebrations (Bullock,
1950: 45, 50).

   Thus, the first censure of local sexual practices by European morality took
place not through the law but through the salvatory mission of Christianity.
But the arrival of pioneer settlements, with the bureaucratic apparatus of civil
and criminal regulation, meant that Christian morality soon had the backing
of a nascent infrastructure. Attempts by missionaries to 'civilize' through the
construction of sin and the regulation of individual bodily practices were supplemented by the developmental requirements of colonial capital – the
bureaucratic regulation of the social body. One instrument inextricably
engaged in this process is the law. The charter of the white settlers provided
that in civil cases between 'natives', the courts were to be guided by 'native
law', only insofar as that law was 'not repugnant to natural justice or morality' (1889 Charter of the British South Africa Company). The process of
deciding what constituted valid 'native law' was not an automatic unfolding
of disinterested facts but an arena in which many contesting interests
attempted to assert their particular claim to truth (Chanock, 1982; 1985).
More significantly, the repugnancy clause meant that homosexual acts would
be criminalized in the same manner as they were criminalized under the
common law of the Cape of Good Hope (which the charter proclaimed to
be the common law of Southern Rhodesia), whatever the situation might have
been under African custom. Thus, the notion of sin became reinforced with
a legal definition of a 'natural' morality, as any act between men which could
be construed as sexual was classified as an 'unnatural offence' under the
Roman–Dutch law of *venus monstrosa*.[2]

LEGAL REGULATION

This prohibition was not something which affected only white men indulging
in a 'decadence' from which black men were miraculously excluded. Indeed

in the very first year of operation of the colonial courts in Southern Rhodesia, the courts heard five cases (1.5% of all criminal court cases that year) of sodomy and indecent assault between males, and none of the people involved was white (Epprecht, in press). Between 1892 and 1923, there were approximately 250 cases of 'homosexual crimes' tried in the magistrates' courts, and of these, only 22 involved white men (Epprecht, in press). Black men were clearly capable of committing these offences without a white co-conspirator. Epprecht's research into prosecutions for 'unnatural offences' between black men in the first 30 years of colonial rule, shows that the relationships between these men varied from casual to long-term, from loving to coercive, from discreet to openly acknowledged, and were certainly not restricted to conditions where men were grouped together in compounds. The constant reference point in all this, is not the race, not the activity and not the type of relationship; the only place in which 'total' exclusions constantly apply is in the prohibition – the law.

The proscription of homosexuality as *venus monstrosa*, under the common law of 'unnatural offences', has remained constant in Zimbabwe since the start of colonial rule. 'Unnatural offences' include three categories of acts: sodomy (anal penetration) between two men; bestiality; and a 'residual group of proscribed "unnatural" sexual acts referred to generally as "an unnatural offence"' (Hunt, 1982: 270). This last category refers to any sexual act between men which does not amount to sodomy, and is deliberately vague in definition in order to serve as a catch-all provision for all imaginable variations of sexual possibilities between males (Phillips, in press). There is no mention of sex involving two women, no case has been prosecuted, and it would seem that the law does not proscribe sex between women (Feltoe, 1980: 246, 251). However, 'unnatural offences' between men are still prosecuted whenever possible (Derks and Anor., 1984; *S* v. *Roffey*, 1991; and also Omerjee *Interview*, 1993), and consent provides no defence. Indeed, the issues of consent, age and privacy are simply taken into account by a trial court as either mitigating or aggravating factors to the main charge of committing an 'unnatural offence'. Thus, the same law is used to punish both consensual and non-consensual acts, and the use of force or violence or a great disparity in ages are all seen as simply aggravating factors to the main charge of the commission of a sexual act between two males (Phillips, in press).

'Unnatural offences' are generally tried in the magistrates' courts where consensual acts between men currently receive sentences which tend to range from a fine to a sentence of two years' imprisonment with labour (*S* v. *Roffey*, 1991; Shadreck Dickson, 1992). As the maximum punitive jurisdiction in the magistrates' courts is seven years' imprisonment, cases of this nature only reach the High Court through the processes of review or appeal. When a sentence of longer than six months is handed down by a magistrate, it is automatically reviewed by a judge of the High Court; but unless the accused is represented or the judge feels that legal argument is necessary, a review is not heard in the High Court itself, but is dealt with by a judge in chambers and so is not published. The court of ultimate appeal is the Supreme Court.

As the common law is established through precedent, legally significant rulings of the High and Supreme Courts are published in the Zimbabwe Law Reports, while all other cases heard in the High Court are only available as cyclostyled judgments on specific request to the High Court. Only a few specialized libraries in the country request these on a regular basis, and they are thus not generally available. A magistrate is expected to apply, rather than set, precedent and so the magistrates' courts records are not published at all but are kept at the courts of origin and then placed in inaccessible regional archives. The crime columns of the local press occasionally report on cases heard in the magistrates' courts, but obviously most attention is focused on cases in the higher courts. There is no annual collation of statistical data on different crimes which could provide an overview of trends in the criminal justice system. Public impressions of conviction trends are therefore based mainly on the cases in the higher courts, as reported through the press and legal publications, usually obscuring indicators in the magistrates' courts from the view of all but those who make a concerted effort to study them.

Epprecht's (in press) research found a predominance of black men convicted in the magistrates' courts for 'unnatural offences' in the first 30 years of colonial rule. This is in direct contrast to the conviction rates of recent years as reflected in law reports. During the 28-year-period 1966–1994,[3] all but three of the 21 convictions for 'unnatural offences' published in the Law Reports and cyclostyled judgments, involve a white man as an offender. The same court records for other sexual offences (such as rape and indecent assault) show no such racial concentration. In a country where white people make up less than 1 percent (and prior to 1980, between 2 and 3%) of the total population, this is remarkable. Without doubt, there are convictions of men who are not white, which took place in regional or local magistrates' courts, but as these did not progress into the higher courts, they remain unpublished, and are kept in restricted archives where they are not readily accessible to the public.[4]

'WHITE MAN'S DISEASE'

There are a number of possible explanations for this disproportionate involvement of white men in 'unnatural offences' cases. First, it must be remembered that there is a disparity in the public reporting of convictions, which should not be confused with a substantive disparity in actual sexual practices. For example, without exception all the reported and cyclostyled convictions in the 14 years prior to Independence in 1980 involve a white man.[5] The judgments in some of these cases make clear that where sex took place between two men of different races the court took a more serious approach to the matter (S v. K, 1972; S v. C, 1976). This was ostensibly on the grounds that the socio-economic differences between the participants vitiated against the defence that consent was freely given.

ZIMBABWEAN LAW AND THE WHITE MAN'S DISEASE   479

> It must be remembered that the appellant was a European of some 52 years of
> age, while the complainant was a humble African domestic servant of 21 years
> of age, the sort of man who would be likely to yield easily to persuasion of this
> sort. . . . I point out, however, . . . that this is not a case where force, or threats
> of force were used in order to induce the complainant to submit. (Beadle, C.J.
> in *S v. K*, 1972, 80E)

While the courts certainly did find themselves obliged to provide protection to workers vulnerable to the unsolicited advances of both heterosexual
and homosexual men, it is impossible, in the context of a society as racist as
white Rhodesia, to ignore the increased 'offensiveness' of inter-racial sex. For
a white man to have sex with a black man was not only construed as taking
advantage of a position of power, and a neglect of the responsibility of
patronage, it also offended directly the racial hierarchy with which all notions
of social behaviour were imbued. To discard one's status and consort with the
underclass in an equalizing act such as sex was to undermine directly an ethos
of racial superiority persistently presented as 'natural'. The efforts of the
courts to protect both vulnerable people and a vulnerable ideology meant that
cases involving two people of different races were more likely to be dealt with
at a higher jurisdiction than those cases involving two men of the same race,
and so would be published in law reports or cyclostyled judgments.

Since 1980, I know of several men, who are not white, who have been convicted of sodomy and unnatural offences but as these prosecutions took place
in the lower courts, they are unreported and go unnoticed. There have been
three published convictions of men who are not white, in courts of a higher
jurisdiction (*S v. Beli Enock Dube*, 1987; *S v. Stanford*, 1992; *S v. Magwenzi*,
1994). *S v. Magwenzi* involved a boy of 8 years old, and *S v. Stanford* involved
a boy of 14 years old, while Beli Enock Dube committed what would amount
to male rape. These disparities in age in *Magwenzi* and *Stanford*, and the
threat of violence in *Dube*'s case, were aggravating factors which led them to
be referred to the High Courts for sentencing and review, and thus led them
to be published in law reports.

In comparison, since 1980, there have been four convictions of white men
dealt with in higher courts and so recorded in law reports (Le Roux, 1981;
Derks & Anor., 1984; Mackie, 1990; *S v. Roffey*, 1991). All of these cases
involved consensual acts and have gone as far as the High Courts (where they
would be published) on review, or on appeal as a result of legal representation. Representation is a luxury few can afford in Zimbabwe, but on
account of their relative economic power many more white men are in a position to do so than are black men. This is one of the main reasons for the disproportionate number of white men whose convictions for 'unnatural
offences', which would normally be dealt with in the lower courts and so
would go unnoticed, proceed as far as the higher courts and are published in
law reports and cyclostyled judgments.[6] Thus, cases involving white men
tend to get into the higher courts far more often on account of their legal representation, while those involving black men tend to get there only on
account of aggravating factors.

The end result of this disparity in convictions is that it contributes to a discourse of discrimination which produces homosexuality as 'a white man's disease'. There is no doubt that some black Zimbabwean men do have sex with each other, and, as with anyone else, this is carried out with varying degrees of furtiveness and openness by men occupying a wide variety of social positions. Yet the cases which go through the higher courts are predominantly those which involve the participation of a white man. This means that the cases passing before the senior judiciary, receiving publicity in the media, being recorded in public law reports, coming to the attention of government, and featuring in the market-place discussions of an insatiably curious populace are those which involve the participation of a white man. Public discussion of homosexuality becomes fueled with racial epithets, and the primary definition of the issue includes the presence of a white man, and the relative obscurity of black men.

SOCIAL ORDER OF BLACK INVISIBILITY

The relativity of visibility is linked to cultural traditions, but not in the actively and resolutely homophobic (or even homovacant) way that has been suggested. Traditional Shona and Ndebele culture were and in many cases still are patriarchal, gerontocratic and polygynous, with women transferred by men into marriage to create links between different kinship networks (Folbre, 1988: 62–7; Jacobs, 1984: 33–4). A system of dowry (*lobola/roora*) lends marriage great significance in local economies and in the fortunes of whole communities. This means that the institution of marriage has social and economic ramifications far beyond just the husband and his wife or wives, as it serves a purpose for all of their extended families. Furthermore, marriage and the production of children is the primary medium through which the independent status and power which constitute adulthood are achieved, and at the heart of marriage is the objective of raising children, rather than the western construction of romantic love.[7] Marriage is therefore more than expected, it is virtually an obligation. It is still unusual to encounter a man or a woman over the age of 30 who is not yet married, and his or her situation is usually greeted with a mixture of surprise and sorrow. The strength of heterosexual marriage as an institution has a number of significant repercussions regarding the visibility of same-sex lovers.

First, it means that most of the black men having sex with men are married. While extramarital heterosexual sex for men is common (but usually discrete), homosexual sex is considerably more furtive as it is both extramarital and same-sex oriented. Second, there is no easy space for a late twentieth-century gay identity to develop (see Note 1). For Shona or Ndebele men to remain unmarried is extremely difficult and often only achieved at the expense of one's kinship ties, support network and the gender-normative power wrought by men in a highly patriarchal society. These kinship ties and communal links are far more pervasive than in western European concepts of marriage and the family. So adopting a gay identity and domestic lifestyle is a remote and comparatively more difficult possibility for black Zimbabweans than it is for white Zimbabweans. This further renders Shona or Ndebele men having sex with other men far less visible than their white counterparts who are less likely to be married and, if they are married, may be happily childless (an improbable combination for a married Shona couple). Third, it means that the possibilities of gay identities and same-sex domestic partnerships are seen by traditionalists as threatening to what is presently established as 'traditional' culture.

This threat is most evident in the case of lesbian relationships. Under customary law, women were perpetual legal minors always subject to the guardianship of their husband, father, uncle or brother. The Legal Age of Majority Act (Act No. 15 of 1982) proclaims any person (black women included) to be legally independent on reaching the age of 18. However, many Zimbabwean families still live by customary law, and most Zimbabwean women therefore find it extremely difficult to assert their independence. Indeed, heterosexual women leading socially, economically and sexually independent lives in the urban areas of Zimbabwe suffer considerable moral censure as a consequence of their autonomy (Seidman, 1984; Morrison, 1995; Jackson, 1993). The few black women who have a visibly lesbian identity find this censure substantially compounded. After the 1996 Book Fair, those black lesbians whose photographs had been published in the press, were harassed at home and work; one woman who was called into a meeting with the local branch of ZANU-PF, ZANU-PF Youth League, and the town mayor, was questioned about her lifestyle and asked which white woman was 'responsible' for this. She was made to feel so threatened that she left the town.

INVENTING ZIMBABWE: 'TRADITION' IN LATE MODERNITY

The clarion call around which issues of gender and sexuality are discussed in Zimbabwe is clearly that of 'tradition' and notions of equity, justice or liberation battle to be heard among the resounding proclamations of what this 'tradition' might be. The strength which notions of 'traditional' culture wield over the discourse around modern Zimbabwean identities owes something both to the entrenched position of those dependent on 'traditional' structures of power (particularly elder men such as chiefs and headmen), and also to the void left by the disappearance of apartheid in South Africa which had previously worked as a cohesive force in Zimbabwean national dynamics. For not only did the apartheid government provide Zimbabwe with an external military, economic and political threat on which to focus, but it presented the Zimbabwean government with a moral high ground easily occupied. Both of these factors provided a moral-political impetus and a certain cohesion to government and society in the newly liberated Zimbabwe, as well as sometimes excusing or distracting from internal problems. However, the new South Africa has a constitution which explicitly premises itself on 'diversity' – the preamble and all that follows make clear the principle that differences between people should never again be used as a force of division, but rather should be seen as a positive asset in building a strong democracy. At its most general, this is illustrated in the torturous process of grieving, recriminating and acknowledging atrocities through the 'Truth and Reconciliation Commission', but it is also more specifically enshrined in Chapter 2 of the Constitution. This is a 'Bill of Rights' which contains the 'Equality Clause' prohibiting discrimination on many grounds including sexual orientation, ethnic origin and language (the constitution recognizes 11 official languages).

This approach to truth and traditions in the new South Africa, is in striking contrast to the current climate in Zimbabwe, where difference or marginality is viewed with suspicion. 'Traditional African culture' is regularly invoked as a monolithic symbol of historical purity, and opinions challenging those of the ruling party are often dismissed as contrary to the national interest. Thus, tradition is widely regarded as a tool of popular homogeneity, rather than a varied expression of overlapping histories. It also serves as a means by which one can rediscover a sense of simultaneously belonging (to the country) and owning (the country); of alternately reclaiming and being reclaimed by history; and of deciding who should be permitted to participate in such a project.

In Zimbabwe there was never any similarly far-reaching and deep-seated attempt to reconcile through the telling of truths and the open discussion of responsibilities. At the end of the liberation war in 1980, the new government under President Mugabe pursued a policy of reconciliation with white settlers, but did nothing so dangerous as to institute a 'Truth Commission'. Initially, with the end of the war, the release from military obligations, the flight of the most racist white Rhodesians, and the lifting of the international isolation of the 1960s and 1970s, the atmosphere was one of euphoria. Social boundaries which had become so definitive during the war were thrown into question, briefly delivering an 'alternative' social scene, more mixed both in terms of sexuality and race, but with the notable absence of black (apart from 'coloured' or Asian) gay men or lesbians (Gay Men *Interviews*, 1991). But by the mid-to-late 1980s, once the honeymoon period was over, it became increasingly clear that this reconciliation had been carried out in such a way that the effect was to paper over the social cracks making differences covert rather than bridged. Zimbabwe continues to be a country riven with enormous social segregation and vast disparities in wealth. The racial transformation of the ruling elite and the creation of a black professional bourgeoisie are evidence of limited reforms rather than extensive restructuring. Disparities in individual wealth remain enormous; the labouring classes are still exclusively black and to be white, Asian or of mixed race is to be middle class. This has significant consequences in terms of the general visibility of different gay men and lesbians, and consequently within the law as well.

Class, Race and Sexual Identity

As the middle classes have ready access to global communications, international developments in sexual politics remain their prerogative. Since white gay men and white lesbians fall so inevitably into this socio-economic sector, they more readily adopt the global paraphernalia of a queer identity. This may be secretive or open to varying degrees, but nevertheless their bourgeois status and the extent to which western Europe is a point of cultural reference, has in the past made sexuality a more self-avowedly constitutive part of their identity. Similarly, as the traditional power of Chiefs is supplanted in urban areas by a developing black bourgeoisie, so sexuality becomes more evocative as a social commodity, a means of measuring worth, a definer of social boundaries and a technique for discovering 'truths' both at an individual level of self-discovery and at a broader level of social politics. Again the corruption that has been 'imported' is not the homosexual act, but rather the growth of the bourgeois notion of sexuality as constitutive of social truths, and the concomitant need to declare and control these truths through such categorical mechanisms as a hetero/homosexual dichotomy. This is a need manifested both by government, in their emphatic censure of homosexuality, and also by those young urbanized Zimbabweans who proclaim their sexuality. These features of contemporary Zimbabwe's changing culture resonate with insights offered by Foucault about the emergence of European sexualities;

> If it is true that sexuality is the set of effects produced in bodies, behaviours, and social relations by a certain deployment deriving from a complex political technology, one has to admit that this deployment does not operate in symmetrical fashion with respect to the social classes, and consequently, that it does not produce the same effects in them. We must return, therefore, to formulations that have long been disparaged; we must say that there is a bourgeois sexuality, and that there are class sexualities. Or rather, that sexuality is originally, historically bourgeois, and that, in its successive shifts and transpositions, it induces specific class effects. (1978: 127)

The relative obscurity but growing visibility of black gay men and lesbians in Zimbabwe owes much to these differing effects of the technologies deployed in the production of sexuality. The negotiation of identity in Zimbabwe's nascent 'lesbian/gay community' is one differently experienced by different individuals within the collective of people having same-sex relationships and, therefore, incorporates varying levels of Afrocentricity and Eurocentricity (a division which is never that clear and unambiguous). What is clear is that there is no mysterious Shona exemption from homosexual desire, for this desire certainly exists and is acted upon. This is illustrated by the increasing number of working-class black men who specifically identify themselves as gay. Communities of young gay men who have either left or been expelled from their families on account of their sexuality are to be found in the larger cities. While some have managed to find employment, or form manufacturing cooperatives in order to generate enough income to survive, others become sex workers on the streets. They are therefore some of the most visible black gay men. Prostitution is illegal in Zimbabwe and these young men are prosecuted for 'unnatural offences'. While their clients range across the spectrum of Zimbabwean men, the most valued tend to be the more 'out' white middle-class men and foreigners. This is on account of their affluence, their ability to supply accommodation (however temporary), and their reliability in terms of payment (Gay Men *Interviews*, 1991). It also means that white men become the most visible employers of gay sex workers, fueling media and public perceptions of homosexuality as a white man's proclivity into which black men are drawn by economic need (*Daily Gazette*, 19/1/93: 1).

Obviously the prosecution of a consensual sexual act between men is complicated by the difficulties of providing evidence. It depends either on the confession of one of the parties or on the evidence of a third party. A vast majority of those cases which come to court are either on account of a dispute over previously agreed payment or alternatively on account of a refusal to succumb to blackmail threatened by one of the parties involved or by a third party. The Director of Public Prosecutions has described blackmail as the main effect of the unnatural offences law, suggesting that an unnatural offence is the easiest and surest means of blackmail in Zimbabwe,[8] and citing a case where this had led to murder (Omerjee *Interview*, 1993). On account of their socio-economic situation, the men most vulnerable to blackmail tend to be white. This is another factor which explains why most convictions for unnatural offences concern white men, and it further increases the public identification of homosexuality as white.

CONCLUSION

The vilification directed at gay men and lesbians in Zimbabwe recently is not the result of an increase in the commission of or convictions for unnatural offences, so much as it is the result of a growth in the visibility of lesbians and gay men. There does not appear to be a marked increase in attempts to arrest or prosecute men for sexual acts. What is being more actively censured, through less formal mechanisms, is the identity of being lesbian or gay, for it is this identification of sexuality as signifying a social truth, and defining a particular lifestyle, which seems to carry the most significance. In both 1995 and 1996, the Zimbabwe International Book Fair were occasions where the government's actions were specifically aimed at silencing people who identified themselves as gay or lesbian.[9] Initially, it was suggested by political commentators that the government was using this identity as a whipping-boy to give vent to its own prejudices and to divert attention away from pressing economic and political problems. A closer consideration suggests the more sinister project of marginalizing a vulnerable minority group to reinforce the frontiers of a consensual hegemonic national identity.

Through a process of exclusion and the defining of an 'other', as outside Zimbabwean identity, there is the concomitant drawing of boundaries.

Boundaries do not just exclude but include patrolling and signifying the normative limits of identity and manufacturing a sense of belonging. By marginalizing an 'other', you consolidate the authority of the normative bloc, building an inclusive consensus and promoting your ascendancy in the balance of forces contesting hegemony. Recent Zimbabwean history would indicate that gay men and lesbians are not the only groups of people vulnerable to this process – students, squatters, street workers, unionists and independent women are just some of those who have undergone state-sponsored marginalization and censure. This involves the use of negative moral and political judgements whose 'general function is to signify, denounce and regulate, not to explain' (Sumner, 1990: 27). In each case, it has been a process of censure orchestrated by a reactionary public discourse conducted through government-controlled press and often articulated by members of government themselves.

In 1994/5 a campaign calling for the boycotting and redistribution of white businesses reopened the question of disproportionate white economic power and caused much racial antipathy to resurface. While the public anxiety over the role and presence of white people in Zimbabwe is clearly grounded in unresolved economic issues, the attack on so-called 'sodomists and sexual perverts' was delivered in this same context. Many of the statements made by Mugabe and his supporters suggest that the vituperation might be more intentionally aimed at demeaning the immorality of western 'European' lifestyles and asserting a new-found sense of 'Africanism'. It is perhaps going too far to suggest that the homophobia is entirely opportunistic, but it is clear that it does present a means towards a broader goal – that of fostering a stronger sense of a normative national identity through the censure of marginal groups and the reinvention of tradition. This is illustrated by one newspaper's celebration of the fact that 'university students and ZANU-PF Women's League have at last found something in common to agree on' (*The Sunday News*, 3/9/95).[10]

Whether the homophobia whipped up in Zimbabwe is a means to an end or an end in itself, the remarks have cost the government dearly in its international reputation, and the response from gays and lesbians in Zimbabwe has been unexpectedly resistant. This included the first public appearances by a significant number of black gay men and lesbians who outed themselves in order to assert their existence and demand recognition, refuting the construction of homosexuality as a white man's disease. The President's remarks also increased the political engagement of white gay men and lesbians who were obliged to assert their identity as Zimbabweans, and further led to the creation of alliances with other local political and civil rights groupings. Such blatant homophobia had bridged what had previously been awkward spaces between diverse communities.

The activities, identities and lifestyles existing in 'the twilight world of the homosexual' have always been shrouded in myth and conjecture. In Zimbabwe the prevalence of the notion that homosexuality is a white man's disease corrupting local innocents has been used to shore up a national identity appropriate to the maintenance of a hegemonic masculinity. This notion is clearly an unsustainable fiction, premised as it is on an absurdity, and ironically patrolled by laws imported with colonialism. The discourse infusing these laws around sex between men is at issue, but as an increasing number of black men and women move from discrete homosexual activity to a more open espousal of same-sex relationships, it will become clear that the real battle concerns an identity which must jostle for space in a dynamic and fast-changing culture. Through their manipulation of public and legal discourse, conservative forces have made themselves the primary definers of a reinvented traditional culture. Such neo-traditionalism will best be countered through the effective combination of revealing the existence of same-sex relationships within a traditional local context and simultaneously emphasizing the indigenous production of those contemporary Zimbabwean identities continually being constructed through participation in a global culture.

NOTES

Much gratitude is due to many people in Zimbabwe, most of whom for obvious reasons shall have to remain nameless, but academic and legal research and advice which made this article possible has been generously given by among others Boyd Carr, Mark Epprecht, Gilles Kleitz-Deissart, Derek Matyszak and Carla Sutherland.

1.   I am unable to enter into a complex definition of terms in this short article. However, in view of the multitude of cultural and personal identities which exist in Zimbabwe and the dangers of falsely projecting a particular consciousness (e.g. 'gay' and 'queer') on an unsuspecting subject, it is necessary to clarify the way I have used terms to describe same-sex love. It is important, first, to recognize that the definition of acts as 'sexual' is not universally shared and, second, to understand that activity and identity are not synonymous. Thus, there are men in Zimbabwe who have some form of sexual contact with other men, but who lead predominantly heterosexual lives and who do not have any conception of themselves as either a 'homosexual' or a gay man – these men shall be included in references to 'men who have sex with men'. Nevertheless, for clarity's sake, where I use 'homosexual act' in this article, it is intended to refer to any act between two men which is proscribed by Zimbabwean law as an 'unnatural offence' (e.g. in Zimbabwean law, a caress between two men could be a sexual act (Phillips, in press)); similarly, 'homosexual' is used to refer to any woman or man regardless of what social identity she or he might choose to assume but whose sexual orientation is exclusively towards people of the same biological sex (thus, derived from the Greek word *homo*, meaning 'same', rather than the Latin word meaning 'man'); 'bisexual' is used to refer to people who openly identify themselves as such and also to men and women who regularly have partners of both sexes; 'gay' or 'lesbian' is ONLY used to refer to those homosexual people who identify themselves as gay or lesbian, consciously acknowledging their sexuality as a significant determinant of their identity, and making them part of a broadbased but particular late twentieth-century sociopolitical community; 'Queer' is only used to refer to those people who have consciously appropriated the label by adopting a political position which problematizes heterosexism and values a multiplicity of differences as in the

Queer politics/theory of the late 1980s and 1990s. These distinctions may seem crudely used here, but it is important to recognize the subjectivity of many of these identities, and the completely blurred and overlapping nature of these analytical boundaries.

2. A category of acts deemed to be 'unnatural' at various stages of the development of Roman–Dutch law were all grouped together as *'Sodomie'*, *'Onkuisheid tegen die natuur'*, or *'venus monstrosa'*. Over the centuries different jurists included various activities within this category, including self-masturbation, heterosexual sodomy, sexual acts between women and heterosexual acts between Jews and Christians (see Hunt, 1982: 266–90).

3. This work was carried out in 1995, allowing for the inclusion of cases up to and including 1994. The 14-year period prior to 1980 was also included, in order to show any differences in the pattern of convictions for equal periods either side of Independence in 1980.

4. Unfortunately, research focused on convictions in magistrates' courts is incomplete, but in the period 1/1/92–30/9/92, of the 88 convicted sexual offenders admitted into Harare Central Prison, five had been convicted of an 'unnatural offence'. None of them was a white man and four of those five had been convicted in a magistrate's court – only the fifth case (*S* v. *Stanford*, 1992, 190) was heard in a higher court and so is recorded in an accessible publication.

5. See Flanagan, 1966, 96; *R* v. *Stephen*, 1966, 271; *R* v. *B*, 1969, 212; Da Silva, 1970, 94; Addison, 1971, 65; Henriques, 1971, 94; Bartlett, 1972, 30; Kladides, 1972, 141; Maritz, 1972, 98; Valades, 1972, 574; Amos, 1974, 98; Jordan, 1975, 7; *S* v. *C*, 1976, 55; *S* v. *Meager*, 1977, 327.

6. In passing, it should also be noted that where the prosecution concerns two consenting adults in a private place, sentences handed down by the High Court appear to be becoming lighter than those in the past (see *S* v. *Roffey*, 1991). However, this reduction in severity is not necessarily reflected in the sentences handed down by magistrates (see Phillips, in press) and whether the High Court will continue on this path in the present climate remains to be seen. Government is clearly in no mood to decriminalize homosexual acts and while the attitudes of the judiciary vary considerably between different judges, interviews with the most senior members of the judiciary suggest that they would not push for such a move.

7. The fundamental significance of children in marriage is demonstrated by the fact that a barren woman may be returned by her husband to her parents, and the *lobola* (bride-price) refunded. While in English the terms of respect for adults are usually Mr and Mrs (denoting marital status regardless of children), in Shona the equivalent forms of respectful address are *Amai* and *Baba* which mean Mother and Father respectively and are accorded only to those who have produced children.

8. The Legal Representative of Gays and Lesbians of Zimbabwe reported that during the first five months of 1996, he had been approached for assistance by five different people threatened with blackmail on account of homosexual activity, and this only accounts for those people who have the confidence to approach GALZ; the most vulnerable to blackmail will be those who are not 'out' and who are unlikely to approach GALZ – suggesting that most of the people being blackmailed are not known about and are unable to defend themselves effectively.

9. For a comprehensive review of the events surrounding the 1995 ZIBF, see Dunton and Palmberg, 1996 : 7–18. At the 1996 ZIBF, the displays of other publishers which contained gay, lesbian and bisexual material were untouched by government. But the Minister of Home Affairs, with the Board of Censors,

488   OLIVER PHILLIPS

attempted (unsuccessfully) to ban GALZ from participating outright regardless of what material they might be intending to display. In the past the Board of Censors has refused applications by GALZ to show such films as the Merchant–Ivory production of E.M. Forster's *Maurice*, but simultaneously allowed far more explicitly gay films to be shown at local film festivals in which GALZ is not involved.

10.   The history of the women's movement in Zimbabwe during the last 15 years provides a useful analogy regarding the assertion of a neo-traditional and xenophobic approach to gender relations. During the war, women had played an active role in the liberation army, and as a result the ZANU government came to power in 1980 with an official commitment to empowering women and promoting sexual equality. As already mentioned, the government commenced by introducing the Legal Age of Majority Act in 1982, according full legal status to all women over the age of 18. However, the reaction from men, particularly chiefs and elder men was so strong that the government backed out of further supporting women's empowerment (Folbre, 1988: 75; Jacobs and Howard, 1987: 32), and indeed became an inhibitor rather than a facilitator of the development of women's position. For example, before coming to power the government had openly espoused the abolition of the dowry system of *lobola*, acknowledging that it had been commodified and inflated with the development of capitalism and so transformed away from its traditional role as a bond between lineage groups into a capitalist and materialist transaction between men. But subsequent to Independence, when discussion arose around its abolition, *lobola* was defended as 'part of the national heritage' which should resist 'western feminism . . . a new form of cultural imperialism' (Seidman, 1984: 432). Similarly, the government attempted to undermine the power of women's groups by remarking on the number of white women, and particularly white South African women involved in women's groups in Zimbabwe, implicitly equating feminism and the empowerment of women not just with 'European' imperialism but with the policy of destabilization practiced by the apartheid government at the time.

CASES CITED

ZIMBABWEAN

Addison AD-65-71.
Amos GS-98-74.
Bartlett AD-30-72.
Da Silva AD-94-70.
Derks & Anor. HC-B-124-84.
Flanagan AD-96-66.
Henriques AD-94-71.
Jordan AD-7-75.
King Kingsley Otis Ndebele SC-135-89.
Kladides AD-141-72.
Le Roux S-172-81.
Mackie HC-B-54-90.
Magwenzi HH-59-94.
Maritz AD-98-72.

Palmer AD-112-73.
R v. B [1969] (2) Rhodesia Law Reports 212.
R v. Masuku 1968 (2) Rhodesia Law Reports 332.
R v. Stephen 1966 Rhodesia Law Reports 271.
Shadreck Dickson R454 Harare, 1992.
S v. Beli Enock Dube HC-B-94-87.
S v. C [1976] (1) Rhodesia Law Reports 55.
S v. K [1972] (2) Rhodesia Law Reports 78.
S v. Macheka [1979] (1) Rhodesia Law Reports 49.
S v. Meager [1977] (2) Rhodesia Law Reports 327.
S v. Roffey [1991] (2) Zimbabwe Law Reports 47.
S v. Simon [1987] (2) Zimbabwe Law Reports 53.
S v. Stanford [1992] (1) Zimbabwe Law Reports 190.
Valades GD-574-72.

SOUTH AFRICAN

R v. Bourne [1952] 36 CR App Rep 125.
R v. K & F [1932] EDL 71.
S v. D [1963] (3) SA 263.
S v. H [1993] (3) SACR 545 (C).

NEWSPAPERS

The Citizen, Johannesburg, South Africa.
The Daily Gazette, Harare, Zimbabwe.
Newsletter of the Gays and Lesbians of Zimbabwe, Issue 11, January 1994.
The Herald, Harare, Zimbabwe.
The Sunday News, Harare, Zimbabwe.

INTERVIEWS

Director of Public Prosecutions (Mr Yunnus Omerjee), 26/1/93.
Gay Men in Zimbabwe, January 1991.
Judges of the High and Supreme Courts of Zimbabwe, 22–25/1/93.
Past Chairman of Zimbabwe Natural and Traditional Healers Association (Professor
    Chavanduka), 28/1/93.

REFERENCES

Bhabha, H. (1994) *The Location of Culture*. London: Routledge.
Bullock, C. (1950) *The Mashona and the Matabele*. Cape Town: Juta & Co.
Burke, T. (1996) *Lifebuoy Men, Lux Women: Commodification, Consumption, and
    Cleanliness in Modern Zimbabwe*. London: Leicester University Press.
Buxton, Jean (1973) *Religion and Healing in the Mandari*. Oxford: Clarendon.

Chanock, M. (1982) 'Making Customary Law: Men, Women, and Courts in Colonial Northern Rhodesia', in M. J. Hay and M. Wright (eds) *African Women and the Law: Historical Perspectives*. Boston, MA: Boston University Papers on Africa VII.

Chanock, M. (1985) *Law, Custom and Social Order: The Colonial Experience in Malawi and Zambia*. Cambridge: Polity.

Colson, E. (1958) *Marriage and the Family among the Plateau Tonga of Northern Rhodesia*. Manchester: Manchester University Press.

De Rachewiltz, B. (1964) *Black Eros: Sexual Customs of Africa from Prehistory to the Present Day* (tr. P. Whigham). London: Allen & Unwin.

Dunton, C. and M. Palmberg (1996) 'Human Rights and Homosexuality in Southern Africa', *Current African Issues* 19. Uppsala: Nordiska Afrikainstitute.

Eaton, M. (1995) 'Homosexual Unmodified: Speculations on Law's Discourse, Race, and the Construction of Sexual Identity', pp. 46–73 in D. Herman and C. Stychin (eds) *Legal Inversions: Lesbians, Gay Men and the Politics of Law*. Philadelphia, PA: Temple University Press.

Epprecht, M. (in press) ' "Good God Almighty, What's This": Homosexual "Crime" in Early Colonial Zimbabwe', in S. Murray and W. Roscoe (eds) *African Homosexualities*. New York: New York University Press.

Evans-Pritchard, E. E. (1970) 'Sexual Inversion among the Azande', *American Anthropologist* 72: 1428–34.

Feltoe, G. (1980) 'A Guide to the Criminal Law', *Zimbabwe Law Journal* 20: 246, 251.

Folbre, N. (1988) 'Patriarchal Social Formations in Zimbabwe' in S. B. Stichter and J. L. Parpart (eds) *Patriarchy and Class: African Women in the Home and the Workforce*. Boulder, CO: Westview.

Foucault, M. (1978) *The History of Sexuality: An Introduction*. London: Penguin.

Greenberg, D. F. (1988) *The Construction of Homosexuality*. Chicago, IL: University of Chicago Press.

Hunt, P. M. A. (1982) *South African Criminal Law and Procedure* (2nd ed.). Cape Town: Juta & Co.

Jackson, L. A. (1993) 'Friday the 13th University of Zimbabwe Mini-skirt Saga', *Southern Africa Political and Economic Monthly* Dec. 92/Jan. 93: 25–6.

Jacobs, S. M. (1984) 'Women and Land Resettlement in Zimbabwe', *Review of African Political Economy* 27/28: 33–50.

Jacobs, S. M. and T. Howard (1987) 'Women in Zimbabwe: Stated Policy and State Action', in H. Afshar (ed.) *Women, State, and Ideology: Studies from Africa and Asia*. London: Macmillan.

Morrison, A. (1995) 'Barking Up the Wrong Tree? Male Hegemony, Discrimination against Women, and the Reporting of Bestiality in the Zimbabwean Press' in C. Caldas-Coulthard and M. Coulthard (eds) *Discourse and Discrimination*. London: Routledge.

Phillips, O. C. (in press) ' "Venus Monstrosa" and "Unnatural Offences": Homosexuality and the Law in Zimbabwe', in R. Green and D. J. West (eds) *Socio-Legal Implications of Homosexual Behaviour*. London: Plenum.

Pittin, R. (1983) 'Houses of Women: A Focus on Alternative Life-Styles in Katsina City', in C. Oppong (ed.) *Female and Male in West Africa*. London: Allen & Unwin.

Seidman, G. (1984) 'Women in Zimbabwe: Post-Independence Struggles', *Feminist Studies*, Fall, 10(3).

Seligman, C. G. and B. Z. Seligman (1932) *Pagan Tribes of the Nilotic Sudan*. London: Routledge.

Sumner, C. (ed.) (1990) *Censure, Politics and Criminal Justice*. Milton Keynes: Open University Press.

Talbot, P. A. (1967) *Some Nigerian Fertility Cults*. London: Frank Cass.

Wilson, M. (1951) *Good Company: A Study of Nyakyusa Age-Villages*. London: Oxford University Press.

[4]

TRANSGENDER JURISPRUDENCE AND THE SPECTRE OF HOMOSEXUALITY[*]

Andrew Sharpe

When such a cavity [vagina] has been constructed in a male, the difference between sexual intercourse using it, and anal or intra-crural intercourse is, in my judgment, to be measured in centimetres.[1]

If the law insists that genetic sex is the pre-determinant for entry into a valid marriage, then a male to female transsexual can contract a valid marriage with a woman. To all outward appearances, such 'marriages' would be homosexual marriages.[2]

An analysis of transgender jurisprudence reveals a number of narrative tropes. This article will consider one, homophobia. While the theme of homophobia is a consistent one within transgender jurisprudence generally, it appears most visibly in cases concerned with marriage, the prime institution of heterosexuality. Judith Butler has suggested that 'it is important to retrace the different routes by which the unthinkability of homosexuality is being constituted time and again'.[3] In suggesting that transgender jurisprudence represents one such 'route', the article will consider the landmark English decision of *Corbett* v *Corbett*[4] where post-operative[5] transgender sex claims were denied for marriage

---

[*] Andrew N. Sharpe, Department of Law, Macquarie University, Sydney NSW 2109. Australia. asharpe@law.law.mq.edu.au

[1] *Corbett v Corbett* (1970) 2 All ER 33 at 49 per Ormrod J.

[2] *Attorney-General v Otahuhu Family Court* (1995) 1 NZLR 603 at 629 per Ellis J.

[3] Judith Butler 'Imitation and Gender Insubordination' in Diana Fuss (ed), *Inside/Out: Lesbian Theories, Gay Theories*, London: Routledge, 1991, 20.

[4] (1970) 2 All ER 33. The *Corbett* decision has been consistently followed in the UK both in relation to marriage (*Peterson* v *Peterson*, The Times 12 July 1985; *Franklin v Franklin* (1990) The Scotsman, 9 November; *S-T (formerly J) v J* (1997) 3 WLR 1287, (1998) 1 All ER 431) and other subject matters (see *Dec C.P. 6/76* National Insurance Commissioner Decisions; *E.A. White v British Sugar Corporation* (1977) IRLR 121; *Social Security Decision numbers R (P) 1 and R (P) 2* (1980) National Insurance Commissioner Decisions; *R v Tan* (1983) QB 1053; *Collins v Wilkin Chapman* (1994) EAT/945/93 (Transcript)) and UK law has been upheld on appeal to the European Court of Human Rights (see *Rees v UK* (1986) 9 EHRR 56; *Cossey v UK* (1991) 13 EHRR 622; *X, Y and Z v UK* (1997) EHRR 143; *Sheffield and Horsham v UK* (1998) 2 FLR 928).

[5] The term 'post-operative' refers to transgender persons who have undergone full sex reassignment surgery (SRS). Crucially, this includes the construction of a vagina (vaginoplasty) or penis (phalloplasty). With the exception of the Australian decision of SRA, which was overturned on appeal, there has been no recognition, anywhere in the common law world, of the sex claims of pre-operative persons (see *Secretary, Department of Social Security v SRA* (1992) 28 ALD 361; (1993) 118 ALR 467). For a discussion of the case see Andrew Sharpe ,'Anglo-Australian Judicial Approaches to Transsexuality: Discontinuities, Continuities and Wider Issues at Stake'(1997) 6:1 *Social and Legal Studies: An International Journal* 23-50.

THE AUSTRALIAN FEMINIST LAW JOURNAL 2000 VOLUME 14

purposes, and the New Jersey decision of *MT v JT*[6] and the New Zealand decisions of *M v M*[7] and *Attorney-General* v *Otahuhu Family Court*[8] where such claims were recognised in the marriage context. While the three latter decisions might, in contrast to *Corbett*, be comprehended in terms of liberal law reform, this article will highlight the ways in which homophobia serves to link all four decisions. That is to say, judicial anxiety over proximity to the homosexual body proves to be a common theme. We will see that this anxiety manifests itself in terms of inquiry into pre-operative sexual practice, transgender desire, gender performance, heterosexual capacity and bodily aesthetics. Accordingly, transgender jurisprudence generally, and marriage law specifically, emerge as a site for gay and lesbian political intervention.

1. MARRIAGE: 'BETWEEN A MAN AND A WOMAN'

The classic legal definition of marriage was stated by Lord Penzance in *Hyde v Hyde and Woodmansee* to be 'the voluntary union for life of one man and one woman, to the exclusion of all others'.[9] This common law definition of marriage contains four distinct requirements. A marriage must be (a) voluntary, (b) for life, (c) between a man and a woman, and (d) to the exclusion of all others. That this definition remains part of the law is apparent not only in judicial statements[10] but finds expression in statutory form.[11] It is, of course, only the third requirement that calls for attention in the present context and which presents itself as the legal issue in the cases to be considered. It is the meaning of the words 'man' and 'woman' which must ultimately determine the marriage possibilities of transgender persons. In view of the silence of statutory enactments, the determination of the meaning of these words has been left to the interpretative practices of the judiciary. These practices have, in different ways, sought to insulate the institution of marriage from the figure of the homosexual and the 'unnatural' practices law maps onto that body.

---

[6]   355 A 2d 204 (1976). It should be noted that more recent decisions in other US jurisdictions have preferred to follow *Corbett* (see *In re Ladrach*, 32 Ohio Misc. 2d 6, 513 N.E. 2d 828 Ohio Probate Ct. 1987; *Littleton v Prange* 288th Judicial District Court, Bexar County, Texas (1999)). Indeed, in the Littleton decision summary judgment was granted on the basis that argument that an M2F was female failed to raise a genuine question of material fact (though see the dissenting judgment of Justice Lopez).

[7]   (1991) NZFLR 337.

[8]   (1995) 1 NZLR 603.

[9]   (1866) LR 1 PD 130; (1861-1873) All ER Rep 175.

[10]   See *Khan* (1962) 3 FLR 496 at 497; *In the Marriage of C and D (falsely called C)* (1979) 35 FLR 340 at 345; *In the Marriage of S* (1980) 42 FLR 94 at 102. In the US context see, for example, *Singer v Hara*, 11 Wash App. 247, 522 P. 2d 1187 (App Ct. 1974); *B v B* 78 Misc. 2d 112, 355 N.Y.S. 2d 712 (Sup Ct. 1974); *Jones v Hallahan*, 501 S.W. 2d 588 (Ky. Ct. App. 1973); *Baker v Nelson*, 291 Minn. 310, 191 N.W. 2d 185 (Sup. Ct. 1971), app. Dism. 409 U.S. 810, 93 S. Ct. 37, 34 L.Ed. 2d 65 (1972).

[11]   In the Australian context see the *Marriage Act 1961* (Cth) sections 46(1) and 69(2); *Family Law Act 1975* (Cth) section 43(a).

2. TRANSGENDER = HOMOSEXUALITY

In mapping the homophobia common to judicial approaches to the sex claims of transgender persons for the purposes of marriage, it is necessary to begin with the landmark English decision of *Corbett* v *Corbett*.[12] In this case the petitioner, Mr Arthur Corbett, sought to have his marriage to April Ashley, a male to female transgender person who had undergone sex reassignment procedures, declared a nullity. While the practical effect of such a legal finding related to questions of maintenance, the key legal question required a determination as to the sex of April Ashley for marriage purposes. In answering this question, Ormrod J. held that 'sex is determined at birth' and by a congruence of chromosomal, gonadal and genital factors.[13]

He made it clear that he was not determining the sex of the respondent, April Ashley, at large, but only within the context of marriage. Crucially, it was within the context of marriage that the *Corbett* test came to be formulated in the (bio)logically and temporally specific fashion that it did. The test was to be applied wherever sex was considered to be an essential determinant of a legal relationship. In Ormrod's view the test could have no more obvious application than to marriage:

> sex is clearly an essential determinant of the relationship called marriage, because it is and always has been recognised as the union of man and woman. It is the institution on which the family is built, and in which the capacity for natural heterosexual intercourse is an essential element. It has, of course, many other characteristics, of which companionship and mutual support is an important one, but the characteristics which distinguish it from all other relationships can only be met by two persons of opposite sex.[14]

However, an emphasis upon the capacity for (hetero)sexual intercourse was not, in and of itself, sufficient to dispense with the respondent's claim that she was a woman, for April Ashley had undergone full sex reassignment surgery so that she now possessed female genitalia and the capacity for (hetero)sexual intercourse. In seeking to understand why Ormrod should wish to invalidate the respondent's capacity for (hetero)sexual intercourse, for the purposes of marriage, one need only focus on the word 'natural' in the above passage. In describing the respondent's vagina as an 'artificial cavity' Ormrod considered its use for sexual intercourse impossible to describe as 'ordinary and complete intercourse' or, and in a reference to Dr Lushington's famous nineteenth century dictum, as 'vera copula of the natural sort of coitus'.[15]

It is the construction of April Ashley's vagina as the locus of the 'unnatural' which is perhaps the most revealing aspect of the judgment. That is to say, Ormrod aimed primarily at insulating the

---

[12] (1970) 2 All ER 33.
[13] Ibid at 48.
[14] Ibid.
[15] Ibid at 49. In doing so he echoed the words of Dr. Lushington from the mid-nineteenth century English case of *D-e v A-g (orse. D-e)* (1845) 1 Rob Eccl 279; 163 ER 1039; 27 Digest (Repl) 273, 2187.

THE AUSTRALIAN FEMINIST LAW JOURNAL 2000 VOLUME 14

institution of marriage from contamination by the 'unnatural'. The coding of April Ashley's vagina as 'unnatural' is, perhaps, especially curious given Ormrod's willingness to assume her to be a woman for the purpose of considering the alternative ground of petition, namely, the question of consummation.[16] The implication of this move appears to be that the vagina of the chromosomal female might also be a locus for the 'unnatural'.[17]

However, in *SY v SY (orse W)* the English Court of Appeal had held that where a wife lacked a natural vagina but could be given an artificial one by surgical intervention then coitus by means of that artificial vagina constituted *vera copula*, so as to consummate a marriage.[18] In coming to this conclusion Willmer LJ. took the view that Dr. Lushington's famous dictum,[19] while being a statement of commanding authority, had to be interpreted in the context of considerable twentieth century advances made in medical science. In a far from satisfactory manner, Ormrod J. distinguished the facts of *SY v SY* from those of *Corbett* on the basis that SY's vagina was abnormal rather than wholly absent.[20] It would seem therefore that Ormrod comprehended the 'naturalness' of the vagina in terms of degree. Yet, perceiving that such an understanding of the vagina posed a threat to the institution of marriage he expressed the view:

> ... by over-refining and over-defining the limits of 'normal' one may, in the end, produce a situation in which consummation may come to mean something altogether different from normal sexual intercourse.[21]

What is clear from Ormrod's judgment is an overriding concern to insulate marriage, the institution of heterosexual intercourse, from the 'unnatural'. In view of this anxiety over the 'natural' it is, perhaps, hardly surprising that Ormrod conflates April Ashley's desires, practices and body with homosexuality. In the first place, Ormrod expressed the following view of April Ashley's vagina:

> When such a cavity has been constructed in a male, the difference between sexual intercourse using it, and anal or intra-crural intercourse is, in my judgment, to be measured in centimetres.[22]

In juxtaposing use of April Ashley's vagina with the practice of anal intercourse, the judgment brings into view the homosexual body and its assumed practices. In a number of other respects, and informed by prevailing medical knowledge, Ormrod's judgment further inscribes homosexuality onto the body of April Ashley. The nature and importance of the references to homosexuality in the judgment must

---

[16]　Ibid.
[17]　The case of *B v B* (1955) P.42; (1954) 3 W.L.R. 237; (1954) 2 All E.R. 598 would seem to provide authority for this proposition.
[18]　(1962) 3 All ER 55.
[19]　Ibid.
[20]　(1970) 2 All ER 33 at 50.
[21]　Ibid.
[22]　Ibid at 49.

TRANSGENDER JURISPRUDENCE AND THE SPECTRE OF HOMOSEXUALITY

be understood in the context of medical knowledge. It must be recognised that in 1970, the contemporary medical story of 'gender dysphoria' had not yet displaced the discovery story of transsexuality as the dominant medical paradigm for understanding transgender bodies.[23] In contrast to the gender dysphoria perspective, which seeks to ascertain the sex in which it is best for a person to live and which is therefore capable of considering suitable for sex reassignment surgery 'effeminate homosexuals' and 'atypical transvestites', the discovery story of transsexuality views these categories as anathema to the 'truth' of transsexuality.[24] Accordingly, surgery is deemed appropriate only for:

> ... those males who are the most feminine, have been expressing this femininity since earliest childhood, have not had periods of living accepted as masculine males, have not enjoyed their penises and have not advertised themselves as males (for example by female impersonation).[25]

In various portions of the judgment the respondent, April Ashley, is contrasted with this picture of the classic or 'true' transsexual. It is made clear that she worked as a female 'impersonator' in Paris for a four year period from 1956.[26] This theme was pursued by Ormrod who considered the respondent's outward appearance at first sight to be 'convincingly feminine'.[27] However, closer and longer examination in the witness box revealed her 'voice, manner, gestures and attitudes (to be) increasingly reminiscent of the accomplished female impersonator'.[28] This judicial postulation of a 'natural' femininity, one that confronts a feminist politics, and perhaps implicates a middle-class gaze,[29] employs the idea of drag as its mode of expression, an idea that in cultural terms continues to issue forth the spectre of homosexuality.[30]

Further, April Ashley is asked in cross-examination 'whether she had ever had an erection, and whether she had had ejaculations'.[31] While she, understandably, refused to answer this question its

---

23 See Dave King, *The Transvestite and the Transsexual*, Aldershot, Hants, UK: Avebury, 1993, Chp 2.

24 Erwin K. Koranyi, *Transsexuality in the Male: the Spectrum of Gender Dysphoria*, Springfield, Il: Charles C. Thomas, 1980, 156.

25 Robert J. Stoller, *Sex and Gender*, NY: Science House, 1968, 251.

26 (1970) 2 All ER 33 at 36.

27   Ibid at 47.

28   Ibid.

29 Carole-Anne Tyler, 'Boys will be Girls: the Politics of Gay Drag' in Diana Fuss (1991) above note 3 at 32–70.

30 During the eighteenth century cross-dressing changed in character in the popular imaginary. From being perceived as disguise or masquerade and as associated with the theatre, albeit with occasional overtones of sodomy, it came to be seen as the signifier of a form of sodomite (see Randolph Trumbach 'London's Sodomites: Homosexual Behaviour and Western Culture in the 18th Century' (1977) Fall *Journal of Social History* 1; Randolph Trumbach 'Sodomitical Subcultures, Sodomitical Roles, and the Gender Revolution of the 18th Century: The Recent Historiography' in Robert P. Maccubbin (ed) *Tis Nature's Fault: Unauthorised Sexuality during the Enlightenment*, Cambridge University Press, 1987; Richard Davenport-Hines, *Sex, Death and Punishment*, London: W. Collins & Sons Ltd, 1990). In the nineteenth century sexology serves to conflate further cross dressing with homosexuality (see George Chauncey, 'From Sexual Inversion to Homosexuality: Medicine and the Changing Conceptualization of Female Deviance' (1982/1983) *Salmagundi* 58/59 ; Gert Hekma 'A Female Soul in a Male Body: Sexual Inversion as Gender Inversion in Nineteenth-Century Sexology' in Gilbert Herdt (ed) *Third Sex, Third Gender: Beyond Sexual Dimorphism in Culture and History*, NY: Zone, 1994).

31 (1970) 2 All ER 33 at 37.

THE AUSTRALIAN FEMINIST LAW JOURNAL 2000 VOLUME 14

purpose seems to have been to establish homosexuality over transsexuality, as in the discovery story of transsexuality, erotic pleasure in the penis does not exist in the 'true' transsexual.[32] Indeed, it was the use of homosexuality primarily, which served to demonstrate the respondent's departure from the 'truth' of transsexuality. Thus in a doctor's letter of 1953, a time prior to sex reassignment surgery, the respondent was described as a 'constitutional homosexual'.[33] This view was shared by two of the medical experts called for the petitioner who described April Ashley as a 'male homosexual transsexualist',[34] the import of which was that she was a male homosexual who had undergone surgical reassignment. In other words, the judgment, in addition to denying April Ashley female status, casts doubt upon the authenticity of her transsexuality on account of her 'homosexuality'.

The construction of the respondent's 'homosexuality' calls for closer attention. The characterisation of April Ashley as homosexual appears to be based on hospital records compiled in 1953 and containing summaries of 'therapeutic' interviews in which she allegedly 'gave some account of various homosexual experiences' had on board a ship while employed by the Merchant Navy.[35] Yet, it is highly unlikely that April Ashley would view these experiences as homosexual as she viewed herself as a woman. Rather, it is more plausible that April Ashley's account referred to pre-operative sexual experiences with men upon which numerous doctors subsequently inscribed homosexuality. Moreover, given Ormrod's penchant for highlighting absence of anal intercourse in discussions of homosexual behaviour it would appear that this practice was either performed, or imagined to have been performed, on the body of April Ashley. In this regard, the scripting of April Ashley as homosexual is an effect of the inability of medicine and law to read anal intercourse as anything other than the locus of homosexual activity. The practice can signify only a particular desire, a particular relation of bodies. It is significant here to note the medical context in which homosexuality, and perhaps also 'promiscuity', is used to deny transsexuality. The 'homosexuality' of April Ashley takes on added significance in the context of a medical epistemology that seeks to discover the 'truth' of her transsexuality.

The concern over the proximity of homosexuality to marriage is also apparent in Ormrod's commentary upon the petitioner, Mr. Arthur Corbett. In the witness box Corbett had apparently informed the court that from a comparatively early age, he had experienced a desire to dress up in female clothes, a desire that had persisted into adult life.[36] As this narrative unfolds in the judgment Ormrod's anxiety becomes more evident:

> From about 1948 onwards his interest in transvestism increased; at first it was mainly literary, attracting him to pornographic bookshops, but gradually he began to make contact with people of similar tendencies and associated with them from time to time in London. This led to frequent homosexual behaviour with numerous men, stopping

---

32   Robert J. Stoller 'Male Transsexualism: Uneasiness' (1973) 130 *American Journal of Psychiatry* 536-9.
33   (1970) 2 All ER 33 at 36.
34   Ibid at 43.
35   Ibid at 36.
36   Ibid at 37.

TRANSGENDER JURISPRUDENCE AND THE SPECTRE OF HOMOSEXUALITY

short of anal intercourse. As time went on he became more and more involved in the society of sexual deviants, and interested in sexual deviations of all kinds.[37]

This passage is revealing for reasons other than the obvious revulsion that this history provokes and the fact that it was through this world of 'sexual deviation' that April Ashley and Arthur Corbett had first met. It is unclear how much of the passage is directly attributable to Corbett and how much reflects Ormrod's interpretation of the facts. The assertion that Corbett engaged in 'frequent homosexual behaviour with numerous men' is, perhaps, not the most persuasive reading of the facts. After all, the passage makes clear that Corbett's 'homosexual behaviour' occurred only after he had met, and by implication with, persons of similar 'transvestic' tendencies. Accordingly, a more convincing reading of the facts would be that the (trans)gender identities of the parties to the 'homosexual behaviour' preclude, or at least problematise, viewing that behaviour as homosexual. Moreover, Ormrod in suggesting that contact with people of similar 'transvestic' tendencies 'led to frequent homosexual behaviour', creates the impression of a causal link between, as well as conflating, the two phenomenon. In the final analysis any distinction is consumed by Ormrod's deployment of the all purpose category for the 'unnatural', 'sexual deviant'. The reference to 'frequent homosexual behaviour' in Ormrod's judgment is of interest in another regard. We are told that Arthur Corbett's 'homosexual behaviour', frequent though it was, 'stopped short of anal intercourse'. That Ormrod brings this fact into play suggests a phallocentric judicial assumption that anal sex is the logical end of same sex sexual activity. In this regard, even while narrating the absence, and the frequency of the absence, of anal intercourse, Ormrod's judgment couples homosexuality with anal intercourse. That is to say, the homosexual body emerges as the site of a particular sexual practice.

In another passage of the judgment Ormrod struggles to comprehend Arthur Corbett's stated desire to both be (like) April Ashley ('[she] was so much more than I could ever hope to be. The reality was far greater than my fantasy') and to have sexual relations with her, a desire which Ormrod described as 'essentially pathetic'.[38] His difficulty arises out of the fact that law assumes a particular, and binary, gendered relationship between the parties to sexual desire. This assumption of an oppositional relation between sexual 'having' and gendered 'being', as both 'natural' and appropriate, is, of course, one that continues to problematise gay and lesbian identities and desires within legal discourse. Indeed, one suspects that the figure of the homosexual again looms large in Ormrod's analysis. It would seem that the cross-dressing practices of Arthur Corbett served to cast judicial doubt on his masculinity. In contrasting the love of a male transvestite for a transsexual with 'the feelings of a full man in love with a girl'[39] Ormrod emasculates the body of Arthur Corbett and juxtaposes it to the 'pastiche of femininity'[40] which he inscribed onto the body of April Ashley. In summing up each of their stories Ormrod expressed the view:

---

37   Ibid.
38   Ibid at 37.
39   Ibid at 38.
40   Ibid at 47.

THE AUSTRALIAN FEMINIST LAW JOURNAL 2000 VOLUME 14

> Listening to each party describing this strange relationship, my principal impression was that it had little or nothing in common with any heterosexual relationship which I could recall hearing about in a fairly extensive experience of this court.[41]

Thus the rejection of April Ashley's sex claims is tied, importantly, to Ormrod's analysis of her pre-operative sexual practice, gender performance and post-operative heterosexual capacity, an analysis that ultimately conflates transgender with homosexuality. This conflation is exacerbated, and indeed replicated, through Ormrod's problematic reading of the sexual practice and desire of April Ashley's marriage partner, Arthur Corbett. While the (bio)logic of congruence of Ormrod's triumvirate of chromosomes, gonads and genitalia has been subject to sustained criticism[42] the suggestion here is that there is more to the Corbett decision than (bio)logic. Indeed, it is perhaps especially significant that homophobia is so evident in a case that inaugurated transgender jurisprudence in the common law world.

3. TRANSGENDER = HETEROSEXUALITY

A judicial rethinking of the transgender/marriage relation can be traced to the decision of *MT v JT*.[43] In this case the Superior Court of New Jersey had to consider the validity of a two year marriage between a biological man and a post-operative male to female transgender person. The court rejected the *Corbett* analysis preferring instead to articulate a test of 'psychological and anatomical harmony'.[44] Accordingly, her body having been brought into conformity with her psychology, MT was considered to be female for the purposes of marriage. Handler J. distinguished the earlier New York decisions of *Anonymous v Anonymous* and *B v B*,[45] where the court had denied transgender sex claims for marriage purposes, on the basis that the transgender persons in those cases were pre-operative and were therefore incapable of (hetero)sexual intercourse. While reference was made to the fact that MT could no longer 'function as a male sexually either for purposes of recreation or procreation',[46] the court placed particular emphasis on her post-operative sexual capacity and desire:

---

41 Ibid at 38.

42 For previous discussion and criticism of the *Corbett* decision see, for example, David Green, 'Transsexualism and Marriage' (1970)120 *New Law Journal* 210; Douglas Smith, 'Transsexualism, Sex Reassignment and the Law' (1971) 56 *Cornell Law Review* 963; Terrence Walton, 'When is a Woman not a Woman?' (1974) 124 *New Law Journal* 501; Henry Finlay, 'Sexual Identity and the Law of Nullity' (1980) 54 *Australian Law Journal* 115; Alec Samuels, 'Once a Man, Always a Man; Once a Woman, Always a Woman – Sex Change and the Law' (1984) *Medicine and Science Law*, 163; John Dewar, 'Transsexualism and Marriage' (1985) 15 *Kingston Law Review* 58; and Jerold Taitz, 'The Law Relating to the Consummation of Marriage where one of the Spouses is a Post-Operative Transsexual' (1986) 15 *Anglo-American Law Review* 141; Michael Kirby, 'Medical Technology and New Frontiers of Family Law' (1987) 1 *Australian Journal of Family Law* 196; John Mountbatten, 'Transsexuals, Hermaphrodites and Other Legal Luminaries' (1991) 16 *Legal Service Bulletin* 223; Vivienne Muller, 'Trapped in the Body – Transsexualism, the Law and Sexual Identity' (1994) 3 *Australian Feminist Law Journal* 103.

43 355 A 2d 204 (1976).

44 Ibid.

45 *Anonymous v Anonymous* 67 Misc. 2d 982; 325 N.Y.S. 2d 499 (Sup. Ct. 1971); *B v B* above note 10.

46 355 A 2d 204 (1976) at 206.

Transgender Jurisprudence and the Spectre of Homosexuality

Implicit in the reasoning underpinning our determination is the tacit but valid assumption of the lower court and the experts upon whom reliance was placed that for purposes of marriage under the circumstances of this case, it is the sexual capacity of the individual which must be scrutinized. Sexual capacity or sexuality in this frame of reference requires the coalescence of both the physical ability and the psychological and emotional orientation to engage in sexual intercourse as either male or female.[47]

The reference to the 'psychological and emotional orientation to engage in sexual intercourse' is significant. It suggests that the creation of a 'functional' vagina is, in and of itself, insufficient for the purposes of legal recognition of male to female transgender sex claims. Rather, recognition for the purposes of marriage proves to be dependent on the additional requirement of heterosexual desire. In this regard, the legal regulation of MT's body is concerned with more than her submission to genital reconstruction. Law desires to know her desire, to know that it is heterosexual, and to be assured through that knowledge as to the authenticity of MT's transsexuality. Indeed, this judicial concern to be assured of heterosexual desire is not confined to marriage cases. Rather, the problematisation of heterosexual desire may lead to the denial of transgender sex claims in other legal contexts given the dominant legal view that transgender persons undergo sex reassignment surgery 'in order that they may enter into heterosexual relationships'.[48]

In relation to MT's sexual functioning the court explored in some detail her genital topography. Drawing on the evidence of Dr Ihlenfeld, MT's medical doctor, Handler J. noted that MT had 'a vagina and labia which were adequate for sexual intercourse and could function as any female vagina, that is, for traditional penile/vaginal intercourse'.[49] There is no reference in the judgment or the medical evidence as to any sexual pleasure that MT might derive from her vagina.[50] Rather, law seeks reassurance that MT's vagina can function as a site of heterosexual male pleasure.

---

[47] Ibid at 209.

[48] *Secretary, Department of Social Security v HH* (1991) 13 AAR 314 at 317 per O'Connor J and Muller. This view is one informed by medicine (see Harry Benjamin, *The Transsexual Phenomenon*, NY: The Julian Press, Inc, 1966; Robert J Stoller above note 32). While some clinicians are now recognising gay and lesbian transgender persons (see, for example, Ray Blanchard, Leonard Clemmensen and Betty W. Steiner, 'Heterosexual and Homosexual Gender Dysphoria' (1987) 16 *Archives of Sexual Behavior* 139-152; Eli Coleman and Walter O. Bockting, 'Heterosexual Prior to Sex Reassignment – Homosexual Afterwards: A Case Study of a Female-to-Male Transsexual' (1988) 12 *Journal of Psychology and Human Sexuality* 69-82; Dorothy Clare and Bryan Tully, 'Transhomosexuality, or the Dissociation of Sexual Orientation and Sex Object Choice' (1989) 18 *Archives of Sexual Behavior* 531-536) the prevalence of non-heterosexual desire tends to be downplayed. Moreover, gay and lesbian transgender identities continue to be viewed negatively in terms of prognosis and therefore access to SRS (see Anne Bolin, *In Search of Eve: Transsexual Rites of Passage*, Massachusetts: Bergin & Garvey Publishers, Inc, 1988; Dave King, 1993, above note 23; Frank Lewins, *Transsexualism in Society: A Sociology of Male-to-Female Transsexuals*. Melbourne: Macmillan Education Australia Pty Ltd, 1995; Jason Cromwell, *Transmen & FTMs: Identities, Bodies, Genders & Sexualities*, Chicago: University of Illinois Press, 1999).

[49] Ibid at 206.

[50] Indeed, a concern with one's own sexual pleasure is not typically read as a sign of 'authentic' transsexual identity within the medical arena. See Harry Benjamin, 1966, above note 48 at 13-14, 54; John Money and Clay Primrose, 'Sexual Dimorphism and Dissociation in the Psychology of Male Transsexuals', in Green and Money (eds) *Transsexualism and Sex Reassignment*, Baltimore: Johns Hopkins Press, 1969, 121-122; Robert J Stoller, 1973, above note 32.

The Australian Feminist Law Journal 2000 Volume 14

Apart from the obvious phallocentric and heterosexist assumptions contained in this approach to the male to female transgender body, law's inspection of MT's vagina serves to highlight a further, though related, legal concern. Thus, judicial evaluation of her vagina, and its sexual adequacy, belie a concern to ensure that MT's body is capable of being the locus of natural pleasure. Thus, and again referring to the evidence of Dr Ihlenfeld, Handler J. pointed out that MT's vagina had been 'lined initially by the skin of [her] penis', that it would, in all likelihood, later take on 'the characteristics of normal vaginal mucosa', that it had a 'good cosmetic appearance and was the same as a normal female vagina after a hysterectomy' and that though at 'a somewhat different angle, was not really different from a natural vagina in size, capacity and the feeling of the walls around it'.[51]

This mapping of MT's genital region suggests a concern to 'naturalise' her vagina, and thereby the practice of heterosexual intercourse. That is to say, medico-legal discourse in emphasising textural, spatial and sensual similarities between MT's vagina and that of biological women, attempts to rearticulate the relation between the transgender body and the 'natural'. This view can be contrasted with Ormrod's view of April Ashley's vagina in *Corbett*. However, even while 'naturalising' MT's vagina for marriage purposes, Handler J., in a passage that suggests judicial anxiety about the coupling of transgender and heterosexuality, felt it necessary to insulate the institution of marriage from 'unnatural' homosexual incursion:

> The historic assumption in the application of common law and statutory strictures relating to marriages is that only persons who can become 'man and wife' have the capacity to enter marriage ... The pertinent statutes relating to marriages and married persons do not contain any explicit references to a requirement that marriage must be between a man and a woman ... Nevertheless ... [it] is so strongly and firmly implied from a full reading of the statutes that a different legislative intent, one which would sanction a marriage between persons of the same sex, cannot be fathomed.[52]

This anxiety over proximity to homosexuality serves to link, seemingly incommensurable, decisions like *Corbett* and *MT v JT*. More recently, the New Zealand judiciary have also rearticulated the transgender/ marriage relation. In *M v M* Aubin J. upheld the validity of a 12 and a half year marriage between a post-operative male to female transgender person and a biological male.[53] In considering M to be female for marriage purposes Aubin J. declined to follow *Corbett*. In rejecting (bio)logical factors as determinative of the issue, and in allusions to the judgments of Ormrod J. in *Corbett* and Nedstadt J. in the South African case of *W v W*,[54] Aubin refused to view M as a 'pseudo-woman',[55] as

---

[51]   355 A 2d 204 (1976) at 206.
[52]   Ibid at 208.
[53]   (1991) NZFLR 337.
[54]   (1976) 2 SALR 308.
[55]   (1991) NZFLR 337 at 344.

TRANSGENDER JURISPRUDENCE AND THE SPECTRE OF HOMOSEXUALITY

a 'pastiche'[56] or as an 'imitation'.[57] Rather, and in purporting to follow the Australian criminal law decision of *R v Harris and McGuiness*,[58] Aubin took the view that, although the question of sex cannot be decided 'merely upon sympathetic or compassionate grounds',[59] a change of sex, 'in a real sense'[60] had occurred in the case of M.

The judgment of Aubin J. is, in the present instance, significant in a number of respects. First, Aubin J. asks rhetorically whether the surgery undertaken by M amounted to 'no more than some ultimately futile attempt to change her from an anguished Mr Hyde into a well-adjusted Mrs Jekyll, producing a kind of hermaphroditic mutant unable to enter into a valid marriage with a man, or indeed with a woman'.[61] This passage is revealing irrespective of, and perhaps despite, the fact that Aubin J. did not view M's sex reassignment surgery as futile. The literary reference to Jekyll and Hyde[62] invokes the notion of the monstrous body. Moreover, it is clear from the reference to 'an anguished Mr Hyde' that it is the pre-operative body that Aubin views as monstrous. This invocation of the figure of the monster is interesting, and perhaps revealing, given the etymology of the term 'monster'. While there is some debate about the term it would appear to come from *monere*, to warn, or *monstrare*, to show forth or demonstrate.[63] Both these words, then, and importantly, refer to signs as well as defective births or malformations.[64] It is contended that one sign that the pre-operative body emits before the legal gaze is the sign of homosexuality. In particular, the male to female pre-operative body is imagined as the locus of sodomy. Thus it is not merely that the coupling of the words 'hermaphrodite' and 'mutant' represent a heightened moment of insensitivity toward transgender and intersexual persons or that Aubin J.'s resort to the 'hermaphroditic mutant' serves to remind us that law cannot, and will not, think sex in any other than binary, oppositional and genitocentric terms that calls for attention. Rather, the invocation of the monstrous serves to issue forth the spectre of homosexuality. This negation of the sex claims, and the homosexualisation, of the pre-operative body serve as prelude to the moment of departure from *Corbett*. That is to say, the depiction of the pre-operative body as monstrous serves to reduce anxiety with regard to the (re)sexing of M's body which the court subsequently sanctions.

In another vein, and in developing the theme of homophobia, Aubin J. notes that 'Mr M was fully aware of his partner's background and accepting of her in a heterosexual relationship'.[65] This statement illustrates judicial anxiety over the possibility of 'fraud'. As in previous decisions the concern

---

56 Ibid.
57 Ibid.
58 *R v Harris and McGuiness* (1988) 35 A Crim R 146.
59 (1991) NZFLR 337 at 348.
60 Ibid.
61 Ibid at 347. This was precisely the view taken of a hermaphrodite by Bell J. in the marriage case of *C and D* (1979) above note 10.
62 Robert Louis Stevenson, *The Strange Case of Dr Jekyll and Mr Hyde*, Der Munchen: Deutscher Taschenbuch Verlag, 1986.
63 See Julia Epstein, *Altered Conditions: Disease, Medicine and Storytelling*, Routledge, 1995, 91.
64 Ibid. In considering the history of the treatment of hermaphrodites, Epstein suggests that their bodies were taken to signify divine wrath.
65 (1991) NZFLR 337 at 348.

over 'fraud' is revealing.[66] It is not clear why transgender persons should be required to 'out' themselves, to confess to the 'truth' about their pre-surgical bodies or indeed, why 'truth' should bear this particular temporal relation to transgender bodies. It would appear, despite judicial emphasis on present psychological and anatomical harmony, that an important, perhaps the important, 'truth' about transgender bodies resides in the past. In this regard, the 'retreat' from *Corbett*, evident in *MT* v *JT*, *M v M* and in other decisions is rendered somewhat inauthentic. It is contended that judicial preoccupation with the revelation of pre-surgical autobiography, particularly within the marriage context, is, in large measure, explicable in terms of fear of coming into contact with the homosexual body. In other words, while law inscribes heterosexuality onto the post-surgical transgender body, as a means of regulating that body and incorporating it within the gender order, this practice of legal inscription appears to be one in relation to which there is some degree of judicial ambivalence.

The case of *M v M* prompted an application by the Attorney-General on behalf of the Registrar of Marriages for 'a declaration as to whether two persons of the same genetic sex may by the law of New Zealand enter into a valid marriage where one of the parties to the proposed marriage has adopted the sex opposite to that of the proposed marriage partner through sexual reassignment by means of surgery or hormone administration or both or by any other medical means'.[67] In that case, *Attorney-General v Otahuhu Family Court*,[68] the High Court purported to follow the legal analyses in *MT v JT*, *R v Harris and McGuiness* and *M v M* insisting that legal recognition of sex claims for marriage purposes was dependent on sex reassignment surgery. The court made it clear that bodily change brought about through hormone administration or other medical means was insufficient in this regard:

> There is clearly a continuum which begins with the person who suffers from gender dysphoria (a state of mental unease or discomfort) but who has not chosen to cross-dress on a regular basis and has embarked on no programme of hormonal modification or surgery, through to the person who has embarked on hormone therapy and perhaps had some minor surgical intervention such as removal of gonads, through to the person who undergoes complete reconstructive surgery ... in order for a transsexual to be eligible to marry in the sex of assignment, the end of the continuum must have been reached and reconstructive surgery done.[69]

Thus, like other common law decisions, the pre or non-surgical transgender body is constructed as necessarily 'outside' to a resexed transgender body that is given a presence within law. However, it would be misleading to suggest that the decision in *Otahuhu* followed, in any simple way, previous

---

[66]   See, for example, *Corbett v Corbett* (1970) above note 1; *B v B* (1974) above note 10; *Rees v UK* (1986) above note 4; *Cossey v UK* (1991) above note 4; *ST (formerly J) v J* (1998) above note 4.
[67]   *Attorney-General v Otahuhu Family Court* (1995) 1 NZLR 603.
[68]   Ibid.
[69]   Ibid at 614–615.

TRANSGENDER JURISPRUDENCE AND THE SPECTRE OF HOMOSEXUALITY

decisions articulating the test of psychological and anatomical harmony. While *Otahuhu* shares much with prior transgender jurisprudence recognising sex claims there is a striking difference. In *MT v JT, Harris and McGuiness* and *M V M* the judiciary had insisted that legal recognition was dependent on, not merely sex reassignment surgery, but also, post-operative capacity for heterosexual intercourse. In *Otahuhu* however, while Ellis J. stated 'that in order to be capable of marriage two persons must present themselves as having what appear to be the genitals of a man and a woman'[70] he insisted that they did not 'have to prove that each can function sexually'[71] for 'there are many forms of sexual expression possible without penetrative sexual intercourse'.[72]

The uncoupling of sex reassignment surgery from the capacity for heterosexual intercourse is significant as it serves to highlight law's concern over bodily aesthetics. While an aesthetic concern over bodies is a consistent theme of transgender jurisprudence it is usually masked, at least partially, by a preoccupation with heterosexual capacity. In the judgment of Ellis J however, law's anxiety over bodily aesthetics is foregrounded. Irrespective of sexual functioning, and guided by an obvious genitocentrism, Ellis J. seeks, and finds, reassurance in the fact that the male to female post-operative body 'can never appear unclothed as a male'[73] and that the female to male post-operative body 'can no longer appear unclothed as a woman'.[74] Absent a concern over sexual functioning, law's view of phallic female, and vaginaed male, bodies as monstrous becomes all the more evident, as does the homosexual sign they emit in the legal imaginary. These monstrous bodies are required to undergo 'a risky surgical procedure'[75] if they are to accord with law's aesthetic sensibility and thereby reduce homophobic anxiety. The decision in *Otahuhu* is significant in another crucial respect. While Ellis J. emphasised that 'the declaration sought is to resolve the capacity to marry and is not intended to resolve questions that arise in other branches of the law such as criminal law, and the law of succession'[76] he departed from previous transgender jurisprudence expressing the opinion that:

> It may be that for other legal purposes, a transsexual who has not had reconstructive surgery or only minimal surgical intervention (such as removal of the testes) could be classified in his or her chosen sex for certain purposes such as employment law, criminal law and the law of inheritance.[77]

---

70 Ibid at 612.
71 Ibid.
72 Ibid at 615.
73 Ibid at 607.
74 Ibid at 615.
75 Ibid at 614.
76 Ibid at 607.
77 Ibid at 615. While no superior court has previously taken this course it should be pointed out that it was adopted by the Administrative Appeals Tribunal in the Australian decision of *Secretary, Department of Social Security v SRA*, a decision that was emphatically overturned on appeal by the Federal Court (see above note 5). For a discussion of the case see Frank Bates, 'When Is a Wife ... ?' (1993) 7 *Australian Journal of Family Law* 274–82; Andrew Sharpe, 'Anglo-Australian Judicial Approaches to Transsexuality' (1997) above note 5.

THE AUSTRALIAN FEMINIST LAW JOURNAL 2000 VOLUME 14

In other words, Ellis J., at the very least, held out the possibility that a superior court might dispense with the requirement of anatomical change. However, while this aspect of the judgment is, perhaps, to be welcomed, the potential for differential treatment of transgender bodies across legal subject matters serves to redraw attention to the bodily aesthetics of law. That is to say, why is it that law can entertain the possibility of creating a legal space in the areas of employment, crime and inheritance for the monstrous body of marriage law? Or to put it another way, why is it that law's aesthetic sensibility cannot be compromised in the marriage context? Such questions might be responded to in a number of ways. One possible explanation might invoke a visibility/invisibility distinction. That is to say, the genital region of the body, which law seeks to police, while visible to parties to a marriage, is not visible in the other contexts referred to by Ellis J. While such an argument may have some explanatory power it appears dubious in the criminal law context where a number of sexual offences would locate the genitalia of non or pre-surgical transgender bodies on the visibility side of the distinction. In any event, to focus on the visibility of the pre-surgical body is to foreground its 'monstrosity' rather than any sign that it may emit.

It is contended that a more convincing explanation for differential treatment of transgender bodies in the marriage context lies in the sexual significance genitals have in/for marriage law. In other words, and as we have already seen, legal anxiety over homosexuality surfaces whenever parties whose genitals are not dissimilar, and therefore not 'complementary', assert heterosexual identity and desire. In sex (genital) reassignment surgery law finds, at least some, assurance that marriage, the institution of heterosexuality, will be insulated from the spectre of the homosexual body. In this sense law produces heterosexuality not only as identity or sexual practice, but as an effect of the present, and of course 'oppositional', anatomical form of the parties to desire.

The concern over proximity of the homosexual body to marriage finds expression in other portions of Ellis' judgment. Thus in a passage that evinces a concern that law should not hinder the heterosexualisation of transgender bodies effected by sex reassignment surgery, Ellis J. expressed the view:

> If the law insists that genetic sex is the pre-determinant for entry into a valid marriage, then a male to female transsexual can contract a valid marriage with a woman. To all outward appearances, such 'marriages' would be homosexual marriages. The marriage could not be consummated.[78]

In this regard legal recognition emerges as a strategy to insulate marriage from contamination by 'homosexuality'. Anxiety over the prospect of 'homosexual marriages' is evident in the fact that Ellis J. problematises the word 'marriages' even though such marriages are quite clearly lawful. Moreover, the homophobia of the judgment is further evidenced by Ellis' assertion that such a marriage 'could not be consummated'. It is curious why reference to consummation should be made given its obvious

---

[78] Ibid at 629.

irrelevance to the law of marriage in New Zealand, a point rendered abundantly clear by Ellis J. in other portions of the judgment.[79] Rather, it would seem that the idea of consummation is deployed against what Ellis J. sees as gay and lesbian transgender persons in order to 'denaturalise' their bodies and desires. This concern over the proximity of the homosexual body to marriage manifests itself in yet another regard:

> From a practical point of view, sex change procedures are unlikely to be undertaken by legitimate medical personnel in New Zealand without the individual having first obtained a dissolution of his or her marriage in the original sex. There is always the possibility that a person could undergo such procedures with less ethical professionals.[80]

This passage of the judgment is revealing. While it is true that psychiatrists are reluctant to refer married persons for sex reassignment procedures and surgeons reluctant to perform those procedures on married persons,[81] that attitude is premised on a view of homosexual desire, a desire which medicine, not unproblematically, inscribes onto married bodies, as inconsistent with transsexuality. It is significant that Ellis J. finds it necessary to delegitimise, and to characterise as unethical, medical practitioners who might be capable of imagining non-heterosexual transgender identities and desires.

4. CONCLUSION

While there are many narrative tropes within transgender jurisprudence this article has sought to tease out and examine one, homophobia. In placing emphasis on this theme the article calls into question a view of the relation between *Corbett* and the line of 'progressive' cases decided in its wake as discontinuous. For homophobia proves to be continuous, linking together ostensibly disparate decisions, be that through inquiry into pre-operative sexual practice, post-operative heterosexual capacity, transgender desire, gender performance and/or a judicial concern over bodily aesthetics. In other words, the figure of the homosexual haunts transgender jurisprudence as a body. Accordingly, the article demonstrates the need to rethink critically relations between cases as a prelude to adequate mapping of this jurisprudence, its trajectories and effects. Moreover, because this nascent jurisprudence emerges as a locus for the denigration and erasure of homosexuality, transgender law reform needs to be placed more firmly on a gay and lesbian political agenda.

---

79   Ibid at 612.

80   Ibid at 619.

81   See Dave King, 1993, above note 23. Indeed, the famous transsexual Jan Morris went to Casablanca for her surgery in 1972 after she was told she must divorce her wife in order to receive surgery in the UK (Jan Morris, *Conundrum: An Extraordinary Narrative of Transsexualism*, NY: Holt, 1986). More recently, Kristina Sheffield stated that she was informed by her consultant psychiatrist and her surgeon that she was required to obtain a divorce as a pre-condition to surgery being carried out (see *Sheffield and Horsham v UK* (1998) 2 FLR 928).

Histories

[5]

RETURNING TO THE SCENE
OF THE CRIME

Uses of Trial Dossiers on Consensual Male
Homosexuality for Urban Research, with Examples
from Twentieth-Century British Columbia

Gordon Brent Ingram

$\mathcal{T}$he transcripts of hearings and trials for consensual homosexuality are a key source for lesbian and gay histories. While trial dossiers are rich troves for social narratives, the documents they contain often include ambiguous and contradictory details. Curiously, discussions on methods of reading and analyzing such sources are rare in studies on sexual minorities. Although trial dossiers can also tell us much about the formation of cities and states, they have been underused in environmental histories and other urban research. The use of such sources to reconstruct maps of shifting homoerotic social spaces, such as gay enclaves and sites of important events, remains underdeveloped, except perhaps in the area of historical preservation. This essay explores ways that trial dossiers can be assessed for applied scholarship and contemporary activism. By returning to the scene of these so-called crimes, and to the repressive activities of police and courts that in the same locations today would be often considered criminal, we can find new ways to understand past and present urban economies of sexualities. I sketch an approach to urban research that explores trial dossiers for policy development, planning, design, and management for physical, social, economic, and cultural aspects of inhabited spaces on various scales, from local sites to metropolitan regions.

The use of trial dossiers in urban research, particularly those in which the state identifies defendants as members of stigmatized and outlawed groups, is problematic. The details presented by either side may be purposefully untrue and, if so, can be considered as competing fictions. But whatever their truth status, the written narratives in a trial dossier are relevant to a range of fields, from history to cultural studies to political economy to geography to urban studies. Trial dossiers examined in terms of urban space over time and drawn on as a basis for activist proposals yield a host of theoretical and methodological questions. At this point in the development of the scholarship on sexual minorities, I argue for multiple readings of trial dossiers—for different, more clearly specified agendas concerning their use. One mark of the success of early sexual-minority social histories— whether global and national or local and focused on aspects of the "specificity of gay life"—is that they have raised new questions that are now being asked.[1] One line of inquiry centers on questions about the formation of urban life and space.[2] In other words, how have homosexuality and homophobia "built" the cities in which we live? Over the last four decades this field has had links to attempts to forge more complete understandings of and defense strategies for public sex. Such examinations of populations, bodies, desires, sites, designed space, political economies, and even queer impacts can lead to more nuanced frameworks, particularly ones intolerant of homophobia and other social inequities, for the planning, design, and management of urban space.

Like the sources with which I work in this essay, my findings are historically and geographically specific, only partly useful for understanding other parts of North America or even the British Empire. Unlike some prominent historians of modern male homosexuality, I do not argue that the information from these trial dossiers is of universal importance to the making of the twentieth-century gay male world. The towns of Victoria and Vancouver, where nearly all of the supposed crimes took place, were among the few relatively stable settlements in British Columbia at the time; crisis-ridden Indian villages and temporary company towns were more typical. Moreover, a plethora of demographic, legal, institutional, and cultural factors made the political economy of sexuality in urbanizing British Columbia distinctive from that of Alberta and parts farther east in Canada, not to mention adjacent areas of the United States, such as Seattle to the south and Alaska to the northwest. First, many parts of the province and the urban neighborhoods of Victoria and Vancouver have had majorities and near majorities of non-European heritages for a century. The comparatively resilient immigration populations of these areas and the economic pressures for higher rates of non-European immigration to them differed from and sometimes prefigured the demographic features of much of urban North America. Second, these areas had a great many more men than women (particularly white women) well into the twentieth century. With massive housing shortages, men often lived in dormitories and slept two and three to a bed.[3] But equating these largely working-class homosocial cultures to nascent homosexual networks remains problematic.[4] Third, few of the aboriginal "First Nations" (labeled "Indians" at the time) were invited (or permitted) to forge treaties, even though they often constituted demographic majorities in many of the rural areas. This institutional obstacle contrasted markedly with the treaty making to the south and east and further destabilized these communities and cultures. Well into the twentieth century this neocolonial landscape had a direct impact on the separate and at times more brutal policing of aboriginal sexual minorities. Fourth, British Columbia's limited independence from Westminster, brought about by the province's entry into the Canadian confederation in 1871, led to a series of racial laws (previously resisted by the Colonial Office in London) that targeted native people ("Indians"), East Asians (especially "China men" and "Japanese"), and later South Asians (often lumped together, regardless of religion, as "Hindoos"). Racial laws, which existed until 1949, coincided with many legal proscriptions against consensual homosexuality between adult males. The particulars of these laws, which marginalized and disenfranchised demographic groups that, when combined, constituted majorities in many communities, and the state apparatus that enforced legal inequities were sometimes unique and asymmetrical in Canada. One example of the unique racialization of the province was that a small community of African Canadians, who were highly influential in the colony's choice to join confederation over the union at the beginning of Reconstruction, were never disenfranchised, in contrast to other demographic groups that were not of European origins. Fifth, British Columbia maintained closer legal ties to Britain than most other parts of North America. These ties, which extended well into the second half of the twentieth century, allowed the law in British Columbia to be more attuned to London in the aftermaths of the Oscar Wilde trials in 1895 and of decriminalization in the 1960s.[5] On account of these conditions, British Columbia has not functioned as a "perfect paradigm" of the social transitions of sexual minorities in Canada, North America, or the British Empire or even as Clive Moore argued Queensland has been for Australia.[6] The value of looking at British Columbia lies in examining local forms of homoerotic networks, repression, resistance, and agency and comparing them with those of other regions. The project of fathoming how these particular margins of empire contributed, if at all, to the making of more global homosexual subcultures remains problematic. For this essay, the work of Rudi C. Bleys, in describing the links between the late-nineteenth- and early-twentieth-century projects of colonialism and imperialism and the construction of a multiplicity of homophobic and ethnic social hierarchies, has been valuable.[7] The "colour line" in British Columbia, though white suprema-

80   **GLQ: A JOURNAL OF LESBIAN AND GAY STUDIES**

cist, was distinctly different from the U.S. color lines explored by Siobhan B. Somerville and, in turn, had different effects on local constructions of sexuality.[8]

What are the most compelling scholarly and activist uses of trial dossiers from such exceptional areas as British Columbia? First, notions of the making of the gay world, as they have been applied to large cities in the United States, are anathema to many, especially those whose cultures, languages, and jurisdictions contrast to those that have predominated on the central East Coast of North America. Today there are regional and neighborhood movements to substitute specificity for earlier generalizations and "loss of locality."[9] In Canada this concept of local-ness was first applied to aboriginal communities and their cultural and nationalist assertions. Local experiences now are of growing interest to some communities and sexual subcultures. Second, the scales of formation of urban space in North America have been fundamentally different among global centers such as New York City, smaller cities such as Toronto, and cities such as Vancouver whose met-ropolitan populations were barely a quarter of a million at the end of World War II. Although tenuous frontier towns until the mid-twentieth century, Vancouver and Victoria did not lack for male homosexuality, public places marked by social net-works of sexual "deviants," or an extraordinary preoccupation on the part of the more urban municipalities with certain kinds of consensual homosexuality.

When we explore local specificity through trial dossiers from British Columbia, some of the region's particularities in relation to its construction of and resistance to imperial, neocolonial, and capitalist projects emerge. Victoria is a mid-nineteenth-century colonial town that initially was better linked economically to San Francisco and other American settlements along the West Coast. But as the economic capital of "the Company Province," Vancouver has been an aggressively capitalist and nationalist city created by the Canadian state in the late nineteenth century during the overlapping neocolonial and early nationalist periods.[10] Built by large corporations, such as the Canadian Pacific Railway, with its near monop-oly and government subsidies, Vancouver has been and remains a strategic point in the flows of European and Asian capital and resources. It has also been, how-ever, a national and North American center for movements contesting the power of capital and the state and for socialist, communist, environmental, and human rights movements, as well as an early staging ground for urban reform initiatives. For example, central Vancouver, where most of the sodomy alleged in the trials took place, was an important base of support for the Industrial Workers of the World (IWW) soon after the organization was formed in Chicago in 1905. In her 1912 articles on the IWW in Vancouver, the pioneering female journalist Agnes C. Laut paints an intriguing picture of the nearly all-male "Wobblie" bases for organizing and sedition and provides clues about the social spaces of activists whom police often brutalized and incarcerated. The IWW, Laut writes, "[aim] to organize in the world of labor the same class that the Salvation Army go after in the religious world. They are what we call 'he-camps,' nearly all homeless and many shirtless."[11] The major organizing hall for the IWW was also in the same central Vancouver neighborhood where most of the trials discussed in this essay took place. Similarly, Vancouver was a national center for sexual radicalism a century ago. More recently, it has been a laboratory for Canadian industrial democracy, social infrastructure, and responsible capitalism, often including tolerance of sexual diversity.

The geopolitical marginality and economic volatility of British Columbia during much of its short history make the state's preoccupation with certain kinds of consensual homosexuality in the first half of the twentieth century intriguing. How were early notions of public and private, along with individual propriety over consensual desires, asserted when the courts were still struggling to define and assert the domain of the state? Why were the municipal police, who constantly complained about inadequate budgets, so interested in homosexuality? What are some implications of early forms of resistance for reconstructing the same locales in the twenty-first century?

Suites of Dossiers of Sodomy Trials as Sources of Information

Throughout the world there are poorly visited dossiers of trials concerning homosexuality, most of them from the nineteenth and early twentieth centuries. It is likely that few such suites of documents, for particular areas, acts, and eras, reveal the events of the trials completely. Most sites of trial dossiers have been subjected to social editing practices, along with erratic transcription, filing, and archiving. Because of tampering and even outright destruction, often decades ago, the records of some trials have effectively been erased, causing others to be highlighted.[12] Moreover, freedom of information and privacy laws often limit access to details. Years after the events and trials, it is sometimes difficult to conclude what information was confirmed, what was fabricated, even what was closeted. Omissions, when they can be confirmed, are sometimes more telling than what was recorded.

The sources used in this essay come mainly from the Office of the Attorney General of British Columbia and date from 1860 in the colonial period to 1967, two years before most consensual homosexuality between two people in a bedroom was decriminalized (but not other kinds of homosexuality). The Office of the Attorney General controls the judiciary of every province, and the attorney general is an elected member of the provincial legislature who is selected by the party's leader to be a cabinet minister, one of whose portfolios is that of attorney general. The attorney general of British Columbia administers federal and provincial laws and historically has had considerable influence over prosecutions. From 1860 to 1967 the attorney general of British Columbia would have kept files on anyone accused under the laws of Canada for sex crimes, with the possible exception of cases involving aboriginals. This suite of dossiers on consensual homosexuality between adults is part of a large set of trial documents on "buggery," "sodomy," and "gross indecency" available for British Columbia. It is entirely possible that, in addition to the examples described in the dossiers, members of a range of social groups were policed but never committed to trial (and therefore were not recorded in this suite of dossiers).

As a consequence of analyzing these sources, I make four observations on their use by scholars who, like myself, are not social historians. First, trial dossiers contain highly ambiguous documents whose interpretation will depend on the agendas of individual researchers and their funding sources. Second, the trial transcripts describe not homophobia specifically but a series of conflicts centered on the power of the individual, the state, police, and the judiciary and encompassing sites of alleged homosexuality, accused bodies, arrests, courtrooms, penitentiaries, and the public space in which hostility to and tolerance of homosexuality can be expressed. Third, consumers of transcripts of the trials of sexual outlaws constantly struggle with questions of objectivity while verging on being historical voyeurs to whom some material is the source of such responses as sorrow, reflection, amusement, and even pleasure. Fourth, these scholarly consumers make up interest groups and stakeholders who sometimes find themselves in competition with each other. The interest of a given scholar in a particular dossier is therefore not necessarily identical to or comparable with the interests of other researchers working with the same sources.

The Search for Dossiers of Sodomy Trials from British Columbia

How can scholars and activists identify the transcripts of sodomy trials? In the present case, an archivist working in what is now the British Columbia Archives and interested in lesbian and gay history, Indiana Matters, had identified a small portion of the relevant files nearly two decades before.[13] In the sources she cited there were leads to many more, often unopened, dossiers. The only subsequent source that prefigured a list of sodomy trials in British Columbia was microfilm reel B00395 at the British Columbia Archives.[14] I located the dossiers of other trials that had not been previously identified by cross-referencing lists of trials, querying gaps in labels and file sequences, and directly examining files when the nature of the charges was particularly unclear. It was necessary to link older lists on microfilm with a more recent, computerized database. The list of sodomy trials used in this essay reflects the most thorough review of trials for sex crimes in the province that might have been undertaken in the 1990s, combined with previous mentions of trials whose dossiers could not be located in the British Columbia Archives.

Dossiers of consensual homosexuality between adults involved trials under three labels, "buggery," "sodomy," and "gross indecency." In reviewing all of these dossiers, I encountered as many prosecutions for pedophilia, same-sex rape, consensual heterosexual anal sex, and interspecies genital contact. The common proscription that linked legal concern over these practices was genital contact in which one or more penises were touching or were inside an orifice other than a vagina. Even in the case of same-sex rape, the notion of consent was poorly defined and of limited interest to prosecutors.

As the urban population and state regulation of sexuality expanded in the twentieth century, so did the number of trials concerning homosexuality. By the 1920s these cases had become so numerous that entire dossiers might not always have been forwarded to the Office of the Attorney General in Victoria. The dossiers of more recent cases, from the 1950s and 1960s, may well have been removed through subsequent application by the parties involved, particularly the defendants. Thus the records from that latter period of prosecutions are less representative than earlier records of the extent of police and court involvement in punishing consensual homosexuality. Nevertheless, it is highly unlikely that a large group of dossiers in the Office of the Attorney General were selectively removed or not archived either by region or by type of crime.[15]

The following list names the hearings and trials whose dossiers have been reviewed for this essay:

1909	*Rex v. Nar Singh*
1910	*Rex v. H——i S——h*
1910	*Rex v. S——n S——h*
1913	*Rex v. Dahn Singh & Franco Rain*
1914	*Rex v. James Valse & Charma Singh*
1915	*Rex v. N——a S——h*
1915	*Rex v. D——p S——h*
1921	*Rex v. William Armitage*
1926	*Rex v. J——M——h*
1929	*Rex v. H——n S——h*

1930   *Rex v. B——e B——r*
1939   *Rex v. O——e G——t*
1939   *Rex v. W——m A——n*
1943   *Rex v. J-y T. P——n*
1943   *Rex v. R——t L——y*
1943   *Rex v. J——n A. P——r*
1943   *Rex v. J—— F——k*
1943   *Rex v. H——y W. M——s*
1943   *Rex v. T——s O. W——e*
1943   *Rex v. E——t J——n*
1943   *Rex v. N——n H——n*
1943   *Rex v. C——t O——y*
1943   *Rex v. L——e D——s*
1943   *Rex v. A——w L——a*
1946   *Rex v. J——h H——r W——r H——n*
1946   *Rex v. J——n D——d H——l*
1947   *Rex v. H——y H——f*
1947   *Rex v. M——n R——n*
1955   *Regina v. J——n E——n S——s*
1963   *Regina v. D——d J——n B——k*
1963   *Regina v. Holte*
1963   *Regina v. Landry*
1963   *Regina v. LaChance*
1963   *Regina v. Bliss*
1963   *Regina v. Desjarlais*
1963   *Regina v. Ferguson*
1963   *Regina v. Herrmann*
1963   *Regina v. Singer*
1966   *Regina v. Del Vecchio*
1966   *Regina v. De Seve*
1967   *Regina v. Boisvert & Regina v. Lupien*

Some of the names above have been obscured because of a requirement of the British Columbia Archives in compliance with the province's Freedom of Information and Protection of Privacy Act.[16] In none of the trial dossiers were there charges against two or more women, even though sex between lesbians was criminalized in Canada from 1954 to 1969.[17] While there was police harassment of identifiable lesbians in this period, no dossiers were located of women prosecuted for specific acts of homosexuality. Given the heavy emphasis on entrapment to obtain sufficient evidence with which to obtain a conviction, combined with the fact that there were few if any female police personnel in the area during this period, it would have been difficult for municipal police to find grounds on which to persuade the Office of the Attorney General to go to trial.

Analysis of Suites of Dossiers of Sodomy Trials

A preliminary examination of a suite of sodomy trial dossiers yields some general patterns. This information warrants cross-referencing with other sources related to those times. The most striking aspect of this suite is that it revealed no trials of *consensual* homosexuality between adults in the nineteenth century. This gap has not been satisfactorily explained, although one of the easiest ways for a man to argue for his innocence would have been to claim that his male sexual partner had assaulted him. The few trials of homosexuality from this period constructed homosexuality as assault. The presence of extensive homosocial institutions on the remote Canadian frontier may have made it difficult to detect and prosecute homosexuality. Adele Perry aptly confirms the dominance of all-male spaces in frontier societies.[18] With much of the male population regularly sharing beds until well into the twentieth century, the lines between consensual, incidental, and situational homosexuality are difficult to define. Only in the decade after the Oscar Wilde trials did a legal basis for prosecuting clearly consensual male homosexuality appear secure in British Columbia.

The paucity of records of trials for consensual homosexuality between adult males in nineteenth-century British Columbia is partly attributable to the difficulty of establishing a criminal justice system on the overwhelmingly male, rough-and-tumble frontier. But by the twentieth century a more comprehensive system of policing and prosecution was in place. While still heavily influenced by Britain, the early-twentieth-century Canadian parliament was increasingly interested in bodies, sexuality, and the regulation of public behavior. The few urban areas had ambitious municipal police forces that worked under the direction of local politicians while enforcing federal laws interpreted by provincial Offices of the Attorney General. By contrast, rural areas were policed by the Royal Canadian Mounted Police (RCMP) and were less under the influence of the provincial governments.

While RCMP officers were expected, under federal law, to police homosexuality, there are no indications of their doing so in rural British Columbia when there was consent between adults. (An exception may have been made for aboriginals, who were effectively wards of the state.) One satisfactory explanation for the gap in prosecutions is that in those rural areas there was not much consensual sex between adult males. This line of thinking suggests that alternative forms of erotic expression, such as sex with animals, were more convenient or desirable. Another explanation is that, given the difficulty and expense of travel in remote areas and the resistance to giving RCMP officers access to private property, it may simply have been difficult to obtain enough evidence to move to trial. A third explanation is that the RCMP had an unwritten, unspoken policy not to seek out and, in effect, to "turn a blind eye" to consensual sex acts between adult males. Two well-attested instances may confirm this explanation. First, the unprecedented crackdown on a network of urban homosexual males in World War II suggests that in Granite Bay, on Quadra Island, there had previously been some awareness and tolerance. Second, there is a credible report of a designated homosexual dormitory in the new industrial town of Kitimat.[19] The Kitimat example points to one of the pressures that might have fostered limited tolerance. British Columbia had an exceptionally fluid, overwhelmingly male workforce in its frontier towns and camps. Workers often left because of the difficult, remote conditions, and consequently there were often labor shortages. Tolerance for sex between men, if it took that to keep them working, would have been one way to maintain a workforce, particularly in areas as difficult as small communities in northwestern British Columbia.

    Not that the state abandoned the regulation of sexuality on the frontier. There appear to have been far more trials for rape of males, per capita, in rural than in urban British Columbia in the period before decriminalization. After World War I there was increasing pressure on the police to protect men, as well as women, from sexual assault, although the line between consensual homosexuality and rape remained poorly defined.[20] For example, the gruesome rape of an eight-year-old boy in a cabin near Prince George in 1933 was tried as buggery and not specifically as (sexual) assault.[21] A decade later in the same town, an adult male was found sucking the penis of a willing adolescent. The adult received a sentence of two years in penitentiary and three lashes.[22] For decades, homosexuality and rape were among the few bases on which wives could charge (and escape from) their abusive husbands. In a 1925 case, a woman from Five Mile Creek, near Princeton, alleged that she had been repeatedly beaten by her husband. She appears to have garnered community and police support less because of the violence supposedly done to her than because of the regular sexual assaults that her husband allegedly made on their eleven-year-old son.[23] By the mid-twentieth century the charge of buggery was rarely used in British Columbia except in cases of sex with animals, as in the 1947 confessions and trial of a man who claimed that he had had regular intercourse with one cow over a three-year period.[24] If more exhaustive searches uncover no records of rural trials of consensual homosexuality, I might conclude that frontier spaces constituted freer zones, where police officers avoided making arrests for consensual erotic acts strictly in private between adult males (who were not aboriginal). However, the full story is unlikely to be that simple.

One additional factor allows trials of consensual homosexuality between adults in British Columbia to be seen as a discourse of regulation of urban space. In remote areas there was not always the level of education and personnel to organize arrests and administer prosecutions unless one of the people engaged in the sex lodged a complaint. With the trials for sex with animals, the evidence came mainly from people who happened to be witnesses to it or, more often, were tired of witnessing it. But there are no indications of rural trials where such complaints were made against consensual homosexuality. As such legal discourses were becoming medicalized, the level of education necessary to conduct such a trial would have taxed most courthouses in British Columbia outside Vancouver and Victoria.

There was, however, a clearer rationale in the larger towns for the state to police sexuality through sodomy trials. Court narratives of consensual homosexuality diverged markedly from those, for example, of men having sex with animals in rural areas. The political anxieties aroused by consensual homosexuality between adult males, as a supposed threat to urban life, are poorly explored in early gay male social histories. In contrast, worries about women's disruptiveness to the urban order and the measures taken to regulate female desire, sexual availability, and access to public space have been explored by Mary P. Ryan, Judith R. Walkowitz, and Elizabeth Wilson.[25] An examination of the dossiers kept by the courthouses of the province leads to a simple and novel conclusion for contemporary gay and lesbian studies. Before the partial decriminalization of 1969, arrests for consensual homosexuality between adult males in British Columbia were part of an almost strictly urban discourse to create, shore up, or reestablish a heteronormative social order.

In British Columbia, most trials of alleged consensual homosexuality between males took place in Vancouver. A few trials were held in the smaller metropolitan area of Victoria, on nearby Vancouver Island. These were the only urban spaces on the West Coast of Canada. The building of these towns and the coincident destruction of Salish-speaking aboriginal cultural centers in the same locales roughly paralleled the emergence and transformation of homosexual identities through the construction of medical and legal frameworks for criminalization.[26]

Nevertheless, these initially homophobic cities contained pockets of opportunity and tolerance. Four factors allowed for the emergence of homosexual subcultures. First, the demographic imbalance between white men and women continued in the early urban centers.[27] It remains to be determined, for particular periods and locales, which was the greater transgression: producing so-called half-breed descendants with aboriginal women or taking part in what in all of the early trial transcripts was referred to as "detestable acts" of homosexuality. There was sometimes a shortage of female prostitutes, which caused their male customers to line up for blocks and wait for hours in the rain.[28] Second, chronic housing shortages led men to sleep two and three to a bed well into the twentieth century. Third, large populations of non-European males asserted their own sexual cultures and proprieties, partly because they were living and working in their native languages, without specific knowledge of or respect for the initially Anglo-Saxon–dominated state's fledgling attempts to regulate consensual homosexuality. Regardless of a particular ethnic group's tolerance of or phobias against certain aspects of homosexuality, it would have been virtually impossible for most people who did not have an extensive command of English to understand exactly which acts and locations were increasingly of interest to the municipal police. From prostitution to opium to immigration, many newcomers to urbanizing British Columbia may have had more pressing worries about the law. Fourth, both Vancouver and Victoria had considerable areas of heavily vegetated open space that made public sex almost impossible to detect.

Keeping in mind the intriguing gap in documentation for consensual adult homosexuality in rural areas, one notices the emergence of some even more striking omissions and possible double standards in the early twentieth century. The selective application of laws against consensual homosexuality relates in part to the racial segregation in these nascent cities. Little more than a year after Vancouver was incorporated in 1886, as a consolidation of logging camps, docks, and declining native villages, a series of anti-Chinese riots broke out. In what was then also referred to as "the Terminal City," mobs of white males, said by local newspapers at the time to be primarily American citizens, tried to create a racially divided city with similarities to those in parts of their own country.[29] Riots in subsequent years led to the further codification of a segregated city, with people of northwestern European heritages predominating on the west side and other groups, particularly Chinese, residing, unless they were servants, on the east side. Consequently, fully recognized British subjects in detente with American citizens of Anglo-Saxon heritage often lived in neighborhoods separated from the multiracial milieus that often comprised majorities of urbanizing neighborhoods. Among the few exceptions to this segregation were furtive social networks and sites of consensual male homosexuality. The emerging town spaces of aboriginals, East Asians (mainly Japanese and southern coastal Chinese), and South Asians (mainly Punjabis) became alternative territories to those where late Victorian notions of race, gender, and sexual propriety were inscribed and more actively enforced.

A number of social groups are not mentioned in the early-twentieth-century trial dossiers for sodomy: aboriginals, people of Chinese and Japanese heritages, and American citizens. These omissions from police and court interest appear to be the result of specific relationships in the regional political economy.[30] All of these groups enjoyed fewer rights than British subjects. Thus these omissions confirm not that the police did not repress homosexuality among these groups but, rather, that defendants had so few civil rights that trials were not necessary. How the police treated homosexual acts between members of these groups, and whether or not such nonsubjects were still the targets of municipally organized entrapments, remains an important question.

The federal government's intrusion into the sexual lives of aboriginals (where provincial and municipal police jurisdictions were somewhat constrained) appears linked to an exceptional lack of treaties, the aboriginals' continued assertion of title and culture in the face of repression, and the vociferous refusal to recognize native governments. Until after the partial decriminalization of 1969, native people were effectively noncitizens who were denied many legal rights. In rural areas, the Indian Agent's tremendous power extended to the suppression of local sexual cultures.[31] The biography of Chief Charles James Nowell of northern Vancouver Island provides clues about conditions on the Pacific Coast. Born in 1870, Nowell recounted the transformation of his formerly cross-dressing lover not long after the anti-potlatch laws of 1885 led to the most systematic legal assault on aboriginal culture: "I guess the Indian agent wrote to Victoria, telling the officials what she was doing. She was taken to Victoria, and the policemen took her clothes off and found she was a man, so they gave him a suit of clothes and cut off his hair and sent him back home. When I saw him again, he was a man. He was no more my sweetheart."[32] As aboriginals migrated to towns, the new urban police forces began to incarcerate them without court proceedings. Laws governing unruly behavior and drinking were easier to enforce than those governing indecency.

Until the mid-twentieth century Chinese and Japanese Canadians were also effectively noncitizens. Throughout the criminalization period and after, East Asians typically accounted for 10–20 percent of the populations of the larger towns. Whether homosexuality in these groups was tolerated, policed internally, or targeted differently is unclear. One of the few references to an East Asian in these trial dossiers was in a 1910 hearing concerning the charge that "Hing (or 'Wing') (Chinaman) at Vancouver on 3rd June 1910 a male person in public did unlawfully attempt to commit an act of gross indecency with Roy Darrah, another male person."[33] In other words, one of the only times that a Chinese Canadian male was prosecuted under the sodomy laws was when he had allegedly made a sexual overture to a male outside his ethnic community. The only other significant reference to a Chinese man and homosexuality dates from 1943, in Victoria. In a public toilet adjacent to the provincial legislature, a "chinaman" warned a group of men engaged in sex of an impending police raid.[34]

In the dossiers of trials against consensual homosexuality, it is curious that none of the defendants seem to have been U.S. citizens. Vancouver and Victoria are within twenty miles of the border. Many Americans worked and settled in Canada while maintaining their original citizenships. When Prohibition was in force in the United States, liquor flowed more publicly in Vancouver, which became a destination for many single men out for a "dirty weekend."[35] Consequently, the lack of court records of male U.S. citizens arrested for homosexuality is curious. In contrast, the police showed interest in, and meticulous records were kept of the citizenship of, the female prostitutes of African heritages who worked around Vancouver's Chinatown. These women were apprehended in the same areas in central Vancouver, and during the same period, that much of the sodomy described in the dossiers supposedly took place.[36] American women who engaged in migrant sex work were quickly sent south, but American men appear to have had more opportunities for social intercourse.

Another intriguing discrepancy is that there are no records of arrests in Vancouver's central urban green space, Stanley Park, even though a subculture of public sex was well established within a few years of the increase in arrests for sodomy during World War I. This is doubly curious given that in Toronto, a much larger Canadian city at the time, there was a program of police response to the (homosexual male) "park problem."[37] In Vancouver the lack of arrests for outdoor sex, before decriminalization, was explained with a joke: the city police were required to keep their boots clean at all times and therefore did not want to venture into the labyrinth of muddy trails. Ironically, during the decades after the partial decriminalization of 1969 (which did not extend to private sex in public parks), there were vigorous police attempts in the same park to criminalize further the behavior of that same subculture of male homosexuals.

So which social groups and nascent subcultures *were* targeted for surveillance and arrest? Well over half of the sodomy trials in the early twentieth century involved at least one partner of non-British heritage. Anxiety about long-term demographic trends that suggested that the Anglo-Saxon power structure was not numerically secure led to the policing both of consensual male homosexuality in general and of interracial homosexuality, a phenomenon that raised the specter of sexually exploited white men. Police entrapment in Vancouver had been fully instituted by 1910.[38] A program of police interest so intense as to verge on sexual engagement initially targeted one group in particular: South Asian men, nearly all of them members of the Sikh religion recently arrived from the Punjab in northwestern India. More than half of the records of trials for consensual homosexuality before the end of World War I targeted Sikhs, sometimes identified in court documents as "Hindoos." This heavy policing of homosexuality occurred at a time when exceptional measures were taken to discourage Indian immigration into British Columbia.[39] In 1909 the South Asian population in British Columbia numbered only in the thousands. Yet Sikh males were defendants in scores of "oriental cases" and in British Columbia's first legal attacks on group and public homosexuality.[40]

The sexual and racial hierarchy evident in the British Columbia dossiers suggests that the imperial project used the criminalization of homosexuality to suppress dissident groups. Conquered only in 1849, Punjabis were asserting their civil and political rights a half century later as British subjects far from India. There was a level of tenacity in Sikh activism in Canada that was consistent with strategies around their minority status in India. Such a disciplined culture of resistance had not been seen before in British Columbia. This heightened level of activism by one colonized group moving into another part of the British Empire generated new anxieties for imperial leaders that, not surprisingly, had dimensions in sexual politics.[41] The documents concerning the anti-Sikh buggery trials reveal two preoccupations. On the one hand, the police appeared to be fascinated with the masculinity of the Sikh and the South Asian male. On the other, they took umbrage at the self-confidence of "oriental" groups, especially at their assertion of sexualities divergent from the Victorian nexus. Neocolonial irritation was exacerbated by the perception of local authorities that groups such as Sikhs were not entitled to settle in British Columbia. The trials of Sikhs appear to have provided the courts with expanded vocabularies with which to talk about the mechanics of homosexuality. There was no shortage of ethnic stereotypes, reinforced through, for example, detailed descriptions of how a South Asian defendant mounted a man of supposedly Greek nationality (while being carefully observed).[42] Two linked trials in 1915, *Rex v. N——a S——h* and *Rex v. D——p S——h*, illustrate this confluence of racism, homophobia, and cultural chauvinism.[43] Two Sikh men, apparently domestic partners, had proposed a foursome to a driver in the Panama Bar in central Vancouver. The driver had informed the police, and an undercover detective had subsequently been introduced as the fourth partner. During the initial pickup conversation one of the Sikhs had mentioned that he had taken part in resisting Canadian Navy operations to keep the *Komagata Maru*, a ship transporting Punjabi immigrants who were British subjects, from docking in Vancouver. In the weeks-long standoff there had been considerable unrest in and resistance from the Indo-Canadian community.[44] So an intricate sodomy entrapment against the same group at the same time was hardly coincidental. After the foursome had begun to have sex by the railroad tracks at the south end of Chinatown, the two men who would soon be arrested were beaten by the undercover detective and by additional police officers whose presence had been arranged previously in this remarkably well-organized operation.

These trials of sexual deviance from 1915 have broader historical significance because witnesses linked both the police and the defendants to the notorious unsolved murder of Bela Singh, who the Sikh community alleged had been the victim of police violence and political murder. In the sodomy trial, the prosecution painted the Sikh defendants as sordid and sexually aggressive. There was particular interest in the defendants' alleged proposition to pay for group sex every Sunday in their shack on the outskirts of the city. Both sides confirmed that the undercover detective had accepted half of 75 cents to be penetrated anally. The first defendant claimed that he had been intimidated by the detective while he, the defendant, was a witness in the Bela Singh case. A great deal was made of the 75 cents paid to the driver and the detective. They argued that because they had given the money back by the time of the court appearance and were producing it in evidence at this time, they had not been unlawfully engaged in homosexuality. Even with the lack of constitutional rights for British subjects in 1915, the particularly "hands-on" approach of this entrapment (with a detective describing in court his having allowed an erect penis to touch his back and buttocks) must have raised legal questions. If not for the police violence that had ensued, the allegations made at trial would have been farcical. There was the testimony of the driver turned informant:

> A. So I got [Detective] Rizzi and introduced him at the tram station as my friend. So at the tram station he [the first defendant] said he would give us seventy-five cents for the two of us and two dollars every Sunday and pay car-fare both ways to Central Park. That is for both of us. . . . We took our pants down, and he had his penis out and everything, and came up on us, and then Mr. S———r [a second police officer whom Detective Rizzi had

arranged to witness the homosexuality secretly] came in a few minutes after that. . . .

Q. Where did that happen?

A. That happened just a little the other side of the Georgia-Harris street viaduct on the [Canadian Pacific Railway] tracks. . . . In the afternoon he [the first defendant] asked me if I would like to fuck. That is just what he said to me, and I said "sure any old thing." . . .

Q. Ever act as stool pigeon for the police?

A. No, sir, never did.

Q. Do you at the present moment?

A. No.

Q. How did you get in touch with Rizzi?

A. I didn't think it was a very just thing that he [the first defendant] was trying to do. I thought the matter should be reported.[45]

Cross-examining one of the undercover detectives, the defense lawyer challenged the same witness:

Q. How did this man [the first defendant] fracture his jaw?

A. I guess he did that when he jumped in the pool of water.

Q. I am advised that you and [Detective] Rizzi held this man up on the street and asked him for money, and that Rizzi hit him over the head with the revolver and he fell down and fractured his jaw?

A. I deny that.

Q. I also tell you very fairly that the tall man [the first defendant] knows Rizzi as well as he knows to see the Magistrate. He has talked to him frequently. Now do I understand you to say that this man came there and didn't know Rizzi as a detective?

A. Yes, sir. Well he didn't say anything about it, but it seems very strange to me that he would try to take down Rizzi's pants and try to go at him.

Q. And you and Rizzi were perfectly agreeable that they should begin?

A. Yes.

Q. For seventy-five cents?

A. Yes.

A broader pattern of intrigue and violence emerged when Detective Rizzi was cross-examined.

Q. Do you mean to say you didn't caution this man [one of the defendants] several times on the occasion of the Bela Singh murder charge?

A. No.

Q. You were a witness on that case?

A. I was.

Q. And he was too?

A. I don't know.

Q. He says he knows you very well indeed, that he saw you frequently in the Bela Singh case, and you cautioned him.

A. He didn't know me that night.

The first defendant took the stand.

N——A S——H Called and Sworn. . . .

Q. What nationality are you?

A. Sikh from India.

Q. Do you know Detective Rizzi?

A. Yes, I know him very well.

Q. When did you first meet Detective Rizzi?

A. I remember him well in the Bela Singh case.

Q. Were you a witness in the Bela Singh case?

A. Yes.

Q. Was Detective Rizzi a witness in that case?

A. Yes.

Q. Did you have occasion to speak to Detective Rizzi during the progress of that case?

A. Very often.

Q. Can you tell us anyone [*sic*] of the conversations that took place?

A. Yes, I can.

Q. Just tell it?

A. I was sitting in the witness room one day and he showed me his pistol and said "If you tell stories about Bela Singh you will get in severe trouble, get seven years in jail."

Q. Now on the night of the 2nd of February did you see Detective Rizzi?

A. Yes.

Virtually every trial dossier has some enigmatic material. For example, a cryptic note recently found in the same file simply states: "whole thing's a frame up! *why* attempted to get easy money! . . . all guilty—and [Detective] Rizzi."

How can one analyze such a rich transcript as the one above and make sense of important historical details? The answer goes back to the scope and goals of particular analyses and the intended uses of their conclusions. For example, the cases outlined above comprise important sources for any history of sexual minorities in British Columbia. But those dossiers are also seminal texts for any account of Sikhs, and more generally South Asians, in Canada and North America. And some of the details might be used to support arguments on how a wider diversity of homosexual subcultures than had been previously recognized was coalescing in the early twentieth century.

Relatively new cities such as Vancouver have changed so much since their first trials for consensual homosexuality that what is often most intriguing and relevant to historical analyses are stable aspects of locations, architecture, and civic space. Greater Vancouver grew by a factor of nearly ten in the second half of the twentieth century, and the city's metropolitan population is now nearly fifteen times greater than it was when the early-twentieth-century arrests took place. Population growth in metropolitan Victoria, though half that of Vancouver, was certainly marked, given the relative stability of the public space used for homosexual cruising. Mapping the locations of the alleged crimes illuminates some striking spatial relationships. Most of the neighborhood spaces where the arrests took place were and continue to be dominated by public transportation, pedestrian and bicycle traffic, and open areas, not by the automobile. The pattern of the male homosexual presence in these urban spaces in British Columbia after World War II contrasts markedly with that of many small North American cities, where the automobile played a direct and positive role in the formation of social space used by sexual minorities.[46]

Vancouver has been particularly vulnerable to flows of capital and economic fluctuations. In any setting, periods of rapid economic change provide opportunities for the erasure of markers of past social relations. With such a market-based city as Vancouver, the regulation of sexuality (like many contentious aspects of urban life) sometimes functions as a way for the state to rationalize itself. Trials for consensual male homosexuality in the first half of the twentieth century give a partial indication of the state's willingness to go into bedrooms and back alleys to justify the expansion of its regulatory powers—almost as a symbolic counterbalance to the emerging freedoms associated with urban capitalist culture.

As a recent analytic framework in lesbian and gay studies, queer theory has supported the identification of social and political economic narratives in fiction.[47] Queer theory, as the dominant investigative framework in lesbian and gay studies over the last decade, has been more effective at illuminating how experiences and social relations inform cultural production than at supporting nuanced understandings of the generation of fictions, as in courtroom assertions, in political economies. But adaptations of queer theory's explorations of the underlying narratives and contexts of literature hold promise for examinations of historical legal documents of conflicts around sexuality. The current gap in analytic tools for historical trial dossiers exists only in part because such documents are not part of conventional modes of cultural production. To understand more clearly the contests among groups identified with homosexuality, homophobia, the state, and resistance, I propose a framework for charting historical landscapes. As arenas for conflicts concerning gender, race, cultures, languages, and sexuality, particular neighborhoods, blocks, streets, buildings, squares, and parks can be reconsidered and reinscribed.[48] Revisiting historical urban spaces as sites of conflict between sexual "stakeholders" ("returning to the scene of the crime") requires examinations of a century-old nexus between the assertion of homosexual desire, homophobia, state intervention, economic decline, and the abjection of sexual minorities. Many of Vancouver's homoerotic sites from the first half of the twentieth century have not been easily integrated into gentrification processes (despite concerted efforts).

In the urban land economy before decriminalization, orderly and middle-class neighborhoods were largely defined as places where so-called indecency was patrolled and largely suppressed. Conflicting notions of sexual propriety played out in urban development, and sodomy trials illustrated contests between relatively insecure social groups. The locations in the trials were marked as undesirable in the urban land economy—especially where interracial contact was confirmed. Better analytic frameworks for mapping urban history could provide a basis for a new activism that expands on earlier liberal and radical notions of democratic public space.[49] Some of the contemporary understandings that can emerge from an exploration of historical documents such as trial dossiers center on the shifting boundaries of public space, privacy, and public displays of desire, along with social and legal definitions of indecency and criminality. Canada has had a long public discourse on the appropriate powers of the police in regulating sex and, increasingly, on the state's obligation to protect sexual minorities from discrimination while providing comparable services. Another activist discourse deals with the identification and management of strategic sites for certain networks of sexual minorities and with the obligations and powers of state and community groups to intervene in and sometimes avoid such places important to certain groups.[50]

Returning to the Scene of the Crime: Theorizing Early Modern Homosexual Resistance in Urban Space

At this point in the development of lesbian and gay studies, one of the more exciting opportunities afforded by examining trial dossiers is the interpretation of early forms of resistance to homophobia. Responses from defendants sometimes embodied notions of autonomous and consensual sexual desire that anticipated more recent notions of corporeal rights. Historical links between these early forms of resistance and contemporary notions of activism remain poorly explored, although frequently the dossiers document urban relationships that prefigured modern resistance to attacks on sexual minorities. While such trials as *Regina v. Butts* (1860), *Rex v. N——a S——h* (1915), and *Rex v. D——p S——h* (1915) evidenced prosecution of outspoken individuals critical of government policy, it took post–World War I concentrations of surplus labor to spark the beginnings of a *culture* of homosexual resistance.

The 1921 trial of William Armitage for gross indecency is indicative of the increasing awkwardness of twentieth-century efforts to control homosexuality. Armitage's defiance foreshadowed the activism that emerged two generations later. He and a man named Joe Wigman had been found having sex in the Great War

Veterans Hostel in the mountain town of Cranbrook. Alerted by noises, a curious neighbor opened the door to their room to find Armitage's face less than two inches from Wigman's erection during or soon after an ejaculation. Enraged at being ejected from the hostel on a cold night, Armitage tried to start a riot. Later that night Armitage resisted arrest while asserting what he believed were his civil rights.[51]

By the 1920s Vancouver's police increasingly invaded men's privacy. In a 1930 case, police had responded to a complaint about a conversation allegedly heard through a wall at 48 1/2 Cordova Street East: "Gee I have swallowed some of this stuff. You are a dirty bugger, it come twice tonight." The police had reported overhearing a subsequent conversation "about different men having big cocks and making great fucking."[52] In a 1939 case concerning "a party amongst men" in Victoria, the defendants freely admitted their group sexual pleasures.[53] However, one of them had gone to the police because, he claimed, he had acquired a sexually transmitted disease from the event. Another defendant went so far as to argue that the anal sex in which some had engaged was private and was or should be legal. However, the intellectual basis of such arguments remained.

One of the most extraordinary examples of the state's interest in prosecuting homosexuality on the West Coast took place at Granite Bay on Quadra Island and in Vancouver in the late 1930s. At a time of mobilization against a possible invasion by Japan, this case was the first and perhaps the only example of a male *couple* charged with gross indecency for simply living together "on affectionate terms." They were incriminated by letters written by others and by their own confessions of a network of their relationships, not by being found having sex. The love story began in Granite Bay. In 1937 the older of the two was still recovering from being gassed in France in World War I. He visited the village to teach spiritualism. His new friend was twenty years old, roughly seventeen years his junior, and came from a well-known Finnish family (which was part of a local political culture often virulently at odds with the state). It would have been impossible to hide the nature of their relationship in such a small village. Five years later the couple was living together in Vancouver, where the younger man drove a taxi before being conscripted. The couple was arrested after an exhaustive investigation conducted across western Canada by military police in search of a homosexual network. Arrested in his barracks, the younger man made a full and unapologetic confession. The older man was sentenced to five years of hard labor—a remarkably harsh sentence during wartime for a disabled veteran. Two other men who admitted to having sex with the first two were also sentenced to one year of hard labor. The Granite Bay case appears to have been the first trial in British

Columbia in which there was broad community support for adult males accused of consensual sodomy. At the height of wartime, residents of Granite Bay organized, wrote letters, and made presentations in hopes that the men would not go to prison or would be given less severe sentences.[54]

There are periodic though poorly confirmed reports of purge trials of homosexual males and females on the West Coast from World War II until the 1960s. The War Measures Act in Canada, which suspended all civil rights, was in force throughout the 1940s and may have removed the need for formal trials of what by then was more often referred to as "gross indecency." No transcripts of hearings and trials concerning consensual homosexuality have yet to be located, most likely because the right of the accused to due process had been removed.

In the 1950s prewar legal frameworks were reconstructed, and the public men's room near the provincial legislature in Victoria once again came under scrutiny. In 1955 there was another series of raids. Although the police claimed to have observed five men having sex in that men's room, only one man, a teacher, appears to have been made an example of for resisting authority. When other men in the washroom were fleeing from the undercover police, the teacher refused to leave his stall. His assertion that it was a private space conflicted with the police accusation that he had been "blowing" a man who was not apprehended, and his assertion was not otherwise confirmed. As a result of the teacher's resistance, the trial transcript contains a legal discussion that turns on the location and dimensions of what today in North America is called a "glory hole" (a gap between toilet stalls through which men can make genital contact). The prosecution argued for conviction on circumstantial evidence—namely, sitting in a stall with such a gap—thereby further conflating homosexual practice with a particular space.[55]

While the homophobic repression of the 1950s and early 1960s was fierce, the courts were no longer viewed as an effective or secure means of attacking sexual minorities for consensual acts. The risk had increased that defendants would find ways to turn trials into circuses for the purpose of embarrassing and making insinuations against the police, the judiciary, and the state. Anecdotal evidence suggests that more instances of broader attacks were occurring, such as the police requesting employers to fire supposedly homosexual employees without recourse. Because discussions of sodomy entrapments often made the police look unprofessional, there was pressure to portray people who supposedly engaged in homosexuality as monsters. The sensational media coverage of one trial and the execution subsequent to it allowed for the continued justification of the criminalization of people engaged in consensual homosexuality. In 1958 Leo Anthony Mantha, a former naval enlistee who had been discharged for homosexuality, murdered his former lover, who was serving at the naval base in Esquimalt, near Victoria.[56] At the trial, numerous homosexual males identified in the murdered man's papers were forced to testify. These men were effectively "outed" and publicly humiliated, with some losing their jobs and committing suicide.[57]

In that brief period of Conservative Party rule, Quebec-born Mantha was the perfect symbol of the homosexual outlaw who deserved no mercy. In the last years of federal cabinets dominated by male, English-speaking Protestant politicians, he was a convenient specter. While this group commuted other capital punishment sentences, they refused to commute Mantha's. It remains unclear why Mantha was chosen to undergo one of the state's final executions. He spoke both English and French and was of a mixed racial background. Depicting him as the predatory and hypermasculine "Homo Sexual," the newspapers whipped up public hysteria.[58] Mantha's mother appealed through the Catholic Church of Quebec when a stay of execution seemed probable, but Prime Minister John Diefenbaker and his cabinet refused to act.

Like much of Canada, British Columbia missed the brunt of the Cold War hysteria against homosexuals until the 1960s. At times the state's interest in men engaged in homosexuality as possible threats to national security may have been more severe on the West Coast than in the rest of Canada. The other supposed security threat was communism, and because so many communists were open and active in British Columbia, it was effectively impossible to charge and incarcerate them. But the extent of antihomosexual operations carried out on the West Coast in the name of national security remains shrouded in mystery. There has been speculation that the extraordinary interest in homosexuality in Victoria after Mantha's hanging reflected the prompting of the U.S. military, which was increasingly influencing its NATO ally. Surveillance appears to have been far more common than arrests. The number of RCMP reports on homosexuals in Canada went from one thousand in 1960–61 to nine thousand in 1967–68.[59] A man's association with a public cruising area or a gay bar was the most predictable basis for RCMP interest. So a full decade before the decriminalization of consensual homosexuality, limited essentially to acts between adults in their bedrooms, the use of sodomy trials was already on the decline in British Columbia because of two contradictory developments. First, surveillance, harassment, and notifying employers had become easier and more effective means of social regulation than going to trial, where police embarrassment was a risk. Second, popular resistance to laws against consensual homosexuality in private increasingly politicized court defenses.

Some of the last trials for consensual homosexuality in British Columbia involved the public toilets at English Bay, in Vancouver.[60] In 1963 eight men were arrested there for gross indecency. This washroom and parts of the nearby park had taken on strategic importance for the national homosexual culture. Some of the defense's arguments, which asserted individual rights, further fueled the decriminalization movement. One of Canada's first homophile organizations had just been formed, and Protestant church groups were increasingly vocal advocates of decriminalization. Such cases were used by homophile and civil liberties advocates to highlight inconsistencies in general policing. Paradoxically, such cases were beginning to be used to reassert the state's rights over sex specifically in public space. The prosecution's weakened logic, along with legal questions about overzealous entrapments, motivated Prime Minister Pierre Trudeau's 1967 advocacy for decriminalization. Today Canadians view Trudeau's assertion that the state has no place in their bedrooms as an important prefiguring of the 1985 Charter of Rights and Freedoms. At the time, however, it was more a compromise that allowed only for the partial dismantling of the antihomosexual bureaucracy.

Paradoxically, more than half of the cases identified in this essay could be prosecuted today, though not on the basis of consensual homosexuality between adults. The same lineage of statutes could be used to criminalize individuals for sex outside the bedroom, especially in effectively private spaces that are still considered public, in certain kinds of group sex (including group sex at private parties), and in anal sex in which at least one partner is an adult and the other is under twenty-one years of age.

The Use of Dossiers of Sodomy Trials for Urban Environmental Histories

The physical locations often described in trial transcripts can be relevant to contemporary social policy and urban planning issues. The information from dossiers is relevant to preservation priorities in Vancouver's Gastown and Chinatown. These neighborhoods are a mix of slums and redevelopment, with shops, sites for social service delivery for the poor, gentrified apartments, lofts, and spaces for cultural production and related education. For example, the alley where Sikh men met other males for standup sex in the early twentieth century is often used today for drug injection and dealing while being adjacent to a major community center. While exploring the implications of these dossiers for policy and decision making, there are unresolved issues of public memory, preservation, and urban design in an inner-city neighborhood ravaged by drug and gang violence, on the one hand, and gentrification, on the other.

In 2001 Alan Herbert, a former city counselor and a self-described gay man who had recently lost his bid for reelection, was asked by the centrist mayor of Vancouver to head a neighborhood renewal project for the city's Chinatown. The Silk Road Task Force was to revive one of Vancouver's seminal neighborhoods, declining because of flight to the suburbs, gang activity, and widespread drug addiction, by making it a cultural destination through historical acknowledgment and public art. A good deal of public money went into highlighting historical sites of importance to the Chinese community. The problem with Herbert's efforts, as maps constructed from the trial dossiers in this suite attest, is that for many years the neighborhood had also been a strategic location, within the region and metropolitan area, for sex workers and sexual minorities. Only recently has the area been dominated by drug use, services for poor people, and often less resilient forms of gentrification.

Little of recent work on lesbian and gay history has explored direct implications for contemporary social policy and urban design. There have been a few efforts to put up commemorative plaques, but rarely has this work acknowledged sites of resistance to criminalization for consensual homosexuality. Yet even for relatively young cities such as Vancouver, these small and conflicted neighborhoods with sometimes localized modes of forming social space by sexual minorities are increasingly of interest. The link between the criminalized past and the volatile present can sometimes be best understood through reflection on the physical and social changes in neighborhoods. The mapping of the scenes of so-called crimes can extend beyond gay tourism and historical plaques to more forward-looking cultural expression, redesigns, and even monuments.[61] And while plaques are useful historical reminders that can sometimes be missed by vandals, the conception, erection, and protection of monuments commemorating sexual minorities and resistance to repression remain highly problematic even in relatively tolerant urban centers such as Vancouver. With these persistent difficulties in mind, a number of practices can be applied to the dissemination of historical data of significance to present and future.

The types of information mentioned above can be compiled on historical maps at neighborhood scales, such as 1:5000. These maps can have additional layers in which various histories and implications for social policy and urban design can be explored. In addition to the marking and decoration of key sites, there are ongoing issues related to safety, security, and service delivery in the vicinity of these historic crime scenes. And there are opportunities for more whimsical or sarcastic treatments of history that could illustrate unresolved tensions. The centennial of Vancouver's first police entrapment of adult males engaged in consensual sexual activities is approaching, and at a time of critical public perspectives on police services. Thus it is unlikely that the entrapment centennial will go unobserved. Similarly, markers of the sites of the first arrests for car sex (and of resistance to police intrusion into private automobiles) in Victoria have some relevance to current discussions concerning a parking lot adjacent to those sites that continues to see regular cruising.[62]

Conclusions: Spatial Narratives of Resistance

The dossiers of sex trials are often as useful for providing details in constructing environmental histories as they are for confirming past erotic cultures. Furthermore, stakeholders such as urban preservationists, policy makers, and designers have an interest in details less important to and sometimes overlooked by social historians. The conflicting cognitive maps evident in trial transcripts can be compiled and cross-referenced to other sources so that new histories and geographies can be constructed for a broader set of uses, social projects, scholarly movements, and audiences.

Despite their value, dossiers of sodomy trials remain ambiguous sources for studies of gay and lesbian life, communities, and historical geographies. But they are important enough to warrant reexamination, reinterpretation, and debate from numerous vantage points. In my reading of trial dossiers from British Columbia, I have outlined the need for greater awareness of the differences among three scholarly projects and types of investigation of such material: general narratives of the social lives of certain sexual minorities; community histories of particular towns, cities, and regions; and applied urban research at various scales, focused on social networks, sites, and neighborhoods linked to questions of public policy, planning, and design. These three modes of investigation require more differentiated and critical practices of reading and analysis.

From today's popular Canadian vantage point, the locations of the crimes are more the courtrooms and the government and police offices (from Westminster to Ottawa to Victoria to Vancouver) than the sites where men may have engaged or did engage in sex. Post-1985 interpretations, based on more robust notions of human rights and social equity, have generated more profound reinterpretations of "the scene of the crime" than the early histories of sexual minorities that arose from the struggle for decriminalization and the initial push for gay rights. In the last thirty years, perhaps the most marked change in the use of trial transcripts on consensual homosexuality has been the proliferation of more specific and less unified agendas. More concerted interventions by sexual minorities in urban spaces make up one of scores of contemporary interests, fields, and social projects. Different readings of the transcripts of the same file can stimulate new dialogues and generate expanded priorities for activism and scholarship about both sex and the city.

Has social conflict related to homosexuality, homophobia, and resistance built and restructured the Terminal City? Yes, but without more careful historical analysis and cognitive mapping, the implications of particular arrests and trials will remain inconclusive.[63] Critical scholarship on past sites of homosexual practice and resistance could alter the direction of future activism and public policy. There is plenty of room for divergent scholarly interpretations.

Much contemporary historical discourse on homoerotic or avowedly queer space has focused on shifting notions of public and private. In fact, much of the theory of sexual minorities in urban space is rooted in comparatively recent theory about the loss of the public sphere. In contrast, the dossiers examined here confirm more dynamic and nuanced transactions in the regulation of bodies, sites, and neighborhoods; they also confirm individual and collective resistance to repression that cannot be reduced to the dialectic of public and private.[64] Conflicts about public sex were muted in the criminalization period, when the courts' rights over the homoerotic extended well into the private. In British Columbia, police and court preoccupation with homosexuality in public space originated more in the mid-twentieth century and in hostile responses by homophobic bureaucracies and police officers to decriminalization.

The sequence of these dossiers suggests pulses of geopolitical and cultural anxiety of which "Homo Sexuals" were convenient targets. In the demographic crisis of some of British Columbia's Anglo-Saxons around World War I, the new public and specifically sexual presence of Sikh men provided the Vancouver police force with an opportunity to repress sexual minorities (and immigrants from South Asia) more broadly. The state's early preoccupation with public assertions of homosexual desire from members of non-European cultures was symptomatic of the anxieties of the ruling circle about the difficulty of populating British Columbia. Subsequently, there were anxieties about men who asserted physical liberties with their bodies while being expected to sacrifice themselves in World War II and in the early Cold War. A dichotomy arose between loyalty to the state and the autonomous expression of sexual, potentially homoerotic, desire. Arresting men for consensual homosexuality was the least contentious way for the state to demonstrate its continued control over male bodies. The policing of men in public washrooms, beginning more systematically in World War II, intensified as public opposition to laws against homosexuality began to emerge. The crisis apparent in the latter trials for consensual homosexuality in British Columbia suggests that popular resistance to such policing and court intervention was not confined to homophile activism. The state's response was to construct a distinction between the less threatening ("good") homosexual, who had sex in private, and the "bad" homosexual, who engaged in public sex and still warranted prosecution. The strength of this logic of "good homosexual/bad homosexual," in part, led the Canadian state in 1967 to abandon its earlier claim on regulating all consensual homosexuality. By getting out of the bedroom, the state salvaged a role for the regulation of consensual sexuality and strengthened its dominion over public places and culture (which still extends to the censoring of books).

Sexual minorities have made gains in recent decades in no small part because of the increased self-knowledge and solidarity engendered by their pioneering histories. The new freedoms after decriminalization have created a new reason to examine homoerotic experiences and explore their implications for neighborhoods and public policy. In British Columbia, the new opportunities for queer scholarship have been so profound that the framework for the production of knowledge has been transformed and expanded. These developments, in turn, have laid the basis for revisiting sources.[65] In today's more critical modes of scholarship, it will be necessary to return periodically to the scene of the crime with new and reformulated questions, research programs, and activist agendas.

Epilogue

Just as this essay was going to press, the International Olympics Committee (IOC) accepted Vancouver's bid to host the 2010 Winter Olympics. What the IOC did not know was that the event would be held during the centennial year of the city's first program of police entrapment for sex between consenting males. The IOC also did not know that many of the sites slated for events and accommodations have historical significance both for early homophobic repression and for homosexual resistance in Canada. Hosting the Olympics concurrently with the entrapment centennial generates new possibilities for and questions about the use of trial transcripts. Historical re-creations and pageants of a hundred years of police entrapment, harassment, and arrests (not to mention the alleged sex acts) might provide some local "colour" between the coverage of skiing and speed skating. If entrapment by municipal police in the metropolitan area continues, as it does today, documentation of such historical and contemporary operations could be blended with the Olympic coverage to suggest that such repressive tactics have become an outdated sport that should be discontinued. And unless the value of such historical events and sites is articulated, many significant places will be destroyed during the redevelopment of central Vancouver in preparation for the Olympics. A few plaques might placate some elements of the gay community while providing work for a few historians, planners, and designers. But closer readings of local history, along with debates, could raise public awareness more substantially about the damage caused by these attacks both to the men engaged in the intimacies and to the course of urban development.

Notes

This essay began as a collaboration with London-based Gavin Brown, who withdrew from the project to focus on his doctoral studies in geography. My greatest thanks go to Carolyn Dinshaw and other colleagues at *GLQ* for their support of this topic and their help in addressing the editorial difficulties raised by the material, and to John Grube and an anonymous reviewer for their guidance in the final revisions. Anne Davis, Ron Dutton, Don Hann, and Indiana Matters provided comments, advice, and editorial support. Funding for this research, on sexual minorities, urban space, and related design issues, was generously provided by the Chicago-based Graham Foundation for Advanced Studies in the Fine Arts and by the Canada Council for the Arts, and material support was provided by a number of friends, including Sarah England, Wahid Gul, Janusz Kowalski, Katherine Laurente, Sally Ogis, Todd Pittson, Cristina Soto, and Lawrence Waterfall. The staff of the British Columbia Archives (BCA) provided access to the restricted files through agreements 97-0043 and 99-0044.

1. Brett Beemyn, ed., *Creating a Place for Ourselves: Lesbian, Gay, and Bisexual Community Histories* (New York: Routledge, 1997), 2.

2. See Jonathan Ned Katz, *Gay American History: Lesbians and Gay Men in the U.S.A.: A Documentary Anthology* (New York: Crowell, 1976); Katz, *Love Stories: Sex between Men before Homosexuality* (Chicago: University of Chicago Press, 2001); and George Chauncey, *Gay New York: Gender, Urban Culture, and the Making of the Gay Male World, 1890–1940* (New York: Basic, 1994).

3. See Adele Perry, *On the Edge of Empire: Gender, Race, and the Making of British Columbia, 1849–1871* (Toronto: University of Toronto Press, 2001), 20–47, 79–96.

4. See Steven Maynard, "Queer Musings on Masculinity and History," *Labour/Le Travail* 42 (1998): 183–97.

5. See Terry L. Chapman, "'An Oscar Wilde Type': The Abominable Crime of Buggery in Western Canada, 1890–1920," *Criminal Justice History* 4 (1983): 97–118.

6. Clive Moore, *Sunshine and Rainbows: The Development of Gay and Lesbian Culture in Queensland* (St. Lucia: University of Queensland Press, 2001), x.

7. See Rudi C. Bleys, *The Geography of Perversion: Male-to-Male Sexual Behaviour outside the West and the Ethnographic Imagination, 1750–1918* (New York: New York University Press, 1995).

8. See Siobhan B. Somerville, *Queering the Color Line: Race and the Invention of Homo-sexuality in American Culture* (Durham: Duke University Press, 2000).

9. See Daniel W. Clayton, *Islands of Truth: The Imperial Fashioning of Vancouver Island* (Vancouver: University of British Columbia Press, 2000), 233–42.

10. See Martin Robin, *The Rush for Spoils: The Company Province, 1871–1933* (Toronto: McClelland and Stewart, 1972).

11. Agnes C. Laut, *Am I My Brother's Keeper? A Study of British Columbia's Labour and Oriental Problems* (Vancouver: Subway, 2003), 27–28.

12. In these transcripts there appear to be gaps between what was said and what was recorded. Some passages seem to lack words that probably were uttered, or the line breaks between questions and answers seem inconsistent. Sometimes it was evidently difficult for a transcriber to hear all that was said. At other times the grammar uttered and recorded was not the King's English, even when the speaker was a judge or a lawyer. Well into the twentieth century there were low levels of formal education on this frontier.

13. Indiana Matters, "'Unfit for Publication': Notes towards a Lavender History of British Columbia" (paper presented at the Sex and the State Conference, Toronto, July 3–6, 1985), on file at the Canadian Lesbian and Gay Archives, Toronto, accession no. 91-258, box 2.

14. BCA BC Attorney General file GR419, vol. 197, file 31, 878–84.

15. The 1963–67 trials, described by the early gay legal historian Douglas E. Sanders, have yet to be located in the collections from the British Columbia Attorney General. See Sanders, "Sentencing of Homosexual Offenders," *Criminal Law Quarterly* 10 (1967): 25–29.

16. The obscuring of certain names was a condition of the research permit that allowed me access to these files. The trials listed with complete names either have been described in other publications, and the information used here is attributed to them, or are no longer subject to confidentiality restrictions.

17. See *Forbidden Love: The Unashamed Stories of Lesbian Lives*, dir. Lynne Fernie and Aerlyn Weissman, National Film Board of Canada, 1992.

18. Perry, *On the Edge of Empire*, 20–96.

19. John Kendrick, *People of the Snow: The Story of Kitimat* (Toronto: NC Press, 1987), 96.

20. For one example of the growing prominence of the narrative of male rape, still under the guise of "gross indecency," in examinations of male homosexuality, see *Rex v. Milton*, BCA GR 2235, Pouce Coupe County Court Criminal Case Files 1931–1949, box 2, file 39/45.

21. *Rex v. Larsen*, BCA GR 2788, Prince George County Criminal Case Files 1914–1949, box 3, file 41/33.

22. *Rex v. Ryan*, BCA GR 2788, Prince George County Criminal Case Files 1914–1949, box 4, file 48/43.

23. *Rex v. Clark/Clark v. Clark*, BCA GR 1957, Penticton County Court Criminal Case Files 1922–1945, box 1.

24. *Rex v. Demco*, BCA GR 2235, Pouce Coupe County Court Criminal Case Files 1931–1949, box 3, file 13/48.

25. See Mary P. Ryan, *Civic Wars: Democracy and Public Life in the American City during the Nineteenth Century* (Berkeley: University of California, 1997); Judith R. Walkowitz, *City of Dreadful Delight: Narratives of Sexual Danger in Late-Victorian London* (Chicago: University of Chicago Press, 1992); and Elizabeth Wilson, *The Sphinx in the City: Urban Life, the Control of Disorder, and Women* (Berkeley: University of California Press, 1992).

26. See Chapman, "'An Oscar Wilde Type'"; and Terry L. Chapman, "Male Homosexuality: Legal Restraints and Social Attitudes in Western Canada, 1890–1920," in *Law and Justice in a New Land: Essays in Western Canadian Legal History*, ed. Louis A. Knafla (Toronto: Carswell, 1986), 277–92.

27. See Adele Perry, "'Fair Ones of a Purer Caste': White Women and Colonialism in Nineteenth-Century British Columbia," *Feminist Studies* 23 (1997): 501–24.

28. Deborah L. Nilsen, "The Social Evil: Prostitution in Vancouver, 1900–1920," Special Collections, University of British Columbia, LE3 B7 1976 A9 N54, 1976.

29. See Patricia E. Roy, "The Preservation of Peace in Vancouver: The Aftermath of the Anti-Chinese Riots of 1887," *BC Studies* 31 (1976): 44–59.

30. Moore, *Sunshine and Rainbows*, x. On other frontiers—in Queensland, for example— a markedly different list of groups was responsible for a "substantial" number of similar offenses against Asian immigrants during the same period.

31. Federal government documents on the targeting of aboriginal sexual minorities during this period, which might have much to say about the calculated assaults on native cultures, have yet to be systematically compiled and assessed.

32. Clellan S. Ford, *Smoke from Their Fires: The Life of a Kwakiutl Chief* (New Haven: Yale University Press, 1941), 130.

33. Charge Book Provincial Gaols in Vancouver, November 1908–December 1911, BCA GR 0602, vol. 3 (C1816), 59.

34. BCA BC Attorney General file GR419, vol. 524, file 77 (1943).

35. Prohibition in British Columbia ran from 1917 to 1921 and in the United States from 1920 to 1933. Thus Vancouver and Victoria were attractive destinations from 1922 to 1933 for people in adjacent parts of the United States who wanted more opportunities to consume alcohol and frequent bars.

36. Nilsen, "The Social Evil," 145–47.

37. See Steven Maynard, "Through a Hole in the Lavatory Wall: Homosexual Subcultures, Police Surveillance, and the Dialectics of Discovery, Toronto, 1890–1930," *Journal of the History of Sexuality* 5 (1994): 232–35.

38. BCA BC Attorney General file GR419, vol. 134, file 50.

39. Letter to A. H. McNeill, Crown Prosecutor, Vancouver, from E. M. N. Woods, Barrister, May 6–20, 1915, included in the dossier with the Crown Brief. *Rex v. —— & ——.* Offense: Attempt [*sic*] Buggery. BCA BC Attorney General file GR419, vol. 197, file 31 (1915).

40. BCA BC Attorney General file GR419, vol. 143, files 48–49.

41. See Anne McClintock, *Imperial Leather: Race, Gender, and Sexuality in the Colonial Contest* (New York: Routledge, 1995).

42. BCA BC Attorney General file GR419, vol. 187, file 91; vol. 197, file 31.

43. BCA BC Attorney General file GR419, vol. 197, file 31.

44. See Hugh Johnston, *The Voyage of the Komagata Maru: The Sikh Challenge to Canada's Colour Bar* (Delhi: Oxford University Press, 1979).

45. This and the following excerpts from the trial transcript are taken from BCA BC Attorney General file GR419, vol. 197, file 31.

46. See Tim Retzloff, "Cars and Bars: Assembling Gay Men in Postwar Flint, Michigan," in Beemyn, *Creating a Place for Ourselves,* 226–52.

47. See William B. Turner, *A Genealogy of Queer Theory* (Philadelphia: Temple University Press, 2000).

48. See Gordon Brent Ingram, "Marginality and the Landscapes of Erotic Alien(n)ations," in *Queers in Space: Communities, Public Places, Sites of Resistance,* ed. Gordon Brent Ingram, Anne-Marie Bouthillette, and Yolanda Retter (Seattle: Bay, 1997), 27–52.

49. See John Grube, "'No More Shit': The Struggle for Democratic Gay Space in Toronto," in Ingram, Bouthillette, and Retter, *Queers in Space,* 127–45.

50. See Gordon Brent Ingram, "'Open' Space as Strategic Queer Sites," in Ingram, Bouthillette, and Retter, *Queers in Space,* 95–125.

51. Constable's deposition, BCA BC Attorney General file GR1623, box 1, file 5 (4/1921).

52. BCA BC Attorney General file GR419, vol. 355, file 10.

53. BCA BC Attorney General file GR419, vol. 476, file 3; vol. 482, file 51.

54. BCA BC Attorney General file GR419, vol. 524, file 78.

55. BCA BC Attorney General file GR419, vol. 686, file 3.

56. See Alan Hustak, *They Were Hanged* (Toronto: Lorimer, 1987), 48–60; and Neil Boyd, "All My Love, Leo," *Angles,* July 1987, 9.

57. John Grube attended one of the sessions of the trial against Mantha and saw gay men forced to testify (pers. com., 2003).

58. Hustak, *They Were Hanged,* 50.

59. For some of the key sources for Canada as a whole and Cold War homophobia see Gary Kinsman, "'Fruit Machines': Towards an Analysis of the Anti-homosexual Security Campaigns in the Canadian Civil Service," *Labour/Le Travail* 35 (1995): 133–61, esp. 134–36nn.

60. Sanders, "Sentencing of Homosexual Offenders," 25.

61. For a whimsical discussion of monuments for Sydney see Marcus O'Donnell and Jamie

Dunbar, "The Illusion of Presence: Missing Monuments," in *Queer City: Gay and Lesbian Politics in Sydney*, ed. Craig Johnston and Paul van Reyk (Annandale, NSW: Pluto, 2001), 42–53.

62. See Robin Perelle, "Victoria Hassles Cruisers: Document Takes Aim at 'Unsavory Activity,'" *Xtra West*, November 14, 2002, 9.

63. See Gavin Brown, "Listening to Queer Maps of the City: Gay Men's Narratives of Pleasure and Danger in London's East End," *Oral History Journal* 29 (2001): 49–62.

64. See Gordon Brent Ingram, Anne-Marie Bouthillette, Brett Josef Grubisic, and Cornelia Wyngaarden, *At the Edge of a Great Forest: The Construction of Public Space by Sexual Minorities in Pacific Canada* (Toronto: University of Toronto Press, in press).

65. Two examples of how the dossiers discussed in this essay can be revisited even by the same researcher are furnished in my upcoming book, *Building the Terminal City: Homosexuality, Homophobia, and Urban Design in a Neocolonial Landscape*, and in a chapter I am contributing to an anthology now in development, *Material World: Research on Sexuality for Urban Policy, Planning, and Activism after Queer Theory*. The concerns and details of the dossiers discussed in these two investigations differ from those discussed in this essay.

[6]

"The Cult of the Clitoris": Anatomy of a National Scandal

Jodie Medd

In Oscar Wilde's *Lady Windermere's Fan,* Cecil Graham insists, "I never talk scandal. *I* only talk gossip." When asked what the difference is between the two, Cecil replies, "Oh! Gossip is charming! History is merely gossip. But scandal is gossip made tedious by morality."[1] Wilde would most likely have agreed that media publicity often accompanies—indeed, amplifies—the tedium of morality as a defining property of scandal. The scandal I want to consider, perhaps the most sensational scandal in Britain during World War I, suitably began with an announcement for a play by Wilde that appeared in the *Sunday Times* newspaper in February 1918:

> OSCAR WILDE'S SALOME
> MAUD ALLAN in private performances by
> J. T. GREIN's INDEPENDENT THEATRE,
> April next.
> Terms of membership from Miss Valetta, 9, Duke Street.

This unassuming notice accompanies other advertisements that evoke Britain's charged cultural atmosphere as it entered its fourth year of war. In the paper's "Social and Personal" section, several personal detectives advertise their services for managing the contemporary misfortunes of "Blackmail, Divorce, Libel or anonymous letters" and for assisting "if you require relief from an embarrassing entanglement, or any delicate matter." The paper also boasts an array of treatments for such modern conditions as shell shock and war neurosis, with cures ranging from hypnotic suggestion to "Hindu Treatment." In the entertainment

Jodie Medd is Assistant Professor of English at Carleton University in Ottawa, Canada. She has published articles on Radclyffe Hall and Virginia Woolf and is currently at work on a book about lesbian legal scandal and the culture of modernism.

MODERNISM /*modernity*

22   notices Madame Taussaud advertises a wax exhibition of "Celebrities of the PAST and
      PRESENT and HEROES of the WAR." The advertisement for Wilde's play, printed
      just above Madame Taussaud's announcement, would become the first document in a
      remarkable legal event which the press ultimately deemed "an unprecedented orgy of
      scandal and disorder."[2] Indeed, as the scandal over *Salomé* unfolded, it encompassed
      the peculiar realms invoked by the other advertisements: detected secrets, blackmail
      and libel, "delicate situations," the nervous disorders of war, hypnotic suggestion, the
      mysteries of the East, and celebrity exhibitions.

      In addition to tedious morality and media publicity, a scandal also requires colorful
      public personalities, a condition satisfied by the above names. In 1918 the name "Os-
      car Wilde" was synonymous with infamy; *Salomé*, written in 1891, was his only drama
      to be banned from public performance in England, and its 1894 English publication
      with Aubrey Beardsley's naughty illustrations kindled a minor literary scandal of its
      own.[3] Maud Allan was a dancer who had become one of London's most famous and
      eroticized performers a decade earlier with her scantily-clad and sexually suggestive
      modern dance, "The Vision of Salome" (fig. 1). Meanwhile, her "intimate yet undefin-
      able" relationship with Margot Asquith, who was rumoured to be a "sapphist," had
      provoked society gossip.[4] J. T. Grein, the play's producer and the owner of the Inde-
      pendent Theatre, was a businessman and dramatic critic of the *Sunday Times*. Active
      in the production of modern and often controversial drama, Grein was the first to
      bring Henrik Ibsen and George Bernard Shaw to the London stage. In 1918, Wilde,
      Salomé, Allan, and Grein were all widely recognized, ideologically charged proper
      names, ripe for scandalous deployment.

      Within less than a week of Grein's advertisement, the front page of a small right
      wing radical newspaper called *The Vigilante* displayed the following cryptic paragraph:

> The Cult of the Clitoris
>
> To be a member of Maud Allan's performances in Oscar Wilde's Salome one has to apply
> to a Miss Valetta, of 9, Duke Street. . . . If Scotland Yard were to seize the list of these
> members I have no doubt they would secure the names of several thousand of the first
> 47,000.[5]

The "Cult of the Clitoris" paragraph then launched the sort of enticing narrative that a
scandal requires and also made its publisher, Noel Pemberton-Billing, a public sensation. In a few weeks, Allan, the play's star, and Grein, its producer, began legal proceedings against Billing on a charge of obscene and criminal libel.[6]

An independent member of Parliament, Billing led the Vigilante Society, whose
mission was to promote "purity" in public life. The Society was particularly dedicated
to rooting out that "'mysterious influence'"—the invisible German presence spreading moral degeneracy in England itself—"which was responsible," Billing claimed,
"for all the British failures in the war" (*SLV*, 3). The "47,000" mentioned in the "Cult of
the Clitoris" paragraph alluded to a previous article by Billing that reported the discovery of a book belonging to "a certain German Prince." This book allegedly compiled reports from "German agents who have infested this country for the past twenty

23

▲

Fig. 1. Photo of Maud Allan performing her dance, "The Vision of Salome." Courtesy of The New York Public Library for the Performing Arts, Astor, Lenox, and Tilden Foundations.

years, agents so vile and spreading debauchery of such a lasciviousness as only German minds could conceive and only German bodies execute" (*VR*, 451). The book's "stupefying contents" provided instruction on "the propagation of evils which all decent men thought had perished in Sodom and Lesbia" and included more than a thousand pages "filled with the names mentioned by German agents in their reports. These are names of forty-seven thousand English men and women" (*VR*, 451–2). Billing's article detailed the methods this "black book of sin" devised for "contaminating" the whole English population through the "carefully cultivated introduction of practices which hint at the extermination of the race" (*VR*, 452). Homosexuality, it seems, was the enemy's secret genocidal weapon. Most threatening to the nation at war was the successful queer invasion of "high politics." Billing warned, "Wives of men in supreme position were entangled. In Lesbian ecstasy the most sacred secrets of State were betrayed. The sexual peculiarities of members of the Peerage were used as a leverage to open fruitful fields for espionage" (ibid.). This book even provided a "glossary" that listed "expressions supposed to be used among themselves by the soul-sick victims of this nauseating disease so skilfully [sic] spread by Potsdam" (ibid.). Under the sub-heading "The Fall of Rome," Billing closed his article with a call for action that exorbitantly merged national, imperial, moral, sexual, and gender panic:

all the horrors of shells and gas and pestilence introduced by the Germans in their open warfare would have but a fraction of the effect in exterminating the manhood of Britain as the plan by which they have already destroyed the first forty-seven thousand. . . . [I]t is a terrible thought to contemplate that the British Empire should fall as fell the great Empire of Rome, and the victor now, as then, should be the Hun. [*VR*, 453]

Thus, "the forty-seven thousand" belonged to a cult of sexual depravity susceptible to the influence, corruption, and exploitation by German agents. Since "The Cult of the Clitoris" paragraph implicated *Salomé* and Maud Allan in the 47,000, associating her with sexual deviance and national sedition, Allan charged Billing with the libel of insinuating that she, her performances, and her audience, were "obscene and indecent," "lewd[,] unchaste and immoral," and "addicted to obscene and unnatural practices" (*VR*, 472). That is, Allan accused Billing of implying that she was a lesbian, and that her performance in Wilde's play would promote sexual perversions among its vulnerable wartime audience, thereby opening "fruitful fields for espionage."

After the initial proceedings at Bow Street Police Court, Billing was committed to trial at the Old Bailey. Six days of sensational court drama then captured the attention of the media, and moreover, captured the popular imagination of a nation panicked, paranoid, and exhausted by the war. Co-opting the courtroom as a space of hystericized spectacle, slinging accusations and fomenting anxiety about the plot of the 47,000, Billing was ultimately acquitted by a jury of his peers and cheered as a hero by a mob of spectators, while press editorials scolded him for exploiting the national atmosphere of war hysteria with his outrageous allegations. Billing claimed the last word by compiling a *Verbatim Report* of the court proceedings for private subscription.

"In Lesbian Ecstasy": Representing the War

Wilde's trial and imprisonment in 1895 brought male homosexuality to the headlines, but the Billing trial signals the first time the discussion of *female* homosexuality obsessed the British popular press.[7] Allan then may be read as a public icon of homosexual danger homologous to Wilde, and her failed libel suit against Billing uncannily echoes Wilde's own libel case against the Marquess of Queensberry that eventually led to his downfall. However, beyond mentioning the trial and Billing's outrageous accusations, social histories of homosexuality have provided little analysis of the relation between the trial, the cultural history of lesbianism, and the gender and sexual dynamics within the cultural history of Great War Britain.[8]

In the two books that deal exclusively with the trial, the question of female sexuality is precluded either by discussions of Wilde or political conspiracies. The title of Philip Hoare's recent book on the trial, *Oscar Wilde's Last Stand* (1998), indicates the study's primary focus of analysis: for Hoare, the "cult" of Wilde and aestheticism were on trial, imagined by Billing as the ultimate threat to the British nation at war. Hoare construes Billing's attack on Wilde's play as a protest against the decadent indulgences that were considered symptomatic of the moral degeneracy and lassitude that put the British nation at risk of defeat by the Germans.[9] In *Salome's Last Veil* (1977), war historian Michael Kettle convincingly argues that Billing's trial was implicated in a political conspiracy of disgruntled British war generals who were trying to block alleged secret peace talks with the Germans and plotting to overthrow Lloyd George's coalition government.

While the trial *did* powerfully evoke the ghost of Wilde's condemned sexuality and artistic practices and *was* deeply enmeshed in the political exigencies of its historical moment, it also crucially introduced the specter of female (homo)sexuality as a locus of national anxiety. Indeed, it was the very conjunction of particular political, literary, and sexual histories that provided the conditions of possibility for such an intriguing utterance as "The Cult of the Clitoris" to come to represent concerns over national security. Unprintable in news reports, the libelous phrase was the open secret of the trial and the phrase upon which Allan's prosecution and Billing's defense hinged.[10] Combining a seductive appeal to sexual fantasy with a whiff of farce, the phrase presented a hermeneutical enigma that recruited the suggestion of female homosexuality into the service of national wartime paranoia. Only recently have critics begun to consider the lesbian significance of the trial. Such work, however, has not had the benefit of the full trial documents and has been primarily interested in the trial's deployment of sexology.[11] In focusing on the lesbian accusation in the trial, I want to consider how a wartime crisis of reading and representation configured national and social anxieties through the operation of lesbian fantasy. The paranoid fantasies that Billing circulated encompassed and exceeded the concerns of Wilde's 1895 trial so that a decadent memory was recalled in order to portend a modern, more frightening manifestation; familiar moral panics were updated with international conspiracy and lesbian terror. Because the suggestion of lesbianism aroused a cultural frisson but lesbianism itself lacked a legal definition, it provided a salient figure of sexual fantasy through which the nation could simultaneously condense and disperse its unrepresentable anxieties about national health and security.

Cultural analyses of World War I tend to agree that when the war violently imposed a radically different structure of national and psychical experience, it demanded new forms to represent this altered condition.[12] This challenge to modes of representation was aggravated by an epistemological destabilization. As the editors of *Women's Fiction and the Great War* contend, "No one knew what was going on throughout the Great War. Censorship, propaganda, and the sheer scale and complexity of the event made it impossible to grasp what was happening at any particular moment."[13] The rise of the daily press had stimulated the public appetite for information, but state intervention into reportage during the war amounted to what Phillip Knightley calls a "sordid conspiracy to keep the truth from the people."[14] Under these circumstances, the British public became disillusioned with the press and increasingly skeptical about the integrity of the printed word.[15] This wartime epistemological blackout was accompanied and exacerbated by a panic over spies "passing" in England and communicating in espionage codes, which raised the anxious hermeneutic question: how does one read or decipher identities—particularly dangerous and subversive ones—during a time of unprecedented uncertainty?

MODERNISM /*modernity*

26   Jacqueline Rose argues in a more conceptual register that in war "something about knowledge or the possibility of acquired and definitive certainty is at stake."[16] In *Why War?* she proposes that, "The familiar destructiveness of war represents not, as is commonly supposed, finality but uncertainty, a hovering on the edge of what, like death, can never be totally known."[17] Billing's plot appropriated the emerging notion of lesbianism as an imaginative form through which to figure this epistemological and hermeneutic dilemma that was engendered by World War I. The very *suggestibility* of lesbianism, with its wide range of connotations and possible manifestations but without a singular consolidated popular image, rendered it a particularly powerful vehicle for figuring the wartime problematic of uncertainty, illegibility, and (mis)representation. Not only are sexual secrets considered commensurate with national ones, but the wartime dilemma of unknowability and uncertainty finds an analogy in the highly suggestive but ultimately unknowable notion of female homosexuality. In other words, if male homosexuality functioned as a figure of the "open secret" in the nineteenth century, as Eve Sedgwick has suggested, then in the early-twentieth century, lesbianism operated as a figure of heightened suggestion and potential-but-always-foreclosed knowledge that enticed only to frustrate the possibility of disclosure or interpretation. What cannot be known or comprehended about the "reality" of the war is translated into a fantasy of the epistemologically elusive category of female homosexuality.

Why lesbianism? Just how unknown or unknowable was it? Certainly, female homosexuality at this time admitted multiple genealogies. Literary (and largely French) representations include the vampiric and decadent "femmes damnées" of Baudelaire, Swinburne, and Balzac; the sapphic revivals of Natalie Barney, Renée Vivien, Michael Field, and Pierre Louÿs; and the indiscriminate courtesan or sexual rake of Zola's *Nana* and Gautier's *Mademoiselle de Maupin*. Medical discourse taxonomized the female sexual invert, while sexual politics aligned lesbianism with the self-exhibiting turn-of-the-century "public woman," a term first applied to prostitutes soliciting on streetcorners and actresses performing on stage that also came to include suffragists protesting in the street and "the New Women" emerging in the public sphere.[18] Such figures of female independence and homosociality, which were linked with anxieties about female homosexuality, became more pronounced during the gender disruption of World War I. In spite of this legacy (notably, a largely literary French one), explicitly scandalous female homosexuality has been considered by many sexual historians as having been essentially "unthinkable" to the British popular imagination emerging from Victoria's reign.[19] In 1918 it is the very inconceivability of scandalous female homosexuality, at its precise historical point of shading into possibility, that constitutes it as the perfect figure for staging the sexualized "Other scene" of wartime. Billing's plot of homosexual invasion and its specific appeal to the emerging cultural recognition of female homosexuality provided a means of representing, through a parodic sexual fantasy, the unrepresentable catastrophe of history. "The Cult of the Clitoris" scandal demonstrates that it is the very connotative suggestibility of lesbianism and its arousal of the imagination that makes Billing's plot so powerfully seductive.

The Spectacle of the Courtroom, The Spectacle of *Salomé*   27

If the narrative leading up to the trial reads like a sensation novel, then the scenes in the courtroom unfold as a dramatic performance that rivals *Salomé*'s own histrionics of fatal desire. Billing admittedly planted the libel in the *Vigilante* to attract legal reaction and media attention, and his introduction to the *Verbatim Report* encourages us to inherit the case as a spectacle whose imaginative appeal exceeds its value as a legal document. He notes that the official *Verbatim Report* does not provide

> those keys to individual and public temper which in the familiar press reports are usually supplied by parenthetical adjectives and nouns, and therefore that such helps to the imagination as "(sarcastically)," "(warmly)," "(great sensation)," and so forth, must be supplied by the reader's own discretion. [*VR*, ix]

Beyond demonstrating Billing's scandal-mongering, this appeal reminds us that we should read the trial not just within a legal or discursive framework, but also according to the operations of imaginative fantasy and interpretative possibility. As Billing writes with sweeping hyperbole, the trial "caused the liveliest stirring of the public mind in all parts of every continent where the English language is understood" (*VR*, iii). Accordingly, he actively "stirred" the public imagination by acting as his own legal representative with theatrical flare (he had four years' experience as an actor), expanding his conspiracy plot to include every member of the court—he accused the presiding judge and the counsel for the prosecution of being among the 47,000—and calling a remarkable cast of witnesses, including Wilde's former lover, Lord Alfred Douglas.

As a theatrical spectacle, the trial takes *Salomé* as its source and inspiration. Billing contended that *Salomé* was "an open representation of degenerated sexual lust, sexual crime, and unnatural passions and an evil and mischievous travesty of a biblical story" which "ministers to sexual perverts, Sodomites and Lesbians" and renders them vulnerable to German influence and blackmail (*VR*, 476, 35). For Billing, the perversions of *Salomé* (both text and character) are the perversions of Wilde are the perversions of Allan are the perversions of the enemy that will destroy the British nation. Billing and his witnesses testify that Salomé's "climax" in kissing/biting the lips of Iokanaan's severed head enacts Wilde's own sexual orgasm of writing—to represent the scene in language is to live the scene. This sexual climax is then transferred to Allan—to represent the scene on the stage is to live the scene, and in turn Allan's performance sexually influences the audience—to witness the scene as spectator is to live the scene. Affective and physical experience is mimetically relayed from one body to another through a simple circuit of representation, performance, and spectatorship. This ease of associative relay and substitution allowed the suggestion of lesbianism in the trial to carry a range of seemingly unrelated wartime anxieties.

Billing's insinuation that Allan's performance is marked by a latent lesbianism trades upon the suggestion that Wilde's own homosexuality seeps into both his title character and the actress performing her. If Salomé embodies Wilde's desire, then she is in effect a gay man masquerading as a sadistic heterosexual woman. Furthermore, if in

28 Billing's reading Salomé's violent passion for and power over Iokanaan reverses conventional heterosexual dynamics of desire by constructing the male body as a feminized object, then she resides somewhere in the undefined territory of masculine female desire, a paradox that easily slips into the shadowy realm of lesbian passion.[20]
And in Billing's chain of associations, if Wilde's betrayal of heterosexual norms is equivalent to a betrayal of state security, then Allan's performance implicates her in a queer
German plot that simultaneously betrays nation and heterosexuality: *"Wives of men in
supreme position were entangled. In Lesbian ecstasy the most sacred secrets of State
were betrayed"* (VR, 452). Any violation of the sacred marriage bond may violate the
sacred secrets of state, and what better figure for representing such a double agent
than the fantasy of "Lesbian ecstasy"?

Billing's deployment of *Salomé* also engages with the play's status as a symbolist
drama. While definitions of literary symbolism vary widely, Charles Chadwick cites
Stéphane Mallarmé's characterization of symbolism as the art of "evoking an object
little by little so as to reveal a mood or, conversely, the art of choosing an object and
extracting from it an 'état d'âme,'" a mood, Mallarmé insists, that "should be extracted
'par une série de déchiffrements'—'by a series of decipherings.'"[21] The object is hinted
at, suggested, gradually revealed. Chadwick considers a companion aspect of symbolism, in which "concrete images are used as symbols, not of particular thoughts and
feelings," but of an ideal world.[22] As Arthur Symons rhetorically asks in *The Symbolist
Movement in Literature* (1899), "What is symbolism if not an establishing of the links
which hold the world together, the affirmation of an eternal, minute, intricate, almost
invisible life, which runs through the whole universe?"[23]

Critics have identified *Salomé* as symbolist in its use of suggestive, mystical, and
highly aestheticized language whose incantatory musicality crosses boundaries of dream
and reality, reference and evasion, representation and affect. However, given the wartime concern over secret agents and codes, any implied mysteries hidden in ambiguous language were suspect. As we will see, the idealized symbolist notion of "links
which hold the world together" finds a parodic manifestation as political paranoia in
Billing's conspiracy theory that connected the *Salomé* production with the "intricate,
almost invisible life" of secret agents and international espionage. In other words, Billing
anchored the possibility of symbolic suggestion to history, politics, and morality by reifying
the "links" that held together Wilde's world of art and Britain's situation in wartime.[24]

In this process of reification, the suggestion of lesbianism functions remarkably like
a symbol in the "symbolist" sense. It operates as a figure for revealing a state of mood
and/or as a material substitute for the intangible, floating, "minute, intricate, almost
invisible" life pervading the British cultural atmosphere of 1918. Indeed, Billing might
have turned the ultimate symbolist phrase, since "The Cult of the Clitoris" purported
to harbor an explicit referential content while simultaneously refusing stable
referentiality in favor of infinite suggestion. It effectively symbolized a complex of
affective relations among war, sexuality, gender, art, and politics that otherwise resist
articulation, achieving this effect through a "series of decipherings," hints, and suggestions. In a Freudian sense, the phrase is a condensation that "represents several asso-

ciative chains at whose point of intersection it is located," while in a Foucaultian sense, it also signals a cultural dispersion with its suggestion that deviant female sexuality is distributed throughout discursive formations and infuses all aspects of political life.[25]

Sexual Sedition: Resurrecting Wilde, Anatomizing Allan

The scandal of "The Cult of the Clitoris" relied upon the scandalous—and seditious—connotations of Wilde's name that had been established through his own trials and imprisonment. As Ed Cohen, Regenia Gagnier, and others have demonstrated, these trials identified Wilde's artistic production, aestheticism, and self-fashioning with his sexual "gross indecency."[26] A rhetoric of national threat conflated aestheticism with national betrayal and displaced anxieties about counterhegemonic sexual activities onto aesthetic movements. Perhaps precisely because Wilde was such an icon of social danger, his presence was recalled and redeployed in the years between his trial and the Billing trial. Most notably, between the spring of 1913 and the autumn of 1914, there were legal battles involving Wilde's biographer, Arthur Ransome, his former lover, Alfred Douglas, and his literary executor, Robert Ross.[27] With the specter of Wilde conjured up particularly close to wartime, his performative invocation and abjection functioned to consolidate national identity and "vigor." We could read Billing's trial as just another addition to this history of early-twentieth-century deployments of Wilde's ghost; however, as I have proposed, in this trial the threat of Wilde was supplemented and perhaps exceeded by the threat of lesbian sexual espionage. While Wilde's infamy certainly underwrote Billing's homosexual plot, "The Cult of the Clitoris" introduced dangerous female homosexuality as a new perversion to be discussed, scandalized, and rallied against.

The very phrase "The Cult of the Clitoris" combines the shock of anatomical reference with the suggestive danger of female sexual and political independence. With limited female suffrage imminent, the phrase traded upon doubts and fears about recent successes in feminism, the gathering of women in political movements and public labor, and the constitution of the female citizen. The phrase actually grafted the aesthetic decadence of "the cult of Wilde" onto the concern that women's citizenship would free them from their traditional role of bearing and raising citizens for the empire.[28] Notably, the primary figure of "The Cult of the Clitoris" was Maud Allan, the most unlikely *and* most suitable figure for effecting this shift from Wilde's aesthetic and sexual threat in the 1890s to women's political-sexual threat in the late war years.

Unlike Wilde's legendary infamy, Allan's public recognition, like her dancing that made her briefly but thoroughly famous, was a fleeting gesture that momentarily entranced audiences, but left little trace of its performance. By 1918 her career was in fact declining, but the trial evoked the cultural memory of her eroticism, aestheticism, mass cultural appeal, and high society affiliations. A North American, Allan studied music in Berlin, then began a dancing career in Europe and Russia; when she performed before King Edward while he was on holiday in Europe, he encouraged her to bring her talent to England (*SD*, 152). Subsequently, clever marketing tactics rendered her dance "The Vision of Salome" a succès de scandale at London's Palace Theatre in

MODERNISM /*modernity*

30   1908, catapulting her to fame, breaking box office records, and gaining her a position
in London society. Reviewers repeatedly deployed the metaphor of hypnosis to convey her mysterious power to seduce, but not offend, her audience with her erotic and
orientalizing dance. Those scandalized by Allan associated her with Wilde's degeneracy, but this hint of perversion only spiced up the gossip about her social affiliations.
With her fame, she secured the patronage and friendship of Prime Minister Asquith
and forged a particular intimacy with his wife, Margot, a relationship which "caused
talk if not open speculation in social, diplomatic, and political circles," and which would
be exploited by Billing in the trial, given rumors of Margot Asquith's unconventional-
ity and lesbian-coded female coterie (*SD*, 176). Inevitably, Allan could not sustain her
hypnotic spell over her audience, particularly once a campaign of demystification was
instigated by the very media that had once promulgated her fascination.[29] A past fad
by 1918, she was most likely attempting to revive her fame by taking her first dramatic
speaking role in Wilde's *Salomé*; however, the very attributes which had once enticed
the Edwardian public had been re-inscribed as national dangers by this time.

Certainly, Allan's artistic and erotic notoriety offended the wartime conservatism in
art and morality. Her popularization of what one reviewer called the "sensuous, decadent, *macabre*" and her training in Germany coded her as suspicious to a country that
blamed French-inflected decadence for the national decay that led to war, and was
intolerant of any hint of German *Kultur*.[30] If her erotic dance had flirted with an association with Wilde's play—and his infamy—a decade earlier, Allan now took the risk,
during a reactionary political climate, of foregoing any difference between her Salomé
and Wilde's. Without a king's sanction to hide behind, her affiliations with the Asquiths
did not help her reputation. Forced to resign as prime minister in December 1916,
Asquith had proved a failure under the exigencies of war, and his continued association with artistic circles had only contributed to doubts about his ability to lead an
aggressive, patriotic campaign.

By 1918, the exoticism, sexual danger, artistic innovation, and political liaisons upon
which Allan had built her earlier fame were attached to a new female archetype: the
sexually and politically dangerous spy-seductress. Just months before Billing initiated
his campaign against *Salomé*, Mata Hari was executed in Paris for espionage. Born
Margeretha Geertruida Zelle, Mata Hari left her notoriously abusive husband in 1904,
changed her identity, embarked on a dancing career even more risqué and orientalizing
than Allan's, and undertook an unapologetic life as a courtesan, taking lovers of the
highest military rank, including German officials.[31] When war was declared, all that
Mata Hari represented came under suspicion: her eroticism, exoticism, refusal of domestic femininity, and sexual promiscuity violated the wartime mood of sacrifice, re-
straint, and conservatism. Accustomed to inventing and reinventing her identity, Mata
Hari mixed her stories and acquaintances one too many times and was eventually arrested. Although little hard evidence was gathered against her, she was swiftly condemned as a spy, and her legend as the female secret service agent par excellence fed
the propaganda machine. Her Eastern identification and sexual repertoire invited an
easy conflation of moral laxity with national deception and foreign difference, and her

role as mistress to men in power elaborated the femme-fatale stereotype into a figure whose sexual power not only destroyed men and threatened marriage, but also imperiled national security.[32] Such fantasies engendered in Mata Hari were directly transferable to Allan at a time when spy-paranoia was escalating.

The Billing trial was situated in and significantly contributed to a volatile period of home front anxieties, manifest in anti-alien sentiment that included both mob violence and official reaction against anything and anyone remotely German.[33] The first months of 1918 witnessed England exhausted and pessimistic about the outcome of the war. The aggressive German offensive in March shook the nation as the stalemate of trench warfare shifted into a campaign of action, including air raids on England. Historians Trevor Wilson and John Terraine concur that as tensions between military leaders and the government increased, the public, denied clear explanations, displaced its anxiety onto a renewed campaign against enemy aliens.[34] Billing's conspiracy of the "47,000" further resonated with war propaganda that explicitly aligned homosexuality with German degeneracy, and the paranoid fantasy of "the enemy within" conflated spy fever with homophobia. Alfred Douglas promulgated this association in his 1915 sonnet, "All's Well with England," which concludes:

> Out there in Flanders all the trampled ground
> Is red with English blood . . .
> . . . Who will count the loss,
> Since here 'at home' sits merry Margot, bound
> With Lesbian fillets, while with front of brass
> 'Old Squiffy' hands the purse to Robert Ross.[35]

"English blood" is spilled "out there in Flanders" while "at home" homosexuality is not only practiced but rewarded by a decadent government. The next year Douglas published *The Rossiad*, which concludes with an appeal to England:

> O England, in thine hour of need . . .
> Raise up the best, hack down the worst,
> Tear from thy heart the thing accurst.
> Two foes thou hast, one there one here,
> One far, one intimately near,
> Two filthy fogs blot out thy light:
> The German, and the Sodomite. [ibid.]

Douglas's conjoining of the "The foe without, the foe within" brings the war "intimately near" by identifying the foreign enemy with the deviant sexuality lurking within the British people.[36] This association of homosexuality, high society, national betrayal, and social decay had a long-standing history, but it was Billing's trial that brought such sentiments into public debate at a particularly vulnerable cultural moment and condensed them into the single cryptic phrase, "The Cult of the Clitoris." As the point of transference for such a range of allusions and connotations, and as the key utterance in the libel charge, the question of "The Cult of the Clitoris"—what it meant, to whom it referred, and who could interpret it—was a primary obsession in the trial.

MODERNISM /*modernity*

32   **Reading Cults and Clits**

The "Cult of the Clitoris" paragraph produces its distinct scandalous effects by staging an irresistible seductive scene of reading that initiates an elaborate sexual fantasy. The detective-reader must sort out the allusions and decode the meaning: Who or what is this cult? Who or what are the 47,000? And perhaps the most puzzling question for many early-twentieth-century readers: What, exactly, is a clitoris? The paragraph compels the reader into a sexy game of reading and allusion—but one that, like a coded war message or a spy-thriller novel, has (for Billing at least) a distinct secret to be deciphered and exposed. The phrase inflames the imagination and provokes interpretation, thus allowing Billing to intervene in the courtroom and unveil the underlying plot. The libel achieves its impact by forcing a convergence of deviant activities that amplifies the panic over national vulnerability while enlisting the most undefined realm of danger, "The Cult of the Clitoris," as the rhetorical gathering point for all other anxieties. As we have seen, in Billing's formulation, the spectacle of *Salomé* occasions a relay of meanings and perversions, from author to actress to audience. Similarly, the phrase, "The Cult of the Clitoris," conjoins the allusions and associations of immorality, national betrayal, homosexuality, and aestheticism. The salience of the phrase rests upon the suggestive invocation of female homosexuality, whose lack of a recognizable popular symbolization renders it most appealing for symbolic appropriation. It is precisely the language of the female body—the female nonreproductive but desiring body—that simultaneously demands and refuses interpretative attention, inciting scandal through its very resistance to representation. Unprintable in the newspapers, the obscene absence of the phrase "Cult of the Clitoris" vexes interpretation. Its lesbian meaning, the prosecution will argue, is obscenely obvious, but a cross fire of courtroom attempts to decipher the phrase culminates in Billing literally retracting the belabored lesbian signified from the range of interpretive possibilities.

In the police proceedings, the counsel for the prosecution, Sir Travers Humphreys, who had also represented Wilde in his trials, introduces the libel with a web of circumlocution. He deems it "an attack of a sort which I hesitate to characterize in language . . . unworthy of any man to have made upon any woman" (VR, 4). Guiding attention to the newspaper, he continues, "I find words which I must read, although I see there are some ladies in Court. I must read them aloud: 'The Cult of the Clitoris.'. . . it is my submission the words themselves are the filthiest words it would be possible to imagine" (ibid.). And yet, he immediately asserts,

> What they mean no one can doubt; no one can doubt who reads the words as they are. . . .
> [T]he coupling of the name of anyone with that cross heading in leaded type . . . can only mean one thing, and that is that the lady whose name is coupled with it, either in her private or in her professional life, approves of that which is sometimes described in perhaps less—I do not know whether it is less objectionable—but less gross language as lesbianism, and a more horrible libel of any woman . . . is impossible to find. [VR, 5–6]

Humphreys claims that the unimaginable title and its association with Allan's name in **33** the paragraph are obvious in their "meaning" and implication, thereby bypassing any interpretive process. According to Humphreys, the "coupling" of a woman's name and a clitoral cult "can only mean one thing," when in fact, the relationship between Allan's name and the title—this "coupling"—hangs suspended in possibility. Humphreys plugs up this epistemological gap with repeated assertions of the transparent meaning of the "coupling." His conspicuous discomfort over uttering the title in the presence of women further codes the phrase as obviously criminally unutterable while maintaining the assumption of female sexual innocence.

Ultimately, his evasion of interpretation culminates in syntactical confusion and referential failure:

> the meaning of that paragraph so far as I have read it is that there is some connection between [Mr. Grein's] proposed production of this play and that cult as it is called, which is the explanation of the paragraph, because that is what it is. Without it, the paragraph is meaningless, it means nothing at all. Under that heavily leaded type heading it means there is some connection with the nameless vice between women, and the performance at the Independent Theatre which is announced. [VR, 6]

The paragraph and its title achieve a singular meaning that cannot be named, a meaning which becomes lost in wandering referents (for example, "because that is what it is"? "Without *it*"? *Which* "it"?). Humphreys compensates for his obscure explanation by emphasizing the "heavily leaded type" of the graphic title (a typographical detail he repeats in this speech), and insisting on its indelible black-and-white obscenity. The lesbian meaning is somehow an effect of the graphic type, so that the ink of publicity stains the reputation of those it names as it does the fingers of its readers. As reference and interpretation fail, words become the things that inscribe them; the materiality of the printed letter stands in for the reference that the utterance itself obscures. Obvious but nameless lesbian meaning occurs as the point of conjunction among title, typeset, names of body parts, and names of actresses.[37] By referring to lesbianism as a "nameless" vice while lamenting the association of Allan's *name* with such a vice, Humphreys performs a move similar to the one that occurred in Wilde's trial, in which Wilde's name was substituted for the terms "sodomy" or "acts of gross indecency."[38] In effect, Humphreys suggests that such a coupling of Allan's proper name with the suggestive but referentially indeterminate title scandalizes Allan's name to a greater degree than if a more explicit accusation had been published. Her name supplies the point of determinate reference that the cryptic title refuses, a coupling which Humphreys both criticizes and exploits.[39]

In his questioning of Allan, Humphreys again asserts the paragraph's criminal offense by evading its explanation. He refuses to repeat the paragraph's title, but asks Allan if she regards it as a libel. "I do," she affirms, and then Humphreys pauses to address the ruling magistrate:

> Sir John, I should like to have your ruling upon this subject. I do not propose to ask the Witness what her understanding is of the libel. I will not ask any further questions unless

34

> there is some matter so obscure to an ordinary person—unless you desire it, Sir, I do not
> think I should ask any more than I have, that she regards that as a libel upon herself; but
> of course it is for you to say. [*VR*, 17–8]

Responding, "Certainly, I agree," the magistrate halts the explanation by admitting to
"know" what Humphreys insists any "ordinary person" would know without naming
(ibid.). The magistrate and Humphreys collude in an interpretive conspiracy of transparent meanings; as "gentlemen," they "hesitate to characterize in language" the "meaning" of Billing's attack, for to do so would violate gender chivalry, according to
Humphreys's characterization of the libel as "unworthy of any man to have made upon
any woman" (*VR*, 4). This unspoken agreement between magistrate and counsel suggests a male homosocial community of knowledge about female deviant desire, a desire whose utterance must be protected from its very object of reference.

The positions of knowing established at the Bow Street Police Court are reoriented
in the criminal proceedings at the Old Bailey, tried before a jury. The counsel config-
ures the jury (who are supposedly, unlike the learned magistrate, *really* "ordinary
people") in a position of innocent ignorance, for in this case to position them as knowing what the coupling means would interpellate them within a community of prurient
knowledge. In the above exchange between Humphreys and the magistrate, the two
agree to share this knowledge in order to protect others' innocence and certainly to
contain interpretation. Lawyer and judge conspire in a shared understanding that the
Old Bailey proceedings then construct as extraordinary, exclusive knowledge.

Ellis Hume Williams, now leading the prosecution for the Crown in the Central
Criminal Court, approaches the libel with the same theatrical caution as Humphreys:
"Gentlemen, I am afraid once and for all, unpleasant as the task is—more particularly
as I see that there are some women in the court—I must describe to you (if these
ladies *will* stay) what the meaning of that phrase is" (*VR*, 57). Again, Williams makes
his point about the danger of Billing's libel by suggesting that it threatens the sexual
innocence of women. To counter Billing's suggestion that women know more and do
more in the nation and in bed than popular culture will admit, the prosecution deliberately constructs the female spectators in the courtroom as most vulnerable in their
ignorance. Williams trades upon and controverts Billing's suggestion that the spectacle of *Salomé* will immorally infect its spectators by now constructing the courtroom
as a space that must be protected from the dangerous influence of Billing's words.
Williams's parenthetical phrase "(if these ladies *will* stay)" reads as a rhetorical aside,
and yet there is a sense in which he suggests that since the ladies *will* insist on staying
in the courtroom then he *must* describe the meaning of the libel, thereby amplifying
the threat of female homosexuality through the very act of interpretation.[40]

Forced to explain the libel, Williams constructs the ability to read it accurately as
dependent upon specific knowledge which he must, unfortunately, disclose:

> You probably may have some idea, but unless you have some physiological knowledge
> you will not appreciate in its fullness what the gross obscenity of this phrase is. . . . [Y]ou
> cannot appreciate the gravity of the charge against this lady unless you appreciate what
> the real meaning is of this horrible phrase. [*VR*, 57–8]

He performatively attempts to short-circuit the paragraph's seductive potential with the intervention of scientific facts, didactically explaining that because clitoral pleasure is unnecessary to procreation, it is necessarily a lesbian vice. In Williams's interpretation, if "clitoris" operates as a metonym for lesbianism, then its utterance in conjunction with a woman's name clearly constitutes the worst accusation to make against any woman: that she indulges a sexual desire extraneous to any biological or social reproduction for the state.[41] In a Darwinian language of natural science, Williams undertakes what must be a first in British legal history: a graphic explanation of the situation and function of the clitoris, and its method of arousal in lesbian sexual practices.[42] With rhetoric that recalls nineteenth-century campaigns against masturbation, Williams denounces lesbian practices as "degrading, repulsive, contrary to nature, and consequently destructive of health—practices which, indulged in to any extent, sap and undermine the sanity and probity and self-respect . . . of those who indulge in them" (*VR*, 58). Ultimately, however, in order to stabilize the offensive meaning of the libel, he must have recourse to male homosexuality:

> If this paragraph had been dealing with men instead of with women and had been headed "The cult of the penis," it would have required no explanation. "The cult of the clitoris" is worse; it means the deliberate perversion of all the natural instincts that nature has implanted in man and woman, to the practice of a filthy, enervating and degrading vice. . . . [reads paragraph aloud] What is the meaning of that? What is the meaning of the heading "The Cult of the Clitoris?" It can have no other reference than to the practice of this Lesbian vice; no other meaning is possible. [ibid.]

Much like Humphreys's argument in the police court, Williams finally just asserts the single possible reading that the title and paragraph make necessary, although here he provides a considerable lesson in anatomy and natural history. His simple declaration that "The Cult of the Clitoris" is worse than "The Cult of the Penis" is devoid of any argument as to why. In fact, the prosecution's strategy here rests upon a paradoxical tautology: an argument that asserts transparent moral obviousness must not be diluted or weakened by argumentation.[43] Within the problematic of interpretation, perhaps "The Cult of the Clitoris" is worse because it requires such lengthy explanation and interpretation. Since the location and "function" of the clitoris is so obscure and not known to the "ordinary" individual, the need for an uncomfortably explicit and protracted translation culminates in an atmosphere of enervated, exhausted shame. Certainly Williams's argument from analogy attests to the phrase's resistance to cultural legibility; supposedly anyone would know what "The Cult of the Penis" means, whereas Billing has manufactured a far more disturbing scene of perversion precisely because it refuses immediate cultural comprehension.

The speculation about "The Cult of the Penis" should also remind us that this scandal over traitorous female body parts occurred at a time when the British male body was being mutilated and dismembered on a scale never before experienced. Men at the front encountered the unprecedented ability of technological warfare to blow the male body into grotesque fragments; those injured bodies that did survive hand grenades,

MODERNISM /*modernity*

36 artillery fire, shelling, and surgical amputations testified to the inconceivable experience of modern war. As Joanna Bourke writes, "The horror of front-line dismemberment was beyond the imagination of many civilians in Britain. They were not, however, totally unaware of its impact on hundreds of thousands of men's bodies."[44] The returned injured soldier provided a corporeal metonym of the war's unimaginable violence against male bodies and masculinity itself. "In war," Bourke writes, "the injured man was not disabled but mutilated. He was the fit man, the potent man, *rendered impotent*. He was mutilated and mutilator in one."[45] Bourke's use of the loaded notion of male impotence alludes to castration as the classic trope of damaged masculinity. Trudi Tate suggests that "the distressing presence of war-injured men" effected a gender crisis by complicating the Freudian schema of gender difference in which the imaginary wholeness of phallic masculinity is constructed in opposition to women's castration.[46] "The Cult of the Clitoris" partakes of this wartime disruption of gender distinction constituted upon visible difference. The phrase dismembers and thus diminishes the female body, but it also invokes the danger of female sexual difference. It gestures to the genital "nothing" that constitutes female sexuality and, since the clitoris has been historically compared to the penis, it also signals the threat of a phallic woman. If masculinity was constructed against femininity's lack, then "The Cult of the Clitoris" confronts the vulnerable masculine body in wartime with a particularly menacing feminine sexual corporeality.

While a seemingly inexhaustible range of connotations emanate from Billing's paragraph, the law had to judge its legal meaning. Whereas Humphreys's speech for the prosecution at Bow Street suggested a vague "connection" or relationship of "approval" between Allan and "unnatural practices," the specific indictment for the Old Bailey trial claimed that the title and paragraph meant

> thereby that the said Maud Allan was a lewd, unchaste and immoral woman and was about to give private performances of an obscene and indecent character so designed as to foster and encourage obscene and unnatural practices among women and that the said Maud Allan associated herself with persons addicted to obscene and unnatural practices. [VR, 472]

Billing's plea of justification then not only stated that this indictment was "true," but further denounced *Salomé* as "an open representation of degenerated sexual lust, sexual crime, and unnatural passions and an evil and mischievous travesty of a biblical story" that was written by "a moral pervert" and was particularly attractive to the German agents' list of the 47,000 (VR, 476). Notably, the prosecution—not the publisher of the paragraph—actually translated for the court what the libel meant; Billing merely claimed that this reading was true and justified, and added the emphasis on the underlying German invasion plot. However, because the indictment alludes to, but does not explicitly *name* lesbianism, it opens a conspicuous gap of interpretive possibilities, a gap which left considerable space for Billing to mount an attack on Allan while evading specific definitions.

Experts and Perverts

When questioned about the meaning of the "Cult of the Clitoris," Dr. Serrell Cooke, an "expert" medical witness, explained that "Clitoris is a Greek word, it is a medical term altogether; it has nothing to do with ordinary language; nobody but a medical man, or people interested in that kind of thing would understand the term" (VR, 259). Semi-clarifying that "that kind of thing" refers to sexual perversion, Cooke concludes, "'The Cult of the Clitoris,' would have been very well understood by all the perverts all over the world. It would not have been understood by ordinary people" (VR, 260). With "clitoris" as a transnational signifier that unites "all the perverts all over the world," Cooke and the defense transforms the "cult" of the clitoris into a cult of readers who can interpret the phrase. In other contexts, Billing referred to the "initiated" as the only readers who could understand the title.[47] This sense of a seductive cult of reading, which recalls the construction of Wilde in his trial, converges with the sexological taxonomies that constituted the homosexual as an exclusive species of shared traits, including shared discourse (recall the glossary in the German Prince's black book). Furthermore, in the war context, the suggestion of secret sects or communities "all over the world" sharing bonds of language, practices, and values that supersede those of national loyalty draws upon and exacerbates paranoid fantasies of spies with shared codes, secret languages, and hidden allegiances. This distrust of nontransparent language feeds into the wartime crisis of knowing and reading, and backs Billing's legal defense.

As we have seen, Allan's lawyers play a game of interpretation with the libel, alternately insisting on the obvious meaning of the paragraph, and then assuming an innocent ignorance of the audience whom they must educate into an appreciation of the libel's unimaginable horror. Billing's defense turns such constructions to his own advantage: how could Allan be innocent if she were able to recognize the phrase as an insult, as a lesbian allusion? In a tactic that relies upon the expert versus pervert opposition, Billing's cross-examination of Allan links knowledge and sexual immorality:

> Billing: Did Mr. Grein explain to you where the libel was and exactly what it meant?
> Allan: I do not think it is necessary for anyone to explain that paragraph to me . . .
> Billing: You are well acquainted with the names that arise in connection with the [alleged libelous] matter?. . . [P]articularly with that one [i.e. the clitoris]?
> Allan: Not particularly at all, Mr. Billing.[48]

Through his questions, Billing ascertains that yes, friends of Allan saw the libel and understood its meaning, but no, neither she nor they are medical students. Billing then triumphantly crows, "Are you aware, Miss Allan, that out of twenty-four people who were shown that libel, including many professional men, only one of them, who happened to be a barrister, understood what it meant?" (VR, 85).

Admitting only two mutually exclusive realms of interpreters, educated professionals and degenerate perverts, Billing demands Allan identify herself in one group or the other. He then collapses the language of homosexual aestheticism with the language of the German enemy when he takes up Allan's autobiography and fixates on her study

38   and milieu in Germany. Reading such passages as "[In Berlin] I came in touch with a broader spirit of what I had best call bohemian bon camaraderie," and "the German tongue was our Esperanto," Billing insinuates that Allan was part of an international "cult" whose adoption of German as its common language marked it as morally depraved danger to the British nation (qtd. in *VR*, 87).

Next, Billing reads passages from *Salomé*, insisting on their perverse sexual meaning. Allan denies such an interpretation, maintaining that Salomé is an innocent girl whose spirituality, not her sexuality, is aroused in her relationship with Iokanaan. Allan's refusal to read the play as remotely erotic belies her untenable position in facing lesbian accusations; she is more on trial than the defendant and must maintain her claim to chastity.[49] Ultimately, Allan's promotion of the play as spiritual and artistic is deployed against her. Billing insists that rather than proving her innocence, Allan's refusal to acknowledge the play's vice betrays her loyalty to the "cult" of readers who find beauty in perversity. Again, much like Wilde's trials, in which Wilde's modes of reading were considered symptomatic of his "gross indecency," Billing attempts to discredit Allan by constructing her as an "extraordinary" reader whose performance of a text by the "high priest" of an "outrageous cult" would appeal to the initiated.

While Allan claims that neither she nor Wilde is responsible for Billing's prurient readings, Billing re-appropriates the same strategy with the claim, "You quite understand that I am not responsible for what you read into the libel," which leads to an explicit comparison of the libel with the play:

> Billing: Which do you think is the most likely to pervert public morals in this country, the witnessing of such a play or the reading of the paragraph complained of. [sic] Which do you think likely to do most harm to the young men and the young women?
> Allan: The paragraph that you have had printed in your paper.
> Billing: Will you tell me why?
> Allan: Because you suggest things to them that they do not know anything about, and the curiosity of man is such that they will go and find out.
> Billing: Are there any suggestions at all in this play?
> Allan: Not that I know; if there are they are so veiled as not to be obvious.
> Billing: You think that that [paragraph] title is unveiled?
> Allan: I think that it is draped from the shoulder.
> Billing: It was meant to be understood by those who could understand it, but was not meant to be understood by others?
> Allan: That is what you say. [*VR*, 113–4]

Allan's apt metaphor of veiled language foregrounds the trial's contest over translation and interpretation, and implicitly evaluates the libel according to symbolist principles. For Allan, the artistic merit and legal defense of *Salomé* rests in its fully veiled language. Signs and symbols are caught up in such a thoroughgoing economy of shifting signification that no phrase holds a single obvious meaning and desire can never be categorized. Billing's libel, however, draped from the shoulder and only half-veiled, insinuates enough that the correspondences it forges intend to communicate vice and trap the vicious. According to Allan, Billing's intention that the reader of "The Cult of the Clitoris" paragraph should arrive at a particular sexual and political meaning renders Billing guilty of the very vice of immoral suggestion of which he is accusing Wilde. Allan's suitably elusive metaphor demonstrates the potential of figurative language with the effect of exposing Billing's attempt to appropriate the symbolist impulse. Billing wants to fasten guilt and shame with knowledge and absolute interpretations, while Wilde's text and Allan's testimony staunchly refuse any such equation.

Veils and draperies here are also telling. Allan's metaphor suggests that Billing's "draping" anticipates a dramatic unveiling, exposing a final, naked body of lesbian meaning. The phrase "The Cult of the Clitoris" cites the perverse materiality of the body—Allan's body—with the intent of digging up Wilde's sentenced body to prove that its criminal corporeality subtends *Salomé*. As Robert Ross wrote in a private letter about the trial, "Kicking the corpse of Wilde has also been a pleasure to the English people even if they disapprove of Billing's methods."[50] Billing's methods include casting suspicion upon Allan and Grein's reading practices by aligning them with the perverted symbolist aestheticism that veils and thus signifies Wilde's condemned homosexual body. Constructing his defense by prosecuting modes of reading, Billing invokes a play of allusion and correspondences which ultimately relies upon and references Wilde's established perversion. Wilde's "corpus" thus functions as the legibly deviant body that anchors and underscores the illegibility of the lesbian accusation.[51]

The Topsy Turvey Language of a Homosexualist

Dr. Serrell Cooke, who defined the interpretive communities capable of understanding the term clitoris, was Billing's most important expert witness. Although a specialist in tuberculosis, Cooke claimed to be an expert in matters of sexual psychology because he had studied Ricard von Krafft-Ebing's *Psychopathia Sexualis* (1886). Supposedly, after he attended the hearings at Bow Street, he read *Salomé*, "consulted several well-known London doctors about the play," and prepared "a detailed medical synopsis of the play, explaining what it was really all about" (SLV, 149). Under Billing's questioning, Cooke offered an extraordinary sexual-linguistic diagnosis that (con)fused the symbolic weight of Wilde with the alleged plot of German queer invasion. He told the court that Grein's testimony exhibited a "rather extraordinary" use of language. "Things which were physical, material, he described as spiritual, poetic, beautiful," Cooke explained, noting that such language "is usually employed by homosexualists" (VR, 248, 249):

> Billing: Is it customary for sex perverts to describe as beautiful and glorious all their perversions? . . . And is it customary for them to read into the distinctly physical acts of sex something spiritual?
> Cooke: Spiritual, poetic, beautiful, pure love; those are their expressions. . . . It is done because they cannot help themselves. I think it is part of their mental condition.[52]

In addition to undermining Grein, Cooke's testimony also reflects back on Allan's cross-examination, as it diagnoses any symbolic mode of reading as "customary for sex perverts."[53]

MODERNISM /*modernity*

40   This perverse mode of interpretation can be appropriated or mimicked, regardless of
the speaker's sexual activity. Much like the instructive glossary in the German black
book, the patois can be learned and deployed. Under cross-examination, Cooke evades
accusing Grein of homosexual *acts* (and thus evades libeling Grein) by making both an
association and a distinction between modes of reading and sexual practices. When
Cooke explains that he considers Grein's language "the language of a sodomist," "Because he describes the sadistic acts [in *Salomé*] . . . as something beautiful, spiritual,
poetic," Williams cautions him, "Do you realise that to bring an accusation against a
man of being a sodomist is the most terrible thing to be said against a man?" Cooke
clarifies:

> Cooke: I have not brought such accusation against any man. . . . It is a curious matter of
> psychology that a man should use such language in the description of this play.
> Williams: Do not you think you left the Jury and the Court under the impression that you
> were intending to convey that the man who used the language of a sodomist used it
> because he was one?
> Cooke: No, I did not intend to leave any such impression on the Jury. [*VR*, 263–5]

Cooke relies upon an analogy that discredits Grein while protecting himself: Grein
reads Wilde "like" a homosexual (because he reads Wilde, likes Wilde, and reads like
Wilde) but this homosexual parlance does not mean Grein *is* a homosexual. The particular claim that to read like a homosexual means to read inversely—physical as spiritual, vice as beauty—insists on a hermeneutics of homosexual contrariness that requires a straight interpreter who could re-invert the claims of homosexual speech in
order to translate them into "ordinary" speech. This logic also assumes a foundational
"ordinary language" of direct reference, in contradistinction to the symbolist mode
where interpretations proliferate but are never resolved. Billing and Cooke's game of
inverse signification easily aligns "speaking like a homosexualist" with both the propagandist portrayal of Germany as a morally inverted culture, and the general panic over
the secret codes of foreign agents.

     This construction of Wilde's inverted language is clinched when the "original" trans-
lator of his play, Lord Alfred Douglas, takes the stand as witness for the defense. He
represents himself as straddling the space between ordinary and extraordinary reading, in the dual position of expert and ex-pervert. He insists that he was "entirely under Wilde's influence" during the writing of *Salomé*, but now recognizes him to be
"the greatest force for evil that has appeared in Europe during the last 350 years" (*VR*,
291, 287). Claiming that, "I translated the play from the French, and I had many
conversations with Wilde about it, and I have a very particular knowledge of what he
meant by the play," he contends that Wilde

> intended the play to be an exhibition of perverted sexual passion excited in a young girl. . . .
> [T]here is one passage which is sodomitic. . . . Wilde was a man who cloaked up those
> things in flowery language. He never used the word "sodomitic." He would express hor-
> ror at such language. Anything like the "Cult of the Clitoris" would fill him with as much

horror as it apparently does Mr. Hume Williams. . . . [Who] share[s] the horror of coarse 41
and vulgar expressions, calling things by their right names. [*VR*, 286]

Here, calling "things" what they *are not*, and an aversion to calling things what they *are*, indicate an inverted sense of sexual morality and a shameful guilt. Douglas's strategy, which privileges "right names," even casts suspicion upon Williams's earlier performance of his offense and disgust at the paragraph title.

With all symbolic modes of reading coded as perverted, Billing and Douglas morally denounce the play's metaphorics, particularly the dialogue's symbolic investment in the moon:

> Billing: In your opinion has Oscar Wilde used the moon as a canvas on which to paint pictures which were almost too revolting to do in any other way?
> Douglas: Yes to paint the situation of the play as it proceeded.
> Judge: . . . Did he use the moon in this version as a canvas on which to paint indecent and abominable pictures?
> Douglas: Yes, he did. Oh, yes.
> Billing: Would he have considered that the most artistic way of doing it? . . . The most intellectual?
> Douglas: To him all that sort of thing, whenever he was going to do anything particularly horrible, it was always disguised in the most flowery language, and always referred back to Art. That was his idea of Art. [*VR*, 292]

When asked about Salomé's desire for Iokanaan, Douglas translates and explicates Wilde's mode of perverse representation:

> Billing: Did Wilde mean [Salomé's desire to touch Iokanaan's body] to be physical or spiritual?
> Douglas: Physical. If anyone calls it spiritual it is a pure misuse of words and making the English language ridiculous.
> Billing: Would you call that language the language of a sodomite?
> Douglas: I think [Wilde] was referring to the language used by people who described it as spiritual. . . . [T]hose sort of people always refer to revolting things under pretty names. They try to disguise the horribleness of the action by giving it such names; they say beautiful, classic, and so on. They will not speak of it by the outspoken English name; they disguise it.
> Billing: Have these people a common patois?
> Douglas: Yes, they have a jargon. I have not had anything to do with them for twenty years. [*VR*, 294]

The lapse of twenty years and Douglas's conversion to Catholicism, conservatism, and homophobia distance him from "those sort of people" and secure his reliability, while positioning him as a privileged interpreter. "Translating" Wilde's perverse slippage between the physical and spiritual world, Douglas arrives at a hermeneutics of absolute inversion:

MODERNISM /*modernity*

Billing: Did Wilde . . . ever give you an idea, when you were doing your translation, that it was anything other than a physical expression of unnatural practices? . . . [D]id he give you to understand that it was a poem dealing with the spiritual love of a young girl finding salvation in the spirit of the Prophet, or a young girl seeking lustfully the body of the Prophet?

Douglas: The point is that that is exactly how he would describe it. He probably did call it spiritual. That was part of the jargon.

Billing: Do you call it spiritual?

Douglas: No. Wilde would call it spiritual; he would say it was a study in the curious passions of the human soul. That was the sort of euphemism he would use. He never used plain coarse words at all. He was always revolted by coarseness of expression.

Judge: He would call spiritual what you call sadism?

Douglas: Yes. With those sort of people evil is their good; everything is topsy turvy; physical is spiritual; spiritual is physical, and so on; it is a perversion, an inversion, of everything. Wilde was a man who made evil his good all through his life. That was the gospel he preached. [VR, 294–5]

With Dr. Cooke's and Douglas's testimonies Billing composes a strategy of inverse translation for reading Wilde, *Salomé*, Grein, Allan, and "those sort of people." Douglas's repeated use of the terms "disguise" and "cloaking up" again figures Wilde's language and reading as covering over the body upon which his sexual guilt is inscribed, and it tropes upon the enemy spy who lurks beneath the disguise of assimilation. Wilde's mode of reading for correspondences marks him as trading in a suspicious economy of counterfeit signifiers, an inverted code of meaning that must be decoded and exposed for its dangerous content. Billing's primary strategy throughout the trial was to queer and discredit Allan's, Grein's, and Wilde's hermeneutic practices; suitably, he finally secured his "innocence" by insisting that Allan's indictment had *misread* his paragraph. Indeed, the ambiguity of the indictment enabled Billing, during the prosecution's concluding argument, to deny that he had ever actually claimed Allan was a lesbian. Throughout the six days of the trial, he allowed the prosecution to educate the audience on lesbians and their clitorises, thus heightening the scandalous effect. However his final disavowal of any lesbian intent renders him innocent of leveling an unforgivable libel against a woman, while maintaining a distinctly queer moral insinuation against Allan and *Salomé*. Having staged a seductive scene of reading that excites the most elaborate lesbian fantasies, Billing can then reassert his authority and officially refuse any lesbian reference. This disavowal, I would propose, actually consolidates and expands the lesbian threat; its banishment from referentiality only confirms its potential ubiquity. Without referential stability, it flourishes in the imagination. The innominate lesbian is the figure of greatest threat precisely because she is "only" what is "read into" the phrase "The Cult of the Clitoris." The symbolist function of "The Cult of the Clitoris" I suggested earlier now requires reassessment to account for Billing's belated disavowal in court. The performative absenting of lesbian reference endows lesbianism with an even more powerful symbolic function through its very referential negation. That is, the erasure of lesbianism from the court record and "The Cult of the Clitoris" achieves a more profound symbolist effect. The symbolic mode is redoubled, so that the *absence* of lesbian reference acts as a figure for revealing a (national) mood or "état d'âme" and becomes a *de*materialized substitute for the intangible, floating, "minute, intricate, almost invisible" life of British anxieties in wartime.

The trial, Wilde's play, and Allan's performance then come to metaphorize, or translate, the crisis of the war into a scene of literary and sexual fantasy. Decadent style represents seditious codes in contrast to the "outspoken English" of the nation; Allan's hypnotic allure is configured as the most insidious form of traitorous influence; sexual betrayal is mapped onto national betrayal; and the violent dismemberment of male bodies at the front lines is reconstituted as the anatomization of female sexual deviancy. The press reports of Billing's acquittal also yoke together the disorder in the court and the high emotions of wartime.[54] The *Daily Mail* reports that when the "not Guilty" verdict was uttered

> the gallery, packed with the public rose, shouting and 'hooraying.' . . . There has never been such an excited throng in the new Central Criminal Court, or one which gave vent to its feelings more vociferously. In vain did the judge try to give an order to suppress the demonstration. His lips were seen moving, but his words stood no chance of being heard.[55]

The voice of the law is literally struck dumb by the force of the crowd, and as the court empties, "Outside a distant murmur of voices and a faint cheer; inside a last hysterical giggle as a woman went and a parting 'Hooray,' deep-toned, from a soldier in hospital blue"—a scene that conjoins feminized hysteria with national service (ibid.).

Newspaper editorials suggested that the trial functioned as a phantasmatic substitute for the war, and even identified it as a manifestation of mass hysteria. The *Times* wrote, "It is safe to say that no lawsuit of modern times has attracted such universal and painful interest as the deplorable libel action which terminated yesterday at the Central Criminal Court"; across England "the daily reports have been read and discussed with almost as deep anxiety as the news of the war itself."[56] The *New Statesman* lamented, "A great battle is raging; armies are bleeding and dying; Paris is at stake; and for a week the interest of the British public has been almost entirely centred upon a trial for criminal libel."[57] According to the *Manchester Guardian*, "Even in the preoccupations of war-time the Pemberton Billing trial is an arresting London event." The reporter specifically diagnosed the public response to the trial as "the most extraordinary expression we have had of war psychology and the feverish distortion of normal beliefs," and the *New Age* considered the trial a demonstration of the "mob-mind."[58] In a letter to the editor of the *Times*, a Labour M. P. insisted that Billing's paranoid conspiracy undermined the psychic health of the nation:

> By far the most serious aspect of the case is the effect upon the great mass of our people, whose minds and thoughts at this moment are concerned with the fate of their loved ones at the front. . . . Reckless assertions . . . entirely unsupported by evidence, and defaming men and women alive and dead, may well have a disturbing effect upon a public opinion already racked with anxiety and tense with emotion.[59]

44   Such a complaint attests to the cultural work performed by the trial. With "loved ones" at the front engaged in a war that defied representation, those at home witnessed a sexualized scene of strife upon which they could displace anxiety and emotion, and the lesbian suggestion afforded a particularly effective conduit for mediating this fantasy. Consequently, even though a lesbian insinuation started the trial, as newspaper commentators noted, "any issue was on trial at most times except the one which was legally at stake."[60] The trial was clearly not *about* female homosexuality; however, lesbianism's combination of *un*representability and potent suggestibility offered a sensationally effective and exquisitely elusive means of figuring Britain's political and epistemological crises of modern history.

Notes

Maud Allan has been a research passion of mine for longer than I'd like to admit. At last I can extend my sincerest thanks and appreciation to a number of people whose suggestions have helped my research, thinking, and writing on this project: Michelle Elleray, Geoffrey Gilbert, Ellis Hanson, Molly Hite, Barbara Leckie, Antonia Losano, Biddy Martin, Natalie Melas, Petra Rau, Lyndsey Stonebridge, Pamela Thurschwell, and Percy Walton. I am particularly grateful to Gabrielle McIntire and Brian Greenspan, whose timely and generous interventions at a critical stage made all the difference.

1. *Complete Works of Oscar Wilde* (Glasgow: Harper Collins, 1994), 451.

2. "The Old Bailey Shocker," *New Statesman*, 8 June 1918, 183.

3. On the composition, banned production, illustration, and publication of *Salomé*, see Richard Ellmann, *Oscar Wilde* (Middlesex: Penguin, 1989), 350–5.

4. Felix Cherniavsky, *The Salome Dancer* (Toronto: McClellend & Steward, 1991), 176; hereafter abbreviated SD.

5. *The Vigilante*, 16 February 1918, reprinted in Noel Pemberton Billing, ed. *Verbatim Report of the Trial of Noel Pemberton Billing, M. P. On a charge of Criminal Libel Before Mr. Justice Darling at the Central Criminal Court, Old Bailey. With report of the preliminary proceedings at Bow Street Police Court, an Appendix of Documents referred to in the Case, Reference index, &c.* (London: Vigilante Office, 1918), 455; hereafter abbreviated VR.

6. Billing did not actually write the paragraph; however, he did take responsibility for it. The novelist Marie Corelli had sent the *Times* advertisement of the play to the *Vigilante* office, with the suggestion that one might find in attendance the members of the 47,000. Captain Harold Spencer, working for Billing at the time, read Corelli's letter and devised the short paragraph just before the newspaper went to press. See Michael Kettle, *Salome's Last Veil: The Libel Case of the Century* (London: Granada Publishing, 1977), 17–8; hereafter abbreviated SLV. Throughout my paper, I will refer to Billing as the author of the libel, as he took full responsibility for it, and had already planted the plot of the 47,000.

7. Wilde's trials actually followed several well publicized trials and scandals regarding male homosexuality that occurred in late-nineteenth-century Britain. See Jeffery Weeks, *Coming Out: Homosexual Politics in Britain, from the Nineteenth Century to the Present* (London: Quartet Books, 1977), 13–21.

8. Weeks mentions the trial in *Coming Out*, 105–6, and H. Montgomery Hyde narrates the trial in *The Other Love: An Historical and Contemporary Survey of Homosexuality in Britain* (London: Heinemann, 1970), 171–6. More recently, Jennifer Travis, Lucy Bland, and Laura Doan have published work on the trial with a specific interest in the legal construction of lesbianism.

9. Hoare's reference to the social representation of the war as an imagined "disinfectant" that would clean up the decline of morals associated with social and artistic decadence reproduces Samuel Hynes's argument that "What the war did was to make the condition of England a social disease for which war was the cure." Samuel Hynes, *A War Imagined: The First World War and English Culture* (New York: Atheneum, 1991), 13.

10. Lord Darling, the judge in the criminal case, directly requested that the press refrain from **45** reporting the "disagreeable details" of the case and emphatically warned that "there is no protection for the publication of indecent matter in any newspaper. . . . [I]f it is indecent there is no protection simply by reason of the fact that it is a report of what is going on in the Court of law" (*VR*, 57–8). The *Manchester Guardian* even printed this warning from the judge, foregrounding, like many other newspapers, the unnamable obscenity of the case. See "Mr Pemberton Billing and Miss Maud Allan," *Manchester Guardian*, 30 May 1918. On the operations of the "open secret," see D. A. Miller's "Secret Subjects, Open Secrets," in *The Novel and the Police* (Berkeley: University of California Press, 1988); Eve Sedgwick's "Epistemology of the Closet," in *Epistemology of the Closet* (Berkeley: University of California Press, 1990); and Michel Foucault's "The Repressive Hypothesis," in *The History of Sexuality*, vol. 1, trans. Robert Hurley (New York: Vintage, 1978).

11. See Jennifer Travis, "Clits in Court: *Salomé*, Sodomy, and the Lesbian 'Sadist,'" in *Lesbian Erotics*, ed. Karla Jay (New York: New York University Press, 1995) and Lucy Bland, "Trial by Sexology?: Maud Allan, Salome, and the 'Cult of the Clitoris' Case" in *Sexology in Culture*, ed. Lucy Bland and Laura Doan (Chicago: University of Chicago Press, 1998). In *Fashioning Sapphism*, (New York: Columbia University Press, 2001), Laura Doan also refers to the trial to frame her discussion of "the visibility of lesbianism in English legal discourse and in the public arena" (32). Notably, none of these analyses use the original trial documents. Their reliance upon Kettle's selective reproductions of passages from the case limits their readings and leads to inaccurate claims about the trial proceedings.

12. See both Samuel Hynes's *A War Imagined* and Paul Fussell's *The Great War and Modern Memory* (London: Oxford University Press, 1975) on how the war impacted on the modern imagination. See also Jay Winter's *Sites of Memory, Sites of Mourning: The Great War in European Cultural History* (New York: Cambridge University Press, 1995) for a nuanced argument that dissents from the notion of the war as a "radical break" and insists on the continuities of tradition in the representation and memorializing of the war. Notably, even though Winter strongly protests the yoking of "modernism" (revolutionary aesthetic practices) and World War I, he calls upon a relatively caricatured notion of modernism as a radical break with the past that wholly disregards traditional forms of representation. My argument attempts to strike a dialogue between the war's simultaneous reliance and innovation upon established historical forms.

13. Suzanne Raitt and Trudi Tate, introduction to *Women's Fiction and the Great War* (Oxford: Clarendon Press, 1997), 1.

14. Phillip Knightley, *The First Casualty: The War Correspondent as Hero, Propagandist, and Myth Maker* (New York: Harcourt Brace Jovanovich, 1975), 109.

15. Knightley points out that censorship of the press was imposed at the outbreak of war, and when war correspondents were allowed at the front, they were strictly regulated so their reports would corroborate the propaganda effort. Appropriately, perhaps, Lord Northcliffe, proprietor of the *Times* and the *Daily Mail*, was also the director of propaganda in enemy countries (Knightley, 82). On the deliberate invention and circulation of lies, false war stories, rumors, and the concealment of actual events, see also Arthur Ponsonby, *Falsehood in Wartime: Containing an Assortment of Lies Circulated Throughout the Nations During the Great War* (London: George Allen and Unwin, 1928). See also Trudi Tate's "Propaganda Lies," in *Modernism, History, and the First World War* (Manchester: Manchester University Press, 1998).

16. Jacqueline Rose, *Why War?* (Oxford: Blackwell, 1993), 21.

17. Ibid., 17.

18. On suffrage, the ideologies of the separate spheres, and the "public woman," see Susan Kingsley Kent, *Sex and Suffrage in Britain, 1860–1914* (Princeton, N.J.: Princeton University Press, 1987), 200.

19. William Cohen argues that male homosexuality, the "unspeakable" crime and most covert of sexual practices during the late Victorian period, is the appropriate locus for an analysis of scandal, while female homosexuality is simply beyond imagination: "While the willful effort to deny female sexuality resulted in celebrated adultery, divorce, and illegitimacy cases, ironically it largely precluded lesbian scandals, which were less unspeakable than unthinkable." William Cohen, *Sex Scandal: The Private Parts of Victorian Fiction* (Durham, N.C.: Duke University Press, 1996), 6.

20. Indeed, most major critical engagements with *Salomé* in the last twenty years have been concerned with her sexual queerness. The most emphatic proponents of reading Salomé as a (gay) man

MODERNISM /*modernity*

46   trapped under transvestic veils are: Gail Finney, *Women in Modern Drama: Freud, Feminism, and the European Theater at the Turn of the Century* (Ithaca, N.Y.: Cornell University Press, 1989); Richard Dellamora, "Traversing the Feminine in Oscar Wilde's *Salomé*," in *Victorian Sages and Cultural Discourse: Renegotiating Gender and Power*, ed. Thais Morgan (New Brunswick, N.J.: Rutgers University Press 1990); Elaine Showalter, *Sexual Anarchy: Gender and Culture at the Fin de Siècle* (London: Bloomsbury, 1991); and Marjorie Garber, *Vested Interests: Cross-Dressing and Cultural Anarchy* (New York: Routledge, 1992).

21. Charles Chadwick, *Symbolism* (London: Methuen, 1971), 1.

22. Ibid, 3.

23. Arthur Symons, *The Symbolist Movement in Literature* (London: Heinemann, 1899), 146.

24. Notably, although *Salomé* clearly pays homage to symbolist drama, the play also self-consciously ironizes the symbolist compulsion in the very moment of enacting it. Thus, Herodias staunchly, even comically, refuses to play the symbolist game of lunar similes with the rebuff, "The moon is like the moon. That is all." Herod likewise ultimately realizes that "It is not wise to find symbols in everything that one sees. It makes life too full of terrors." *Salomé*, in *The Portable Oscar Wilde*, ed. Richard Aldington and Stanley Wientraub (New York: Penguin, 1981), 407, 419. In this sense, as much as the drama exploits the symbolist compulsion, it also foregrounds its maddening potential and keeps an ironic distance from the very paranoid associative chains of meaning that Billing forges in 1918.

25. Jean Laplanche and J.-B. Pontalis, *The Language of Psychoanalysis*, trans. Donald Nicholson-Smith (New York: W. W. Norton, 1973), 42.

26. For analyses of Wilde's trial, see Ed Cohen, *Talk on the Wilde Side: Toward a Genealogy of a Discourse on Male Sexualities* (New York: Routledge, 1993); Regenia Gagnier, *Idylls of the Marketplace: Oscar Wilde and the Victorian Public* (Stanford, Calif.: Stanford University Press, 1986); and Michael Foldy, *The Trials of Oscar Wilde: Deviancy, Morality, and Late-Victorian Society* (New Haven, Conn.: Yale University Press, 1997).

27. In the spring of 1913 Douglas charged Ransome with libel for his literary biography of Wilde, which referred to the expurgated sections of *De Profundis* and largely blamed Douglas, without naming him, for Wilde's suffering. See Ransome, *Oscar Wilde: A Critical Study* (New York: Mitchell Kennerley, 1913). Douglas lost the case when the jury decided that the words complained of did constitute a libel, but were true. Notably, Justice Darling was the judge presiding over the case, the same judge who presided over Billing's case.

28. In fact, "The Cult of the Clitoris" not only gestures to the "cult" of Wilde (and the Dandy as the "cult of the self"), but also to the cult of Sappho practiced by the all-women salons of Natalie Barney and Renée Vivien or represented in Pierre Louÿs's *Songs of Bilitis*. The phrase suggestively overlaps the decadent Sappho-revival of Baudelaire, Louÿs, Vivien, Barney, and Swinburne with the political reaction to the successes of the feminist movement. On the sapphic revival in Paris, see Shari Benstock, *Women of the Left Bank: Paris, 1900–1940* (Austin: University of Texas Press, 1986) and Catherine Van Casselaer, *Lot's Wife: Lesbian Paris, 1890–1914* (Liverpool: Janus Press, 1986).

29. While the journal *Academy* published an enthusiastic review of her debut in March 1908, less than two months later it published another review that questioned Allan's legitimacy and dismissed her fame as the effect of crass self-promotion. J. C. F., "Miss Maud Allan's Salome Dance," *Academy*, 21 March 1908, 598–9; Christopher St. John, "All We Like Sheep," *Academy*, 2 May 1908, 736.

30. "The New Dancer," *Times Literary Supplement*, 26 March 1908, 102. By 1918 German composers had been wiped off of British concert programs, and the war against Strauss was particularly violent. See Hynes, *A War Imagined*, 75.

31. Mata Hari fabricated an identity as a Javanese dancer, claiming to give authentic expression to Javanese and Indian sacred dances, which she performed in little or no clothes. Capitalizing on the same Salomania as Allan, Mata Hari performed her own "Dance of the Seven Veils," was constantly compared to Salome, and urged her agent to ask Strauss to produce a *Salomé* performance for her. Julie Wheelwright, *The Fatal Lover: Mata Hari and the Myth of Women in Espionage* (London: Collins and Brown, 1992), 17.

32. Mata Hari was immediately mythologized and her story exploited by war propagandists. An example of this is Henry de Halsalle's, *The Life Story of Madame Zelle, The World's Most Beautiful*

MEDD / *"the cult of the clitoris"*

Spy (London: Skeffington and Sons, 1917), a sensational, fictionalized account of Mata Hari's life as a **47** German agent.

33. The First Sea Lord, Prince Louis Battenberg, whose father had been a German prince; Lord Haldane, whose German education and diplomatic ties made him a target of public hostility; and the vice-consul in Rotterdam, A. G. Holzapfel, who was British-born with an unfortunate appellation, were all forced to resign because of popular anti-alien sentiment. See John Terraine, *The Impacts of War 1914 and 1918* (London: Hutchinson, 1970). See also David French, "Spy Fever in Britain, 1900–1915," *The Historical Journal* 21.2 (1978): 355–70, for a discussion of the prewar and wartime history of popular sentiment and official legislation regarding "aliens" and spies.

34. Trevor Wilson speculates that the public, unable to dispense with its political and military leaders at this time, displaced its anxiety onto a renewed campaign against enemy aliens in Britain. Terraine concurs, diagnosing a vehement hatred and righteous indignation against the Germans as a desperate civilian attempt to combat the "flagging of the spirit as the war dragged on," and which found its most explosive expression in anti-alien activity. Terraine, *Impacts of War*, 177.

35. Qtd. in *SLV*, 15. The purse refers to money raised in support of Robert Ross while he was undergoing his legal battles with Douglas.

36. Qtd. in Philip Hoare, *Oscar Wilde's Last Stand: Decadence, Conspiracy, and the Most Outrageous Trial of the Century* (New York: Arcarde, 1998), 22. Douglas's representation of homosexuality as national sedition resonates with Allied anti-German propaganda that connected homosexuality and German moral degeneracy. Propagandist works published during the war such as Henry de Halsalle's *Degenerate Germany* (London: T. Werner Laurie, 1917) and de Halsalle and C. Sheridan Jones's *The German Woman and Her Master* (London: T. Werner Laurie, 1916) expressly aligned sexual perversity in Germany with the country's moral degeneracy, citing in particular "the unspeakable Eulenburg affair," in which a group of "advisers and confidants of the Emperor" were exposed as indulging in *le vice allemand* (155–6).

37. Allan's position as an actress actually feeds into the lesbian suggestion. Havelock Ellis includes the theatre along with girls' schools, prisons, and "lunatic asylums" as the breeding ground for female homosexuality. Havelock Ellis and John Addington Symonds, *Sexual Inversion* (1897; New Hampshire: Ayer Company, 1994), 83–4.

38. Cohen makes this point in "Typing Wilde," in *Talk on the Wilde Side*.

39. What might be the significance that lesbianism is "nameless" and not "unnamable," the common nominal refusal of sodomy? This is not the love that dare not speak its name, but a love that *has no name* or does not know what name to speak.

40. Here we encounter what Stuart Hall et al would characterize as a signification spiral; that is:

> a way of signifying events which also intrinsically escalates their threat. . . . The signification spiral is a self-amplifying sequence within the area of signification: the activity or event with which the signification deals is escalated—made to seem more threatening—within the course of the signification itself.

Stuart Hall, Chas Critcher, Tony Jefferson, John Clarke, and Brian Roberts, *Policing the Crisis: Mugging, the State, and Law and Order* (London: MacMillan Press, 1978), 223.

41. Here is the full passage of Williams's instructive interpretation:

> [Y]ou cannot appreciate the gravity of the charge against this lady unless you appreciate what the real meaning is of this horrible phrase. . . . [T]he fact is that this particular part of the female organization is open to treatment, let us say, other than by normal means which nature intended. And, hence, there has come into this wicked world undoubtedly a practice. . . .— recognised as a vice which is supposed to have originated in the Island of Lesbos where there were women and no men—a vice by which the clitoris can be excited (*six words omitted*) and ways other than those which nature intended. And there do exist in the world vicious practices where men are able to gratify their passions with men, and women with women—degrading, repulsive, contrary to nature, and consequently destructive of health—practices which, indulged in to any extent, sap and undermine the sanity and probity and self-respect . . . of those who indulge in them. [*VR*, 58]

M O D E R N I S M / *m o d e r n i t y*

48   The notion of the clitoris as extraneous will not only be elaborated by Freud, but has a history stretching back to the middle ages. On the discursive history of the clitoris, see Valerie Traub, "The Psychomorphology of the Clitoris," *Gay and Lesbian Quarterly* 2 (1995): 81–113 and Thomas W. Laqueur, "Amor Veneris, vel Dulcedo Appeletur" in *Fragments for a History of the Human Body, Part Three,* ed. Romona Naddaff and Nadia Tazi (New York: Zone, 1989), 90–131.

42 Notably, the *Verbatim Report* makes a point of omitting the "sixty-one words" in which "The learned counsel explained in a very clear manner the precise situation and function of the clitoris" and also "six words" in which he explains how the clitoris can be excited (57, 58). It seems worthwhile to note that Marie Stopes's *Married Love* was first published at the end of March 1918, reviews of which can be sometimes found alongside editorials about the Billing trial. An accessible and immmensely popular book for the lay public on sexuality, it proposed the ground-breaking argument that sexual knowledge, education, and instruction were all necessary for a healthy marriage. Stopes explicitly and simply explained the importance of the clitoris for female pleasure and argued vehemently for the benefits of female sexual satisfaction (beyond reproduction). The trial, then, is poised at, and contributes to, a revolutionary moment in the knowledge of female body parts and configurations of female sexuality.

43. My thanks to Ellis Hanson for calling my attention to this tautology.

44. Joanna Bourke, *Dismembering the Male: Men's Bodies, Britain, and the Great War* (Chicago: University of Chicago Press, 1996), 34.

45. Ibid., 37–8.

46. Tate, *Modernism, History,* 97–9, 117–8.

47. Billing's defense at the police trial had been that his libel could not have posed a threat to public order, as only the "initiated" or medical experts would understand the meaning of the phrase. Either the understanding reader would already be corrupted, or would be a medical expert, and thus incorruptible (*SLV*, 20).

48. *VR*, 84–5. Jennifer Travis similarly points out how Billing tried to use Allan's knowledge of terms as "sadism" to prove her sexual immorality. See "Clits in Court."

49. One of Allan's repeated tactics for deflecting a sexual reading is an appeal to orientalism, so that Wilde's curious phrases, such as "gilded tigers," are shifted from the language of sexuality to the language of the East; it is the authenticity of Wilde's orientalizing play that accounts for its indecipherability and which an ignorant reader might misconstrue as sexual. Allan thus attempts to intervene another "expert" position, one of cultural and artistic knowledge, to cleanse the play of inherent sexual transgression and consign Billing's reading to prurient scandal-mongering.

50. Letter to Cecil Sprigge; qtd. in Hoare, *Oscar Wilde's Last Stand,* 137.

51. My thanks to Natalie Melas for pointing out this relationship.

52. *VR*, 249. Hoare briefly cites some of this exchange and claims,

> The exchange between Billing and Cooke rehashed all the old shibboleths of the Wildean era; only now, prejudice masqueraded as pseudo-medical 'evidence.' It was the barely cloaked philistinism of an age whose cultural horizons were foreshortened by war and desperate blind patriotism. In 1918—nearly two decades into the twentieth century and the modern era— these words were a direct reversion to Victorian values and hypocrisy. [Hoare, *Oscar Wilde's Last Stand,* 145]

I am arguing that we cannot dismiss such exchanges, as blatantly outrageous as they appear now, as simply philistinism. The concern with modes of reading seems a crucial context for the trial's ability to connect issues of artistic practices, national security, sexual practices, and moral codes.

53. Cooke's exchange with Billing regarding sex perverts who "describe as beautiful and glorious all their perversions," particularly when in a courtroom, seems to be referencing Wilde's elegant account of "The Love that dare not speak its name" in his own criminal proceedings. For Wilde's speech, see H. Montgomery Hyde's *The Trials of Oscar Wilde* (New York: Dover Publications, 1962), 256.

54. That the unimaginable experiences of war at the front found an analogue in Billing's trial is graphically suggested by the press's juxtaposition of photographs and reports of the trial alongside maps of the battles at the front. See for example, the *Daily Mail,* 1 June 1918, where a photo of witnesses "who have given remarkable evidence in the Billing trial" is positioned directly under a map

MEDD / *"the cult of the clitoris"*

of the front and the photo headline "Huns Gain in France and Flanders." The *Times'* report of the trial on 3 June, "Mr. Billing's Trial," frames a map of "Great Battles Between the Oise and the Marne," while the *Manchester Guardian's* report of the "Frantic Demonstrations" at Billing's acquittal borders a map of the front lines. The *Daily Mail's* photo of the crowd cheering Billing's acquittal appears directly beside a photo of "The War Council of Versailles," with a photo headline that links the two: "Billing Trial—After the Acquittal. Versailles Council."

49

55. "The Billing Trial," *Daily Mail,* 5 June 1918, 3.

56. "A Scandalous Trial," *Times,* 5 June 1918, 7.

57. "The Old Bailey Shocker," *New Statesman,* 8 June 1918, 183.

58. "Study in War Psychology," *Manchester Guardian,* 5 June 1918, 4; untitled editorial, *New Age* 23.7 (13 June 1918): 99.

59. J. H. Thomas, "Common Sense and the Billing Trial: To the Editor of the *Times*," *Times,* 5 June 1918, 7.

60. "A Scandalous Trial," *Times,* 5 June 1918, 7.

Part II
Locating Sexual Identity in Law

The State

[7]

POLICING THE STATE

ANNJANETTE ROSGA, PH.D.*

> It is a widespread but fatal trap—precisely, a trap of 'liberal opin-
> ion'—to split analysis from action, and to assign the first to the
> instance of the 'long term,' which never comes, and reserve only the
> second to 'what is practical and realistic in the short term.'... Oscar
> Wilde once said that it is an outrage for reformers to spend time asking
> what can be done to ease the lot of the poor, or to make the poor bear
> their conditions with greater dignity, when the only remedy is to abolish
> the condition of poverty itself.... So if someone says to us: 'Yes, but
> given the present conditions, what are we to do now?' we can only
> reply, 'Do something about the "present conditions." '
>
> Stuart Hall[1]

INTRODUCTION

What are the "present conditions" that bring us here, to a symposium on hate crime and state accountability? Those of us who are concerned with the problem of hate crime are seeking to explore two interrelated questions. The first is one of articulation: how are we to describe the relationship between state power and violence in the United States? That is, how much responsibility, if any, should the state bear for the violent actions of non-state actors? The second question is one of strategy: *how*, rather than *whether*, to hold the state accountable.

Before we can address these questions, however, we must examine several assumptions upon which they rest. First is the belief that the state is responsible for maintaining the conditions that make hate crime and domestic violence available as forms of violent expression. If this is true, then the state must likewise be responsible for the elimination of those conditions. As a result of this assumption, the more expansive first question—how to articulate the relationship between the state and violence by non-state actors—is answered only indirectly. Rather than having its tendrils teased apart and carefully examined, the relationship of the state to hate crime and domestic violence is taken for granted. The second assumption is that it makes strategic or epistemological sense to separate the state's responsibilities with regard to hate crime from its responsibilities for

* AnnJanette Rosga holds a doctorate in the History of Consciousness from the University of California, Santa Cruz. She is currently an assistant professor of Sociology and Anthropology at Knox College in Galesburg, Illinois. She thanks Diane Chin and Alice Miller for conversations important to the development of arguments presented here, and to Tom Kuczajda and the other editors of *The Georgetown Journal of Gender and the Law* for assistance with revisions. Rosga also extends her gratitude to Meghan Faux, Melissa Goldberg, and others responsible for the First Annual Gender, Sexuality, and the Law Symposium; as well as to the University of Minnesota's Center for Advanced Feminist Studies for a "Visiting Scholar" fellowship which supported the writing of this essay during the summer of 1998.

1. STUART HALL, ET AL., POLICING THE CRISIS: MUGGING, THE STATE, AND LAW AND ORDER ix-x (1978).

other kinds of violence, such as child abuse, gang-related homicides, widespread homelessness, vigilante "justice," the massive expansion of prisons, and the vastly disproportionate rate of imprisonment for young men of color. The third assumption underlying these questions is that there is substantive agreement on what "the state" is, and that conceiving of it as an entity separate from "us" is useful and appropriate. I think that most of my fellow participants agree either with the observation that such assumptions do exist, or with the suggestion that each assumption may itself be worthy of scrutiny. Nevertheless, for the most part, the validity of these assumptions has escaped sustained discussion.

I do not claim to have made an exhaustive analysis of these assumptions, or to have found a satisfactory means of addressing hate crime. However, I do suggest that the reluctance to examine these assumptions, to broaden and multiply our *levels* of action and analysis, is itself a manifestation of our present conditions. In my view, we are at an historical moment in which the increased use of state power and the legal reification of identity are more likely than not to have detrimental effects over the long term. For the purposes of this essay, I will forego speculation about the forces that have produced this moment. Rather, I will offer some anecdotes from my own research, which focuses on the concrete effects of the institutionalization of hate crime, both in the law and in the popular lexicon of late twentieth century United States.[2] I will also discuss my fieldwork with law enforcement agencies in two east coast suburban counties. This research has led me to conclude that individuals both within and outside of law enforcement mobilize the term "hate crime" in indirect but powerful negotiations over police

---

2. For the past ten years I have analyzed hate crime from the perspective of an academic researcher, activist, and volunteer for anti-hate crime organizations. I have also served as an educator in several different public and law enforcement venues. Tension between the goals, languages, strategies, and identities of the positions of researcher, activist, and educator are unavoidable and palpable. In each case, I have been both participant and observer. This dual role has made me painfully aware that each realm can call into question the very foundations of another.

For instance, I have written about the epistemological assumptions necessary to the current concept of hate crime, including the assumption that identity categories are static and finite enough to be expressed as factors in a mathematical equation. *See, e.g.*, Adrien Katherine Wing, *Brief Reflections Toward a Multiplicative Theory and Praxis of Being, in* CRITICAL RACE FEMINISM: A READER 27-34 (Adrien Katherine Wing ed., 1997) (arguing that the traditional "additive" view of people's multiple identities does not adequately reflect their "multiplicative" nature). In turn this suggests that the categories used in identifying hate crime are significantly comparable (anti-immigrant = anti-gay = anti-Asian). In this sense, "hate crime" requires the assumption that individuals are neatly contained packages separable from their social environments. This makes the parameters of guilt for causing harm to another appear confinable to the individual perpetrators. It also presumes that "bigotry" or "hatred" is the underlying cause of hate crime. My point here is not so much to challenge these assumptions as to point out how opening them up to examination is often incompatible with current anti-hate crime initiatives.

Studying the epistemological assumptions underlying the term "hate crime" makes it difficult for me to recall the cogency of proposals that call for teaching police officers to correctly define the term "prejudice" on demand. (For instance, among the most basic curricular goals of the U.S. Department of Justice's law enforcement training program for the collection of hate crime data is a review of terms. "Prejudice" is one of these terms; the definition is drawn from GORDON ALLPORT, THE NATURE OF PREJUDICE 6-8 (1954). Allport's text is also cited as recommended reading for officer trainees. U.S. DEP'T OF JUSTICE, TRAINING GUIDE FOR HATE CRIME DATA COLLECTION (1991).

identity, and by extension, over state accountability.[3]

It is my hope that some critical reflection on the category hate crime as it works in practice will provide tools with which to open new, less well-rehearsed, conversations about the relationships between law, the state, identity, and violence. To that end, Part I of this essay describes three different phases of my early research that eventually drew my focus to the concept of hate crime in law enforcement contexts, and that led me to see the problems raised by framing hate crime as an issue to be addressed by criminal law.[4] In Part II, I offer three more accounts—this time drawn directly from my recent research with police—which illuminate some of the shortcomings in common sense constructions of the problem of state accountability.[5] Finally, Part III turns to an examination of tensions between feminist critique of the state and activist efforts to address hate crime.

I. HATE CRIMES AND LAW ENFORCEMENT

The materialization of hate crime as a concept has produced an unprecedented number of encounters between the police and groups with which the police have had fraught relationships. Such encounters require communication between

---

3. As part of my research, I spent two years doing ethnographic fieldwork with law enforcement agencies in two east coast suburban counties. I observed recruit training sessions on hate crime and multicultural sensitivity, accompanied officers when they gave presentations on hate crime, attended law enforcement conferences on bias-related violence, and conducted in-depth interviews with officers involved in hate crime investigations. Portions of the material presented here have been adapted from AnnJanette Rosga, Policing The State: Violence, Identity And The Law In Constructions of Hate Crime (1998) (unpublished Ph.D. dissertation, University of California (Santa Cruz)) (on file with author).

4. In the process of laying out these reflections, I have at times found it unwieldy to do without the misleadingly opposed terms "activists" (or "non-profit/advocates") and "police" (or "law enforcement" or "the state" more generally). In advance then, I want to register my increasing dissatisfaction with these terms. I think the dichotomy is more often obfuscating than useful. I worry that it is enabling us to make widely generalizing claims—about police, about activists, and about policy—that may hinder the development of effective policies. Furthermore, dividing those who desire to find ways of using state power from those who reject state-centered strategies serves to defer crucial discussions about how to define effective and just law enforcement.

5. The extent to which it even makes sense to talk about "the state" in a world in which national and political boundaries are increasingly permeable has been critically reviewed by many. For a good sampling of this work, see the articles collected in POLITICAL THEORY TODAY (David Held ed., 1991) [hereinafter POLITICAL THEORY TODAY] and CULTURE, GLOBALIZATION AND THE WORLD-SYSTEM: CONTEMPORARY CONDITIONS FOR THE REPRESENTATION OF IDENTITY (Anthony D. King ed., 1997). For the purposes of this essay, however, in which so much that seems solid is, if not melted into air, at least significantly dispersed, I have chosen to maintain the government-nation homology. The article in this issue by Alice Miller and Meghan Faux provides an effective undermining of the steadfastly domestic blinders that often limit discussions of state accountability in the United States. See Alice Miller & Meghan Faux, Reconceiving Responses to Private Violence and State Accountability: Using an International Human Rights Framework in the United States, INAUGURAL GEO. J. GENDER & LAW 67 (1999); see also David Held, Democracy, the Nation-State and the Global System, in POLITICAL THEORY TODAY, supra, at 197, 204 (arguing that "[t]erritorial boundaries demarcate the basis on which individuals are included in and excluded from participation in decisions affecting their lives . . . but the outcomes of these decisions frequently 'stretch' beyond national frontiers. Regional and global interconnectedness contests the traditional national resolutions of the central questions of democratic theory and practice. The very process of governance seems to be 'escaping the categories' of the nation-state.").

widely divergent perspectives and vocabularies. They are forums in which narrative possibilities are crafted, both for police interpretation of crimes and for activist interpretations of police. Not all of these narratives are progressive, and none are benign. Hate crimes are potent symbols of the challenges faced by a multicultural nation, symptoms of various social ills and a pressure gauge on the limits of the accommodation of difference. Police officers, as our most noticeable daily representatives of the state, play an enormously critical role—both materially and in the national imaginary—in shaping what will count as social order.

A. EDUCATING

In 1987, I was hired by the New York City Mayor's Office to work on a sensitivity training video for police officers.[6] The video was intended to offer an educational exploration of the issue of anti-gay violence, and was designed for use in recruit training and patrol officer in-services. As a researcher and editorial assistant for the video, my job was to locate and screen interviewees.

Our task was to make visual the human effects of anti-gay violence because, we were told, police had a hard time seeing gay people as legitimate victims who were deserving of their services. Police also failed to identify such violence as particularly harmful to gay and lesbian communities. Officers tended to miss the significance of bias clues and consequently would treat anti-gay or anti-lesbian crimes as standard assaults or murders, without fulfilling departmental requirements to flag these crimes for special investigation by the Bias Crimes Unit. As educational filmmakers, our goal was to establish anti-gay and lesbian violence as acts that are as serious for police-community relations and as terrorizing to their victims as racist or anti-Semitic violence. In the course of this work, we found that "hate crime" and "bias-related violence" out-performed "anti-gay violence" in establishing conceptual similarities between racism, anti-Semitism, and homophobia.

Establishing such analogies was crucial because, though they may not have elicited particularly effective policy responses, incidents of racist and anti-Semitic violence were viewed as social problems warranting public condemnation. Anti-gay violence (and still less, anti-lesbian violence) had not, before the mid-1980s, developed the contours and visibility of a problem. Thus, it was nothing less than a profound rearticulation of reality to correlate this violence with racist and anti-Semitic violence.[7]

---

6. The project arose out of meetings between the director of the New York Lesbian and Gay Anti-Violence Project, the Mayor's Office Liaison to the Gay and Lesbian Community, and officers in the New York City Police Department's Bias Crimes Unit. It was funded and coordinated by the Mayor's Office.

7. This, of course, is my own personal and retrospective understanding of the reasons behind the gradual increase in the use of the term "hate crime" particularly by gay and lesbian communities and media outlets. This perspective finds some support in VALERIE JENNESS & KENDALL BROAD, HATE CRIMES: NEW SOCIAL MOVEMENTS AND THE POLITICS OF VIOLENCE (1997). The book discusses the processes by which social movement organizations effectively transformed anti-gay and anti-lesbian

In retrospect, the most significant impact of the rearticulation of anti-gay violence may have been its implicit shift in the definition of an attacker and in the social acceptability of his violence. Thanks to the civil rights movement, by the 1980s, perpetrators of racist violence were not generally embraced publicly as models of citizenship. An unsanctioned category for such people had developed: the "bigot." To categorize an individual as a bigot was to marginalize and disempower him. By linking anti-gay violence to racist and anti-Semitic violence, its perpetrators too could occasionally be stripped of their previously assumed justifications.[8] The grassroots fight for the recognition of hate crimes in general, and against gay men and lesbians in particular, offered a newly empowered response to old varieties of violence.[9]

This is one possible history to tell about the category of hate crime. A supplemental history would tell of new coalitions between identity groups under the banner of mutual victimization.[10] A less optimistic history, however, would emphasize hate crime's exclusions; it would explore how the model of oppression (conceived as majority vs. different minority) has, among other things, tended to exclude violence against women.[11] Such a history would trace the term's susceptibility to individualized models of oppression through its mobilization of personal, psychological notions of prejudice and hatred. It would call attention to the ways in which the legal prohibition against hate crimes has had the paradoxical effect of reinforcing static identity boundaries and has contributed to the naturalization of difference.[12]

---

violence into a social problem. Jenness and Broad also describe the early stages of efforts to incorporate violence against women into the hate crime framework.

8. One such justification was the "homosexual panic defense," with which a defendant could be acquitted for assault, or even murder, on the grounds that he had committed the crime in self-defense against a homosexual advance. This defense was used successfully, for example, in a 1986 Kalamazoo, Michigan case to acquit a man accused of an anti-gay murder. *See* NATIONAL GAY AND LESBIAN TASK FORCE, ANTI-GAY VIOLENCE, VICTIMIZATION, AND DEFAMATION IN 1986 9 (1987). In good part because of the widespread publicity accorded hate crimes, including those against gay men and lesbians, this defense has been, if not eliminated, at least widely discredited. An excellent literary analysis of the "homosexual panic" notion can be found in EVE SEDGEWICK, THE EPISTEMOLOGY OF THE CLOSET 18-21 (1990).

9. For historical accounts of racial, anti-Semitic, anti-gay and anti-lesbian violence in the United States prior to their consolidation within the category "hate crime," see JONATHAN KATZ, GAY AMERICAN HISTORY: LESBIANS AND GAY MEN IN THE U.S.A. (1976); MICHAEL NEWTON & JUDY ANN NEWTON, RACIAL AND RELIGIOUS VIOLENCE IN AMERICA: A CHRONOLOGY (1991); EDWIN NEWMAN, ED., THE HATE READER (1964); IDA B. WELLS-BARNETT, ON LYNCHINGS: SOUTHERN HORRORS, A RED RECORD, AND MOB RULE IN NEW ORLEANS, 1892 (1969); Steven A. Rosen, *Police Harassment of Homosexual Women and Men in New York City 1960-1980* 12 COLUM. HUM. RTS L. REV. 159 (1981).

10. An excellent first contribution to this kind of history, focusing on anti-gay/lesbian violence and violence against women, is provided in JENNESS & BROAD, *supra* note 7.

11. *See* Pamela Coukos, *Deconstructing the Debate Over the Gender and Hate Crimes Legislation*, INAUGURAL GEO. J. GENDER & LAW 11 (1999) (describing civil rights legislation protecting against bias violence on the basis of race, ethnicity, and religion).

12. *See generally* MARTHA MINOW, MAKING ALL THE DIFFERENCE: INCLUSION, EXCLUSION, AND AMERICAN LAW 49, 50 (1990) (stating that "[d]ilemmas of difference appear unresolvable . . . Difference can be recreated in color or gender blindness and in affirmative action; in governmental neutrality and in governmental preferences . . . The probability of reiterating difference, whether by acknowledgment or nonacknowledgment, arises as long as difference itself carries stigma and precludes equality.").

150   THE GEORGETOWN JOURNAL OF GENDER AND THE LAW   [Inaugural:145]

B. ADVOCATING

Transformed in many ways by the experience of working on the police training video, I began both to focus on hate crime in my scholarly writing, and to volunteer with a series of anti-hate crime organizations. To begin with, my scholarship and volunteer work were for the most part complementary. In both capacities I was actively engaged in the quotidian task of producing knowledge about hate crimes. However, as a volunteer activist, the truths I conveyed were disseminated and contested much more widely than anything in my academic speaking and writing experience.

As an advocate for anti-hate crime programs in the late 1980's and early 1990s, I used the expertise I developed as a scholar to argue 1) that hate crimes exist, 2) that they are identifiable as such and are increasing in frequency, and 3) that they pose particularly unique dangers not posed by "regular" crimes. For example, I even referred to hate crimes as acts of terrorism, citing, of all the sources I never expected to draw upon for support in my activism, the Federal Bureau of Investigation.[13] Quite self-consciously, I deployed the discourse of terrorism to argue that an attack motivated by prejudice targets not only its individual victim, but by its symbolic weight, effectively targets a whole group of marked individuals. As such, it is another step in a violent marking process. It functions, in other words, to reduce complex, multi-faceted individuals into one-dimensional, victimized identity categories.

Thus, I invoked the fears born by the term terrorism, along with its vast set of associations with internal versus external nationalities and affinities. I allowed the connotation of attacks upon the nation to circulate, unchallenged. I deliberately suppressed my own association of the term with its law enforcement usage against civil rights groups (Black Power activists, resisters of U.S. intervention in Central America, and others). I did this because terrorism quickly conveyed the idea of an effect larger than any single attack or crime; it captured the peculiar combination of randomness and politicized special selection that characterizes many hate crimes. Most of my opportunities to advocate publicly for anti-hate crime measures were constrained by time, and by the limited range of words that I could count on meaning the same thing to me as they would to my audience. For these reasons, the production of dramatic narrative was often the easiest and most effective tool with which to unsettle and persuade audiences.

I was by no means alone in reaching this conclusion. Examples of the dramatic narration strategy are prevalent in articles on hate crime, whether in legal, popular press, or social scientific publications. Such articles often begin with a vivid description of a hate crime.[14] "On [date], [name], a [member of identity-

---

13. AnnJanette Rosga, Proposal to the Santa Cruz County Board of Supervisors by the Santa Cruz County Hate Action Limitation Team (1992) (on file with author) [hereinafter HALT report].

14. For examples of the use of a dramatic narration strategy in writing about hate crimes, see James Jacobs, *Should Hate Be a Crime?*, PUB. INTEREST 3-4 (1993); Charles H. Jones, Jr., *An Argument for Federal Protection Against Racially Motivated Crimes: 18 U.S.C. § 241 And the Thirteenth Amendment*, 21 HARV. C.R.-C.L. L. REV. 689, 689-690 (1986); Beatrice von Schulthess, *Violence in the Streets:*

group(s)], was violently [beaten, assaulted, murdered] by [perpetrator(s) who were members of identity group(s)]." The description is often followed by a dramatic narration of the incident's details and of its consequences for the victim.

Indeed, toward the end of the 1980s legal scholars associated with critical race theory began issuing powerful calls for more victim-centered storytelling.[15] This strategy has emerged out of the specific context of legal argumentation, in which unmarked norms (purportedly neutral with regard to sex, race, class, or other status) tend to privilege those who are white, male, or middle-to-upper class. By treating all victims alike under supposedly neutral standards, such scholars argue, the non-normative victim's experience is often rendered invisible or nonsensical. Delgado writes:

> Traditional legal writing purports to be neutral and dispassionately analytical, but too often it is not. . . . [T]he received wisdoms that serve as [legal writers'] starting points [are] themselves no more than stories. . . . Stories are useful tools for the underdog because they invite the listener to suspend judgment, listen for the story's point, and test it against his or her own version of reality.[16]

Delgado claims no greater level of objectivity for "underdog" accounts. Instead, he seeks an acknowledgment that legal principles do not emerge out of socially neutral contexts, and he proposes that a proliferation of stories, especially by "outgroups," will pluralize the law and help "lead the way to new environments."[17] Robin West also urges a corrective privileging of subordinated voices, arguing that the life experience of individuals without access to hegemonic forms of social power is more likely to produce just and humane legal interpretations.[18]

Interestingly, during the same period legal scholars were formulating calls for narrative and the articulation of oppressed perspectives, other feminist and anti-racist scholars were engaged in critiques of how identity categories and narrative—the story form itself—function to repress and distort non-hegemonic experiences.[19] Scholars engaged in this more literary and historical writing have attended to the ways in which subjects' own narrations of themselves are fundamentally shaped (though never fully contained) by available modes of

---

Anti-Lesbian Assault and Harassment in San Francisco, in HATE CRIMES: CONFRONTING VIOLENCE AGAINST LESBIANS AND GAY MEN 65-66 (Gregory M. Herek & Kevin T. Berrill eds., 1992).

15. *See* Richard Delgado, *Storytelling for Oppositionists and Others: A Plea for Narrative,* 87 MICH. L. REV. 2411 (1989); Mari J. Matsuda, *Public Response to Racist Speech: Considering the Victim's Story,* 87 MICH. L. REV. 2320 (1989).

16. Delgado, *supra* note 15, at 2440-41.

. 17. *Id.* at 2440.

18. Robin West, *Relativism, Objectivity and Law,* 99 YALE L.J. 1473 (1990). For a critical response to West's article, see Barbara Hernnstein-Smith, *The Unquiet Judge: Activism without Objectivism in Law and Politics, in* RE-THINKING OBJECTIVITY 289, 293-311 (Alan Megill ed., 1994).

19. *See, e.g.,* "RACE," WRITING, AND DIFFERENCE (Henry Louis Gates ed., 1986); Teresa deLauretis, *The Violence of Rhetoric: Considerations on Representation and Gender, in* THE VIOLENCE OF REPRESENTATION 239-58 (Nancy Armstrong & Leonard Tennenhouse eds., 1989).

expression.[20] For example, Joan Scott poses challenging questions for any strategy that relies solely on victims' stories:

> [Experience] serves as a way of talking about what happened, of establishing difference and similarity, of claiming knowledge that is 'unassailable.'. . . Experience is at once always already an interpretation and is in need of interpretation. What counts as experience is neither self-evident nor straightforward; it is always contested, always therefore political.[21]

Unfortunately, the scholarly contexts in which legal advocates of storytelling and theorists of narrative, identity, and representation in the humanities cross paths are relatively few.[22]

In the more concrete world of public policy, however, intersections abound between, on the one hand, modes of presentation that deliver dramatic, experiential narrative as urgent self-evidence, and on the other hand, modes of listening that assume cynical or manipulative intent. Consider my own experience with the Santa Cruz County Criminal Justice Council, an organization composed of judges, police chiefs, district attorneys, prison officials, and social workers. On behalf of an organization seeking the Council's endorsement, I presented a proposal for a hate crimes prevention program.[23] I suspected that to the majority of this Council's members I would be seen as the spokeswoman for yet another "interest group" asking for "special rights." Thus, in the ten minutes I had been allotted, I was willing to take the risk that when I spoke of a rise in numbers of hate crimes, my audience would envision hordes of dark-skinned thugs or "white trash" Aryan-Nation provocateurs, searching every town and suburb for innocent victims on whom to vent their prejudices. My group needed the endorsement, and, if necessary, I was ready to invoke the threat of widespread civil unrest to get it.

---

20. *See* DAVID THEO GOLDBERG, RACIST CULTURE (1993) (exploring the racialization of social subjectivity and fundamental categories of western thought). For a critique of the idea of self-as-subject, especially as it is expressed by and through identity categories, see Judith Butler, *Contingent Foundations: Feminism and the Question of 'Postmodernism'*, in FEMINISTS THEORIZE THE POLITICAL 3-21 (Judith Butler & Joan W. Scott eds., 1992) [hereinafter FEMINISTS THEORIZE].

21. Joan Scott, *Experience*, in FEMINISTS THEORIZE, *supra* note 20, at 22.

22. *See, e.g.*, PATRICIA WILLIAMS, THE ALCHEMY OF RACE AND RIGHTS (1991) (providing one of the earliest examples of legal writing that simultaneously integrates storytelling, problematizes identity, and critiques legal epistemology). *See also* Toni M. Massaro, *Empathy, Legal Storytelling, and the Rule of Law: New Words, Old Wounds?*, 87 MICH L. REV. 2099 (1989); AFTER IDENTITY: A READER IN LAW AND CULTURE (Dan Danielsen & Karen Engle eds., 1995); JUDITH BUTLER, EXCITABLE SPEECH (1997); HENRY LOUIS GATES ET AL., SPEAKING OF RACE, SPEAKING OF SEX (1994).

23. From October 1991 to February 1993, I conducted participant-observation fieldwork with two grass-roots anti-hate crime organizations in north central California. In the course of my work with one of these groups, the Hate Action Limitation Team (HALT), I drafted a proposal for a public "Commission for the Prevention of Hate Action" in Santa Cruz County, California. In that capacity I made presentations to such governmental bodies as the Human Resources Administration, the County Criminal Justice Council, and the County Board of Supervisors. *See* HALT report, *supra* note 13.

My actions in this context, however, were not merely strategic. Hate crime, when inadequately addressed by law enforcement, often *does* lead to wider community conflicts.[24] Furthermore, I was—and am still—compelled by the argument that the term terrorism conveys something intrinsically accurate about hate crimes. Alas, my terrorism was not really their terrorism—our nightmares and fears are not likely to have been the same. I was aware of this, and maybe so were they. But the meeting progressed and since we were, after all, speaking the same language, we could willfully attempt to outwit each other by pretending our words meant the same thing.[25]

C. STUDYING

I began researching the social construction of hate crimes in the late 1980s when some of the most volatile struggles concerned the inclusion of sexual orientation in hate crime legislation.[26] At that time, my primary interest was in how activists were mobilizing the term hate crime to draw attention to anti-gay violence; therefore I conducted the majority of my research on grassroots and non-profit organizations that focused on the issue of bias-related violence. From the beginning, I approached the category hate crime as a social construction, interested as much or more in its political effects than in any intrinsic value it might have as a meaningful descriptor of events. For the most part, I supported the political aims of such groups: increasing research on the causes and consequences of hate crime, promoting public awareness of the ongoing effects of cultural and socioeconomic subordination, and crafting legal efforts to treat hate crime victims as seriously as otherwise similar crime victims from majority social groups.

Nevertheless, by the early 1990s, my experiences with anti-hate crime efforts—particularly legal ones—had already begun to raise questions about the wisdom of advocating new criminal laws against bias-related violence. First, these strategies allowed the very identity categories enforced by hate violence to be

---

24. *See, e.g.,* Brian Levin, *A Practical Approach to Bias Crimes for Police*, 10-11 (unpublished manuscript on file with author) (quoting a police lieutenant who cautions that "[t]hese incidents have great potential to escalate in numbers and severity"). Levin goes on to note that [i]n the three weeks following a well-publicized attack where minority youths were robbed and painted with white shoe polish the NYPD documented double the previous years [sic] average. After a fatal mixed race auto accident in Brooklyn in August 1991, 1500 NYPD officers were needed to contain the resulting rioting which lasted for four days and resulted in 180 arrests." *Id.* (citations omitted).

25. As in so many struggles for social policy reform, we prevailed in this small skirmish only to lose in the later, more significant battle. The Criminal Justice Council endorsed our proposal, and the County Board of Supervisors passed it after intense lobbying. To my knowledge, however, it was never implemented due to lack of funding.

26. Among the longest running battles over the inclusion of "sexual orientation" in laws against bias crime has been in the state of New York. As early as 1985 the Governor's Office urged inclusion of sexual orientation in state anti-discrimination policies. NEW YORK GOVERNOR'S TASK FORCE ON BIAS-RELATED VIOLENCE, 218 (1988). For a review of the five-year battle in the U.S. Congress over the inclusion of sexual orientation in the federal Hate Crime Statistics Act, see Joseph M. Fernandez, *Bringing Hate Crime into Focus—The Hate Crime Statistics Act of 1990, Pub. L. No. 101-275,* 26 HARV. C.R.-C.L. L. REV. 261-93 (1991).

written into law, and thereby reinforced hegemonic notions of mutually exclusive, internally undifferentiated, bio-social groups. Second, these anti-hate crime efforts conceded the necessity of equalizing a wide variety of events in the neutral language of law so that, for instance, an "anti-white" crime is rendered the exact reverse counterpart of an "anti-Latino" crime. Moreover, they invoked the force of a criminal justice system that has repeatedly proven itself to both rely upon and exacerbate structural inequities mapped upon the social body.

Not by coincidence, the criminal justice system's inequities fall along the very axes of identity that are fundamental to the concept of hate crime, most prominently race.[27] My doubts proliferated in the face of legal articles on the problems with hate crime sentence enhancement laws, and of sensationalistic mainstream media portrayals of hate crime.[28] But the aspect of anti-hate crime activism that disturbed me most was the emphasis on criminal justice-related solutions that seemed to result from coalition-building among progressive groups under the banner of hate crime. While such coalitions have been promising in many respects, they also have disadvantages. They run the risk of erasing historical specificity of identity formation and socioeconomic inequality on the one hand, and they risk consolidating support for conservative expansions in retributive models of law and order on the other.

The focus on criminal justice remedies became acutely apparent to me in the concrete, day-to-day prevalence of discussion about police within the organizations that I was studying. In part, the pervasiveness of police talk[29] in anti-hate crime groups can be explained by the historical coincidence of steadily increasing anti-hate crime activities in the early 1990s and the 1991 police beating of Rodney King in Los Angeles. However, this linkage between hate crime and police discrimination and brutality pre-dates the events surrounding the infamous Los Angeles Police Department incident. The problem of police brutality has long been inextricable from efforts to address police racism and other forms of

---

27. While no reliable data are yet available, anecdotal evidence suggests that young men of color may be charged with hate crime with a frequency that is disproportionate to the percentage of hate crimes they are reported to have committed. Telephone Interview with Diane Chin, Director, Racial Violence Project of San Francisco Lawyers' Committee for Civil Rights, in San Francisco, Cal. (Aug. 2, 1993). This may be related to a phenomenon of reporting noted by several anti-hate crime workers with whom I have spoken. As Greg Merrill, Victims Services Coordinator for Community United Against Violence remarked, "[m]ost of our reports [of anti-gay or anti-lesbian violence] come from white gay men. I think there are many possible reasons for that. White gay men probably have the resources to be more 'out,' and that leads to them being targeted more often. People of color often don't feel as comfortable coming to us with hate crime reports—in part because they may need to stay in the closet for family or job reasons. And women and people of color are probably more desensitized to violence in their lives—it doesn't seem exceptional enough to report it." Interview with Greg Merrill, Victims Services Coordinator for Community United Against Violence, in San Francisco, Cal. (Oct. 16, 1991).

28. For a few examples on television alone, see *Hate on Trial: A Bill Moyers Special* (CBS television broadcast, Mar. 5, 1992), *Lone Star Hate* (BBC television broadcast, July 22, 1997), *48 Hours on Hate Street* (CBS television broadcast, Mar. 26, 1992).

29. "Police talk" included both formal and informal conversation about how group members had seen, heard, or believed that police mistreated minorities, and about how police responded to bias-related incidents.

discrimination.[30] Many post-World War II race riots received their initial sparks from police abuse of force.[31] Additionally, police officers have been implicated in countless incidents across the country that would likely be termed hate crimes if committed by civilians.[32]

The members of anti-hate crime groups I observed seldom distinguished violence perpetrated by police from bias-related crime committed by civilians. Thus, by the early 1990s it had become clear to me that, within the realm of these activist groups, police were the most central figures in both action and talk about the problem of hate crime. In order to understand how this attention was received by police, I shifted the focus of my fieldwork to law enforcement sites and to the interpretive frameworks guiding police engagement with this newly-named category of crime.

---

30. James Richardson noted that "American public opinion has traditionally supported arbitrary police behavior against unpopular minorities" and he asserted that police departments and racist organizations often had coextensive memberships. JAMES RICHARDSON, URBAN POLICE IN THE UNITED STATES 17 (1974). "Politically, policemen have long had a penchant for joining extremist, right-wing organizations. . . . In the 1920s policemen in southern and northern cities became members of the revived Ku Klux Klan; in the early 1960s a considerable number of the Dallas police force were reputedly Klan members. In [the early 1970s] the John Birch Society . . . attracted many policemen, either as members or strong sympathizers." *Id.* at 144. For a more recent discussion of connections between law enforcement and white supremacist activities, see "Good Cop/Bad Cop: Refashioning Law Enforcement as the Thin Blue Line Between Bigotry and Tolerance," in Rosga, *supra* note 3, at 272-312. For excellent resources on the role of police in enforcing particular social arrangements, see PAUL CHEVIGNY, EDGE OF THE KNIFE: POLICE VIOLENCE IN THE AMERICAS (1995), and STEVE HERBERT, POLICY SPACE: TERRITORIALITY AND THE LOSE ANGELES POLICE DEPARTMENT (1997).

31. The link between excessive force by law enforcement and civilian violence has been most noticeable in clashes between police and largely Latino and/or African American communities. The history of policing in the United States is riddled with examples of police actions setting off larger social disturbances; recall, for example, the 1965 "Watts Riots" in California. KERNER COMMISSION ON CIVIL DISORDERS, REPORT OF THE NAT'L ADVISORY COMM'N ON CIVIL DISORDERS 93 (1970). A quarter century later, in May of 1991, a black police officer shot a Latino in the Mount Pleasant area of the District of Columbia, home of a large community of Central American immigrants, and the confrontation sparked "the Mount Pleasant riots" over perceived police discrimination against Hispanics. *See* Nancy Lewis and James Rupert, *D.C. Neighborhood Erupts After Officer Shoots Suspect: Crowd of Hundreds Confronts Police, Sets Cruisers Ablaze in Mt. Pleasant*, WASH. POST at A1 (May 6, 1991). In recent years, police use of deadly force has continued to trigger widespread protests. Nationally publicized cases include the beating of alleged illegal immigrants by sheriff's deputies in Riverside, California. *See* Abigail Goldman et al, *Beatings Spur U.S. Investigation and a National Debate*, L.A. TIMES, Apr. 3, 1996, at A1; Kevin Flynn, *The Louima Case: The Commission; U.S. To Hear Complaints About Police*, N.Y. TIMES, May 26, 1999, at A1 (discussing the torture of Abner Louima); Michael Cooper, *Officers in Bronx Fire 41 Shots, And an Unarmed Man Is Killed*, N.Y. TIMES, Feb. 5, 1999, at A1 (discussing the fatal shooting of Amadou Diallo by officers of the New York City Police Department).

32. *See, e.g.*, INDEP. COMM'N ON THE LOS ANGELES POLICE DEP'T, REPORT 32-59 (1991) (describing the Christopher Commission's findings of police abuse of force in their report on the L.A.P.D., following the videotaped beating of Rodney King in March of 1991). In the wake of King's beating, several reports of police brutality, predominantly against U.S. racial minorities, emerged in the press. *See also Police Brutality*, CQ RESEARCHER, Sept. 6, 1991, at 633-56; Elizabeth Gleick, *The Crooked Blue Line*, TIME, Sept. 11, 1995, at 38-42; *Beating Crime: The Los Angeles Police*, THE ECONOMIST, Mar. 23, 1991, at 28-29; *Law and Disorder on the Beat*, TIME, Apr. 1, 1991, at 3-25; *Brutality on the Beat*, NEWSWEEK, Mar. 25, 1991, at 32-33; *Police Brutality!*, TIME, Mar. 25, 1991, at 16-19.

II. "COPS JUST DON'T GET IT"

There are two concrete reasons why law enforcement agencies have been central targets of educational campaigns on the recognition and response to hate crime. First, throughout the history of organized policing—long before the likes of Sergeant Stacey Koon and Mark Furhman[33] took center stage—police officers frequently have been accused of discriminatory conduct and civilian abuse.[34] According to some representations advanced by activists, hate crime signifies discriminatory police conduct; thus, law enforcement officers are explicitly accused of perpetrating hate crimes. When this is not the case, police are seen by many activists as inadequately responsive to hate crimes by civilians, and as bearing central responsibility for the fact that many perpetrators go unpunished.

Second, police officers play an important role in the treatment and success of hate crime prosecution. Initial police reporting is often, in fact, the determining factor in whether or not bias-related attacks are officially recognized as "bias-related." An officer's interpretations and written accounts of an incident play an essential role in directing if, how, and by whom that incident will be investigated.[35] If an officer does not recognize an event as bias-related, the crime may fail to catch the attention of subsequent players in the criminal justice system. Indirectly, then, the officer's initial response can affect the level of punishment a convicted perpetrator will receive.[36]

---

33. Sergeant Stacey Koon was the highest ranking of four Los Angeles Police Department officers charged in the March 1991 beating of Rodney King. INDEP. COMM'N ON THE LOS ANGELES POLICE DEP'T, REPORT 5 (1991). Detective Mark Furhman was among those involved in the Los Angeles Police Department investigation of the murder of Nicole Simpson. His testimony was discredited in the globally televised criminal trial of O.J. Simpson in 1995 after an audiotaped recording was introduced by defense attorneys in which Furhman could be heard making racist comments to an interviewer. *See* Jim Newton & Bill Boyarsky, *Witnesses Tell Jury of Fuhrman's Racial Epithets; Simpson trial: Ex-detective disparaged interracial couples and bragged about making up charges, two women say. Session ends with playing of writer's tapes*, L.A. TIMES, Sept. 6, 1995, at A1.

34. *See Police Brutality, supra* note 32, 28-29; Gleick, *supra* note 32, at 38-42; *Beating Crime: The Los Angeles Police, supra* note 32, at 3-25; *Brutality on the Beat, supra* note 32, at 32-33; *Police Brutality!, supra* note 32, at 16-19.

35. In conjunction with a federal hate crime statistics collection program, increasing numbers of police departments (particularly those in large cities) maintain hate crime reporting systems and policies for special investigative procedures in cases involving alleged hate crimes, though their levels of implementation vary widely. BIAS CRIME: AMERICAN LAW ENFORCEMENT AND LEGAL RESPONSE (Robert J. Kelly, ed., 1993); S. Walker & C.M. Katz, *Less Than Meets The Eye: Police Department Bias-Crime Units*, XIV AMER. J. POLICE 29-48 (1995).

36. This would be the case, for instance, if sentence enhancement laws for bias-related crime are in force within the jurisdiction. Most such laws are based upon a model developed by the Anti-Defamation League of B'nai B'rith. The model includes several components, the most significant of which for the purposes of this essay is its "penalty enhancement" provision in cases of intimidation or assault. The law is written as follows:

A. A person commits the crime of intimidation if, by reason of the actual or perceived race, color, religion, national origin or sexual orientation of another individual or group of individuals, he violates Section _____ of the Penal Code (insert code provision for criminal trespass, criminal mischief, harassment, menacing, assault and/or any other appropriate statutorily proscribed criminal conduct).

Furthermore, any statistics on the prevalence of hate crime that are generated by local police departments are in turn processed by the national Bureau of Criminal Justice Statistics and used to evaluate the need for legislation and resources. Thus, police discretion is a crucial element in determining the perceived seriousness of the hate crime problem. Many grassroots organizations and law enforcement associations have recognized the importance of police interpretation, and have raised concerns about how it may be affected by the fraught history of discriminatory conduct and abuse of force by police. As a result, both internal and external efforts at change have focused on increasing police sensitivity to the problem of hate crime, and at improving law enforcement's relationship to "minority" communities.

Concrete examples of such measures include an annual hate crime conference for law enforcement officers that has been held in Towson, Maryland for the past five years, as well as training programs conducted by the Department of Justice on hate crime investigation and statistics-keeping throughout the nation.[37] Moreover, most, if not all, police departments in the country include a "diversity training" or "community relations" unit as part of new officer training academies.[38] Furthermore, as a measure of the concern over police sensitivity to issues of multiculturalism, the national law enforcement magazine *The Police Chief* has had regular articles and commentary on diversity training programs.[39] Likewise, a number of governmental and non-governmental bodies send trainers into law enforcement agencies to work with officers on their understandings of,

---

B. Intimidation is a _____ misdemeanor/felony (the degree of criminal liability should be made contingent upon the severity of the injury incurred or property lost or damaged)

JEFFREY P. SINENSKY, HATE CRIME STATUTES: A RESPONSE TO ANTI-SEMITISM, VANDALISM AND VIOLENT BIGOTRY App. A (1988).

In other words, when someone commits what is already designated a relevant crime under this provision, and does so against a victim because of "bias" against a group defined by one of the named categories, that person may be charged with a more serious crime and given a harsher sentence. If responding officers do not identify the incident as potentially bias-related, however, and if complainants do not press for the case to be investigated as a hate crime, no such charges are likely to be filed. Unless the prosecutor makes a special effort to discover bias-motivation and can gather enough evidence to make a hate crime charge feasible, the perpetrator will not receive an increased sentence upon conviction. In states like California, where the hate crime law will in some instances transform a misdemeanor charge into a felony charge, the difference in consequences for the perpetrator can be substantial. *See* CAL. PENAL CODE § 422.16 (West Supp. 1993).

37. Interview with Jim Nolan, Federal Bureau of Investigation, Uniform Crime Reporting Unit, in Washington, D.C. (Apr. 29, 1996). *See also* DEP'T OF JUSTICE, TRAINING GUIDE FOR HATE CRIME DATA COLLECTION (1996).

38. Stephen M. Hennessy, *Cultural Sensitivity Training, in* MULTICULTURAL PERSPECTIVES IN CRIMINAL JUSTICE AND CRIMINOLOGY 347-83 (James E. Hendricks & Brian Byers, eds., 1994).

39. *See, e.g.,* Terry Bickham and Allison Rossett, *Diversity Training: Are We Doing the Right Thing Right?,* THE POLICE CHIEF, Nov. 1993, at 43-47 (discussing the role of department leadership in diversity training); Paul A. Pomerville, *Popular Myths About Cultural Awareness Training,* THE POLICE CHIEF, Nov. 1993, at 30-42 (addressing ineffective methods of implementing training); Elsie L. Scott, *Cultural Awareness Training,* THE POLICE CHIEF, Nov. 1993, at 26-29 (discussing the proper focus and content of cultural awareness training); Jane A. Torres, *Making Sensitivity Training Work,* THE POLICE CHIEF, Aug. 1992, at 32-33.

and responses to, hate crimes.[40]

Interestingly, the pivotal role of law enforcement officers emerged as a significant issue at this symposium.[41] Several participants noted that while various legal strategies for dealing with hate crime and domestic violence have been implemented, the first point of application of those strategies is often between police and either victims or perpetrators. Audience members repeatedly asked questions about how officers are (or are not) trained, how they do (or do not) successfully adapt to new procedures, and whether innovative legal approaches would be undermined by the fact that some officers may sympathize more with perpetrators of hate crime and domestic violence than with their victims. Presenters and members of the audience alike seemed to share the worry that, too often, as one audience member put it, "cops just don't get it."

The remainder of this section offers three brief examples from my research, each of which belies any suggestion that police agencies are monolithic in their relationship to anti-hate crime projects. Each presents a slightly different (and usually underrepresented) picture of how hate crime is taken up by law enforcement officials in different contexts. The first includes a bias-crime perpetrator's account of his interrogation by police, the second recounts a moment from a law enforcement presentation to elementary school children on the topic of hate speech, and the third describes a law enforcement conference on hate crime.

A. HATE CRIME PERPETRATORS AND POLICE

In 1996, I spent several months working as the researcher and editorial consultant for a documentary on men who had committed anti-gay murders. In the course of this work, I accompanied the film's director, Arthur Dong, to several prisons across the United States to assist with interviews of inmates.[42] Like many of my informants from anti-hate crime organizations, several inmates clearly viewed police as unconcerned with the victims of (at least, anti-gay) hate crime and even as occasionally sympathetic with perpetrators. Jeffrey Swinford, imprisoned for his 1993 murder of twenty-three year old Chris Miller in Little Rock, Arkansas, illustrated this feeling, when he explained why he believed attacking and robbing gay men to be a fairly risk-free crime:

---

40. Throughout the 1980s and 1990s, law enforcement training sessions have been conducted by most large gay and lesbian anti-violence projects (e.g., New York Anti-Violence Project, San Francisco's Community United Against Violence, and an anti-violence project of the National Gay and Lesbian Task Force in Washington, D.C.), by a number of state and local human relations departments (e.g., Los Angeles, Cal., Alameda County, Cal., and Montgomery County, Md.), and by legal NGOs such as the Lawyer's Committee for Civil Rights. For an ethnographic account of such trainings, see Rosga, *supra* note 3, at 132-221.

41. *See* Diane T. Chin, *Power and the Civil Suit: Using Civil Remedies in the Battle Against Hate Violence*, INAUGURAL GEO. J. GENDER & LAW 115 (1999); Deborah Epstein, *Redefining the State's Response to Domestic Violence: Past Victories and Future Challenges*, INAUGURAL GEO. J. GENDER & LAW 127 (1999).

42. Videotape: Licensed to Kill (DeepFocus Productions 1996) (on file with author).

To me, not too many people in the world care about a homosexual. And the police are the same way. Police ain't gonna do nothin', in Little Rock, to help 'em. I know. I know this. I know police officers. Y'know? They just ain't . . . interested.[43]

Donald Aldrich, on death row in Huntsville, Texas for his part in the 1993 murder of Nicholas West, a twenty-three year old gay man, was aware of the same vulnerabilities of gay men who cruise in public parks.[44] Not only would the victims of assault and robbery be unlikely to report the crime because of their fear of being publicly identified as homosexual, but they would also choose cruising areas that by definition are seldom patrolled by police:

The homosexuals make themselves easy targets . . . It don't matter what city you go to; you can find 'em in parks . . . There's no cops around because they generally pick a spot where cops don't go to because the police will bust 'em for . . . public indecency, what have you.[45]

Remarks such as these certainly resonate with progressive groups' generally suspicious attitudes toward police, and they offer plenty of allusive support for claims about state complicity in hate crime. On the other hand, such generalizations by both hate crime opponents and perpetrators can miss important contradictions in the manifestations of state power. Shortly before Donald Aldrich and his co-defendants committed the murder of Nicholas West, Texas became one of a number of states to pass a hate crime sentence enhancement law that included sexual orientation.[46] Aldrich blames his death sentence on a strategic error: he was mistaken in his assumption that the investigating officers would go easier on him if they understood that his victim was a homosexual:

[The reason my] crime came out to what it was—it was because I knew how the police felt about homosexuals back in Tyler. I turn around and tell them I hated homosexuals and that certain things were done because of this, it was supposed to help me out. But because of the new hate crime statutes, it backfired on me. [The police said], "Well, this is what could happen, and even if it wasn't capital murder, it could be upgraded to capital murder because of the hate crime . . ." I'm like, "What hate crime?" In other words, if I'da known about the new hate crime statutes, I'da prob'ly never said any of that.[47]

Contrary to his original statement to police, Aldrich assured us he felt no

---

43. *Id.*
44. *Id.*
45. *Id.*
46. *Id.*
47. *Id.*

160   THE GEORGETOWN JOURNAL OF GENDER AND THE LAW   [Inaugural:145

animosity whatsoever toward homosexuals. He was operating under his well-established assessment of police officers' aversion to gays. The crime itself was not anti-gay; it was merely an attempted robbery that "got out of hand."[48]

This account, of course, can be interpreted in a number of different ways. I do not include it to suggest anything about the validity of claims that the murder of Nicholas West was or was not an actual hate crime. Nor do I present it as evidence that the state, while no one was looking, has quietly transformed itself into a staunch avenger of the disenfranchised victims of hate crimes. Rather, it serves as an example of how very difficult it can be, in practice, to assess the meaning and value of the turn to state power—a turn that hate crime laws seem to represent.

B. POLICE AND *POTENTIAL* HATE CRIME PERPETRATORS

During fieldwork in 1995 on police use of the category hate crime in an east coast suburb, I spent some time observing county law enforcement officials as they made bias crime prevention presentations in the local public schools.[49] The exchange described here took place during a visit by two law enforcement officers to a predominantly white suburban elementary school. The officers' primary goal was to discourage children from making fun of one another on the basis of race, color, language, religion, or country of origin. As part of their effort to make this arguably advanced message accessible to a group of first and second graders, the officers showed clips from a Sesame Street video promoting multiculturalism and inter-group tolerance.

The class listened to three different songs sung by an upbeat cast of children and brightly colored muppets. The melodious chorus of one song contained these lyrics: "yes, in some ways, we're different, as different as can be. But in some ways we're the same . . . you can look at the difference if that's what you want to do, but I'd rather find the ways that I'm like you."[50] A second tune accompanied a cinematic montage of happy children of different races playing together on a playground. The background voices sang:

> No matter what you look like, no matter where you live . . . when you're happy you giggle, when you're sad you cry a lot . . . you shiver when it's cold out, when it's warm out, you get hot . . . no matter the shape of your nose . . . no matter what . . . brown or yellow, short or tall . . . when it comes to feelings, your body doesn't matter at all. . . .[51]

---

48. *Id.*

49. These visits were undertaken jointly by law enforcement agencies in two neighboring counties. They made up one element of a statewide response to bias-related incidences that originated in 1981. Two consecutive governors in this state formed advisory councils on the problem of bigotry which sought to evaluate and coordinate the efforts of law enforcement, human relations commissions, elected officials, and community groups. *See* Fieldnotes by AnnJanette Rosga, Multicultural Awareness Sessions for Police Recruits (on file with author).

50. *Id.*

51. *Id.*

After the songs, one of the officers turned the tape off and asked the class, "what were [these songs] trying to say about kids?" A child answered:

"That they're not different because of their skin or their homes."

"That's right," Officer One responded enthusiastically. "They're more alike than they are different, like the horse and cow [muppets that you saw were] both animals."

A boy bouncing excitedly in his seat called out, "some people are different and some are the same!"

Hesitating, Officer One glanced quickly at his partner, "that's right, but aren't we all more alike than we are different?" Without waiting for a response, he announced, "sure we are!"

Officer Two backed him up, asking, "we all like pizza, don't we?"

The kids cheered, "yeah!!"[52]

Officer Two then began the lesson in earnest. "Every one of us in this room, unless they're a Native American Indian, came from somewhere different. My parents are Italian, German, Irish, and English. I'm a regular Heinz 57! We're all immigrants here. That's how this country was founded. That's why this is the best country in the world!"[53]

Not to be distracted from the fact that these were, after all, police officers in uniform standing at the front of their classroom, a child in the front of the room shouted,

"One time, a burglar tried to get in our house!" Another instantly offered,

"Yeah, and my mom? Her car got broken into!"

Order disintegrated in a chorus of pleas to see, touch, or hold the officers' guns.[54]

C. POLICE AND BIGOTS

During this same period of fieldwork, I attended a law enforcement conference entitled "The Impact of Hate."[55] The event was attended by more than seven hundred law enforcement officers from over one hundred and twenty-five federal, state, and local agencies. Coincidentally, the conference took place only three weeks after the bombing of the Murrah Federal Building in Oklahoma City. While conference organizers had planned long before the bombing to focus on the dangers of hate speech, the Oklahoma City tragedy was seen as so strikingly relevant that they chose to reorient the day's events toward a discussion of the

---

52. *Id.*
53. *Id.*
54. *Id.*
55. Conference, The Impact of Hate in the Twentieth Century and Beyond, at Goucher College, Towson, Md. (May 9, 1995).

bombing as an "anti-government hate crime."[56]

By establishing the Oklahoma City bombing as a point of urgent departure, the conference speakers implicitly assumed a set of understandings about the bombing and about the recently publicized anti-government patriot movement. Several presenters interpreted the motives of the two men charged with the bombing, both of whom had been affiliated with the "patriot movement," as quite specifically directed. They suggested, with varying levels of explicitness that the bombers viewed the Murrah Federal Building as the embodiment of federal accommodations to difference and of governmental efforts on behalf of those with minority status in the United States. The bombing, then, was implicitly framed as an attack upon the nation. In a significant departure from mass media representations, in which the attack was described as expressing general anti-government sentiment, these speakers inferred a more particular motive: it was not the government in general that had been targeted, but a government perceived to support ethnic and cultural diversity. More specifically, the audience of law enforcement officers was likened to the bombing victims, and by extension, to the more general category of hate crime victims. As the final step in this series of associations, the officers were addressed as part of an implied category of state actors whose difficult and dangerous job it would be to save our multicultural nation from the swelling tide of organized, well-armed bigots.[57]

D. COUNTER-HEGEMONY

When I began my research on the category hate crime, I approached it as a term in the rhetoric of resistance to state power. As my research progressed, I came to see that, in actively constructing what will count as hate crime, those who represent the state (law enforcement officials and others) mobilize fairly traditional models of the United States as a multicultural nation. This nation is comprised of clearly delineated, equally empowered, internally uniform identity groups, protected from one another—or from extremists and deviants—by a benign and neutral state. In spite of the rather predictable paternalism of such

---

56. *Id.* The originally planned subtitle for the conference had been "When free speech becomes a safety issue."

57. One speaker announced, "you guys are getting killed as much as anybody else by these guys. They see you as race traitors and tools of ZOG (the Zionist Occupied Government). Law enforcement is the number one enemy of white supremacists." The term "ZOG" is frequently used by white supremacist organizations to refer to their conspiracy theory that the U.S. government is controlled by Jews and other "mud people"—a term denoting, depending on the speaker, people of color, Jews, homosexuals, and/or all those not considered part of the "white race." *Id.* The effect of reorienting this conference in relation to the Oklahoma City bombing was to dramatically highlight—and significantly rearticulate—several elements long present in efforts to craft the U.S. "state" as the source behind what is projected as a national image of successful multicultural pluralism. In particular, speakers at the conference rearticulated the identity of police officers by narratively positioning them on the front line between hate criminals and the rest of us. *See* AnnJanette Rosga, *Good Cop/Bad Cop: Refashioning Law Enforcement as the Thin Blue Line Between Bigotry and Tolerance, in* HOME GROWN TERRORISM: "AMERICA" AND POLITICAL VIOLENCE IN THE 90s (Lucinda Cole & Richard G. Swartz eds., forthcoming) (on file with author).

models, I think it is worth noting the ways in which the characteristics of those positioned as "deviant" or "extremist," and by implication, the traits of our patriotic selves, are shifting via the discourse of hate crime.

In the first anecdote, a perpetrator describes himself as literally caught mid-shift. Donald Aldrich expects the police to recognize the relative lack of harm done by the murder of a homosexual. Surprisingly, the police use this very expression of solidarity-through-homophobia against him. While it is impossible to know whether or not these particular officers had come to view homophobic violence as a more serious crime as a result of the new hate crime law, it certainly seems safe to surmise that officers can and do see hate crime sentence enhancement laws as one more useful tool in keeping criminals locked up for as long as possible, and in some cases, in putting them to death.[58]

The second anecdote is perhaps the most complicated. Here, the state-as-law-enforcement is not simply acting in its traditional capacity as the "repressive state apparatus" of policing, but is also functioning as part of the "ideological state apparatus" of public schools.[59] Two law enforcement officers from two different agencies cooperated in a project to reduce bias-related harassment in the public schools with the enthusiastic support of principals and teachers. Their message, that name-calling leads to hate violence which leads to getting in trouble, was ill-equipped to disrupt the entrenched cultural calculus that one student articulated so well: "some people are different and some are the same." In this algorithm, any distinctions between race and culture are effectively erased, the world is divided up into normal and different ways of being, and identity categories like race, sexual orientation, gender, and class are constructed as ahistorical givens, as matters of purely synchronic—as opposed to diachronic— relations of difference.[60]

---

58. One officer I interviewed, in discussing charges brought against two white men accused of committing a racially-motivated attack upon two black women, had this to say about the value of a hate crime sentence enhancement law in his state: "I mean, when I come to work, I don't go out and say, I'm gonna catch somebody doin' a hate crime. I mean, that's just not realistic . . . I'll say to myself, I'm gonna go out and catch a burglar, but . . . if he is doin' a burglary because he wants to get this white victim, or he wants to get this black victim, or whatever, that makes it all, that makes it sweeter. That we snag that guy for doin' that. That's icing on top of the cake." Interview with "Officer Len Richards" (pseudonym), Towson, Md. (Oct. 24, 1996). For additional research on police uses and interpretations of hate crime law, see Susan E. Martin, *"A Cross-Burning Is Not Just An Arson": Police Social Construction Of Hate Crimes In Baltimore County* 33 CRIMINOLOGY 303-26 (1995); Susan E. Martin, *Investigating Hate Crimes: Case Characteristics and Law Enforcement Responses,* 13 JUSTICE QUARTERLY 455-80 (1996); Elizabeth A. Boyd et al., *Motivated by Hatred or Prejudice: Categorization of Hate-motivated Crimes in Two Police Divisions,* 30 L. & SOC'Y REV. 819-50 (1996).

59. *See* Louis Althusser, *Ideology and Ideological State Apparatuses, in* LENIN AND PHILOSOPHY AND OTHER ARTICLES 127-86 (Ben Brewster trans., 1971).

60. Synchronic and diachronic are terms borrowed from the study of linguistics. They refer to the different ways in which the meanings of words emerge from their relationships with other words. To say that the words of a language acquire their meaning synchronically is to say that they do so in relation to other words at a single moment in time, in abstraction from history. A diachronic description of language would be one that attends to how the meanings of words change over time. The word "write," for instance, which conveys a rich abundance of meaning in English, requires both synchronic and

A vivid example of how diachronic relations of difference are erased in common talk about race and culture is illustrated by a multicultural awareness session for police recruits which I observed in the course of my fieldwork.[61] A county human relations trainer handed out a sheet of paper to each recruit. The sheet had two simple drawings on it, one a crude staircase, the other a curvy line. The trainer told the group that this exercise was to help them evaluate their cultural assumptions, values, and norms. The trainer explained that the drawings represented two different cultural models: the staircase culture and the roller coaster culture.

> In the staircase culture, people believe that if you work hard, you'll move to the top. They are future-oriented, and change is valued. The people in this culture can choose not to work hard, but then they will suffer the consequences of not moving up. Everything is up to the individual. Rules are informal and communication is direct. In the roller coaster culture, on the other hand, people believe that nothing ever changes: what goes up must come down. Outside forces control things. The individual is not important; the group is more important, and interrelatedness among different members is emphasized. It is a very rule-bound culture where hierarchy, roles, and status are extremely important. Communication is indirect.[62]

The trainer next led the recruits in a discussion of imagined encounters between the two cultures described, where the metaphorical quality of the exercise broke down. Very quickly it became apparent that both the trainer and the recruits understood the "staircase culture" to represent U.S.-born whites and the "roller coaster culture" to represent everyone else.[63]

It is not just history, writ large, that is erased in this presentation. Also eclipsed

---

diachronic structures to be meaningful. In its most simple, concrete sense, to write is to trace or form characters on a material (such as paper), with an instrument (such as a pen). It conveys this meaning in part through its historical relationship to older, related words. It has developed over time from a cognate of an Old Saxon word "writan" meaning among other things "to cut." The structures through which "writan" has become "write" are diachronic. Similarly, the connotations of "write" can vary even at a given moment in time. It can be a command: "Write your name here;" or it can describe the act of communicating: "I write to him every week." The word's synchronic relationship to other words in the sentence determines, in part, which sense(s) of the word predominate in a given utterance. *See* FERDINAND DE SAUSSURE, A COURSE IN GENERAL LINGUISTICS (Charles Ballyh & Albert Sechehaye eds., 1959).

Since language will always be structured both synchronically and diachronically, distinguishing between them is an artificial imposition, useful mainly for temporary analytical clarity. In this context, I use the terms to emphasize both the artificiality of distinguishing between histories of identity formation and current expressions of differences between "groups." To describe intergroup relations synchronically is to present "now" as "always" it is to describe a located, culturally contingent account as a universal truth. It is to assert that the groups in question have always had the same contents and boundaries, and that solely inherent traits (inevitably and transparently observed) define them.

61. Fieldnotes by AnnJanette Rosga, Multicultural Awareness Sessions for Police Recruits (on file with author).

62. *Id.*

63. *See id.*

is the corollary implication that differences—or the circles "we" draw and the contents "we" choose to place within them—are always constructed, changing over time, and subject to all manner of disruption and internal contradiction.

The third example, from the conference on the Oklahoma City bombing, indicates an emerging law enforcement construction of hate crime that specifically uses that term to elide accusations of police bigotry. Further, hate crime is taken up as a central term in the formation of a new extremist Other, the white-supremacist, anti-government, militia-member patriot, whose existence will justify increased police powers.[64]

When this is the case, I contend, it is no longer possible to speak of the fight against hate crime as a purely counter-hegemonic project. An examination of common usage, even among progressive scholars, would find that hegemony often appears as a synonym for "dominant culture," or "the state's" version of reality. My ethnographic tracking of the category hate crime—as a legal innovation, as a sensationalist term in the mass media, and as a coalition mobilizer for many identity-based organizations—has made it evident that hate crime is regarded as a leftist (or liberal), grassroots-oriented term. In the common usage sense then, the struggle against "hate" is widely understood to be a counter-hegemonic struggle. Indeed, it is easy enough to tell the history of the institutionalization of the term hate crime as a story of disenfranchised identity groups successfully countering the state's failure to systematically address bias-related violence. In many ways, that story is true.

It is also true, however, that the people and agencies that have played a role in the gradual institutionalization of this category can't be easily separated into camps like "the community," or "grassroots," and "the state." For virtually its entire history, the term hate crime has been recognized by progressive grass-roots groups, non-governmental organizations (those with and without substantial governmental lobbying powers), legislators at every level of government, and law enforcement officers from varying ranks. This is not to say that the push for anti-hate crime laws has not met with resistance ranging from outright rejection to benign neglect. Nevertheless, many of the earliest, most visible, and determinative fights over the term have taken place within the state. As a result, it seems misleading to conceptualize the fight against hate crime as a simple narrative of disenfranchised progressives battling for recognition and protection by the behemoth of the United States government.

In fact, I have come to conclude that the law enforcement response to hate

---

64. For instance, as far back as 1976, the Maryland State Police were monitoring white supremacist activities in their state. It was a coalition of State Police and Human Relations Department officials who spearheaded a proposal for bias incident reporting by police. As Captain John Cook, of the Maryland State Police Department explained, "you've got to have the government buy in. In Maryland, the Governor at the time was Hughes, Governor Hughes, and [he backed a law applying] to all state agencies" that would mandate the collection of data on "RRE [racial, religious, and ethnic] bias-related incidents." Interview with John Cook, Captain, Maryland State Police (May 5, 1996). The Maryland Bias Incident Reporting Law went into effect in the summer of 1981, making Maryland the first state in the country to have a hate crime reporting law. See MD. CODE ANN., [STATE GOV'T] § 88B(9)(a)-(b) (1998).

crime actually makes up one strand of a hegemonic project: the articulation of the U.S. as a tolerant, multicultural nation. In making this argument, I am borrowing Stuart Hall's definition of hegemony:

> "Hegemony" implies: the struggle to contest and dis-organize an existing political formation; the taking of the "leading position" (on however minority a basis) over a number of different spheres of society at once—economy, civil society, intellectual and moral life, culture; the conduct of a wide and differentiated type of struggle; the winning of a strategic measure of popular consent; and, thus, the securing of a social authority sufficiently deep to conform society into a new historic project. It should never be mistaken for a finished or settled project. It is always contested, always trying to secure itself, always "in process."[65]

I do not argue that the crafting of a tolerant multicultural national identity is an all-encompassing, internally homogenous, or even fully successful, hegemonic project, nor that there aren't forces hostile to this project that could be seen as equally hegemonic. I will assert, however, that this renegotiation of U.S. identity is nonetheless one of our country's current and foremost hegemonic projects.[66] I derive this conclusion, in part, from my observation that the state's role as a mediator of relations between inhabitants from many different races, religions, political formations, cultural identities, and linguistic groups is under specific and dramatic contention in law enforcement responses to hate crime.

In other words, it is a mistake of vision to see anti-hate crime efforts as solely—or even primarily—about hate crime, and to treat "hegemony" as a synonym for domination by the elite. No doubt we need progressives who will want to take active part in this ongoing hegemonic construction of the United States as a successfully multicultural nation, if only to prevent its becoming a whitewash of structural inequities, both present and historical, and to foreclose the reduction cultural difference to food. (Throwing out the melting pot for a violently mixed metaphor of a "tossed salad" with mostly "Heinz 57's" spiced up by freeze-dried packets of ethnicity, and unified by the shared love of pizza and ice cream, will only take us so far.) On the other hand, we should also pay relentless attention to the ways in which anti-hate crime efforts are being perversely rearticulated in the service of increasing police power and reducing complex social problems to matters of individual criminality.

III. USING THE STATE AGAINST ITSELF

In her book *States of Injury*, Wendy Brown critically analyzes a late twentieth century U.S. political culture in the United States that she sees as reifying

---

65. STUART HALL, HARD ROAD TO RENEWAL: THATCHERISM AND THE CRISIS OF THE LEFT 7 (1988).
66. *See* AnnJanette Rosga, *Bias Before the Law: The Rearticulation of Hate Crimes in* Wisconsin v. Mitchell, NYU REV. L. & SOCIAL CHANGE (forthcoming Dec. 1999) (on file with author).

relationships between identity and injury in efforts to achieve state recognition of both.[67] She is critical of what she calls "a tendency toward . . . [a] kind of moralizing politics" that "turn[s] away from freedom's pursuit," and she seems to identify hate crime laws as paradigmatic of this tendency:

> [A tendency that] is perhaps nowhere more evident than in the contemporary proliferation of efforts to pursue legal redress for injuries related to social subordination by marked attributes or behaviors: race, sexuality, and so forth. This effort, which strives to establish racism, sexism, and homophobia as morally heinous in the law, and to prosecute its individual perpetrators there, has many of the attributes of what Nietzsche named the politics of ressentiment.[68]

For the purposes of this symposium "the state" referred to legal, judicial, and criminal justice systems in the United States and focused on these systems' responses to domestic violence and hate crime. Whatever else those who combat hate crime and domestic violence may or may not share, they do hold in common the general aim of creating more effective "legal redress for injuries related to social subordination by marked attributes or behaviors."[69] I take seriously Brown's suggestion that such efforts may be, at best, counterproductive:

> While the effort to replace liberalism's abstract formulation of equality with legal recognition of injurious social stratifications is understandable, legal "protection" for a certain injury-forming identity [may entrench] the injury-identity connection it denounces. Might such protection codify within the law the very powerlessness it aims to redress? Might it . . . collude with the conversion of attribute into identity, of a historical effect of power into a presumed cause of victimization?[70]

In addition to reifying the connection between identity and injury, Brown argues, the "effort to 'outlaw' social injury powerfully legitimizes law and the state as appropriate protectors against injury, [and figures them] as neutral arbiters of injury rather themselves invested with the power to injure."[71] Instead, Brown insists, we must learn to articulate alternative models for collective life, rather than engaging in struggles that risk "bartering political freedom for legal protection."[72] We must take advantage of the opportunities offered by postmoder-

---

67. WENDY BROWN, STATES OF INJURY: POWER AND FREEDOM IN LATE MODERNITY (1995).

68. *Id.* at 27. Although Brown goes on to mention anti-discrimination laws and laws that attempt to ban or restrict hate speech, the range of her critique remains somewhat unclear. She does not specifically name hate crime sentence enhancement laws, but it seems fair to assume that she would include such laws as examples of the tendency toward a politics of ressentiment.

69. *Id.*

70. *Id.* at 21.

71. *Id.* at 27.

72. *Id.* at 28.

nity to "decide 'what we want' rather than derive it from assumptions or arguments about 'who we are'" as, she contends, do current legal approaches to hate crime and hate speech.[73]

Brown is certainly not alone in arguing that attempts to construct legal remedies for identity-based injury always have the paradoxical effect of reifying the power of identities already enshrined within the law, whether implicitly or explicitly. Feminist legal scholars have been grappling with this problem for many years.[74] Notably, in taking up this paradox as one fundamental to all freedom-seeking projects, Brown neither assumes a solution to the problem must be found in the law, nor reduces this paradox to a dialectic, in which thesis and antithesis can be resolved into synthesis. Crucially, she refuses easy generalities about state power:

> Insofar as "the state" is not an entity or a unity, it does not harbor and deploy only one kind of political power. . . . Any attempt to reduce or define power as such . . . obscures that, for example, social workers, the Pentagon, and the police are not simply different faces of the state . . . but different kinds of power. Each works differently, . . . produces different effects, engenders different kinds of possible resistance . . . [E]ach emerges and operates in specific historical, political, and economic relation with the others.[75]

On the other hand, while Brown's criticisms of identity-injury based laws may be entirely persuasive in the abstract, they do not reflect the nuance of her own theories of state power. Efforts to engage the state in a fight against hate crime are, in practice, less homogenous, more critical of state power, and often shrewdly discerning of the varying operations of that power, than Brown's critiques of them would seem to suggest. My research indicates a relentless confusion of boundaries between the state and its putatively dissociated interlocutors. The varied manifestations of anti-hate crime efforts clearly illustrate the complexity involved in any effort to designate "progressive" or "regressive" labels for social change strategies that call upon the power of the state.

Certainly both activists and law enforcement officers are using the category hate crime to classify certain types of crime, to identify a (contested) selection of incidents as deriving from, and/or enacting, social prejudices.[76] However, social

---

73. *Id.* at 49.

74. The so-called "equality-difference" debates are concerned with this paradox. *See, generally* Joan Williams, *Deconstructing Gender*, 87 MICH. L. REV. 797 (1989), *reprinted in* FEMINIST JURISPRUDENCE 531-58 (Patricia Smith ed., 1993); MINOW, *supra* note 12.

75. BROWN, *supra* note 67, at 175. Brown also provides an extremely nuanced description of how state power is gendered through to its very roots, while not reducing that analysis to a claim that the state is purely or simply "male," or that it operates only in the interests of actual men. *Id.* at 177.

76. The problem of the "nature" of hate crime, and its meaning as an event, is extremely complex and cannot be fully addressed in this essay. Suffice it to say, however, that there are two predominant

actors situated both within and outside of law enforcement are also mobilizing the category hate crime in negotiations over police—and metonymically state—identity. In arguing for or against particular elements of hate crime's definition, in supporting or rejecting policies that will affect police procedure, interested advocates from across the political spectrum contribute to the ongoing construction of the function and roles of law enforcement officers. It is worth closely examining, rather than dismissing on theoretical grounds, the labors of activist and non-profit organizations that have historically occupied a place of resistance to state power in general, and to police persecution in particular.[77] Hate crime, as a recently emergent social problem, has produced what may be an unprecedented number of settings in which police and those who often view them as bigots, are required to communicate with one another, and to establish cooperative relationships.

Furthermore, sometimes representatives of law enforcement themselves actively resist the construction of the state as a benign force. Law enforcement officers, as representatives of the state, are both the subjects and objects of the battle against hate crimes. While I recorded numerous encounters in my observations of police that would support the assessment that "cops don't get it," I also found that law enforcement responses to anti-hate crime measures are less monolithic than they are frequently perceived to be. Certainly, when police officers don't "get it," their failure to do so manifests itself in different ways, and is occurring for different reasons.

In a later passage concerning the discourse of legal rights, Brown acknowledges the need for more specific analyses of power and resistance in relation to the state. "[W]e can see quite clearly the impossibility of saying anything generic about the political value of rights: it makes little sense to argue for them or against them separately from an analysis of the historical conditions, social powers, and political discourses with which they converge or which they interdict."[78] I would argue that the same should be said for hate crime laws and

articulations of the meaning of hate crime, one that emphasizes its causes and another that focuses on its effects. Causal articulations tend, implicitly or explicitly, to privilege the notion that hate crime derives from social prejudices—whether or not the prejudices themselves have been produced by structural economic, psychological, political, and/or historical factors. These articulations appear most often in literature that either focuses solely on delineable criminal acts (assault, vandalism, etc.), or that broadly addresses all bias-related incidents, including those that are non-criminal (for example, instances of "hateful speech"). Models that attempt to articulate the effects of bias-related incidents appear more frequently in literature specifically on "hate speech," descriptions of the effects of such speech are usually emphasized to support efforts to move hate speech into the realm of punishable hate crime, or of otherwise legally redressable harm.

77. Organizations that support lesbian and gay rights, as well as civil rights groups working against racial and ethnic discrimination, fall into this category. In notable contrast, however, the Anti-Defamation League of B'nai B'rith has long been in the forefront of movements to pass hate crime legislation. While this group certainly concerns itself with abuses of state power, with regard to hate crime its position has always been one that sees the state as that which can protect Jews and other groups from abuses of non-state actors.

78. *See* BROWN, *supra* note 67, at 98.

that Brown's otherwise persuasive analysis of the current political moment fails to appreciate the subtlety of some attempts to make the state speak, as it were, against itself.

CONCLUSION

To the extent that the state does emerge as a benign and neutral arbiter from these sites of intense negotiation, I hope the examples above have demonstrated how those constructions may be intentional and strategically prevaricated, or unintentional but serendipitously productive. Continuous rhetorical labor is necessary to maintain the state's historically gendered and racialized character as unmarked or neutral. It seems apparent that both state and non-state actors often collude in this construction of the state, not naively, but with troubled awareness of the dangers inherent in the strategy. Those who figure the state as "neutral arbiters of injury" are not necessarily unaware, or deliberately incognizant, of the fact that the state and its manifestations in hate crime law are "themselves invested with the power to injure."[79]

Instead of tacitly accepting, or rejecting wholesale, strategies that are state-focused, we would do well to ask what conditions make it difficult to conceptualize *non*-state-centered strategies: what conditions make criminal justice strategies so compelling to activists? Are such strategies sometimes successful in disrupting the state's apparent neutrality, albeit in limited and contradictory ways? Do they create spaces of possibility for mobilizing state power in more just and responsible ways? What are the limits to those spaces?

I believe there are enough transformations of power and knowledge in law enforcement's response to bigotry and hate violence that one could make the argument either way: involving the criminal justice system in the effort to reduce hate crime can either be seen as hegemonic or counter-hegemonic. The way in which we view it makes a significant difference, however, and ultimately I believe that the former view is more accurate and has significant strategic advantages over the latter.

To view the implementation of anti-hate crime laws as counter-hegemonic is both a misreading of the current political climate, and an oversimplification of relations of power. "The state" is neither wholly progressive, nor wholly conservative—if indeed these labels continue to be meaningful at all. To position the state as only the target of positive change, rather than as a partial agent in such change is to accept a number of terms that constrain substantive efforts to improve intergroup relations in the United States. It is to fight harder for the presence or absence of training like that described above, than for a reconsideration of either policing itself or the appropriate role for governing bodies of

---

79. *Id.* at 27.

multicultural citizens. Finally, it functions to. prevent us from asking more directly what role it is we think police should play, and what other roles the state might play, in the effort to move toward more peaceful, more truly democratic collectives.

[8]

'A Stranger to its Laws':[1] Sovereign Bodies, Global Sexualities, and Transnational Citizens

CARL F. STYCHIN*

This article examines the importance of mobility in the historical and ongoing constitution of lesbian and gay subjectivities. While the state in the past frequently sought to restrict the movement of sexual dissidents across national borders, current developments in an array of jurisdictions suggest a more permissive attitude, particularly in the case of the 'unification' of same-sex couples. These legal and political developments are interrogated with respect to the construction of 'acceptable' homosexualities and, more broadly, in terms of cosmopolitan and communitarian visions of sexual citizenship.

INTRODUCTION

This article is about mobility, migration, and sexuality. I seek to build upon a body of work that has considered the centrality of free movement and mobility to the constitution of lesbian and gay subjectivities, both historically and currently. Mobility has been a powerful dimension in the

1 'A state cannot so deem a class of persons a stranger to its laws': *Romer* v. *Evans* 517 US 620 (1986), per Kennedy J (invalidating the Colorado state constitutional amendment repealing provisions that barred discrimination on the basis of sexual orientation).

Department of Law, University of Reading, Whiteknights, PO Box 217, Reading RG6 6AH, England

Funding for this research was provided by an ESRC funded research project, 'Strategies of Civic Inclusion in Pan-European Civil Society', within the 'One Europe or Several' research programme, award no. L213252002, and is gratefully acknowledged. Thanks to Jon Binnie, Davina Cooper, Didi Herman, Jo Shaw, and Alex Warleigh for their extensive comments. Earlier versions of this paper were delivered at the Socio-Legal Studies Association Conference (Belfast, April 2000), the American Law and Society Conference (Miami, May 2000), and at a workshop on European Citizenship and Social and Political Integration of the European Union (organized by the University of Sassari, and held at Alghero, Italy, June 2000). Many thanks to participants at those gatherings for questions and comments.

construction of the lesbian and gay subject but, at the same time, movement across national borders historically has produced anxieties within the nation state which have been articulated to highly sexualized discourses, deployed in part in order to control and curtail mobility, not only of sexual dissidents, but of a wide range of people. Thus, I will consider migration and movement from (at least) two quite different vantage points: as enabling and empowering, but also as producing an historically hostile response. I then go on to discuss current legal and political developments with respect to same-sex relationships which cross national borders as an example.

I consider as well the related question of whether legal recognition symbolizes 'progressive' change in social attitudes and a hegemonic shift, particularly in an era characterized by increasingly reactionary responses to migration more generally, most obviously in the context of refugee movements. In a time in which the nation state responds to perceived globalization through a selective tightening of border control, how might we understand what appears to be a liberalizing of legal and political responses to the movement of lesbians and gay men, especially when migration is aimed at facilitating unification with a same-sex partner? In other words, how might we 'map' what appear to be liberal and progressive developments onto a genealogy of legal and political responses to the sexuality-migration nexus? And, finally, I consider what these developments might suggest regarding broader concepts of citizenship, community, and cosmopolitanism, and notions of inclusion within civil society and the state. In keeping with the transnational focus, my analysis will itself take a somewhat 'nomadic' approach. Examples will be drawn from a range of national and geopolitical contexts to answer these questions.

MOBILIZING SEXUALITY

I begin by clarifying some concepts integral to my argument. I use the term 'mobility' to refer to the idea of 'uprooting'; a concept closely tied to freedom of movement and, more generally, associated with the nomadic subject – the crosser of borders and boundaries (whether by 'necessity' or 'choice'). Thus, mobility is used not only in terms of a legal right to free movement, but also to suggest wider connotations with respect to sexuality.[2] Mobility provides a useful lens through which to analyse sexual identities, and here it is connected to migration and travel more generally: movement towards a new place and a new life(style). The connections between travel, mobility, and sexuality have a long and complex history which I want now to trace, albeit in an admittedly abbreviated form.

---

2 For an exploration of these connections in the context of 'gender', see R. Braidotti, *Nomadic Subjects: Embodiment and Sexual Difference in Contemporary Feminist Theory* (1994).

The significance of migration in the constitution of lesbian and gay subjectivities is increasingly documented, particularly from within the discipline of geography.[3] It is a recognized historical phenomenon, especially noteworthy in the United States of America.[4] For example, Kath Weston's ethnographic work on the 'Great Gay Migration' to American cities of the 1970s and early 1980s suggests that this period saw the movement of tens of thousands of people, and the importance of the imaginative, aspirational processes associated with this migratory flow cannot be underestimated.[5] Moreover, Weston describes how the gay imaginary has come to be spatialized, with the city providing 'a beacon of tolerance and gay community, the country a locus of persecution and gay absence'.[6] The creation of gay urban spaces is crucial to this narrative of migration, as is the way in which those spaces were and continue to be constituted.[7]

Central to this imaginary is movement and travel, and the importance of a literal escape from the constraints of locality, family, and history.[8] In this regard, 'home' has often been an ambiguous signifier for lesbians and gays, suggesting for some a place not of refuge but from which they need to escape, thereby leading to the appropriation of a more nomadic or diasporic identity. Although I certainly would not universalize this experience, it does seem to resonate with many. Yet, at the same time, as lesbian and gay identities became increasingly 'ethnicized' (in part through a spatial imagining of the city and gay presence within it), lesbians and gays could increasingly see themselves (and be seen by others) as trying to construct a 'homeland' within an urban setting. But, of course, the appropriation of space around an identity in this way can also be (and has been) highly exclusionary. As Weston suggests, 'from its inception, the imagined community incarnated in gay neighborhoods has been gendered, racialized, and classed'.[9] Ironically,

3 See J. Binnie, 'Invisible Europeans: Sexual Citizenship in the New Europe' (1997) 29 *Environment and Planning A* 237; J. Binnie and G. Valentine, 'Geographies of Sexuality – A Review of Progress' (1999) 23 *Progress in Human Geography* 175.
4 See, for example, J. D'Emilio, *Sexual Politics, Sexual Communities* (1983); G. Chauncey, *Gay New York* (1994).
5 K. Weston, 'Get Thee To a Big City: Sexual Imaginary and the Great Gay Migration' (1995) 2 *Gay and Lesbian Q.* 253.
6 id., p. 262.
7 See, for example, M. Castells, 'Cultural Identity and Urban Structure: The Spatial Organization of San Francisco's Urban Gay Community' in *Urban Policy under Capitalism*, eds. N.I. Fainstein and S.S. Fainstein (1983) 237. But see, also, L. Knopp, 'Sexuality and Urban Space: Gay Male Identity Politics in the United States, the United Kingdom and Australia' in *Cities of Difference*, eds. R. Fincher and J.M. Jacobs (1998) 149, at 172, who underscores how forms of urbanization are also highly culturally specific, in his comparison of American and British developments, suggesting that 'territorially based economic and political practices' are more feasible in some countries than in others.
8 See B. Cant, 'Introduction' in *Invented Identities?: Lesbians and Gays Talk About Migration*, ed. B. Cant (1997) 1.
9 Weston, op. cit., n. 5, p. 270.

though, as lesbian and gay identities become geographically grounded through urban migration, these places themselves come to be simultaneously 'delocalised';[10] part of a 'worldwide network of "gay villages"' possessing a homogeneity and familiarity across place and time.[11]

While bearing in mind the very important point that choices regarding travel and migration (and the two often raise very different issues) are always highly constrained – in particular by money – the discourse of migration is shaped as well by an array of variables, such as relationship to family, kin, and place. While some seek escape from the constraints of family, for others family continues to be a place of refuge from a hostile world.[12] Moreover, narratives of travel and migration with respect to sexuality may be a particularly western (or, indeed, American) phenomenon. However, the impact of globalization, time-space compression, and increased labour mobility is wide ranging. As Jon Binnie suggests, 'contemporary transformations of the global economy have created new possibilities for the transformation of sexual cultures', and this is occurring in a range of cultural locations, and shaped as a phenomenon by an array of identities and constraints.[13] My aim is to heed Binnie's criticism that 'awareness of migration as the underpinning of sexual-dissident consciousness is often overlooked in studies of sexuality and space',[14] and to suggest that legal discourse is not immune from that point either. Escape, displacement, and the search for place are important elements in lesbian and gay consciousness, and I think provide a partial explanation for the role of sexual mobility issues in legal discourse today. As Oliva Espín suggests, regarding lesbian (as well as heterosexual) women, 'the crossing of borders through migration provides the space and "permission" to cross boundaries and transform their sexuality and sex roles'.[15] Although much of the history of gay mobility has an American focus (and is internal to the nation state), Binnie suggests, for example, that 'the development of a European economic superpower [could] have consequences for the social and cultural politics around sexuality', in which the need for labour mobility has necessitated rights of free movement for workers between members states of the European Union.[16] Thus, I cautiously suggest that lesbian and gay migration issues may well have an increasing importance, and that they are facilitated by wider economic, political, and cultural developments. At the same time, I believe that an analysis of lesbian and gay migration can illuminate the experience of immigration more generally.

10 G.B. Ingram, 'Marginality and the Landscape of Erotic Alien(n)nations' in *Queers in Space: Communities, Public Places, Sites of Resistance*, eds. G.B. Ingram, A.-M. Bonthillette, and Y. Retter (1997) 27, at 50.
11 D.T. Evans, '(*homo*)Sexual Citizenship' in *Gender Perceptions and the Law*, eds. C.R. Barker, E.A. Kirk, and M. Soh (1998) 117, at 141.
12 This may have particular importance in the context of racial and ethnic minorities.
13 Binnie, op. cit., n. 3, p. 242.
14 id., p. 241.
15 O.M. Espín, *Women Crossing Boundaries: A Psychology of Immigration and Transformations of Sexuality* (1999) 5.
16 Binnie, op. cit., n. 3, p. 242.

But the importance of movement and travel in relation to the constitution of sexual identities has other dimensions as well, especially outside of the context of the increasingly clearly delineated gay spaces of urban America. The recognition of the importance of sexuality within tourism studies, for example, has underscored the nexus between tourism and sexual identity.[17] Holidays may be significant in the construction of sexual identities; reinforcing again the relationship between identity and consumption. But a more complex connection is also apparent. Identity can be understood not only as literally *being* a tourist, but also more broadly as experiencing an identity (for those living outside the gay village) which is located away from where most of life is lived; by physically leaving one's immediate environs through travel, for example, to a gay space which may be *far* from 'home'. Travel thus can serve as a metaphor for identity. The search for identity and 'self' becomes a form of tourism. Identity is constituted through visits to the 'scene' (being a tourist there), and in this way, it is through travel that one finds one's place – a homeland – which is removed from the everyday constraints of home. Mobility thus can signify freedom, and it also signifies a *need* to leave – to escape – which suggests inhospitability, danger, and violence; dangerous journeys undertaken before reaching a (safe) destination.

Mobility has other metaphorical resonances as well. In relation to gender, Rosi Braidotti has argued that 'mobility also refers to the intellectual space of creativity, that is to say, the freedom to invent new ways of conducting our lives, new schemes of representation of ourselves'.[18] Indeed, the experience of migration can provide 'a metaphor for the crossing of borders and boundaries that all lesbians [and gay men] confront when refusing to continue living in old ways'.[19] Furthermore, these migratory processes are operating on a virtual level. Research has shown how 'one of the most common benefits of the Internet to the gay community, according to the interviewees, is that it permits geographically dispersed minority individuals to interact with one another as if they were a local majority' (which may be reducing, in the process, the importance of physical travel to identity).[20] Finally, not surprisingly, mobility can be discursively appropriated in a negative reaction to its empowering potential for lesbians and gays. The perceived frequency of lesbian and gay travel has been deployed in the construction of gays as an

17 See, for example, J. Binnie, 'Trading Places: Consumption, Sexuality and the Production of Queer Space' in *Mapping Desire: Geographies of Sexualities*, eds. D. Bell and G. Valentine (1995) 182; H. Hughes, 'Holidays and Homosexual Identity' (1997) 18 *Tourism Management* 3.

18 Braidotti, op. cit., n. 2, p. 256.

19 Espín, op. cit., n. 15, p. 159.

20 J.D. Weinrich, 'Strange Bedfellows: Homosexuality, Gay Liberation, and the Internet' (1997) 22 *J. of Sex Education and Therapy* 58. See, also, the essays on the 'Cybersexual' in *The Cybercultures Reader*, eds. D. Bell and B.M. Kennedy (2000) 391–467.

'undeserving' (because privileged) minority, who do not 'deserve' what are described as 'special rights', because of their *upward mobility*.[21]

Yet, mobility should not be 'celebrated' as the unproblematic basis for the constitution of a lesbian or gay identity. First, as I have already suggested, mobility is constrained from the outset by its central relationship to consumption and class, which are all too frequently closely connected to race and gender. Thus, mobility is a limited and limiting basis for identity, and moreover, in analysing gay migration processes, there is a constant danger of 'centring' the affluent, more likely male, middle-class, able-bodied, healthy, 'cosmopolitan' citizen. Relatedly, there is a tendency to assume that lesbian and gay migrants are necessarily economic migrants who choose to move, thereby forgetting that many migration experiences may be more closely analogous to – or, indeed, in fact may be – those of refugees. Second, while movement may involve travel to a more congenial place and life, this also opens up the possibilities for disappointment with what one finds in the search for 'roots' and a 'home'. Migration involves loss as well as opportunity, and transnational migrants (especially when members of a racial or ethnic minority) are subject to intense surveillance from the state, as well as from within migrant communities, particularly when they are women – both heterosexual and lesbian.[22] Language also provides a severe constraint on participation and acceptance. Moreover, while migration may facilitate the expression of a sexual identity, it may involve a sense of leaving other identities behind. Finally, the relationship between mobility in the context of transnationalism and globalization, and the constitution of sexual identities, is politically highly ambiguous. It has been argued, for example, that globalization is contributing to the imposition of a modernist, Eurocentric, universalist sexual subjectivity and a formulaic picture of sexuality.[23] That is, a 'Stonewall' model of liberation based upon the closet and 'coming out' is universalized as *the* foundation for same-sex sexual identities, which is assumed to be culturally constituted in the same way everywhere. Mobility as the basis of identity can be seen as part of that same narrative, and indeed, physical mobility may well help to entrench it through the expansion of the gay global village, as a result of which spaces for local articulations are increasingly constrained.[24] This also impacts upon migrants and the way their sexual identities are constituted. After all, sexual

21 D. Herman, *The Anti-Gay Agenda: Orthodox Vision and the Christian Right* (1997) 111–36.
22 Espín, op. cit., n. 15, p. 6.
23 M.F. Manalansan, 'In the Shadows of Stonewall: Examining Gay Transnational Politics and the Diasporic Dilemma' (1995) 2 *Gay and Lesbian Q.* 425.
24 See, also, G. Valentine, 'An Equal Place to Work? Anti-Lesbian Discrimination and Sexual Citizenship in the European Union' in *Women of the European Union: The Politics of Work and Daily Life*, eds. M.D. García-Ramon and J. Monk (1996) 111, at 122, who argues that with the likely expansion of the European Union eastward and the growth of transnational mobilization, an Anglo-American 'imperialism' can result through the imposition of an equality agenda modelled on individual rights.

cultures are also culturally specific. In her analysis of lesbian migration, Oliva Espín has found, for example, that:

> many women who identified as lesbian before the migration have to learn to be lesbian in their new cultural context. If a lesbian is from a non-European background, she also faces acculturation as a (so-called) minority person.[25]

The problems of tourism in relation to sexuality also need to be critically considered. Here again, global travel and time-space compression may be liberating for some: for those with the money to found their identity on mobility. It can result in the sexual exoticization of the 'southern' and 'eastern', economic exploitation, and can impact negatively on local identities through a 'backlash' by the post-colonial state in response to the (sometimes rightly) perceived decadence of western gay tourism (the docking of gay cruiseships provides an apt example).

Thus, this article aims not to celebrate migration for its own sake, but rather, I attempt to respond to the observations of queer geographers Jon Binnie and Gill Valentine that 'the significance of migration in lesbian and gay lives and identities needs to receive greater attention'.[26] As they go on to point out, 'sexualities and the state are mutually constituted at different spatial scales': the local, national, and increasingly, the transnational and global.[27] Sexualities have long served in the project of state and nation building, and it is to such constructs that I now turn.

BORDER ANXIETIES AND THE GOOD HOMOSEXUAL

Mobility often triggers social anxieties and fears of disorder centred on a lack of social control of subjects who are not 'in place'.[28] This is most obvious in the context of reactions to travelling and nomadic peoples, particularly when movement is perceived, not as the product of *individual* exile, but rather of group migration:

> travel is very much a modern concept, signifying both commercial and leisure movement in an era of expanding western capitalism, while displacement refers to the more mass migrations that modernity has engendered.[29]

The latter certainly continues to produce severe social anxieties: fears of loss of control, of a loosening of national identity, anxieties about the non-assimilable 'other', and so on. Those reactions have a long genealogy within the western nation state.

However, this raises another important distinction, in terms of the degree to which movement involves the literal crossing of borders. It is the

25 Espín, op. cit., n. 15, p. 156.
26 Binnie and Valentine, op. cit., n. 3, p. 179.
27 id.
28 I recognize that these reactions may be culturally specific, and I would not claim that these observations are universally true.
29 C. Kaplan, *Questions of Travel* (1998) 3.

transgression of political boundaries which may be crucial to understanding social anxieties. The boundary represents the demarcation of space, and suggests that what is within, as well as what is outside, can be contained. As a consequence:

> movement within nation-states is called mobility and is highly desirable [for governments and corporate interests]. Movement between nation-states is called migration and is extremely undesirable. At the borders of nation-states the virtue of flexibility mutates into the vice of potentially criminal immigration.[30]

Thus, movement within nation states is often positively encouraged. Market flexibility demands the movement of factors of production, such as labour, to where the jobs are; and such mobility is often facilitated by the state. On the other hand, the crossing of nation state borders to achieve the same end is frequently seen as illegitimate, and leads to the construction of the identity of the 'economic migrant'.

Indeed, it is the fear of migration, and the connections that are drawn between migration, crime, jobs, and social insecurity, amongst other anxieties, that produce what has been described in the United Kingdom context as a 'pathological focus' on border control.[31] Adrian Favell suggests that this heightened anxiety is closely related to his claim that 'Britain is not and has never been a monocultural nation-state' and that it is 'not strictly bound to any cultural "imagined community".'[32] Although *Britain* may lack such a monocultural identity, Eve Darian-Smith has convincingly shown how border control remains connected to identity and space in the context of *Englishness*:

> modern English identity is, above all, about inclusion and exclusion, which was intricately mapped onto the British state's spatial expression as an isolated island-nation. In turn this necessitated and confirmed the need for constant military defence of what was constructed as a national cultural space.[33]

Again, border control seems central to understanding reactions to migration. It also explains national anxieties and tensions around free movement in the context of the European Union:

> with the free movement of ideas, goods and peoples defining the essential character of a new borderless Europe, the rising salience of territorial control emerges to oppose this characterization, particularly in the security and transportation areas.[34]

---

30 U. Beck, 'The Cosmopolitan Perspective: Sociology of the Second Age of Modernity' (2000) 51 *British J. of Sociology* 79, at 93.

31 A. Favell, *Philosophies of Integration: Immigration and the Idea of Citizenship in France and Britain* (1998) 202.

32 id., p. 102.

33 E. Darian-Smith, *Bridging Divides: The Channel Tunnel and English Legal Identity in the New Europe* (1999) 89.

34 id., p. 75.

One could add control with regard to immigration, particularly third-country nationals, and especially refugees and asylum-seekers. The tension between movement and control is thus central to the relationship between post-national forces and the nation state.[35]

My claim in this article is that that these dynamics are important to an understanding of reactions by the state to sexual dissidents; that there are close connections between the historical desire for social control of homosexuality, and control over movement and borders more generally. In this regard, the figure of the illegal alien provides a useful analogue to the homosexual. Both are produced as outside the bounds of normalcy, and law, and they are strangers, but also the most dangerous strangers of all, in that they are *essentially* different, but also able to 'pass' undetected in the absence of close surveillance.

A metaphor of bodily containment thereby becomes relevant.[36] Both the homosexual and the illegal alien (or, indeed, the 'bogus' refugee claimant) are constructed as threats to the coherence and boundedness of the national body, and as a threat to knowledge of the national self, producing a heightened state of anxiety in response. As Jessica Chapin suggests in the context of United States-Mexican border patrols:

> The failure of the border patrol to control entrances into the body politic gives rise to anxieties that are frequently articulated in terms of the vulnerability to penetration, and hence the feminization, of a symbolically masculine body. The defense of the nation, like the defense of hegemonic forms of masculine heterosexuality, is framed as a rigorous policing of boundaries, in this case against an onslaught of immigrants at America's 'back door'.[37]

In both anti-immigration and anti-gay discourses, we find tropes of bodily production and waste, in/visibility, the threat of penetration of borders, the power to 'pass' undetected, to defy and to undermine knowledges of the self. Both the immigrant and the homosexual become problems of self-knowledge, necessitating heightened surveillance. Opening the door to either will lead down a slippery slope: if homosexuality, to a slippery slope of vices threatening the existence of the heterosexual family; if immigration, opening the door to offspring, cousins, and in-laws, which threaten the essential cultural heritage of the nation state.[38] The importance of reading and controlling bodies thereby becomes central.

These 'genealogical linkages' have been well documented in the United Kingdom context by Anna Marie Smith in the particular circumstances of the

---

35 Favell, op. cit., n. 31, p. 245.

36 I have considered the role of containment metaphors in the constitution of nation state and sexuality in more detail elsewhere; see C.F. Stychin, 'New Labour, New "Britain"?: Constitutionalism, Sovereignty, and Nation/State in Transition' (1999) 19 *Studies in Law, Politics, and Society* 139.

37 J. Chapin, 'Closing America's "Back Door"?' (1998) 4 *Gay and Lesbian Q.* 403, at 412.

38 id., p. 414.

1980s.[39] Smith shows how 'traditional articulations' concerning race and immigration get rearticulated in the context of the 'dangerous queer', in which both racism and homophobia serve as 'symbolic nodal points' from which linkages are then made.[40] These links centre on disease, foreign invasion, and the threat of unassimilable 'other' cultures, dangerous criminality, and so on. Such tropes are heavily dependent upon viral and bodily metaphors. They are also highly spatialized. Thus, with respect to sexuality, we see described the 'heterosexual nation as if it were a body whose immune system had to ward off the dangerous homosexual virus which threatened to invade the nation from the immoral outside'.[41] So too with immigration, as 'the unwanted foreign populations install themselves in the heartland of the "mother country's" body and establish the flow of nutrients back to the foreign bodies'.[42] Thus, border control is metaphorically linked to the skin and immune system:

> the British obsession with border controls against continental rabies is in this sense an important precursor to the hegemonic discourse on AIDS. The representation of disease as originating in foreign elements also mobilizes the militarization of discourse on immigration.[43]

Both become invasions of the social from outside and from within. There is also a connection to the idea of containment; both migration and homosexuality have an unfixity and an excessiveness that needs to be contained to prevent invasion: this is a dangerous difference that threatens order, consensus, nation state, and way of life.[44] Like migrants more generally, the (particularly male) homosexual has been a threat because of an inability to know *his* borders, and these tropes were also closely

---

39 A.M. Smith, *New Right Discourses on Race and Sexuality* (1994).
40 id., p. 17.
41 id., p. 25.
42 id., p. 159.
43 id., p. 200.
44 The manipulability of these tropes is readily apparent in the context of CJD, a deadly human disease which may well have a link to 'mad cow disease', which was caused by unsafe practices in the production of animal feed in the United Kingdom. Here we find the export of disease from the island state (which is hardly a new phenomenon, as the history of imperialism and the spread of disease to indigenous peoples demonstrates), and it is also a disease which could be articulated to similar discourses as have been prevalent around HIV. Yet, within the United Kingdom, the dominant tropes surrounding CJD are trivialization ('only a few cases'), resolution ('problem now solved; no more worries'), and historical accident (a trope rarely employed within dominant discourses around HIV). Moreover, CJD itself becomes associated with foreignness and a European 'plot' against Britain in the attempts by continental European countries to foreclose the importation of British beef. Rhetorical tropes are then deployed to suggest that things are more unsafe 'there' than 'here', where only the highest standards of food safety are employed. Thus, in a turn of events, the threat to nation state sovereignty comes from the European Union in the attempts by EU member states to protect public health and safety.

connected to the idea of the homosexual as security risk in the context of the Cold War.[45]

But, I want now to take the analysis further, and rather than considering the similarities in the discursive construction of homosexuality and migration, to consider the construction of homosexual as migrant. Of course, it is not surprising that given the genealogical linkages between discourses of homosexuality and migration, and given the way in which, as I suggested in the previous section, migration has played a key role in the construction of sexual identities, the state has sought explicitly to control migration of those who identify with or practice same-sex sexual acts. Although it is important to recognize that transnational movements are not uniform as between different cultural locales, and that there is an uneven politics of mobilization around migration which varies as between nation states, numerous examples can be deployed to demonstrate the relevance of migration in several different national contexts. Certainly, in the United States of America, the history of the exclusion of homosexuals from the nation state is extensive, and it was originally linked, not to discourses of national security, but to concerns about the health of the body politic.[46] There were close genealogical connections to race-based exclusions in immigration law, turning on a eugenic justification for the control of immigration.[47] Later, the homosexual exclusion would be linked to anti-Communist discourses, but those too were articulated to threats to health and to the immune system. Once again we find clear links between nation, borders, race, immigration, sexuality, mobility, health, immunity, infection, and containment.

For example, until 1991, homosexuality was a ground for exclusion from admission to the United States pursuant to s. 212(a)(4) of the Immigration and Nationality Act. However, the Immigration Act (1990) eliminated 'sexual deviancy' as a basis for exclusion, and this occurred through a remarkably 'low key' and largely unnoticed legislative reform.[48] Although I would not want to exaggerate the point, the timing did coincide with the so-called fall of Communism, and it demonstrates how the most blunt use of juridical power in controlling the movement of lesbians and gay men gave way to liberal reform (to be replaced, I will argue, by more subtle disciplinary mechanisms of power).[49]

45 See L. Edelman, *Homographesis* (1994).
46 R.J. Foss, 'The Demise of the Homosexual Exclusion: New Possibilities for Gay and Lesbian Immigration' (1994) 29 *Harvard Civil Rights – Civil Liberties Law Rev.* 439, at 446.
47 id., p. 445.
48 id., p. 462.
49 The exclusion provision itself though operated as part of a system of procedures 'for administering sex in relation to multiform objectives (that concerned not only sex but also gender, race, class, and constructions of nation)': E. Luibheid, ' "Looking Like a Lesbian": The Organization of Sexual Monitoring at the United States-Mexican Border' (1998) 8 *J. of the History of Sexuality* 477, at 479.

Of course, the use of juridical power certainly has not disappeared in the context of same-sex sexuality and migration. The American immigration ban on persons with HIV undoubtedly is underpinned by both racist and homophobic ideologies, which reproduce the discourses of containment, infection, and fears of loss of control of the body politic.[50] Of interest here also is the fact that the HIV exclusion is accompanied by a 'waiver' provision which allows persons with HIV to immigrate to the United States if they have a 'qualifying relationship' with a United States citizen or permanent resident (spouse, parent or child), and if the applicant can prove that he or she is not likely to become a 'public charge'.[51] The waiver is not extended to same-sex relationships. It underscores the extent to which even the powerful language of disease, containment, and the transgression of national borders can give way to the discourse of relationships and their reunification, particularly with regard to 'spouses'. When that spousal nexus is explicitly grounded in the privatization of financial responsibilities for support, its attraction seems overwhelming.

The repeal of the homosexual exclusion in immigration law may foreshadow the extent to which we are witnessing at least the beginnings of a hegemonic shift at the turn of the century, and mobility provides a useful vantage point from which to investigate changing conceptions of sexuality within dominant discourses. In particular, I want to interrogate the continuing relevance of Anna Marie Smith's 'good homosexual', which she contrasts to the 'dangerous queer' construction in 1980s Britain. Smith argues, drawing on Parliamentary debates regarding s. 28 of the Local Government Act, that speakers who argued in support of legal restrictions on the 'promotion of homosexuality by local authorities' 'spoke again and again of a law-abiding, disease-free, self-closeting homosexual figure who knew her or his proper place on the secret fringes of mainstream society'.[52] This becomes an imaginary figure who, because completely discrete and closeted, has no public identity at all. Thus, the scope for social acceptance of homosexuality was limited to the subject who completely respected the public/private dichotomy, and thus facilitated the elimination of all traces of homosexuality (and certainly any 'positive images') from public view.

Undoubtedly, Smith's analysis of the good homosexual resonated strongly in the context of the Thatcher government's tropes around sexuality in 1980s Britain. However, can we detect shifts in the construction of the good homosexual in present day 'Cool Britannia' and elsewhere? If such shifts *are* occurring (and I will suggest that there are at least signs that they are) what,

---

50 Foss, op. cit., n. 46, p. 451.
51 L.S. Soloway, 'Challenging Discrimination Against Gays and Lesbians in U.S. Immigration Law: The Lesbian and Gay Immigration Rights Taskforce' (n.d.) <http://www.girtf.org/html/about.html>.
52 Smith, op. cit., n. 39, p. 18.

in turn, does that suggest about the continuing relevance of the notions of containment, nation, place, and surveillance? Do these concepts continue to leave *their* 'traces'?

The importance of mobility in current political and legal developments is readily apparent. Freedom of movement, for example, is a central constitutional right in the context of the European Union legal order, and it is a powerful enabling force in the construction of identity; although it is a right which undoubtedly most favours 'affluent professional lesbians and gay men with marketable skills'.[53] And, as I have argued, mobility is also vitally important in understanding anxieties which lead to a range of restrictive and repressive measures by the state in an effort to control and contain what are perceived to be threats to the nation state and its borders.

Thus, although much attention up to now in lesbian and gay legal strategies has been focused on the empowering potential of a discourse of equality and equal rights as a key to the achievement of full citizenship and social inclusion, one could argue that it is through claims around mobility rights and freedom of movement that we can find a powerful legal 'toolkit', through which claims to citizenship can be made, and with a fairly high degree of success. At the same time, the limitations of rights discourse, and its potential for the *disciplining* of the lesbian and gay subject, certainly do not disappear in the context of claims to mobility. Even with this 'freedom' seems to come requirements for responsibility, which are closely connected to changing ideas of what constitutes the good homosexual. In this regard, many developments concerning mobility claims are tied to the legal recognition of same-sex relationships, and it is here where we may particularly witness hegemonic shifts. A liberal, 'progressive' acceptance and social inclusion is accompanied by an increasingly disciplinary regime which accompanies legal recognition; in which implicitly an excluded 'other' is constructed who can then be re-placed outside the borders of a body politic in which inclusion is symbolized by relationship recognition. This reconstruction of the good homosexual, I want to argue, is linked to wider social and political currents concerning the privatization of financial responsibility within the family, in which 'good' relationships more generally are defined in terms of their cost-saving capacity for the state. Thus, the centrality of paid employment to citizenship and inclusion (which is increasingly facilitated by mobility across national borders) is combined with the encouragement of stable relationships which are supported because they are perceived to be the basis of good citizenship.

53 D. Bell and J. Binnie, *The Sexual Citizen: Queer Politics and Beyond* (2000) 120.

CITIZENSHIP AND THE UNIFICATION OF 'SPOUSES'

> Nothing throws the question of the different ways in which formations of sexual citizenship are constructed by nation-states into greater relief than migration policies.[54]

Mobility and sexuality increasingly conjoin in legal discourse in the context of the recognition of same-sex partnerships which involve geographically complex facts, but which appear to replicate the legally recognized institution of marriage. The complexity arises from the fact that the relationship is between a 'full citizen' and a 'foreign national', and the latter seeks to migrate to the country of the former in order to fully 'perform' their marriage-like relationship.[55] These claims for reunification increasingly are being recognized in a number of western nation states through immigration law and special administrative concessions.

The issue brings together a number of different cultural currents which on their face one might think would produce a politically explosive combination. First, it raises the spectre of the legal recognition of same-sex relationships, a major political question in the west today. As Manuel Castells has argued:

> the yearning for same-sex families became [in the past few years] one of the most powerful cultural trends amongst gays and lesbians ... extending the value of family to non-traditional, non-heterosexual forms of love, sharing, and child rearing.[56]

In addition, it relates to globalization, transnationalism, mobility, and travel. It underscores the increasing possibilities for the crossing of borders, and the forming of relationships internationally, suggesting a cosmopolitanism that comes with travel.

As a consequence, we might expect to find a hostile reaction grounded in the fears of spatial, territorial, and sexual transgression. Here we find a transgression of the nuclear family and marital relationship through its replication (and worse, the attempt to obtain legal recognition for such 'pretend' families through immigration law), as well as transgression of the physical boundaries of the nation state through the 'importation' of a homosexual relationship. The struggle for recognition of these relationships thus might well lead to a potent combination of discourses: national territory; border controls; sexual deviancy; immigration 'fraud'; and the opening of floodgates to sexual deviants.

Given the centrality of migration and travel in the constitution of lesbian and gay identities, it is not surprising that this issue has assumed an

---

54 id., p. 119.

55 In the context of the European Union, the interesting issues revolve around relationships between a 'Citizen of the Union' and a 'third country national'.

56 M. Castells, *The Power of Identity* (1997) 219.

increasingly central place on the lesbian and gay legal reform agenda. What is particularly interesting to me is the extent to which legal change is occuring with relatively little 'backlash'. Of course, the symbolic and material meanings of migration differ widely across national cultures, but generally, liberal law reform appears to be occurring in this arena (as in many others) with an almost inevitability.

Australia provided an early example, and something of a model for what is occurring in other jurisdictions. As far back as 1991, recognition of same-sex relationships for immigration purposes occurred by administrative regulation, described as 'non-familial relationships of emotional interdependency'.[57] This allowance for ministerial discretion in immigration with respect to same-sex couples followed an intensive lobbying campaign by the Gay and Lesbian Immigration Task Force (GLITF). Although decision making ultimately rested with the cabinet minister responsible for immigration, the Task Force 'screened' applicants to ensure a 'commitment to monogamy and lookalike heterosexual relationships'.[58] The Minister relied on the Task Force 'to ensure that genuine and monogamous relationships were presented by the couples'.[59] Same-sex migration has become increasingly institutionalized in Australia over the period since it was introduced by ministerial discretion, although admittedly not always in increasingly liberal and enabling ways.[60] Those applying in the 'interdependency visa category' are now required to demonstrate cohabitation for a year previous to the application:

> It is necessary to prove that 'for the period of 12 months immediately preceding the date of application' you had a 'mutual commitment to a shared life'; 'the relationship between you was genuine and continuing and you had been living together; or not living separately and apart on a permanent basis'.[61]

The institutionalization and normalization of same-sex immigration, however, as is clear from the Australian example, occurs with a requirement to replicate an idealized model of heterosexual romance, centred upon monogamy, cohabitation, and extreme interdependency. Of course, the Australian experience has to be placed in context: it is itself a national culture in which migration is highly normalized, and where the 'tyranny of distance' may create a *somewhat* more sympathetic context in which

---

57 J. Hart, 'A Cocktail of Alarm: Same-Sex Couples and Migration to Australia 1985–90' in *Modern Homosexualities: Fragments of Lesbian and Gay Experience*, ed. K. Plummer (1992) 121, at 122.

58 id., p. 131.

59 id., p. 126.

60 See C.F. Stychin, *A Nation by Rights: National Cultures, Sexual Identity Politics, and the Discourse of Rights* (1998) 217, fn. 13.

61 GLITF, 'Gay and Lesbian Partnership Migration' (1999) <http://www.glitf.org.au>. Effective 1 November 1999, the visa is no longer referred to as the 'interdependency visa', the name having been changed to a 'partner visa'.

reunification of partners can occur.[62] Yet, at the same time, an undercurrent of 'self-discipline' has informed the history of same-sex migration. The early role of the Task Force was to ensure that only 'proper' relationships were placed before the Minister for the exercise of his discretion. Thus, while on the one hand, same-sex couples were strongly encouraged to mimic the supposedly 'private' institution of marriage as the prerequisite for obtaining immigration status on the basis of their relationship, in so doing, the couple subject their relationship to detailed surveillance and examination, in order to determine whether it *sufficiently* copied an imagined and imaginary model.

Very similar patterns are now occurring in other national contexts. In the United Kingdom, new immigration guidelines were implemented by the Labour government on 10 October 1997; one justification being the concern, as expressed by the Immigration Minister, that previous guidelines (which made virtually no provision for same-sex couple reunification) may have breached human rights law.[63] The 'concessions' which have been introduced (which operate outside the immigration rules themselves), make clear the requirements which must be met before an application will be considered:

> (i) the applicant is the unmarried partner of a person present and settled in the United Kingdom or who is on the same occasion being admitted for settlement; and (ii) any previous marriage (or similar relationship) by either partner has permanently broken down; and (iii) the parties are legally unable to marry under United Kingdom law (other than by reason of consanguineous relationships or age); and (iv) the parties have been living together in a relationship akin to marriage which has subsisted for four years or more; and (v) there will be adequate accommodation for the parties and any dependants without recourse to public funds in accommodation which they own or occupy exclusively; and (vi) the parties will be able to maintain themselves and any dependants adequately without recourse to public funds; and (vii) the parties intend to live together permanently; and (viii) the applicant holds a valid United Kingdom entry clearance for entry in this capacity.[64]

The guidelines underscore the extent to which relationships must meet an 'idealized' vision of cohabitation, and they also demonstrate the extent to which marriage-like relationships are assumed to carry with them a financial responsibility grounded in interdependency. The message in the guidelines is clear: with recognition comes responsibility, through the privatization of all costs of the migrant onto the relationship, rather than onto the state. Yet, while the expectation is that the couple will act 'responsibly' (primarily in a financial sense), through such mechanisms as ownership of a family home, it

62 Hart, op. cit., n. 57, p. 121.
63 'Britain Eases Immigration for Gay Partners' (n.d.) <http://religioustolerance.org/hom_0055.htm>.
64 Home Office, 'Concession Outside the Immigration Rules for Unmarried Partners' (1999) <http://www.homeoffice.gov.uk/ind/concess.htm>.

also has been made clear by the government that these 'concessions' to same-sex couples should not be taken to suggest that the relationships are on a 'par' with marriage. At the same time, they are required to act in a way which replicates both an idealized version of marriage and an idealized, class inflected, model of familial economic relations. Those who are legally able to marry are foreclosed from taking advantage of the concession. As the Immigration Minister, Mike O'Brien, explained:

> It has been a fundamental principle of the Immigration Rules that someone already settled in the United Kingdom may bring their spouse into the United Kingdom to join them, subject to meeting clear tests as to the genuineness of the marriage and the financial capacity of the couple. The policy which was announced on 10 October is a concession outside the Immigration Rules for those unmarried partners who are legally unable to marry. This retains the special position of marriage. There are no current plans to incorporate this concession into the Immigration Rules.[65]

But such a focus on privatization of financial responsibility is very much in keeping with a broader ideology which underpins the goverment's immigration policies. The Immigration and Asylum Act 1999 affects all those who migrate on the basis of sponsorship by a family member:

> a sponsor's failure to support will be a criminal offence, and there will be no state support for sponsored immigrants, even in the direst of emergencies. The only exception will be destitute asylum-seekers, who can be provided with accommodation and support at a price. The asylum welfare system will be run by a new Home Office agency, in a completely segregated regime featuring compulsion and surveillance. Although the Home Office says its plan is to develop 'clusters' of asylum-seekers in areas where local refugee communities already exist, the Bill expressly prohibits either location or the asylum-seeker's preference from being taken into account in allocating accommodation.[66]

Thus, the overwhelming drive is for the privatization of the costs and responsibility of migration, combined with heightened surveillance of those who require the aid of the state. The family is idealized, not only in terms of emotional support, but also as the provider of financial assistance. Yet, even in those cases where sponsorship by a same-sex partner is offered, relationships remain subject to intense surveillance by immigration officers, often with continuing fears of deportation.[67] In Foucauldian terms, the gaining of the concessions may produce 'the appearance of advancement in the fight for equality',[68] while in its everyday application, the immigration system gives rise to surveillance, regulation, and control of those seeking to

---

65 M. O'Brien, 305 *H.C. Debs.* col. 720w (4 February 1998).
66 CARF, 'Exclusion: New Labour Style' (1999) <http://www.carf.demon.co.uk/feat24.html>.
67 See, for example, 'Nightmare for Immigration Pair' (2000) 622 *Pink Paper* 2.
68 L.G. Beaman, 'Sexual Orientation and Legal Discourse: Legal Constructions of the "Normal Family"' (1999) 14 *Cdn. J. of Law and Society* 173, at 185.

migrate. Thus, the decision by the government to create the concession to same-sex migrants is not surprising, as it fits very well with New Labour ideology. The government explicitly justifies its actions on the basis of conformity with human rights, but only by further entrenching the principle of privatization of the financial costs of migration onto 'stable' relationships based on (inter)dependence.[69] Liberal law reform occurs, but only within a strict set of constraints as to the requirements which are imposed as the price of recognition for the good homosexual. Recognition rights, as opposed to redistributive politics, are inexpensive for the neo-liberal state.

However, this is not to suggest that more overt anti-gay discourses, which easily articulate to issues of migration, have disappeared. The construction of the 'dangerous queer' described by Smith continues to resonate, albeit from a somewhat more marginalized vantage point.[70] Here we find attacks on the heterosexual space of marriage linked to literal concerns about border control and the protection of the space of the nation state, which is constructed in heterosexual terms. Thus, right-wing Conservative party reaction to the concession was all too predictable:

> It is clear that the Government's policy is to place sodomite marriage on the same standing as the honourable estate of matrimony. Presumably now we will have to endure a succession of real or alleged homosexual partners being brought in to avoid our immigration rules (Lord Tebbit).

> [The regulation] undermines marriage and undermines immigration control. The Labour party have managed to deal a severe blow at both in one fell swoop (Ann Widdecombe MP).[71]

In addition to the tropes of border control and containment which are explicit in these criticisms of the concession, we find fears of 'passing' by the inauthentic in the perpetration of both an immigration fraud and a fraud on the institution of marriage.[72] Of course, the linking of migration to fraud is common within anti-immigration discourse. It is also connected to the idea of passing and of being undetectable (which is also deployed in anti-immigration discourse). Finally, critics of the concession expressed 'fears that "millions" will pretend to be gay in order to qualify'.[73] Here we find anti-gay and anti-immigrant tropes merging seamlessly through a floodgates

---

69 The employment of a discourse of 'human rights' contains an irony. Presumably, the human right which justifies the concession is the right to the enjoyment of 'private life'; but the impact of the concession is to require of same-sex couples a public acknowledgement, and an openness about their relationship for the purposes of surveillance and regulation.

70 Smith, op. cit., n. 39. The vociferous reactions of sections of the public to the proposed repeal of s. 28 of the Local Government Act underscores this point.

71 op. cit., n. 63.

72 The irony is that the absence of such a concession leads to widespread 'passing' as heterosexual through fraudulent 'immigration marriages'.

73 op. cit., n. 63.

argument grounded in the importance of controlling borders against a torrent of inauthentic immigrants seeking to take advantage of a concession, but who cannot meet the requirements contained within the rules.

Although I do not want to minimize the impact of these rhetorical tropes, particularly in their ability to draw upon heightened anti-immigrant, border-control sentiment, they do appear to be increasingly located outside of the mainstream. Although the good homosexual may have been a construct which, in 1980s Britain, could only be appropriated by the completely closeted homosexual who was good precisely because no public identity was assumed, two decades later, we may see at least the beginnings of a shift towards a somewhat different construct of the good homosexual. The importance of financial in(ter)dependence is emphasized, as is stability in relationships, and the replication of key signifiers of privatized responsibility, such as home ownership. Yet, while the responsibilities of citizenship are demanded, recognition is extremely limited: marriage remains an unattainable option, as do most of the material benefits which flow therefrom. Official recognition may allow reunification across national frontiers (with accompanying surveillance and regulation), but it seems to be justified implicitly, not on a discourse of human rights (one of the official justifications), but on the importance of stable relationships in the fulfilment of the responsibilities of citizenship. This move fits New Labour's focus on the importance of stable family life as both a prerequisite to success in a global marketplace, and as a response to 'the individualizing self-interest' of that same marketplace.[74]

This construction of the good homosexual *citizen* also can be demonstrated by turning to another example; this time, a national culture in which issues of migration are tied to constitutional rights: South Africa. In keeping with my claim that migration issues have assumed a heightened priority in sexuality politics, it is worth noting that one of the most important constitutional challenges to South African laws on sexuality has centred on the issue of migration of same-sex partners, and it has been the subject of a test case before the Constitutional Court.[75] This appeal dealt with the constitutionality of s. 25(5) of the Aliens Control Act 96 of 1991, which allows preferential treatment to be given to a foreign national applying for an immigration permit, who is 'the spouse ... of a person permanently and lawfully resident in the Republic', but not, in the words of the Constitutional Court, 'to a foreign national who, though similarly placed in all other respects, is in a same-sex life partnership with a person permanently and lawfully resident in the Republic'.[76] The challenge to the law was brought by the national lesbian and gay rights lobbying group, in

74 Bell and Binnie, op. cit., n. 53, p. 111.
75 *National Coalition for Gay and Lesbian Equality* v. *Minister of Home Affairs* [2000] 1 B.C.L.R. 39 (CC).
76 id., para. 15.

combination with a number of applicants claiming on behalf of their 'alien' same-sex partners.

It was determined by the Court that, given the wording of the statute, it could not be construed as including foreign same-sex partners.[77] Therefore, at issue was its constitutionality in terms of the rights of the South African partners. Interestingly, the Court explicitly left open the question whether the provision was unconstitutional in relation to the mobility rights of the citizen 'spouse',[78] instead focusing on the violation of equality rights: 'overlapping or intersecting discrimination on the grounds of sexual orientation and marital status'.[79] The Court found the failure to recognize same-sex partnerships within the statute to be unconstitutional and, in the process, it went to great length to demonstrate a *knowledge* of homosexual relationships, thereby underscoring law's continuing production of the truth of homosexuality. According to Justice Ackermann for the unanimous Court, such relationships are defined as: 'a life partnership which entails a conjugal same-sex relationship, which is the only form of conjugal relationship open to gays and lesbians in harmony with their sexual orientation',[80] which is 'not distinguishable in any significant respect from that of heterosexual spouses'.[81] Unmarried heterosexuals are left to one side in the case, as the remedy ordered by the Court is the 'reading in', after the word spouse, of the words: 'or partner, in a permanent same-sex life partnership'.[82]

But with legal recognition comes requirements of disclosure and surveillance, as the Court proceeds to define (or 'produce') a permanent same-sex life partnership which is indistinguishable from opposite sex marriage. The Court finds that while conventional marriage – because of its legal recognition as a status – 'is capable of easy and virtually incontestable proof', same-sex relationships are not.[83] Thus, implicit again in the judgment, despite its very liberal and 'progressive' tenor, is a fear of fraud through 'pretended' relationships. Consequently, Justice Ackermann makes plain that:

> it would … be permissible for Parliament and the executive to take reasonable steps to prevent persons falsely purporting to be in same-sex life partnerships from evading the provisions of the Act.[84]

Finally, the Court explicitly defines the meaning of 'permanence' in relationships, producing the idealized relationship against which all others can be measured:

77 id., para. 26.
78 id., para. 28.
79 id., para. 40.
80 id., para. 36.
81 id., para. 53.
82 id., para. 86.
83 id., para. 84.
84 id., para. 85.

Without purporting to provide an exhaustive list, such facts would include the following: the respective ages of the partners; the duration of the partnership; whether the partners took part in a ceremony manifesting their intention to enter into a permanent partnership, what the nature of that ceremony was and who attended it; how the partnership is viewed by the relations and friends of the partners; whether the partners share a common abode; whether the partners own or lease the common abode jointly; whether and to what extent the partners share responsibility for living expenses and the upkeep of the joint home; whether and to what extent the partners have made provision for one another in relation to medical, pension and related benefits; whether there is a partnership agreement and what its contents are; and whether and to what extent the partners have made provision in their wills for one another. None of these considerations is indispensable for establishing a permanent partnership. In order to apply the above criteria, those administering the Act are entitled, within the ambit of the Constitution and bearing in mind what has been said in this judgment, to take all reasonable steps, by way of regulations or otherwise, to ensure that full information concerning the permanent nature of any same-sex life partnership, is disclosed.[85]

The decision neatly exemplifies Lori Beaman's insight about the production of the truth of homosexual relationships through legal discourse:

> the public confession of one's sexual orientation becomes a part of the process of the production of the truth of sex. The 'outed' party is rewarded for his/her public declaration with the promise of equality. The law becomes the confessional, the gay or lesbian couple the penitents, properly controlled by framing their requests within the confines of legal boundaries.[86]

The conditions of recognition for the transnational couple include the requirement to approach the idealized status of marriage in the organization of the relationship, largely through the appearance of permanence, stability and location in a particular *place* (preferably an owner-occupied home). The transnational, nomadic potentiality of the relationship is constrained by the act of recognition through a disciplinarity of geography and place which is imposed in order to forcibly provide roots to the relationship, as the reciprocal side of the claiming of recognition rights. This ironically occurs, in the South African example, within a national context in which, historically, marriage and the family often did not comport with such a narrow model because of the forced mobility which the apartheid system imposed upon so many families. Indeed, spousal relationships often survived distance and severe dislocation and the 'standards' which the Court is now imposing would themselves have appeared 'alien' to many marital relationships. Instead, those requirements (such as common abode, pension rights, wills, and so on) resonate in the language of financial privatization of responsibility, constructing an image of the good homosexual which seems to be strongly inflected by a class-based and perhaps race-based construction of homosexuality. That is, implicit in the Court's imagining of the good homosexual may be an understanding of

85 id., para. 88.
86 Beaman, op. cit., n. 68, p. 186.

homosexuality as a white, middle-class phenomenon and, as a consequence, a wide array of ways of living come to be erased.[87]

Processes of legal liberalization through recognition seem to come at a price, and that is in how the homosexual must be put in *place* through the disciplinarity of relationships centring upon the privatization of financial responsibility for oneself and one's 'life partner'. Historically, as I have suggested, the homosexual may have been constituted as the stranger, the nomad, the outsider, and the excess, in which homosexuality was foreign to the nation state. However, with changing times, we find that the good homosexual can be incorporated and assimilated into a space that is 'not-marriage' (which remains a special symbolic heterosexual space), and presumably in which children are simply *assumed* not to enter the picture, but in which a relationship is recognized which possesses the imagined characteristics of marriage and which can be interrogated and subjected to surveillance on that basis. While relationship recognition in all of these cases may be a result of increased mobility, legal 'success' produces a requirement to *settle down*, and to disidentify with the disorder and lawlessness associated with undisciplined migratory flows.

The disciplinarity of legal recognition has been observed by others. As Lori Beaman argues, drawing on a feminist analysis:

> the discussion of this one form of relationship as though it were the ultimate *raison d'être* in human relations is extremely misleading. Marriage is arguably the most efficient means by which men have been able to 'protect' and control what is theirs.[88]

So too, as Jon Binnie cautions:

> discussion of law reform in the area of migration can lose sight of the desirability of different forms of relationships. Many would-be immigrants are not in long-term relationships, and recognising same-sex relationships for the purpose of immigration would reinforce the ideal of long-term relationships ... [and would] ... further the agenda of those activists who favour the politics of assimilation.[89]

Yet, this process of legal recognition, as I have argued, seems to be 'progressing' inexorably. Finally, this is evidenced by a European Commission proposal for a Directive on the right to family reunification, which would facilitate migration by 'third country nationals', including same-sex partners.[90] Thus, moves which up to now have been occurring at the national level are beginning to 'filter up' to the transnational arena, where we may well witness EC law in the future.

---

87 The racial construction of same-sex sexualities in South Africa is a complex issue, beyond the scope of this article; see generally, Stychin, op. cit., n. 60, pp. 52–88.
88 Beaman, op. cit., n. 68, p. 191.
89 Binnie, op. cit., n. 3, p. 246.
90 EU Commission, 'Press Release: Proposal for a Directive on the Right to Family Reunification' (IP/99/920) (1999) <http://europa.eu.int/rapid>.

CONCLUDING THOUGHTS

It is surely no coincidence that mobility has assumed such a central role in claims to sexual citizenship today. Both citizenship and mobility articulate to inclusion and exclusion. The hegemony of free movement in economic discourses of globalization under late capitalism has proved a useful discourse upon which to graft sexual citizenship demands. However, the complexity of processes of economic globalization is no less apparent in the context of sexuality. Global capital, as Jon Binnie argues, desires urban spaces which are 'business-friendly controlled environments',[91] but not obviously queer cultural hotspots; underscoring how sexual citizenship has 'a mixed relationship with advanced capitalism'.[92]

Claims regarding mobility also provide new insights and further problematize simple binaries concerning cosmopolitan and communitarian visions of citizenship, thereby underscoring the inadequacies of such a stark choice.[93] On the one hand, citizenship claims centred on mobility rights appear intuitively to emanate from the cosmopolitan citizen, and suggest a 'transition from a nation-state world order to a cosmopolitan world order'.[94] Rights are deployed in universal terms, such that they can be claimed across national frontiers, trumping local hostility and opposition in their path. Moreover, recognition rights further the flow of factors of production across borders; localism again becomes an anti-modern hindrance to globalizing forces and, ultimately, the creation of a more transnational civil society. In this way, the lesbian or gay subject, who claims citizenship rights in part on the basis of freedom of movement, becomes the quintessential cosmopolitan citizen. This seems appropriate given the centrality of migration, movement, and travel to the constitution of a gay identity – what Jon Binnie describes as a 'queer cosmopolitanism' based on 'knowingness and sophistication'.[95]

However, I also have suggested in this article that such an analysis is problematic. Rights which are being advanced, which stem from mobility, are claimed, not so much as a means to advance the values of cosmopolitanism, but as a means of social inclusion within a local/national community, where recognition within the confines of community is seen as central to citizenship. This is the desire for incorporation within a specific local culture in resistance to the historical construction of lesbians and gays as outsiders to national culture and as non-citizens.

---

91 J. Binnie, 'Cosmopolitanism and the Sexed City' in *City Visions*, eds. D. Bell and A. Haddour (2000) 166.
92 E. Isin and P. Wood, *Citizenship and Identity* (1999) 71.
93 See R. Bellamy and A. Warleigh, 'From an Ethics of Integration to an Ethics of Participation: Citizenship and the Future of the European Union' (1998) 27 *Millennium: J. of International Studies* 447.
94 Beck, op. cit., n. 30, p. 83.
95 Binnie, op. cit., n. 91, p. 166.

It is perhaps ironic that mobility provides the basis upon which such communitarian based claims are made, given that these claims are often justified through cosmopolitan discourses, such as international human rights and globalization. Although they are resisted, to some degree, in the language of localism and community, this may become increasingly marginalized. The success of these claims may facilitate mobility, free movement, and 'transnational' relationships (all of which may be associated with cosmopolitanism), but more importantly perhaps, the goal is inclusion within national civil societies through the power of law. But this, in turn, also underscores the contradictions thrown into relief by the relationship between globalization and sexual citizenship. While strong, traditional families may be seen as a corrective to the insecurities of the global marketplace, globalization has facilitated the emergence of transnationalism in the politics of sexual citizenship. However, that development clearly centres the already privileged within the lesbian and gay communities; which reproduces the construction of lesbians and gays as affluent, independent, unconstrained by family, and selfish. Yet, the political and legal claims that these sexual 'dissidents' make are claims for recognition as 'couples' located within particular communities, in which the presumed benefits of family life for communities are being reproduced. In this way, cosmopolitanism and communitarianism become inseparably intertwined.

My aim thus has been to interrogate how recognition, civil inclusion, and citizenship claims come at a price, in terms of the demands of assimilation, normalization and disciplinarity in several different guises (for example, market-place; monogamy; traditional patterns of gendered relationships; home ownership), and to underscore the role which law plays in these constructions. Clearly, changes in civil society resulting from transnational social and economic processes are shaping citizenship claims and are having a material impact on people's lives. But, at the same time, legal discourse also operates to 'tame' them; to take cosmopolitan subjects of rights and put them in their place: that is, within a recognizable, manageable, and normalizable guise (and, if not normalizable, to exclude them).

This analysis also raises the wider question of whether alternative ways of imagining a legal regime that recognizes spousal-type relationships is possible. In the absence of open borders, is the disciplinary and normalizing function of law an inevitable result of relationship recognition? Of course, it has been the privileging of marriage in immigration law that has led to highly effective resistance and subversion of that institution through 'marriages of convenience'. In a more 'liberal' regime, will the 'unattached' form same-sex relationships of convenience? And what would be the reaction to such relationships from 'authentic' same-sex couples? It bears reiterating that with discipline inevitably comes resistance in unpredictable forms. The ability of law to manage and to discipline is never totalizing, and subjects are not necessarily as docile nor as unimaginative as we may sometimes think. Finally, consideration should be paid to the legal status of the migrating 'dependent' who, by definition, is cast in a non-autonomous (and sometimes highly precarious) position. As a normative matter, should law produce such a status? Should lesbian and gay law reform campaigners be encouraging the reproduction of a subject position grounded in dependence? However, in the absence of greater openness to independent migration, there are no easy answers. What current developments do underscore, though, is the way in which law, and the language of citizenship, prove again to be both constraining *and* enabling in their deployment around issues of sexuality.

The Criminal Justice System

[9]

After Dunblane: Crime, Corporeality, and the (Hetero-) Sexing of the Bodies of Men

RICHARD COLLIER*

The human mind is the most complex and delicately balanced of all created things. Wisdom cannot foresee all the consequences of its sickness. The most that wisdom can do is shield society from some of the possible consequences . . .

(Dr. Robert Runcie, Archbishop of Canterbury, speaking at the Memorial Service for the Hungerford victims 1987).[1]

According to the experts [mass] killers, who are invariably male, are unlikely to be mentally ill but are likely to have achieved very little and, as a result, harbour grudges and resentment that can develop into violent fantasies.

(*Guardian* 29 April 1996, following the murder of thirty-two people in Tasmania by Martin Bryant)

INTRODUCTION

This article is an exploration of responses to a series of murders which in recent years, in Britain and elsewhere, have become known as 'lone-gunman' or 'spree' killings.[2] The particular focus is the legal, political, criminological, and media reception to the events which took place in Dunblane, Scotland in March 1996 where sixteen children and their teacher were murdered, and seventeen others injured,[3] by the forty-three year-old man, Thomas Hamilton. The article will argue that the experience of the 'lone gunman' or 'spree

* Newcastle Law School, University of Newcastle upon Tyne, 22–24 Windsor Terrace, Newcastle upon Tyne NE1 7RU, England

Earlier versions of this paper were presented to the Law and Society Association Annual Meeting, Glasgow, 1996, the Socio Legal Studies Association Annual Conference, University of Southampton, 1996, the Centre for Gender and Women's Studies, University of Newcastle upon Tyne, 1996, the Law School, University of Keele, November 1996, and Kent Law School, January 1997. I would like to thank all who participated in discussion for their comments and, in particular, the anonymous reviewers for the *Journal of Law and Society* for their helpful suggestions. I am indebted to conversations with Bea Campbell on aspects of the argument.

killer' is, both in its generic construction and its practice, a gendered and distinctly masculinized phenomenon. The central aim of the article is to (re)read the spree killing in such a way as to reposition the *sexed* male body within discourses around crime. It is my intention to surface the inadequacy of simply adding 'men' or 'gender' empirically to the study of crime by investigating the epistemological implications of what it might mean to theorize the masculinity/crime relation in the light of recent approaches which have sought to dissolve the integrity of the gendered 'identity' of the subject.[4] In so doing, I wish to explore the ways in which the (sexed) bodies of men continue to be constituted as an 'absent presence' within contemporary discourses around crime and criminality. I want to surface, that is, the significance of sexual difference in engaging with the criminal(ized) bodies of men in cultural and psychical terms.[5]

The first part of the article explores the content of press discourse constructions of the 'spree killing' and, in particular, representations of the gunman Thomas Hamilton in the aftermath of the Dunblane massacre. My concern is with what has been 'seen' and 'unseen'[6] within a range of 'crimino-legal'[7] constructions of the men/crime relationship. The second part of the article explores the genealogy of this silencing of the sexed specificity of the Dunblane massacre. In investigating the gender order of the signifying complex which surrounds the phenomenon of the spree killing this article is, ultimately, about Thomas Hamilton, not as a 'monster', 'pervert' or personification of 'evil', but as a *man*.

Defining the 'spree killing': a note on Dunblane

There has over the last few years been an increasing fascination, reflected in the rapid spread of the term within diverse cultural artefacts, with the phenomenon of the 'lone gunman' or 'spree killing'. The spree killing refers to the murder of several victims over a period of minutes, hours or days in one or more different locations '. . . by an impulsive killer who appears to make little effort to evade detection . . . At completion of the sequence this type of killer is unlikely to kill again; many commit suicide or are killed in shootouts with the police'.[8] The victims of the spree killing, it has been argued, appear to have some symbolic significance for the offender and are killed in a 'frenzied' attack, whether planned in advance or on the 'spur of the moment'. Though details in each case differ, a number of recent murders have been classified as examples of the spree killing. In Britain, prior to Dunblane, the most notorious of these was the case of Michael Ryan, who shot dead sixteen people in August 1987 in Hungerford, England. Internationally, and within weeks of the Dunblane massacre, in April 1996 the twenty-eight year old Martin Bryant slaughtered thirty-five people in Tasmania[9] in the worst spree killing on record. Opinion remains divided as to whether the spree killing should be considered a separate form of multiple murder.[10] What is agreed, however, is that 'almost all mass and spree murders are male with a racial composition "that closely approximates that of the population itself".[11]

It is not my intention, in writing of Dunblane in the detached terms of social theory,[12] to '. . . trivialise the horror felt by the majority of people' at such a crime.[13] Certainly, 'the following analysis seeks neither to inflame . . . strongly felt emotions nor to hold them up to criticism or ridicule.'[14] It seeks, rather, to develop a deeper understanding of the event by addressing what remains the most obvious, taken-for-granted, yet curiously unexplored fact about not just the murders at Dunblane but crime generally: '. . . that it is almost always committed by men'.[15] Engaging with this fact is, I shall argue, essential if '. . . we are ever going to act in a way that loosens that paralysing grip of guilt and helplessness'[16] in the face of such horrific crimes.

CRIMINO-LEGAL RESPONSES TO THE SPREE MURDER: THE PRESS DISCOURSE IN THE AFTERMATH OF DUNBLANE

On March 13 1996 Thomas Hamilton, a forty-three-year-old man, fatally shot sixteen five- and six-year-old children and their teacher in the gymnasium at Dunblane Primary School in Scotland. Seventeen others were injured before Hamilton eventually put one of the guns to his own head. How are we to begin to make sense of the press discourse around such a horrific event? There exists a rich literature[17] concerned with exploring how, as unique cultural products, newspapers and other media outlets tell us much about the social, political, and moral order of our culture and, as such, play an important role in the development of an individual's sense of self.[18] However, constructing a reading from something as diffuse and complex as the press discourse is notoriously problematic.[19] The apparently random nature of the spree killing, like the serial murder, runs counter to the general assumption that crimes have 'motives' and can be presented as a deviant form of instrumental rationality. It is, nonetheless, possible to locate a certain homogeneity to the press response. A number of themes emerge and recur within the national and international media coverage of the Dunblane massacre as a transition takes place from initial shock and incomprehension at what had happened to a growing demand for answers and explanations.

1. *The vocabulary of evil – Thomas Hamilton as 'inhuman' and 'beyond reason'*

The tone of the media reporting in the immediate aftermath of the massacre was encapsulated by the powerful and moving comments of the headmaster of Dunblane Primary School. 'Evil', he stated, 'visited us yesterday . . . We don't know why, we don't understand it, and I guess we never will.' This notion that 'only the Vocabulary of Evil could explain what happened at Dunblane'[20] set the course for the following press coverage in which Thomas

Hamilton was commonly described as an 'evil freak of nature'';[21] whilst 'Dunblane returned to God',[22] he would surely '. . . Burn in Hell'[23] – 'His evil is now where it belongs – in the fires of hell'. Notwithstanding differences between tabloid and 'quality' newspapers in their representations of crime,[24] for each the language of 'good' and 'evil' appeared initially as the only available vocabulary through which the event might be described. Just as Robert Thompson and Jon Venables, the two ten-year-old boys convicted of the murder of James Bulger in 1993, had been described as the embodiment of 'unparalleled evil and barbarity',[25] the good/evil binary here suggested a possibility, if not a firm belief, that there may be no defence to some propensities of the human condition. However, this immediately poses problems for a secularized crimino-legal sphere which demands explanation and account in terms of liberal notions of human nature. In the context of Dunblane, what was being constituted at this point as a social problem? Clearly some issues were immediately comprehensible as being 'within' understanding. By the end of the day of the massacre the questions of school security and reform of gun laws had emerged as the dominant 'social problems' raised by the case. Hamilton's maleness, in contrast, did not figure in the 'pre-existing categories for rational problem-identification and problem-solution.'[26]

The terms 'evil' and 'human wickedness' promote a construction of Hamilton as a 'monster' or 'grotesque' which is misleading in several respects. First, it rests uneasily with the very *familiarity* of the 'spree killing'. If Dunblane was exceptional in terms of the age and vulnerability of the victims, it was, none the less, readily identifiable as a generic crime. The lone gunman is a recognizable phenomenon of the late twentieth century.[27] Thomas Hamilton was placed immediately within an established frame of reference. The use of 'evil' has a second, related, consequence. The vast majority of spree killers, like offenders generally, are men. Yet the ontology of Hamilton as 'inhuman' robs both the act of the murders and the body of the murderer of its sexual specificity. Hamilton is transformed into something 'beyond human', his actions emblematic of an inhumanity beyond comprehension and understanding. This banishing of Hamilton from the social, however:

> '. . . erodes . . . responsibility for understanding and challenging the individual and social forces that have produced such an . . . event. To demonise . . . removes the [act] from the realm of social action.'[28]

The expunging of the social does not simply individualize crime. It also underwrites and legitimates feelings of despair and helplessness which are commonplace responses to particularly horrific crimes: 'We cannot even begin to grasp', it was declared, what could have driven Hamilton to act as he did '. . . and there is no point pretending we can'.[29]

Crimes, even the worst and most seemingly inexplicable, do not happen in a vacuum.[30] In order to reconfigure Thomas Hamilton as a man, it is necessary to relocate his actions by contextualizing the atrocity within the gendered social framework in which he lived and died. It is necessary, that is, to reframe the relationship between men, women, and children in such a way as to problematize the ideas of hetero-masculinity which were, I now wish to suggest, central to, and the sub-text of, press reporting of the Dunblane massacre.

2. *Sexing the social: configurations of community, class, and 'otherness'*

The ontological importance given to the 'family' as the institutional source for the preservation and reproduction of moral order has been central to the discursive construction of the social within modernity.[31] It is in the context of this social/familial frame that Thomas Hamilton was systematically represented as a 'loner.' On the one hand he appeared to have few friends. No person, no locale appeared willing to claim him as one of their own. He was, on one level, 'not acceptable'. Yet his place as an outsider to this 'social' is ambiguous. It is also clear from newspaper reports that Thomas Hamilton was *known* within the community in which he lived. The numerous testimonies to his character, his 'eccentricities' and family background belied the notion that he was a stranger in the midst of an otherwise homogenous community. There exists a tension between, on the one hand, the (readily accessible) knowledge of Hamilton (who he was, what he was 'like') and, on the other, a desire to expunge him from that community, and from the sociality more generally, through reference to his status as grotesque, 'inhuman' monster and so forth. The former places him within a broader community. The latter ensures he is rendered outside the social.

Within this process, of course, something is being said about the community of which Thomas Hamilton was deemed to be not one. In this respect, press representations of the town of Dunblane reveal much about the ways in which the discursive construction of the social has been configured through reference to crime, criminality and the ontological importance of the family referred to above. One newspaper declared:

> *it would be easier for us* if Thomas Hamilton was simply a madman who came out of nowhere. But what if [he] . . . comes out of a society which itself is showing signs of deranged and violent breakdown?[32]

This is an engagement with the social. It focuses on such issues as the role of the media in promoting crime, the availability of guns, questions of school security, and so forth. Yet, each of these conversations about 'society' stop short of any engagement with the relationship between sex, gender, and crime. What results is a 'desexing' of Hamilton's maleness by fusing two ideas; that of a phantasmatic (non-criminal) *community* secured as such by reference to a historically specific *iconography of male otherness.*

(a) A space of crime: the (non-)criminal community

To clarify: the town of Dunblane was routinely depicted, almost without exception, as a place to which crime was a stranger. It appeared at the other end of a spectrum from the communities more traditionally associated with high-profile crimes.[33] It is Britain's 'dangerous places'[34] which have come to symbolize social breakdown, moral atrophy, and increasingly, notably in the context of the 'criminal' city, crimes by and against children. Dunblane, in contrast, symbolized something very different. It did not translate into familiar representations of region and place. It was, if anything, a place 'too good to be true'. An editorial in the *Guardian* captured the general assumption being made about the conflation of space and crime. Like Hungerford, the scene of the previous spree killing by Michael Ryan in 1987, Dunblane was:

> . . . the last place where one would expect random violence to erupt: small attractive country towns with strong community ties and none of the alienation associated with larger cities. Both killers lived within the communities they devastated. Both are described as lonely, secretive, friendless people. Neither was being treated for any mental disorder. Yet both committed indiscriminate and irrational violence on a massive scale. Why?[35]

This image of (non-criminal) community is fleshed out by accounts of the minutiae of everyday life. Dunblane was a town where 'nothing ever happens', a place where '. . . if a child fell in the street, three people would rush to pick them up'.[36] Interestingly, even the children who lived in the town appeared at times to be qualitatively different from their counterparts in the criminal(ized) city.[37] *Time* magazine noted:

> . . . the names [of the children] . . . were as familiar and as evocative of middle-class Scottish family life . . . Ordinary names, pretty names, the names on teachers' attendance lists, on captions of school pictures, on programs for school pageants, on line-ups for school games.[38]

On one level this mythologizing of locale, involving a conflation of certain assumptions about family life and socio-economic privilege, is a familiar phenomenon. What results is a powerful evocation of a (crime-free) world we all, it is implied (and not just the citizens of Dunblane), have lost:

> A generation of professionals – doctors, lawyers, journalists – had dreamed of somewhere the air is so crisp you can actually smell the smoke from a chimney or from a gentle puffing biddy on the street corner; where fearsome things come in picture books; where the water of life is softly reassuring as it falls – or golden, as it washes the back of the throat. Dunblane was that dream incarnate.[39]

However, it is not simply the (well-documented) association of class, crime, and notions of 'respectability' which is being made here. The 'space' of men's crime is itself, on closer examination, bound up with assumptions which betray the centrality of the family to this construction of the social. The dominant image of the community of Dunblane itself as embodiment of comfortable, crime-free existence rests upon, and derives from, a heterosexual familial frame signified as such by virtue of the presence of *children*.[40] Dunblane is presented as a place where 'families moved' and where 'children would be safe'.

(b) Thomas Hamilton as Other: the single male outsider

It is against this background that Hamilton appears outside the parameters of the familial. He *appeared* to be of this community. In 'reality' he failed to belong – he was an outsider, an impostor. Yet the depiction of his otherness involves, simultaneously, the representation of both a familiar and unfamiliar figure. Much was made of his 'peculiar' upbringing, a knowledge juxtaposed with the 'normality' of the family life of the Dunblane children, and his sexual status as a single (unpartnered) man. The *Independent*, for example, noted that:

> Loners like Hamilton are where *benign singleness* festers and turn poisonous, where being alone creates the space in which paranoia flourishes to burst out in violence' (my emphasis).[41]

It is estimated that, by the year 2001, lone men will form the largest group of one-person households in Britain.[42] Increased social atomization has brought into focus and prompted considerable research, notably under the umbrella 'crisis of masculinity', into the ways in which distinctive communities of 'lone men' are forming. It is men who are increasingly seen to be '. . . either drifting into despair, illness or break-down, or are aggressively asserting another kind of masculine identity through law-breaking and crime.'[43] The *Guardian* noted how

> The back streets of the shabbier ends of every British town are evidence of the elaborate communities of fantasy that men create as substitutes: martial arts centres, porn shops, tattoo parlours. Plus the erotica, often spiced up with violence, on the top shelf of your neighbourhood newsagent's or video store. Plus the extraordinary ease of buying drink almost everywhere, to help you sit at home and brood on all this.[44]

This, it is implied, was the habitat of Thomas Hamilton, a world symbolically far away from, though physically cheek-by-jowl with, the non-criminal and familial community of Dunblane. Quite explicitly it was stated that 'Hamilton *did not belong* to the manicured world of Dunblane. His home was a scruffy, damp council maisonette on a joyless estate in Kent Road, Stirling, five miles away.' Nor had he '. . . enjoyed the stable, happy childhood apparent in some of the children at Dunblane primary school'.[45]

The 'horror' of the criminal(ized) urban which is said to 'pursue us even here' is symbolized not just by the failure to 'escape' from crime. Within the present reconfiguration of the familial, the figure of the single male outsider has increasingly come to appear as an embodiment of social disorder, normlessness, and dislocation. However, importantly, the inadequacy of this iconography of male otherness to *consistently* depict Hamilton as 'outside' the social becomes glaringly apparent as its very familiarity at times comes to evoke rather different images of the masculine. He is, on one level, immediately recognizable (and is recognized) as a *particular type* of man. In other contexts, other genres, he would be the 'very stuff' of pulp fiction:

> . . . unmarried, 43, a thwarted scoutmaster with an obsessive interest in guns and a habit of photographing very young boys naked from the waist up . . . a familiar but dislocated story, the kind usually set in dreary rooming houses across the Atlantic – narratives pieced together after the grisly, ground-breaking crimes that are an American genre.[46]

A rich vocabulary exists, known to adults and children alike, through which to depict his otherness. Testimonies range from the relatively benign accounts of Hamilton as a 'quiet "anorak" type',[47] a 'strange moonfaced man'[48] who lived in a 'shabby bachelor apartment',[49] to the more overtly dangerous and troubling depictions of a 'vengeful misfit'[50], a '"Mr. Creepy" or "Weird" man'[51] who was driven by 'monsters of the psyche'.[52] It is the very familiarity of these images which betrays the contingency and fluidity of the overarching framework of hetero-masculinity which would depict him as beyond society, outwith the social. Ultimately, as only few accounts noted, Thomas Hamilton:

> . . . was not a loner at all. He was the exact opposite. He wanted to run boys clubs. He wanted to run Scout camps. He belonged to a gun club. He wrote peeved letters to everyone. He had his own business. Lots of people knew him. Some loner.[53]

Far from having distinguishing marks, the stigmata of his imputed paedophilic intent, Hamilton lived in a community unsuspected. He was *known*. Reading Hamilton as 'other' is far from straightforward when his 'normality' as a man seeps through in representations which reveal much about the dualisms through which ideas of normal masculinity have been constituted in the first place. As a man with 'two sides',[54] a 'caring son' whose apparent normality betrayed the 'darker truth' of a 'mummy's boy', a 'repressed homosexual', representations of Hamilton's otherness draw on a complex discourse of hetero-masculinity[55] which is multi-layered and open-ended.[56] Yet, once again, in this process important questions are left begging around why it should be *men* whose responses to the 'bottling up' of emotions should routinely take such violent forms. Violence is banished to the criminal space of those such as Thomas Hamilton (the world of the misfit, the loner).

Such accounts are, quite simply, inadequate. In order to develop an analysis of Hamilton's sexed specificity at the level of (social) structure and (individual) psyche it is necessary to explore further how this iconography of otherness played out in terms of notions of the spree killer as social 'failure' – and why men's reaction to that failure should so frequently be understood to take such violent and destructive forms.

CONFIGURING HETERO-MASCULINITY: THOMAS HAMILTON AS REPRESSED 'FAILED MAN'

The 'classic psychological profile' of the spree killer

Though it varies from case to case (Hungerford, Dunblane, Tasmania) a number of key features recur around the image of the lone gunman as a failed man '. . . lonely, angry, resentful and ready to snap':[57]

> The classic profile of the killer as a single, lonely and obsessive man who is unable to articulate his emotions and is desperate for some form of recognition. Very few of these people are psychotic.[58]

There is some overlap with the dominant representation of the serial murderer as a 'resentment killer' out to take revenge on society for some past trauma. Like multiple murderers and serial killers, the spree killer is not generally understood to have been 'ill', at least not in the sense of suffering from schizophrenia, manic depression, and so forth. The following comments are not atypical of those made after Dunblane:

> Where you look in terms of background is at things like isolation, whether he is a loner with a possible desire for revenge, desire for status, a desire to be famous, or infamous, a desire to be a soldier or a commando who idolises guns. [59]
>
> The Man could well be someone who people thought of as odd but not mentally ill who has killed for the sake of it. People who go on spree killings . . . bottle it up until it all explodes in catastrophe . . .They harbour resentment for a long time while on the face of it they put up with being laughed at.[60]
>
> They obviously have major problems communicating their feelings and are likely to have all sorts of anger and aggression.[61]

Each of these comments draw on an emotional framework familiar to men and women. After all, 'we all know fear, uncertainty, desire and envy'.[62] In this model, rationality and intentionality is imputed to the spree killer. He decides to take 'revenge' on a society which has somehow 'rejected' him.

Such social failures, however, have a distinctly *gendered* dimension. Within a range of popular cultural texts of the 1980s and 1990s (plays, novels, films[63]), for example, these are emotions associated with a distinctively masculine (and arguably a white, ethnically specific)[64] psychology. It is white men who are, at the present moment, increasingly presumed to be experiencing these kinds of life experiences in a particularly acute form[65]. The press discourse in the aftermath of the Dunblane massacre shared, and drew on, this more general notion of masculine failure and crisis. Hamilton was an inadequate nobody, '. . . unable to succeed in society – financially, socially, sexually, academically, in sport or in their work'. Yet within this (gendered) model the *sexed specificity* of Hamilton continues to be erased, no less powerfully than it had been within the quasi-religious binary of good/evil. The dominant psychological profile model is gendered both in terms of *cause* (what is constructed as the source of rejection and failure in the first place: sexual, social, work failure) and its *effects* (in the recourse to

185

specifically masculinized forms of violence as response: for example, the use of guns and weapons). There is, moreover, a contradiction emerging here. On the one hand, we have seen, it was said to be 'almost impossible' to pinpoint reasons for the lone gunman's actions. Like the serial murder, the spree killing does not take place in a pre-given rationally ordered society. However, the failed man narrative introduces an emotional framework in which notions of masculine failure are not just accessible and readily understandable; it also imputes an intentionality which is deeply familiar. It can, it would seem, be understood.

Ultimately, this framework serves to normalize (if not excuse) men's criminality. It does so because it remains within the positivist and modernist crimino-legal frame which seeks causes in terms of 'maleness'; but *it does not make the sexed specificity of crime explicit*. The dualism of normal/deviant fixes Hamilton as the latter; but there is no engagement with masculine subjectivity as itself being in any sense fluid and contradictory (or that men may shift between different subject positions). It negates any analysis of what Hamilton may have *shared* with other men at the very moment that it calls upon a normative masculinity by way of explanation for his actions. The failed man model places the spree killer within an understanding of crime as a deviant form of instrumental rationality. The means-ends relation which typifies crime as a modernist discourse thus remains in place. Yet, what would happen if we were to re-frame the question asked by the model in such a way as to make sexed specificity problematic? Why should it be that *his* social failures take such spectacularly violent and destructive forms?[66] Why is it, in the vast majority of cases, *men's* anger and despair (and not women's) which manifests itself, with apparently increasing frequency, in the murder of so many 'strangers'?

In the remainder of this article I wish to present a reading of the performative strategies in and through which Thomas Hamilton, as a (sexed) subject in a specific (social) location may have sought to constitute himself as 'a man'. In highlighting the performativity of masculinity it is possible, I shall argue, to interrogate the interface between the contexts in which Hamilton lived at the level of social structure and the specificities of his own life-history.

THE FANTASIZED MASCULINE AND THE (A)SOCIAL MASCULINE: (RE)CONSTRUCTING THE SEXED BODY OF THE LONE GUNMAN

Thomas Hamilton's life, from what is known, had been dominated by two principal activities: first, an involvement in the scouting and youth club movements, and secondly, by an involvement in gun clubs. In re-reading each of these activities in terms of how masculinity is performed in specific contexts, both the youth movement and the gun club can each be seen, in different and overlapping ways, as sites for the (hetero)sexing of the male body as 'masculine'.

1. *Thomas Hamilton as surrogate father: childhood, the scouting movement, and the youth club*

The dominant, indeed exclusive, representation of childhood in the press discourse around the Dunblane massacre is one of 'spotless innocence and hope'.[67] It is an innocence captured in two images extensively reproduced in television and newspaper accounts. The first is the photograph of Class P1 of Dunblane Primary School with their teacher, Gwen Mayor. This was to become a central icon, the reference point for the construction of childhood innocence around which all other images circulated.[68] The second is a freeze-frame taken from a home video recording showing Thomas Hamilton with young boys in a gymnasium assisting them in vaulting over a wooden-horse[69]. They are disturbing, haunting, and culturally familiar. It is through our subsequent knowledge, what we now 'know', that they come to tell other, more dangerous stories: of childhood destroyed by a stranger, of evil's destruction of innocence, of a woman who lost her life attempting to protect the children in her class, of a man who sexually desired those in his charge and who should not have been allowed to get into such a position of trust, authority, and power in the first place.

Such were the dominant interpretations of these images within the press discourse. Yet if each representation is reframed in a context which renders problematic the sociality of masculinities what else comes into view? I have argued above that the representation of Hamilton as both (quasi-religious) 'evil' 'grotesque' *and* (secularized) 'social failure' divert attention from the sexed specificity of the social context in which he lived. With regard to these images this is a context in which men's presence with children is *per se* presently considered problematic in certain scenarios and situations. It is a context in which, moreover, key elements of normative hetero-masculinity are constituted, not through contact or association *with* women and children, but via a range of activities primarily located as beyond the familial sphere and which take men *away* from shared physical space with women and children. The British primary school, in many ways the embodiment of a 'feminized' social space,[70] epitomizes this gendering of institution, space, and body in terms of a hierarchical structuring of sexual difference. At issue here are more general and pervasive questions, anxieties, and concerns about cultural representations of the paternal relationship which pervade the crimino-legal in its responses to Dunblane. In the case of the press discourse, the problematic nature of this relationship was consistently effaced notwithstanding the fact that it was central to the social context of Thomas Hamilton's life and actions.[71]

Hamilton was, the psychologist Paul Britton has written, neither '. . . an altruistic youth leader nor an uncomplicated paedophile' but, rather, '. . . a person who grew to need to guide, direct and control young boys; to influence how their bodies and morals developed'.[72] In so doing he was not alone. A range of institutions have historically sought to discipline, guide, direct, and control the bodies of young boys.[73] Such disciplining has been secured historically by facilitating boys' subjection and bodily proximity to the (suitable) authority of an older man or men. In a more contemporary variant, the search for appropriate male role models for young boys is seen, at a time of widespread 'father-absence', as essential to instilling in male youth non-criminal behaviour. Far from transgressing societal norms, his concern with disciplining and rendering subject to masculine authority potentially 'wayward' male youth is in fact in keeping with the British government's understanding of young men's socialization 'into crime'.[74]

It is not, in other words, because of any concern to 'discipline' boys *per se* that Hamilton's actions are seen as problematic. The youth clubs he set up exist within a terrain 'outside' the family. They are, however, no less regulated by codes of a familial ideology which ascribes to men particular social roles and functions (as disciplinarian, authority figure, protector, and 'friend'). It was by virtue of Thomas Hamilton's imputed sexual transgression that this authority was breached. The symbolic dominance of the father-figure ideal of this authority, however, remains in place. In the freeze-frame image of a man assisting boys in the gymnasium, Thomas Hamilton encapsulates a paternal presence which is, in other contexts, deemed desirable (as being, for example, a central strategy in crime prevention). As both 'surrogate father' in the youth club and 'rogue male' in the primary school Thomas Hamilton appears the embodiment of, at the same time as he makes visible, the pervasive *absence of men* from the lives of children whether in their capacity as (biological or social) fathers or as 'caregivers' to children and welfare workers across a range of institutions and organizations.[75] The 'normality' of men's relationships with young boys is deeply contested (to be regulated, policed, and rendered subject to surveillance). Indeed, the relationship between men and children constitutes, at present, a major political conversation[76] which rests, in part, on a consciousness of men as potential threats to the safety, integrity, and autonomy and, ultimately, to the lives of children. These threats cannot be confined to the extra-familial, though it is significant how at present a whole range of stories – hitherto subjugated knowledges – are articulating the point that 'strangers' have been a significant problem in the lives of many young men in terms of sexual abuse in locations such as the youth club, the school, and the church. It is arguably *within* the parameters of the (hetero-)sexual family that the rupture between men and children is being most rigorously and pervasively experienced in late modernity/postmodernity. It is, none the less, the pervasiveness of a threat of the 'dangerous' male which more generally transcends (and in so doing disturbs) the utility of the public/private dualism as a meaningful distinction in seeking to locate the crimes of men.

As such, the representation in the press discourse of the community of Dunblane as being somehow beyond, or without, crime assumes a particular significance in terms of its relation to the familial. The dominant image of childhood was, we have seen, one of 'innocence destroyed'. The innocence of childhood secures the body of the child within a particular configuration of the social. Whereas the serial killer, it has been argued, chooses as his victims individuals or groups who can be seen to be somehow 'outside' the social (down-and-outs, hitch-hikers, and so on),[77] Thomas Hamilton chose as his victims the very subjects – children – who constituted the sociality of Dunblane as a phantasmatic community. The representation of Hamilton as a straightforward paedophile appears to restore the order of the (familial) community. It *appears* to efface the rupture caused by a breach of men's (surrogate) paternal trust. Increasingly, however, the family of modernity is being displaced as institutional source for the preservation and reproduction of moral (sexual) order. It is in this context that the problematic nature of the relationship between men and children becomes something which cannot be sutured by reference to certainties and securities evoked by essentialist representations of masculinity constituted through the concepts, categories, and binaries which have marked the gender order of modernity. That which is considered 'dangerous' about men has, it would seem, moved somewhat closer to 'home'.

2. *The cultural framework of idealized masculinity: the 'copycat' spree killer and the gun club*

> There are calls for the gun club in a basement under the House of Lords to be scrapped as an example to the nation and turned, of all things, into a créche.
>
> (*South China Morning Post*, 22 March 1996)

Alongside his involvement in youth clubs Thomas Hamilton had one other abiding interest: a fascination with handguns, many of which he had obtained over a twenty-year period. In the months following the massacre, culminating with the publication of the Cullen Report in October 1996, an at times intemperate and heated debate over the legal regulation of firearms has been rarely out of the news in Britain.[78] It was, and is, a debate in which gender is systematically silenced. Both the 'sporting' and 'lone' gunman appear routinely as de-sexed figures. The debate, it seems, has *nothing* to say of men and masculinity. Certainly, the sport of firearms shooting attracts both women and men among its participants. However, it is an activity framed by a particular gender politics and order.[79]

The above comment in the *South China Morning Post* that, 'of all things', there were calls for the gun club in a basement under the House of Lords to be 'turned . . . into a créche' appears a throwaway comment. It suggests that in Britain the debate over gun control has become far removed from 'reality'. Yet it does, albeit unintentionally, capture an important point. The fact that a decision had been made to install in the basement of Britain's second legislative chamber a gun club, as opposed to any provision for the care of children, is indicative not just of the priorities of those who made that decision. It would be misleading to suggest simply that 'times have changed'. It symbolizes the hierarchical structuring of power, resources, and access to decision-making positions in terms of sexual difference which cannot be confined to one institution (such as Parliament) or organization. In the case of the gun club this was, in terms of (empirical) membership/ involvement and prevailing ethos, a pervasively *masculinized* culture.[80] The Cullen Inquiry noted how the authorities had shown a 'tacit sympathy' towards the prevailing gun culture; the attitudes of the police and gun licensing officers had been 'coloured' by this 'official' (legitimate) gun culture.[81] Shooting remains a popular pastime amongst members of the men-dominated legislature and judiciary.[82] Notwithstanding subsequent tightening of the law regulating firearms ownership in the light of Cullen's recommendations, this broader culture highlights a tension between the purported deviance of Thomas Hamilton's involvement with firearms and the 'normality' of *other* men's actions and attitudes, a tension exemplified by the press discourse as it sought to understand the spree killer in terms of the phenomena of 'copycat' violence.[83] Had Hamilton, having witnessed the 'fame' (however fleeting) accorded to other lone gunmen in recent years, sought to kill in order to achieve his own '. . . status, a desire to be famous, or infamous . . .'?[84]

Such a question individualizes crime at the moment it negates consideration of the wider social context in which men's relationships to violence are established in particular ways. As an editorial in the *Independent* noted, 'Hamilton's story, like the story of so much violence in our society, is a tale of men and weapons, sex . . . power and revenge.'[85] The culture which encircles schools is one of incessant violence in which, it is estimated, 30 per cent of boys between the ages of fourteen and fifteen carry weapons and where a third of teenage boys and two-thirds of girls fear physical attack.[86] The broader framework which surrounded Thomas Hamilton and the school is itself encoded by representations of potency, privilege, and empowerment associated with traditionally public locations for the achievement of idealized heterosexual masculinity – locations, that is, such as the gun club (or, indeed, the office, the legislature, the sports field or the university).

3. *The 'criminal man' as social (hetero-sexed) subject*

The following encapsulates the dominant reading within the press discourse of the events in Thomas Hamilton's life in the weeks prior to the massacre (a reading with which the Cullen Report was to subsequently concur). Hamilton had forcefully resisted the term 'pervert' with which, he proclaimed, he had been unjustly labelled. In a sense he 'fought back', protesting his 'normality' to everyone from the Queen to the Ombudsman in a series of '. . . articulate but increasingly obsessive'[87] letters complaining of his 'damaged reputation.' It was only when this strategy of resistance 'failed' that he finally 'snapped'.

It is possible, I wish to suggest, to read the 'resistance' of Thomas Hamilton in a rather different way. In his account of the murder of James Bulger, *Destroying the Baby in Themselves*, David Jackson has noted how Jon Venables and Robert Thompson, the two ten-year-old boys convicted of the murder, existed '. . . for much of [the] time within the constraining framework of adult authority, regulation and surveillance.'[88] Thomas Hamilton, in relation to his work, home, family and, it seems, sexuality, may also be seen to have been a dis-empowered subject. However, unlike two ten-year-old children, as an adult male he had access to a range of institutional resources through which he might seek to establish and exercise power and control over his own (and other) lives. In seeking to carve out an identity for himself '. . . in a different framework that seemed to offer . . . some status and self-respect'[89] he turned to a range of organizations and behaviour, in and through which he might constitute claims to other sources of power, other subject positions and definitions of masculinity from those through which his 'failure' as a man was otherwise being repeatedly confirmed.

In this active renegotiation of existing frameworks of masculine identification (in the form, for example, of his participation in youth work and gun clubs) Thomas Hamilton's (sexed, specific) *male* body is connected with, and ascribed meanings through, notions of sexualized violence and potency. Far from setting him apart, this connected Thomas Hamilton to those other men and boys who on a daily basis, in Jackson's words, long to associate themselves with the power and conventionality of masculine identity '. . . because of the dominating position that heterosexual masculinity occupies in our Western culture. Practically, this means trying to *heterosexualise* and *masculinise* their . . . bodies.'[90] This is a culture pervaded by images of hypermasculine toughness, which valorizes, in multifarious ways, the male body acting on space in conjunction with the skilled use and technical knowledge of weapons, be they guns or knives. Many boys routinely carry weapons. It is not hard to envisage how images of masculine bodies, bulging muscles, and empowered actors might be enticing and seductive for those who lack, in so many other respects, any commanding presence and status in the world. Through the use of weaponry, indeed, the male body is itself transformed. Far from seeing the build-up to the massacre as one of Hamilton losing control therefore, it is to locate the offence as a means of *taking* control.[91] As Cullen himself concluded about Hamilton:

> . . . he lacked any real insight into the fact that his (own) conduct had led to the decline in his fortunes . . . he turned his fantasy into reality in order to achieve control in one final and terrible manner.'[92]

This was, however, a taking of control which was – most importantly – profoundly masculinized. To adapt and re-write Jackson's argument, this is to see the actions of Thomas Hamilton as closely connected to a '. . .

desperate struggle to become masculine . . .'.[93] Although Thomas Hamilton's killing of sixteen children and their teacher '. . . was exceptional in degree and intensity, he was not a one-off, devilish, "freak of nature". He shared many of the learnt tendencies of aggressive, heterosexual manliness that many insecure young boys and men are desperately striving for today. Although representing a heightened, extremely unusual form of these tendencies, Thomas Hamilton existed firmly within the common continuum of male violence.[94]

To recap the argument at this point: Thomas Hamilton, in trying to masculinize himself within the ideals of traditional heterosexual masculinity, can be read as attempting to forge a more commanding and potent sense of himself as a man.[95] He did this, I have argued, through his involvement in (at least) three major activities. First, in his participation in the youth clubs, in which he is constituted as (surrogate) father-figure. Secondly, in his involvement with firearms and gun clubs, in which his subjectivity is empowered (however fleetingly) through the constitution of the body as 'masculine'; and, finally, and by way of a combination of each of the above, in his ultimate invasion, re-framing, and destruction of the largely feminized space of the Primary School at Dunblane which resulted in the death of sixteen children and their teacher.

CONCLUDING REMARKS: RECONSTITUTING THE CRIMES OF MEN *AS MEN*

> What is it about our world that impels men such as Thomas Hamilton to go on random, apparently motiveless killing sprees? This is a new kind of crime, not much more than a decade old, and signs were available long before its emergence.[96]

I have argued that a number of oppositions pervade the press discourse in its constructions of Thomas Hamilton. The result is a rich iconography of masculine otherness far more complex than the initial focus on good/evil, normal/deviant binaries would suggest. As a single (unpartnered) man he is not a 'family man' for he is of no family. Yet he is understood as other *through* the family. The crisis of representation of the paternal relation which surrounds the case results from the reconfiguration taking place within postmodernity of the sociality and contingency of those oppositional categories through which hetero-masculinity has hitherto been constituted as a naturalized, essentialist phenomenon. In this process, the broader heterosexual matrix which has historically framed understandings of men's crimes and criminality itself appears as, I have suggested, a phantasmatic ideal. The representation of Thomas Hamilton's 'dangerousness' embraces a range of images, behaviours, and demeanours which cannot be confined to the 'pervert/paedophile'-'normal' binary. Nor does it fit in which any straightforward representation of Hamilton as a (self-evident) 'psychopath'.

In the suggestion that there is something new and distinct about the spree killing, that it is a 'new kind of crime', it is envisaged that crime has 'transformed itself and mutated'. Crime appears as '. . . a law unto itself, outside the law, an outlaw'.[97] Outside the law, beyond reason, a space opens up for speculation about the dark side of 'human nature' which marked so much of the media coverage of Dunblane. Yet what, I have argued, constitutes a more plausible reading of the symbolic power of Dunblane is to locate representations of Thomas Hamilton in relation to a transformation in the discursive experience of the social. With this in mind, it should not surprise that the present re-configuration of men's relationships with children (all too evident in contemporary 'law and order' debates) should also involve a reframing of hitherto self-evident 'dangerous' masculinities of men and boys. For what is at issue here is ultimately the concept of childhood itself and the way in which it relates to the idea of the social. From the child's post-Enlightenment positioning as an unequivocal source of love, the child of postmodernity has come to signify simultaneously both a 'nostalgia' for an innocence-lost[98] and, notably in the form of the criminality of male youth, destructive social breakdown and moral dislocation. Following the investment of the innocence of childhood with no less than grounding a sense of sociality at a time of intolerable and disorientating change, it is no wonder that the abuse and destruction of such innocence should then be seen to strike at the remaining vestigages of that social bond; nor, as in the aftermath of the deaths of the Dunblane children (and, indeed, James Bulger), that what should surface should be such an intense expression of collective pain at the loss of that social identity.[99] In contrast to Hamilton's embodiment of 'evil', the Dunblane children appear as permanent and dependable, the incarnation of a 'nostalgic' vision of the child which has increasingly come to preserve no less than the meta-narrative of society itself.[100]

Where does this leave the politics of masculinity, the relationship between masculinity and crime? In this article I have presented an interpretative genealogy of how the 'silencing' of masculinity is achieved in one particular context. I have taken the press coverage of Dunblane as illustrative of the broader phenomenon whereby the sociality of men's crimes *as the actions of men* is routinely effaced. This is a question traditional political discourse appears incapable of addressing, something which says much about contemporary understandings of the relation between the crimes of men and the idea of the social. Faced with the events at Dunblane even the eloquence of politicians seemed to fail: '. . . some public catastrophes', it was stated, 'are out of public reach.'[101] For others the 'pain for the grieving silenced [traditional] politics.'[102] That which was evacuated, silenced from the very outset was, I have argued, any analysis of Thomas Hamilton not as a 'lone gunman', 'spree killer' or 'monster' but *as a man*. For all the limited engagement it contains addressing Thomas Hamilton's 'character and attitudes', his 'mood' and 'psychological and psychiatric evidence', there is no trace of any such questions in the Cullen report.[103] 'Traditional' politics seemed to sense, but barely express, the feeling of the betrayal of the vulnerable which run through the crimino-legal response to Dunblane and, more generally, to crimes against children. The terms 'no evidence' and 'no action taken' were repeated constantly during the Cullen inquiry. Certain assumptions about men and crime pervade this lack of response to those mothers who made complaints about the actions of Thomas Hamilton.[104] What had happened to the knowledge which so clearly existed about his actions (and was so evident in the accounts of women and children)? How was it, in a sense, 'neutralized'? The dominant representation of the spree killer as (asocial) other fed into a valorizing of childhood innocence which, perhaps ironically, itself served to silence the voices of those children who sought to speak of, and be heard in, their testimonies of the crimes of men.

To re-configure the relationship between masculinities and crime leads, ultimately, to a transformation in how crime is imagined. It leads to a set of different questions and issues which ill-fit the traditional formulations of liberal political and crimino-legal thought (in terms, for example, of public/private, mind/body). In one sense Thomas Hamilton is a 'one-off'. Yet from such '. . . so called "aberrant" cases' much can be learnt about the crimes of men more generally. Indeed, it is arguably all the more pressing to locate the thread which links such crimes with the fantasies and actions of 'normal' men. We have yet, it appears, to be challenged by what Thomas Hamilton may have shared with other men.[105] It is precisely such questions which raise important and difficult issues about the responses to and reception of the life and death of Thomas Hamilton. To dismiss the lack of response on the part of 'the Authorities' to 'do something' about his activities as *simply* a bureaucratic failure or regulatory matter (of firearms, school security)[106] is to misread – and to negate analysis of – the pervasive masculinism of state institutions themselves in terms of their assumptions, prevailing culture and, importantly, conceptualization of whether other 'subordinated' masculinities are, or are not, perceived of as actually or potentially 'criminal'.[107] In order to develop an understanding which might 'shield society from the consequences' of men's criminality, it is necessary to 'reflexively re-configure the relationship between the social and subjectivity'.[108] Far from being a 'one-off', exceptional and not-to-be-repeated event, in (re)locating the 'lone gunman' within a broader framework of idealized masculinity, the recent instances of spree killings can be seen as highlighting, not just a failure to protect women and children from the depredations of 'psychopathic' males, but as also raising important, and disturbing, questions about the boundaries of what constitutes 'acceptable' male behaviour in the first place.

NOTES AND REFERENCES

1 Quoted in the *Guardian*, editorial, 14 March 1996.
2 These are distinct from the phenomena of 'serial killing', on which see, further, J. Stratton, 'Serial Killing and the Transformation of the Social' (1996) 13 *Theory, Culture and Society* 77–98. On non-politically motivated homicides, including the spree killing, see D. Gresswell and C. Hollin, 'Multiple Murder: A Review' (1994) 34 *Brit. J. of Criminology* 1–14.
3 A detailed account of the events can be found in the *Report of the Public Inquiry into the shootings at Dunblane Primary School on 13 March 1996* (1996; Cm. 3386; Chair, Lord Cullen) - hereafter, the Cullen report. An outline of the events can be found in 'Minutes of Mayhem that took 17 Lives: Dunblane Inquiry' *Guardian*, 30 May 1996. The details of what happened will be considered further below.
4 In relation to theorizing masculinity, see, further, S. Gutterman, 'Postmodernism and the interrogation of masculinity' in *Theorizing Masculinities*, eds. M. Kimmell and M. Kaufman (1994); D. Saco, 'Masculinity as Signs: Poststructuralist Feminist Approaches to the Study of Gender' in *Men, Masculinity and the Media*, ed. S. Craig (1992).
5 See, for example, J. Butler, *Gender Trouble* (1990); J. Butler, *Bodies that Matter* (1993); E. Grosz, *Volatile Bodies: Towards a Corporeal Feminism* (1994); M. Gatens, *Imaginary Bodies* (1996). Also J. Butler, 'Against Proper Objects', (1994) 6(2/3) *Differences: J. of Feminist Cultural Studies* 1–27; 'Gender as Performance: An Interview with Judith Butler' (1994) 67 *Radical Philosophy* 32–9 (interviewed by P. Osbourne and L. Segal). For an excellent introduction to queer legal theory see, further, C. Stychin, *Law's Desire: Sexuality and the Limits of Justice* (1995): L.J. Moran, *The (Homo)Sexuality of Law* (1996).
6 A. Young, *Imagining Crime* (1996) 112.
7 My use of 'Crimino-legal' here delineates, following Young, id., more than simply 'criminology', 'criminal justice' or 'criminal law' but, rather, '. . . all of these together with the popular discourses that are manifested in the media, cinema and advertising, in order to convey the sense that "crime" has become (been made?) a potent sign which can be exchanged among criminal justice personnel, criminologists, politicians, journalists, film-makers and, importantly, (mythical) ordinary individuals' (id., p. 2).
8 Gresswell and Hollin, op. cit., n. 2, p. 3.
9 See, for example, 'Slaughter in the Sun' *Guardian*, 29 April 1996: N. Rufford and P. Arthur, 'The Misfit Behind the Massacre' *Sunday Times*, 5 May 1995.
10 K. Busch and J. Cavanaugh, 'The Story of Multiple Murder: Preliminary Examination of the Interface Between Epistemology and Methodology' (1986) 1 *J. of Interpersonal Violence* 5–23; R. Rappaport, 'The Serial and Mass Murder: Patterns, Differentiation, Pathology' (1988) 9 *Am. J. of Forensic Psychiatry* 38–48; M. Rowlands, 'Multiple Murder: A Review of the International Literature' (1990) 1 *J. of the College of Prison Medicine* 3–7.
11 Gresswell and Hollin, op. cit., n. 2, p. 3.
12 M. King, 'The James Bulger Murder Trial: Moral Dilemmas and Social Solutions' (1995) 3 *International J. of Children's Rights* 167–87.
13 See, for example, Young, op. cit., n. 6, p. 111: '. . . personal reactions to it are as strong as they ever were . . . in writing this chapter I have had frequent bad dreams and have felt a deep sense of horror'. Also, King, id., p. 168.
14 King, id., p. 168.
15 T. Newburn and E. Stanko (eds.), *Just Boys Doing Business? Masculinity and Crime* (1994) 1.
16 D. Jackson, *Destroying the Baby in Themselves: Why did the two boys kill James Bulger?* (1995) 3.
17 See, for example, R. Ericson, P. Baranik, and J. Chan, *Visualising Deviance: A Study of News Organisation* (1987); R. Ericson, P. Baranik, and J. Chan, *Negotiating Control: A*

    Study of News Sources (1989); R. Ericson, P. Baranik, and J. Chan, *Representing Order: Crime, Law and Justice in the News Media* (1991).

18 K. McEvoy, 'Newspapers and Crime: Narrative and the Construction of Identity' in *Tall Stories? Reading Law and Literature*, eds. J. Morison and C. Bell (1996).

19 See, further, A. McRobbie, *Postmodernism and Popular Culture* (1994).

20 *Time Magazine*, 25 March 1996.

21 *Daily Express*, 20 March 1996.

22 *Daily Mirror*, 20 March 1996.

23 *Sun*, 20 March 1996.

24 The 'quality' (broadsheet) press tends to seek more liberal, rational explanations in contrast to the more sensationalizing tendencies of the tabloids. Given the latter's (considerably) greater circulation, it is open to question what effect this has on the framing of public opinion. Notwithstanding these differences, each tended to share an initial depiction of Hamilton in terms of 'evil'; compare *Daily Mirror*, 20 March 1996. On the day Dunblane primary school re-opened, it was stated that 'the evil has gone.' (*Sun*, 23 March 1996).

25 Mr. Justice Moreland, summing up in the James Bulger murder trial (*Guardian*, 25 November 1993). On the Bulger case see, further, Young, op. cit., n. 6, p. 111: Jackson, op. cit., n. 16.

26 King, op. cit., n. 12, p. 167–8.

27 Features of the spree killing have been taken up in the representation of other crimes: see, for example, accounts of the apparently random knife attack by a shopworker in Birmingham, England, which left one person dead and nine injured (*Guardian*, 30 July 1996).

28 Jackson, op. cit., n. 16, p. 4.

29 Editorial comment *Daily Mirror*, 14 March 1996.

30 P. Barker, 'Loner in Our Midst' *Guardian*, 15 March 1996.

31 Stratton, op. cit., n. 2, p. 78.

32 *Guardian*, 15 March 1996.

33 Compare with the representation of community in the aftermath of the murder of James Bulger; Young, op. cit., n. 6, p. 120.

34 B. Campbell, *Goliath: Britain's Dangerous Places* (1993).

35 *Guardian*, 14 March 1996.

36 E. Fergurson, D. D. Harrison, and R.McKay, 'Dunblane: the Story That Need Never Have Been Told' *Observer*, 17 March 1996.

37 See, for example, 'Fear Rules in No Go Britain: A Report on the parts of the country most people would rather not think about - never mind live' *Independent on Sunday*, 17 April 1994.

38 *Time*, op. cit., n. 20.

39 *Observer*, op. cit., n. 36.

40 A number of reports noted how the adults who lived in Dunblane, a commuter town, tended not to be familiar with each other. The children, in contrast, *knew* each other and the primary school had come to be a focus of life in the town. It brought people, who otherwise lived very separate lives, together. As such, the mass murder of the children took on a particular resonance in its symbolic violence against the idea of a community which had seemed crime-free.

41 *Independent*, 16 March 1996. Hamilton had been brought up to believe his natural mother, to whom he was very close, was in fact his sister: see, further, Cullen report, op. cit., n. 3, para. 4.2, p. 20.

42 Barker, op. cit., n. 30.

43 Jackson, op. cit., n. 16, p. 17.

44 Barker, op. cit., n. 30.

45 Fergurson, Harrison, and McKay, op. cit., n. 36. My emphasis.

46 *Guardian*, op. cit., n. 32.

196

47 *Independent*, 18 March 1996.

48 *Time*, op. cit., n. 20.

49 id.

50 *Chicago Tribune*, 20 March 1996.

51 *Guardian*, op. cit., n. 35.

52 *Time*, op. cit., n. 20.

53 D. Campbell, 'He was a loner: he kept his cliches to himself' *Guardian*, 13 July 1996.

54 *Guardian*, 31 May 1996

55 id.

56 A similiar reading informs A. Young's discussion of the mothers of Jon Venables and Robert Thompson, the two boys convicted of the murder of James Bulger (Young, op., cit., n. 6, p. 125).

57 *Guardian*, 29 April 1996.

58 id.

59 Gerard Bailes, Novik Clinical Forensic Unit, quoted in G. Younge 'He Just Shot Everyone Coming In', id.

60 Ian Stephen, quoted in Younge, id.

61 Clive Meux, Senior Lecturer, Institute of Psychiatry, London, and consultant at Broadmoor Top Security Hospital, quoted in Younge, id.

62 P. Hoggett, 'A Place for Experience: A Psychoanalytic Perspective on Boundary, Identity and Culture' (1992) 10 *Environment and Planning: Society and Space* 345–56, at 345.

63 See, in particular, on the 1993 film *Falling Down*, C. Clover, 'White Noise' in *Sight and Sound*, May 1993, 6–9.

64 According to Clover (id., p. 9), the 'Average White Male' '. . . is the great unmarked or default category of western culture, the one that never needed to define itself, the standard against which other categories have calculated their difference'; 'No Travis Bickle this, *Falling Down*'s story is precisely that of *Taxi Driver* . . . its whole effect depends on seeing D-Fens [the principal character in the film, played by Michael Douglas] not as a vet descending into madness, but as a tax-paying citizen whose anger allows him to see, with preternatural clarity, the madness in the society around him' (p. 8).

65 See, further, R. Collier, '"Coming Together?": Post-Heterosexuality, Masculine Crisis and the New Men's Movement' (1996) 4 *Feminist Legal Studies* 3–48.

66 In relation to urban disorder, see Campbell, op. cit., n. 34.

67 *Time*, op. cit., n. 20.

68 Compare with representations of school photographs in the Bulger case, notably in relation to representing the innocence of James Bulger himself: Young, op. cit., n. 6, p. 116.

69 The video was to later form the basis of a BBC *Panorama* documentary on Dunblane, broadcast 16 September 1996.

70 Men remain rare in primary school teaching, except as the Head of School. Even before the emergence of high-profile debates around school security in the 1990s, following a number of murders and attacks inside and outside school grounds, the very presence of an unknown man in any school is enough to arouse suspicion.

71 In July 1973 Thomas Hamilton became a leader in the Boy Scouts movement. In 1974, at the age of twenty-one, he was subsequently dismissed as leader of a local troop for 'inappropriate behaviour.' In the intervening years he made frequent attempts to be allowed to re-enter the organization, the last in 1988: he was rebuffed on every occasion.

72 P. Britton in the *Sunday Times*, 17 March 1996. Notwithstanding that the Cullen inquiry heard from 171 witnesses unrestrained by libel laws, hard evidence linking Hamilton with sexual abuse of children remained meagre (*Guardian*, 11 July 1996).

73 See, further, A. Parker 'The Construction of Masculinity Within Boys' Physical Education' (1996) 8 *Gender and Education* 141–57.

74 The stated aims of the 'boot camps' introduced by the British government as a way of instilling military discipline for young offenders, for example, emphasize similar concerns

with the disciplining, surveillance, and regulation of male bodies. C. Murray, *The Emerging British Underclass* (1990). In the British context, see N. Dennis and G. Erdos, *Families Without Fatherhood* (1991).

75 C. Skelton, 'Sex, Male Teachers and Young Children' (1994) 6 *Gender and Education* 87–93. Also K. Pringle, *Men, Masculinities and Social Welfare* (1995).

76 A. Burgess and S. Ruxton, *Men and Their Children: Proposals for Public Policy* (1996).

77 Stratton, op. cit., n. 2, p. 82.

78 By way of an exception, see B. Campbell, 'The Problem With Arms and Men' *Guardian*, 23 July 1996.

79 On the gender politics of the gun lobby, see, further, R. Connell, 'Politics of Changing Men' (1995) 25 *Socialist Rev.* 135–59, at 146–7.

80 Note, for example, the Masonic links it was suggested Thomas Hamilton had made (*Scotsman*, 22 March 1996).

81 *Guardian*, 11 July 1996.

82 'Who Are the Judges?' (1987) 76(1) *Labour Research* 9–11.

83 For example, 'Gun Man Obsessed by Hungerford shot 17 bystanders' *Times*, 25 May 1996.

84 G. Bailes, quoted in Younge, op. cit., n. 59.

85 *Independent*, 16 March 1996.

86 The results of a survey of 24,000 teenagers in 1996 (J. Balding, *Young People: Tenth Report* (1996).

87 *Times*, 15 March 1996. On the events preceding the massacre, see Cullen report, op. cit., n. 3, ch. 5.

88 Jackson, op. cit., n. 16, p. 9.

89 id., p. 16.

90 id., p. 32.

91 See N. Eastman, 'Madness or Badness?' *Guardian*, 22 October 1996.

92 Cullen report, op. cit., n. 3, para. 5.46.

93 Jackson, op. cit., n. 16, p. 24.

94 This section re-writes, in the context of Dunblane, Jackson's analysis of the Bulger murder (id., p. 4).

95 id., p. 28.

96 Editorial, 'They Deserve Our Answers' *Independent on Sunday*, 17 March 1996.

97 Young, op. cit., n. 6, p. 6.

98 C. Jenks 'The Postmodern Child' in *Children in Families: Research and Policy*, eds. J. Brannen and M. O'Brien (1996).

99 id., p. 20.

100 id., p. 21.

101 H. Young 'Many Questions, No Answers' *Guardian*, 14 March 1996.

102 *Independent*, Editorial, 15 March 1996.

103 See, for example, paras. 5.2, 5.25–5.28, 5.37–5.49. Government strategy continues to be to regulate the body of the paedophile in quite specific ways: see the consultation paper, *Sentencing and the Supervision of Sex Offenders*, published 17 June 1996.

104 See, for example, Cullen report, op. cit., n. 3, ch. 4.

105 For a rare exception to this, in another context, see J. O'Sullivan, 'We're still in the dark over West's madness' *Independent*, 12 September 1996.

106 Which is, in effect, what the Cullen report concludes. A senior police officer subsequently resigned in the wake of the comments made on bureaucratic failings in the report.

107 It is an interesting question as to whether, had the complaints being made about Thomas Hamilton come from men, rather than women, they would have met with a similar reception in terms of identification of men's dangerousness.

108 T. Jefferson, Review (1996) 36 *Brit. J. of Criminology* 323.

[10]

Violence and the Law: The Case of Sado-Masochism

LESLIE J. MORAN

University of Lancaster

On 11 MARCH 1993, the Judicial Committee of the House of Lords sitting as the final court of appeal in England and Wales published a collection of opinions known as *R* v. *Brown*,[1] dealing with the legality of a series of acts that were described by the court as acts of homosexual sado-masochism (hereinafter referred to as S/M). The acts had been performed with full mutual consent in private homes. A majority of the judges in the House of Lords (3–2) concluded that these acts were unlawful, being assaults occasioning actual bodily harm or acts of unlawful wounding.[2] The publication of these judicial opinions is the most important recent event[3] in a series of encounters between various institutions and practices of English law and the bodies and desires of the men who engaged in these consensual acts. Throughout these encounters have had an exorbitant quality. They continued over a considerable period of time, beginning in 1987.[4] Over £3 million was spent on the extensive police investigation, codenamed 'Operation Spanner' (Farshae, 1993; Kershaw, 1992), that brought these acts before the law. Over 100 gay men were interviewed. Over 40 men were arrested. Sixteen men were charged and found guilty. As a result of the criminal proceedings 14 of the 16 defendants lost their jobs, several lost their homes and some lost their good health (Kershaw, 1992; *R* v *Brown*,[5] CAR: 310). The original sentences imposed upon the individuals who performed these consensual acts included terms of imprisonment of over four years.

The general focus of this analysis is upon the juridification of the male body and its desires that has taken place during these encounters. In particular, the analysis will proceed by way of a consideration of the judicial opinions that are to be found in the judgment of the English Court of Appeal[6] and in the majority and minority opinions in the final appeal court, the House of Lords. The judicial opinions presented in these judgments are of particular significance. First, they provide evidence of the legal practices through which the performances undertaken by the defendants are made legible within the law and thereby subject to the law. Second, they provide an opportunity to explore the particular intelligibility by which the sense and non-sense of these bodies and desires is made in the law. Third, they provide an opportunity to study a theme that dominates the judicial attempts to make sense and non-sense of these bodies and desires; the relationship between law and violence. Fourth, they provide a demonstration of the way the law/violence distinction is used within legal practice in order to represent the practice of law itself. Finally, the essay will use the analysis of this juridification of the male body and its desires to develop a critique of the law.

VIOLENCE

The Court of Appeal decision and the judgments of majority in the House of Lords provide elaborate expositions of the S/M practices. Not only does violence have a particular importance in these attempts to make sense and non-sense of the male bodies and their desires that are the object of attention but the judges proceed according to the requirements of a specific logic of violence. Thus we are told that S/M is a violence that is unpredictably dangerous. These acts are not to be thought of as isolated transactions but as performances that have a certain contagious quality; they will breed cruelty (HL: 236H). They are ascribed with the ability to generate 'increasing barbarity' (HL: 235F). They are invariably described as activities that will 'get out of hand' (HL: 255H). They are exhibitions where there is an absence of control (HL: 236B); 'no referee is present' (HL: 238F). According to the requirements of this particular intelligibility, S/M as violence is that which will escalate, escape, overstep boundaries. These S/M bodies, desires and practices are produced in law according to a logic of loss of control, loss or absence of the authority figure, the controller. In general these S/M bodies are made legible according to a logic of violence as unruly escalation.[7]

This particular logic of violence is also represented through metaphors of blood, wounds and disease. We are told that in S/M practice 'blood will flow free' (HL: 246A); '[w]ounds ... easily become septic' (HL: 246A); one person may infect another (HL: 246A). Each symbolizes a violence having particular qualities: communicability, incrementality and uncontrollability. These themes also operate through metaphors of sex, drink and drugs. Thus we are told that 'an inflicter who is carried away by sexual excitement or by drink or drugs could easily inflict pain and injury beyond the level to which the receiver consented' (HL: 246B); '[S]ado-masochistic activity under the powerful influence of sexual instinct will get out of hand ... will involve a danger of infection' (HL: 255G–H). In turn, the themes of communicability and incrementality are repeated in references to S/M as a practice that arises out of corruption (HL: 235G, 255F and 275C) where that corruption is brought about by a process of education (HL: 235F–F and 275C).

A further manifestation of the theme of S/M as unruly, escalating violence appears in various references to the law. The law or, more specifically, various images of the corruption of the law, are put to work as images of S/M's violence. Here S/M's violence is portrayed as that which, in the first instance, is other to the law and as that which in its proximity will pervert the law and thereby render law indistinct. An example of the operation of this theme is to be found in responses to the defendants' argument that the acts of S/M were consensual and thereby not unlawful. In response, Lord Templeman argued that to accept consent and thereby to bring these practices within the law is to bring S/M's violence within the law. The effect that this would have upon the law is presented in various ways. For example, to accept the consensual nature of these performances would also be to change the law. Here 'change' has a particular significance. It is not merely a movement from one point to another. It is a crossing of boundaries: to cross from judgment as a declaration of law to judgment as making the law. It renders indistinct the distinction between applying the law and making the law (HL: 234H). In turn, to accept the claims of the defendants threatens to confuse the distinction between law and policy as it is presented as crossing from law to policy. Furthermore, we are told that to set a 'new' boundary between the lawful and the unlawful would not, in this instance, clarify the law but would introduce a new complexity into the law and thereby make the law less clear; more opaque. The task of instructing the jury would become more difficult. The prospects of conviction would recede (HL: 245). Within this narrative law appears twice. First, it is presented as that which is always already above and beyond violence and that which is in opposition to violence, both threatened by and resistant to violence which will pervert, infect and corrupt it. Law appears a second time as an image of law corrupted by violence. On this occasion the image is one of the conflation of violence and law. Here law infected by violence is perverted: it has changed its nature and lost its way. Here law as corruption appears by way of all of those attributes that the judiciary wish to associate with S/M; law is confused, inarticulate, opaque, unruled and thereby unable to achieve its goals.

Here the judges tell a very specific story about the nature of law and violence and about the relationship between them (Sarat and Kearns, 1991). It is an economy of law and violence that creates a distance between S/M as violence and the law. Within this particular economy of law and violence there can be no public interest in the lawful consent to S/M practices. In this scheme of things law is associated with order, predictability, reason, rule, control, limit. The body and its desires as violence is presented as its opposite: disorder, the unruly and unruled, unbounded, irrational and unpredictable. This embodied violence is that which is outside the law, and that which defies the law. On the other hand, this economy demands a certain proximity between law and violence. Violence is the object of law's attention. According to this story, violence stands immediately before the law. As such it beckons the law and demands a response. Here embodied violence is law's point of departure. In its proximity to S/M as violence law appears as a promise to overcome this embodied disorder (Sarat and Kearns, 1991: 221).[8] This story of law and embodied violence focuses on law's majesty, on its value-declaring, rights enhancing and community building aspects (Sarat and Kearns, 1991: 218). Within this scheme of things, the body and its desires as contagious and unruly threaten law and, thereby, social order. This particular legibility of the body and desire demands that the law respond to the disorder that S/M is made to stand for. It is within the confines of this discursive economy that the law promises to bring unruly violence to an end; to re-establish order in the face of escalating embodied disorder.

THE DEFENCE OF CONSENT: REPRESENTING THE LAW

In producing the S/M body and its desires by way of this particular economy of law and violence, the judges paint a very specific picture about the nature of legal practice. In this section I want to turn to the judicial analysis of the law by which the acts of the defendants were criminalized in order to develop a critique of the way legal practice represents itself. The judicial exegesis arises in two institutional contexts. In the Court of Appeal it was framed by way of an appeal against conviction. In the House of Lords it was performed in response to a specific question formulated by the Court of Appeal:

> Where A wounds or assaults B occasioning him actual bodily harm in the course of a sado-masochistic encounter, does the prosecution have to prove lack of consent on the part of B before they can establish A's guilt under section 20 or section 47 of the Act of 1861.[9]

Throughout the Court of Appeal and the House of Lords, judicial practice represents itself as a tireless search for authentic sources of law which demands the expenditure of extravagant amounts of time and effort. Lavish attention is paid to these authentic sources in order to expose the reason that will not only control but dictate specific outcomes producing a predetermined order. It is a judicial practice that portrays rules as that which are both knowable and known. It portrays language as an effective guide and limit to action. As such these rules and legal language are capable of orienting official action towards rational ends and imposing a limit on the exercise of that action. Here the juridical performance celebrates judicial passivity, painting a portrait of the judge as a mere conduit. It presents an impression that law is impersonal and temperate rather than terrifying and painful (Sarat and Kearns, 1991: 217).

However, while the appeal judges in both the Court of Appeal and the House of Lords tell this story about law and perform it through their resort to numerous citations, their exegesis also presents another side of legal practice. It is revealed in various instances, for example in their deliberations on the question of the legal relevance of consent. In the Court of Appeal Lord Lane begins his observations with the following statement: 'Generally speaking, the prosecution, in order to bring home a charge of assault, must prove that the victim did not consent to the defendant's actions, an assault being any unlawful touching of another without that other's consent.' This suggests that consent is an ingredient of the offence. This is swiftly followed with the statement that in 'certain circumstances . . . the law does not permit a defendant to rely, so to speak, on the victim's consent' (CAR: 498 D–E). Here, in the movement from one sentence to the next, Lord Lane appears to move from the lack of consent as an ingredient of the offence to consent as a defence. In the House of Lords, with the exception of Lord Jauncey, the matter attracts little attention. When addressed by Lord Jauncey, the exposition of the law mirrors the conflicting positions presented in the Court of Appeal by Lord Lane. Lord Jauncey noted that evidence of the relationship between consent and assault in judicial pronouncements produced 'conflicting data' (HL: 246H). On the one hand, he noted that in *Attorney General's Reference (No 6 of 1980)*,[10] which raised the question of assault and consent in the context of an agreement between two men to resolve a dispute by means of a fist fight in a public street, Lord Lane had declared:

> We think that it can be taken as a starting point that it is an essential element of an assault that the act is done contrary to the will and without the consent of the victim; and it is doubtless for this reason that the burden lies on the prosecution to negative consent. (718E)

On the other hand, he found that in the earlier case of *R* v. *Coney*,[11] which raised the issue of assault and consent in the context of proceedings against individuals who were members of an audience watching an illegal prize fight in a public place and charged with aiding and abetting an assault, Stephen J had referred to consent as being no defence (549). Finally and more recently, Lord Jauncey noted that in the case of *Collins* v. *Wilcock*[12] (1177F) which involved an assault by a police officer upon a member of the public, Goff LJ had referred to consent as a defence to battery. Having assembled the conflicting citations, Lord Jauncey proceeded to resolve the conflict in a particular way. First, he concluded that it is not necessary to resolve the conflict. Then, contrary to expectations, he proceeded to resolve the conflict in the following terms; 'If it were necessary . . . to decide which argument was correct I would hold that consent was a defence to but not a necessary ingredient in assault' (HL: 575A). While this may resolve the conflict, no attempt is made to provide an explanation or to give reasons for this conclusion. In the final instance, contrary to the expectations generated by the representations in law that the citation of authorities will produce a single answer to the problem, the practice of law demonstrates that citations may produce a number of different answers to the problem. Thus citation, rather than imposing a particular outcome upon judicial deliberations, may leave the judge with no clear guideline. The resolution of the matter of the relationship between consent and assault then appears to be not so much a practice that slavishly follows the dictate of a previously existing rule but, at best, a practice that must forget the ambiguity cited and proceeds as nothing more than an arbitrary judicial assertion.[13] The attribution of authority and source to a citation is something that at best follows the citation rather than something that precedes it.

In the final instance, Lord Jauncey's assertion that consent ought to be read as a defence echoes the assumption that informs the analysis undertaken by the other judges.[14] In proceeding on this basis, the judges moved on to address a series of questions about the defence of consent. The questions posed by the judges gave rise to a problem of some complexity. In part this complexity comes from the fact that English law seeks to regulate offences against the person by way of an elaborate taxonomy of forbidden acts. When set within the context of this taxonomy the availability of consent as a defence may depend upon the allocation of the act within the hierarchy of offences against the person. For example, the judges noted that it is well established that consent is always a defence to the minor (summary) offence of common assault. At the other extreme Lord Lane noted that consent is never available as a defence to a killing (CAR: 498E). The events that were the subject of the charges in *R* v. *Brown* raised a question as to the boundary between those actions where consent is a defence and those where no defence is possible. In an attempt to resolve the issue, observations made by the eminent Victorian legal scholar and judge, Sir James Fitzjames Stephen (referred to in the House of Lords' judgments as this 'high authority') (HL: 262D) were cited. Stephen's *Digest of the Criminal Law* suggested that consent was available as a defence to acts of violence in all but the most extreme situations. 'Everyone has a right to consent to the infliction upon himself of bodily harm not amounting to a maim' (Stephen, 1894: art 227)[15] (a maim suggests an extreme and permanent injury, for example the severing of a limb, which deprives the King of an able-bodied subject). These observations appeared to be a commentary upon, and an elaboration of, statements made by him in the earlier prize-fighting case, *R* v. *Coney*, said to be the 'classic authority' on the availability of consent as a defence (QB: 498F).

In the House of Lords, these observations were rejected as an accurate expression of the law. The most detailed study of the point was undertaken by Lord Jauncey. First, he noted that while the *Digest* might clarify the observation on consent made by Stephen J in *R* v. *Coney* the statement in the *Digest* had to be dismissed, as *R* v. *Coney* was a case of no great assistance (HL: 241G). Secondly, the statement in the *Digest* had to be rejected as it had been the subject of adverse comment in the 1934 Court of Criminal Appeal case of *R* v. *Donovan*[16] which dealt with the question of assault and consent in the context of a trial court judge's direction to a jury arising out of an incident where a man beat a woman with a cane. During the course of the judgement in that case Swift J had stated that the statement by Stephen J was to be subject to considerable qualification. The reason being that what might be acceptable violence in 1883 was not acceptable in 1934 (507). Lord Jauncey supported this conclusion.[17] The reasoning that ultimately underpins the acceptance of *R* v. *Donovan* and application of that case by Lord Jauncey to the present situation and the rejection of Stephen J's argument is, in the final instance, no more than the banal fact that 1883 is neither 1934 nor 1993 and the peculiar fact that 1934 is 1993.

The imposition of this assertion and the logic that supports it had important effects. It shifted attention away from a generous interpretation of consent as a defence, where consent was a defence to all but the most extreme acts of maim and unlawful killing, and relocate the consent as defence debate at the lower threshold between common assault and actual bodily harm and wounding.[18] Thereby the meaning of bodily harm assumed particular significance. Various previous decisions were cited as the source of authoritative definitions of bodily harm. For example in the case of *R* v. *Coney*, relating to aiding and abetting assault in the context of a public prize-fight, Cave J defined bodily harm as a blow 'struck in anger or which is likely to do corporal hurt' (539). In the same case, Stephen J suggested that bodily harm was an injury that 'is of such a nature, or is inflicted under such circumstances, that its infliction is injurious to the public as well as to the person injured' (549). A further definition is to be found in *R* v. *Donovan*. Swift J defined bodily harm as a hurt or injury that 'need not be permanent, but must, no doubt be more than merely transient and trifling' (509).

While all of these citations refer to previous examples of attempts to draw a clear line between less serious and more serious forbidden acts, various commentators have noted that they are problematic. The definitions include words or phrases that are vague and capable of wide interpretation (Hughes, 1962: 685). Rather than providing clear distinctions, the language of the law has been said to make the definitions 'capable of discretionary application' (Leigh, 1976: 138). Finally, the definitions have been criticized on the basis that they are tautologous (Williams, 1962: 156). These criticisms have been echoed not only in academic commentary but also in judicial analysis of the definitions. For example, in the case dealing with a fist fight in a public place, *Attorney General's Reference (No. 6 of 1980)*, Lord Lane concluded that the reasoning in *R* v. *Donovan* was tautologous (718H). In *R* v. *Brown* Lord Jauncey found the observations in *R* v. *Coney* of no great assistance as the case was not concerned with a statutory offence and was, unlike *R* v. *Brown*, concerned with violence that involved a breach of the peace (HL: 241G). Likewise, Lord Lowry concluded that *R* v. *Coney* provided 'little help' and as a source of law was inconclusive and contained conflicting statements (HL: 250E–F).

In an attempt to bypass this impasse a further question was considered. Did consensual S/M practices fall under one of the existing exceptions within the law recognizing consent as a defence? *The Attorney General's Reference (No. 6 of 1980)* provided the main authority relating to the recognized exceptions that allow consent as a defence to bodily harm. In that case Lord Lane had attempted to provide a summary of the law in the following observation:

> . . . it is not in the public interest that people should try to cause, or should cause, each other actual bodily harm for no good reason. . . . Nothing which we have said is intended to cast doubt upon the accepted legality of properly conducted games and sports, lawful chastisement or correction, reasonable surgical interference, dangerous exhibitions, etc. These apparent exceptions can be justified as involving the exercise of a legal right, in the case of chastisement or correction, or as needed in the public interest, in the other cases. (719)

When applied to the facts of *R* v. *Brown* in the Court of Appeal, Lord Lane declared that consent was not a defence to an assault conducted during an S/M performance. His reasoning took the following form:

> What may be 'good reason' it is not necessary for us to decide. It is sufficient to say, so far as the instant case is concerned, that we agree with the learned trial judge that the

satisfying of sado-masochistic libido does not come within the category of good reason. (QB: 500)

His reasoning at this point has interesting qualities. While in the earlier case Lord Lane appeared to demonstrate an ability to name a common denominator that brought the various examples together, when faced with the application of his earlier observations to S/M he demonstrates that he was neither capable of explaining the meaning of 'good reason' and 'public interest' nor capable of explaining the distinction between S/M and these other acts. As such, his conclusion is a mere assertion.

When considered by the judges in the House of Lords we find that the opinions contain a more extensive consideration of the exceptions that fall under the good reason/public interest justification for the defence of consent. Perhaps the most extensive analysis of this aspect of the law is undertaken by one of the minority judges, Lord Mustill. He began his analysis by way of a search for a common theme that informed the various examples of good reason/public interest. However this project was swiftly abandoned. He concluded:

> For all the intellectual neatness of this method I must recognise that it will not do, for it imposes on the reported cases and on the diversities of human life an order they do not possess . . . either all or almost all the instances of the consensual infliction of violence are special. They have been in the past, and will continue to be in the future, the subject of special treatment by the law. (HL: 259)

Having abandoned any attempt to establish a common denominator that might be used to guide the judges in their consideration of the application of the defence of consent to S/M, he then adopted a different approach. He proceeded to catalogue each example of the defence of consent in order to discover the principle that informed each exception. Having discovered the principles of the law he would then be in a position to respond to the new challenge of S/M.

He began his search with a consideration of the defence of consent in the context of the law's response to death and dueling. He concluded that: 'There is nothing to help us here' (HL: 262B). The second example considered is maiming. Again, he concluded that the law's response to the defence of consent in this context, and in particular the observations made by Sir James Fitzjames Stephen, was of no assistance as the crime is 'antique'. He then proceeded through a list of further examples that include boxing, 'contact' sports, surgery, lawful correction, dangerous pastimes, bravado, mortification, rough horseplay, prostitution and 'ordinary' fighting. Some, he concluded, such as lawful correction, were irrelevant as they have nothing to do with the defence of consent (HL: 267B). Other exceptions, such as surgery, were of no assistance as it could only in part be explained by reference to consent. Furthermore, the example of surgery was of no assistance as it is 'in a category of its own' (HL: 266H). Of the other examples, such as dangerous pastimes, bravado and mortification, he concluded that these exceptions were of no assistance as the practices had little in common with each other or with the matter before the court. No further advantage was to be gained in exploring them (HL: 267 C–D). Where, as in rough horseplay, an explanation appeared to be forthcoming, his analysis frustrates expectations. Thus he noted that the underlying reason for the exception is nothing more than 'a matter of policy . . .' (HL: 267F). Furthermore, that policy was rendered obscure as the assumptions that were expressed therein would not remain constant (HL: 267G). The exception of boxing was explained on the basis that 'society chooses to tolerate it' (HL: 265H). By way of a general conclusion to the analysis of the examples of consent as a defence to assault, he noted that 'public interest may sometimes operate in one direction and sometimes in the other. . . . Sometimes the element of consent will make no difference and sometimes it will make all the difference. Circumstances must alter cases' (HL: 270F). In the final instance, he came to the conclusion that the statutes and cases cited failed to provide any guidance. The House of Lords was free to consider the matter entirely afresh (HL: 270F–G).

In general, the judges variously conclude that the sources of law, the Offences Against the Person Act, and the case law dealing with assault and consent, lack clarity: 'the language of the statute is opaque, and the cases few and unhelpful' (HL: 258F). The law contains 'conflicting data' (HL: 246G–H and 250E–F). It is 'inconclusive' (HL: 250E–F). It demonstrates inconsistency (HL: 267G). Long-standing authorities are unable to guide; they are of no assistance (HL: 241G). Well established rules are 'antique . . . obsolete' (*Brown*, 1994: 262F–H). The same rule may 'sometimes operate in one direction and sometimes operate in the other' (HL: 270D–E). In addition, while the judgments of the Court of Appeal and the House of Lords cite statutes and case law in support of their conclusions and offer an analysis of those sources of law in an attempt to resolve the various enigmas relating to the relationship between assault and consent, the analysis makes little or no progress. As the above analysis of the opinions demonstrates, the citation of cases and statutes as sources of law does not provide a single, clear, precise guide or dictate particular conclusions. Nor do the works cited appear to evidence an underlying and unfolding reason at work. The language of the law, offered in this legal practice as a limit to official action and as a guide that reduces or erases the possibility of arbitrary action and thereby seeks to put law on the other side of violence, is shown to be unhelpful, inconsistent, contradictory, ambiguous and opaque. The judicial exegesis invariably proceeds by way of citations that are ambiguous, tautologous or, at best, empty of reason, being nothing more than bold assertion. As such the law appears to operate within the decision as the unknown and unknowable. At best the statutes and cases cited as source reason and cause of the decision are citations whose authority and control is not so much something that precedes the judicial exegesis but is a product and an effect of that practice of citation.

Judicial practice reveals itself to be not so much a practice that resolves the enigma of the meaning of the law but a practice that defers the resolution of the enigma and displaces it, reformulates it and repeats it. Here the enigma travels from the question of lack of consent as a requirement of the offence, to consent as a general defence, to the search for the borderline between those acts where consent is always a defence and those where it is unavailable, to those specific situations where consent is a defence in exceptional circumstances, to the meaning of good reason and public interest (Barthes, 1990; Moran, 1991). As demonstrated in the reasoning that informs Lord Jauncey's application of *R* v. *Donovan* (1993 is not 1889), judicial practice rather than being a practice that is limited by language, rule based and reason bound, shows itself to be at best a form of domination performed through the arbitrary imposition of an empty assertion.

VIOLENCE AND THE LAW

These characteristics of the practice of law displayed in the judicial opinions in *R* v. *Brown* have a particular significance. They problematize the place of law within the economy of law and violence represented in the judgments, that seeks to place law in opposition to violence. When the language and the rules of the law are shown to be incapable of either providing clear guidelines or imposing strict limits upon action, the law begins to appear as a practice that is not so much a thing in opposition to violence but as a practice that has many characteristics that have been associated with violence. Thus law appears now as an arbitrary practice of domination rather than a practice controlled by language, rule and reason. Without the guidance arising from an authentic source of law, decision making might get out of hand. Without rule or reason judicial practice appears to be a practice without a referee or a controller. Legal practice no longer appears to be benign and impartial controlled by the rigorous demands of language, rule or reason but appears to be a practice of co-coercion more closely associated with the whim of those who have access to it. Thus law appears to take up a position similar to that previously allocated to the embodied violence that is said to be the S/M performance. The practice of the law has come to resemble a practice of unruly violence (Deleuze, 1989; Derrida, 1987). In the final instance this is not only a violence of domination through the imposition of an idiosyncratic view of the world and its enforcement by way of an arbitrary decisions, but also the more familiar violence that is punishment, in this instance the sentences ranging from four and a half years to two years, and the violence in the act of arrest and in the process of detention for interrogation, in subsequent loss of jobs, homes and good health.

The Western legal tradition has long recognized that violence as physical and conceptual domination and a practice of pain through punishment is part of the function of law and also one form (Rose, 1992: 141) of the law. This draws attention to the fact that law and legal practice have been represented not only by way of the oppositional relationship between law and violence but also by way of a story of the dual nature of violence. According to the latter story, while the violence of the law closely resembles the violence that is the object of its concern, criminal violence (Girard, 1979: 1, 37), the violence of the law is said to be separate and different from that other violence that is placed before and outside the law. Within this economy of dual violence, the violence of the law is presented as beneficial violence or good violence to be carefully distinguished from harmful or bad violence (Sarat and Kearns, 1991: 221–4; Derrida 1992: 39;

Girard, 1979: 37). Bad violence is presented as either a greater violence or a violence with the potential to generate greater violence and thereby is more destructive than the violence of the law. The (good) violence of the law is presented as a different type of violence. For example, it is violence of limited availability; not only does the law seek to monopolize violence but it will only be performed by designated individuals. Further, it is a violence operated according to a strict economy. As such it is violence that has been tamed and harnessed (Sarat and Kearns, 1991: 221–70). The violence of the law is named the lesser evil. Furthermore, the violence of law is a regime of legitimate violence (Sarat and Kearns, 1992: 4). It is a violence perpetrated in the name of the community (Devlin, 1965: Preface and Ch. 1) in order to protect that community. It protects it not only from the violence that is located outside the community but also it is a violence that is said to channel and redirect other violence that is scattered throughout the community. As such it protects the community by providing a substitute for the violence within the community (Girard, 1979: 8–10, 1986). Thereby, it is a violence that creates the bonds of community rather than being a violence that destroys community. Finally, the violence of the law is public vengeance. It differs from the private vengeance that is associated with bad violence as the latter is characterized by its capacity to escalate, to generate further violence. The violence of public vengeance is presented as a violence without reprisal or reciprocal vengeance; a violence without escalation. The violence of the law does not suppress violence; rather it purports to effectively limit it to a single act of reprisal, enacted by a sovereign authority specializing in this particular function thereby bringing violence to an end (Girard, 1979: 13–16). As such it is a curative violence. It is a violence that is said to rationalize revenge, limiting and isolating its effects in accordance with social demands. The violence of the law is said to be a practice that offers to treat the social disease of unruly, escalating violence without fear of contagion and presents itself as a highly effective technique for the cure and, as a secondary effect, the prevention of violence (Girard, 1979: 22).

Girard draws attention to the fact that these characteristics of the law in general and the judicial system in particular have a form and function similar to the institution of sacrifice.[19] As a sacrificial practice, legal practice is not only a practice of violence but it is a practice of violence that requires a particular object of that violence – a victim. The victim of sacrifice is produced according to particular requirements: as one without social bonds and without the capacity to establish the same; as one who is exterior and marginal to that community. These attributes are important as they suggest that the physical or civil death of the victim will not automatically generate a reciprocal act of revenge (Girard, 1979: 13). Here the violence of the law demands the marginality and vulnerability of the object of violence so that the violence might be exercised without fear of reprisal. In order to represent that marginality, the victim is made to depict characteristics of physical and/or moral monstrosity. While this is an essential requirement of the constitution of the sacrificial victim, the production of marginality also threatens to frustrate the sacrificial rites.

If sacrifice is to be successful there must be a substitution; the victim must be made to stand as a substitute for the members of the community who are the actual possible objects of intra-community violence serving as the one against whom violence is channeled in the name of protecting the community from its own violence. If this is to succeed the object of collective violence must also be constituted as the one that is the same as those that are to be named the community: its double (Girard, 1979: Ch. 6). It is their interchangeability that makes possible the act of sacrificial substitution. This draws attention to a fundamental requirement of the production of the sacrificial victim. The sacrificial victim must be both the double and the monster. While the final representation will tend to emphasize only one aspect (usually the monstrous aspect) in order to minimize the other this ought not to detract from the requirement that both are necessary. This also draws attention to the fact that sacrificial substitution implies a degree of misunderstanding. Its vitality as an institution depends on its ability to conceal the displacement upon which the rite is based – from intra-community violence to a violence that threatens from outside the community and from the victim as one within the community to the victim as one without the community. Once attention is focused on the sacrificial victim, the individuals of the community who were originally singled out for acts of intra-community violence fade from view. However, sacrifice must never lose sight entirely of the original object, or cease to be aware of the act of transference from that object to the surrogate victim; without that awareness no substitute can take place and the sacrifice loses all efficiency (Girard, 1979: 5).

S/M AS VICTIM

It is within the context of the insights provided by Girard's analysis of sacrificial violence and the place of the victim within that scheme of things that we return to the representation of the male bodies and desires that were the object of the proceedings in Brown. The investigation, trial and appeal proceedings have produced and organized an immense verbosity about (homosexual) S/M. The exorbitant history of the 'Operation Spanner' investigations and court proceedings suggests that all responded with enthusiasm to the contiguity of (homosexual) S/M and the law. The representation of (homosexual) S/M in the law is the effect of various practices of the police, prosecuting authorities, defence lawyers and judiciary, that have extorted admissions and confidences, accumulated endless details through examinations and insistent observation; contacting bodies, caressing them with their eyes, intensifying areas, electrifying surfaces, dramatizing trouble moments, wrapping these bodies in the law's embrace (Foucault, 1978: 44). What had, prior to these events been a minority practice, performed within a limited closed community, largely invisible to all including the various practitioners of the law, has been made public and been given a public potential which prior to the 'Operation Spanner' investigations and the Brown proceedings had been largely absent. The exorbitant nature of the proceedings show a determination to speak publicly of (homosexual) S/M and to hear it spoken about, and to cause it to speak through explicit articulation and endlessly accumulated detail. Through these practices these (homosexual) S/M bodies and desires were portrayed as unruly contagious violence.

At the same time, the opinions of the appeal court judges reveal another side to this will to knowledge: a systematic blindness. They demonstrate a refusal to know concerning the very thing that they purport to bring to light and whose formulation has been so extravagantly solicited (Foucault, 1978: 55). Evidence found in the various judgments and beyond suggests that the (homosexual) S/M that stands before and outside the law seems to bear little resemblance to the representations of (homosexual) S/M that are produced and enforced within the law. Thus, these practices appear to be so much acts in which consent is impossible but rather performances where consent is central (HL: 236 B–C). Rather than being a world of enforced silence, of abject and involuntary submission, of the impossibility of participation and dialogue, it is a world of participation and dialogue:

> If the two people don't talk about what they want to do and how they want to do it, the relationship won't work. . . . The starting point of all S/M relationships, then, is talk of the most intimate kind. The talk is about what S/M play gets the potential partners off: who will assume which role; whether other people may be included. (Tucker, 1991: 18–19; see also Califia, 1988)

They are acts in which the giving and receiving of pain has nothing to do with violence: 'Consensual sado-masochism is about *safely* enacting sexual fantasies with a consenting partner. Violence is the epitome of non sensuality, an act perpetrated by a predator on a victim' (Tucker, 1991: 30). Thus rather than a world made up of acts of animosity and hatred it is a practice without animosity, without aggression, devoid of personal rancour (HL: 258 A–B), without hostility (HL: 244B). It is a world of sensuality without victims (HL: 236B).[20] It is a world where the infliction of bodily harm is not the end of pleasure but essential to the production and satisfaction of pleasure. The thrill of power and the thrill of helplessness are not to be denied or avoided but have become the very reason for the performance. Here pleasure is derived from giving or receiving pain and humiliation (HL: 236B). Rather than a world devoid of institutions it is a highly organized world, of bars, meeting places, safe houses, organizations, publications, guidebooks, style manuals (HL: 245E; Rubin, 1993: 15–18; Brodsky 1993). It is a communication network with a self-regulating potential:

> The reputations of people who have harmed their play partners travel quickly on the greasy S/M community grapevine. It doesn't take long before everybody knows F had a partner wind up on the emergency room, and suddenly F can't find anybody to play with. (Tucker, 1991: 30)

It is a world of spoken and unspoken preparatory negotiations (Tucker, 1991: 19), of agreements, of contracts, where activities are undertaken in a well ordered (HL: 245E) and highly controlled manner (HL: 238E). Rather than a world of unruly violence it is a world of risk management and risk reduction (HL: 238E; Brodsky, 1993; Lee, 1983). Here the instruments of pain are clean and sterilized. Thus the limit of pain is negotiated, defined and enforced through verbal (the code word) and non-verbal signs that terminate the performance. It is a world where cruelty has been replaced by a particular etiquette of civility (HL: 255H).

Here S/M begins to exhibit an uncanny resemblance to those qualities which the narratives of law and violence and of good violence and bad violence associate with the law. S/M is not so much unruly violence but a practice that is concerned with an end to cruelty and revenge, where cruelty and revenge have been banished by the requirement of prior agreement and contract. It is here a legitimate and legitimated economy of pleasure. It seeks to subject the performance to strict limitations, negotiated by the involvement of all participants in advance. S/M practice is not so much an unruly practice devoid of purpose but one that is always oriented to a very specific objective; the production of pleasure. The failure to manage the performance towards this goal will inevitably result in the failure of the performance. Here S/M does not appear so much as a performance of violence and, as such a performance, devoid of ethical considerations and in opposition to law's ethical claims, but appears as a social practice in which ethical considerations can and must play a fundamental role. Furthermore, in the context of the display of the unruly and unbounded nature of legal practice in *R* v. *Brown*, S/M appears as a social practice that is antithetical to the arbitrary violence of the law; it is the good violence to the bad violence of the law. Here the relationship between S/M and the law appears to be the inverse of that painted in the judgments of *R* v. *Brown*. The body and desire that is S/M appears as an ethical space of social relations where the fundamental problems of pleasure, participation, dialogue, respect, trust, community, are explored and resolved. Law appears in contrast to this as a practice of domination, subordination, fear, silence, unwilling victims, and of potentially unlimited violence.

The official portrait of these (homosexual) S/M bodies and desires as unruly, contagious violence, produced through the manifold practices of law as evidenced in the majority appeal judgments, suggests that these bodies and desires have been made to appear according to a very particular narrative of law and violence. As such the appearance of these bodies and desires through the practices of law is an effect of censorship (the prohibition of an unconscious wish), and the imposition and enforcement of a very particular interpretation. Rather than bringing meaning to an end this censorship has been central to the construction of meaning. It has been put to work upon a mass of material to authorize and enforce a particular arrangement of things. Elements of a situation are selected, added to, (re)organized. Thereby the portrait of (homosexual) S/M is fabricated according to particular comprehensibility, by way of a particular scenario, that organizes details producing a particular spurious unity, a connectedness, an idiosyncratic intelligibility within the field of law (Laplanche and Pontalis, 1988: 65–6, 314–19, 412). One theme that is central to these considerations of intelligibility is the opposition between law and violence. In this instance the violence of the law is displaced (Laplanche and Pontalis, 1988: 118–21) and (re)appears as law's opposite, the embodied practices of S/M as violence. In a second theme, the opposition between good violence and bad violence, the violence of the law returns as a celebration of justice and just deserts, forged into an abstract principle that all are obliged to uphold and respect. Again the embodied practices of S/M remain in opposition to this good violence as bad violence.

The appeal judgments present three important aspects of the production of (homosexual) S/M as the sacrificial victim. First, in the final instance, the distinction between the sacrificial victim and the other members of the community is an effect of the violence of the law itself, as the imposition and enforcement of a particular meaning, that bestows the attribute of victim on these bodies and desires, the previously invisible consensual acts of S/M, which are only the pretext for a conflict. As such it is futile to look for the secret of the sacrificial victim in the 'truth' of the distinction that is drawn between the surrogate victim and the other members of the community. Anyone can play the part of the surrogate victim. Second, the whole process of the interpretation of (homosexual) S/M is dominated by the production of (homosexual) S/M as the monstrous double. It is made in the image of moral monstrosity in its representation as unruly (bad) violence in contrast to the rule bound rationality (good violence) of the law. It is made in the image of physical monstrosity in its representation as scarred and broken bodies, as open and weeping wounds. But it is also as violence that (homosexual) S/M is produced as the double of a violence that lies elsewhere. The appeal decisions evidence the place and nature of this other violence. It is revealed in the analysis of the distinction that is drawn in the judgments between the impossibility of consent in the context of (homosexual) S/M and the possibility of consent as a defence in the context of other acts of violence: 'contact' sport, boxing and rough horseplay. The judges note that an ethos of physical contact is deeply entrenched in each. More specifically, they demonstrate how each involves deliberate bodily contact of particular force. Thus 'contact' sport may involve 'what would otherwise be a painful battery . . . conceivably of sufficient severity to amount to grievous bodily harm' (HL: 266). In boxing,

> . . . each boxer tries to hurt the opponent more than he is hurt himself, and aims to end the contest prematurely by inflicting a brain injury serious enough to make the opponent unconscious, or temporarily, by impairing his central nervous system through a blow to the midriff, or cutting his skin. (HL: 265D–F)

Rough horseplay between male youths is explained by reference to *R* v. *Terence Jones*.[21] In that case a group of male youths seized two others. In the case report we are told that the latter were grabbed, pulled to the ground, punched, kicked and thrown in the air on three separate occasions. On falling to the ground they suffered substantial injury: a ruptured spleen and a broken arm. Both required immediate and extensive hospital treatment. The activities were described by the court as rough and unruly. The appeal judgment notes that the violence was treated by the defendants as a joke. The protests of the victims and their demands that the violence cease were ignored. The court concluded that consent to these acts of violence was a possible defence that should have been put to the jury. This case is of interest not only because of the way it reveals the degree of male to male violence that the law is willing to tolerate but also because of the court's approach to the matter of consent. The judgment draws attention to the fact that in this instance the law does not require the actual consent of the person who is the object of the defendant's acts. It is sufficient that there be a genuine belief by the defendant. Nor does the law require that the belief be reasonably held. This approach to consent refuses to recognize the importance of the voice of the one who is the object of the defendant's acts and thereby gives greater protection to the one who performs those acts of violence. Here the violence that is later projected on to S/M (in the process of its misrecognition) in order to condemn it, is institutionalized, normalized and celebrated 'as boys do' (377). Thus, at the same time as the judicial exegesis seeks to separate these acts of violence out from the idea of violence that is to be associated with (homosexual) S/M, it produces, through that projection, the connection between the two.

(Homosexual) S/M as double is also produced through another connection. A point common to the judicial consideration of all of the categories of acceptable violence, though one that is never overtly referred to, is the fact that they are only ever discussed as all-male practices, manly sports. Homosexual reproduces this manly attribute in the context of S/M. However, at the same time homosexual works to render this connection largely invisible. This is achieved by way of homosexual(ity) as another image of monstrosity. While the relevance of homosexual is formally denied in the judgments it is repeatedly referred to (Stychin 1994). Its formal disavowal and repeated citation in the judgments is significant in two respects. First, it marks the place of the requirement of a misunderstanding that must accompany the process whereby the victim is made to stand as a substitute for the other men in the community who are the actual possible objects of intra-community violence. That misunderstanding relates to the homosocial[22] nature of the actual intra-community violence. Here homosocial violence is misnamed homosexual violence. Thereby legal practice both recognizes the nature of homosocial violence which is a violence that requires unwilling victims, uses coercion, refuses to acknowledge the cries of the victim, achieves subordination and produces inequality, and projects it on to homosexual (S/M). In doing so it produces homosexual as the double of homosocial, creating the possibility of the substitution at the same time as it creates homosexual as monstrosity. At the same time it works to install a systematic blindness with regard to homosexual (S/M) denying it the possibility of being a practice of equal players, where each respects the other, of willing participants, of negotiation, contract and mutual pleasure.

The third important feature of legal practice is the function of 'guilt'. The attribution of guilt to those who performed S/M, that henceforth passes for the 'true' of those practices, differs in no way from those attributes that will henceforth be regarded as 'false' except that in the case of 'true' guilt no effective voice is raised to protest any aspect of the charge. Through 'guilt' a particular version of events succeeds in imposing itself. It loses its polemical nature in becoming the 'truth' itself. In 'guilt' one voice alone makes itself heard (Girard, 1979: 78). Through 'guilt' the machinery of legal practice as a sacrificial practice disappears from sight. The attribution of 'guilt' also works to conceal – even as it reveals – the resemblance of legal practice to acts of vengeance. In fact, the system functions best when everyone concerned is least aware that it involves retribution (Girard, 1979: 21–2). Rather than covering over the sacrificial nature of legal practice, in *R* v. *Brown* the 'guilt' of the defendants works to reveal that aspect of law. In *R*. v. *Brown* 'guilt' is problematic as the actions of the defendants have generated no victims: these acts were consensual. In *R* v. *Brown* all of the S/M practitioners are before the law. There are no victims other than the defendants themselves and they are made victims by the law, for the law. Production of the guilty as victims draws attention to the importance of public vengeance and recognizes the practice of law as a sacrificial practice. It is as sacrificial victim that the monstrosity of (homosexual) S/M as contagion (a violence that is both an essential part of the identity of those subjected to the law but also a sort of fluid substance that flows everywhere and impregnates on contact) and infection (with particular reference to HIV and AIDS (HL: 246A–B); as a practice of escalating vengeance; is celebrated so loudly in *R* v. *Brown*, at the same time as its manifestation as none of these is passed over.

Conclusion

Deleuze (1989: Ch. VII) has drawn attention to some of the distinctive characteristics of the challenge that S/M generates for law. It is to be found in the irony that the tyrant lies in the law rather than beyond the law. The tyrant speaks the language of the law. As De Sade observes: 'I have infinitely less reason to fear my neighbour's passions than the law's injustice, for my neighbour's passions are contained by mine, whereas nothing stops the injustices of the law' (quoted in Deleuze, 1989: 86). The apparent obedience of the masochist conceals another critique and a provocation. The masochist participates in the law by diligently observing the very letter of the law. Here the very law that forbids the satisfaction of a desire under the threat of subsequent punishment is the thing that precedes pleasure, that makes pleasure possible. Masochism provides a demonstration of the absurdity of law. The violence with which the English law has responded to S/M suggests that there is a recognition that S/M embodies a very distinctive challenge to the law.

The analysis of this case draws attention to another dimension of the challenge of homosexual S/M. The homosexual(ity) that is so regularly recited and denied in *R* v. *Brown* raises the spectre of an erotics of male/male relations that is denied in homosociality. Furthermore, *R* v. *Brown* raises the spectre of a homoerotics that provides a critique of homosocial violence. The violence of the decision in *R* v. *Brown* points to the troubling proximity and radical difference of homosexual S/M.

Reading the legal practices demonstrated in *R* v. *Brown* as sacrificial practices draws attention to another matter: the use of law's violence. If the violence of the law as sacrifice is to be successful there must be a substitution: the victim must be made to stand as a substitute for the members of the community who are the actual possible objects of intra-community violence. The sacrificial victim acts as the one against whom this intra-community violence is channelled in the name of protecting the community from its own violence. As sacrificial victims (homosexual) S/M in general, and the defendant practitioners in particular, are a substitute for a male to male homosocial intra-community violence that lies elsewhere. They might also be a substitute for another violence – a heterosocial violence of men against women. Various references in the judgments point to this heterosocial violence. For example, it is suggested in the definition of consent discussed in the context of 'rough horseplay' in *R* v. *Jones*. It is a definition that echoes the definition of consent found in the context of another manifestation of male violence: rape (Duncan, 1994). As many feminist scholars have pointed out, the law is not only tolerant of acts of violence between men but also tolerant of acts of violence by men upon women.[23] While the judgments in *R* v. *Brown* do not deal directly with violence by men against women, there is evidence in the judgments that this is also part of the intra-community violence that finds its substitute in the body and desires of (homosexual) S/M. Two references are made in the judgments to legal condonation of violence in a heterosocial context. The first is the case of *R* v. *Clarence*.[24] In that case the accused had consensual intercourse with his wife, he knowing and she ignorant that he had gonorrhea, with the result that she was infected. The law condoned this act of violence against the wife accepting that the act was not actual bodily harm, grievous bodily harm or an unlawful wounding. The reason given in support of this conclusion was that this act was not an assault and therefore not unlawful. The second case referred to is *R* v. *Donovan* where the accused beat a woman with a cane. While this decision appears to deny the possibility of consent to acts of violence, and thereby might be thought of as a decision that protects women, it should not be forgotten that the man who beat the woman in this instance successfully appealed against conviction on the basis of the trail judge's misdirection to the jury and remained unconvicted.

These cases draw attention to the other site of intra-community violence. It is not only the violence of homosociality (between men) but also the violence of heterosociality (by men against women). (Homosexual) S/M as victim is put to work as a substitute for the men and women of the community who are the actual possible objects of this homosocial and heterosocial violence. (Homosexual) S/M acts as the one against whom this intra-community violence is channelled in the name of protecting the community from its own violence. In the process of making (homosexual) S/M the monstrous double the judgments also demonstrate another feature of sacrificial practice; the production of difference. Here it is not so much the difference between violence and non-violence or the difference between bad violence and good violence. The homosocial and heterosocial contexts draw attention to the fact that these practices of sacrifice are also implicated in the production of the difference between homosexual and heterosexual. As such the violence of the law is deployed for a particular sex, sexual and gender hierarchy (Girard, 1979: Ch. 3).

Three events subsequent to the final judgment in *R* v. *Brown* are of importance. The first event occurred on 16 May 1993,[25] a little over two months after the House of Lords decision. *The Pink Paper* a (UK) national newspaper for lesbians and gay men, reported that 38 men had been arrested in a police swoop on a gay party in Hoylandswaine, a small village in the North of England. The raid, conducted by 26 police officers in a squad of nine police cars and vans, followed an anonymous tip-off that men had been seen entering and leaving a house with large bags. Having, on the basis of this information, obtained a warrant to search for stolen goods, the police entered the property. There they discovered a party. The party host described the scene immediately prior to the arrival of the police as 'merely a party for my gay friends', where the guests were standing around chatting and drinking. As a result of the raid all the party-goers were arrested and taken to the police station. All were subsequently released on bail. At the time of the report none of the men had been charged. When asked what the charges against the men might be, a Chief Inspector with the South Yorkshire Police informed the newspaper that 'the charges being brought would depend on "what the men said"'.

R v. *Brown* seems to have been of particular significance in this intervention and temporary incarceration. Various factors suggest that the activities of the police were in some way informed by and invested with the recent judgment of the House of Lords. First, the Hoylandswaine investigation has an interesting history. We are told that it was inaugurated by an anonymous telephone call not to the local police, the South Yorkshire force, but to the Metropolitan Police. In the first instance, a call to the Metropolitan Police about an incident relating to the handling of stolen goods taking place in a village several hundred miles away from their jurisdiction makes little sense. It makes more sense when set in the context of the police investigation that gave birth to the *Brown* proceedings: 'Operation Spanner'. The surveillance and investigation of the men that took place under 'Operation Spanner' was in part inspired and largely conducted by the Metropolitan Police (Obscene Publications Squad). Second, in sharp contrast to the description of the party given by the party host, the police tell a very different yet specific story of the party scene they apparently discovered upon their arrival. For the police it was not so much a party where men stood around chatting and drinking, but one where some men were tied up, some were handcuffed and some wore masks. Third, as a result of the raid for stolen goods the police seized particular items: leather jackets, leather and rubber trousers, sex-toys, masks and a sling. Under English law any lawful seizure depends upon a connection being made between the items seized and a criminal offence. None of the items seized appear to have been stolen, the original justification for the search. Nor is it an offence in itself to possess or wear leather jackets, leather trousers and so on within the context of an all-male gathering. Nor, after *R* v. *Brown*, is it specifically an offence to wear such items as part of a sado-masochistic performance provided that there is consent and those acts amount to no more than common assault. However, the seizure, if it is to be lawful, suggests that the leather jacket, leather and rubber trousers, mask, sex toy and sling had to be paraphernalia of unlawful practices. As such they might be read metony-mically: each alone and together are made to stand for an illegality that is elsewhere. The decision in *R* v. *Brown* makes these items capable of being read as signs of an illegal practice. That the legal practices performed by way of the police seizure might have given a meaning to these items that deployed the sense and non-sense of the body and desire so insistently demonstrated in *R* v. *Brown* is shown in one observation made by the police, that decisions relating to any charges and prosecutions flowing from the raid would have to take account of the *Brown* decision.

Other factors suggest that the raid might evidence another aspect of the post-*Brown* practice of the law. When set in the context of evidence of the history and current practice of police harassment of gay men, be it in the specific form of raids on gay parties or in other forms,[26] the Hoylandswaine raid does not suggest any particular connection between the police action and the *Brown* judgment. The raid can be read as just another example of the routine policing of gay men. In turn, it is important to recognize that the artifacts seized as a result of the raid have long been encoded as metonyms of perverse and thereby illegal sexual practices. Thus, when placed in the context of a group of gay men, these items might be read as the trappings of unlawful (homo)sexual practices in general. This possibility is evidenced in the Hoylandswaine incident in the reported suggestion that the men might be charged with the (homosexual) offence of conspiracy to commit gross indecency. As such, the seizure of these items might be read merely as part of the routine of policing sexual relations between men.

Thus, as meaningful elements that signify unlawful acts, the items seized are capable of at least two readings: one that relates to sado-masochism in particular and one that relates to unlawful (homo)sexual practices in general. On the one hand, it is important to recognize the gap that separates the two expressive systems through which the leather jacket, etc. may evidence illegal activity. On the other hand, it is also important to recognize their proximity. The signs of different illegalities are capable of being produced through the same paraphernalia. Homosexual and S/M may function as one and the same, representations of perverse sexualized bodies and desires (Stychin, 1994). This draws attention to the way that, on the one hand illegal homosexual relations might be read as both separate from sado-masochism and, at the same time, be read as the same as sado-masochism. The similarity between the portrait of homosexuality that haunts the imagination of the Common Law and the portrait of S/M suggests that the former may well be reduced to the latter in the wake of the House of Lords decision. As such, *R* v. *Brown* may work in general to recriminalize sexual relations between men as it works to name sado-masochism as unlawful violence and to equate homosexuality to sado-masochism. The raid on a bungalow in Hoylandswaine is perhaps a pertinent reminder of this aspect of *R* v. *Brown*.

The Hoylandswaine incident also problematizes one of the attributes said to be associated with the good violence of the law – that it brings violence to an end. The Hoylandswaine incident suggests that the violence of the law performed in the trial and appeal procedure is not so much brought to an end in those decisions but institutionalized. The invasion of the party by the police and the incarceration of the party-goers is the repetition of that violence. Thus, the violence of the law is not so much an act of violence to end violence, but an act of violence to inaugurate a new regime of lawful violence.

A second series of events also problematizes the suggestion that the violence of the law brings other violence to an end. Subsequent to the *Brown* decision, there has been an escalation in violence towards gay men, in particular during the summer of 1993 several gay men were murdered (Stychin, 1994). Between 1992 and 1993 the number of male rapes reported to the London police doubled (*The Pink Paper*, 1 April 1994). This evidence draws attention to the problematic nature of any suggestion that the measured violence of the law will end violence within the community into the law, or channel it through the law. Here the violence of the law in *R* v. *Brown* appears more as an invitation to channel violence against gay men in the community and an invitation that is regularly taken up.

The third incident subsequent to the Brown decision is the publication of a consultation paper which reviews the various judicial opinions in *R* v. *Brown* in particular, and the issue of consent and violence in general (Law Commission, 1994; Bamforth, 1994). Perhaps the most interesting feature of the Law Commission's preliminary analysis is the way the structure and content of the analysis mimics that of the judicial analysis in *R* v. *Brown*. The analysis proceeds on the basis that (homosexual) S/M is violence in opposition to the law. It perpetuates the myth of guilt of the consensual S/M and of the designation of one of the consenting participants as 'victim' of their own violence (Law Commission, 1994: 1, 5ff). It repeats the belief in legal practice as a rule bound, rational, limiting and limited practice at the same time that it reveals its arbitrary, unruly and unlimited potential.

It differs from *R* v. *Brown* in the outcome that is proposed. The consultation paper suggests that certain consensual acts that were criminalized under the *Brown* decision would no longer be criminal by virtue of the fact that under the terms of earlier proposals put forward by the Commission for the reform of the criminal law (Law Commission, 1993: paras 15.1–15.31). Provided the acts did not amount to 'serious injury', consent would absolve the accused. However, the decriminalization of such consensual acts is far from clear. Even in its proposals for reform the Law Commission celebrates the arbitrary nature of law. Thus the new key concept in law, 'serious injury', is said to involve 'an element of judgment'. The Law Commission notes that 'serious injury', 'will not give a potential injurer a conclusive answer in every case as to whether he should act on a particular consent of the victim' (Law Commission, 1994: paras 10.19–10.22). In the final instance, the meaning of 'serious' is to be left to the jury and as such it can only be known *post hoc* (Law Commission, 1994: para. 15.8).

While the Commission appears to be able, albeit very tentatively, to recognize boxing as an institutionalized celebration of male-to-male violence and urges that its legality be reviewed (Law Commission, 1994: paras 10.19–10.22), the other forms of institutionalized violence are to be called 'healthy recreation' (Law Commission, 1994: para. 44.4). Thereby, the essence of sport would appear to be a violence that is conducted according to rules, which are not simply made up, or alleged to have been made up, by the participants as they go along, but violence according to well established rules (Law Commission, 1994: 6, 270ff). As such, the violence of sport appears to disappear the further it is institutionalized only to reappear projected on to S/M, which is presented as the other to 'healthy' violence.

Perhaps the greatest weakness of the review is its failure to take seriously those forms of intra-community violence that are supported by the law. One conspicuous silence in this respect is the escalating violence that is perpetrated against homosexuals. While the judgments in *R* v. *Brown* and in turn the Law Commission seek to disavow the relevance of homosexual, it ought not to be forgotten that, while the relevance of homosexual was denied in *R* v. *Brown*, it was repeatedly referred to throughout the proceedings and functioned as a sign of the law's sacrificial victim. In turn, subsequent events draw attention to the way that the violence of the law against homosexuals is not so much a violence that ends violence, but violence that is copied in the day-to-day practices of violence against those who are thought to be homosexual.

The meeting between law and sado-masochism not only demands that we acknowledge the violence of the law, but that we recognize its particular qualities. As such, it is important to recognize that law's violence is concerned with coercion, terror, fear, domination, hostility, subordination, silence and inequality. Furthermore, the ethical features of a practice of homosexual S/M draws attention to the capacity of S/M to function as a vehicle through which a critique of law's violence may be embarked upon. The ethical dimensions of S/M practice enable us to display the ethical impoverishment of law's violence. This may be of particular significance where there is the recognition that law and violence are necessarily connected. More specifically, it raises questions about the nature of law's violence; about the relationship between law's violence and desire, pleasure, dialogue, participation and consent. Where law's violence is denied, all ethical considerations of law's violence are silenced. A recognition of law's violence opens up a new ethical space in law. As such a recognition of the law's violence is to be welcomed and not to be denied. Unless the Law Commission and modern legal scholarship in general can cope with the fact that retaliatory vengeance, ritual sacrifice and punishment, are capable of intersecting in legal practice, little light will be shed on the ethical questions of violence, law and order. The problem of homosocial and heterosocial violence will remain invisible and particular bodies and desires will be sacrificed in the name of law and order.

NOTES

Many people have contributed to the genesis of this article. Particular thanks are due to David Greenberg for his helpful references, Peter Rush for his usual insightful comments and suggestions and the anonymous referees who provided encouragement and helpful suggestions.

1.   *R* v. *Brown* [1994] A.C. 212. All subsequent page references to this report will be referred to by the prefix HL.
2.   In addition to the charges relating to assault occasioning actual bodily harm and unlawful wounding, and charges of aiding and abetting these assaults upon themselves, some defendants were charged with keeping a disorderly house, aiding and abetting the same, publishing an obscene article, and the taking and possession of an indecent photograph of a child.

3. Subsequent to the publication of these opinions the English Law Commission, a statutory body created under s.1 of the Law Commissions Act 1965, has conducted an investigation into consent and offences against the person which is dominated by a consideration of *R v. Brown*. A consultation paper has been published. At the time of writing the Law Commission is considering the responses to the consultation paper. This paper has been submitted to the Law Commission as part of that consultation process. The final report will be published in due course.

4. Many different stories have been told about the origins of the investigation (see Richardson, 1992). The activities of the men preceded the investigation by several years dating from at least 1978.

5. *R v. Brown* (1992) Cr.App. R. 302. All subsequent page references to this report will be referred to by the prefix CAR.

6. *R v. Brown* [1992] 1 QB 491. All subsequent page references to this report will be referred to by the prefix QB.

7. It would be wrong to conclude that this portrait of S/M as a particular type of violence is peculiar to the majority judges in the House of Lords. For example, it is found in the writing of legal scholars; see Wilson, 1993 and Edwards, 1993 (cf. Bibbings and Alldridge, 1993). It can also be found in certain feminist writings on S/M; for example, see Herman, 1994; Jeffreys, 1994; Linden, 1982.

8. See also Sarat and Kearns (1992); Derrida (1992); Cover (1986); Scarry (1985) and Douzinas and Goodrich (1993).

9. S. 20 provides: 'Whosoever shall unlawfully and maliciously wound or inflict any grievous bodily harm upon any other person, either with or without any weapon or instrument . . . shall be liable . . . to imprisonment . . . for not more than five years.' Section 47 provides: 'Whosoever shall be convicted on indictment of any assault occasioning actual bodily harm shall be liable . . . to imprisonment for not more than five years.'

10. [1981] QB 715.

11. (1882) 8 QBD 534.

12. [1984] 1 WLR 1172

13. In *Christopherson* v. *Bare* (1848) 11 QB 473, Lord Denman CJ declared that: ' . . . it is a manifest contradiction in terms to say that the defendant assaulted the plaintiff by his permission.' In the same case Patteson J stated: 'An assault must be an act done against the will of the party assaulted; and therefore it cannot be said that a party has been assaulted by his own permission' (478). Both observations can be read as evidence that in the Common Law the lack of consent is a fundamental requirement of assault. However, the case received no consideration either before the Court of Appeal or the House of Lords. See also Williams, 1962: 76. The practice of judgment as assertion has been noted by other commentators; see Murphy and Rawlings, 1981.

14. Lord Slynn is the exception. He gives the point consideration and concludes, contrary to Lord Jauncey, that consent is an ingredient of the offence (HL: 281 B–D).

15. In the House of Lords reference is made to the 1883 edition of the text. In that edition the right to consent to bodily harm short of maim is to be found in art. 206.

16. [1934] 2 KB 498.

17. The application of this assertion is not unique to Lord Jauncey (see also HL: Lord Templeman, 230–2; Lord Lowry, 251; Lord Mustill, 262F; and Lord Slynn, 280). In law assertions are not formally acknowledged as good argument. Their rejection is usually based upon the fact that they provide no evidence to support the assertion. An example of this argument used against the appellants is to be found in Lord Templeman's opinion (HL: 235E–G).

18. It would be wrong to conclude that these two categories of forbidden action

248   Leslie J. Moran

represent separate and distinct offences. Lord Lowry notes the criticisms that have been made over the codification of acts of violence to be found in the Offences Against the Person Act 1861. The categories have been variously described as imprecise, untidy, cumbersome, obscure, illogical, a rag-bag, and inconsistent as to substance or as to form (HL: 248D–F).

19.   Girard continues 'but the judicial system is infinitely more effective' (Girard. 1979: 23). (On sacrifice and the law, see Haldar, 1995.)

20.   The use of 'victim' which draws attention to the problematic use of the term, suggests a use of the word other than as a term that refers to one who has been misused and abused. The use of victim should be contrasted with the use of 'receiver' which has none of the connotations of lack of consent, misuse, abuse and so forth. It is important to note that in the review undertaken by the Law Commission, the problematic use of 'victim' to designate one of the parties to S/M practice is noted but passed over without any consideration being given to its wider significance for an understanding of the nature of either the law or the way the law has and is likely to continue to understand the practice of S/M (The Law Commission, 1994: 1, 5ff).

21.   (1986) 83 Cr. App. R. 375. A more recent case dealing with the same point is *Aitken* where the court concluded that a defence of consent was viable where during the course of a party the defendants poured lighter fuel over a colleague, overpowered his resistance and set light to the fuel, causing extremely severe burns, with 35 percent of his body sustaining superficial burns of a life threatening nature [1992] 1 WLR 1006.

22.   'Homosocial is a word occasionally used in history and social sciences, where it describes social bonds between persons of the same sex; it is a neologism obviously formed by analogy with "homosexual" and just as obviously meant to be distinguished from "homosexual". In fact it is applied to such activities as male bonding which may, in our society, be characterised by intense homophobia, fear and hatred of homosexuality' (Sedgwick, 1985: 1).

23.   There is now a massive literature on the various dimensions of violence against women and the tolerance of law to acts of violence against women. The following is a short illustration of the diversity of this material. For example, in the context of rape, see Adler (1987); Brown (1993); Brownmiller (1975); Edwards (1981); Marsh (1982); Matoesian (1993); Tempkin (1987). On heterosocial violence in familiar settings, see Bourlet (1990); Edwards (1989); Hague (1993); Russell (1990); Dobash (1992). For examples in the context of pornography, see Kappeller (1986); Dworkin (1981). On violence and the law, see Mackinnon (1987, 1989); Young (1990). Much less has been written on violence against lesbians and gay men and little has yet been written on the tolerance of that violence by the law, but see Comstock (1991); McMullen (1990).

24.   (1888) 22 QBD 473.

25.   Another police raid was reported in *Gay Times* in July 1993: 'Herts police seize gay man's SM paraphernalia'. Another report in *Capital Gay* (30 July 1993), 'Police step up on SM raids', referred to further police raids in North London.

26.   This takes many forms: raids on bookstores selling lesbian and gay material, such as 'Gays the Word' in London; police surveillance of public toilets (using agent provocateurs and optic fibre equipment) and public places (sometimes with infra-red surveillance equipment) used by gay men to meet other men; police raids on discos; all of which is catalogued regularly in the lesbian and gay press.

Cases Cited

Attorney General's Reference (No 6 of 1980) [1981] QB 715.
Christopherson v. *Bare* (1848) 11 QB 473.

Violence and the Law   249

Collins v. *Wilcock* [1984] 1 WLR 1172.
R v. *Aitken* [1992] 1 W.L.R. 1006.
R v. *Brown* (1992) Cr. App. R. 302.
R v. *Brown* [1992] 1 QB 491.
R v. *Brown* [1994] A.C. 212.
R v. *Clarence* (1888) 22 Q.B.D. 23
R v. *Coney* (1882) 8 Q.B.D. 534.
R v. *Court* [1987] Q.B. 156
R v. *Donovan* [1934] 2 KB 498.
R v. *Terence Jones* (1986) 83 Cr. App. R. 375.

References

Adler, Z. (1987) *Rape on Trial*. London: Routledge.
Bamforth, N. (1994) 'Sado-Masochism and Consent', *Criminal Law Review* 661–5.
Barthes, R. (1990) *S/Z* (tr. R. Miller). Oxford: Blackwell.
Bibbings, L. and P. Alldridge (1993) 'Sexual Expression, Body Alteration, and the Defence of Consent', *Journal of Law and Society* 20(3): 356–70.
Bourlet, A. (1990) *Police Intervention in Marital Violence*. Oxford: Open University Press.
Brodsky, J.I. (1993) 'The Mineshaft: A Retrospective Ethnography', *Journal of Homosexuality* 24(3/4): 233–52.
Brown, B. (1993) *Sex Crimes on Trial: The Use of Sexual Evidence in Scottish Courts*. Edinburgh: Edinburgh University Press.
Brownmiller, S. (1975) *Against Our Will: Men, Women and Rape*. London: Secker and Warburg.
Califia, P. (1988) *The Lesbian S/M Safety Manual*. Boston, MA: Alyson Publications.
Comstock, G.D. (1991) *Violence against Lesbians and Gay Men*. New York: Columbia University Press.
Cover, R. (1986) 'Violence and the Word', *Yale Law Journal* 95: 1601–29.
Deleuze, G. (1989) 'Coldness and Cruelty', pp. 9–143 in *Masochism* (tr. from the French by J. McNeil). New York: Zone Books.
Derrida, J. (1987) 'Devant le loi', pp. 128–48 in A. Udoff (ed.), *Kafka and the Contemporary Critical Performance: Centenary Readings*. Bloomington, IN: Indiana University Press.
Derrida, J. (1992) 'Force of Law: The "Mystical Foundations of Authority"', pp. 3–67 in D. Cornell, M. Rosenfeld and D. Gray Carlson (eds), *Deconstruction and the Possibility of Justice*. London: Routledge.
Devlin, P. (1965) *The Enforcement of Morals*. Oxford: Oxford University Press.
Dobash, R. (1992) *Women, Violence and Social Change*. London: Routledge.
Douzinas, C. and P. Goodrich (eds) (1993) 'Special Issue: Violence and the Law', *Law and Critique* IV: 131–252.
Duncan, S. (1994) 'Law as Literature: Deconstructing the Legal Text', *Law and Critique* V(I): 3–29.
Dworkin, A. (1981) *Pornography: Men Possessing Women*. London: Women's Press.
Edwards, S. (1981) *Female Sexuality and the Law*. Oxford: Robertson.
Edwards, S. (1989) *Policing Domestic Violence: Women, the Law and the State*. London: Sage.
Edwards, S. (1993) 'No Defence for a Sado-Masochistic Libido', *New Law Journal* 19 (143): 406–8.
Farshae, K. (1993) *Countdown on Spanner Information Pack*. London: Countdown on Spanner.

Foucault, M. (1978) *The History of Sexuality. Volume 1: An Introduction*. London: Penguin.

Girard, R. (1979) *Violence and the Sacred* (tr. P. Gregory). Baltimore, MD: Johns Hopkins University Press.

Girard, R. (1986) *The Scapegoat* (tr. Y. Freccero). Baltimore, MD: Johns Hopkins University Press.

Hague, G. (1993) *Domestic Violence: Action for Change*. Chelthenham: New Clarion Press.

Haldar, P. (1996) 'Words with the Shaman', in S. McVeigh and P. Rush (eds), *Criminal Legal Practices*. Oxford: Oxford University Press, forthcoming.

Herman, D. (1994) 'Law and Morality Revisited', paper presented to the Canadian Learned Law and Society Conference June, and to the American Law and Society Conference.

Hughes, G. (1962) 'Consent and Sexual Offences', *Modern Law Review* 25: 672–86.

Jeffreys, S. (1994) *The Lesbian Heresy*. London: Women's Press.

Kappeller, S. (1986) *The Pornography of Representation*. Cambridge: Polity Press.

Kershaw, A. (1992) 'Love', *Weekend Guardian*, 28 November: 6–12.

Krafft Ebing, R. von (1965) *Psychopathia Sexualis*. New York: Stein and Day.

Laplanche, J. and J. B. Pontalis (1988) *The Language of Psychoanalysis*. London: Karnac Books.

Law Commission (1993) *Legislating the Criminal Code: Offences against the Person and General Principles*. No. 218. London: HMSO.

Law Commission (1994) *Consultation Paper No. 134. Criminal Law: Consent and Offences against the Person. A Consultation Paper*. London: HMSO.

Lee, J. A. (1983) 'The Social Organisation of Sexual Risk', pp. 175–93 in T. S. Weinberg and G. W. Levi Kamel (eds), *S and M: Studies in Sadomasochism*. Buffalo, NY: Prometheus Books.

Leigh, L. H. (1976) 'Sado-Masochism, Consent and the Reform of the Criminal Law', *Modern Law Review* 39: 131–46.

Linden, R. R. et al. (1982) *Against Sado-Masochism: A Radical Feminist Analysis*. San Francisco, CA: Frog in the Well.

Mackinnon, C. (1987) *Feminism Unmodified: Discourses on Life and Law*. Boston, MA: Harvard University Press.

Mackinnon, C. (1989) *Towards a Feminist Theory of the State*. Boston, MA: Harvard University Press.

Marsh, J. C. (1982) *Rape and the Limits of Law Reform*. Boston, MA: Auburn House.

Matoesian, G. (1993) *Reproducing Rape: Domination through Talk in the Court Room*. Cambridge: Polity Press.

McMullen, R. J. (1990) *Male Rape: Breaking the Silence on the Last Taboo*. London: Gay Men's Press.

Mezey, G. C. and M. B. King (1992) *Male Victims of Sexual Assault*. Oxford: Oxford University Press.

Moran, L. J. (1989) 'Indecent Assault: What Is Indecency?', *Liverpool Law Review* X(1): 99–109.

Moran, L. J. (1991) 'Justice and its Vicissitudes', *Modern Law Review* 54: 146–61.

Murphy, W. T. and R. W. Rawlings (1981) 'After the Ancien Regime', *Modern Law Review* 44: 617–57; 45: 34–61.

Richardson, C. (1992) 'Myths, Half-Truths and Fantasies', *Gay Times* February: 14–16.

Rose, G. (1992) *The Broken Middle*. Oxford: Blackwell.

Rubin, G. (1993) 'Preface', pp. 15–19 in G. Baldwin (ed.), *Ties that Bind: The SM/Leather/Fetish Erotic Style; Issues, Commentaries and Advice*. Los Angeles, CA: Deadalus.

Russell, D. (1990) *Rape in Marriage*. Bloomington, IN: Indiana University Press.

Sarat, A. and T. Kearns (1991) 'A Journey through Forgetting: Towards a Jurisprudence of Violence', pp. 208–73 in A. Sarat and T. Kearns (eds), *The Fate of Law*. Ann Arbour, MI: University of Michigan Press.

Sarat, A. and T. Kearns (1992) 'Making Peace with Violence', pp. 211–50 in A. Sarat and T. R. Kearns (eds), *Law's Violence*. Ann Arbour, MI: University of Michigan Press.

Scarry, E. (1985) *The Body in Pain*. Oxford: Oxford University Press.

Sedgwick, E. Kosowsky (1985) *Between Men*. New York: Columbia University Press.

Stephen, Sir James Fitzjames (1894) *A Digest of the Criminal Law*. London: Macmillan.

Stychin, C. (1994) 'Unmanly Diversions: The Construction of the "Homosexual" Body (Politic) in Law', paper presented to the Canadian Learned Societies Conference and the Law and Society Conference, June; the American Law and Society Association Conference, June.

Tempkin, J. (1987) *Rape and the Legal Process*. London: Sweet and Maxwell.

Tucker, S. (1991) 'The Hanged Man', pp. 1–36 in M. Thompson (ed.), *Leather Folk: Radical Sex, People, Politics and Practice*. Boston, MA: Alyson Publications.

Weinberg, T. S. and G. W. Levi Kamel (1983) 'Introduction', pp. 17–24 in T. S. Weinberg and G. W. Levi Kamel (eds), *S and M: Studies in Sadomasochism*. Buffalo, NY: Prometheus Books.

Williams, G. (1962) 'Consent and Public Policy', *Criminal Law Review* 74–83; 154–9.

Wilson, W. (1993) 'Is Hurting People Wrong?', *Journal of Social Welfare and Family Law*: 388–97.

Young, A. (1990) *Femininity in Dissent*. London: Routledge.

[11]

Sexual Preference, Crime and Punishment

Diana Fishbein

ABSTRACT. The homosexual behavior of male inmates has been extensively studied; however, similar behaviors by female inmates, other than descriptions of the role of masculinity in prison settings, has been virtually ignored. Observations suggest that the incidence of both lesbianism and unusual masculinity among females may be higher in prisons and jails than in the general population. This study surveyed both heterosexual and homosexual female detainees to determine whether lesbian inmates, particularly those with a masculinized appearance, are more prone to violent or antisocial behavior, than heterosexual females without masculine features and, if so, whether this relationship is a function of biological conditions or sociological influences. Results indicated that lesbian detainees had more masculine traits, more feelings of hostility and anger, and experienced more physical child abuse than did heterosexual detainees. Although they did not report significantly more violent crimes, they were more often detained for longer periods of time. And while self-reported symptoms of Attention Deficit and Conduct Disorders were more prevalent in lesbian detainees, other conditions of biologic origin were not related to sexual preference. These findings suggest that lesbian detainees are treated more harshly by the criminal justice system and that further research is needed to sort out the various biological and social contributors to behavioral and attitudinal differ-

Diana Fishbein, PhD, is affiliated with the Transdisciplinary Behavioral Science Program, Research Triangle Institute, 6110 Executive Boulevard, Suite 420, Rockville, MD 20852.

The author would like to recognize the conscientious efforts of Shawn Ellerman who routinely visited the Baltimore City Detention Center for the unusually difficult chore of data collection for this project. The author would also like to express my gratitude to Commissioner LaMont Flanagan who approved this research and to Gwen Oliver of the Women's Detention Center who so kindly granted me access to her population.

ences. *[Article copies available for a fee from The Haworth Document Delivery Service: 1-800-342-9678. E-mail address: getinfo@haworthpressinc.com <Website: http://www.haworthpressinc.com>]*

KEYWORDS. Lesbian inmates, lesbian detainees

Several years of research and clinical work in prisons and jails throughout the Washington, D.C. region led to the observation that there is a disproportionate number of females with self-reported lesbianism in correctional facilities relative to the general population. Many openly report a preference for female companionship, although prostitution is routine for many in this population, e.g., "sex for drugs." There also appears to be an increased incidence of a masculinized physical appearance amongst these females. Masculine traits are considered to include unusual hair growth on the face and chest, a large musculature, small breasts, deep voice, preference for male attire, and frequent and persistent aggressiveness. Excessive testosterone production, a male hormone, has been associated with both masculine traits and aggressiveness in females, although only one study has reported an indirect association between testosterone and lesbianism thus far (Pearcey et al., 1996). Nevertheless, there is a possibility that masculine traits are more pronounced in this population of lesbians and that their presence may be a function of sex hormone influences which may, in turn, increase aggressive or antisocial tendencies.

Social forces may also play a role in the behavior, attitudes and criminal tendencies of this lesbian population, possibly even contributing to their sexual preference and/or their increased likelihood of being apprehended and incarcerated, explaining their disproportionate representation in a jail population. Specifically, many of the female inmates in this population reported experiencing sexual and physical abuse perpetrated by males early in life; hence, their dislike for the opposite sex. Is it possible that their sexual preference is to some degree a function of these experiences? While these experiences cannot account for masculine physical traits, they may partially explain their aggressive-defensive demeanor and preference for female companionship. It is also possible that their physical appearance may provoke sexual or physical attacks, either by family members rejecting of a masculine appearing female relative or by strangers who may taunt them. A history of male-perpetrated abuse may explain both the antisocial behavior and the sexual preference in this subgroup of female offenders. Although there is research to show that abuse is related to behavioral disorders (Snell, 1994; OJJDP, 1996), no literature could be found to elucidate relationships between abuse and tendency to lesbianism.

Thus, the question arose as to whether lesbian inmates, particularly those with a masculinized appearance, are more prone to violent or antisocial behavior, than heterosexual females without masculine features and, if so, whether this relationship is a result of biological conditions or sociological influences. Certainly, not all lesbians are masculine in appearance, nor are all heterosexual females without masculine features. This study, however, focused upon masculinized lesbians for two reasons: (1) they are more prevalent in jail/prison than in the general population; and (2) to test the hypothesis that their appearance may play a role in their sexual identity and official responses to them.

BACKGROUND

Pervasive homosexuality among male and female prisoners has been well-documented over the past several decades; however, its occurrence has been depicted as serving quite different purposes in male as opposed to female institutions. Relationships between women in prison are often defined as either familial or connubial (Pollack-Byrne, 1990), while male homosexuality in prison is thought to serve the purpose of establishing dominance, manifesting aggressive tendencies, economic gain and providing a sexual outlet. According to most reports, only a small portion of women who engage in homosexuality in prison are committed to this orientation as a lifestyle (Pollack-Byrne, 1990). Because jails differ greatly from prisons, particularly with respect to the amount of time in residence and the extent to which physical and emotional needs must be met over time, the incidence of homosexual behavior among heterosexual women is probably lower during a short jail term than for prison inmates. Thus, homosexual behavior among women in jail is more likely to be a lifestyle preference rather than a function of incarceration, suggesting that a subgroup of female offenders enters correctional facilities already having an established sexual preference for women.

Surprisingly, other than descriptions of lesbian relationships within a prison environment, there is very little research on ways in which preexisting self-defined lesbian offenders may differ from heterosexual female offenders with respect to behavioral patterns, criminality, family histories, childhood experiences or biological conditions (Freedman, 1996). And although most visitors in a female institution will readily notice the unusual proportion of masculine-appearing inmates relative to the general population, there has been very little attention paid to appearance in relation to sexual orientation and behavioral patterns. Moreover, there has been no research to examine relationships between these factors: lesbianism, masculinity and criminal behaviors.

Ward and Kassebaum (1965) and Toigo (1962) both reported a tendency of females with masculine characteristics to engage in homosexuality to acquire power and privileges, and to maintain control and dominance, similar to the structure within male institutions. Many of these early researchers argued that women acquired these roles to avoid being victimized and to maintain some semblance of order. The possibility that a subgroup of these women either became homosexual on their own accord or that they were naturally (biologically) inclined to this sexual orientation was not considered. Further discussions of those with masculine features were limited to ways in which these features served a purpose within the facility. As a result, the literature has neglected female offenders with an established preference for homosexuality in favor of examining the greater numbers of female inmates who engage in homosexuality in response to their imprisonment.

The extent to which differences in behaviors and criminal histories can be explained by biological influences cannot be directly addressed in this study due to the inability to collect blood samples. Yet, the striking relationship observed between lesbianism, unusual masculinity, and criminality compels this research to examine indirect measures of potential biological influences. The release of male hormones, or androgens, in utero are primarily responsible for anatomical sex differences (Ehrhardt and Meyer-Bahlburg, 1981; Valzelli, 1981). The relative absence of androgen activity, in particular testosterone, in the normal female fetus and its presence in the male results in notably dissimilar anatomical features, including those of the brain (Hedge et al., 1987). Exposure of a female fetus to heightened levels of androgens, or a genetic hypersensitivity in the brain's receptor sites to these hormones, during this developmental phase can masculinize the fetus by altering both the neuroanatomy and the physical constitution (Ellis and Ames, 1987; Hoygenga and Hoygenga, 1979; Nyborg, 1984; Simon and Whalen, 1986). Strong evidence exists for the influence of male hormones on a masculine physique, a masculine self-identity and increased aggressiveness both in adult males and females (see Ellis, 1988; & Fishbein, 1992).

Prenatal drug exposures, genetic defects, neurotransmitter imbalances, certain medical conditions and even social factors can all affect sexual development and identity by altering sex hormone influences. Thus, masculine features, aggressiveness, and homosexuality may be related in a subgroup of female offenders. Dabbs et al., for example, have reported high levels of testosterone among violent female inmates relative to those considered nonviolent (1988). Similar to males, unusually high testosterone levels in females may contribute to the increased incidence of mesomorphy among female offenders and may function to reinforce aggressive tendencies under certain environmental conditions.

Hormonal influences can also produce similar effects later in the development of a female. For example, the medical condition called Polycystic Ovary Syndrome is characterized by unusually large increases in male androgen release during puberty in the female. Given that puberty is a developmental phase in which profound sexual differentiation occurs, the heightened release of androgens during this stage can result in masculine physical and behavioral features—a process known as androgenization. Typically, women with this disorder develop normally until puberty, although hirsutism (abnormal facial hair growth) may develop before menarche. Menses may be irregular and many patients are infertile. Others may have dysfunctional bleeding and endometrial changes. Many affected women, particularly those underserved by the medical community, remain undiagnosed. Thus, it is impossible to estimate the prevalence outside or within a correctional environment. Nevertheless, given the strong association between elevated levels of androgens in females, masculine features and aggressiveness, it is possible that its incidence may be greater in this subgroup of female offenders.

The possibility was also considered that lesbianism is not strictly a biological phenomenon in this population, but may have some profound social precursors. Studies suggest that the incidence of physical and sexual abuse is pervasive among female offenders, particularly those responsible for violent crimes, relative to male offenders and the general population (Snell, 1994; OJJDP, 1996). There is evidence that female offenders are often victims of severe and inconsistent parenting techniques, dysfunctional families, inappropriate physical contact by relatives, rape, and neglect during childhood. Furthermore, investigators speculate that these early experiences are precursors to later concomitant behavioral disorders, including depression, aggressiveness, hostility, drug dependency and co-dependent relationships (Bays, 1990; Testa et al., 1991). Several reports suggest an increased vulnerability among women, relative to men, to behavioral and psychological dysfunction in response to these traumatic events (e.g., Covington, 1985; Dornfield and Kruttschnitt, 1992; Robertson et al., 1987; Widom, 1991). As a result, women with this history may be prone to behaviors that place them at risk for criminalization, e.g., drug abuse and perpetrators of, or accessories in, crime. The tendency to reject men, the primary perpetrators of these experiences, increases the likelihood that some may also prefer female partners for intimate relationships. Interestingly, one study showed that homosexual women with histories of sexual abuse were more satisfied with their present intimate relationships than women without histories of abuse, suggesting that a change in sexual orientation may be an effective coping mechanism (Weingourt, 1998). Anecdotal reports from scores of female inmates express their hatred of men given both the abandonment and abuse they had experienced since early childhood, and their subsequent preference for female companionship.

Another aspect of the relationship between criminal offending and sexual preference involves the possibility that systemic reactions to lesbians in general, and particularly those with a masculine appearance and demeanor, may influence their status within the criminal justice system (CJS) and perhaps even increase the likelihood of their incarceration. In other words, their homosexuality, appearance and demeanor may play a role in their stigmatization, resulting in negative reactions by the CJS. Certainly, there is strong historical evidence for stereotyping lesbian inmates (Freedman, 1996). Such differences between lesbian and heterosexual female offenders may be reflected in length of sentence, number of times jailed or detention as opposed to release on recognizance. There are certainly numerous reports of discrimination in sentencing and correctional responses on the basis of race, gender and even attractiveness (Cavior et al., 1974; Frazier,

1979; Frazier et al., 1980; Leventhal and Krate, 1977; Moyer, 1981; Rosenbaum and Chesney-Lind, 1994). Moreover, entire texts have been devoted to the topic of CJS labeling and discretionary decision-making in cases involving women who do not appear to be feminine or "nice girls" according to the prevailing social expectations (e.g., Feinman, 1986; Pollack-Byrne, 1990; Weisheit and Mahan, 1988). Is it possible that lesbians, particularly those with a masculine appearance, are more likely to be incarcerated, explaining in part their disproportionate representation in correctional facilities?

The specific hypotheses tested by this study include: (1) Lesbian inmates tend to have more masculine physical traits than heterosexual female inmates; (2) Lesbian inmates perceive themselves to be more masculine than the other inmates; (3) Lesbians are more likely to commit violent offenses; (4) Lesbian inmates experience more male-perpetrated sexual or physical abuse in their lifetimes; (5) There is a greater incidence of symptoms indicative of Polycystic Ovary Syndrome, reports of prenatal complications during gestation, and symptoms of ADHD and CD in lesbian inmates; (6) Sentencing of lesbian offenders is more severe than nonlesbian or more feminine offenders. This latter hypothesis is based on speculation that their demeanor and/or appearance may unfavorably influence both informal relationships and court decisions. It is critical to note that the findings reported below reflect inmate *perceptions* of their differences, their behaviors and their experiences. However, given that one of the purposes of this study is to examine the differential social and criminal justice-related experiences of lesbian or masculine female inmates, perceptions are most informative.

DESIGN AND METHODS

Approximately 300 females were housed at the Baltimore City Detention Center at the time of this study. The majority were African-American (82%) and the remainder were largely Caucasian (17%). Their ages ranged from about 15 to 60. Female inmates in this facility are generally responsible for a wide variety of crimes, from petty property crimes to murder. The overwhelming majority of female inmates, however, are charged with drug-related offenses (e.g., "sex for drugs," drug possession, drug distribution, and accessories in drug dealing) and, while there are no precise estimates, many of these inmates are addicted to heroin, crack cocaine and/or alcohol in order of prevalence.

Announcements to recruit subjects for this study were made to the general population during classes available through the facility, throughout the cell blocks and by the program administrator. Forty-one female inmates from the Baltimore City Detention Center volunteered to be interviewed and to complete a self-report survey regarding their backgrounds, criminal activities, and medical and psychological problems. They were informed that the study was of relationships between their health status and personal problems. The average age was 29.4 (7.13 sd). Eight of the females were white, twenty-nine were African-American, three were Native American and six were "other." The average number of times sent to jail was 4.05 (4.7 sd) and the average number of days spent in jail in their lifetimes was 278 (473.7 sd). A total of 26 (63%) of this group reported a heterosexual orientation, while 15 (37%) reported a preference for homosexuality.[1]

Categories included in the survey questionnaire were constructed in the following format. "General Information" inquired about age, sex, race, number of days spent in jail or prison, and number of times mandated to jail or prison. The "Medical Status" section queried subjects for information on hospitalizations, chronic medical problems, medications, head injuries, prenatal conditions and mother's status while pregnant, and reproductive health. "Family/Social Relationships" included items regarding partners and intimate relationships, childhood environment particularly with respect to physical and sexual abuse, and sexual preferences. Questions regarding perceptions of psychological problems were included in the section called "Personal Status," and questions regarding crimes committed in addition to general assaultiveness and hostility were included in the "Legal Status" section. Under the section entitled "Childhood History," items attempted to solicit responses about childhood traits and experiences before the age of twelve, including symptoms of Conduct Disorder (CD) and Attention Deficit Hyperactivity Disorder (ADHD; American Psychiatric Association, DSM-IV). Similar questions were then posed in a subsequent section regarding adulthood traits and experiences which also included items pertaining to the histories of close family members. The "Drug Preference" section inquired about the use of various illicit drugs and alcohol, including age of onset and relationship to criminal activity. Finally, the section entitled "Sexual Preference" included items regarding intimate sexual relationships and comfort levels about their sexual preferences and appearance. From these items, a determination of whether the subject was lesbian *irrespective of her incarcerative status was made.*

Subjects completed this questionnaire in small groups (from 4-5 per group) in a quiet room. No correctional officers or other facility staff were present. Inmates were read consent forms explaining that results were confidential and anonymous, the jail was uninvolved in the study and would not have access to individual records or results, and that data would be reported in aggregate, not individual, form. The consent form described the study as an attempt to determine whether medical condition, childhood experiences and social relationships were related to criminal activity and criminal justice response. The questionnaire form was favorably received by inmates; there were no complaints and they appeared to enjoy completing the instrument.

RESULTS[2]

Subjects were classified as masculinized by two independent raters if they displayed at least five of the following features: unusual hair growth (on the face or chest), large musculature, deep voice, irregular menstrual cycle, difficulty becoming or maintaining a pregnancy, high aggressiveness, and a mandatory feature that she considered herself to be masculine. There was 100% reliability between raters. Strong support for the first question regarding a relationship between masculine traits and lesbianism was found, with lesbians significantly more likely to appear masculine than heterosexual female inmates (Chi Sq = 20.99; $p < 0.00001$); in fact, all of the lesbians in this analysis had masculine traits, while only 2 of the female heterosexuals were so classified. Not surprisingly, lesbian subjects also reported much more dislike for men in general than heterosexual subjects (Chi Sq = 14.2, $p < 0.0005$) and they indicated that they "felt different" from other women (Chi Sq = 7.6, $p < 0.01$).

Analyses of variance (ANOVAs) were performed to identify group differences in criminal histories between female inmates with and without lesbianism (see Table 1). Lesbians were jailed significantly more times (X = 6.6, sd = 6.4) than other subjects (X = 2.7, sd = 2.8; F = 7.01, $p < 0.01$). Lesbians reported a tendency to commit their first crime at an earlier age (X = 17.6, sd = 4.8) than did heterosexual

TABLE 1. Analysis of Variance to Distinguish Between Female Inmates with Different Sexual Preferences

Variable	Heterosexual Mean (sd)	Lesbian Mean (sd)	F Ratio	P Value
Age of First Crime	21.3 (6.05)	17.6 (4.8)	3.73	0.06
Number of Times Jailed	2.7 (2.8)	6.6 (6.4)	7.01	< 0.01
Total Number of Days Spent in Jail	210 (362)	387 (624)	1.09	ns
Violent Crimes	.56 (1.04)	1.21 (1.3)	1.3	ns
Property Crimes	1.7 (3.3)	1.9 (2.5)	0.034	ns
Assaultiveness	4.3 (4.6)	11.4 (12.2)	5.8	0.02
Physical Abuse	2.35 (1.72)	3.78 (1.6)	4.7	< 0.05
Sexual Abuse	1.6 (1.6)	2.3 (1.5)	1.7	ns
Conduct Disorder	4.65 (4)	9.7 (8.6)	6.5	< 0.05
Attention Deficit	3.77 (3)	4.5 (2.3)	0.53	ns
Family History	6.27 (3.8)	6.92 (3)	0.31	ns
Home History	2.31 (1.97)	1.23 (2.2)	2.55	0.12
Learning Disability	.22 (.42)	.29 (.47)	0.2	ns

female inmates ($X = 21.3$, sd = 6.05; $F = 3.73$, $p = 0.06$). Interestingly, lesbians did not report more arrests for violent crime ($F = 0.13$, $p = 0.76$) or property crime ($F = 0.034$, $p = 0.6$) than heterosexual subjects.

Given the finding that, in spite of the near equality of arrests for violent and property crimes between lesbian and heterosexual subjects, lesbians were jailed more frequently, a stepwise discriminant analysis[3] was conducted to assess the interaction between number of times jailed and number of arrests for violent and property crimes. Number of times jailed significantly predicted group assignment ($F = 7.01$, $p < 0.01$) relative to number of arrests, which did not enter the equation. Lesbians also spent many more days in jail during their lifetimes (mean = 387) than heterosexuals (mean = 210), but because of the large standard deviations and small Ns, this difference was not significant.

One additional analysis was performed to account for possibilities of inaccurate reports of arrests and for the misleading nature of self report arrest data in general. In addition to using reports of number of arrests, various indicators of assaultiveness and hostility were examined. Subjects were asked about the presence of a violent temper, a "tougher" attitude than other females, a generalized angry state in both childhood and adulthood, and a history of acting aggressively when disrespected or when bothered by others, becoming violent when using drugs, engaging in fights, using a weapon and injuring others. Composite responses to these items were calculated. Results of the ANOVA showed that lesbians were significantly more likely to perceive themselves as assaultive and aggressive ($X = 11.4$, sd = 12.2; $F = 5.8$, $p < 0.05$) than heterosexual subjects ($X = 4.3$, sd = 4.6).

In order to determine whether lesbians reported experiential differences from heterosexual inmates, additional Chi Squares were computed. The purpose of this analysis was to determine whether, throughout their lives, they may have been subjected to different experiences or social interactions, possibly as a result of their appearance or demeanor. The groups differed in several ways. For example, lesbians reportedly were "hit hard" more often during childhood than heterosexual inmates (Chi Sq = 4.0, $p < 0.05$). Lesbians reported more childhood physical abuse in general than heterosexuals (Chi Sq = 4.68, $p < 0.05$). Consistently, this group was more likely to report being raised in a violent home (Chi Sq = 3.6, $p < 0.05$). However, there were no significant group differences in male-perpetrated sexual abuse during childhood. While there was only a trend for the lesbians with masculine features to have been raped (Chi Sq = 2.8, $p = 0.09$), they were reportedly more likely to have been forced by a man to have sexual intercourse against their will (Chi Sq = 4.4, $p < 0.05$). While coerced intercourse is defined by most in our society as rape, women in this population often do not employ similar definitions. Thus, the question was asked in different ways, i.e., "rape" versus "forced sexual intercourse." The same is true for "child abuse"; if asked about abuse in childhood, many inmates will deny its occurrence. However, if asked about the incidence of being beaten, hit until marks are left, unconscious, or bloody, many more will respond in the affirmative.

Consistent with the composite measure employed in the above ANOVA, the masculine lesbian group perceived themselves to be more violent than the others (Chi Sq = 10.4, $p < 0.001$), they were more likely to have used a weapon (Chi Sq = 4.36, $p < 0.05$), and they reported the tendency to become more violent while using drugs (Chi Sq = 4.5, $p < 0.05$). They did not differ in perceptions of the "stability" of their home environment, in the incidence of being "spanked" as a child, shyness, or bad temper, feelings of depression, hyperactivity, engagement in prostitution, violent neighborhood, single parent homes, hospitalizations, or incidence of head injury.

In a stepwise discriminant analysis to distinguish lesbians from heterosexuals on the basis of childhood experiences to determine their relative contributions, six composite background factors were entered as independent variables: (1) reports of childhood physical abuse, (2) reports of sexual abuse, (3) dysfunctional home environment, (4) adverse family histories (criminal behavior, mental illness, drug abuse and assaultiveness), (5) self-reported symptoms of CD, and (6) self-reported symptoms of Attention Deficit Hyperactivity Disorder (ADHD). Reports of physical abuse as a child ($F = 9.98$, $p < 0.01$) and symptoms of CD ($F = 13.09$, $p < 0.005$) significantly discriminated between those with different sexual preferences. And while ADHD was not related to preference independently, once CD entered the equation, ADHD became significantly related to the dependent variable ($F = 6.08$, $p < 0.01$).[4] This finding suggests that ADHD is only related to sexual preference in the presence of CD. In a multivariate test of significance, physical abuse, and symptoms of CD and ADHD strongly predicted sexual preference ($F = 7.8$, $p < 0.0005$) as seen in Table 2.

The possibility that biological conditions influence the behavior of lesbians could not be tested directly in the absence of biological measures. Instead, an indirect test using ANOVA was performed to determine whether lesbians had a greater number of symptoms of polycystic ovary syndrome, a masculinizing disorder associated with higher levels of circulating male hormones in puberty. Group differ-

TABLE 2. Relative Contributions of Childhood Experiences to Sexual Preference: Stepwise Discriminant Analysis

Variable	Heterosexual	Lesbian	F to Remove	Total F	Significance
Physical Abuse	2.08 (1.6)	3.67 (1.49)	9.98	7.77	p = .0005
Sexual Abuse	1.62 (1.6)	2.08 (1.5)			
Home History	2.37 (1.9)	1.08 (2.2)			
Family History	6.33 (3.7)	6.92 (3.3)			
Conduct Disorder	4.04 (3.3)	7.83 (5.1)	13.09		
ADHD	2.87 (3.48)	3.67 (3.2)	6.08		

ences were insignificant. In addition, an ANOVA was performed to determine whether their mothers experienced a greater incidence of prenatal or perinatal complications than comparison group mothers. Once again, the results were insignificant.[5] The most compelling indication of a biological influence is the obvious differences in physical appearance between groups which cannot be socially constructed. Given the limitations of this study, however, there was no way to assess the origins of these morphological differences, nor was there a way to determine whether the mechanisms underlying morphological traits are further associated with behavioral or temperamental differences.

CONCLUSIONS

There is a glaring absence of systematic research on lesbianism among offenders in spite of numerous anecdotal reports and observations that they comprise a distinct subgroup of female inmates. This neglect is likely due to opposing political and social forces which promote discomfort about issues regarding sex differences in general and homosexuality in particular (Freedman, 1996; Schuklenk and Ristow, 1996). Rather than perpetrate this neglect or add to findings of dated literature which studies lesbianism in a socially biased or narrowly constructed fashion, it is necessary to account for self perception of sexual preferences and behavioral differences, and identify relative contributions of the social and biological environment.

To summarize these findings, lesbian detainees differed in several ways from heterosexual female detainees. Lesbians were more likely to exhibit hyper-masculine traits, a dislike for men and perceptions of being different from other women. They also perceived themselves to be more assaultive and hostile, have a greater temper and become more violent under the influence of drugs. A measure of social influence that included items pertaining to childhood experiences showed that child physical abuse, violent home environments and coerced sexual intercourse significantly discriminated between groups. The question of whether official criminal justice responses to lesbians differ from responses to heterosexual females was tested by a discriminant analysis which suggested that lesbians are more often jailed and for longer periods of time than heterosexual female inmates in spite of similarities in reported official criminal histories. Thus, while lesbians perceive themselves to be more aggressive, they did not report the commission of more violent crimes. Perhaps this self perception contributed to a more hostile demeanor and, therefore, a harsher criminal justice response (Frazier et al., 1980; Moyer, 1981).

The hypothesis that lesbian offenders commit more violent crimes as a result of an underlying biological disorder, that may also be reflected in their physical appearance, was not directly supported or refuted by this study. Although the role of biology could not be directly addressed by this investigation, a test of relationships between antisocial behaviors and symptoms of polycystic ovary syndrome and reports of prenatal and perinatal trauma were insignificant. Despite obvious physical differences, these analyses did not yield significant findings. Only one test of a possible biological contribution to group differences yielded positive results. Assessment of the relationship between lesbianism, and self-reported symptoms of CD and ADHD was included, given the ample literature which suggests that CD and ADHD have biological origins and putative genetic markers (see Comings, 1995; Comings et al., 1996). The stepwise discriminant analysis showed significant differences between groups in number of symptoms of CD and ADHD. Reports of sex hormone influences in learning disabilities (see Geschwind and Galaburda, 1985) that often antedate antisocial behaviors suggest the need for further research into linkages between sexual orientation, sex hormones and related behaviors.

These findings provide support for the contention that masculine females may receive a level of criminal justice treatment more typically provided to male offenders, which tends to be harsher (Snell, 1994). For instance, male offenders often receive longer sentences than female offenders given similar criminal charges (Snell, 1994). Studies suggest that "perception of oneself as highly masculine or feminine does not in itself determine whether one will engage in criminal activity" (Campbell et al., 1987). Instead of gender identity being predictive of criminal tendencies, Campbell and colleagues (1987) argued that gender identity might predict type of crime in the presence of criminal tendencies. Masculine appearing lesbians included in the present study, however, did not report greater levels of more serious criminal activity than heterosexuals, but differed in perceptions of their attitudes and demeanor. Thus, it is likely that the official response to masculine female offenders is more severe even in the presence of a relatively equivalent criminal history. In other words, the demeanor of these offenders may provoke a negative response from police and courts, while female offenders engaged in similar behaviors who are more compliant and "feminine" may avoid criminal justice processing.

Further research is necessary on several levels. First, biomedical research on women with an unusually masculinized constitution is recommended to identify the presence of possible underlying hormonal influences given the treatment implications–both by the medical and criminal justice systems.[6] Such studies should attempt to identify the prevalence of polycystic ovary syndrome in masculinized female offenders, in addition to other endocrine sources of these traits, including both heritable and acquired mechanisms. A study reported in *Science* (Gladue et al., 1984) found that exclusively homosexual males produced hormonal responses to the injection of a female hormone more similar to the "typical" female response than to the normal male hormonal response. A replication of this study in lesbians could easily be conducted. Once the prevalence of underlying biological conditions associated with sexual preference or masculine traits in female offenders is estimated, the link between these conditions and offending behaviors must be established. If there is no significant relationship, then the incidence of these biological conditions amongst female offenders should not concern the criminologist.

Additional research establishing the relationship between physical appearance, demeanor and both the societal and criminal justice response, however, does concern the field of criminology. There is ample literature to suggest that the incidence of victimization, both physical and sexual, among lesbians is higher than for the larger community (e.g., Otis and Skinner, 1996; Hall, 1996; Harrison, 1996) and that the psychological consequences often involve depression and other indications of compromised well being. How such victimization among lesbians contributes to offending is, at present, unknown, although there is evidence that such abuse leads to risk factors associated with substance abuse, suicide, prostitution, running away and school problems (Grossman and Kerner, 1998). Findings indicative of such discrimination should compel the criminal justice system, and society-at-large, to identify potential sources of bias and readjust official responses to women with varying sexual preferences and appearances.

NOTES

1. No attempts were made to recruit inmates with any specific characteristics.

2. The sample sizes differ slightly between analyses due to random missing data points.

3. The sample size for the lesbian group is small for meaningful discriminant analyses. Thus, these results should be interpreted as provocative, rather than conclusive.

4. ADHD and Conduct Disorder are significantly related with a Pearson R Correlation of 0.58.

5. Although it is unlikely that knowledge or recollection of their mothers' pregnancies would be entirely accurate, group differences may still surface.

6. The presence of lesbianism in the absence of a clinical disorder or associated behavioral disturbance has no treatment implications–a homosexual orientation is, by itself, not considered to be a disorder requiring treatment.

REFERENCES

Bays, J. (1990). Substance abuse and child abuse. Pediatric Clinics of North America, 37: 881-904.

Campbell, C.S., MacKenzie, D.L., Robinson, J.W. (1987). Female offenders: Criminal behavior and gender-role identity. Psychological Reports, 60: 867-873.

Cavior, H.E., Hayes, S.C. and Cavior, N. (1974). Physical attractiveness of female offenders: Effects on institutional performance. Criminal Justice and Behavior 1: 321-331.

Comings, D.E. (1995). Genetic Mechanisms in Neuropsychiatric disorders. In: Handbook of Psychoneurogenetics, Edited by Blum, K., Noble, E.P., Sparks, R.S. and Sheridan, P.J. CRC Press, Boca Raton, FL.

Comings, D.E., Wu, H., Chiu, C., Ring, R.H., Gade, R., Ahn, C., MacMurray, J.P., Dietz, G., and Muhleman, D. (1996). Polygenic inheritance of Tourette syndrome, stuttering, attention deficit hyperactivity, conduct and oppositional defiant disorders: The addictive and subtractive effect of three dopaminergic genes–DRD2, DβH, and DAT1. American Journal of Medical Genetics (Neuropsychiatric Genetics) 67: 264-288.

Covington, J. Gender differences in criminality among heroin users. Journal of Research in Crime and Delinquency, 22: 329-354, 1985.

Dabbs, J.M., Ruback, R.B., Frady, R.L., Hopper, C.H. and Sgoutas, D.S. (1988). Saliva testosterone and criminal violence among women. Personality and Individual Differences, 9: 269-275.

Dornfield, M., and Kruttschnitt, C. Do the stereotypes fit? Mapping gender-specific outcomes and risk factors. Criminology, 30: 397-419, 1992.

Ellis, L. (1988). Neurohormonal bases of varying tendencies to learn delinquent and criminal behavior. In E. Morris and C. Braukmann (Eds.) Behavioral Approaches to Crime and Delinquency, New York: Plenum.

Ellis, L. and Ames, M.A. (1987). Neurohormonal functioning and sexual orientation: A theory of homosexuality-heterosexuality. Psychological Bulletin, 101: 233-258.

Erhardt, A.A. and Meyer-Bahlburg, H.F.L. (1981). Effects of prenatal sex hormones on gender-related behavior. Science 211: 1312-1318.

Feinman, C. (1986). Women in the Criminal Justice System. New York: Praeger.

Fishbein, D.H. (1992). The psychobiology of female aggression. Criminal Justice and Behavior 19: 99-126.

Frazier, C.E. (1979). Appearance, demeanor, and backstage negotiations: Bases of discretion in a first appearance court. International Journal of the Sociology of Law, 7: 197-209.

Frazier, C.E., Bock, E.W., Henretta, J.C. (1980). Pretrial release and bail decisions: The effects of legal, community, and personal variables. Criminology, 18: 162-181.

Freedman, E.S. (1996). The prison lesbian: Race, class, and the construction of the aggressive female homosexual, 1915-1965. Feminist Studies, 22: 397-422.

Geschwind, N. and Galaburda, A.M. (1985). Cerebral Lateralization. Biological mechanisms, associations and pathology: III. A hypothesis and a program for research. Archives of Neurology, 42: 634-654.

Gladue, B.A., Green, R., Hellman, R.E. (1984). Neuroendocrine response to estrogen and sexual orientation. Science, 225: 1496-1499.

Grossman, A.H. and Kerner, M.S. (1998). Self esteem and supportiveness as predictors of emotional distress in gay male and lesbian youth. Journal of Homosexuality, 35: 25-39.

Hall, J.M. (1996). Pervasive effects of childhood sexual abuse in lesbians' recovery from alcohol problems. Substance Use and Misuse, 31: 225-239.

Harrison, A.E. (1996). Primary care of lesbian and gay patients: Educating ourselves and our students. Family Medicine, 28: 10-23.

Hedge, G.A., Colby, H.D. and Goodman, R.L. (1987). Clinical endocrine physiology. Philadelphia: W.B. Saunders.

Hoyenga, D.B. and Hoyenga, K.T. (1979). The question of sex differences. Boston, MA: Little and Brown.

Levanthal, G. and Krate, R. (1977). Physical attractiveness and severity of sentencing. Psychological Reports 40: 315-318.

Moyer, I.L. (1981). Demeanor, sex and race in police processing. Journal of Criminal Justice, 9: 235-246.

Nyborg, H. (1984). Performance and intelligence in hormonally different groups. Progress in Brain Research, 61: 491-508.

Office of Juvenile Justice and Delinquency Prevention (1996). Training and Technical Assistance Program to Promote Gender-Specific Programming for Female Juvenile Offenders and At-Risk Girls. Washington, D.C.: National Institute of Justice.

Otis, M.D. and Skinner, W.F. (1996). The prevalence of victimization and its effect on mental well being among lesbian and gay people. Journal of Homosexuality, 30:93-121.

Pearcey, S.M., Docherty, K.J., Dabbs, J.M., Jr. (1996). Testosterone and sex role identification in lesbian couples. Physiology of Behavior, 60: 1033-1035.

Pollock-Byrne, J.M. (1990). Women, Prison and Crime. Pacific Grove, CA: Wadsworth.

Robertson, R.G., Bankier, R.G., and Schwartz, L. The female offender: A Canadian Study. Canadian Journal of Psychiatry, 32: 749-755, 1987.

Rosenbaum, J.L., Chesney-Lind, M. (1994). Appearance and delinquency: A research note. Crime and Delinquency, 40: 250-261.

Scheklenk, U. and Ristow, M. (1996). The ethics of Research into the cause(s) of homosexuality. Journal of Homosexuality, 31: 5-30.

Simon, N.G. and Whalen, R.E. (1986). Hormonal regulation of aggression: Evidence for a relationship among genotype, receptor binding, and behavioral sensitivity to androgen and estrogen. Aggressive Behavior, 12: 255-266.

Snell, T. (1994). Women in Prison. Bureau of Justice Statistics Bulletin. Washington, D.C.: U.S. Department of Justice, March.

Testa, M., Miller, B.A., and Downs, W.R. (1991). The long-term impact of childhood and adulthood victimization on Women's Mental Health. Paper presented at the annual meeting of the American Society of Criminology, San Francisco, November.

Toigo, R. (1962). Illegitimate and legitimate cultures in a training school for girls. Rip Van Winkle Clinical Proceedings 13: 3-29.

Valzelli, L. (1981). Psychobiology of aggression and violence. New York: Raven.

Ward, D. and Kassebaum, G. (1965). Women's Prison: Sex and Social Structure. Chicago: Aldine-Atherton.

Weingourt, R. (1998). A comparison of heterosexual and homosexual long-term sexual relationships. Archives of Psychiatric Nursing, 12: 114-118.

Weisheit, R., and Mahan, S. (1988). Women, Crime and Criminal Justice. Cincinnati, Ohio: Anderson Publishing Co.

Widom, C.S. (1991). Childhood victimization: Risk factor for delinquency. In M.E. Colten and S. Gore (Eds.) Adolescent Stress. Causes and Consequences. New York: Aldine De Gruyter.

Public Places

[12]

GOVERNING BODIES, CREATING GAY SPACES

Policing and Security Issues in 'Gay' Downtown Toronto

Mariana Valverde and Miomir Cirak*

In contrast to criminological studies of gay-specific hate crimes, this study focuses not on crimes but on the governance of security in a major global centre of lesbian/gay community life, namely Toronto's gay village, with security defined as the attempt to guarantee order mainly by governing space and time. Based on interviews with community activists, business owners and police officers, as well as examinations of criminal justice data, gay and mainstream newspapers, and the files of the Alcohol and Gaming Commission of Ontario, the authors document the complex layers of private (both formal and informal) policing that uneasily coexist with the actions of the public police and of regulatory officials such as municipal licensing officers. The research site consists of two kinds of spaces: the commercial spaces of bars and baths, which have their own unique systems for ensuring security for the patrons and for the premises, and the streets, particularly the legal space that is created through municipal and provincial permits during Pride Day celebrations. In general, the authors document a growing trend toward self-policing in both businesses and community events, and a commercialization of security services that extends to the public police, insofar as many public police work as 'paid duty officers' and act like security guards for the organization holding events. The implications of this study for theoretical work on governance relations, particularly on the governance of security, are developed throughout.

This article is not a comprehensive account of policing and security issues in Toronto's gay village. It simply uses a few issues to develop some insights into the workings of the constellation of public and private authorities that maintain security in a socially specific site. We argue that these insights are contributions not only to empirical studies of minority urban communities but also to theoretical and legal discussions of governance relations (Valverde *et al.* 1999). It must first be noted that unlike those who document specific patterns of crime (gaybashing, for instance), our focus is not on crime, but rather on security. 'Crime', including the ordinary crimes that any neighbourhood has and the crimes that are characteristic of the gay village, is a process focused on *individuals*— perpetrators and victims, mostly. Crimes are also temporally distinct from 'normal' everyday life. By contrast, our investigation corroborates the literature's emerging insight that 'security' work, while sometimes involving the coercive policing of particular 'problem' individuals, is a much broader, not necessarily coercive, often unremarkable, everyday process that works through the organization of space and time more than on the control of individuals, and that looks not to punish past deeds but to ensure order-liness, risk minimization, and safety *for the future* (Bayley and Shearing 1996; Crawford 1997; Shearing 1992; Shearing and Stenning 1985). Security and crime control are of course not mutually exclusive. Individuals and stigmatized groups end up being

GOVERNING BODIES, CREATING GAY SPACES

governed through security measures, directly or indirectly, in Toronto's gay village as in American gated communities (Davis 1992: ch. 4); and threats to security can end up being policed and punished with the traditional, past-oriented tools of the criminal justice system. But the ultimate goal of security procedures is to generate safe and orderly *spaces* (Cooper 1998)—to reduce criminogenic opportunities, more than to investigate criminal intentions and acts.

In the case at hand, security processes work upon three kinds of spaces: the commercial space of bars, clubs, and baths; the public, city-controlled space of 'the street'; and the equally public space of parks. Security processes aimed at parks, and public debates about gay men's actual or perceived tendency to use parks as sexual spaces, are a key dimension of the governance of gay male sexuality, in Toronto as in other major urban centres (see e.g. Leap 1999); but, partly because there is virtually no park space within the boundaries of the 'gay village' downtown (cruising-friendly parks are, with one small exception, outside the downtown area), we are leaving the problematic of parks for a future study.

The current study of city spaces, of bars and streets and of the regulatory systems that constitute and govern them, draws on two main types of scholarly sources. First, we have borrowed insights from the criminological literature on policing, particularly studies of the relations between private policing and public police (Shearing and Stenning 1985; Johnston 1995; Johnston 1999; Kempa *et al.* 1999; Shearing 1992). Second, we have drawn on studies by queer urban geographers and sociologists of the ways in which certain spaces can acquire a moral reputation and a sexual orientation of their own, as it were (Bell and Valentine 1995; Dangerous Bedfellows 1996; Leap 1999). This study thus contributes both to the literature on the governance of security and to the emerging field of queer urban studies. We hope that this necessarily preliminary study shows policing scholars and others analysing trends in security governance that it is very important to study not only 'mainstream' spaces and institutions such as gated communities but also the activities of culturally marginalized communities. Gay communities are generally urban communities, and they have specific patterns of security needs and security services quite unlike those obtaining in, say, poor African-American urban communities. We suggest that it is important for scholars of security to be aware of how urban communities that have historically had an antagonistic relationship to the public police despite being, generally speaking, racially and economically privileged, have in the recent past come to develop complex internal structures that as well as promoting a cultural identity, also promote or ensure security.

The information assembled to generate the analysis in this article was collected through the following means: interviews with three police officers and with eight community activists; interviews with three managers of 'gay' businesses; attending numerous community meetings; analysing crime data obtained from Toronto police and from the Canadian Centre for Justice Statistics; and searching the holdings of the Canadian Lesbian and Gay Archives and the current 'establishment files' of the Alcohol and Gaming Commission of Ontario.[1] As well, back issues of *Xtra!*, the local gay weekly,

---

[1] The Alcohol and Gaming Commission of Ontario keeps extensive files on each licensed establishment, with information gathered through liquor inspectors' visits, complaints from neighbours and customers, police reports, etc. Twelve establishment files from both gay and straight sexually oriented establishments were accessed under a research agreement.

proved extremely useful, in part because of the lively and often reflexive debates about security, safety, and 'decency' carried on in the letters to the editor page.

As Clifford Shearing and others have pointed out, 'policing' is not just about catching those who break the law, and it is as such never just the job of 'the police' (Shearing 1992; Bayley and Shearing 1996; Jones and Newburn 1998; Johnston 1995). What the public police do when they arrest someone is only the proverbial tip of the iceberg. The fundamental role of police—a role that they by no means monopolize—is *the maintenance of order and the guaranteeing of security.* Thus, volunteer marshalls can be said to be engaged in 'policing' the parade floats during the annual June LGBT[2] Pride Day parade, while the men who do the laundry at the baths similarly police the street youth that try to sleep in the bathhouse lobby—whether or not any coercive measures are used or threatened. In both cases there is a certain 'order' that has to be maintained and whose continuation has to be guaranteed by some kind of authority.

In most cases, the authorities that guarantee security and ensure the maintenance of order in Toronto's gay village are non-government bodies. Community activists, the gay media, and other grassroots groupings are fond of denouncing Big Brother: and in this they are usually supported by left-wing academics, often operating within a social-control paradigm, who join in the denunciations of police raids or other Big Brother-type activities. While Big Brother continues to be active in Toronto's gay village, we nevertheless feel it is important to begin studying the ways in which community-based organizations, privately owned businesses, and unorganized community members police and self-police the spaces, the times, and the bodies that make up Toronto's gay village. While homophobic police raids continue, it is nevertheless important to document the less obvious mechanisms by which order is maintained and guaranteed on an everyday basis.

The gay village whose heart is the intersection of Church and Wellesley streets, just a block from Toronto's main artery, Yonge Street, now has a very complex social organization that did not exist, say, at the time of the December 1978 raid on the gay s/m bar, The Barracks—a police raid that greatly contributed to the formation of the contemporary Toronto gay/lesbian movement. The village, whose boundaries are, like those of Toronto's numerous ethnic districts, indistinct, is recreated every day through the routine activities of a large number of organizations, business, and informal groupings. Walking up and down Church Street (which runs one block east of Toronto's main street, Yonge Street) for five or six blocks, from Isabella Street in the north to Gerrard Street in the south, one sees numerous bars, mostly populated by white gay men, restaurants, souvenir shops selling 'gay' t-shirts and souvenirs, and such specialty businesses as health shops catering to HIV+ people. Rainbow flags are everywhere, and the numerous apparently heterosexual passers-by seem to accept the gay flavour of the neighbourhood as a fact of life. Nevertheless, signs of lingering security concerns can be observed. Sitting in the coffee shop generally considered to be 'the heart' of the village, the Second Cup—on whose expansive front steps groups of people congregate to chat and people-watch regardless of weather or time of day—one can look across the street and see the large, busy offices of the weekly gay paper, *Xtra!* and reflect on the fact that

---

[2] 'LGBT' stands for 'Lesbian, Gay, Bisexual and Transgendered'. To avoid this cumbersome term we will more often use the term 'queer'.

GOVERNING BODIES, CREATING GAY SPACES

even in the heart of the village, both the lesbian/gay weekly and the local gay/lesbian bookstore have thought it wiser to rent second-floor premises to minimize the risk of homophobic vandalism.

Looking through the pages of *Xtra!* or examining the bulletin boards at the local, gay-oriented Community Centre, one can read about the activities of a myriad cultural organizations—three gay and lesbian choirs, an organization providing programmes for gay youth, softball and soccer leagues, outdoor and hiking clubs, organizations geared to gays and lesbians from a variety of ethnic groups, from Portuguese to South Asian, a very large organization providing services to people with HIV (the Aids Committee of Toronto), a number of organizations catering to leather enthusiasts, s/m practitioners, drag queens, and such community institutions as the Judy Garland Memorial Bowling League. Again, 'gay pride' seems to be everywhere: but the community's visibility and pride are still punctuated by evidence of safety and security concerns, from promises of anonymity for those fearful of joining groups to signs at the 519 Community Centre asking for information about gay-bashing incidents.

The activities generated by formal and informal gay village institutions have security dimensions that have not received the same attention, even from queer scholars, as the actions of the public police. As a community—or more accurately, a loose coalition of communities—Toronto's gay village has from its inception in the late seventies been keenly aware of the need to provide itself with security. The Gay Community Patrol, a volunteer self-defence organization developed around 1980 to protect drag queens participating in the grand Halloween parade that used to take place on Yonge Street, may be the earliest instance of self-policing on an organized basis. But as we shall see in the mini-case study of nudity at Pride Day, self-policing is not always simply an effort to prevent gaybashing: it is in some cases a positive effort to constitute a particular kind of gay/lesbian order, a well-ordered, 'civilized' community. On Pride Day, which has become the community's main way of signifying itself to the larger heterosexual public, gaybashing is no longer a concern: more typical security worries include the theft of sound equipment and street decorations, and ensuring the orderly progression of the parade through crowds that have reached close to a million people. While the early activists of the 1978–81 period rightly focused their energies on documenting and fighting back against the actions of the public police (Kinsman 1996), the size and complexity of current organizations and spaces justifies studying the way in which the community itself defines orderliness and actively creates a civilized and secure community. Those who live, spend time, work or own businesses in the gay village are not passive recipients of 'policing'. They are key actors in the formation and in the governance of spaces of leisure and community events, and through often intuitive responses to perceived 'disorder' and risk, they too use 'policing' to shape the spaces and activities of gay[3] leisure time.

---

[3] We use 'gay' here because the space of the gay village is largely inhabited by gay men and generally reveals a distinct 'gay' sensibility. Lesbians too, and to a lesser extent transgendered people, find it a friendly neighbourhood, but most of the spaces, commercial and public, are distinctly 'gay'. Similarly, while there are significant numbers of people of colour who use the village, the space has a distinctly 'white' and even WASP feel; again, listings in *Xtra!* do include some groups, activities, and businesses by and for people of colour, but these are marginal, and not only quantitatively.

VALVERDE AND CIRAK

Securing Pride: Pride Day as a Security Problem

In North America, lesbian and gay literature from the 1950s and 1960s can be thought of as a series of variations on the theme expressed in John Rechy's classic novel, *City of Night* (1963). The importance of a certain time—night time—and of a certain space—the (usually sleazy) bar—is also documented in all the major works of gay and lesbian history (Chauncey 1994; Davis and Kennedy 1993). In North American cities, lesbian and gay culture developed in places such as private house parties, theatres, beaches, and public bathrooms, but the downtown sleazy bar in the evening hours had pride of place in the process by which modern queer identities were formed.

In this context, efforts to organize daytime activities celebrating lesbian/gay life and love can be seen as a radical attempt to literally displace the community. In Toronto, Gay Days, celebrated in 1978 on a sunny August Sunday in the park behind the provincial legislature, with lots of balloons and much fear about potential gaybashers, was one of the formative events. That was one of the key early moments in which lesbians and gays stepped out of the bars and into the public space of the city, 'out in the open'. The innocuous picnic atmosphere gave outsiders few clues about the profound radicalism of the temporality of the event: for perhaps the first time in Toronto's history, gays and lesbians were meeting *as gays and lesbians, in the daytime,* in an atmosphere resembling that of an ethnic community picnic. People who had previously only seen each other in the relative seclusion of bars or indoor political meetings at safe venues were seeing each other, in many cases for the first time, outdoors and in the light of day.[4]

That event, and similar celebrations held in subsequent years, nevertheless took place in a downtown park that, on a Sunday, had very little pedestrian traffic. Even this modest intrusion into the space/time of civic respectability, however, was not easy: organizers had to fight with the Parks Department to obtain the appropriate permits. But the crucial turning point, in terms of the symbolic politics of time and space, was Pride Day 1985. That year, Kyle Rae, now a city councillor and then executive director of the 519 Community Centre, was entrusted with the task of securing municipal permission to close off—that is, to mark as 'gay space'—part of Church Street. This spatial designation requires two permits: one from the city office for 'Street Closures', and one from the police for a parade. Entry into the political scene is thus possible only for those who can work the complex system. Apart from persuading the right officials to issue the permits (after having located the right personnel, a difficult task in the days before bureaucracies had web pages), a further requirement raised the barrier to public visibility even higher: only groups with liability insurance could be issued with a street closure permit (this is still the case today). Needless to say, the Pride Day committee was then not incorporated and was in no position to get insurance. What finally allowed the first street-based Pride Day was the fortunate fact that the 519 Centre, of which Kyle Rae was the director, was itself a municipal agency, and could thus draw on the city's own insurance policy to then ask the city for permission to have the street closed to vehicles. (Even then, however, a police constable in charge of by-law enforcement attempted to claim that the street could not be closed, a claim that had to be counteracted with threats to call municipal officials.)[5]

---

[4] The best source of information on gay activism in Toronto in the 1970s and 1980s is the huge website assembled by Rick Bebout, 'Promiscuous affections: a life in bars' [www.rbebout.com].

[5] Interviews with Councillor Kyle Rae, June and August of 2000.

GOVERNING BODIES, CREATING GAY SPACES

One moral of this story is that politics is not only a matter of heroic public actions, but also a matter of finding ways to satisfy the complex bureaucratic requirements imposed (in Toronto, and probably elsewhere as well) by a welter of municipal by-laws, public police regulations, and commercial insurance policies. It may not be too far fetched to see that 1985 permit-getting activity as the end of the era of spontaneous street marches and physical fights with police—the end of that first era, and the beginning of the contemporary Toronto gay/lesbian movement, a movement characterized by excellent commercial, public-relations, legal and bureaucratic know-how. What might appear to the average news consumer as a spontaneous outburst of celebratory energy is the carefully assembled product of numerous regulations and clever manoeuvres to use or circumvent those regulations.

The Privatization of Pride Day Policing?

In 1997, Pride Day was a huge success from the point of view of numbers—some estimates went as high as a million participants and spectators. But only 241 volunteers were available for marshalling and volunteer security, while organizers claimed that 500 was the minimum number needed. Volunteer shortages are important not only because of volunteers' role in enhancing safety—preventing accidents, deterring potential gaybashers, etc.—but also because the more self-regulated a community event is, the less money has to be spent on paid-duty police officers. Back in 1993, for example, (a year for which *Xtra!*'s estimate of attendance was only around 10,000) Toronto police had asked the Pride Day committee to pay for three additional officers (at a total cost of $3,500) in order to close two extra city blocks: the committee's protests, however, succeeded in having Pride Day declared 'a community event', a designation that meant that the costs of traffic control and security patrols would be borne by the police itself.[6]

This happy situation did not last. Whereas the early lesbian/gay actions and demonstrations on issues such as the 1977 high-profile charges against the magazine *The Body Politic*, The Barracks raids of December 1978, and the multiple bath raids and mass arrests of February 1981 were policed for free, as it were, the increasingly commercial nature of Pride Day created a new situation. As Sergeant Rob Knapper clarified for us in an interview, the Police Services Act states that revenue-generating events (even if put on by non-profit organizations) are not entitled to free policing. The parade is policed free of charge, as demonstrations are; but for the street closure, the organization needs to provide what are known as 'site security' officers to prevent damage to the group's property, to regulate crowds and avert traffic problems, and to ensure that unauthorized vehicles do not enter sites that have been closed by means of a municipal 'street closing' permit.[7] Thus, in recent years Pride Day has come to be policed not like an old-time demonstration but rather like a large construction site.

The cost of paid-duty officers—whose number is determined by the police itself, according to subjective calculations of the risks inherent in any particular event—has

---

[6] Information compiled from back issues of *Xtra!* and interviews with Rae and with two anonymous Pride Day organizers.

[7] Interview with Sergeant Knapper, September 2000, and with anonymous Pride Day organizer designated as 'K', September 2000. See also 'We love a parade', *Xtra!*, 9 July 1993.

VALVERDE AND CIRAK

more recently been one of the key reasons behind the Pride Committee's decision to hire a private security firm, First Nations Security: the more paid (non-volunteer) security the committee hires, the fewer paid-duty officers that will be required.[8] At this point it is difficult to judge whether the racial specificity (i.e. aboriginality) of the private security firm employed will prove a significant factor in the evolution of Pride Day security, but one can hazard a guess that the firm, which is, unusually in the sector, run by a woman, is more likely to provide more conciliatory and lower-key services than its larger, mainstream competitors.

The continued hiring of private security is also favoured by the fact that private security is often demanded as a condition for a special-occasion liquor licence by the Alcohol and Gaming Commission (ACGO). In 1999, the Pride Day committee attempted to get a 'street licence' to supplement the 'garden' licence, basically to extend the cramped space within which it was legal to stand around with a drink, and it was thought that showing the AGCO that private security staff were in place would facilitate this. The AGCO eventually refused the request for the unusual licence. The hiring of private security, therefore, while not specifically requested by any government body—either the police or the provincial liquor board—was nevertheless a way of attempting to meet, in advance, the evolving expectations of these state agencies in regard to self-policing, particularly the largely unwritten and discretionary expectation that professional rather than volunteer security staff be employed.

If, in a fit of nostalgia for the more politically pure eighties, the Pride Day committee had decided to take a strong line against private security, this would have had negative consequences: more money would have had to be spent on paid-duty officers, and the liquor licence might prove more difficult to obtain or might have had more restrictive conditions attached to it.[9] Whether or not professional paid security resulted in better security or not, their mere presence nevertheless helped the organizers to satisfy the liquor board and other licensing bodies that security was being professionally provided rather than carried out by politically motivated volunteers. It also saved money: the hourly wage of police officers is much higher than that of private security personnel, and in addition, paid-duty officers—who are dispatched by Traffic Services—get time and a half or even double time. The cost of paid-duty officers for Pride 2000 was estimated by one organizer at $60,000, and this figure would have been even higher without the private security.[10]

Thus, one can summarize the recent evolution of Pride security by concluding that there is a dual process of privatization: (a) a commercial security firm is being used (albeit a small, aboriginal-owned and operated company); (b) some of the uniformed officers present are there to do 'site security' for the organizing committee, and to that extent are providing a paid service rather than engaging in beat-patrol activities. In earlier years, volunteer-event marshalls (usually, hardened politicos) saw their relation to the police as one of complete antagonism. Nowadays, however, although the

---

[8] Interview with anonymous Pride Day organizer 'C', August 2000.

[9] Licensing decisions are highly discretionary, and although they can be appealed to a court, judicial review is not a practical option when a group is asking for a special occasion permit.

[10] 'Are police trying to pick Pride's pockets?' *Now*, 14 June 2000. Whether the police are acting legally in arbitrarily imposing financial burdens on community groups is unclear to us, but no consistent guidelines are being provided to groups holding events requiring security.

GOVERNING BODIES, CREATING GAY SPACES

antagonism still continues, the gay community is simultaneously just another customer of an organization formerly known as 'the force' but currently called 'police *services*'.

Two elements can be seen to have been involved in this partial commercialization. First, the Pride Day committee is literally a customer, just like film studios that operate on public streets and are obligated to hire paid-duty officers. Second, in the past ten years or so, a small but significant group of 'community liaison' officers have been active in the police division within which the gay village is located (52 Division). This group, which has significant support among higher management, is often undermined by other sections within the police—the plainclothes 'whisky dicks' within 52 Division, the morality squad, and perhaps most importantly today, the police union—but its existence fits with the new neoliberal logic of police as 'service providers', a logic which now has the Ontario Provincial Police literally contracting out its services to a number of Ontario municipalities (Wood 1998).

The commercialization of the work of public policing is of course also in keeping with the growing commercialization of Pride Day itself. As letters to the *Xtra!* editor regularly point out, Pride Day is starting to look like nothing but a huge opportunity for corporate sponsorship, particularly from beer and liquor companies. In respect to commodities like vodka and services such as policing, we are all customers now. Significantly, even during confrontational community meetings held in the wake of raids on The Barn and The Bijou in the spring of 2000, many gay people stood up not only to denounce raids but also to demand that the cops take more aggressive action against drug sellers, panhandlers and prostitutes—a law-and-order, 'gays-are-respectable-too', that was never even contemplated, much less voiced, at meetings of the late-seventies activist group, the Right to Privacy Committee.[11]

In years to come, it is likely that the role of paid private security will be a greater one: they provide licensed workers who don't require training, who won't suddenly desert their post, and who will (one presumes) be counted when the police make their thus far secret calculations about how many paid-duty officers need to be present. Given that First Nations security is a newcomer to Pride Day, it is too early to draw any conclusions about how their participation affects volunteer participation. In general, the relationships among these three very different groups would repay a much closer and detailed study than is possible here. But our study does show that the specific mix of public, paid, and volunteer security is to a large extent under the control of the organizers themselves, since the participation of public police is (partially) determined by the committee's prior arrangements with paid and volunteer security providers.

The complex relations among the various branches of the public police, private security and volunteer security are partly shaped by the community's own activity; but to a large extent they are also shaped by existing legal relations. In the next section we will go on to explore the overlapping legal jurisdictions that exist in the gay village not only on Pride Day but everyday, and that invisibly shape our lives even when nothing special is happening.

---

[11] Personal observations, meetings of the Church-Wellesley police community advisory committee, June and July, 2000. For the Right to Privacy Committee's activities, see Rick Bebout's website [www.rbebout.com]

Law, Urban Space, and Security

When is a street not a street? Pride Day organizers who have had to understand and implement that Alcohol and Gaming Commission's byzantine rules for the governance of 'beer garden' know that a street is sometimes not a street at all, but rather a 'licensed establishment', subject to unpublished, complex rules that contradict people's basic assumptions about the nature of public urban space. To give but one example: although children are welcome at Pride Day, liquor licensing rules prohibit children from being inside the barriers marking off the beer 'garden' (which is not a garden at all but a section of the carriageway of a street). During Pride 2000, one of the stages on Church Street was located so that one could only comfortably watch the outdoor show from the beer garden. Any people under 19 who wanted to hear the gay and lesbian chorus performing on the stage were forced to stand on the sidewalk and try to see something through the crowds milling on the sidewalk. A good number of adults brought kids to the event, and of course there were many LGBT teenagers present; but they could not watch gay and lesbian culture in relative comfort.

Going about one's business on downtown streets, whether on Pride Day or a 'normal' day, people constantly cross invisible boundaries, only some of which are physically marked by barriers or signs. These boundaries are created by administrative and legal regulatory processes whose character and origins are often shrouded, as English judges love to say, in the mists of 'time immemorial'. But what is most important to point out is that like all other forms of licensing, provincial liquor licensing regulations do not operate externally and coercively on the citizens in a top-down manner. The regulations and conditions formally or informally attaching to licences impose a whole series of onerous obligations on those holding the licence, and among them the obligation to themselves police the patrons is foremost (Reich 1964; Hogan 1983).

Licensing is, in general, a legal technology to carry out and regulate, at a distance, the work of governing activities, occupations, and spaces. In a beer 'garden', the licence holder is obligated not only to keep children out but also to get all of the servers to regulate patrons, for instance to ensure that intoxicated customers are not be served. This creates a situation in which the policing of disorder is subcontracted—first to the licence holder and then by him/her to all of the servers, who are expected to watch for and stop drug selling, to refuse service to minors and intoxicated adults, and generally to enforce the myriad regulations of time, space, and bodies that the province of Ontario has historically held to be necessary for the smooth governance of public leisure (Levi and Valverde 2001).

The subcontracting of policing through the legal mechanism of 'the licence' has a number of effects that happen to fit very nicely with the community's own self-image as a well-regulated, self-policing community.[12] If volunteer security people stop someone from leaving the Pride Day beer 'garden' with a half-full glass of beer, for instance, this action is simultaneously enforcing the province's liquor regulations *and* demonstrating

---

[12] The organizers of the lesbian bath house raided by police in September 2000 and charged with 'disorderly conduct' under the provincial Liquor Licence Act, for example, explained in some detail that all customers are asked for ID and issued with a list of legal dos and don'ts involving both sex and liquor. All bars and baths appear to have policies—not always written down for customers—strictly regulating customers' conduct. During our interviews, several people involved in such establishments volunteered comments to the effect that some other place was 'asking for trouble' because they did not sufficiently police their patrons.

GOVERNING BODIES, CREATING GAY SPACES

that gay people too believe in keeping drinking under spatial control, thus preventing 'excess' and disorder. State regulation and community autonomy are thus not necessarily at odds.

To take another site upon which one can see how state regulation meshes with the community's own sense of orderliness, let us turn for a moment to the baths. Baths have of course received much negative police attention in the past: but this does not mean that they always have a negative relationship with the police. One bath owner told us about an incident in which a 'street kid' assaulted the owner with a knife, in a robbery attempt. The police were called. After dealing with the particular crime in question, the police took steps to ensure the security of the bath patrons regularly: they now routinely patrol the lobby area and the stairs at the back of the building, keeping a particular watch on 'street kids'.[13] This is an excellent example of the relatively new role of gay establishments as customers of police services rather than as targets of police raids. Being so well served by the public police, this bath does not employ private security staff, relying instead on laundry and other workers to impose order when required (e.g. when patrons come in drunk from the bars). And because this bath, unlike some others, does not have a liquor licence, they are able to control when police come into the premises in a way that other places cannot: the police only have automatic right of entry into licensed establishments.

Other baths employ a minimal number of private security staff, mostly to control the entry area and the space immediately outside: but these businesses also deploy laundry and cleaning personnel to 'keep an eye on anyone destroying property or disturbing clients'.[14] One manager told us about a tactic he uses to preserve order: if faced with a drunk client, the manager will offer free food, a free room and a free shower. This way of risk-managing a situation so as to prevent any future disorder is of course a classic instance of modern security practices. It fits the thesis generally accepted in criminology circles that law enforcement and security is shifting away from punishing past deeds and toward managing future risks, a shift pioneered by commercial private security firms but now visible even in the state sector (O'Malley 1992, 1996; Shearing 1992; Bayley and Shearing 1996).

While bathhouses that do not have a liquor licence have a freedom to determine their own policing not enjoyed by those that have a licence, they are nevertheless subject to public health regulations, under the licence that they must obtain from the city in order to operate. This licence does not carry with it detailed norms and regulations in the same way as a liquor licence, but it nevertheless subjects the space of the bathhouse—often celebrated by gay men as a space of total freedom—to the intrusive gaze of municipal officials and public health inspectors. While in Toronto this gaze has been largely benevolent, in San Francisco and elsewhere in the United States baths were closed down on the grounds of health concerns related to AIDS, something that should remind us that the criminal law is not always the most coercive tool of the state. By-laws, public health regulations, regulations imposed by municipal bodies granting licences to bathhouses and 'adult entertainment parlours', liquor regulations . . . those are the tools used to reproduce order and security on an everyday basis, in the gay village as in the rest of the city.

---

[13] Interview with anonymous bathhouse manager 'D', May 2000.

[14] Interview with anonymous bathhouse manager 'F', August 2000. 'The X Bath does its own policing', Mr F told us proudly.

In contrast to baths, bars generally employ private security, thus adding another level to the already complex structure of policing/security. They do this partly for the same security reasons that lead heterosexual clubs to hire bouncers, and partly because police have made it clear that a certain amount of sexual activity in gay bars can only be tolerated if all customers are clearly warned before they go in about the nature of the establishment. Bar patrons are thus policed through several simultaneously operating mechanisms: (1) the actions of private security/bouncers; (2) the Alcohol and Gaming Commission, whose liquor inspectors are rarely seen but whose rules are continually enforced by the bar staff themselves; (3) the public police, acting either to enforce liquor regulations or to enforce the Criminal Code provisions on 'bawdy houses' and on indecent exposure and indecent acts.

But despite this complex layering of policing and security mechanisms, some bar patrons feel that there is not enough policing. The 'establishment file' of one well-known gay bar contains some letters to the Alcohol and Gaming Commission written (in 1995) by self-defined gay people who went there to have a drink after a meeting but who were turned away by staff because women were part of the group.[15] The bar was between a rock and a hard place. On the one hand, if women were allowed in, they might be offended by the male-male erotic activity going on and initiate complaints that could result in a licence suspension. On the other hand, if they are not allowed in, complaints of discrimination could also be lodged with the Commission, again with negative potential effects for the business. In that particular case, the gay group in question wrote to the Commission to complain about gender exclusion; this led to a site visit by a liquor inspector. The inspector, however, reported seeing at least one woman among the customers, and decided that no further disciplinary action was required.

The mapping of the complex legal, regulatory, and policing mechanisms that pervade the gay village could be continued at much greater length. But the general point has perhaps already become clear: that rather than being clearly and simply divided into 'public' and 'private' spaces, the gay village, like the city within which it is located, is in fact a complex network of overlapping regulatory systems, each of which has a certain policing or security dimension. Some of these are formal and backed by state resources; others are much more informal and backed only by a small private capital or by volunteer energy. Each type of site within the gay village—streets, bars, baths, parks—has its own particular mix of governing authorities, its own security system, as it were. And even the most coercive of these authorities never work on their own—there is always participation, sometimes even enthusiastic participation, from the ordinary people of the village.

Putting bodies in their place: debates about nudity

In 1996, some men belonging to the gay nudist group TNT marched naked in the Pride Day June parade. Some complaints were apparently made to the police about this, and the media coverage of the event included some negative remarks made by spectators. During 1997 and in the run-up to Pride '98, the police apparently asked the organizers to be the first line of defence—that is, to police their own community. This move may have

---

[15] We thank the Alcohol and Gaming Commission for giving us access to 12 current establishment files. Under the research agreement we are not allowed to reveal identifying information about any establishment.

GOVERNING BODIES, CREATING GAY SPACES

been prompted by lobbying carried out by the conservative group REAL Women of Canada: their lobbying was directed first at Police Chief Boothby and then at 52 Division, moving on to the Attorney General of Ontario's office when told by Superintendent James Parkin of 52 Division that the public nudity section of the Criminal Code requires permission of the Attorney General to prosecute.[16] Be that as it may, Pride Day Security Co-chair Laurie Bryson was quoted as saying: 'The police made it very clear . . . that the onus was on Pride security to take the front line—to be policing our own. I did get the sense that they would step in if things got out of control, but there was a reluctance with the police to move in.'[17]

Perhaps not knowing that the police were less than keen to prosecute nudity, some organizers took the informal subcontracting of police work very seriously. One senior organizer personally watched the TNT contingent, telling security volunteers that if they saw any nudity they should inform the people in question that they were at risk of being arrested and, furthermore, that Pride Day's 'parade licence' was at stake.[18] This vigilance was for nought, however, for when complaints were brought by Pride volunteer security to the police, the police took no action at all. Another key organizer complained that after training the volunteers to report nudity to the police, 'the police captain was informed and that was it.' As one of the main organizers, this activist obviously felt obliged to protect Pride's licence to march in the streets: apart from monitoring potential nudity, he also actively participated in the request made to one of the s/m oriented floats to modify the s/m performance on the float so that the whip being brandished was not actually used on anyone. But in addition to wanting to defend the organizing committee against possible criminal or by-law infraction charges, this organizer was motivated by a belief that 'nudity in and of itself is not a gay thing' and 'has no place in the Pride parade'. Nudity is all right at private parties, such as the one regularly held once a month by the TNT group, but not on a public street, he told us.

This self-policing was, however, contested strongly by another key organizer who has been very active from 1993 onward. Her view is that the gay community contains a great deal of internal diversity and that we should not be afraid to show this diversity to the Toronto public lining the streets to watch the Pride Parade. She was thus very critical of the actions of the man cited above, and was of the opinion that volunteer security should not have been instructed to remove naked people from the parade, as happened when, in 1998, Pride volunteers actively participated in the arrest of a naked woman.[19] This particular woman, described by all people interviewed as a nuisance,[20] breached not only the Criminal Code provisions on indecency but the rather more draconian provisions of the provincial Licensing Act: she insisted on climbing over the fence into the 'beer garden'.[21] There were a number of criticisms afterward from within the community about overzealous enforcement of moral codes.

---

[16] 'Fig Leaf follies at Toronto Gay Pride Day', in the on-line newsletter of REAL Women, July/August 1998; thanks to Kevin Beaulieu for forwarding this story.

[17] 'What's right and wrong: Pride holds secret post mortem?' *Xtra!*, 30 July 1998.

[18] Interview with 'C', August 2000.

[19] Interview with 'M', August 2000.

[20] One organizer claimed that she was 'under the influence' of an unspecified substance. Interview with 'K', September 2000.

[21] We were unable to obtain reliable information on whether this woman was indeed charged and if so under what statute.

In 1999 and 2000 there were rumours that if TNT men or any other group or individual took all their clothes off at the parade, charges would be laid; but this never took place.[22] In both of these parades, the police did not respond either to complaints by volunteer security or to being provoked by some of the TNT men marching in the parade, who although wearing a fig leaf, took it off when passing by uniformed officers standing on the sidewalks. Thus, if nudity is policed in the future, it will probably have to proceed as an explicit community-norm project rather than as a necessary measure to pre-empt arrests.

A proper place for nude bodies: the beach?

An interesting development related to the issue of public nudity on Pride Day is the opening of Toronto's 'clothing-optional' beach at the traditionally gay pleasure ground of Hanlan's Point, on Toronto Island. Kyle Rae was one of the city councillors who spearheaded the move to create this nude beach (or rather, to restore it, since there had been a nude beach on Hanlan's many decades earlier[23]). In doing so, he was aiming (he told us in an interview) to provide a sort of nudity safety valve, telling us in an interview that 'nudity belongs on the beach, not on Yonge Street'. The intricate details of the zoning and other regulations required to set up and police this very specific space, a space which in typical bureaucratic parlance is designated as 'clothing-optional' rather than as 'nude', do not concern us here. What is of interest is that this novel space, the largely gay nude beach at Hanlan's Point, is hardly the exuberant, unregulated space of ludic excess that one might imagine. The public police, who have over the decades laid numerous indecency charges against gay men on the beach at Hanlan's, of course take a continuing interest in this space, although they have been legally frustrated in their efforts to actually lay charges. But, like the space of Pride Day, the space of the 'nude' beach is hardly one of anarchy and liberty even when no police are present.

The box on the next page shows just some of the regulations imposed on this space of freedom not by Big Brother but by the 'Hanlan's Beach Naturists'. As the flyer distributed to users states, in language evoking the 'Toronto the Good' stereotype, 'nude is not lewd.'

As if this list of rules were not sufficiently clear, the other side of the leaflet states, in larger type, 'Naturists are ordinary people who want to be nude in a non-sexual environment . . .'

Apart from the nude beach, the one other space frequented by gay men in which nudity has been permitted is the monthly gathering of TNT men at The Barn. This again is a highly regulated event. It has always been conducted in relative secrecy, with someone posted at the door to ensure that no unsuspecting passers-by looking merely to have a beer wander in, and has at the same time been subject to all of the regulations of the Liquor Licensing Act as well as the informal regulations imposed by TNT men themselves. This high degree of self-policing seemed to suffice for a long time: but in the spring of 2000, during the same time period that certain police officers said to be closely supported by the police union were raiding the raunchy porn-film bar The Bijou, the gay

---

[22] For further analysis, see David Walberg, editorial, *Xtra!*, 1 July 1999, and Nancy Irwin, 'Topless in Toronto' *Xtra!*, 10 August 2000.
[23] See Peter Simm, 'The wiles of the sea vamp', *Xtra!*, 15 July 1999 (a detailed historical study of nude beaches).

GOVERNING BODIES, CREATING GAY SPACES

FREE BEACH ETIQUETTE

Many people will insist that rules for proper behaviour are not necessary since any decent or intelligent person should know how to act . . . We want to leave no doubt as to what kind of people are advocates of clothes-optional recreation! Naturists are nice people . . .

- SHOW RESPECT FOR OTHERS. Glancing is OK, but staring or sitting next to a person without getting an invitation or making sexually suggestive remarks is very offensive. We would be very happy to have a quiet talk with these individuals and discuss beach etiquette. Also, if you intend to wear your clothes or swimsuit, please consider using the regular beaches. Naturists are not exhibitionists for others to stare at!
- USE YOUR TOWEL for sanitary reasons when sitting on park benches at the beach
- NO OVERT, EROTIC, OR HIDDEN SEXUAL ACTIVITY. Nude is not lewd, but combined with public sex, it undermines our public image. Sexual activity belongs in the bedroom, not on the beach or nearby public areas.
- HELP WITH LITTER by bringing along a trash bag . . .
- PRIVACY IS FUNDAMENTAL! Many are at the beach for a quiet time and don't want to be disturbed. Beach Romeos and Juliets are people who can't take 'I would like to read my book for a while' for an answer . . .
- SPEAK UP FOR STANDARDS. If a person seems unaware of beach etiquette, they may be first timers, so give them a nice welcome to the beach and give them a copy of 'Free Beach Etiquette' or tell them their behaviour is inappropriate.

Most people you meet here are great . . . let us know about the others!

---

male bar The Barn was raided during TNT parties. These raids were said to be 'routine liquor licence inspections'. After the second one, a meeting between 52 Division head Superintendent Aidan Maher and Councillor Kyle Rae developed a sort of protocol ensuring even greater 'privacy': it was agreed that tickets would have to be sold in advance clearly declaring the nature of the event. Thus, even gay men fully aware of and in sympathy with the goals of the TNT group could not spontaneously decide to attend this event: they would have to plan carefully in advance to take their clothes off at a later specified time, a style of governance rather in conflict with the idea that taking off one's clothes involves diminishing inhibitions! But even this careful set of regulations did not suffice to keep the particular officers in question away: they went back again, and proceeded to lay a single charge under the Liquor Licensing Act's notoriously vague provision targeting licensees who are found to be 'permitting riotous, quarrelsome, violent, or disorderly conduct'.

The use of Liquor Licensing statutes to police not 'the establishment' but rather nudity or other acts by individuals is curious, to put it mildly, since if charges were to be laid under the Criminal Code, it is highly unlikely that a court would convict the particular men in question of committing an indecent act in public—as Superintendent Maher, the head of 52 Division, himself admitted in a public meeting. This questionable legal manoeuvre—repeated in a raid in September of 2000 of the women's Thursday night bathhouse that led to charges of 'disorderly conduct' under the Liquor Act— brings us to the last section of this article.

Governing Through Alcohol

The truce between local police and gay institutions that prevailed in the early nineties was broken in 1996, when the strip bar Remington's was raided after a few months of undercover morality squad investigation. In this case, two kinds of charges were laid: (1) bawdy house charges (which were later withdrawn), and (2) charges under the 'indecent theatrical performance' section of the Criminal Code, the section generally used against heterosexual strip bars and lap-dancing establishment.[24] In 1999, the Bijou—a licensed 'porn bar' in which much sexual activity was tolerated, without much effort to confine sex behind partitions or other contraptions to simulate 'privacy'—was also raided by police (morality squad officers, reportedly backed by the police union), and 30 criminal charges of committing an indecent act in a public place were laid, some long after the actual raid. However, these charges, like most of the Remington's charges, were later dropped, and several newspapers reported that it was police management itself that told the Crown to drop the charges.[25] The police then changed tactics, leaving the Criminal Code on the shelf and using instead the huge discretionary power granted to them (and to liquor inspectors) under the provincial Liquor Licensing Act. Instead of charging individuals with morals offences, they chose to charge the business with infractions of the Licensing Act—specifically, 'permitting disorderly conduct'.[26]

This type of tactic was later used against The Barn (in order to pressure them to eliminate the nude events hosted by TNT men) and more recently against the women's group hosting lesbian bathhouse events on a regular basis at a men's spa. Like the men's bar The Barn, the women's event (licensed only for the evening under a special occasion permit) also led to charges under the 'permitting disorderly conduct' section of the provincial Licensing Act. While the liquor-inspection police visits to the Bijou were short and relatively well-mannered, the 15 September 2000 raid on the women's event was clearly designed to intimidate customers and close the business: five plainclothes officers, all male, spent an hour and a half walking around and reportedly even going into individual rooms whose doors were closed.[27]

It seems, then, that the sector of the police force that continues to be intent on harassing gay and lesbian establishments has shifted its tactics, tending now to avoid the Criminal Code in favour of administrative law. Laying criminal charges against individuals engaged in consensual indoor activities is often frowned upon by higher police management these days, since the general approach is to target street soliciting while tolerating indoor sex work. In addition, individuals who are charged, regarded by a large part of the public as victims of Big Brother, often generate a political outcry. To make matters worse for the rogue officers, criminal charges often result in high-priced

---

[24] R. di Manno, 'Raid on gay troupe in "salacious" act cited as regressive', *Toronto Star*, 26 February 1996: A7; S. Pazzano, 'Gay club owner slapped with fine, kept bawdy house, allowed stage sex', *Toronto Sun*, 20 January 2000: 27; 'Caught in Dragnet' *Toronto Sun*, 20 August 1999: 24; R. di Manno, 'Is cop scandal just a feud?' *Toronto Star*, 18 August 1999 [no page number given in online version]; Christie Blatchford, 'Judge rejects experts' view in "sperm attack" case', *National Post*, 16 December 1999: A4.

[25] Brenda Cossman, 'Indecency is an easy trap', *Xtra!*, 26 August 1999; 'Bijou customers fear cops', *Xtra!*, 10 February 2000; Vern Smith, 'Things are cookin': a game of hot potato with the Bijou' *Xtra!*, 12 August 2000. In the last of these stories, the Crown in charge told *Xtra!*, that it was not the defence lawyers for the men who had made the request to drop the charges—a statement which would seem to imply that it was higher management within the police that had a quiet word with the Crown.

[26] Vern Smith, 'Bathouse busted', *Xtra!*, 13 Jan, 2000; Vern Smith, 'What's going on? Bathouse owners and cops hold closed-door shindig', *Xtra!*, 27 January 2000; Scott Anderson, 'Liquor quicker' *Now*, 21 December 2000.

[27] Interviews with two anonymous women's bath house customers, 17 and 18 September.

GOVERNING BODIES, CREATING GAY SPACES

talent being employed by the businesses to cross-examine arresting officers in court, something which the average police officer would rather avoid. By contrast, administrative law offers the police greater discretion and less public scrutiny and allows for faster effective sanctions, in that the Liquor Board can relatively quickly order a suspension of the licence, a penalty that has huge financial consequences for the business.[28]

The use of liquor statutes by the police to enforce moral codes—something that the liquor board itself is no longer keen to do—is nevertheless not a straightforward matter if the establishments in question are licensed by the city as 'bath houses' as well as by the province as drinking establishments. Although lap dancing was declared to be criminally indecent by the Supreme Court of Canada in the 1997 decision in the *Cheaters Tavern* case, *Mara and East*, subsequent developments in case law have resulted in a situation where lap dancing—and thus some non-penetrative sexual activity—is not only tolerated but actually licensed. Generally, a licence to operate an 'adult entertainment parlour', like all other licences, ensures that a particular business can carry on with the city's blessing, as long as it meets certain requirements (e.g. for lap dancing, touching is only tolerated if taking place behind a partition, such that the dancer and one customer can be said to be 'in private'). The Licensing Commission of Toronto has in recent years assumed responsibility for governing and monitoring sexually oriented entertainment and sexually oriented services such as massages in all establishments, those with liquor licences and those without, while the Alcohol and Gaming Commission, which in former years exercised draconian control over every minute detail of life in the bars, no longer sees itself as having a responsibility to regulate entertainment or otherwise shape the morals of Ontario's drinkers.[29]

It is a curious development that just as the draconian powers of the provincial liquor authorities are fading away, some Toronto police have taken it upon themselves to use the antiquated machinery of the Liquor Licensing Act to continue enforcing moral codes that can no longer be easily enforced with the Criminal Code. Some might say that homophobia will find any legal tools to pursue its target; and indeed, much has been made in the local gay press of the discriminatory character of liquor-law enforcement within the boundaries of 52 Division. This charge of discrimination is of course well founded, as has been documented in the case of the Bijou, the Barn, and the women's bath house. But there is more here than simple discrimination. A look at police charge statistics for the past few years, for the downtown police stations, reveals that the Liquor Licensing Act is routinely used to govern street 'disorder': charges of being drunk in public make up between 10 per cent and 25 per cent of all charges laid (see appendix B). The people caught by this antiquated legal machinery are much more likely to be the poor and the homeless than the respectable customers of gay businesses: governing through alcohol, while a useful strategy for homophobic police officers, is not unique to the gay village.

---

[28] The files of licensed establishments consulted suggest that suspensions have come to be relatively rare, and often now extend to a mere five days rather than the previous standard two-week period. However, the LLBO can, and still does, impose any number of conditions on a licence: they can order an establishment to stop selling alcohol after 8 pm, for example, a move with serious financial implications, or they can demand that private security personnel be hired.

[29] See correspondence from ACGO's legal counsel and other documents in the Cheaters Tavern file (AGCO current files). Other files show that the liquor board leaves prostitution to be controlled by the police and stripping to be regulated by the city.

Conclusion

The seventeenth-century political theorist Thomas Hobbes pointed out that peace, namely the absence of violence or war at a particular time, was not sufficient to meet people's basic needs. What people need and want, he stated, is 'security'—a situation in which one can reasonably expect to be able to plan one's activities without fear of violence from others (Hobbes 1651/1968: 186).

The notion of Time is to be considered in the nature of War; as it is in the nature of Weather. For as the nature of Foule weather lyeth not in a shower or two of rain, but in an inclination thereto of many dayes together: so the Nature of war, consisteth not in actuall fighting; but in the known disposition thereto, during all the time there is no assurance to the contrary.

Security, in that Hobbesian sense of peace of mind about the future, is something that individuals and communities continue to need and want. While Hobbes argued that the need for security is so strong that people will agree to be ruled by a tyrant just to obtain it, contemporary studies of policing and security issues by contrast emphasize that the Big Brother state is no longer regarded as the only source of security (if it ever was). There is a growing trend toward commercialized security—not only private security in the usual sense, but such phenomena as paid-duty officers ensuring 'site security' for community groups and businesses. Contemporary studies also document the phenomenal growth of services, tools and advice to enable individuals to monitor their own risks and maximize their own security without state interference—from home security systems and cell phones to the numerous flyers and pamphlets on protecting oneself, one's family, and one's property that are distributed by police, by community groups, and by commercial security firms.

Ensuring security—security for individuals going about their political or their bodily pleasures, and security for businesses, for state authorities, and for community organizations organizing major events—is thus a complex process in which the public police play a part that may be diminishing. Of course the part they play is in some senses unique: as Max Weber famously pointed out, governance is conducted at many sites, but only the state holds a monopoly over the legitimate use of force. But in Canada, the monopoly that the state has over force and over sanctions such as fines is exercised cautiously. Much state governance is conducted at a distance, for example through the ubiquitous Anglo-Saxon legal technique of 'the licence'. Activist as well as academic writers on gay issues have thus far focused on coercive state actions against gay individuals and communities, but we believe it is high time to undertake analyses of the ways in which state, commercial, and volunteer agencies and groups interact in the governance of everyday life, in the gay village as elsewhere in the city.

Pointing out that the development of a large and lively gay village has involved a multiplication of governance and a proliferation of systems of control should not be taken to imply that we live in an Orwellian society or that freedom is impossible. If, in Toronto, one can only be 'gay and proud' by means of a series of permits and licences, this does not mean that there is some kind of state conspiracy to control lesbian and gay lives: it means simply that, like every other urban space in every other highly developed society, the gay village is *both* a space of freedom—the freedom to find sex, the freedom to consume products, the freedom to engage in politics—*and* a dense network of regulation. And in many cases the freedoms that we have come to enjoy over the past 10 or 15 years can be

GOVERNING BODIES, CREATING GAY SPACES

shown to be the direct products of regulation (Rose 1999). Abolishing regulation has always been a myth: and denouncing control and regulation as such has prevented many of us from engaging in more mature reflections about just what sort of regulation we need and want. Such reflections will be furthered if both scholars and activists participate in disseminating information about the often obscure processes through which urban spaces are governed and secured.

APPENDIX A

Enforcement of Indecency Laws—1998 Data[30]

Vancouver	169 incidents (30 per 100k population)	19 men, 2 women charged	7 cleared
Montreal	390 incidents (22 per 100k population)	93 men, 1 woman charged	41 cleared
Toronto	552 incidents (22 per 100k population)	198 men, 71 women charged	21 cleared

Note 1: 'Incidents' does not mean individuals: one individual could be charged with five counts of an offence and this would show as five incidents. Also, an establishment could be charged, typically with allowing 'an indecent theatrical performance'. The incidents are counted from police occurrence reports.
Note 2: An incident reported in Dec. 1997 might lead to a charge in 1998, and so on. The charges laid, however, are such a low percentage of the incidents reported for that year, in all three cities, that the overlap between years can be disregarded if what one wants is a rough sense of how indecency laws are enforced.

Analysis

The most significant fact about indecency law enforcement that emerges from this admittedly partial data is that a large number of incidents do not seem to result either in a charge or in the incident being cleared. For Toronto, 71 adult females, 3 male youths, 1 female youth and 140 male adults were charged in 1998: this gives a total number of 165 individuals charged. Since the total number of charges was 198, we can deduce that 33 charges were laid either against establishments or against already charged individuals. The question is then: if over 500 incidents were documented by the police as involving 'indecency', why weren't more charges laid? A police source suggested that the low number of incidents that result in either clearance or charging is caused by the fact that women might be indecently grabbed by an unknown person, say in the subway. An alternative explanation might be that customers of bars, bath houses, and individual sex trade workers are having their particulars taken down by police at the time of an occurrence, with this information being held in limbo, without clearance and without charges. It is impossible to obtain the kind of breakdown of indecency incidents that would allow these hypotheses to be tested, but for now we can at least conclude that the gay/lesbian movement's working hypothesis, namely that police are collecting information on those involved in semi-public sex for the mere purpose of intimidation, is not disproved by the available data.

Be that as it may, citizens of Toronto have a significantly higher chance of actually being charged as a result of police investigations of 'indecency'.

---

[30] Data obtained from the Canadian Centre for Justice Statistics.

Vancouver	19 charges/169 incidents = 11 %
Montreal	93 charges/390 incidents = 24 %
Toronto 198	charges/552 incidents = **36 %**

APPENDIX B

Liquor Licensing Law and Urban Disorder

For the years 1996–99, charges under the Liquor Licensing Act constituted about 25 per cent of all non-traffic charges in two selected downtown police divisions, 14 and 52 (52 includes the gay village, 14 includes most of Parkdale). This contrasts with figures of 10–18 per cent in police divisions further from downtown.

But how much of this activity is directed at establishments? A breakdown of the police charge data for the division including the gay village (52) and for a division responsible for a low-income area with much heterosexual prostitution and drug activity (14), tells us that the liquor licensing provisions are being overwhelmingly used against individuals, not spaces.

1997 Data (selected from data provided by Toronto Police Services Corporate Communications)

	Sell liquor to intoxicated person	Selling liquor to a minor	Consume alcohol not on licensed premises	'Drunk'
52 Division	0	0	493	356
14 Division	4	1	718	662

1998 Data (selected from data provided by Toronto Police Services Corporate Communications)

	Sell liquor to intoxicated person	Selling liquor to a minor	Consume alcohol not on licensed premises	'Drunk'
52 Division	0	29	852	357
14 Division	1	43	660	527

Liquor licensing laws, therefore, are key instruments in the regulation of street disorder, particularly in the downtown areas.

REFERENCES

BAYLEY, D. and SHEARING, C. (1996), 'The Future of Policing', *Law and Society Review* 30/3: 585–606.

BELL, D. and VALENTINE, G. (1995), *Mapping Desire: Geographies of Sexualities*. London: Routledge.

CHAUNCEY, G. (1994), *Gay New York: Gender, Urban Culture and the Making of the Gay Male World 1890–1940*. New York: Basic Books.

COOPER, D. (1998), *Governing out of Order: Space, Law, and the Politics of Belonging*. London and New York: Rivers Oram Press.

CRAWFORD, A. (1997), *The Local Governance of Crime: Appeals to Community and Partnerships*. Oxford: Clarendon.

GOVERNING BODIES, CREATING GAY SPACES

DANGEROUS BEDFELLOWS, eds. (1996), *Policing Public Sex: Queer Politics and the Future of Aids Activism.* Boston: South End Press.

DAVIS, E. and KENNEDY, M. (1993), *Boots of Leather, Slippers of Gold: The History of a Lesbian Community.* New York: Routledge.

DAVIS, M. (1992), *City of Quartz: Excavating the Future in Los Angeles.* New York: Vintage.

HOBBES, T. (1651/1968) *Leviathan,* edited by C. B. MacPherson. Harmondsworth: Penguin.

HOGAN, D. (1983), 'The effectiveness of licensing', *Law and Human Behavior,* 7(2/3): 117–38.

JOHNSTON, L. (1995), *The Rebirth of Private Policing.* London: Routledge.

——(1999), 'Private policing in context', *European Journal on Criminal Policy and Research,* 7/2: 175–96.

JONES, T. and NEWBURN, T. (1998), *Private Security and Public Policing.* Oxford: Clarendon Press.

KEMPA, M, CARRIER, R., WOOD, J. and SHEARING, C. (1999), 'The evolving concept of "private policing"', *European Journal on Criminal Policy and Research,* 7/2: 197–223.

KINSMAN, G. (1996), *The Regulation of Desire.* Montreal: Black Rose Books.

LEAP, W. (1999), ed. *Public Sex, Gay Space.* New York: Columbia University Press.

LEVI, R. and VALVERDE, M. (2001), 'Knowledge on tap: police science and common knowledge in the legal regulation of drunkenness', *Law and Social Inquiry,* 26/4, 819–46.

O'MALLEY, P. (1992), 'Risk, power and crime prevention', *Economy and Society,* 21/2: 252–75.

——(1996), 'Indigenous governance', *Economy and Society,* 25/3.

RECHY, J. (1963), *City of Night.* New York: Grove Press.

REICH, C. (1964), 'The new property', *Yale Law Journal,* 73/5: 733–87.

ROSE, N. (1999), *Powers of Freedom: Reframing Political Thought.* Cambridge: Cambridge University Press.

SHEARING, C. (1992), 'The relation between public and private policing' in M. Tonry and N. Morris, eds., *Modern Policing,* 399–434. Chicago: University of Chicago Press.

SHEARING, C. and STENNING, P. (1985), 'From the panopticon to Disney World: the development of discipline' in A. Doob and E. Greenspan, eds., *Perspectives in Criminal Law,* 335–49. Toronto: Canada Law Books.

VALVERDE, M., LEVI, R., CONDON, M., SHEARING, C. and O'MALLEY, P. (1999), *Democracy in Governance: A Socio-Legal Framework,* Report for the Law Commission of Canada.

WOOD, J. (1998), Reinventing governance: a study of transformations in the Ontario Provincial Police, PhD thesis, Centre of Criminology, University of Toronto.

The Workplace

[13]

A Legal Perspective on Sexuality and Organization: A Lesbian and Gay Case Study

Paul Skidmore*

This article argues the case for incorporating legal discourse into social theories relating to sexuality and organization. The central theme around which this argument is constructed is that of the heteronormativity of the workplace which is critically interrogated by adopting perspectives of lesbian and gay workers. The processes through which this heteronormativity is maintained are examined with particular emphasis on how notions of public and private are strategically deployed to this end. The legal case study evaluates judicial discourse in court judgments noting how it contributes to and reinforces heteronormative practices. Examples are drawn from litigation in the UK and in Germany, illustrating the broad range of discursive techniques in use which in part vary according to the qualities of the legal norm at issue.

Keywords: lesbian and gay, legal discourse, organization, heteronormativity

Introduction

Over the past 20 years or so social scientists have become increasingly interested in sexuality in organizations. The workplace has been recognized as an important locus in organizational and spatial terms for sexualized performances by individual subjects. This approach argues that 'work' — here taken to be labour, usually paid and outside the household, whether in terms of the task to be performed or the function of workers in the production process — can be better understood when sexuality is taken into account, a perspective which additionally opens up new insights into the power relation of gender. This permits both the enrichment of the study of

Address for correspondence: *Paul Skidmore, Humboldt Universität zu Berlin, Juristische Fakultät L.S. Baer Unter den Linden 6, D-10099 Berlin, Germany, e-mail: paul.skidmore@rewi.hu-berlin.de

work by incorporating the sexuality perspective but also, in the other direction, it permits reflection on how the social structure of the workplace can have a disciplining and shaping effect on the lived experience of sexuality.

This article will argue that the dual relation, sexuality/organization, organization/sexuality, needs to be interpreted in the context of a heteronormative society. The heteronormative axis around which work is constructed, organized and managed needs to be exposed and revealed in order to develop an understanding of how scripts of gender and sexuality are embedded into the workplace. While for many workers compliance with the heteronormative hegemonic scripts poses problems, for example, for reasons of race, class, religion or political beliefs, the perspective adopted here is one restricted to issues arising from lesbian and gay standpoints. It is merely illustrative of the problems created by a heteronormative ideology and acknowledges that many similar issues could be raised by considering other perspectives.

The explicit questioning of the heterosexual norm in the theorizing of work in this fashion offers the opportunity to connect with the limited volume of empirical research in western Europe into the workplace experience of lesbians and gay men. In this way narratives of lesbians and gay men describing their negotiation of sexuality at work on an everyday basis can be related more closely to the cultural environment and structures of the workplace. An exploration of the disciplining effects on lesbians and gay men of the behaviour of co-workers and of management demands and attitudes will enrich lesbian and gay studies and also provide a more nuanced and refined account of sexuality at work.

In seeking to deepen our understanding of the reciprocal relation, sexuality/organization, this article introduces a new dimension generally overlooked or ignored. It incorporates into the analysis the legal discourse through which the formal boundaries for the behaviour of employers and workers are set. The discourse of legal 'rights' places spatial and temporal constraints, in formal terms at least, both on the employer's freedom to manage and on the individual's freedom of self-expression. Whilst no claim is advanced as to the impact of legal discourse on the agency of any particular individual it is contended that it contributes to the discursive parameters both of organizational behaviour, in the sense of workplaces, and of individuals' lived sexualities. Whatever the weaknesses and shortcomings of law as a regulatory apparatus it cannot be simply disregarded when considering the production of cultural norms. Furthermore an analysis of legal discourse with regard to the regulation of the workplace is helpful in shedding further light on the public/private debate, revealing the contingent, ambiguous and at times contradictory nature of this binary.

The norms of labour law which illustrate the contribution of the law to the sexuality/organization relation are many and varied. Thomson (1996) and Sheldon (1999) have shown that health and safety rules, formally adopted to protect human reproductive capacity from dangerous chemicals at the workplace, sexualize men and women in very different terms despite similar levels of biological risk. Statutory entitlements to maternity, paternity and parental leaves reveal the embodied sexualized constructions of parents and workers with which law operates, with knock-on effects for the gender hierarchy (Collier, 1999). The case study chosen for investigation in this article, however, reflects the aim of foregrounding lesbian and gay perspectives. While the interests of lesbians and gay men clearly do not always overlap (Humphrey, 2000), for the purposes of this article emphasis will be placed on areas of common ground. Judicial discourse in court cases brought by lesbians and gay men where their sexuality was at issue will be considered. Two reasons exist for this choice. Firstly, it provides an excellent opportunity to expose the general heteronormativity of the workplace. Secondly, it offers many obvious examples of the way the law (re)produces cultural norms as to the behaviour 'appropriate' to men and women at work and highlights some of the difficulties faced by all those who, for whatever reason, depart from these norms.

Sexuality in organizations

Mainstream organizational theory for many years failed to consider that workplace subjects are sexualized individuals (Burrell and Hearn, 1989). However with the increasing volume of research into the gendered nature of work and organizations it became clear that the individual subjectivities of men and women workers needed to be brought into the analysis of workplace culture and processes. Whilst there is no single agreed definition of the exact relationship between the concepts of sex, gender and sexuality, all the more so following the work of Butler (1990, 1991), as acknowledged recently by Parker in this journal (2002), the notion of sexuality to be explored here relates to the corporeal desires, attractions and erotic behaviour which are sewn into the fabric of everyday working life (see, for example, Brewis, 2002; Brewis and Sinclair, 2000). The individual agency involved in these performances is, of course, constrained by a social system of economic imperatives and the patriarchal power structure which constructs male and female unequally (Jackson, 1996). Thus, while sexuality is not the same as gender, it cannot be understood without reference to it (in the context of organizations, Hassard *et al.*, 2000).

Early work naming and recognizing sexuality in organizations includes that of McKinnon (1979) in her analysis of sexual harassment and of Pringle (1989), which explores the dimensions of the secretary/boss relationship. These analyses tended to view sexuality as incidental to the economic interests of the organization. Others have gone further. Acker (1990) argues that both jobs and workers are gendered and 'bodied'. The abstract, bodiless worker does not exist, although in general men come closer to fulfilling this ideal type than do women. The sexualized, embodied form inscribed on women is often used, so she argues, in justifying patterns of gender segregation. Adkins (1995) takes the economic argument a stage further, arguing that women's labour market participation is generally contingent on their performance of sexual services, which is not required of men. By this she does not mean that a woman has to perform sex acts, as a prostitute would, but that her labour is nevertheless subjected to a sexualized discipline and gaze.

The lens through which this sexualized labour is brought into focus is a heteronormative one, one which is shaped by a particular form of masculinity, described by Connell (1995) as hegemonic. This dominant discourse of heteronormativity sets the framework conditions under which labour is generally supplied, both in terms of relations with customers and also with co-workers and managers. Empirical evidence provides support for the existence of this heteronormative discourse in many sectors of the economy. Halford *et al.* (1997) illustrate how managers in banking and local government intentionally organize mixed-sex workgroups based on heteronormative assumptions in order to channel and direct the performance of sexuality in accordance with employer needs. In the leisure sector investigated by Adkins (1995) women were expected, as part of their job, to respond in a sexualized fashion to male customers, and thus their embodied appearance as women was, in practice, a condition of employment. Similarly, the experience of women working in the male-dominated City of London was one in which they were very conscious of the limits and possibilities presented by the need to perform as embodied workers subject to a male gaze (McDowell, 1997). Men, too, can be aware of the heteronormative scripts of the workplace, especially when working in non-traditional occupations (Cross and Bagilhole, 2002). For example, the mapping of male/female to doctor/nurse, constructed within the heteronormative paradigm, is fractured by men who work as nurses (Halford *et al.*, 1997). To accommodate this fracturing, men working as nurses are often assumed to be gay. This, in turn, poses challenges for those men who identify as heterosexual and yet work as nurses (Isaacs and Poole, 1996).

Whilst this evidence usefully supports theoretical accounts of sexuality in organizations inscribed within a heteronormative frame, the focus of these studies has been on workers identifying (or presumed to identify) as heterosexual. Implications for lesbian and gay workers have to be 'read off' from the initial analysis. This marginalization of lesbian and gay issues reflects mainstream concerns with exploring heterosexuality, patriarchy and hegemonic masculinity (acknowledged in Burrell and Hearn, 1989, p. 21) where the principal research question has not been drawn up with lesbians or gay men in mind. Only when the relation is reversed and the organization of sexuality is addressed does empirical evidence begin to emerge with a more definite focus on lesbians and/or gay men, which in part considers how organization — for our purposes the workplace — in spatial and temporal terms shapes the lived experience of sexuality.

Organizing sexuality at work

By reason of its normative qualities the heteronormative workplace has, by definition, an impact on all workers, albeit to differing extents. Even those workers identifying as heterosexual may have difficulty in complying with the particular version of heteronormativity prevailing in their workplace (Lee, 2000). In focusing in this article on the experiences of lesbians and gay men, however, the contours of the heteronormative workplace are thrown into somewhat sharper relief than would otherwise be the case. Nevertheless, much of the research on lesbians and gay men at work has to be carefully unpicked before this heteronormativity is fully visible. Many of the accounts are of a biographic nature, investigating 'coping' strategies at work (Burke, 1993; Dunne, 1997; Hall, 1989; Maas, 1999; Zillich, 1988). The subjective behaviour adopted, for example, techniques of (non-)disclosure, assertiveness or over-identification with the employer's objectives, tends to be emphasized over and above the structural features of the workplace. The possibility of viewing the relationship between the worker and the workplace as a dynamic one is rarely addressed. Discursive workplace practices in terms of language, appearance, demeanour, expected and accepted patterns of interaction with customers and co-workers have not been adequately incorporated into accounts of lesbian and gay performances at work.

Yet the need to do this is underscored by the social geographer, Nancy Duncan, who states:

> [a]lthough many would think of workplaces as generally asexual . . . these are nevertheless also heterosexual, often heterosexist spaces. Nearly invisible because it is universalized and naturalized, heterosexuality is inscribed in public as well as private spaces. . . . [I]t is difficult to make heterosexuals aware that their spaces invoke a sexuality. (Duncan, 1996, p. 138)

It is, of course, not only heterosexuals who need to be aware of how space invokes sexuality. A sensibility for the workspace and its particular set of power relations will help enrich social constructionist accounts of all sexualities. By exploring and mapping the multiple dimensions of this space the axes along which heteronormativity is exerted will be revealed. This, in turn, helps identify the disciplining practices which, as will be seen below, are often reinforced and reproduced through legal discourse.

The heterosexual workplace

One of the most obvious ways in which the 'space' of work disciplines lesbians and gay men is by seeking to control and 'normalize' physical appearance, particularly through dress codes and grooming requirements (Skidmore, 1999). These practices demand worker performances according to essentialized masculine and feminine scripts, in particular requiring women workers to satisfy a male definition of attractiveness (Adkins, 1995). This encoding makes sense only within a heteronormative paradigm. While the possibility of their transgression and subversion should not be ignored (Taylor and Tyler, 2000, p. 90: Bell *et al.*, 1994 are, however, more critical than Taylor and Tyler of the proposition that breaching dress codes is transgressive) their very existence suggests a 'compulsory heterosexuality' at work (Rich, 1980). In certain jobs, for example in traditional 'male' manual work, such as that of a mechanic, the whole cultural construction of the job itself imposes sufficient discipline in a heteronormative sense, so that a (gendered) dress code is unnecessary. As Dunne's (lesbian) respondents pointed out, the mere embodiment of being a woman in such a job was sufficient to be labelled as a 'dyke' (Dunne, 1997). The heteronormativity of the workplace was so strong that this was the only plausible 'explanation' of a woman's presence. While for some women this disciplining force eventually meant that they left to find another job, others preferred this 'outlaw' status to the regime of femininity which would be imposed upon them in secretarial or retailing work.

Another technique to enforce heterosexuality is to exclude and alienate lesbians and gay men from the social fabric of the workplace *because of their sexuality*. This operates at many different levels. At its most extreme, lesbians and gay men may be denied access to the workplace. The employer refuses to hire them because of their known or perceived sexuality (Knoll *et al.*, 1997, pp. 44–8; Palmer, 1993, p. 6). Similarly dismissal may be motivated by sexuality (Palmer, 1993, pp. 7–8). Less severe, but often equally distressing, is ostracization (Burke, 1993; Dunne, 1997; Humphrey, 1999; Snape *et al.*, 1995). This can take many forms, depending on the nature of the work. Its dimensions can be quite corporeal, for example, refusing or avoiding direct physical contact with a lesbian or a gay man, even where this is a necessary part of the job, or refusing to share changing facilities, communal showers or sleeping accommodation. (For evidence from the armed forces see Homosexuality Policy Assessment Team, 1996). In other jobs, exclusionary practices may be more subtle, ranging from a refusal to speak to a lesbian or gay co-worker or to engage with his/her sexuality, or lack of management support for lesbian and gay workers (Humphrey, 1999), to 'social' events which take place in overtly 'straight' locations, for which non-attendance is unofficially sanctioned.

In addition, exclusion takes place through the medium of language. This is not simply a question of insults or offensive 'jokes', undermining lesbian and gay self-worth. (Survey evidence points to this being one of the commonest forms of harassment reported: Knoll *et al.*, 1997; Palmer, 1993). In the 'small talk' of social interactions, an integral part of any job which involves interpersonal relationships with customers or co-workers, assumptions are made by all participants as to some degree of commonality of cultural knowledge and shared identity in order that the conversation can be understood by all. For any worker who does not share this assumed commonality of knowledge or identity this practice is likely to be alienating. For lesbian and gay workers this scenario tends to arise where the conversation is based upon a tacit assumption of shared heterosexuality, a regular occurrence when families, relationships and many social and cultural phenomena are being discussed. To counter this by talking about unambiguously lesbian and gay people, places, events or issues thus making visible the heteronormativity of the dominant discourse is not always easy because of the misplaced but often quoted response that this is 'ramming it [homosexuality] down the throats' of straight co-workers (for similar evidence, see Humphrey 1999, pp. 138–40).

For lesbians and gay men who have integrated themselves into a lesbian or gay subculture outside work, the workplace, whether the office, the factory, the shop or the building site, is often the most constant and obvious reminder of 'heterosexual space' and of its disciplining pressures. Given the economic imperative of work, this is space which is not easily avoided, although certain professions and jobs, in addition to the possibility of becoming self-employed, offer opportunities to create alternative forms of workspace.

A further dimension to the heterosexuality of work is often the impermeability of this space to same-sex couples. This can arise in a formal manner through employer policies denying benefits (sometimes of considerable pecuniary worth: for example, medical insurance, 'marital' supplements, pensions for dependants and travel concessions) in respect of same-sex partners, but which are granted to opposite sex partners (Equal Opportunities Review, 1997). The invisibility of the same-sex partner may also be achieved through informal norms and practices, making it difficult to talk about a partner, put his/her picture up in the office, bring him/her along to 'social' functions (ver.di, 2002). Similarly crises, break-ups or bereavements in same-sex relationships may not receive the same level of support from co-workers or the same discretionary leave granted by line managers as would similar problems experienced by those in opposite sex relationships. In terms of career progression the invisibility of the same-sex partner can put lesbians and gay men at a disadvantage. Where in practice a senior position in an organization requires 'a man with an appropriate female partner' servicing his and (indirectly) the organization's needs, a lesbian or gay man with a same-sex partner is rarely seen as functionally equivalent (Dunne, 1997, pp. 168–9; Knoll *et al.*, 1997, pp. 41–3; Palmer 1993, p. 7).

Thus the 'place' in which the heterosexuality of work is constructed and played out is a 'leaky' one in spatial terms. It is not bounded by the four walls of the office, factory, call-centre or similar. It also includes 'leisure' venues where required socializing between co-workers takes place and situations in which clients are being courted, won and entertained, often away from the formal workplace (McDowell, 1997, pp. 174–7). It can perhaps be better encapsulated in relational terms, encompassing those encounters subject to both formal and informal control of the employer and of co-workers, where certain types of scripted behaviours are required. What distinguishes 'work' from other *loci* of adult interactions are both its confines and the nature and range of sanctions for deviating from the script.

While for some lesbians and gay men their autonomy is limited by both economic and cultural factors such as class and ethnicity, others have the opportunity to order their domestic and social life so as to maximize the opportunities to live openly as a lesbian or gay man. For many this involves a move to a big city (Bell and Binnie, 2000; Binnie and Valentine, 1999, pp. 176–9), promising not only anonymity, less scrutiny by neighbours, the possibility of severing or loosening of ties with family and previous acquaintances but also the prospect of having access to the well-established infrastructure of a subculture. In this way some, but by no means all, of the social sanctions applied to lesbians and gay men can be avoided, or their impact reduced. Some of the threats posed by 'public' space nevertheless remain (Moran *et al.*, 2001; Myslik, 1996; Valentine, 1996). However, in comparison with 'work' these encounters on public transport, in the street or in shops are often more random and therefore particular individuals are more likely to be avoided. For many workers a distinguishing feature of the workplace is the regular, if not daily, contact with a group of co-workers with whom one is obliged to interact. The temporal, as well as spatial boundaries, of work means that these interactions cannot easily be escaped. Work, therefore, remains for many lesbians and gay men a location for the repeated (re-)negotiation of their relationship with heterosexuality (Humphrey, 1999). One of the discursive frames regulating these patterns of interaction is that of the legal discourse relating both to the relationship between employer and employee and between co-workers.

Legal regulation of work: public/private questions

Within legal academic discourse, relatively little attention has been paid to how legal rules and doctrines discursively shape the workplace experience of lesbians and gay men (Skidmore, 1999). Feminist and other critical accounts have shown how legal regulation of work has been shaped around a male (Conaghan, 1999; Fredman, 1997; Owens, 1997) and an able-bodied norm (Gooding, 1994). The particular experiences of ethnic minority women have also been highlighted (Ashiagbor, 1999). However, the heterosexuality of employment law has not been adequately exposed. Writing on lesbians and gay men, as treated by employment law, has in the main been positivistic (for example, Byre, 1993; Harrison, 1996; Waaldijk, 1993, pp. 104–14; contrast, however, Chapman, 1995), with certain exceptions in relation to the military's exclusion of lesbians and gay men (McGhee, 1998; Stychin, 1995, chapter 5).

Those seeking to explore and critique law's heteronormativity have tended to pick on the 'easier' targets of criminal, family, education and local government law, all of which have offered fertile ground for analysis in the British context (Beresford, 1998; Collier, 1995; Evans, 1989; Monk, 1998; Moran, 1996). Despite the importance of the workplace in the everyday lives of lesbians and gay men as they negotiate their sexuality, the legal discourse which operates upon it has barely been addressed. This is regrettable. An analysis of legal discourse relating to the workplace helps reveal its heteronormativity. Furthermore it provides a further opportunity to reflect on the falsity of the public/private duality around which much traditional analysis of work and sexuality is constructed.

Critical analysis of the public/private duality has revealed its inherent instability, arising from multiple and conflicting meanings of 'public' and 'private' (Warner, 2000). These tensions are instructive in exploring the heteronormative nature of the legal discourse constructed with regard to the workplace. Paid work, typically carried out away from the home, has conventionally been seen as falling within the 'public' sphere of activities. According to this model, sexuality is a 'private' matter which has nothing to do with the workplace (O'Donovan, 1985). This position is, however, complicated by the conventional legal approach to regulating the individual employment relationship as developed in the 19th century, which in the overwhelming majority of cases regards it as a *private* contractual arrangement, subject to the basic rules of *private* law (Wedderburn, 1986). Even where the relationship is formally classified as a public law one, it is nevertheless a relationship of subordination, whereby the worker's freedoms are restrained. Thus, for the purposes of this article, analysis will be focused on this tension between the characteristically 'private' (employer) regulation of what is perceived to be a 'public' sphere.

Public policy has limited its intervention into the norms and shapes of this private relationship. Its terms are set by the private parties, conceptualized as autonomous legal individuals, who are endowed with 'freedom of contract'. In practice, however, the economically dominant party — invariably the employer — sets the parameters of the employment relationship (Fox, 1974) which can have significant implications for the playing out of the sexuality/organization relation. This arises out of the confluence of public and private discourses. Whilst on one reading, the workplace is 'public' space into which sexuality does not normally intrude, except, of course, for the universalized and hence invisible heterosexuality, on another reading this is in the 'private' domain which the employer can structure as it sees fit.

Legal discourse on the workplace is highly saturated with its deployment of these public and private tropes. Firstly, the argument concerning the 'private' autonomy (and prejudices) of employers is widely used to resist the very introduction of legislation to grant workers rights (Epstein, 1984; contrast Mückenberger and Deakin, 1989). Even when enacted, judicial interpretation of such measures, for example the British law on unfair dismissal, often reflects a desire to defend the employer's private interests (Collins, 1992). Secondly, the 'public' qualities of the workplace are at other times emphasized, where especially women's sexuality must be restrained, as can be seen in certain sexual harassment cases (Fredman, 1997, pp. 322–4; McColgan, 1995). Intrusions by non-normative sexualities are seen as disruptive to the 'neutral' work environment. Similarly, liberal versions of anti-discrimination law adopt this perspective, seeking to render sexuality 'irrelevant' at work, without questioning the in-built heteronormative paradigm (from a gender equality perspective, see Lacey, 1987). Despite the incoherence of work being conceptualized as both public and private, as a rhetorical device this duality is alive and well in legal discourse.

In the context of our case study a few preliminary observations can be made relating to the deployment of 'public' and 'private'. In respect of behaviour between co-workers, the workplace is essentially coded as 'public'. It is not the private domain of any worker. Hence the standards of behaviour expected between workers are those which apply more generally in other areas of 'public' space and are regulated by the general rules of criminal (public) law and private law as it creates civil liability between strangers (in the context of bullying, see O'Donnell, 1999). In this one sense then, the workplace is no different from other 'public' spaces in which law discursively constructs sexualities.

However, once the employer is brought into the picture, the tension between 'public' and 'private' becomes more difficult, with competition between different discursive regimes. Public norms overlay the private norms set down by the employer. Sometimes the externally imposed public norms are weak, effectively allowing the employer's 'private' justice system to prevail. As a result, employers are generally free to set their own rules, both formal and informal, with regard to behaviour and discipline within the managerial prerogative (Fox, 1974). The lack of external control exerted in particular by the law on dismissal (Collins, 1992) permits the employer considerable power in regulating everyday (*inter alia* sexualized) interactions. Where the public norms are stronger, the employer's private rules may not prevail. Thus, for example, English law makes the employer responsible for a worker's health and safety, which includes protecting the worker from her co-workers (Deakin and Morris, 2001, pp. 316–21). In a similar fashion, the law on harassment also makes employers responsible for upholding public standards in their 'private' realm. Nevertheless, the courts have restricted this liability, permitting employers to argue that the conduct of the workers was their own 'private' matter and hence beyond employer control and responsibility (Fredman, 1997, p. 325). This judicial task of delimiting the scope of a worker's private conduct has not been made any easier by the fluid boundaries of work.

It is these difficult, contradictory and sometimes overlapping meanings of public and private which make the contribution of legal discourse to the relationship of organization and sexuality so rich and so compelling, as the case study below demonstrates.

Case study evidence: litigation by lesbians and gay men

The methodology used here is to consider judicial discourse in litigation by lesbians and gay men as evidence of a legal contribution to the heteronormativity of the workplace. The focus is not the substantive outcome of the cases, but the courts' construction of lesbians and gay men and the nature of the workplace. For, even in cases which can from a certain perspective be seen as a 'victory' for lesbians and/or gay men, the discourse invariably fails to challenge workplace heteronormativity. Germany and the UK were chosen for investigation (for a benchmarking of the German position, see Skidmore, 2001). The choice of these two legal systems reflects a desire to illustrate how, within 'mature' market-orientated European societies, law operates in a similar discursive fashion. While within the 'science' of law, emphasis is placed on pointing out differences in legal method between the 'common law' (English) and 'civil law' (Continental European) traditions (Zweigert and Kötz, 1998), when viewed as a discursive regulatory regime it is the similarities that are easier to spot. Despite the richness of data which the comparative method can produce (Kilpatrick, 2001) this approach is not without its dangers. National boundaries in legal science are often extremely tightly drawn, placing the comparative scholar at considerable risk of misinterpreting the 'foreign' system (Kahn-Freund, 1974; Wedderburn, 1995, chapter 6). The aim of using the comparator of the German legal system is limited to refuting any suggestion that the (re)production of heteronormative legal discourse is unique to English law, or the Anglo-American legal system. Whilst the *substantive details* of legal discourse do vary considerably, according to the nature of the legal provision in question and to the judicial method utilized, the evidence suggests that the main argument regarding law's discursive contribution to the organization/sexuality relation nevertheless holds true.

Four differing paradigms will be put forward in interpreting and organizing the case law to illustrate varied discursive techniques employed. Firstly, the technique of exclusion, by which a lesbian or gay presence is treated as incompatible with the workplace, will be examined. The second situation is one of the law's collusion in ostracizing lesbians and gay men from the workplace. In these circumstances, the discourse is one of 'hand-wringing', expressing regret with regard to homophobic behaviour, but refusing to reach interpretations which would offer lesbians and gay men any legal redress. A third variation involves a discourse which fails to valorize lesbians or gay men, or fails to take full account of their lives, for example, by not 'seeing' their same-sex partners. Finally, the liberal discourse of 'tolerance' or 'equality' will be interrogated, according to which lesbians and gay men are accepted into the workplace provided that they do not disturb the heterosexual hegemony.

Exclusion

'Exclusion' is the oldest and most obvious legal technique for ensuring the primacy of heterosexuality at work. According to this approach, the law sanctions an employer's refusal to hire, or decision to sack, a lesbian or gay man for a reason related to her/his sexuality. In this way an explicit employer choice to enforce heterosexuality is sustained and upheld. Whilst in recent years there is less evidence of this practice, 20 years or so ago this discourse was more prevalent.[1] Two British cases illustrate this approach (Bamforth, 1997, pp. 43–4). Where it became known that a maintenance worker at a holiday camp for children was gay, his employer sacked him because of the impact this would have on clients. His tribunal claim for unfair dismissal failed. The Appeal Tribunal upheld this decision. It concluded that the initial tribunal had applied the correct test to determine the fairness of the dismissal, asking itself how a 'reasonable employer' would have reacted on discovering that their employee was gay. It had been deduced from a psychiatrist's evidence that:

> a considerable proportion of employers would take the view that the employment of a homosexual should be restricted, particularly when required to work in proximity and contact with children. (*Saunders* v. *Scottish National Camps* [1980] IRLR, 174)

The Appeal Tribunal commented approvingly: 'That evidence the Tribunal were entitled to accept and it appears to have coincided with their own knowledge and experience.' Here popular prejudice, exercised by members of the initial tribunal and employers at large, was treated as sufficient legal justification for the dismissal.

Similarly where a lesbian was dismissed for wearing a consciousness-raising badge, 'lesbians ignite', the Appeal Tribunal upheld the employer's managerial prerogative to shape and discipline the workplace. It concluded that:

a reasonable employer, who is after all ultimately responsible for the interests of the business, can be allowed to decide, what upon reflection and
mature consideration, could be offensive to the customers and to fellow-
employees. (*Boychuk* v. *Symons* [1977] IRLR, 395, 396)

In this case, as in *Saunders*, the employer shied away from explicitly citing the
employee's sexuality as *the* reason for dismissal. However such a subterfuge
should not divert us from noting the courts' heteronormative discourse.

In the early 1980s German courts (approved by the highest labour court)
took a similar view with regard to the dismissal of a gay psychologist
employed by a family therapy centre controlled by the Protestant Church.
He was 'outed' when a third party revealed that he had been spotted in
'unambiguous' bars (in the words of the Law Report),[2] had formed a relationship with an 18 year-old man and was involved in a gay activist group.
The employer's view that its employee's homosexuality posed a 'danger'
and was incompatible with church teachings *per se* was accepted at face
value. Judicial deference to the employer permitted its subjective view of
'appropriate' conduct to prevail. In delimiting the scope of church employees' duty of obedience the court agreed that the decisive criterion was
'endangering the credibility of the church' (Malt, 1991; *NJW*, 1984, 1917).

In these cases, not only did the courts accept normative views with regard
to sexuality, treating 'deviant' (homo)sexuality as incompatible with the
workplace, but they also explicitly supported the religious employer in
enforcement of these norms. The confluence of 'public' and 'private' discourses can be thus observed in the exclusion of sexuality from the 'public'
sphere, combined with the employer's power to regulate its own 'private'
space.

The significance of this judicial reinforcement of social norms goes beyond
the fate of the lesbians and gay men directly affected. Whilst the cases were
decided many years ago, the iterative nature of legal discourse means that
they cast a long shadow. Legal commentators incorporate the judicial discourse into their 'authoritative' works, setting out what the law 'is' (Smith
and Thomas, 2000, p. 467). As a result, in subsequent cases courts are likely
to accept and reproduce the existing discourse until they find a route of interpretation which enables them to go beyond the earlier position.[3] Furthermore, the dearth of legal academic interest in the experience of lesbians and
gay men at work means that these cases and a few similar cases, to be
explored below, are the principal representation which lesbians and gay men
achieve within employment law.

'Regret'

The trope of 'regret' has been observed on several occasions in British
judicial discourse in recent years (no examples have been found in German

judicial discourse). It has emerged most clearly in situations where lesbians and gay men have sought to hold their employer responsible for workplace homophobic or lesbophobic harassment. Whilst upholding heteronormative practices, thereby erasing lesbian and gay experience, judges have on occasions tempered this with some palliative comment. For example, in relation to a campaign of abuse by pupils against a lesbian teacher which her school did nothing to prevent, referred to as a 'catalogue of unpleasant-ness' (judicial understatement), Mr. Justice Burton expressed his regret. He noted:

> [p]lainly we have, as would anyone, very considerable sympathy . . . for anyone who has suffered discrimination or abuse on grounds of his or her sexual orientation. But there is not yet a law proscribing such conduct . . .
> (*Pearce* v. *Governing Body of Mayfield School* [2000] IRLR, 548)

Comments of this nature arose in cases dealing with the interpretation of sex discrimination legislation. Legal advisers of lesbians and gay men have tried to persuade tribunals that it can be interpreted and extended to cover harass-ment and other forms of detriment suffered on grounds of sexual orienta-tion. The issue on which these cases have, however, foundered relates to the characteristics of the comparator (an essential element in discrimination law) with whom the applicant must be compared. In simple terms, where the applicant is a lesbian she has argued that her treatment should be compared with that accorded to a straight man and not a gay man (Skidmore, 1997). The logic utilized here depends upon the principle of sex discrimination law designed to isolate the difference of sex. It requires the comparator to be of the *opposite* sex, with all other 'relevant circumstances' unchanged. The stick-ing point lies, however, in the construction of the 'relevant circumstances.' If the characteristic at issue is seen as 'desiring a woman', then the comparison works and a woman attracted to another woman can be compared to a man attracted to a woman. Wintemute (1997) has demonstrated the soundness of this argument, recognized by Lord Prosser, dissenting, in the Scottish Court of Session (*Advocate General for Scotland* v. *McDonald* [2001] IRLR, 431) and by Lady Justice Hale in the Court of Appeal (*Pearce* v. *Governing Body of Mayfield School* [2001] IRLR, 669).

It is, however, also possible to treat 'homosexuality' as a relevant circum-stance of the applicant, and therefore to demand it as a characteristic of the comparator. This has been the approach taken by tribunals, leading to les-bians being compared with gay men, which results in reduced legal protec-tion under sex discrimination law in the case of homophobic or lesbophobic harassment. Only in much more limited circumstances have the courts granted statutory protection. For example, where a lesbian has suffered *worse* treatment than a gay man (or vice versa), this may give rise to unlawful sex discrimination (*Pearce* v. *Governing Body of Mayfield School* [2000] IRLR, p. 548). Similarly it has been held that sex discrimination law applies where a gay man is treated less favourably than a woman, *because he is a man*, but not because he is gay (*Smith v. Gardner Merchant* [1998] IRLR, p. 510).

The political choice made by the courts between these two alternative interpretations of the statutory provision has protected employers from bearing financial responsibility for the detriment that their lesbian and gay employees have suffered on grounds of sexual orientation. Whatever the judicial motivation for preferring the less lesbian/gay-friendly interpretation, and however it is linguistically dressed up as being a factual rather than a legal issue, the outcome in terms of organization/sexuality is stark. The legal silence or erasure of homosexual harassment is indicative of judicial support being offered to 'appropriate' heterosexuality. Heterosexuality at work is actively managed, ensuring that hegemonic masculinity is not permitted to become too unruly. Hence judicial discourse pays at least lip-service to some women's claims of harassment (if they fulfil certain stereotypes of femininity: Flynn (1996) and Schultz (1998) on her reading of US case law). However, harassment of lesbians and gay men is a constituent element in the practice of heteronormativity. From this perspective it would be unnecessary and counter-productive for law to intervene, valorizing lesbian and gay experience. Judicial 'regret' camouflages the power relations at stake. By pretending to be power*less*, unable to help lesbians and gay men, the judiciary are in fact exercising considerable power, helping to perpetuate the heteronormative *status quo*.

Refusal to valorize

Through a discourse which refuses to valorize, courts do not express 'regret' for not seeing lesbians or gay men, but indicate clearly that they consider them to be 'second-class' workers, who should not expect their 'lifestyle' to be valorized. This forceful assertion of a heteronormative ideology can be seen in two parallel sets of proceedings, one wholly within the German system and the other which began in the British courts at around the same time and which was subject to the adjudication of the European Court of Justice.

Both cases concerned the rights of lesbians and gay men to have their same-sex partners 'seen' through the eyes of employment law. In the German case, a gay civil servant failed in his claim to have a 'marital supplement' paid in respect of his same-sex partner (Federal Labour Court, *BAGE*, 85, 375; Federal Constitutional Court: EzA, Art 3 GG Nr 72a). This supplement was paid to married workers only. At the time, same-sex 'domestic' or 'registered' partnerships did not exist in German law, nor could same-sex couples enter a civil marriage (Rauhofer, 1998; Schimmel and Heun, 2001). All the courts seised of the case took essentially the same view. They held that, notwithstanding the constitutional rights of lesbians and gay men, neither the state, employers, nor 'social partners' were obliged to grant them, in the context of a same-sex relationship, the same benefits enjoyed by heterosexual married couples. The parties to the collective agreement, in setting the rates of pay, were free to treat married employees more favourably. Such a preference was fully in accordance with the weight attached to marriage and the family in the Constitution. The legal rights and duties concomitant with marriage could not be compared with those of an unmarried couple (straight or gay). Not satisfied with this formal distinction between marriage and other relationships of cohabitation and/or mutual support, the Federal Labour Court launched into an essentializing diatribe on the function of marriage, demonstrating its heteronormative perspective (noted with approval by legal commentators Marschner [1998] and Marhold [1998]).

> . . . [A] same-sex relationship is in practical terms in at least one respect not comparable with marriage. It is in contrast to marriage not suited to the reproduction of the population. It is in these circumstances of no great importance that not all marriages are concluded with this aim [of reproduction] in mind and that also some marriages remain involuntarily childless. The parties to the collective agreement in their setting of norms were permitted to generalize. This generalization by which only relationships which are as a rule presumptively capable of reproduction are benefited is objectively justifiable and takes into account that marriage is above all constitutionally supported because it is designed to facilitate the partner's legal protection when founding a family by having children together. (Federal Labour Court, BAGE, 85, 375, 379)

The Court's valorizing of heterosexual marriage, insisting on its hierarchically superior position to a same-sex relationship, is a clear illustration of this discursive use of law in promoting heterosexuality. The Court expressed no sympathy for the gay litigant, and indicated clearly to the social partners that they, too, need feel no shame in ignoring the domestic partners of lesbian and gay employees. A further twist on the interpretation of 'public' and 'private' arguments can be discerned barely below the surface in this case. Whereas same-sex relationships are banished to the 'private' sphere and erased from the workplace, opposite-sex relationships which are sealed with marriage are affirmed. Marriage is not treated as a private contractual relationship, but is given a 'public' function because of its support for reproduction, which is in the general interest.

The European Court of Justice took a similar approach in assessing the staff travel policy of a British train operator (*Grant* v. *South West Trains* case C-249/96 [1998] ECR, I-621, discussed in Armstrong [1998]; Bell [1999]; Barnard [1999]). The employer refused concessionary rail travel for the same-sex partner of an employee, whereas an opposite-sex partner (married or not) was so entitled. In upholding the employer's policy, the Court of Justice reflected upon the case law of the European Court on Human Rights, which had repeatedly confirmed the second-class status of lesbians and gay men with regard to marriage and the 'family'. Applying this it stated:

> It follows that, . . . stable relationships between two persons of the same sex are not regarded as equivalent to marriages or stable relationships outside marriage between persons of the opposite sex. Consequently, an employer is not required by Community law to treat the situation of a person who has a stable relationship with a partner of the same sex as equivalent to that of a person who is married to or has a stable relationship outside marriage with a partner of the opposite sex. (*Grant*, judgment of the Court, para. 35)

It thus upheld, as already noted by Advocate-General Elmer in his Opinion in the case, the employer's private morality (*Grant*, Opinion of AG Elmer, point 40). It refused to penetrate this domain of private regulation, supporting the employer's choice not to 'see' lesbians. The message was very clear: the Court was unwilling to valorize homosexuality and used its discursive technique to support heteronormative practices.

'Tolerance'

The final technique to be considered here is that of 'tolerance', where homosexuality is both simultaneously recognized and denied by the courts. This approach emerges clearly from German courts in their application of Constitutional principles affording some protection to lesbians and gay men (Skidmore, 2001). The 'rights' of the individual lesbian or gay man are acknowledged, while disturbing the dominant heterosexual ideology as little as possible. For example the Federal Labour Court held that it was a breach of the contractual good faith norm to dismiss a gay man during his probationary period, *solely* on grounds of sexuality (Federal Labour Court, *NZA*, 1994, p. 1080). However it made clear that if the worker's sexuality had 'disturbed' the heterosexuality of the workplace, the dismissal would not necessarily have been in breach of contract. It offered several reasons why, had they been put forward by the employer, the applicant's sexuality might have been relevant:

> Given the facts (as found by the lower court) requirements of the defendant potentially capable of justifying its conduct — for example, the effects of the applicant's lifestyle on his ability to work together with co-workers, the atmosphere of the workplace, relationships with customers, etc. — cannot be assumed. The defendant has not as yet sought to rely on such arguments (p. 1082).

It took the view that (homo)sexuality *per se* was a private matter and not a relevant matter for the employer. It went on:

> Design of the private sphere lies outside the scope of the employer's influence and is restricted by duties arising out of the employment contract, only in so far as private conduct has an effect on the employment sphere and leads to its disruption (p. 1082).

The German court's ideological separation of public and private fails to take into account heterosexuality's intrusion into the 'public' sphere. The normalization of heterosexuality has rendered it invisible in this judicial discourse. Thus 'tolerating' lesbian and gay workers accommodates them only in so far as they 'fit in' by obeying heterosexual norms. Although it is not as extreme a technique as excluding lesbians and gay men from the workplace, nevertheless it permits their participation only to the extent that the space and interests of others are not infringed. Furthermore, it may discipline those who appear to the employer to be lesbian or gay.

This public/private distinction can also be observed in a decision to allow a gay man to begin a training contract in a residential home for disabled children controlled by the Catholic Church (Lörrach Labour Court, *AuR*, 1993, 151). The defendant had argued that the applicant's previous conduct during an internship, in once having a nocturnal male visitor and once walking hand in hand with his boyfriend out of the home's grounds into the nearby village, was a 'demonstrative representation' of homosexuality. This was said to be incompatible with Catholic theology and rendered him unsuitable for a training contract. In the first instance the court concluded that this 'private' conduct could be separated from the applicant's workplace *persona*. Essentializing greatly, it treated homosexuality as a fixed biological phenomenon, comparing it to the orbiting of the planets, which the church had to recognize. On appeal, the Regional Labour Court of Baden-Württemberg (*NZA*, 1994, p. 416) was more explicit in its discussion of the public/private distinction. It found insufficient evidence that the worker had lived 'openly' as a gay man or had represented homosexuality in public, such as to contravene Catholic teachings.

The applicant was clearly a 'good' homosexual who could be 'tolerated' because he would not destabilize the heterosexuality of the workplace. Indeed, he led evidence to this effect. It is not known whether this was a strategic choice for the purposes of litigation (in another context, see Beresford, 1998) or whether he himself believed in the public/private distinction (as did some of the interviewees of Maas [1999]). Whatever his motivation, however, this litigant offered to live off the premises away from the children's home. Furthermore his evidence, that he had never in any way demonstrated his homosexuality at work, was not contradicted by the employer. Thus, as his sexuality was sufficiently hidden and non-threatening, his 'rights' could be accommodated.

The importance of this technique of 'tolerating' lesbians and gay men for the maintenance of heterosexuality through law must be recognized. It is a discourse which liberals, if unchallenged, are likely to present as positive, emerging as it does from the interpretation of provisions embodying the values of equality and respect for human dignity and personality. However such discourse must be seen in the context of the 'public' heterosexualized space of work. To uphold equality or rights to human dignity against a backdrop which is not neutral, but heteronormative, is highly problematic. It demands that lesbians and gay men in exercising such rights, 'leave their sexuality at home' in the same way that heterosexuals are (erroneously) believed to do. Thus a discourse of neutrality, tolerance and rendering sexuality 'irrelevant' in reality maintains the *status quo* of the workplace and leaves the dominant ideology intact.

Conclusion

This case study has illustrated some of the varied facets of legal heteronormative discourse. As was stated at the outset, these are not the only examples to be found. An analysis of equal pay or sexual harassment case law is very likely to reveal further veins of heteronormativity. For many readers this outcome has probably caused no great surprise. Given the pervasiveness of heteronormativity it would have been more surprising to discover that judicial discourse is immune from its influence.

What is important, once armed with the results of the case study, is to interrogate afresh the reciprocal relation of organization/sexuality in an attempt to incorporate the legal paradigm. When viewed from the perspective of sexuality in organizations we can note that judicial discourse produces an image of organizations in which certain constructions and manifestations of sexualities are considered to be alien and incompatible. The employer's (economic) interest in regulating and disciplining sexuality is in the circumstances seen as prima-facie legitimate. Thus, the picture emerges of a legal construction of organization which does not significantly differ from that put forward by social science theory and practice, as discussed earlier in this article. Within this construction embodied sexualities are actively managed and harnessed as part of the organizational culture.

Turning the matter on its head, we can also see law's discursive organization of sexuality. Not only does sexuality become incorporated into organizational practice, but equally sexuality becomes organized through the workplace. The evidence of the case study shows judicial discourse rejecting certain ontological forms of sexuality as being deviant and unacceptable. Lesbians and gay men were generally constructed as being in principle dangerous, although as 'victims' (of their own sexuality) they could at times be pitied or even tolerated, especially if they appeared in other respects to conform to the heteronormative world-view. This style of legal discourse is well-known in other contexts, particularly as regards the criminal law and its construction of male sexuality (Moran, 1996). What is interesting here is the confluence of the public policy discourse expressed through the judicial voice with that of the employer/organization in constructing hierarchies of sexualities. Often the employer's private view was given a public seal of approval.

This system of legal discourse consisting of legislation, judicial interpretation and academic comment should not be seen as sealed, but as permeable. It allows ideas and constructions to pass in both directions, albeit that meanings and interpretations attached to them may well vary considerably depending on context. Accounts of organization and of sexualities already in circulation can enter into legal discourse. Equally, legal doctrine and discourse can filter through into non-expert discourses and become part of cultural knowledge. It is not possible here to go into greater depth and consider the full complexity of the dynamic and reciprocal relationship between legal and non-legal discourses. It is sufficient for the present to acknowledge that legal discourse co-exists along with, and is interdependent upon, other frames of reference (Teubner, 1989). Future theorizing of the organization/sexuality relation would benefit from taking this into greater account.

The argument presented here cannot easily be universalized. The role played by legal discourse varies between cultural locations. The western view of the 'law' is likely to be inappropriate in other societies. Similarly, the theorizing of sexualities has been shown to be historically and culturally specific (Weeks, 1989). The world of work, too, as analysed in the writings of Acker (1990) and Adkins (1995), is contingent on a particular set of economic production relations. Notwithstanding these caveats, in the systems considered here where legal discourse clearly produces constructions of organization and sexualities located in their respective cultures it would be foolhardy to ignore a legal perspective. Those of us interested in the place and process of work, its meanings for men and women, its norms and their transgression, whether as students of geography, sociology, organization studies, or law have much to learn from one another. This problematizing of the sexuality/organization relation, as illuminated by the judicial discourse relating to the treatment of lesbians and gay men at work, is but one way to begin the dialogue between law and other paradigms of inquiry.

Acknowledgments

This research has been supported by a Marie Curie Fellowship of the European Community programme, 'Improving Human Potential', under contract number HPMF-CT-2001-01176. An earlier version of this paper was presented at the Law and Society Conference, Budapest, July 2001. The author is grateful to Davina Cooper, Iain McDonald and Tonia Novitz and the journal's anonymous referees for their comments on earlier drafts.

AuR	Arbeit und Recht
BAGE	Bundesarbeitsgerichtentscheidungen
ECR	European Court Reports
EzA	Entscheidungen zum Arbeitsrecht
IRLR	Industrial Relations Law Reports
NJW	Neue Juristische Wochenschrift
NZA	Neue Zeitschrift für Arbeitsrecht

Notes

1. There is no clear precedent in British law which indicates that this approach is no longer sustainable.
2. All translations from the German are the author's own.
3. While the common law approach takes a stricter view with regard to the doctrine of precedent than the German civil law system, the role of previously decided cases and academic comment thereupon cannot be underestimated in either system.

References

Acker, J. (1990) Hierarchies, jobs, bodies: a theory of gendered organisations. *Gender and Society*, 4, 139–58.

Adkins, L. (1995) *Gendered Work: Sexuality, Family and the Labour Market*. Buckingham: Open University Press.

Armstrong, K. (1998) Tales of the Community: sexual orientation discrimination and EC law. *Journal of Social Welfare and Family Law*, 20,4, 455–68.

Ashiagbor, D. (1999) The intersection between gender and 'race' in the labour market: lessons for anti-discrimination law. In Morris, A. and O'Donnell, T. (eds) *Feminist Perspectives on Employment Law*. London: Cavendish.

Bamforth, N. (1997) *Sexuality, morals and justice: a theory of lesbian and gay rights law*. London: Cassell.

Barnard, C. (1999) Some are more equal than others: the decision of the Court of Justice. In *Grant* v. *South-West Trains Cambridge Yearbook of European Legal Studies*, Vol. 1, 147–73.

Bell, D. and Binnie, J. (2000) *The Sexual Citizen: Queer Politics and Beyond*. Cambridge: Polity Press.

Bell, D., Binnie, J., Cream, J. and Valentine, G. (1994) All hyped up and no place to go. *Gender, Place and Culture*, 1, 31–47.

Bell, M. (1999) Shifting conceptions of sexual discrimination at the Court of Justice from *P* v. *S* to *Grant* v. *SWT*. *European Law Journal*, 5,1, 82.

Beresford, S. (1998) The lesbian mother: questions of gender and sexuality. In Moran, L., Monk, D. and Beresford, S. (eds) *Legal Queeries*, pp. 57–67. London: Cassell.

Binnie, J. and Valentine, G. (1999) Geographies of sexuality — a review of progress. *Progress in Human Geography*, 23,2, 175–87.

Sexuality and Identity

Brewis, J. (2002) 'When a body meet a body . . .': experiencing the female body at work. In McKie, L. and Watson, N. (eds) *Organising bodies: Institutions, Policy and Work*, pp. 166–84. Basingstoke: Macmillan.

Brewis, J. and Sinclair, J. (2000) Exploring embodiment: women, biology and work. In Hassard, J., Holliday, R. and Willmott, H. (eds) *Body and Organisation*. London: Sage.

Burke, M. (1993) *Coming Out of the Blue: British Police Officers Talk about their Lives in The Job as Lesbians, Gays and Bisexuals*. London: Cassell.

Burrell, G. and Hearn, J. (1989) The sexuality of organization. In Hearn, J., Sheppard, D., Tancred-Sherriff, P. and Burrell, G. (eds) *The Sexuality of Organization*, pp. 1–28. London: Sage.

Butler, J. (1990) *Gender Trouble: Feminism and the Subversion of Identity*. London: Routledge.

Butler, J. (1991) Imitation and gender insubordination. In Fuss, D. (ed.) *Inside/Out*, pp. 13–31. London: Routledge.

Byre, A. (1993) Equality and non-discrimination. In Waaldijk, K. and Clapham, A. (eds) *Homosexuality: a European Community Issue*, pp. 207–19. Dordrecht: Martinus Nijhoff.

Chapman, A. (1995) Sexuality and workplace oppression. *Melbourne University Law Review*, 20,2, 311–49.

Collier, R. (1995) *Masculinity, Law and the Family*. London: Routledge.

Collier, R. (1999) 'Feminising' the workplace? Law, the 'good parent' and the 'problem of men'. In Morris, A. and O'Donnell, T. (eds) *Feminist Perspectives on Employment Law*, pp. 161–81. London: Cavendish.

Collins, H. (1992) *Justice in Dismissal*. Oxford: Oxford University Press.

Conaghan, J. (1999) Feminism and labour law: contesting the terrain. In Morris, A. and O'Donnell, T. (eds) *Feminist Perspectives on Employment Law*. London: Cavendish.

Connell, R.W. (1995) *Masculinities*. Oxford: Polity.

Cross, S. and Bagilhole, B. (2002) Girls' jobs for the boys? Men, masculinity and non-traditional occupations. *Gender, Work & Organization*, 9,2, 204–26.

Deakin, S. and Morris, G. (2001) *Labour Law*. 3rd. edn. London: Butterworths.

Duncan, N. (1996) Renegotiating gender and sexuality in public and private spaces. In Duncan, N. (ed.) *Bodyspace: Destabilizing Geographies of Gender and Sexuality*, pp. 127–44. London: Routledge.

Dunne, G. (1997) *Lesbian Lifestyles*. Basingstoke: Macmillan.

Equal Opportunities Review (1997) Equality for lesbians and gay men in the workplace. *Equal Opportunities Review*, 74, 20–7.

Epstein, R. (1984) In defense of the contract at will. *University of Chicago Law Review*, 51,4, 947–82.

Evans, D. (1989) Section 28: law, myth and paradox. *Critical Social Policy*, 27, 73–95.

Flynn, L. (1996) Interpretation and disputed accounts in sexual harassment cases: Stewart v. Cleveland Guest (Engineering) Ltd. *Feminist Legal Studies*, 4,1, 109.

Fox, A. (1974) *Beyond Contract: Work, Power and Trust Relations*. London: Faber and Faber.

Fredman, S. (1997) *Women and the Law*. Oxford: Oxford University Press.

Gooding, C. (1994) *Disabling Laws, Enabling Acts: Disability Rights in Britain and America*. London: Pluto.

Halford, S., Savage, M. and Witz, A. (1997) *Gender, Career and Organisations: Current Developments in Banking, Nursing and Local Government*. Basingstoke: Macmillan.

Hall, M. (1989) Private experiences in the public domain: lesbians in organisations. In Hearn, J., Sheppard, D., Tancred-Sherriff, P. and Burrell, G. (eds) *The Sexuality of Organization*, pp. 125–38. London: Sage.

Harrison, V. (1996) Using EC law to challenge sexual orientation discrimination at work. In Hervey, T. and O'Keeffe, D. (eds) *Sex Equality Law in the European Union*, pp. 267–80. Chichester: Wiley.

Hassard, J., Holliday, R. and Willmott, H. (2000) Introduction: the body and organization. In Hassard, J., Holliday, R. and Willmott, H. (eds) *Body and Organization*, pp. 1–14. London: Sage.

Homosexuality Policy Assessment Team (HPAT) (1996) *Report of the Homosexuality Policy Assessment Team*. London: Ministry of Defence.

Humphrey, J. (1999) Organizing sexualities, organized inequalities: lesbians and gay men in public service occupations. *Gender, Work & Organization*, 6,3, 134–51.

Humphrey, J. (2000) Cracks in the feminist mirror? Research and reflections on lesbians and gay men working together. *Feminist Review*, 66, 95–130.

Isaacs, D. and Poole, M. (1996) Becoming a man and becoming a nurse: three men's stories *Journal of Gender Studies*, 5,1, 39–47.

Jackson, S. (1996) Heterosexuality as a problem for feminist theory. In Adkins, L. and Merchant, V. (eds) *Sexualizing the Social: Power and the Organisation of Sexuality*, pp. 15–33. London: Macmillan.

Kahn-Freund, O. (1974) On the uses and misuses of comparative law. *Modern Law Review*, 37,1, 1–27.

Kilpatrick, C. (2001) Gender equality: a fundamental dialogue. In Sciarra, S. (ed.) *Labour Law in the Courts*, pp. 31–130. Oxford: Hart.

Knoll, C., Edinger, M. and Reisbeck, G. (1997) *Grenzgänge: Schwule und Lesben in der Arbeitswelt*. Munich: Profil.

Lacey, N. (1987) Legislation against sex discrimination: questions from a feminist perspective. *Journal of Law and Society*, 14,4, 411–21.

Lee, D. (2000) Hegemonic masculinity and male feminisation: the sexual harassment of men at work. *Journal of Gender Studies*, 9,2, 141–55.

Maas, J. (1999) *Identität und Stigma-Mangement von homosexuellen Führungskräften*. Wiesbaden: Deutscher Universitäts-Verlag.

Malt, M. (1991) . . . *ist unstreitig homosexuell: Diskriminierung von Lesben und Schwulen in Arbeits-und Zivilrecht*. Hamburg: Frühlingserwachen.

Marhold, F. (1998) untitled case note in loose-leaf collection: *EzBAT § 29 BAT Nr. 22*.

Marschner, A. (1998) untitled case note in loose-leaf collection: *Entscheidungen zum Arbeitsrecht GG Art. 3 Nr. 72*.

McColgan, A. (1995) Sexual harassment, sex discrimination and unfair dismissal. *Industrial Law Journal*, 24,2, 181–6.

McDowell, L. (1997) *Capital Culture: Gender at Work in the City*. Oxford: Blackwell.

McGhee, D. (1998) Looking and acting the part: gays in the armed forces — a case of passing masculinity. *Feminist Legal Studies*, 6,2, 205.

McKinnon, C. (1979) *Sexual Harassment of Working Women*. New Haven: Yale University Press.

Monk, D. (1998) Beyond section 28: law governance and sex education. In Moran, L., Monk, D. and Beresford, S. (eds) *Legal Queeries*. London: Cassell.

Moran, L. (1996) *The Homosexual(ity) of Law*. London: Routledge.

Moran, L., Skeggs, B., Tyrer, P. and Corteen, K. (2001) Property, boundary, exclusion: making sense of hetero-violence in safer spaces. *Social and Cultural Geography*, 2,4, 407–20.

Mückenberger, U. and Deakin, S. (1989) From deregulation to a European floor of rights: labour law, flexibilisation and the European single market. *Zeitschrift für ausländisches und internationales Arbeits-und Sozialrecht*, 3,3, 157–206.

Myslik, W. (1996) Renegotiating the social/sexual identities of places. In Duncan, N. (ed.) *Bodyspace: Destabilizing Geographies of Gender and Sexuality*. London: Routledge.

O'Donnell, T. (1999) The sweat of the brow or the breaking of the heart? In Morris, A. and O'Donnell, T. (eds) *Feminist Perspectives on Employment Law*, pp. 61–88. London: Cavendish.

O'Donovan, K. (1985) *Sexual Divisions in Law*. London: Weidenfeld and Nicolson.

Owens, R. (1997) Working in the sex market. In Naffine, N. and Owens, R. (eds) *Sexing the Subject of Law*. Sydney: Law Book Company.

Palmer, A. (1993) *Some are More Equal than Others*. London: Stonewall.

Parker, M. (2002) Queering management and organization *Gender, Work & Organization*, 9,2, 146–66.

Pringle, R. (1989) *Secretaries Talk: Sexuality, Power and Work*. London: Verso.

Rauhofer, J. (1998) The possibility of a registered partnership under German law. In Moran, L., Monk, D. and Beresford, S. (eds) *Legal Queeries*, pp. 68–80. London: Cassell.

Rich, A. (1980) Compulsory heterosexuality and lesbian existence. *Signs: Journal of Women in Culture and Society*, 5,4, 631–60.

Schimmel, R. and Heun, S. (2001) The legal situation of same-sex partnerships in Germany: an overview. In Wintemute, R. and Andenaes, M. (eds) *Legal Recognition of Same-Sex Partnerships*, pp. 575–90. Oxford: Hart.

Schultz, V. (1998) Reconceptualizing sexual harassment. *Yale Law Journal*, 107,6, 1683–805.

Sheldon, S. (1999) ReConceiving masculinity: imagining men's reproductive bodies in law. *Journal of Law and Society*, 26,2, 129–49.

Skidmore, P. (1997) Sex, gender and comparators in employment discrimination. *Industrial Law Journal*, 26,1, 51–61.

Skidmore, P. (1999) Dress to impress: employer regulation of gay and lesbian appearance. *Social and Legal Studies*, 8,4, 509–29.

Skidmore, P. (2001) Improving the position of lesbians and gay men at work in the light of the framework directive for equal treatment in employment: a German case study. In Dashwood, A., Spencer, J., Ward, A. and Hillion, C. (eds) *Cambridge Yearbook of European Legal Studies*, Vol. 3, pp. 425–55.

Smith, I. and Thomas, G. (2000) *Smith and Wood's Industrial Law*. 7th edn. London: Butterworths.

Snape, D., Thomson, K. and Chetwynd, M. (1995) *Discrimination against Gay Men and Lesbians*. London: Social and Community Planning Research.

Stychin, C. (1995) *Law's Desire*. London: Routledge.

Taylor, S. and Tyler, M. (2000) Emotional labour and sexual difference and in the airline industry. *Work, Employment and Society*. 14,1, 77–95.

Teubner, G. (1989) How the law thinks: towards a constructivist epistemology of law. *Law and Society Review* 23,5, 727–57.

Thomson, M. (1996) Embodying the body: the reproductive body and employment exclusion *Social and Legal Studies*, 5,2, 243–67.

Valentine, G. (1996) (Re)negotiating the 'heterosexual street'. In Duncan, N. (ed.) *Bodyspace: Destabilizing Geographies of Gender and Sexuality*. London: Routledge.

Ver.di (2002) *ver.di-Report Lesben und Schwule Bisexuelle und Transgender* no. 12. Ver.di: Berlin.

Waaldijk, K. (1993) The legal situation in the member states. In Waaldijk, K. and Clapham, A. (eds) *Homosexuality: a European Community Issue*, pp. 71–130. Dordrecht: Martinus Nijhoff.

Warner, M. (2000) Zones of privacy. In Butler, J., Guillory, J. and Thomas, K. (eds) *What's Left of Theory?* pp. 75–113. Routledge: New York.

Wedderburn, B. (Lord) (1986) *The Worker and the Law*. 3rd. edn. Harmondsworth: Penguin.

Wedderburn, B. (Lord) (1995) *Labour Law and Freedom: Further Essays in Labour Law*. London: Lawrence and Wishart.

Weeks, J. (1989) *Sex, Politics and Society: The Regulation of Sexuality since 1800*. 2nd. edn. London: Longman.

Wintemute, R. (1997) Recognising new kinds of direct sex discrimination: transsexualism, sexual orientation and dress codes. *Modern Law Review*, 60,3, 334–59.

Zillich, N. (1988) *Homosexuelle Männer im Arbeitsleben*. Frankfurt am Main: Campus.

Zweigert, K. and Kötz, H. (1998) *An Introduction to Comparative Law*. 3rd. edn. Oxford: Oxford University Press.

[14]

SOME REFLECTIONS ON THE STUDY OF SEXUAL ORIENTATION BIAS IN THE LEGAL PROFESSION

William B. Rubenstein*

The [U.S. Court of Appeals for the] Ninth Circuit takes pride, justifiably, in the fact that it is the first federal court to have conducted a study of gender bias in the judicial system. We voted at our 1993 conference to conduct a similar circuit-wide study of racial, ethnic and religious bias in the judicial system. However, when a lawyer raised the subject of bias based on sexual orientation, an embarrassed silence followed. Finally, the chief judge stepped in and explained that we couldn't take on too many problems at one time. It is doubtful that the answer convinced anyone. The subject just made our judges and lawyers too uncomfortable.[1]

I. INTRODUCTION

In the past seven years, eleven bar associations have undertaken studies and issued reports about sexual orientation bias in the legal profession. It is fair to assume that this is only a beginning, and that calls for such studies will continue to escalate in the coming years. This is, therefore, an opportune time to evaluate what has been accomplished to date and to consider how future efforts can be even more efficacious. In what follows, I describe the contexts from which the sexual orientation bias studies arise (Part II); look at how the reports have been sponsored and issued (Part III); describe the methodologies that have been used and analyze their strengths and weaknesses (Part IV); re-

---

    * Acting Professor, UCLA School of Law. For their thoughtful comments and assistance, I am indebted to Rick Abel, Jennifer Durkin, Maryann Gray, Ruth E. Harlow, and Arthur Leonard.
    1. Stephen Reinhardt, *The Court and the Closet; Why Should Federal Judges Have to Hide Homosexuality?*, WASH. POST, Oct. 31, 1993, *available in* 1993 WL 2091078.

count and consider the meaning of the findings that have been documented (Part V); consider the recommendations that have been issued (Part VI); and, finally, provide a set of suggestions for future efforts (Part VII).

The three primary conclusions that I draw, discussed more fully below, are the following. First, the bar is to be commended for the initial steps it has taken in surveying sexual orientation bias — no other profession can claim this degree of self-analysis and concern. Yet the studies conclusively demonstrate just how preliminary these steps have been. No judiciary has yet to issue a report on sexual orientation bias. All eleven reports have been issued by bar associations, and by bar associations in only a handful of large cities. As Judge Reinhardt's statement above implies, it would be an important step for the judiciary to embrace the normative message of these studies and to lend its imprimatur — nationwide — to ensuring equal justice for all Americans regardless of their sexual orientation.

Second, these reports constitute a significant portion of all of the existing empirical work about anti-gay bias. Yet methodological problems with surveying gay people, coupled with the fact that it is so obvious that such bias exists, lead to the conclusion that future studies should focus more on making concrete, achievable recommendations; on developing model sexual orientation policies; and on the perpetuation of such programs, rather than on the task of quantitative analysis which will, inevitably, never satisfy its critics.

Finally, these bias studies have the potential to produce more justice for gay people, not just more professional stability for queer attorneys. To this end, the studies should be geared towards culminating with judicial education programs and such programs should be developed, tested, and implemented.

Pro-gay advocates can be emboldened by the fact that sexual orientation bias is already outlawed by canons of judicial ethics. Society knows that sexual orientation bias exists and has largely accepted that it is bad. The time has come to devote energy to doing something about it by training judges to provide more justice and, simultaneously, by propelling gay people onto the bench.

II. THE CONTEXT IN WHICH SEXUAL ORIENTATION BIAS STUDIES ARISE

The sexual orientation bias studies emerge out of several distinct contexts. First, the studies emulate similar efforts to study gender and racial bias at the bar and in the courts. The first gender bias study was conducted by the New Jersey court system in 1982. By 1988, the Conference of Chief Justices and the Conference of State Court Administrators had adopted resolutions "urging every state supreme court chief justice to establish a task force 'devoted to the study of gender bias in the court system.'"[2] Within a decade, more than thirty state judiciaries had convened task forces on gender bias and nearly thirty reports had been issued.[3] In the early 1990s, spurred in part by congressional encouragement,[4] the United States Courts of Appeals for the D.C. and Ninth Circuits established task forces to study gender bias in the federal courts and nearly all of the Circuits have since followed.[5] Interestingly, studies of racial bias in the courts and bar came later;[6] the first race bias studies appeared in the

---

2. Lynn Hecht Schafran, *Gender and Justice: Florida and the Nation*, 42 U. FLA. L. REV. 181, 186 (1990) [hereinafter Schafran, *Gender and Justice*] (quoting Conference of Chief Justices, *Resolution XVIII, Task Forces on Gender Bias and Minority Concerns* (adopted Aug. 4, 1988), *published in* 26 CT. REV. 5 (1989); Conference of State Court Administrators, *Resolution I, Task Forces on Gender Bias and Minority Concerns* (adopted Aug. 4, 1988)).

3. *See* Vicki C. Jackson, *Empiricism, Gender, and Legal Pedagogy: An Experiment in a Federal Courts Seminar at Georgetown University Law Center*, 83 GEO. L.J. 461, 462 n.5 (1994) ("By 1994, task forces on gender bias had started in at least 38 state court jurisdictions, and 28 had issued reports."); *see also* Judith Resnik, *Ambivalence: The Resiliency of Legal Culture in the United States*, 45 STAN. L. REV. 1525, 1544-46 (1993) (listing 24 gender bias reports) [hereinafter Resnik, *Ambivalence*].

4. Title IV of the Violent Crime Control and Law Enforcement Act of 1994, codified at 42 U.S.C.A. § 14001 (West 1995), now encourages the circuit judicial councils to conduct studies of gender bias in their circuits and to implement recommended reforms, requires the Administrative Office of the U.S. Courts to serve as a clearinghouse for such reports, and authorizes the Federal Judicial Center to develop model programs on gender bias issues.
Jackson, *supra* note 3, at 464 n.11.

5. *See* Special Comm. on Race and Ethnicity, *Report of the Special Committee on Race and Ethnicity to the D.C. Circuit Task Force on Gender, Race, and Ethnic Bias*, 64 GEO. WASH. L. REV. 189, 198 n.12 (1996) [hereinafter *Special Report*] ("In addition to the D.C. Circuit, nine circuits currently have task forces operating."). On the reluctance of the federal courts to pursue studies of bias, *see* Judith Resnik, *"Naturally" Without Gender: Women, Jurisdiction, and the Federal Courts*, 66 N.Y.U. L. REV. 1682, 1685-89 (1991) [hereinafter Resnik, *"Naturally"*].

6. This is interesting because we tend to think of the 1970s women's rights movement efforts following on the heels of the black civil rights movement of the 1960s. It is less usual to uncover an area of progressive activity that has commenced

late 1980s.[7] By 1996, nineteen states had formed task forces devoted to studying racial and ethnic bias and nine studies had been completed.[8]

The sexual orientation bias studies not only follow from these earlier efforts, they often overlap with them. A lesbian fired from her job may find it difficult to determine whether her employer was sexist or homophobic.[9] More generally, homophobia, by forcing particular gender roles on individuals (e.g., women should sexually desire men), can be seen as a manifestation of sexism.[10] Thus, many individuals who fall at the intersection of these identity categories may find themselves the subjects of a number of different types of bias studies.

While sexual orientation, gender, and race studies arise out of similar concerns about bias in the legal profession, neither the bar nor the bench has been as quick to embrace studies of anti-gay bias.[11] Two factors may explain this disparity. By the time judiciaries embraced the study of gender and race bias, legal

---

in the women's rights movement and then been replicated by race-based civil rights efforts.

7. *See Special Report, supra* note 5, at 197 n.6 ("The first state task force to study race and ethnicity was formed in Michigan in 1987; a final report was issued in 1989.").

8. *See id.* at 196-97. The Information Service of the National Center for State Court maintains a website containing a bibliography of "Materials from States and Individual Task Forces and Commissions on Racial and Ethnic Bias in the Courts." *See* Information Serv. of the Nat'l Ctr. for State Courts, *Racial and Ethnic Bias in the Courts Bibliography* (last modified April 1997) <http://www.ncsc.dni.us/is/Bib2_1.htm>.

9. For example, participants to one sexual orientation bias study stated:
I had one highly negative evaluation that can probably be most directly attributed to my open feminist politics rather than homophobia (although the fact that as a female employee, I didn't act stereotypically toward supervisor complicates analysis).

It's difficult to be a rainmaker without a husband to drag to dinner. On the other hand this is a problem for all single women, not just lesbians.
Committee on Lesbian and Gay Men in the Legal Profession, *Report on the Experience of Lesbians and Gay Men in the Legal Profession*, 48 Rec. Ass'n B. City N.Y. 843, 855, 870 (1993) [hereinafter *ABCNY 1993 Report*].

10. *Cf.* Price Waterhouse v. Hopkins, 490 U.S. 228 (1989) (holding that gender role deviation constitutes sex discrimination). *See generally* Francisco Valdes, *Queers, Sissies, Dykes, and Tomboys: Deconstructing the Conflation of "Sex," "Gender," and "Sexual Orientation" in Euro-American Law and Society*, 83 Cal. L. Rev. 1 (1995).

11. *See* Reinhardt, *supra* note 1; *see also supra* text accompanying notes 3-8 (discussing 30 gender and 20 race/ethnicity bias studies performed by judicial systems, as compared to approximately 12 sexual orientation studies produced only by local bar associations).

norms outlawing such bias were an accepted part of the American legal landscape.[12] Laws prohibiting discrimination on the basis of sexual orientation have not yet achieved such widespread acceptance.[13]

A second factor that spurred judicial involvement in gender bias work was the institutional support for such studies. NOW Legal Defense and Education Fund made this a priority in the 1970s and devoted significant resources to making these studies happen.[14] Moreover, in 1985, the National Association of Women Judges (775 members-strong at that point) created a National Task Force on Gender Bias in the Courts "to encourage the formation of state task forces on gender bias throughout the country and to provide technical assistance to enable these task forces to perform their functions as efficiently and effectively as

---

12. These studies began proliferating in the 1980s, some two decades after Congress' enactment of the Civil Rights Act of 1964.

13. *See* WILLIAM B. RUBENSTEIN, CASES AND MATERIALS ON SEXUAL ORIENTATION AND THE LAW 469 (2d ed. 1997) (citing nine state sexual orientation bias laws and noting absence of federal law). New Hampshire enacted a gay rights law in 1997, thus bringing the current total to 10 states. *See New Hampshire Governor Signs Gay-Rights Measure*, L.A. TIMES, June 7, 1997, at A17, *available in* 1997 WL 2217897.

14. Lynn Hecht Schafran, long the director of NOW's efforts in these areas, writes:

> The catalyst for the gender bias task force movement was an effort, conceived in 1969 and formally inaugurated in 1980, to introduce information into state and national judicial education programs about the way gender bias affects decisionmaking and court interaction. In that year, the National Organization for Women Legal Defense and Education Fund (NOW LDEF) established the National Judicial Education Program to Promote Equality for Women and Men in the Courts (NJEP) and invited the newly organized National Association of Women Judges to become the project's cosponsor. The inspiration for NJEP came from women litigators whose personal experiences in the courts demonstrated that many judges were unaware of the social issues confronting women and that these judges were undermining the promise of the remedial legislation in areas such as domestic violence and divorce. . . . From its inception [NJEP] realized the importance of developing specific information about gender bias in the court of each state in which it was teaching. Local data was [sic] necessary to demonstrate that gender bias was in fact a problem in each jurisdiction and to minimize the denial that is an inevitable aspect of raising this sensitive issue.

Schafran, *Gender and Justice*, *supra* note 2, at 183-84 (footnotes omitted); *see also* LYNN HECHT SCHAFRAN & NORMA JULIET WIKLER, OPERATING A TASK FORCE ON GENDER BIAS IN THE COURTS: A MANUAL FOR ACTION (1986) [hereinafter NJEP MANUAL]; Norma Juliet Wikler, *On the Judicial Agenda for the 80s: Equal Treatment for Men and Women in the Courts*, 64 JUDICATURE 202 (1980).

possible."[15] These efforts were then embraced by established institutions of the bench and bar.[16] Similarly, in 1988, the National Consortium on Task Forces and Commissions on Racial and Ethnic Bias in the Courts was formed to coordinate the efforts of the state bias commissions.[17]

The initial examinations of sexual orientation bias within the legal profession are a consequence of a growing awareness of such bias at the bar, but they are occurring without significant, centralized, institutional support.[18] Awareness of sexual orientation bias commenced in the late 1970s, following the formation of the first gay law student groups. In the early 1980s, law schools began adopting policies prohibiting discrimination on the basis of sexual orientation. By 1990, the AALS had adopted a policy that member schools not discriminate on this basis nor allow on-campus recruiting by employers who discriminate on the basis of sexual orientation.[19] Typically, law firms that recruit at law schools must sign pledges agreeing to comply with these requirements. It is probably fair to assume that, as of this writing, nearly all medium and large size law firms in the United States have signed such a pledge. An increasing number of firms also offer same-sex partner benefits.[20]

---

15. NJEP MANUAL, *supra* note 14, at [introductory page from The Nat'l Ass'n of Women Judges].

16. Evidence of this is contained in guidebooks published by such institutions. *See, e.g.*, MOLLY TREADWAY JOHNSON, FEDERAL JUDICIAL CTR., STUDYING THE ROLE OF GENDER IN THE FEDERAL COURTS: A RESEARCH GUIDE (1995); NAT'L CTR. FOR STATE COURTS AND THE STATE JUSTICE INST., ESTABLISHING AND OPERATING A TASK FORCE OR COMMISSION ON RACE AND ETHNIC BIAS IN THE COURTS (1993).

17. *See* Todd D. Peterson, *Studying the Impact of Race and Ethnicity in the Federal Courts*, 64 GEO. WASH. L. REV. 173, 174 n.4 (1996) (citing Arline S. Tyler & Steven Montano, *State Panels Document Racial, Ethnic Bias in the Courts*, 78 JUDICATURE 154 (1994)).

18. The following information is extracted from William B. Rubenstein, *In Community Begins Responsibility: Obligations at the Gay Bar*, 48 HASTINGS L.J. (forthcoming 1998).

19. *See* Gene P. Schultz, *The Inclusion of Sexual Orientation in Nondiscrimination Policies: A Survey of American Law Schools*, LAW & SEXUALITY, Summer 1992, at 131, 140. The ABA also requires law schools to have such policies as a condition of accreditation.

The AALS Directory of Law Teachers now also includes a list of "Gay, Lesbian and Bisexual Community Law Teachers." *See* ASS'N OF AM. LAW SCHOOLS, THE AALS DIRECTORY OF LAW TEACHERS 1997-98 1335-36 (1997).

20. *See, e.g.*, COMM. ON SEXUAL ORIENTATION ISSUES, B. ASS'N OF SAN FRANCISCO, BASF REP. ON EMPLOYMENT POLICIES FOR GAY AND LESBIAN ATTORNEYS 45 (1996) (reporting that 28% of the 64 San Francisco law firms that responded to

Gay-oriented legal institutions also expanded rapidly in the late 1980s and early 1990s. For example, between 1985 and 1995, Lambda Legal Defense and Education Fund grew from one lawyer in a one-room office into a nationally-renowned legal institution with offices in New York, Chicago, Los Angeles, and Atlanta. By the late 1970s, small private law firms dedicated to serving the lesbian and gay community also started to dot the legal landscape. By the late 1980s, they had proliferated. For example, the Los Angeles Gay and Lesbian Yellow Pages contains forty-two pages of attorney listings that includes sixty different law firms.[21] The growth of the gay bar is reflected in the growing number of local lesbian and gay bar associations as well as the expanding National Lesbian and Gay Law Association. In 1988, the latter group held its first national law conference, Lavender Law I, in San Francisco. Five Lavender Law conferences have followed, each generally attracting hundreds of practicing attorneys from across the United States.

Notwithstanding the growth and accomplishments of the gay bar, the major gay legal organizations have not yet had the opportunity to devote the kind of serious attention to the bar association bias work that NOW Legal Defense Fund did in the 1980s. With few laws or cases protecting against sexual orientation discrimination itself, these groups' attention has understandably been trained elsewhere. Further, there are only two small organizations of gay judges in the United States, both only five years old, and each with only a few dozen judges on their mailing lists.[22] No organization acts as a clearinghouse for these studies. No established institutions of the bar or bench have underwritten guidebooks to help others undertaking them. Such institutional constraints, coupled with the nascent character of pro-gay legal norms, have limited the pace at which sexual orientation bias studies have been undertaken.

Not only is the quantity of sexual orientation bias studies limited, the reports have come from relatively few geographic locations. Four of the eleven studies undertaken to date come from California, one from the state, two from San Francisco, and

---

the survey offered health benefits to partners of lesbian/gay employees) [hereinafter BASF REPORT].

21. *See* 98 Gay & Lesbian Community Yellow Pages 47-90 (1998).

22. E-mail from Judge Michael R. Sonberg, President, *Association of Lesbian & Gay Judges*, to William Rubenstein, Acting Professor, *UCLA School of Law* (Jan. 30, 1998) (on file with author); *see also ABCNY 1993 Report, supra* note 9, at 863 n.24.

one from Los Angeles. Another three emanate from New York City. The remaining three were conducted by organizations in Seattle, Minneapolis/St. Paul, and Boston. That the studies commenced in these places is not surprising, given the concentration of lesbians, gay men, and bisexuals in major metropolitan areas. What is more surprising is that these efforts have spread so slowly to other areas. After the first gay civil rights laws were passed by municipalities in the early 1970s, and the first domestic partnership ordinances were enacted in the early 1980s, such efforts quickly were adopted in localities widely dispersed throughout the United States.[23] Indeed, today, gay activism is quite diffuse, with important efforts raging from Hawaii to Maine, and most places in between. In light of the fact that other gay rights issues have aroused interest across the country, the short list of cities where studies of sexual orientation bias in the legal profession have been conducted is striking.

These bar efforts may have spread more slowly than legislative efforts for another important reason: there has been relatively little empirical investigation of sexual orientation discrimination anywhere in the United States.[24] Efforts to enact a federal gay rights law have been hampered by, among other factors, this absence of empirical data. Moreover, in places where gay rights laws have been enacted, they have not produced large numbers of reported discrimination complaints.[25] The dearth of efforts to examine sexual orientation bias makes these bar studies more meaningful than they might otherwise be. Not only do they document bias against gay people in the legal system, they also provide some of the most important existing information about sexual orientation discrimination occurring anywhere. In this sense, the studies may contribute not only to bettering the situation of gay attorneys, but also to the promulgation of wider societal antidiscrimination principles.

---

23. For a listing, see NAN D. HUNTER ET AL., THE RIGHTS OF LESBIANS AND GAY MEN: THE BASIC ACLU GUIDE TO A GAY PERSON'S RIGHTS 204-08 (3d ed. 1992).

24. *See* M.V. Lee Badgett, *Vulnerability in the Workplace: Evidence of Anti-Gay Discrimination*, ANGLES: POL'Y J. INST. FOR GAY & LESBIAN STRATEGIC STUD., Sept. 1997, at 1, 1-4 (summarizing results of a national survey and twenty local studies but concluding that "little systematic research exists").

25. *See generally* GENERAL ACCOUNTING OFFICE, SEXUAL-ORIENTATION-BASED EMPLOYMENT DISCRIMINATION: STATES' EXPERIENCE WITH STATUTORY PROHIBITIONS (1997).

III. Sources of Sexual Orientation Bias Studies

All of the sexual orientation bias studies to date have been conducted by state or local bar associations. Not a single sexual orientation bias study has been completed by the judiciary.[26] By contrast, gender and racial bias studies have largely been undertaken by courts, not bar associations. Most data on sexual orientation discrimination outside the bar has been collected by lesbian and gay political organizations, usually in efforts to persuade legislators to enact civil rights protections.[27] The bar association studies of sexual orientation discrimination are an important step forward because they represent efforts to study this problem by non-gay institutions, although often it is the gay members of such institutions who have pushed for the studies to be undertaken. That these efforts have been conducted by non-gay institutions indicates growing acceptance of the principle that sexual orientation discrimination is wrong. While this alone is encouraging, a final report published by the judiciary itself would place the state's imprimatur on efforts to uncover sexual orientation bias. Judith Resnik has characterized such official sponsorship of gender bias studies as "radical,"[28] writing that the bias report conclusions,

> are officially authored by chief justices and leading jurists and lawyers (and not "only" by academic lawyers and social scientists, and not "only" by members of the group against whom the discrimination runs) and are published in reports literally stamped with a court's seal.[29]

Judicial reports on sexual orientation bias would similarly send a strong message that the government acknowledges that such bias

---

26. The Chief Justice of the Supreme Court of New Jersey has convened a Task Force on Gay and Lesbian Issues that is currently in the process of undertaking such a judicially-sponsored study of sexual orientation discrimination. *See* Letter from Deborah T. Poritz, Chief Justice, *Supreme Court of New Jersey*, to Ruth E. Harlow, Esq. (June 30, 1997) (on file with author). Similarly, the Judicial Council of California, the chief policy making agency of the California judicial system, is currently conducting a study through its Sexual Orientation Fairness Subcommittee. *See* Donna J. Hitchens, *California Studies Sexual-Orientation Bias*, Fam. Advoc., Summer 1997, at 29.

27. *See* Lee Badgett et al., National Gay & Lesbian Task Force Pol'y Inst., Pervasive Patterns of Discrimination Against Lesbians and Gay Men: Evidence from Surveys Across the United States (1992). *See generally* Matthew A. Coles, Try This at Home!: A Do-It-Yourself Guide to Winning Lesbian and Gay Civil Rights Policy 200-02 (1996) (discussing the benefits of discrimination surveys in efforts to enact civil rights laws).

28. Resnik, *Ambivalence, supra* note 3, at 1529.

29. *Id.* at 1533.

is unacceptable and that it is willing to take the initial steps toward ending it.

IV. COMMON METHODOLOGIES OF SEXUAL ORIENTATION BIAS STUDIES

The abstracts of sexual orientation bias studies printed herein demonstrate that the strategies for conducting this work have been fairly uniform. Most of the reports follow from the distribution and collection of survey instruments; some involve the use of focus groups; other studies simply analyze previously-collected data and reports.

Most of the surveys were aimed at lesbian, gay, and bisexual members of the legal community and sought information about their individual experiences. Some of the studies took a broader focus. For example, one done by the Association of the Bar of the City of New York surveyed all Legal Aid attorneys, only 12% of whom were gay, to ascertain their sense of the barriers that lesbian, gay, and bisexual attorneys might confront in the courts, and hence the profession. The California State Bar included questions about sexual orientation in a demographic survey of more than 14,000 randomly-chosen members. In both San Francisco and Los Angeles, law firms were surveyed about the presence of bias in their workplaces and about any steps they had undertaken to address such bias.

The methods employed to date raise several interrelated concerns. The first involves the scope of the studies.[30] Studies of gender and race bias have examined at least three relatively distinct phenomena: (1) judicial bias in substantive legal rulings concerning women and minorities; (2) discriminatory animus expressed by court officials (attorneys, paralegals, courthouse employees, jurors, litigants, etc.) against court users (attorneys,

---

30. One interesting note about the scope of all of these types of studies is their use of neutral language — thus, the study of "gender bias" in the courts rather than "sex discrimination." One explanation of this is linguistic — that employment of the term "gender" is meant to indicate that what is being studied are the socially constructed, not natural, differences between the treatment of men and women. *See* Judith Resnik, *Gender Bias: From Classes to Courts*, 45 STAN. L. REV. 2195, 2201 (1993). A second aspect is that the term is meant to capture bias against men as well as women, though perhaps "sex discrimination" is traditionally thought of as applicable only to harms women face. *See* NJEP MANUAL, *supra* note 14, at 7. Most generally, though, the term "gender bias" is employed because these studies are meant not simply to document the discrimination women (or men) face in the legal profession or court system, but rather how *gender* affects justice at all levels.

witnesses, litigants, etc.); and (3) bias within the legal profession that impedes professional opportunities. Gender and racial bias studies have therefore often extended beyond the bar to consider the experiences of users of the penal and legal systems, and they have looked at the lives of law students. They have also considered how substantive law embodies gender and race bias.[31] By contrast, the sexual orientation studies have generally attempted to analyze only one thing: bias faced by attorneys (and sometimes law students). These studies have not typically looked at bias throughout the legal system (including, for instance, police forces) nor analyzed the content of judicial decisions.

The fact that it is often difficult to know who "is" gay leads to a second methodological concern about sexual orientation bias studies — the randomness of sampling methods and the statistical significance of responses.[32] There is no fixed definition of what constitutes sexual orientation,[33] and even those individuals

---

31. For example, Vicki Jackson writes:
These reports looked into how women attorneys were treated by judges and other lawyers, and how women parties — especially (i) women in family court cases involving divorce, custody, support and alimony, (ii) women as victims of crime including domestic violence and sexual assault, and (iii) women as criminal defendants — were treated. Some task forces looked at the awards of civil damages and tort recoveries, for women and men. Many looked at the employment and appointment of women and men in court systems and the legal profession as a whole. Some considered legal education and its impact on women and men. Even for studies limited to the courthouse, there are many different participants whose treatment and behavior can be and have been studied — lawyers, parties, courthouse employees, witnesses, jurors, and judges.
Jackson, *supra* note 3, at 462 n.5; *see also* 42 U.S.C.A. § 14001(b) (1994) (outlining 12 areas of study for federal court undertaking gender bias reports); COMMISSION TO STUDY RACIAL AND ETHNIC BIAS IN THE COURTS, SUPREME JUDICIAL COURT OF MASS., EQUAL JUSTICE: ELIMINATING THE BARRIERS (1994) (considering, inter alia, jury composition, sentencing, appointment of judges, and employment in the courts); JUDICIAL COUNCIL OF CAL., FINAL REP. OF THE CAL. JUDICIAL COUNCIL ADVISORY COMM. ON RACIAL AND ETHNIC BIAS IN THE COURTS (1997) (considering, inter alia, treatment of counsel, language and cultural barriers in the courts, sentencing); *Special Report*, *supra* note 5 (discussing, inter alia, the composition of the courthouse work force, including judges, law clerks, ADR panels, and the racial composition of the judicial conference).

32. *See generally* Los Angeles County Bar Ass'n Ad Hoc Comm. on Sexual Orientation Bias, *The Los Angeles County Bar Association Report on Sexual Orientation Bias*, 4 S. CAL. REV. L. & WOMEN'S STUD. 295, 377-79 (1995) [hereinafter *LACBA Report*].

33. *See* EDWARD O. LAUMANN ET AL., THE SOCIAL ORGANIZATION OF SEXUALITY: SEXUAL PRACTICES IN THE UNITED STATES 292-93 (1994) (discussing construction of a study of homosexuality into three distinct dimensions: behavior, desire, and identity).

who identify as lesbians, gay men, and bisexuals are not visually identifiable as such.[34] The ambiguity of sexual orientation and its apparent invisibility present unique problems for those attempting to define what actions evidence bias and to assess the precise quantity of such bias. Given such a starting point, it is difficult, if not impossible, to conduct random population "sampling" because a surveyer can never know what constitutes the proper population to be "sampled" nor what a good "sample" of that population would consist of.

Not surprisingly, then, few of the sexual orientation bias studies even attempted to collect information through random sampling methods. Most of the studies have gathered information by targeting their surveys to people known to be openly gay, such as members of gay bar associations.[35] Nearly all the studies rely on voluntary responses and most of these responses were of "self-reported" instances of bias which are "inherently subjective."[36] These approaches inevitably skewed the studies' empiric reliability. However, in the absence of some accepted index, the ways in which the results are inaccurate is difficult to ascertain. On the one hand, many people who have experienced sexual orientation bias are not members of gay organizations and thus are rarely reached by these surveys. Thus, there might be underreporting of the magnitude of bias.[37] On the other hand, those who are members of these gay organizations are probably openly gay, and therefore may be more likely to face overt discrimination, creating a risk of the incidence of bias being over-represented.[38] In addition, organizations that are identified as "gay" often consist of more men than women, more whites than people of color.

---

34. *See* Comm. on Lesbian and Gay Issues, B. Ass'n of San Francisco, Creating an Environment Conducive to Diversity: A Guide for Legal Employers on Eliminating Sexual Orientation Discrimination 1 n.1 (1991) [hereinafter BASF Report] ("It is important to note that collection of data documenting this form of discrimination is particularly problematic because many gay and lesbian law students and attorneys are reluctant to reveal their sexual orientation, and many legal organizations are reluctant to collect data on the numbers of openly gay and lesbian law students and employees.").

35. The L.A. County Report collected information from a large cross section of bar association members, thus leading it to conclude that the data it received from the *heterosexual* attorneys were drawn from a random sample. *See LACBA Report*, *supra* note 32, at 377.

36. *Id.* at 378.

37. *See ABCNY 1993 Report*, *supra* note 9, at 851.

38. Of course, those who are closeted are more likely to face the discriminatory attributes of forced hiding, characteristics which may be underreported given the methodologies employed by the studies.

Thus, one would expect that the responses to bias surveys distributed through such organizations would be skewed along these divides.[39]

Indeed, a third methodological issue concerns the fact that none of the studies to date has looked separately at bias affecting gay men and bias affecting lesbians, nor considered sexual orientation bias in the context of race or class.[40] Traditionally, most of the gender studies did not distinguish the treatment of white women from that of women of color,[41] but recently some have begun to do so.[42] Of the nine reports from race and ethnic bias task forces, two looked specifically at issues concerning minority women.[43] Unless studies are designed to account for the effect of gender, race, and class, sexual orientation bias studies might be thought to have as their only subject white gay men.[44] As noted above, this concern begins with the fact that surveys are often

---

39. *See ABCNY 1993 Report*, *supra* note 9, at 851.

40. The ongoing California judicial study states as one of five of its guiding principles that it "will identify and address the interests and needs of lesbians and gay men who have historically suffered from multiple biases such as race, gender, and disability." Hitchens, *supra* note 26, at 29.

41. The NJEP Manual acknowledged that "race, ethnicity, economic status and age certainly affect the treatment of women in the courts and compound the effects of sexism" and urged that task forces "reflect awareness of how these additional factors interrelate with gender." NJEP MANUAL, *supra* note 14, at 6. Yet the Manual warns that "attempting simultaneously to investigate all forms of racism and other kinds of bias in addition to sexism at an appropriate level of detail would be impossible within the constraints imposed on a Task Force," *id.*, and thus concludes that *separate* task forces on racial bias are necessary. *Id.* at 8.

42. *See, e.g.*, JUDICIAL COUNCIL ADVISORY COMM. ON GENDER BIAS IN THE COURTS, ACHIEVING EQUAL JUSTICE FOR WOMEN AND MEN IN THE COURTS, REPORT OF THE JUDICIAL COUNCIL ADVISORY COMMITTEE ON GENDER BIAS IN THE [CALIFORNIA] COURTS 14 (1990). *See generally* Resnik, *Ambivalence*, *supra* note 3, at 1539 n.65 ("Of the 24 reports on gender considered here, only a few discuss, sometimes briefly, the distinctive status of being both a woman and of color.").

43. *See Special Report*, *supra* note 5, at 198 n.15 (*citing* WASHINGTON STATE MINORITY AND JUSTICE TASK FORCE, FINAL REPORT 63-75 (1990); 2 REPORT AND RECOMMENDATIONS OF THE FLORIDA SUPREME COURT RACIAL AND ETHNIC BIAS STUDY COMMISSION, "WHERE THE INJURED FLY FOR JUSTICE" 49-60 (1991)).

44. As the historian Lisa Duggan has written:
   any gay politics based on the primacy of sexual identity defined as unitary and "essential," residing clearly, intelligibly and unalterably in the body or psyche, and fixing desire in a gendered direction, ultimately represents the view from the subject position "twentieth-century, Western, white, gay male."
Lisa Duggan, *Making It Perfectly Queer, in* SEX WARS: SEXUAL DISSENT AND POLITICAL CULTURE 155, 162 (Lisa Duggan & Nan D. Hunter eds., 1995). *See generally* Kimberlé Crenshaw, *Mapping the Margins: Intersectionality, Identity Politics, and Violence Against Women of Color*, 43 STAN. L. REV. 1241 (1991) (demonstrating how race discrimination law is constructed with black men in mind, sex discrimina-

distributed through organizations that may not be representative of women and people of color.[45] Further, the questions posed in such surveys might be skewed along race or gender lines. Finally, as will be noted below, the written reports issued from the studies may only be able to discuss the particular features of these distinct intersectional biases if the survey methodology is, at the outset, sensitive to them.

Given all of these limitations, it would be a mistake to attempt to draw definitive conclusions about the quantity of sexual orientation bias in the legal profession from these reports. They are most helpful in providing support for the argument that such bias exists[46] and in giving voice to the nature of that bias.[47]

V. Findings of Sexual Orientation Bias Studies

Not surprisingly, the studies paint a disheartening portrait of the professional lives of lesbian and gay attorneys. The statistics indicate that many lesbians, gay men, and bisexuals have suffered discrimination. Nearly half remain closeted at work, anxiously micro-managing the performance of their sexual identities to their colleagues, supervisors, clients, and judges. Many lack mentors and support systems and feel excluded from the social network of the bar and firm life by their forced single status, if not by their sexual orientation. Almost no gay attorneys receive equal pay for equal work, as their benefit packages do not extend to their partners and partners' children. These factors typically combine to impede progress in the profession in various ways including job satisfaction; progress to partnership; pay equity; firm and bar leadership positions; and elevation to the bench. The California demographic study[48] provides concrete data about pay differentials between gay and non-gay attorneys. The

---

tion law around white women, and hence how the situation of women of color — those at the intersection of these subjects — is neglected).

45. *See supra* text accompanying notes 36-39.

46. *See, e.g.,* Badgett, *supra* note 24, at 1-2 ("Identifying a precise level of discrimination is impossible given [the self-reporting survey] method, but such consistent findings across time and region reflect gay employees' beliefs that their workplaces are unfair or hostile.").

47. The limitations of survey analysis in these settings are summarized in the NJEP Manual, *supra* note 14, at 35-37.

48. SRI Int'l, 1991 Demographic Survey of the State B. of Cal.: Comparisons of Gay and Non-gay State B. Members (1994) [hereinafter Cal. Study]. Given the size and random nature of this study, this data is among the more reliable quantitative information contained in any of the studies. Compare *supra* text accompanying notes 32-39.

study shows that 50% of non-gay attorneys over forty make more than $100,000 per year, compared with only 25% of gay attorneys. After ten years in the profession, 54% of non-gay attorneys earn more than $100,000 while only 33% of gay attorneys earn that much. After ten years in the profession, 38% of non-gay attorneys were law firm partners while only 26% of gay attorneys were.[49]

It is worth noting that there are some encouraging findings in this data, as well. Approximately 15% of those polled in New York believe that being gay was a positive factor in the hiring process: "[E]mployers affirmatively told applicants that they seek diversity in the workplace and welcome a gay and lesbian perspective."[50] This finding is in stark contrast with the fact that only a decade ago, a gay fundraising event held at a major New York law firm could not be photographed by the *New York Times* because of the fears of those present.[51]

There are three aspects of these results that bear comment. First, the primary site of concern for most queer law students and attorneys is the closet. While this is not surprising, it suggests the unique dynamics of sexual orientation discrimination.[52] A major component of the suffering that lesbian, gay, and bisexual attorneys endure is the emotional anxiety that attends the performance of their sexual orientation.[53] They must constantly scrutinize how much to reveal and how much to conceal of their

---

49. *See* CAL. STUDY, *supra* note 48, at 3; COMM. ON SEXUAL ORIENTATION DISCRIMINATION, THE STATE B. OF CAL., REP. AND RECOMMENDATIONS REGARDING SEXUAL ORIENTATION DISCRIMINATION IN THE CAL. LEGAL PROFESSION 2 (1996). These distinctions might be due in part to different career paths voluntarily chosen by gay attorneys. For example, lesbian/gay identified attorneys are more likely to provide legal services to indigent clients and to spend more hours on pro bono work than are non-gay attorneys. *See* CAL. STUDY, *supra* note 48, at 4-5. Still, the different earning levels could reflect the fact that openly gay attorneys feel compelled to pursue different career paths, even if they do so in what appears to be a voluntary fashion.

50. *ABCNY 1993 Report*, *supra* note 9, at 853; *see also* Special Comm. on Lesbians and Gay Men in the Profession, *Rep. on the Experience of Lesbians and Gay Law Students in New York Metropolitan Area Law Schools*, 51 REC. ASS'N B. CITY N.Y. 145, 148 (1996) (discussing how being openly gay can "have a positive impact on success in [law] school").

51. *See* E.R. Shipp, *Concern Over AIDS Helps Rights Unit*, N.Y. TIMES, May 3, 1987, at 43, *available in* LEXIS, News Library, Nyt File.

52. *See generally* EVE KOSOFSKY SEDGWICK, EPISTEMOLOGY OF THE CLOSET (1990).

53. *See, e.g.*, *LACBA Report*, *supra* note 32, at 337-43 (discussing dynamics of closet); *ABCNY 1993 Report*, *supra* note 9, at 847 (discussing the "psychological" impact of sexual orientation discrimination).

personal lives in their myriad day-to-day interactions. The closet is meant to render gay attorneys invisible and where it does so successfully, the resulting anxiety harms their productivity, undermines their ability to network with one another, and thwarts their career trajectory.[54] The absence of openly gay persons also "serve[s] to suppress discussion of sexual orientation bias generally and to suppress complaints about sexual orientation discrimination in particular."[55] Measures aimed at easing sexual orientation bias must address these particular features of that discrimination if they are to have a meaningful impact.

A second conclusion to draw from these reports is counter-intuitive: concerns that keep attorneys closeted may be *less* pervasive than is commonly acknowledged. It is true that an individual's coming out often continues to have negative ramifications. For example, even where anti-gay bias may be perceived as wrong, coming out is simply reconceptualized as "bad judgment" and then the error in "judgment," rather than the coming out itself, is used as the explicit basis of termination.[56] However, a particularly invidious aspect of the closet is how it succeeds precisely because it operates as a site of fear. Thus, even irrational fears of coming out are rendered real because an isolated lawyer, ignorant about how her coming out might be received, simply remains closeted. Interestingly, queer attorneys' fears about coming out in fact may actually be undermined by some of the statistics found by these studies. Although 70% of the participants in a New York City study stated that they were not out on their resume, nearly 88% reported that at no time during the hiring process "did an interviewer or employer's representative ever make statements or pursue lines of inquiry which had or could have had the effect of excluding gay and lesbian applicants."[57] Further, nearly 60% of the participants in that survey were out to most of their coworkers, 88% to some coworkers, and nearly 90% reported that they were never asked to conceal their sexual

---

54. *See LACBA Report, supra* note 32, at 337-38.
55. *Id.* at 337.
56. One report states:
    Despite the easy acceptance of heterosexual relationships, the routine introduction of a gay attorney's same-sex domestic partner is still viewed by many as "flaunting" one's "sexuality." One gay attorney wrote, "I have been the object of critical statements about 'dragging in' my 'personal' life because I mentioned my life partner."
    Id. at 347; *see also* Shahar v. Bowers, 114 F.3d 1097 (11th Cir. 1997) (en banc), *cert. denied*, 118 S. Ct. 693 (1998).
57. *ABCNY 1993 Report, supra* note 9, at 885.

orientation in the workplace.[58] The Los Angeles study suggests that non-gay participants think the consequences of coming out are less significant than gay participants do.[59] Because heterosexual participants create the consequences of coming out, this finding might be read to provide comfort to gay lawyers. Nonetheless, a rational lawyer might not rely on statistics alone as a basis for risking a job or even a career. The cruel quality of fear is that it prevails simply by existing.

The perception that there will be negative consequences if a lawyer comes out is also evident in responses of employers when they are asked about having lesbian, gay, and bisexual attorneys in their firms. Just as a gay attorney contemplating coming out generally anticipates that her employer will react negatively, employers, in turn, often automatically assume that clients, judges, and other third parties, will behave poorly. One study found that, "[w]hen it comes to matters relating to a gay or suspected gay colleague, heterosexual attorneys often act on the assumption that clients, judges, and others will have a problem with that attorney's sexual orientation."[60] At times, the employer's projection may be valid. The Los Angeles study demonstrates that "approximately 15% of the . . . participants said that clients of their office have expressed a preference not to work with gay attorneys."[61] Yet some of the employers' concern is just fear itself. This same statistic also suggests that 85% of firms report that their clients have *not* expressed anti-gay sentiments. Indeed, some clients are themselves gay. Others, particularly corporate clients, may be struggling with these same issues and might be relieved if their counsel proved knowledgeable about them. But within the regime of the closet, employers, like their employees, enforce silence, constantly fearing, whether correctly or not, that open discussion will provoke negative reactions.

Beyond noting how the closet is a central figure in these texts, and examining some of the dynamics of how the closet operates here, a third reflection on these documents concerns their style. One of the most dramatic aspects of these reports is how boring they are to read. Judith Resnik has observed that the gender bias reports constitute a "howl of pain" that nonetheless has

---

58. *See id.* at 886-87.
59. *See LACBA Report, supra* note 32, at 340-42.
60. *Id.* at 321.
61. *See id.* at 320 & n.78.

not resulted in "profound transformation."[62] While the sexual orientation bias studies represent a howl of pain, they present something different. The humanity of their narratives is lost in the dry, clinical presentation of the material, replete with repeated statistics and flat bureaucratic language:

> A troubling degree of sexual orientation discrimination exists in the employment of attorneys in Los Angeles County.[63]

> Many interviewees reported that private law firm partners consider same-sex sexual orientation an undesirable factor.[64]

> All legal employers, especially private firms and corporations, risk losing employees and potential employees by failing to take strong affirmative steps to eradicate both the perception and the underlying reality of discrimination.[65]

These reports provide a cathartic opportunity for their subjects by furnishing a forum in which the lawyers can tell their stories.[66] But after identities have been stripped and stories have been transcribed, analyzed, and placed within the dispassionate framework of a "sexual orientation bias study report," the human pain is gone, the entreaty to the heart buried. What remains are intellectual appeals containing only traces of real lives. It is nearly impossible to reconstruct from these ashes the slights, the unfulfilled expectations of ruined careers, the anguish.

VI. Recommendations of Sexual Orientation Bias Studies

The recommendations derived from these studies fall into four broad categories:[67] (1) recommendations concerning general employment policies (e.g., firms should adopt written policies affirming their opposition to sexual orientation discrimination); (2) specific recommendations concerning recruitment and hiring (e.g., firms should send recruitment letters to gay student groups at local law schools); (3) recommendations concerning retention, advancement, and compensation (e.g., firms should provide men-

---

62. Resnik, *Ambivalence, supra* note 3, at 1534.

63. *LACBA Report, supra* note 32, at 297.

64. Lesbian and Gay Issues Subcomm., Hennepin County B. Ass'n, Legal Employers' Barriers to Advancement and to Economic Equality Based Upon Sexual Orientation 15 (1995).

65. *ABCNY 1993 Report, supra* note 9, at 873.

66. On the psychological values of participatory story-telling, see, for example, E. Allan Lind et al., *Discovery and Presentation of Evidence in Adversary and Nonadversary Proceedings*, 71 Mich. L. Rev. 1129 (1973).

67. These are drawn from BASF Report, *supra* note 20, at 8.

tors or permit employees to work on gay pro bono cases); and (4) recommendations concerning employee benefits (e.g., firms should provide benefits for the partners of their lesbian and gay employees). Some of the reports' recommendations were re- markably concrete, others strikingly vague. Perhaps the most im- pressive work in the remedial area is the longitudinal work done by the Bar Association of San Francisco. In 1991, the Associa- tion published a report with twenty-three specific recommenda- tions. In 1995, the Association undertook a follow-up survey to assess whether its recommendations had been adopted. Only 20% of the firms responded to the follow-up study, and these firms were likely to be those that had made the most progress. Yet importantly, the Association did not consider its work done with the completion of its initial report and recommendations. The follow-up survey, even where not returned, served as a re- minder to firms of the Association's earlier recommendations and served to shame noncompliant firms.

An initial reflection on the recommendation aspects of these reports flows from this San Francisco experience: that effort demonstrates that the recommendations, and their enforcement, are perhaps more important than information gathering. The documentation phase of these studies does, arguably, serve im- portant purposes. The statistical data provides some rare empiri- cal evidence of sexual orientation bias, the studies offer a forum for subjects to tell their stories, and sometimes the evidence that is gathered provides crucial support for calls for change. How- ever, as discussed above, the surveys suffer from methodological problems, are often difficult to read, and may not be persuasive to those who do not want to be persuaded. Anti-gay bias may be so obvious, and the recommendations so normatively appropri- ate, that the importance of surveying pales in comparison to the significance of enforcement. At the very least, the Bar Associa- tion of San Francisco's work demonstrates that an initial bias study is just a start. True change comes through continued pres- sure over time.

True change in the legal system also requires an enlightened judiciary. NOW Legal Defense Fund's efforts in the gender bias studies grew out of the experiences of women attorneys con- fronting sexist judges.[68] NOW identified these judges as an ob-

---

68. See Schafran, *Gender and Justice, supra* note 2, at 183-84; *see also* NJEP MANUAL, *supra* note 14, at Author's Preface.

stacle to women's equality and sought a method to teach the judges when and how they were being sexist. The gender bias studies were seen as instrumental to this end — by demonstrating that bias existed in the court system, women's advocates could establish that training programs were needed to educate judges about sexism.[69]

By contrast, few of the sexual orientation bias reports have linked their explicit findings to recommendations for judicial education. While this goal may animate some of the sexual orientation bias work, most of it reads as an indictment of the private bar. Judges are surprisingly absent here. Yet although judges are ethically barred from discriminating on the basis of sexual orientation,[70] few of them are familiar with sexual orientation issues. There is probably not a sitting judge in the entire United States who took a course on sexual orientation law in law school. And there are few developed programs of judicial education on sexual orientation issues.[71] Perhaps because these reports have not been issued by the judiciary, they lack a judicial focus in their recommendations.

A final reflection on the reports' recommendations is more theoretical. These recommendations can be seen as suggestions about what gay people want. In that sense, they provide a particular image about what constitutes queer equality. Building from the explicit recommendations made in these reports, the image of equality that emerges is one in which (1) gay people couple as heterosexuals do and seek to be recognized in the same ways (e.g., listed in the company's directory with their partner's names; encouraged to bring a partner to firm social events, etc.); (2) gay people exist as a distinct identity-based group, with their own bar associations to which firms are urged to underwrite dues; and (3) gay people are seen to have unique perspectives such that we should be represented on hiring committees and firm newsletters should include "items of particular interest to lesbian and gay employees." That such recommendations would follow from reports that grow out of an identity-based political movement in the first place is unsurprising. Nonetheless, the confident tone

---

69. Schafran, *Gender and Justice, supra* note 2, at 183-84.

70. *See* ABA MODEL CODE OF JUDICIAL CONDUCT Canon 3(B)(5)-(6) (1990).

71. *See* Nancy D. Polikoff, *Educating Judges About Lesbian and Gay Parenting: A Simulation*, LAW & SEXUALITY, Summer 1991, at 173, 175 (reporting knowledge of only two judicial education programs in history that address lesbian and gay parenting issues).

with which these goals are expressed contrasts rather starkly with debates among lesbians, gay men, and bisexuals about who we are and what we want.[72] The reports and their recommendations, therefore, raise interesting questions about whether sexual orientation bias will, ultimately, be ameliorated by embracing gay identity, or whether the goal should be a world in which the distinction between heterosexuality and homosexuality simply does not exist.[73] Those who espouse the latter goal might take an entirely different approach to making recommendations to end sexual orientation bias.

VII.   Lessons for the Future

My review of the studies of sexual orientation bias has led to the following recommendations for those involved with such efforts:

1. *Establish a clearinghouse.* Community institutions should take a leadership role in coordinating sexual orientation bias studies. NOW LDF's work in the field of gender bias studies provides a valuable model of community organizing that produces concrete, verifiable results — not only for women within the legal profession, but for women in the justice system generally. Lambda Legal Defense Fund has begun to devote some staff resources to these efforts and, specifically, to the development of judicial education programs. The National Lesbian and Gay Law Association, the new associations of gay judges, or both, might consider how they can actively encourage, coordinate, and perpetuate this work. By providing continuity over time, such institutional support could help enable a wider geographic distribution of this work; the development, refinement, and employment of better empirical investigative techniques; and more systematic long-term implementation of recommendations, including judicial education.

2. *Aim higher.* First, gay attorneys and their allies should seek studies sponsored by the judiciary itself. Second, the studies

---

72. *See generally* William B. Rubenstein, *Divided We Litigate: Addressing Disputes Among Group Members and Lawyers in Civil Rights Campaigns*, 106 Yale L.J. 1623 (1997).

73. *See, e.g.*, Judith Butler, *Imitation and Gender Insubordination, in* Inside/ Out: Lesbian Theories, Gay Theories 13 (Diana Fuss ed., 1991); John D'Emilio, *Making and Unmaking Minorities: The Tensions Between Gay History and Politics, in* Making Trouble: Essays on Gay History, Politics, and the University 181 (1992).

ought to cast a broader net. For example, the studies might consider how lesbians and gay men are treated when they are victims or defendants in the criminal justice system,[74] what happens to lesbians and gay men in custody disputes, and why so few gay people are on the bench.

3. *Address the multiple identities of subjects.* The studies should grapple more explicitly in their methodology, summary, and recommendations with the multiple identities of many of their subjects. The ongoing California bench study that promises to "identify and address the interests and needs of lesbians and gay men who have historically suffered from multiple biases such as race, gender, and disability"[75] is encouraging because it identifies as a goal this multidimensional analysis. This effort may yield models that can be replicated in future studies or at least provide information for the continued refinement of these efforts.

4. *Increase the professionalism of the studies.* Methodologically, those producing these reports should strive for the fewest surveying problems possible. To this end, social science experts must be employed. Such experts should carefully evaluate earlier studies of gender, race, and sexual orientation bias. Again, this is an instance where a clearinghouse could provide vital coordination. Given the effort that goes into these studies, and the care that should be given to their methodology, they would benefit enormously by more professionally-written final reports. This is not meant to disparage the attempts of the existing studies. But lawyers and social scientists are trained to present dispassionate arguments in cold type. Bias studies that are deftly drafted and substantively engaging might be considerably more effective.

5. *Emphasize positive findings.* Reports should highlight good stories as well as bad. Given the layers of quiet fear that sustain the closet, real life narratives with positive outcomes could have a beneficial effect in raising the courage of gay and non-gay lawyers alike.

---

74. *See, e.g.*, Florida Supreme Court Racial and Ethnic Bias Study Comm'n, *Report and Recommendations of the Florida Supreme Court Racial and Ethnic Bias Study Commission*, 19 FLA. ST. U. L. REV. 591, 634-44 (1992) [hereinafter *Florida Report*] (discussing the interaction of law enforcement officers with racial minorities).

75. Hitchens, *supra* note 26, at 1.

6. *Study employer compliance.* Judges and bar associations should study employer compliance efforts as much as they study employee problems. Studying what employers have or have not done to ameliorate sexual orientation bias appropriately centers attention on the locus of discrimination. This approach also rewards firms that have made strides at alleviating bias and thus presents models for others. Finally, studying compliance publicly shames those that have not addressed these problems. Longitudinal studies are especially helpful as they raise the levels of pressure and humiliation by demonstrating continued noncompliance.

7. *Involve and educate the judiciary.* The point of these studies should not solely be to analyze and make recommendations concerning the professional lives of queer lawyers. Their purpose must also be to help produce more justice for lesbians and gay men. If they are to have such an effect, more systematic judicial education programs must follow from their publication. Lambda's initial efforts at developing and implementing model judicial education programs that can follow from, and secure the gains realized by, these efforts are encouraging. A single pioneering, sympathetic, state Supreme Court justice could make an enormous difference by taking the initiative and giving judicial imprimatur and resources to developing such a model program.

8. *Change the make up of the judiciary.* While judicial education is helpful, gay and lesbian judges are also vital. Only one Article III judge in the entire United States is openly gay, federal district court judge Deborah Batts, and her sexual orientation was probably unknown to the senators who confirmed her. While there is no exact count of gay and lesbian state court judges, there are approximately 30,000 state court judges in the United States[76] and the gay judges' association has only a few dozen members. This suggests that roughly one in every 1,000 state court judges is gay.[77]

---

76. Resnik, "*Naturally,*" *supra* note 5, at 1705 n.91.

77. Of course, some gay judges might not be part of the gay judges association, yet that underrepresentation would only slightly diminish this rough estimate. By way of comparison, consider Judith Resnik's analysis on the quantity of women judges:

> As of April 1, 1990, senior and active article III judges — on all levels of the federal courts — numbered 978. Of the 9 who serve on the United States Supreme Court, 1 was a woman (11.1%). Of the 216 who served at the appellate level, 198 (91.7%) were men and 18 (8.3%) women. All 69 of the senior appellate judges were men. At

This is an appalling statistic. The gay bar and its allies ought to invest more time and effort into preparing gay attorneys to be judges and into pushing for the nomination and appointment of lesbian and gay jurists. Too little attention has been paid to this issue. A single editorial piece written five years ago by Judge Stephen Reinhardt of the United States Court of Appeals for the Ninth Circuit is the full extent of the literature.[78]

9. *Continually reappraise the goal.* Having made these recommendations from a position of identity-based politics, it is, finally, interesting to consider whether society would be better were there no recognizable sexual orientation categories. Many of the identity-based recommendations that have issued from these reports seem necessary to the short term goal of ensuring protection for lesbian, gay, and bisexual attorneys. But would it make more sense, in the long run, if benefit plans did not turn on the nature of one's sexual relationship or if it could not be assumed that there were certain luncheon speakers who would be of particular interest to gay employees? These identity-based efforts strive to change the conditions under which we all live. Yet the constant questioning of strategies and tactics — particularly at these sites of confrontation — may prove valuable, even if alternative approaches are ultimately rejected.

VIII.   Conclusion

Interest in sexual orientation bias within the justice system is appropriate, important, and compelling. The Florida Supreme Court prefaced its study of racial and ethnic bias with one of Aesop's fables that captures the essence of this point well:

> A swallow had built her nest under the eaves of a Court of Justice. Before her young ones could fly, a serpent gliding out of his hole ate them all up. When the poor bird returned to her nest and found it empty, she began a pitiable wailing. A neighbor suggested, by way of comfort, that she was not the first bird who had lost her young. "True," she replied, "but it is not only my little ones that I mourn but that I should have

---

the trial level there were 753 article III judges, of whom 702 (93.2%) were men and 51 (6.8% women). Of the 223 senior trial judges, 219 (98.2%) were men and 4 (1.8%) women. Twelve (92.3%) of the 13 judges who sit on the Court of International Trade were men; 1 (7.7%) was a woman. Data from state courts may produce a helpful context in which to read these numbers. Woman are estimated to be about 8% of all state court judges.
Id. at 1705-06 (footnotes omitted).
   78. *See* Reinhardt, *supra* note 1.

been wronged in that very place where the injured fly for justice."[79]

With some important exceptions, courts have not been a refuge providing justice to lesbian, gay and bisexual Americans. As NOW Legal Defense Fund recognized three decades ago, the potential that bias studies provide is the potential to reform the judiciary. Sexual orientation bias studies can educate judges about the lives and experiences of lesbians, gay men, and bisexuals and can inspire them to dispense more justice. These are, therefore, important efforts that should be perpetuated and perfected.

---

79. *Florida Report, supra* note 74, at 608 (*quoting* M. FRANCES McNAMARA, 2000 FAMOUS LEGAL QUOTATIONS 129-30 (1967)).

Hate

[15]

Measuring Gay Populations and Antigay Hate Crime*

Donald P. Green, *Yale University*

Dara Z. Strolovitch, *University of Minnesota*

Janelle S. Wong, *University of Southern California*

Robert W. Bailey, *Rutgers University*

Objectives. The study of crime directed at gay and lesbian targets is hampered by two measurement problems: Police agencies provide unreliable data on hate crime, and tract-level census data contain no direct information about gay or lesbian population density. This article attempts to gauge two quantities that cannot be measured directly or unambiguously: the size of the gay and lesbian populations and the number of hate crimes directed at gay and lesbian targets. *Methods*. Population data for New York City were gathered from market research lists and from a special tabulation of the 1990 Census. Hate crime data were obtained from the Anti-Violence Project and the New York Police Department. Confirmatory factor analysis was used to assess the reliability of each measure and the correlation between latent population density and hate crime. *Results*. Each of these measures offers a reliable means by which to assess cross-sectional differences in the population density and victimization of gay men. Census and police data prove to be inferior indicators of lesbian population density and antilesbian hate crime. For both men and women, population density is strongly correlated with the incidence of hate crime. *Conclusions*. Despite the fact that advocacy groups record many more antigay incidents than do the police, both sources of data are in agreement about where hate crimes occur. The strong correlation between population density and hate crime against gay men implies that Census data could be used to forecast the occurrence of hate crime in areas where no police records exist.

The study of hate crime—that is, criminal conduct motivated by prejudice—is fraught with measurement problems. Nowhere are these problems more evident than in the study of hate crime directed at gay men and lesbians. In addition to the usual uncertainties of ascertaining whether criminal

*Direct all correspondence to Donald P. Green, Department of Political Science, 124 Prospect St., New Haven, CT 06520-8301 <donald.green@yale.edu>. The data and programs used here may be obtained at <http://pantheon.yale.edu/~gogreen>. We are grateful to Sean Strub, the Bias Unit of the New York Police Department, and the Anti-Violence Project for sharing their data. This research was supported by grants from the Institution for Social and Policy Studies at Yale and the National Science Foundation.

conduct is motivated by prejudice (Boyd, Berk, and Hamner, 1996; Jacobs and Potter, 1998) are the vagaries of data collection. Victims of antigay attacks may be unwilling to report their experiences because they fear publicizing their sexual orientation, distrust the people or agency to whom the report would be made, or believe that little would be achieved through reporting (Berk, Boyd, and Hamner, 1992; Comstock, 1991; Herek, 1989). Critics of law enforcement statistics contend that, as a result, only a fraction of all incidents are reported to police agencies (Herek, 1989). In an effort to address the underreporting problem, organizations such as the New York City Gay & Lesbian Anti-Violence Project (AVP) have sought to gather their own data on what they classify as heterosexist incidents, but these data are criticized by police agencies because they encompass incidents such as name calling that do not necessarily involve criminal conduct (Comstock, 1991).

Equally difficult is the problem of measuring gay and lesbian population density. Although a great many studies have examined the economic, cultural, and political geography of the homosexual population, quantitative inquiry has been hampered by the paucity of reliable data. In contrast to racial, linguistic, or class characteristics, sexual orientation is not tracked by the government surveys or administrative records. Other surveys, such as public opinion polls, seldom ask about sexual orientation, and when they do, the number of respondents who report a gay or lesbian orientation is too small to support any meaningful spatial analysis at small levels of aggregation, such as zip code or police precinct.

Beset by measurement problems, scholars are at a loss to answer even basic descriptive questions. It is unclear, for example, whether the statistics that police gather on hate crime, particularly antigay/antilesbian hate crime, are sufficiently reliable to support comparisons within a given jurisdiction. Equally unclear is the question of whether gay population density can be inferred from census information concerning household composition, age, and occupation (Glick, 1988:867). Finally, scholars have been at a loss to estimate the correlation between rates of hate crime and the population density of gay men and lesbians. Is victimization more common in areas with a high proportion of gay/lesbian inhabitants, or is it less common?

This article proposes and tests new methods for gauging the incidence of hate crime and the population density of gay men and lesbians. Using zip code–level hate crime reports from the AVP and Bias Unit of the New York Police Department (NYPD) and population data from commercial mailing lists and a special tabulation of the 1990 Census data, we perform a multimethod, multitrait analysis (Campbell and Fiske, 1959) that makes allowance for measurement error in each of these indicators. We show that despite the infirmities of the hate crime data derived from police reports and monitoring organizations, each provides a surprisingly reliable account of zip code–level variation. Moreover, we find that a carefully defined special tabulation from the decennial Census provides a reliable means by which to measure the population density of gay men in New York City, a finding that suggests the feasibility of more broad-ranging analyses that look across time or to different locations. Unfortunately, the same approach performs less well when used to assess the population density of lesbians.

Conceptualization of Latent Variables: Population Density and Hate Crime

Defining and measuring homosexuality for purposes of empirical research presents an array of difficult issues. Definitions are complicated by the fact that same-sex sexual *behavior*, same-sex erotic *appeal*, and gay or lesbian sexual *self-identification* need not be coterminous (Laumann et al., 1994). A man, for example, may harbor sexual fantasies about other men but not engage in sexual contact with men. Further complicating matters is the fact that both the standards by which behavior is categorized as homosexual and the manner in which sexual identities form vary across time and place.

These definitional uncertainties are compounded by a dearth of direct measures. Except in the case of small, self-selecting samples, measures of sexual behavior, fantasies, and identities are difficult to obtain. As a result, operationalizations inevitably fall back on indirect measures, raising questions about validity and reliability. Not all same-sex roommates are gay, regardless of whether the standard is one of identities, fantasies, or sexual behavior; not all of those who might otherwise be classified as gay have same-sex roommates.

The severity of these methodological problems is mitigated by two factors. First, the proxy measures tested here are used to gauge the characteristics of aggregate spatial units, not households or individuals. Each of the indirect measures to be applied will introduce an error of its own, but our methodological approach is to use measures with different sources of error so as to triangulate on the latent trait of interest. Second, this latent trait itself is less recalcitrant in its complexity than the tripartite distinction between sexual identity, appeal, and behavior might at first suggest. Prior work (e.g., Laumann et al., 1994) has shown that appeal, behavior, and identity form something of a Guttman scale. They are highly correlated, but erotic appeal is more common than same-sex behavior, which is in turn more common than a fully integrated sense of gay/lesbian identity. Thus, it is plausible to think that any measure of gay population density will be *proportional* to density of those who harbor same-sex fantasies, engage in same-sex sexual contact, or regard themselves as gay. Such a measure will be context-specific in the sense that the levels observed for any time and place will reflect the social forces that make expressions of gay orientations more or less acceptable; within any localized environment, however, one can draw inferences about areas in which homosexuality, however defined, is more or less prevalent.

Conceptualization of antigay hate crime presents thorny problems of its own. Although definitions and statutes vary, hate crime is typically defined as unlawful conduct motivated by animus against the victim's perceived race, religion, ethnicity, or sexual orientation (Wang, 1994). Note that according to this definition, *perceived* homosexuality is what matters, not actual homosexuality. One need only think of the many instances in which boys who are rumored to be "fags" are beaten up in school to appreciate the distinction between perception and reality. For this reason, and also because many hate crimes involve graffiti and other property crimes, the presence of gay people is not a necessary condition for antigay hate crime to occur in a neighborhood.

Since the definition of hate crime involves a judgment about the perpetrator's beliefs and motivations, it is sometimes difficult to establish that a given unlawful act constitutes a hate crime. From a legal standpoint, the simple fact that a gay person was victimized by a straight perpetrator is not sufficient. Extrinsic evidence (e.g., name calling, a history of harassment by the perpetrator) is required to establish that the perpetrator perceived the victim to be gay or lesbian and attacked out of hatred.

A less-exacting standard is applied to the classification of "heterosexist incidents," a term used by community organizations such as the AVP. This category encompasses acts motivated by prejudice that do not necessarily cross the threshold of illegality. Name calling or threats that fall short of criminal harassment, for example, would be considered heterosexist incidents, although they would not meet the police definition of hate crime. Thus, in principle, antigay hate crimes as classified by the NYPD constitute a subset of all heterosexist incidents classified by the AVP, and one might suspect the frequency with which the two occur to be proportional. We will see below that this is in fact the case.

Measures

The present investigation focuses on the 152 zip codes of New York City with at least 5,000 inhabitants. Like many other large American cities, New York contains enclaves that harbor gay institutions and business establishments (see Bailey, 1999, on parallels with other U.S. cities) but is one of the few cities in which police agencies and community organizations have gathered hate crime statistics over a period of several years.

Census

The idea of using Census data to measure gay residential concentration is not new (Glick, 1988) but neither is there a published literature on how best to do it. We requested a special tabulation of the 1990 Census for the five boroughs of New York City at both the zip code and tract level consisting of three key variables. The concentration of gay male households was tabulated by counting the number of households composed of two unrelated males over the age of 30. We further specified that neither resident of the household could be enrolled in school. The number of lesbian households was estimated similarly by counting households containing two unrelated, nonstudent women over 30. To generate a denominator for the purpose of calculating rates, we tabulated the number of unrelated, over-30, opposite-sex households, married or unmarried, with neither household resident enrolled in school. Population density was calculated as the fraction of all households that fit the criteria listed above.

Direct Mail Database

The other data used in this study come from Strubco, Inc/Metamorphosis, a data collection and direct-mailing firm based in New York City. Strubco compiled a direct-mail list created from nearly 100 smaller regional lists and a number of national lists (Bailey, 1999, ch. 5). Names on the list were supplied by local community groups, health groups, gay press subscriptions, donor lists from some lesbian and gay identified political candidates, HIV/AIDS service organizations, several national organizations (e.g., the National Gay and Lesbian Task Force, the Human Rights Campaign, and the Victory Fund), nightclubs, gay and lesbian bookstores, newspaper subscribers, and other lists. Thus, the Strubco database is less a direct-marketing list than a compilation of names associated with gay and lesbian groups, enterprises, and organizations from 1990 to 1996. Population density was computed as the ratio of Strubco names (men or women, as the case may be) to the total Census population living in each zip code.

Hate Crime Reports to the New York Police Department

One source of hate crime data is the NYPD's Bias Incident Investigative Unit, which since 1985 has documented and investigated unlawful acts committed against a person, group, or place because of the race, religion, ethnicity, or sexual orientation of the victim. Our data include antigay and lesbian incidents that were reported by patrol officers or detectives to this unit during 1994 and 1995. These incident counts are divided by total population in each zip code.

Heterosexist Incidents Reported to the Anti-Violence Program

Additional hate crime data come from the AVP. The AVP is a victim service agency, providing advocacy and information services primarily to gay, lesbian, bisexual, and transgender crime victims in the New York area. The AVP also documents violence motivated by hate against lesbians and gays, collecting information on hate crime from individuals who contact the agency for victim service provision. Heterosexist incidents are defined by the

AVP as acts motivated in whole or in part by the offender's bias against lesbian, gay, bisexual, or transgender people. Those who contact the agency provide information about an incident on the AVP's Incident Report Form. We organized the data obtained through these forms according to case (incident, not individual victim), sex, precinct, and type of crime. We tabulated the heterosexist incidents that took place during 1994 and 1995 and divided these incident counts by total population in each zip code.

Units of Aggregation

Our measures of gay and lesbian population density are available at the zip code level, whereas our measures of hate crime are available at the level of police precincts. In order to use all the measures in the same analysis without losing any cases when aggregating up to larger units (precincts), we devised a system for converting the precinct-level data into the smaller zip code units, which had an average population of 46,486 with a standard deviation of 22,477. Superimposing transparent maps of each borough's zip code and precinct boundaries, we determined the correspondence between zip codes and precincts, assigning fractions of precincts to zip codes where necessary. To estimate the number of hate crimes in a given zip code, we multiplied the total number of antigay incidents in a precinct by the proportion of the geographic area that the zip code comprised, and, for zip codes that cross precinct boundaries, added up the resulting values. We next gauge the reliability of this and other measures.

Measurement Model to Gauge Reliability

By what standard does one judge the quality of a measuring device? The most straightforward way is to compare its assessments to quantities that are known in advance. If three stones are known to weigh 50, 100, and 150 pounds, but the bathroom scale puts them at 40, 90, and 140 pounds, we have reason to complain about the calibration of the scale on the grounds that it seems to be *biased* downward by 10 pounds. On the other hand, the scale gives a highly *reliable* assessment of weight, in the sense that the true and measured weights correlate at 1.0. Note that the same would be true if the measured weights were 25, 50, and 75 pounds. Again, there is a downward bias, because the bathroom scale obeys a metric in which 2 true pounds = 1 measured pound. Nevertheless, the measures are perfectly reliable, because there is a correlation of 1.0 between the true and observed scores. Since we lack a means for calibrating our measures against known quantities of gay population density or hate crime, bias is an irreducible problem, and we focus instead on the reliability of each measure, that is, its correlation with the latent trait that it gauges.

Measurement Model of Gay Population Density

Let us begin by considering a one-factor model in which the ξ_i denote the latent proportion of gay households among all households in region i. The observed measures of the gay population proportion may be treated as manifestations of this latent trait:

$$X_{1i} = \lambda_{11}\xi_i + \delta_{1i}$$

$$X_{2i} = \lambda_{21}\xi_i + \delta_{2i}$$

Here $\{X_{1i}, X_{2i}\}$ represent, respectively, the measures derived from the Census and mailing list, each deviated from its sample mean. Centering the data in this way (in effect, discarding information about absolute levels) reflects the fact that we take no position on the issue of whether homosexuality should be defined narrowly or broadly. The $\{\delta_{1i}, \delta_{2i}\}$ represent errors of measurement for each observed indicator. The scaling factor that translates these true scores into measured scores are the λ_{pq}. Error is the discrepancy between the observed score and the scaled true score.

The key statistical assumption that makes it possible to differentiate trait variance from error is that different measures make unrelated mistakes when measuring the gay population of a given zip code. Formally, we assume that in large samples the covariance of δ_{ji} and δ_{ki} is zero. Furthermore, we must assume that errors of measurement are independent of the trait to be measured (ξ_i), an assumption that would be violated if, for example, a given measure tended to overestimate the gay population of areas where the true gay population is larger than average.

Measurement Model of Antigay Hate Crime

A similar logic applies to the relationship between true levels of hate crime in each zip code (denoted η_i) and our two observed indicators, hate crime incidents reported to the AVP (Y_{1i}) and NYPD (Y_{2i}).

$$Y_{1i} = \lambda_{11}\eta_i + \varepsilon_{1i}$$

$$Y_{2i} = \lambda_{21}\eta_i + \varepsilon_{2i}$$

And as before, ε_{1i} and ε_{2i} are assumed to be random error, uncorrelated with one another and with true rates of hate crime (η_i). It is further assumed that the errors made in measuring gay population density are unrelated to errors made in detecting hate crime.

Interfactor Correlations

In theory, if the latent variables "gay population density" and "antigay hate crime" are correlated, the parameters of the measurement model become estimable using confirmatory factor analysis. In practice, the estimation will fail if the observed measures should turn out to be weakly correlated with one another, resulting in empirical underidentification (Bollen, 1989).

What, then, is the correlation between population density and hate crime? Studies of hate crime have to date focused almost entirely on racially or ethnically motivated crime. Emphasizing the importance of demographic factors, such as the population balance of different racial groups and the rate at which this balance changes over time, such studies (Green, Strolovitch, and Wong, 1998; Tolnay and Beck, 1995) suggest a wide range of hypotheses that may or may not generalize to hate crime directed against gay men and lesbians. Is it the case, consistent with historical studies that find a positive correlation between antiblack lynching and the population density of blacks in Southern counties (Blalock, 1957), that antigay hate crime is more frequent in areas with a higher population density of gay men and lesbians? Or does antigay hate crime resemble instead contemporary hate crime directed against racial minorities (Green, Strolovich, and Wong, 1998), which occurs with greater frequency in areas where minorities are greatly outnumbered by whites?

Among scholars of gay and lesbian communities, intuitions about the relationship between population density and victimization differ. Some argue that antigay hate crime tends to occur more frequently in areas with high concentrations of gay or lesbian households, because their reputation as such attracts perpetrators seeking lesbian and gay victims (Comstock, 1991). Others portray the "gay ghetto" as a safe haven, suggesting that hate crimes against gay men and lesbians occur most often outside areas of high residential concentration, where the protection of other gay men and lesbians is unavailable (Levine, 1979). Assessing the relationship between hate crime and gay/lesbian population density is an important first step toward understanding the nature and origins of hate crime.

Thus, the correlation between hate crime and population density is both substantively interesting and methodologically crucial. A rough assessment of this correlation can be derived from graphical displays. The apparent correlation between population density and hate crime is strongly positive. Figure 1 displays the correlation (.74) between the Census tabulation and the NYPD reports for gay men, and Table 1 reports the full range of correlations among each of the measures. In each instance, graphical inspection of the data reveals a strong relationship, the most notable of which is the remarkable .97 correlation between alternative measures of hate crime against gay men (Figure 2).

The correlations among our measures are influenced by a relatively small number of observations that tend to have both high rates of hate crime and large populations of gay men. To make the analysis more robust, it is useful to work with rank-order correlations, which transform these metric variables into a series of ranks. This approach greatly diminishes the influence of par-

FIGURE 1

Association between Hate Crime (NYPD)
and Population Density of Gay Men (Census)

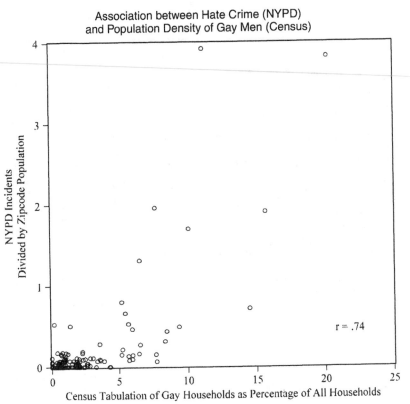

Census Tabulation of Gay Households as Percentage of All Households

ticular observations while at the same time making it easier to generalize from an analysis of New York City to other areas that may not have neighborhoods comparable to Greenwich Village. As shown in Table 1, when rank-order correlations are employed, the Spearman rho correlation between the two measures of hate crime falls to .72, and the correlation between alternative measures of gay population density is .65.

Repeating the analysis for the population density and victimization of lesbians, we find somewhat weaker correlations. The Pearson correlation between the alternative measures of hate crime is .81, but the correlation between the two measures of population density is only .57. Looking at the interfactor correlations, we find a strong correlation of .84 when examining mailing list and AVP indicators but just .31 when looking at Census and NYPD measures. The Spearman correlations paint an even less promising picture: The correlation between alternative measures of hate crime drops to .52. The two measures of population density correlate at just .29. As we

TABLE 1

Correlations between Measures of Hate Crime, Population Density, and Other Demographic Variables

Gay men	(1)	(2)	(3)	(4)
1. Census tabulation per household	1.00	.65	.54	.57
2. Strubco names per capita	.90	1.00	.62	.56
3. AVP incidents per capita	.79	.83	1.00	.72
4. NYPD bias crimes per capita	.74	.76	.97	1.00
5. Percentage of population that is white	.19	.24	.20	.16
6. Percentage of population under age 5	−.40	−.46	−.38	−.35
7. Median household income in 1989	.09	.17	.11	.06
8. Proportion of population in poverty	−.03	−.11	−.08	−.06
Lesbians	**(1)**	**(2)**	**(3)**	**(4)**
1. Census tabulation per household	1.00	.29	.36	.10
2. Strubco names per capita	.57	1.00	.54	.35
3. AVP incidents per capita	.46	.84	1.00	.52
4. NYPD bias crimes per capita	.31	.73	.81	1.00
5. Percentage of population that is white	.00	.25	.18	.26
6. Percentage of population under age 5	−.17	−.44	−.33	−.27
7. Median household income in 1989	−.03	.18	.04	.14
8. Proportion of population in Poverty	.08	−.11	−.05	−.12

NOTE: Pearson correlations are included below the diagonal row of 1.0s; Spearman's rho is above the diagaonal in italics. $N = 152$.

show more rigorously below, the Census and NYPD measures in particular seem to have low reliability.

Covariates

Our basic measurement model is augmented by covariates, that is, variables that may or may not be correlated with gay population density and rates of victimization. Such ancillary variables are not strictly necessary for estimation, but by introducing additional degrees of freedom, covariates help reduce the biases associated with misspecification of the model, particularly the model's assumption that all errors of measurement are white noise. Covariates also serve a useful diagnostic role. If just one measure of the gay population, for example, should bear an unexpectedly high correlation with affluence—higher than we would expect based on the estimated reliability of the measure—we would suspect that the indicator suffers from nonrandom error associated with social class.

Measuring Gay Populations and Antigay Hate Crime 291

FIGURE 2

Association between NYPD and AVP Reports of Bias Crimes
and Heterosexist Incidents Directed at Gay Men

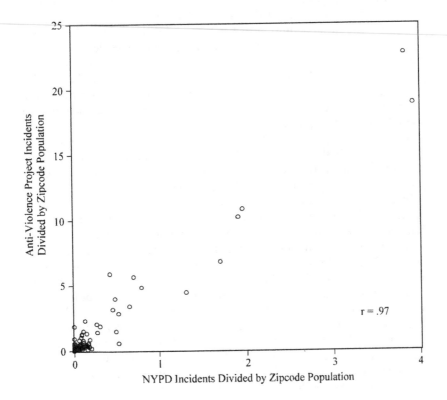

Results

Population Density of Gay Men and Rate of Incidents Directed against Them

Confirmatory factor analysis provides estimates of both the reliability of each measure and the correlations among the latent factors. The reliability estimates suggest that both measures of population density perform adequately. Reliability estimates of .78 and .67 imply that approximately 22% of the variability in the rank-ordering of zip codes based on the market research lists is measurement error, as compared to 33% of the variability in the Census ranking. The reliabilities of the hate crime measures are similar in magnitude: .69 for the AVP reports and .61 for the police reports.

Despite the fact that the AVP typically reports a much higher number of incidents in each zip code, these two measures are surprisingly comparable in terms of reliability. Interest groups and police agencies frequently criticize each other's data-gathering efforts. The AVP laments the many incidents that seem to escape notice of the police, which in turn regards the AVP as too permissive in its definition of heterosexist incidents. Yet, when viewed cross-sectionally, the two measures are virtually interchangable. (It should be noted as well that when the two hate crime measures are examined longitudinally—on a monthly basis from January 1994 through December 1995— they show a strong .62 correlation.) Despite the uncertainty surrounding the measurement of hate crime, these measures seem to track each other in ways that cannot simply be attributed to shared reporting errors.

The relationship between hate crime and gay population density is a powerful one. As shown in Table 2, net of measurement error, the rank orderings for population density and hate crime are highly correlated ($r = .83$), indicating that areas with higher density of gay men experience substantially higher rates of hate crime. As might be expected from a correlation of this magnitude, population density and hate crime bear similar, but not identical, correlations to other socioeconomic characteristics. Each is negatively correlated with the proportion of people under the age of five ($r = -.38$ and $-.34$, respectively) and only weakly correlated with poverty rates ($r = .06$ and $-.07$). On the other hand, hate crimes correlate more strongly than population density with median household income ($r = .20$ vs. .04) and the white proportion of the population ($r = .30$ vs. .12), which could reflect a class-related reporting bias or a concentration of gay institutions and establishments in somewhat more affluent neighborhoods. Either way, the correlations with income and race remain fairly weak.

Overall, the fit between data and model specification is quite good. The root mean square residual—more or less the average discrepancy between the observed and predicted correlation matrix—is just .02. The adjusted goodness of fit index (AGFI) is .95. Moreover, the results are robust across alternative specifications, such as those omitting the four socioeconomic variables.

Population Density of Lesbians and Antilesbian Hate Crime

As one might expect based on the interitem correlations, the statistical results are less propitious as we turn our attention to lesbian population density, as Table 3 confirms. The Census measure proves to be unreliable, with approximately 80% of its variance attributable to mismeasurement. The Strubco measure, though superior, is by no means outstanding, given its reliability of .48. Neither a tabulation of roommates nor an accumulation of mailing lists, by itself, seems to offer an accurate means by which to assess the spatial arrangement of the lesbian population.

TABLE 2

Confirmatory Factor Analysis: Population Density of Gay Men and Antigay Hate Crime

	Standardized Factor Loadings		Reliabilities
	Hate Crimes per Capita: Gay Men	Population Density of Gay Men	
AVP incidents per capita	.882		.777
NYPD bias crimes per capita	.818		.669
Census tabulation per household		.782	.611
Strubco names per capita		.833	.694

Correlations among latent factors

Hate crimes per capita	1.000					
Population density: Gay men	0.831	1.000				
Percentage white	0.300	0.116	1.000			
Percentage under age 5	−0.341	−0.379	−0.560	1.000		
Median household income	0.199	0.042	0.731	−0.559	1.000	
Percentage in poverty	−0.073	0.059	−0.752	0.547	−0.938	1.000

FIT STATISTICS: Root mean square residual = .020; goodness of fit index = .988; adjusted GFI = .953; chi-square with nine degrees of freedom = 7.07.

NOTE: n = 152.

Corresponding assessment of the hate crime measures produces mixed results. The AVP measure performs admirably; its reliability is .72. The NYPD measure, on the other hand, does not fare well when transformed into a series of ranks. As noted above, a large proportion of all zip codes lack any NYPD reports, a fact that contributes to the low reliability of .37. These erratic correlations account for the fact that the goodness of fit indices are poorer for the measures of lesbian population density and antilesbian hate crime.

Although the Census and NYPD measures could not suffice on their own, they do perform an important function as redundant indicators in our confirmatory factor analysis model. Without them, it would be difficult or impossible to gauge the reliabilities of the AVP and Strubco indicators, an exercise necessary to determine the interfactor correlation between population density and hate crime. This correlation turns out to be a remarkable .90, suggesting that, measurement error aside, hate crimes occur where concentrations of lesbians are greatest. Although on the whole the measures of population density and hate crime concerning lesbians are inferior to the corresponding indicators for gay men, the overall conclusion is very much the same: A powerful statistical link exists between population density and hate crime.

TABLE 3

Confirmatory Factor Analysis: Population Density
of Lesbians and Antilesbian Hate Crime

	Standardized Factor Loadings		Reliabilities
	Hate Crimes per Capita: Lesbians	Population Density of Lesbians	
AVP incidents per capita	.848		.719
NYPD bias crimes per capita	.610		.372
Census tabulation per household		.431	.186
Strubco names per capita		.693	.481

Correlations among latent factors

Hate crimes per capita	1.000					
Population density: Lesbians	0.901	1.000				
Percentage white	0.302	0.139	1.000			
Percentage under age 5	−0.345	−0.438	−0.560	1.000		
Median household income	0.177	0.081	0.731	−0.559	1.000	
Percentage in poverty	−0.061	0.041	−0.752	0.547	−0.938	1.000

FIT STATISTICS: Root mean square residual = .049; goodness of fit index = .975; adjusted GFI = .900; chi-square with nine degrees of freedom = 15.19.

NOTE: n = 152.

Conclusion

The capacity to measure the population density of gay men and lesbians has far-ranging implications for policymaking and social science inquiry. Given the high correlation between population density and hate crime, knowledge of where gay men and lesbians live provides a map for law enforcement agencies and community organizations that seek to deter such incidents. This link is fortuitous, since little or no systematic effort is made to gather data on antigay hate crime in many jurisdictions. A similar logic applies to other policy interventions, such as those aimed at HIV prevention, as well as efforts at political mobilization and redistricting (Bailey, 1999). Knowing where gay men and lesbians live is crucial to an efficient allocation of effort.

The difficulty to date has been the dearth of official data charting the gay and lesbian populations. At least in the case of gay men, this problem may be solved by means of a special tabulation of Census data. This measure, though not flawless, is sufficiently reliable to support statistical analysis at levels of aggregation as low as the zip code. Although these data currently require a rather expensive special tabulation, they are not proprietary (as are the Strubco data), and they may become more readily available and timely as the American Community Survey gets underway. Unlike mailing lists,

Census measures are in principle comparable across time and place. One could, for example, chart patterns in same-sex habitation over time or compare gay population density across cities (Bailey, 1999).

Our research also sheds light on certain nagging issues concerning the measurement of hate crime. Given the difficulties of defining and identifying hate crime, encouraging victims to come forward, and compiling meaningful records of when and where incidents occur, there is understandable skepticism about the reliability and validity of hate crime data. One cannot compare jurisdictions that use different reporting standards or have different levels of commitment to the monitoring of hate crime. But what about comparisons within jurisdictions? If one cannot compare the incidence of hate crime among sections of a city, then the prospects for quantitative analysis of hate crime seem bleak.

Prior to gathering the data for this study, we were skeptical that hate crimes directed at gay men and lesbians could be studied reliably. Judging from the total numbers of incidents reported to the press, official police statistics seemed altogether unlike the statistics gathered by monitoring groups. What we discovered is that when arrayed spatially, police statistics and those compiled by the AVP are more or less proportional to one another. Although it is true that these police figures cannot be compared directly to those collected by monitoring groups, they each offer a similar spatial (and temporal) depiction of hate crime within the city. This fact does not help resolve the question of how much authentic hate crime actually occurs, but it does offer reassurance to those who seek to analyze and explain variability in rates of hate crime.

REFERENCES

Bailey, Robert W. 1999. *Gay Politics, Urban Politics: Identity and Economics in the Urban Setting*. New York: Columbia University Press.

Berk, Richard A., Elizabeth A. Boyd, and Karl M. Hamner. 1992. "Thinking More Clearly about Hate-motivated Crimes." Pp. 123–43 in Gregory M. Herek and Kevin T. Berrill (eds.), *Hate Crimes: Confronting Violence against Lesbians and Gay Men*. Newbury Park, Calif.: Sage.

Blalock, Hubert M. 1957. "Per Cent Non-White and Discrimination in the South." *American Journal of Sociology* 22:677–82.

Bollen, Kenneth A. 1989. *Structural Equations with Latent Variables*. New York: Wiley.

Boyd, Elizabeth A., Richard A. Berk, and Karl M. Hamner. 1996. "'Motivated by Hatred or Prejudice': Categorization of Hate-Motivated Crimes in Two Police Divisions." *Law & Society Review* 30:819–50.

Campbell, D. T., and D. W. Fiske. 1959. "Convergent and Discriminant Validation by the Multi-Trait-Multimethod Matrix." *Psychological Bulletin* 56:89–105.

Comstock, Gary David. 1991. *Violence against Lesbians and Gay Men*. New York: Columbia University.

Glick, Paul C. 1988. "Fifty Years of Family Demography: A Record of Social Change." *Journal of Marriage and the Family* 50:861–73.

Green, Donald P., Dara Z. Strolovitch, and Janelle S. Wong. 1998. "Defended Neighborhoods, Integration, and Racially Motivated Crime." *American Journal of Sociology* 104:372–403.

Herek, Gregory M. 1989. "Hate Crimes against Lesbians and Gay Men: Issues for Research and Policy." *American Psychologist* 44:948–55.

Jacobs, James B., and Kimberly Potter. 1998. *Hate Crimes: Criminal Law and Identity Politics.* New York: Oxford University Press.

Laumann, Edward O., John H. Gagnon, Robert T. Michael, and Stuart Michaels. 1994. *The Social Organization of Sexuality: Sexual Practices in the United States.* Chicago: University of Chicago Press.

Levine, Martin. 1979. "Gay Ghettos." *Journal of Homosexuality* 4:363–77.

Tolnay, Stewart E., and E. M. Beck. 1995. *A Festival of Violence: An Analysis of Southern Lynchings, 1882–1930.* Chicago: University of Illinois Press.

Wang, L. 1994. *Hate Crime Laws.* New York: Clark, Boardman, Callagan.

[16]

NOT OUR KIND OF HATE CRIME

GAIL MASON

ABSTRACT. Implicit in hate crime is the premise that certain types of violence can be usefully articulated through the concept of hate. This article seeks to raise some questions about hate as a heuristic device for understanding homophobic violence. It sets the scene for this discussion by providing a brief overview of the ways in which the concept of hate has been introduced into Australian legislation. In many accounts of homophobic violence hate is reduced to a question of fear, to the perpetrator's fear of his own homosexual desires. Drawing upon the specific example of violence by heterosexual men towards lesbian women, the article argues for a somewhat different angle on the relationship between hate and fear. In highlighting the significance of narratives of heterosexual love to anti-lesbian violence, it asks, what kinds of fear might we see if we looked at homophobic violence through the concept of love? To do so does not require us to reject the concept of hate but, rather, to acknowledge that love and hate are intimately entwined with each other.

KEY WORDS: fear, hate, homophobic violence, lesbian, love

INTRODUCTION

Academics are often ambivalent about conferences. We love to attend them but we also love to avoid them. We vacillate. We feel like we missed out if we did not go to 'the' conference that everyone is talking about. Yet, we often come away from a conference asking ourselves whether it was worth the long trip. Should we have remained at home and done some 'real' work instead? Did we have any fun? Part of the appeal of a conference, however, is found in the fact that we cannot predict these things in advance. Often, it is the odd encounters, the behind-the-scenes experiences that attract us, stray thoughts that we do not mention to anyone at the time, tucking them away for the future. Of course, such experiences always re-emerge, usually when we sit down to write. This has happened to me several times now.[1] When I started to write this paper I was not surprised to find myself remembering a conference that I had organised on hate crime in 1999 at the University of Sydney. What did surprise me was the way that my thoughts kept returning to an encounter that took place before the conference even

---

[1] Recently, this happened when I started to write a paper on the relationship between homophobic violence and discourses of visibility. See G. Mason, 'Body Maps: Envisaging Homophobia, Violence and Safety', *Social and Legal Studies* 10(1) (2001), 23–44.

began.[2] Eventually I realised that this incident had come to symbolise the sense of reservation that I have about the concept of hate crime. In effect, it has compelled me to articulate these concerns. For this reason, I believe it is worth repeating.

The idea of the Hate Crime Conference was to bring together academics, community workers, and government agencies to explore the concept of hate crime in an Australian context. Given this diversity, we decided to organise a community consultation forum prior to the actual conference: an informal venue where people could offer suggestions and ideas for the conference. The forum was a huge success. The idea of hate crime was taken up in the broadest possible sense. There were discussions of racist violence, homophobic violence, anti-Semitic violence, gendered violence, violence towards sex workers, and violence towards transgender people. There was a real buzz in the air, a sense of potential, of what might happen if we really did all talk, and listen, to each other. It reminded me of a queer dance party: a hot, tight space where people's diversities and idiosyncrasies were encouraged to come out, step around each other, converge momentarily, only to return to their own corner with a renewed sense of what an encounter with otherness might actually feel like. It was inspiring.

When it came to inviting speakers to the conference, one of the first places I started was the panel of the people who had addressed this forum. Having received an enthusiastic response to my first few calls, I found myself hesitating at one name on the list. Despite the infectious atmosphere of the forum, I had noticed on the night that this particular speaker, who had spoken on a form of ethno-religious violence, had seemed less than enthusiastic every time someone talked about gay, lesbian, transgender or sex worker issues. I was concerned that she may have found the forum rather confronting, perhaps even unpalatable. However, I did not want to let my own assumptions prevent me from inviting her. So, I rang. She remembered me. When I asked her if she would like to speak at the conference she politely replied: 'No, I don't think so. It's not our kind of hate crime.' I persevered: might anyone else in her organisation be interested? Quickly and firmly, she said 'No', again assuring me that: 'It's not our kind of hate crime.'

It is not our kind of hate crime ... an odd statement. Despite the fact that I half expected it, I was taken aback. I felt put in my place, although I was not certain where that place might be. Without being rude, the woman on the other end of the telephone had managed to draw a line between

---

[2] *Hate Crime: Politics Practice Power* Conference, Department of Gender Studies and the Institute of Criminology, The University of Sydney, Australia, 9–10 December 1999.

'her' kind of hate crime and 'our' kind of hate crime. I mulled it over. The word 'kind' had connotations of types of people, types of perpetrators and types of victims; a comment on whom belongs with whom. Was she really saying 'they're not our kind of people'? Perhaps. But who were we and who were they? As for the word 'our', it seemed to have a possessive, almost territorial, tone to it. Can someone own hate crime? Did her words signal a distinction between hate which is considered to be serious and hate which is not serious and, hence, not even real hate crime (like 'our' hate crime)? My speculations were endless.

Despite the fact that I was disappointed by this woman's response, I am not especially interested in reproaching her. I suspect that she may have found it a genuinely disconcerting experience to be in a room full of queers, trannies and sex workers. However, I am interested in the fact that she chose to convey this to me by emphasising the differences between various forms of hate crime. Implicit in hate crime is the premise that certain types of violence embody a material expression of the hate that some groups of people feel towards other groups of people. In turn, the codification of hate crime in law implies that such violence can be usefully articulated – defined and identified – via the concept of hate. Hate crime is thus designed to highlight the violent manifestations of particular regimes *of* difference, such as those of race, ethnicity, religion, sexuality, and so on. Yet, like all umbrella terms, it can so easily obscure the important differences *between* these specific forms of violence. Irrespective of the actual sentiment that prompted this woman to demarcate 'her' kind of hate crime from 'our' kind of hate crime, her comments remind me that we cannot afford to be complacent about these differences.

My purpose in this article is quite simple. I wish to raise some questions about hate as a heuristic device. I set the scene for this discussion by providing a brief overview of the ways in which the concept of hate has been introduced into Australian legislation. I ask, what explanatory links are we encouraged to see when we look at violence through hate? What are we less likely to see?[3] I explore these questions as they relate to one specific form of hate crime: violence that is directed towards lesbians and gay men and which involves anti-homosexual sentiment. I take the violence that heterosexual men direct towards lesbian women as a specific example upon which to centre my analysis.[4] In many accounts of such

---

[3] My purpose is not to establish what it is that the concept of hate tells us about these forms of violence. Instead, I focus on the kinds of things that hate does *not* tell us. What does it leave out?

[4] Heterosexual women are far less likely than heterosexual men to act violently towards lesbian women. It is more common for women and girls to verbally abuse lesbians. Violence by women may well require another line of analysis.

256   GAIL MASON

violence hate is reduced to a question of fear, particularly to the perpetrator's fear of his own homosexual desires. Drawing upon examples of
violence towards lesbians prompts me to look for a slightly different angle
on the relationship between hate and fear. In particular, when I consider
the way in which such violence is infused with narratives of heterosexual love, I am prompted to ask what kinds of fear might we see if we
looked at anti-homosexual violence through the concept of love? To do
so does not demand that we reject the concept of hate. Instead it requires
us to acknowledge that love and hate are intimately entwined with each
other.

The governing modes of conceptualising both love and hate are deeply
influenced by psychology and/or psychoanalytic theory. This makes it
impossible to explore such concepts without engaging with these bodies of
knowledge. Yet, in many ways I am wary of this literature. I am sceptical
of its preoccupation with the individual, with the self that is said to lie
'within'.[5] To put it simply, this search for internal causes, for deeper and
deeper origins, leaves me cold. Thus I come to the literature on love and
hate as an outsider, as someone who seeks only to make my way across its
surface, to trace its principal contours with a specific strategy in mind.
I want to see what different theorisations of hate can, and cannot, tell
me about violence towards lesbians and gay men. By both necessity and
choice, then, my reading of psychology and psychoanalytic theory is one
that respects the epistemological paradigms within which it is produced
but which unashamedly translates these premises into my own terms.

HATE IN LAW

It is generally accepted that the term hate crime was coined in the 1980s in
the United States. It came to national prominence through the federal *Hate
Crime Statistics Act* (1990) which required the US Department of Justice to
collect and publish statistics on the prevalence and nature of crimes where
there was evidence of prejudice based on race, religion, sexual orientation,

---

It is also important to note that my discussion here is confined to the specificities of
gender and sexuality between perpetrator and victim. It does not address differences of
race, ethnicity or class. For a discussion of the ways in which racial difference, particularly
between Anglo perpetrators and Asian victims, shapes the enactment and experience of
homophobic violence see G. Mason, *The Spectacle of Violence: Homophobia, Gender and
Knowledge* (London: Routledge, 2001), Chapter 3.

[5] Obviously, psychology and psychoanalytic theory are different from each other.
However, as someone whose work is positioned at the intersection of poststructuralism and
feminism, I have a broad scepticism about the type of human subject that each presupposes
and the methods of analysis that are used to investigate this.

or disability.[6] Since then more than half the state legislatures, as well as the federal legislature, have enacted hate crime laws. Most of these focus upon enhancing the sentence if an offender's 'motive manifests in a legislatively designated prejudice.'[7] However, some states have also created substantive new offences under the rubric of hate crime.[8] As of 1998 the main protected category under US hate crime legislation was race, with sexual orientation featuring in just over fifty percent of laws, and gender in about forty percent.[9] Goldberg suggests that this emphasis on hate emerged 'in direct response to the recognition in the 1980's of the return of visceral racism in the public sphere.'[10] In contrast, Jacobs and Potter suggest that the anti-hate crime movement has been generated, not by 'an epidemic of unprecedented bigotry' but by 'heightened sensitivity to prejudice and, more importantly, by our society's emphasis on identity politics.'[11]

Australian jurisdictions have not enacted the same kinds of criminal law provisions. However, words and images that incite hatred towards particular groups of people are now outlawed at federal and state (and territory) level. Primarily, this has taken place through discrimination law, where the conduct that constitutes the legal wrong is referred to as 'vilification' or, in the federal legislation, 'racial hatred'.[12] Drawing upon international covenants to help frame the law,[13] New South Wales was the first Australian jurisdiction to introduce such legislation in 1989.[14] In this

---

[6] *Hate Crime Statistics Act* (1990).

[7] J. Jacobs and K. Potter, *Hate Crimes: Criminal Law and Identity Politics* (New York: Oxford University Press, 1998), 6.

[8] For example, in California, it is against the law to 'wilfully injure, intimidate, interfere with, oppress, or threaten' another person, by force or threat of force, from the free exercise or enjoyment of rights and privileges secured via the Constitution or US laws because of the person's 'race, color, religion, ancestry, national origin, disability, gender, or sexual orientation'. See California Penal Code 422.7, as cited in V. Jenness, *Law and Critique* 12(3), 279–308 (this volume).

[9] Jacobs and Potter, *supra* n. 7 at 20.

[10] D.T. Goldberg, 'Afterword: Hate, or Power?', in R.K. Willock and D. Slayden, eds., *Hate Speech* (California: Sage, 1995), 268.

[11] Jacobs and Potter, *supra* n. 7 at 4.

[12] Unlike other forms of discrimination, vilification and racial hatred are not restricted to particular areas of activity, such as employment, education or the provision of goods and services.

[13] N. Hennessy and P. Smith, 'Have We Got It Right? NSW Racial Vilification Laws Five Years on', *Australian Journal of Human Rights* 1(1) (1994), 250. It is interesting to note that the word 'hatred' is used in both the International Covenant on Civil and Political Rights, Article 20(2) and the International Covenant on the Elimination of all Forms of Racial Discrimination, Article 4.

[14] However, Jones notes that the much earlier federal *Racial Discrimination Bill* proposed to outlaw 'offences of incitement of racial disharmony and dissemination of ideas

state it is 'unlawful for a person, by a public act, to incite hatred towards, serious contempt for, or severe ridicule of' a person or group of persons on the grounds of homosexuality,[15] transgender,[16] race[17] or HIV/AIDS[18] status. Most states and territories in Australia now have broadly similar provisions.[19] In 1995 the federal race discrimination laws were amended by the *Racial Hatred Act 1995* (Cth) to 'prohibit certain conduct involving the hatred of other people on the ground of race, colour or national or ethnic origin'.[20] To date no other grounds have been included in the federal law. Significantly, in a number of states there are additional provisions for 'serious vilification'. For example, in New South Wales, these allow a complaint to be referred to the police for criminal prosecution.[21] The key ingredient of serious vilification is a perpetrator who threatens, or incites

---

based on racial superiority or hatred'. By the time the bill became law in 1975 these provisions against hate speech had been dropped. It was only after subsequent inquiries – into racist violence, aboriginal deaths in custody and multicultural legal issues – highlighted the problem of racial intimidation and harassment that the federal government sought to provide remedies for the expression of ideas involving racism and other types of group prejudice: M. Jones, 'The Legal Response: Dealing with Hatred – A User's Guide', in C. Cunneen, D. Fraser and S. Tomsen, eds., *Faces of Hate: Hate Crime in Australia* (NSW: Hawkins Press, 1997), 217–218.

[15] *Anti-Discrimination Act* 1977 (NSW) (ADA (NSW)) ss 49ZS–49ZTA, as amended by the *Anti-Discrimination (Homosexual Vilification) Amendment Act* 1993 (NSW).

[16] ADA (NSW) ss 38R–38T as amended by the *Transgender (Anti-Discrimination and Other Act Amendment) Act* 1996 (NSW)).

[17] ADA (NSW) ss 20B, 20C and 20D as amended by the *Anti-Discrimination (Racial Vilification) Amendment Act* 1989 (NSW).

[18] ADA (NSW) ss 49ZXA–49ZXC as amended by the *Anti-Discrimination Act* 1994 (NSW)).

[19] *Racial Vilification Act 1996* (SA), *Anti-Discrimination Act 1991* (Qld), *Discrimination Act 1991* (ACT).

[20] *Racial Hatred Act 1995* (Cth) (RHA) Long Title. The RHA was inserted into the *Racial Discrimination Act 1975* (Cth) (RDA) Part IIA Prohibition of Offensive Behaviour Based on Racial Hatred and became operable in October 1995. The legislation states that it 'is unlawful for a person to do an act, otherwise than in private,' that is 'reasonably likely, in all the circumstances, to offend, insult, humiliate or intimidate another person or a group of people', if the act is 'because of the race, colour or national or ethnic origin of the other person or of some or all of the people in the group.' RDA s18C(1)(a), (b). It is interesting to note that the *Racial Hatred Bill 1994* (Cth), which preceded the RHA, included criminal provisions against the incitement of racial hatred. Whilst racial hatred was not defined in the bill it was said to carry its 'ordinary meaning of intense dislike or enmity'. See K. Eastman, 'Drafting Vilification Laws: Legal and Policy Issues', *Australian Journal of Human Rights* 1(1) (1994), 287–288.

[21] Serious vilification is prohibited in the last of each vilification section in the ADA (NSW): s20D race; s49ZTA homosexuality; s49ZXC HIV/AIDS status; and s38T transgender.

others to threaten, physical harm towards a person or their property on the basis of one of the grounds listed above.

There are important distinctions between the various statutory definitions of vilification, serious vilification and racial hatred in Australian law. It is notable, however, that in all states, vilification encompasses not only acts which incite serious contempt or ridicule for groups of people, but also those which are said to incite hatred towards these groups.[22] Whilst the term hatred is not used to define the proscribed behaviour under the federal legislation the title and aim of the act suggest that it is intended to prohibit conduct involving hatred. In this sense it is fair to say that the concept of hate has already been introduced into Australian law, albeit in restricted ways. Of course, as legal wrongs, vilification and racial hatred are not the same as hate crime; they have more in common with the notion of hate speech and are often referred to as such. Nevertheless, the prohibition of serious vilification in some jurisdictions does suggest a certain willingness of Australian legislatures to entertain the possibility that incitement to hatred warrants a specific response by the criminal law. Indeed, the New South Wales Law Reform Commission has recently recommended that the serious vilification provisions in that state be relocated to the criminal law.[23] Moreover, the connection between vilification law and hate crime has long been emphasised by those who argue that vilifying speech encourages and incites violence and hostility: outlawing the speech is said to enable us to attack the attitudes that make hate crime possible.[24] In short, despite the fact that hate crime laws have not been enacted in Australia, the wider debates that surround their utility have a particular pertinence. Only by engaging in these debates can we bring a critical eye to the current legal situation and participate in informed dialogue about the desirability of enacting hate crime legislation in the future.

Although there are multiple legal and social definitions of hate crime,[25] they each share a common denominator; one that is also shared by the

---

[22] In commentary on the legislation, it has been suggested that incitement to hatred represents an extreme form of vilification: T. Solomon, 'Problems in Drafting Legislation against Racist Activities', *Australian Journal of Human Rights* 1(1) (1994), 265, 266.

[23] Recommendation 96 of the New South Wales Law Reform Commission Report No. 92 states, among other things: 'Remove s20D from the ADA and relocate the offence of serious vilification in the *Crimes Act 1900* (NSW)': New South Wales Law Reform Commission, Report No. 92, *Review of the Anti-Discrimination Act 1977 (NSW)* (Sydney: New South Wales Law Reform Commission, 1999), 553.

[24] For example, see C. Puplick, 'Achieving an Equilibrium: A Reply to David Marr', *Australasian Gay and Lesbian Law Journal* 9 (2000), 22–36.

[25] For example, there is considerable variation between the ways in which hate crime has been formulated in US law. Not all laws expressly use the language of hate, bias or

concept of vilification. Hate crime characterises certain forms of behaviour as a physical expression of the emotion of hate. The behaviour that is outlawed is behaviour that is directed towards a person or persons on the basis, even if only in part, of a perceived *group* characteristic of that person (for example, they are homosexual, black, or Jewish); hate crime is not a question of individual dislikes or hatreds. In turn, the perpetrator (or respondent, in Australian discrimination law) is assumed to have acted because he or she holds stereotyped, prejudicial or less than favourable images of that group of people. Hate crime thus encourages us to assume that the notion of hate has considerable explanatory force. In turn, the enactment of legislation against hate crime codifies this same psychological model of behaviour – this causal link between hate and violence – as a legal wrong. One of the ways in which we can contribute to current debates about the merits of hate crime legislation is to consider the effects of privileging this particular conceptual link at law. Can this link between violence and hate adequately account for all kinds of violence that are grounded in prejudicial or stereotyped attitudes? Might other concepts be just as helpful for understanding, or legislating against, some types of violence? Only by being cautious about the kinds of concepts that we introduce into legislation can we reduce the chances that law will be 'unable to solve the mischief it was designed to address.'[26] I would like to take up these issues through the specific example of anti-homosexual violence, particularly as lesbian women experience it.

ANTI-HOMOSEXUAL VIOLENCE

For some time I have been engaged in research into verbal hostility and physical violence that is perpetrated by heterosexual men towards lesbian women and which involves negative attitudes towards homosexuality.[27] When lesbian women describe such violence they recount many different experiences. At the risk of over-simplification, I believe it is possible to divide these experiences into two main types. First, there are those incidents that look very similar to the primary kinds of violence that gay

---

prejudice: see Jenness in this volume. There is also considerable variation in the ways in which the concept has been put into sociological, activist, and government discourse. For different academic definitions of hate crime see: J. Levin and J. McDevitt, *Hate Crimes: the Rising Tide of Bigotry and Bloodshed* (New York: Plenum, 1993); C. Cunneen, D. Fraser and S. Tomsen, eds., *Faces of Hate: Hate Crime in Australia* (NSW: Hawkins Press, 1997).

[26] M. Jones, 'Empowering Victims of Racial Hatred by Outlawing Spirit Murder: Outlawing Racist Speech', *Australian Journal of Human Rights* 1(1) (1994), 145–146.

[27] See Mason, *supra* n. 4.

men report: attacks in public places by young men, often acting in groups, who are strangers to the victim/s. Second, there are those encounters with violence that, on first glance, appear to have more in common with the experiences of heterosexual women: a more personalised form of violence from one man who is known to the woman. Although random stranger attacks are believed to be the most common form of violence towards gay men, recent research suggests that there may be two main types of violence at play for gay men too. In his research on gay killings, Tomsen reveals that such homicides do not only occur in the context of a random attack. They also erupt in more personal situations where one man has made a non-violent sexual pass at another, which then becomes the impetus for the latter to kill the former.[28] Hence, it is probably fair to say that both lesbians and gay men are subject to attacks by strangers and to attacks that occur in the context of existing, even if short-lived, relationships.

I would like to illustrate the types of violence that lesbians encounter by presenting two scenarios. These scenarios do not represent the actual experiences of particular women. They are reconstructions, compositions of different stories, put together from my research into this kind of violence. They are neither exhaustive nor mutually exclusive of each other. The first scenario depicts a typical incident of stranger violence:

A woman, Barbara, leaves a gay bar alone, late at night in Oxford Street, a well-known queer entertainment area of Sydney. She is dressed in lots of leather, has very short hair, and wears no make-up. Some might say that Barbara 'looks like a dyke'. A couple of young men, Bruce and Bazza, are hanging around the backstreets. They see Barbara and decide to give her a hard time. They walk over to her, calling her a 'butch dyke' and a 'dirty leso' as they approach. They ask her whether she is a boy or a girl. Barbara retaliates with a few insults of her own. They push her around, up against the side of her car. Their intention is clearly to intimidate and frighten her. They leave, saying something like: 'Can't you get a man?'

The second scenario depicts a situation in which a woman experiences violence by a man she knows:

Jenny and John have been married for 5 years. They have two children. They are in the process of getting divorced. Jenny has initiated the split. She has been having an affair with a woman at work. Although this is a catalyst for her decision to leave John, it is far from the only reason. Whilst John is devastated about the divorce, he has been coping to date. However, when John finds out that Jenny is involved with a woman he goes out and gets very drunk. He visits Jenny and forces her to have sex with him. During the rape he says he does not believe that Jenny is a lesbian, that lesbians are all revolting man-haters, that it is wrong to be a lesbian, and so on. Later, he says he is sorry and that he would never intentionally do anything to hurt Jenny because he loves her.

---

[28] Stephen Tomsen, 'Sexual Identity and Victimhood in Gay-hate Murder Trials', in C. Cunneen, D. Fraser and S. Tomsen, eds., *Faces of Hate: Hate Crime in Australia* (NSW: Hawkins Press, 1997), 97–114.

In both scenarios the violence appears to be tied to the idea that lesbian sexuality embodies a rejection or repudiation of the conventional systems of sexual and gendered order.[29] The use of insulting words such as dirty and butch hint at John, Bruce and Bazza's belief that this is an unacceptable state of affairs. They imply that lesbians inhabit unhygienic, potentially polluting, bodies. Their desire to engage in sexual acts with other women is read as a sign of a confused gender identity, perhaps a distorted form of masculinity. It is as if in expressing love or sexual desire towards other women Jenny and Barbara threaten or mock the presumption that femininity is, by its very nature, intrinsically heterosexual. Hence, such violence is rarely a question of anti-homosexual sentiment alone. It is usually a product of the ways in which negative attitudes towards homosexuality are refracted through regimes of gender. This interaction between sexuality and gender also shapes violence towards gay men, where expressions of anti-homosexual sentiment are often coloured by anxieties about masculinity.[30] However, it is important to note that the actual processes at work in anti-homosexual violence will differ according to whether the victim is a lesbian or a gay man. This is most apparent in scenarios of personalised violence. When violence erupts in the context of a sexual advance by one man towards another, such violence appears to be a means for the perpetrator to reject the homosexual overtures of another. When violence erupts in the context of an existing relationship between a heterosexual man and a lesbian woman, it appears to be tied to the assumption that the woman has rejected, or might reject, the sexual overtures of the perpetrator. In other words, violence by heterosexual men towards gay men may be a reaction to the suggestion that the *perpetrator* is homosexual, whereas violence by heterosexual men towards lesbian women may be a reaction to the belief that the *victim* is homosexual. In both cases, the violent repudiation of homosexuality may ultimately facilitate an affirmation of heterosexuality. The gender of the victim, and whether it differs from the gender of the perpetrator, will determine how this affirmation is effected.

I would like to flesh out the significance of this distinction for my exploration of the heuristic capacity of hate. This requires me to consider the variables that tend to be privileged in theorisations of hate. Specifically, I look at hatred towards homosexuality as a question of homophobia

---

[29] For a more detailed discussion of the kinds of discourses that make violence towards lesbians possible see Mason, *supra* n. 4, Chapter 2.

[30] Tomsen, *supra* n. 28 details the interaction between homophobia and masculinity in relation to homicides of gay men.

which, as I shall suggest, links violence towards lesbians and gay men to a particular understanding of fear.

HATE AND THE FEAR OF DIFFERENCE

Although psychologists and philosophers continue to debate whether hate is an emotion, an attitude or a sentiment, it is possible to broadly define it as an intense dislike, extreme aversion or hostility.[31] Winborne and Cohen suggest that hate ranges from milder to stronger forms of negativity.[32] They capture this fluidity in a grid-like model with two intersecting dimensions: 'passive to active' and 'thought to behavior'.[33] Group hate occurs when these emotions are directed towards a whole class of persons. Thus it is not unusual for the notion of group hate and the notion of prejudice to be used interchangeably.[34] Despite an even greater profusion of definitions, Duckitt concludes that prejudice is now generally understood to be a 'negative intergroup attitude'.[35] This kind of negativity is entwined with stereotypes about the groups of people to which it is directed.[36] To this way of thinking group hate and prejudice are both rooted in hierarchies of inter-personal alterity. That is, they are thought to emerge from the exclusionary kinds of logic – the oppositions of self/other – through which the differences between social groups are constructed. Such logic values

---

[31] W. Winborne and R. Cohen, 'Hating those Different from Ourselves: The Origins of Racial, Ethnic, and Religious Hatred', in S. McElhaney and T. Gullotta, eds., *Violence in Homes and Communities: Prevention, Intervention, and Treatment* (California: Sage, 1999), 159.

[32] See A. Soble, *The Structure of Love* (New Haven: Yale University Press, 1990); A. Ben-Ze'ev, *The Subtlety of Emotions* (Massachusetts: The MIT Press, 2000).

[33] Winborne and Cohen, *supra* n. 31 at 162–163.

[34] Jacobs and Potter suggest that hate crime is 'not really about hate, but about bias or prejudice', *supra* n. 7, at 11. Whilst I do not have a problem with the emphasis that they place on prejudice and bias, I am less convinced by the suggestion that hate crime has nothing to do with hate. To my mind, this sets up a distinction between hate and prejudice that is difficult to maintain. Given that we do not talk about 'prejudice crime', I believe that any discussion of the pros and cons of hate crime demands that we address what it is that the concept of hate can and cannot tell us about certain types of violence. This does not mean, however, that we can safely ignore the concept of prejudice. As I have suggested, the two are closely connected. It should become apparent in the following discussion that when it comes to homophobic violence, whether we adopt the language of hate or the language of prejudice is ultimately less important than the ingredients that are said to go into anti-homosexual sentiment.

[35] J. Duckitt, *The Social Psychology of Prejudice* (Westport, CT: Praeger, 1992), 23.

[36] Winborne and Cohen, *supra* n. 31, at 165.

264   GAIL MASON

certain identities and certain subjectivities at the expense of others: for example, heterosexuality over homosexuality.

Many accounts of hate and prejudice are also concerned with the ways in which alterity functions in an *intra*-personal sense. Put very simply, this means that they are influenced by a more psychic or internal sense of the self/other binary, particularly with the idea that we all have a deep-seated fear of the differences that reside within us.[37] Drawing upon psychoanalytic theory, this way of looking at hate and prejudice came to the fore in the work that appeared on anti-Semitism in the aftermath of World War II, particularly that which emanated from the Frankfurt School.[38] The influence of this approach to prejudice has been extensive. For example, in his 1946 account of anti-Semitism Sartre argued that hate is based not so much upon a fear of Jews but upon the anti-Semite's fear 'of himself, of his conscience, ... of change, of society and the world; of everything except the Jews.'[39] Thus, the anti-Semite's desire to confirm 'his' difference from those who are Jewish is not just about an aversion to the external threat that Jewishness supposedly represents to 'his' quality of life, it is also tied to the vulnerabilities and disappointments that 'he' carries within himself.[40] This idea – that group hate has its origins in a fear of the differences that lie

---

[37] Van Pelt provides a detailed discussion of intra-psychic alterity by reference to Lacan's notion of the decentered Other. He juxtaposes this to the ways in which otherness is used to denote inter-personal alterity: T. van Pelt, 'Otherness', http://muse.jhu.edu/journals/postmodern_culture/v010/10.2vanpelt.html, 1–4.

[38] Werz describes the five volume series entitled Studies in Prejudice, which also emanated from the Frankfurt School during this period, as a materialist project with a 'social-psychological orientation': M. Werz, 'Personality, Authority, and Society: Remarks on the Analysis of Authoritarianism and Prejudice in the Social Science', *Social Thought and Research* 21(1–2) (1998), 90, 88. An example of this is found in Adorno and Horkheimer's integration of Freudian psychoanalytic theory with Marx and Weber in their 1944 book, *Dialectic of Enlightenment*. This socio-psychological approach is also evident in the subsequent development of the concept of the authoritarian personality: see T. Adorno, E. Frenkel-Brunswick, D.J. Levinson and R.N. Sanford, *The Authoritarian Personality* (New York: Harper, 1950). Bell traces the influence of this body of work in contemporary debates about identity and mimesis: V. Bell, *Feminist Imagination* (London: Sage, 1999).

[39] Jean-Paul Sartre, 'Portrait of an Anti-Semite', *Partisan Review* 13(2) (1946), 177. The anti-Semite displaces 'his' fears onto Jews: Jews do not cause those fears. Thus, the Jew is 'only a pretext, elsewhere it will be the Negro, the yellow race': at 178.

[40] In Sartre's account the anti-Semite takes pleasure in reciting his hatred for the Jews. It enables him to condemn the Jewish other for the very things that he longs for himself, for the things he imagines that other to have or to be (a point I will return to in the following section): Sartre, *supra* n. 39, at 166. Bell spells out this connection between pleasure, hate and desire for the other through the notion of mimesis, and critiques Sartre in the process: Bell, *supra* n. 38, at 96.

within, and not just outside, of us – continues to be emphasised in contemporary accounts of hate. These differences are said to threaten or erode our sense of identity as particular types of people; we live with the fear that we may become the other.[41] This is particularly apparent in the significance that accounts of group hate often place on the process of 'projection'.[42] Here we are said to project unpalatable parts of our selves onto others in order that they may experience these qualities in themselves. The object of our projection thus becomes inferior and repellent, a container for our fears and anxieties.[43] He or she becomes someone to hate who, in turn, enables us to discriminate against, or be violent towards, them.[44] Hence, hate is often understood as a passion which facilitates the hater's sense of a cohesive identity, anger that is said to excite the self more than the emotion of love.[45]

Fear of oneself is emphasised in much of the literature on anti-homosexual sentiment. Consider, for example, the term homophobia itself. Popularised in the 1960's, the word initially referred to an irrational fear of homosexuality, particularly to heterosexuals' dread of being in close quarters with homosexuals.[46] The source of this loathing is said to be a fear, not just of homosexuality in others, but also of one's own homo-

---

[41] For example, Eisentein argues that 'the psychic dimensions of hate borders on fear': Z. Eisenstein, 'Writing Hatred on the Body', *New Political Scientist* 30/31 (1994), 5. Eisenstein is careful to point out that racial hatred is also a response to the fears of daily life, a product of the imagined construction of the other who is commonly named as foreigner, immigrant, or stranger. Such anxieties are generated by the sense of ambivalence and uncertainty that we feel about racial difference. Ultimately, however, she argues that we can only come to terms with hate if we look at it in Lacanian terms. That is, if we recognise that hate is tied to a fear of our own lack or incompleteness; a fear that we project onto others: at 8–9.

[42] S. Clarke, 'Splitting Difference: Psychoanalysis, Hatred and Exclusion', *Journal for the Theory of Social Behaviour* 29(1) (1999), 24. Clarke details the mimetic and paranoid aspects of this process. He also links it to the Kleinian mechanism of projective identification, suggesting that the critical theory of the Frankfurt school provides a 'theoretical bridge' between Freudian theory and the work of Melanie Klein. For Clarke, this provides a 'starting point for the consideration of a contemporary psychosocial theory of hatred and exclusion,' at 21.

[43] J. Bird and S. Clarke, 'Racism, Hatred, and Discrimination Through the Lens of Projective Identification', *Journal for the Psychoanalysis of Culture and Society* 4(2) (1999), 332–333.

[44] *Ibid.*, 333.

[45] L. Langman, 'I Hate, Therefore I Am', *Social Thought and Research* 21(1–2) (1998), 172–174. Langman, draws upon the work of Erich Fromm to make this argument in the context of fascism.

[46] G. Weinberg, *Society and the Healthy Homosexual* (New York: St. Martin's Press, 1972).

sexual desires.[47] Despite much criticism,[48] including attempts to promote alternative terms,[49] homophobia is now the most popular means of signifying all forms of negativity towards homosexuality. With some prominent exceptions,[50] this model of fear dominates explanatory accounts of anti-homosexual sentiment and, in turn, of violence towards lesbians and gay

---

[47] In this sense, homophobia is partially rooted in the Freudian idea that paranoia stems from the repression of homosexual desire: Richard Golstein, 'The Hate that Makes Men Straight: Psychoanalysts Probe the Roots of Homophobia', in R. Baird and S. Rosenbaum, eds., *Hatred, Bigotry, and Prejudice: Definitions, Causes and Solutions* (New York: Prometheus Books, 1999), 169.

[48] Some of these criticisms have come from within psychology. For example, the social psychologist Gregory Herek has sought to establish that prejudice towards homosexuals is not a phobia in the clinical sense of the word. He has argued instead that negativity and violence towards homosexuality serve a number of psychological functions: G. Herek, 'The Social Psychology of Homophobia: Toward a Practical Theory', *Review of Law and Social Change* 14(4) (1986), 923–934. Outside of psychology, Kinsman argued some time ago that although homophobia may be an accurate description of the panic that some heterosexual men experience in the company of gay men, the location of this reaction within a psychological framework 'individualizes and privatizes gay oppression and obscures the social relations that organize it': G. Kinsman, *The Regulation of Desire: Sexuality in Canada* (Montreal: Black Rose, 1987), 29. Kinsman chooses to reserve the word homophobia for particularly virulent personal responses to homosexuality, the types that are more likely to engender violence.

[49] For example, the term heterosexism has been promoted by a number of commentators. It was originally coined by Morin and Garfinkle in 1978: see S. Morin and E. Garfinkle, 'Male Homophobia', *Journal of Social Issues* 34(1) (1978), 29–47. Taking their lead from sociology, rather than psychology, Morin and Garfinkle used heterosexism to describe a belief system founded upon the assumption that heterosexuality is superior to homosexuality. Herek has advocated the use of heterosexism, which he redefines as an 'ideological system that denies, denigrates, and stigmatizes any nonheterosexual form of behavior, identity, relationship, or community': G. Herek, 'The Context of Anti-Gay Violence: Notes on Cultural and Psychological Heterosexism', *Journal of Interpersonal Violence* 5(3) (1990), 316. Herek divides heterosexism into cultural heterosexism and psychological heterosexism. More recently, Herek has favoured the term 'sexual prejudice'. Emphasising the functional nature of anti-homosexual sentiment, he uses sexual prejudice to refer to 'all negative attitudes based on sexual orientation, whether the target is homosexual, bisexual, or heterosexual'. As a negative attitude, evaluation or judgement directed at a social group, sexual prejudice signifies hostility or dislike but is designed to avoid the value judgements and assumptions about the underlying motivations of anti-gay attitudes: G. Herek, 'The Psychology of Sexual Prejudice', *Current Directions in Psychological Science* 9(1) (2000), 19–22.

[50] In Herek's work on negative attitudes towards homosexuality, affirmation of the perpetrator's heterosexual identity through a violent rejection of the homosexual other is only one of the psychological functions of anti-gay violence. All of the functions that he identifies do, however, presuppose an intolerance of difference: see Herek, *supra* n. 48, n. 49; G. Herek, 'Can Functions Be Measured? A New Perspective on the Functional Approach to Attitudes', *Social Psychology Quarterly* 59(4) (1987), 285–303.

men; it is not a question of whether or not a given account recognises this fear but, merely, of the degree to which it privileges it.[51] For example, Iris Young suggests that homophobia is one of the 'deepest fears of difference precisely because the border between gay and straight is constructed as the most permeable.'[52] For Young, this 'border anxiety' is rooted in the possibility that an individual *could* be gay, even if he or she identifies as heterosexual. She notes that this kind of aversion is also found in prejudice towards people who are elderly or disabled: it is a fear of becoming the other.[53] Prejudice, hostility and violence enable an individual to confirm his or her difference from the homosexual other and thereby confirm a sense of heterosexuality. In a not dissimilar way, Moss suggests that homophobia comes about when a 'man's' sense of 'his' heterosexuality is threatened and requires defending.[54] This anxious sense of aversion towards homosexuality operates in conjunction with an anxious identification with one's own heterosexuality.[55] By keeping the phobic object at a distance, the individual who feels threatened is able to identify more closely with others who are like 'himself' (that is, heterosexual). 'He' is able to transform the fear that 'he' has of 'his' own homosexual desire into

---

[51] It is interesting to note that recent violence prevention campaigns by the New South Wales Gay and Lesbian Anti-Violence Project reinforce, at the same time that they question, the idea that hostility towards homosexuality is grounded in fear. These campaigns promote the slogan 'Homophobia: what are you scared of?'

[52] I.M. Young, *Justice and the Politics of Difference* (Princeton: Princeton University Press, 1990), 146.

[53] Young appropriates Kristeva's work on abjection – particularly in terms of dirt as that which marks the precarious nature of one's subjectivity – to analyse homophobia. She suggests that homosexuality is often understood as an in-between or ambiguous form of sexuality, one that represents a disruption to the sexual order of contemporary western societies. If this sexual order is to be maintained homosexuality must be expelled from the realms of respectable sexual practices. Naming it as 'dirty' provides the rationalisation for this to happen. In other words, once homosexuality is said to be unclean, the sense of personal revulsion that follows ensures that it will be excluded from legitimate social and political spheres. *Ibid.*, 146–147.

[54] In Moss's theory of hatred in the 'first person plural' the border between sexuality which is safe and that which is dangerous is blurred. This results in a paranoid search for new borders and new distinctions: see D. Moss, 'Introductory Thoughts: Hating in the First Person Plural: The Example of Homophobia', *American Imago* 49(3) (1992), 278.

[55] *Ibid.*, 283. For Moss, it is the threat that homosexuality poses to established systems of sexual order, to one's heterosexual identity, that engenders the emotion of hatred. In this way, hatred is dependent upon order. Those who are hated are constant reminders that order can easily be 'scuttled'. Moreover, hatred towards homosexuality is critical to the dominant sexual order because it enables the boundary between heterosexuality and homosexuality to be maintained.

268　　　　　　　　　GAIL MASON

a hatred of the homosexual other. Quite simply, the phobic self will be safe 'as long as it can avert the dangerous object' of homosexuality.[56]

Although these accounts of hate and prejudice emerge from diverse, sometimes conflicting, schools of thought, they share a common proposition. Broadly speaking, they all explain group hate as a fear of difference and, particularly, a fear of being or becoming the other that is assumed to embody this difference. To look at violence towards lesbians and gay men in this way is to see it as the end product of a process that goes something like: 'I fear myself, therefore I fear you, therefore I hate you.' Or, as Donald Moss puts it: 'It is we, myself and people like me, who must protect ourselves from that, there, which we both fear and hate.'[57] It suggests that such violence represents a material mode of rejecting difference, a casting out of that which is fearful because it threatens the perpetrator's own fragile sense of sexual identity. It is not difficult to picture acts of violence by heterosexual men towards gay men in this light. Violent rejections of homosexuality provide a means for the perpetrator to demonstrate his difference from the homosexual other and, in the process, reaffirm his heterosexuality (both in his own eyes and in the eyes of others). Such affirmation simultaneously functions as a sign of the perpetrator's masculine credentials.[58] This way of looking at hate, fear and violence also offers some insight into violence that is directed towards lesbians. For example, there are expressions of extreme dislike and aversion towards homosexuality in the scenarios of anti-lesbian violence that I presented earlier: lesbians are too butch, too dirty, too masculine or too man hating. It is not difficult to imagine that John, Bruce and Bazza feel threatened by homosexuality, irrespective of whether it is in a woman or a man. Indeed, it is possible that Bruce and Bazza would be just as eager to attack a gay man as a lesbian woman. It may be that all three perpetrators are able to minimise their own anxieties by violently creating a distance between the 'abnormality' of the homosexual other and the 'normality' of heterosexuality.

---

[56] *Ibid.*, 282. I am intrigued by the use of a masculine pronoun in a number of the accounts that I have discussed so far in this article. This is not simply a case of sexist language that invites condemnation (always a fairly pointless exercise when it comes to texts written over fifty years ago). Instead, it suggests to me that the benchmark relationship for analysing the connections between prejudice and fear, or homophobia and fear, all too often imagines that the subject who fears and the imagined object of that fear are both male.

[57] *Ibid.*, 282–283.

[58] See Tomsen, n. 15; J. Harry, 'Conceptualising Anti-Gay Violence', *Journal of Interpersonal Violence* 5(3) (1990), 350–358.

However, the border that John, Bruce and Bazza police is not just the border between homosexuality and heterosexuality. As I suggested earlier, negativity towards homosexuality is also shaped by the assumption that heterosexuality is the privileged sexual mode of expressing 'normal' masculinity and femininity. This means that gender always comes into play in violence towards lesbians and gay men: for example, in Bruce and Bazza's question, 'are you a boy or a girl?'[59] However, it does this in ways that are specific to the gender dynamics of the actual incident itself. According to the explanatory accounts set out above, violence by a heterosexual *man* towards a gay *man* is rooted in the perpetrator's fear of his own (homo)sexual desires. In violence by heterosexual men towards homosexual women, gender works in a slightly different way. Lesbianism means that a woman's sexual attention is turned away from men. Bruce and Bazza are only too aware of this. Their taunt of 'can't you get a man' seems like a weak response to their belief that Barbara has rejected the kinds of love and sex that they have to offer. This may induce fear into their hearts. But surely the basis of this fear cannot be reduced to a question of their homosexual tendencies. This is even more pronounced in John's violence towards Jenny. Here, the sexual nature of the violence hints at the possibility that Jenny's homosexuality makes John anxious because she is no longer available to him. John may well fear something, but this appears to have much to do with losing Jenny, with the fact that she does not love him any more. Indeed, in his violent expression of anti-lesbian sentiment John makes a declaration of love for Jenny. In trying this declaration to a denunciation of lesbianism, John implies that in not choosing him to love, Jenny has chosen not just the wrong person, but the wrong *type* of person, to love: a woman.

To assert that there are different kinds of hate crime is, in effect, to assert that there are different kinds of hate. The version of hate that dominates the literature on violence towards gay men and lesbians is one that privileges a particular understanding of fear. Yet, a somewhat different kind of fear also appears to be at play in the types of violence that lesbians experience. Indeed, the thing that strikes me about scenarios of anti-lesbian violence is the consistency with which they are coloured by narratives of sex and love. This prompts me to speculate whether we might come closer to recognising this fear if we momentarily take a step back from the notion of hate itself. In particular, I wonder what such fear might look like if we examine it through the conceptual lens of love. This is not an attempt to analyti-

---

[59] Sedgwick points to the heterosexist assumptions that inhere in the very concept of gender; a bias that gives 'heterosocial and heterosexual relations a conceptual privilege of incalculable consequence': E. Kosofsky Sedgwick, *Epistemology of the Closet* (Berkeley: University of California Press, 1990), 31.

270   GAIL MASON

cally sever anti-lesbian violence from anti-gay violence. As I shall suggest, notions of love and notions of hate are inevitably implicated in each other. It is just that some kinds of hate may also have a lot to do with love.

LOVE IN VIOLENCE?

As with hate, so too are there many competing interpretations of love. Generally, love is said to be an emotion, particularly an attachment or a way of relating to others, that brings us pleasure.[60] There are different, yet interacting, experiences of love: familial love for parents and siblings; social love for a way of life; or sexual love for another individual. Whilst the desire for sex may exist outside of the desire for love, sexual love refers to the specific desire to give and/or to receive sexual pleasure: 'I am in love with you and I want to have sex with you'.[61] Here, desire represents the condition of wanting or wishing for sexual love.[62] When one individual experiences sexual love with another, the latter becomes an object of desire for the former. Thus, sexual love is itself the object of desire, an experience that people want: 'I wish I was in love'. Although, sexual love can be experienced without being returned, the presence or absence of reciprocity is integral to the quality of this experience: 'Do you love me?'; 'Why don't you love me?'[63] As we shall see, reciprocity is one of the keys to understanding the transformation of love into hate.

These connections between love, sex, desire and pleasure mean that it might be fruitful to look at violence through any or all of these concepts. I have, however, chosen to engage primarily with the notion of love and,

---

[60] See Ben-Ze'ev, *supra* n. 32; Soble, *supra* n. 32; Ian Suttie, *The Origins of Love and Hate* (London: Free Association books, 1988, first published 1935).

[61] Soble, *supra* n. 32, at 245.

[62] The accounts of love that I discuss in this section pay only minimal attention to defining desire. Generally, they employ desire to denote the experience of wanting something or someone. For example, Soble's philosophical account of love and hate uses desire to distinguish the two. He asserts that love is the desire to benefit or do good towards the object of one's love, whilst hate is the desire to harm or diminish the welfare of the object of one's hate: Soble, *supra* n. 32, at 137. Although I also use desire to denote the experience of wanting or wishing for something in particular, I am aware that desire has become a highly contested concept. For example, the psychoanalyatic version of desire as lack has been rejected by Foucault (who preferred the notion of pleasure) and critiqued by Deleuze, who interprets desire as a relational force between individuals and objects that produces modes of subjectification: see E. Probyn, *Outside Belongings* (London: Routledge, 1996), 39–62.

[63] Reciprocity is integral to Suttie's theory of love: Suttie, *supra* n. 60, at xlvii. For Soble, the issue of reciprocity is much more uncertain: 'the desire for reciprocity, as a matter of logic, can exist only when one already loves somebody; it is the desire to be loved by the particular person one loves.': Soble, *supra* n. 32, at 247.

indeed, have highlighted it in my reconstructed scenarios of anti-lesbian violence. This is because of the intimate relationship that the concept of love has with the concept of hate. As I shall suggest, this nexus provides us with a means of recognising that violence against gay men and lesbians may be the product of fears that are linked both to hate and to love.

Nonetheless, my decision to look at violence through the concept of love may seem a little contrary from a feminist perspective. Many feminists have been at pains to show that men's violence towards women is not a physical expression of love.[64] Indeed, feminism has a long history of arguing that men's violence is an expression of misogyny or hatred towards women;[65] which may partly explain more recent arguments that gendered violence is just as much a form of hate crime as racist or homophobic violence.[66] It is hardly necessary to rehearse why feminists have taken this line. They are motivated by scenarios of violence with which we are all too familiar: scenarios where men seek to explain their violence by saying that they did it out of love, that their violence is in fact a sign of their love. Many have argued that this enables men's violence to be justified in the name of 'love, protection, and help':[67] 'he wouldn't do it if he didn't care'; 'he wouldn't do it I loved him more'. Others have argued that this rationalisation only works, that women and men only believe it, because it is backed by long-standing discourses that construct heterosexual relations as a form of love in which women 'assume a particular part – that of the possessed.'[68] To this way of thinking, there is nothing natural or pure about the emotion of love. Just as history and culture tell us that there are preferred objects of hate, so too do they tell us that there are

---

[64] I came across a recent example of this in a postcard produced by the Women's Health Information Resource Association to advertise a Day of Action Against Sexual Assault in New South Wales. The postcard consists of a number of loose sketches of hearts and an abstract image of a woman's face in profile against a blue background. The woman's mouth is open and she is speaking the words, 'there is no love in violence'.

[65] For example, see A. Dworkin, *Woman Hating* (New York: Dutton, 1974); P. Kellett, 'Acts of Power, Control and Resistance: Narrative Accounts of Convicted Rapists', in Whillock and Slayden, *supra* n. 10, 142–162.

[66] K. Gelber, 'Hate Crimes: Public Policy Implications of the Inclusion of Gender', *Australian Journal of Political Science* 35(2) (2000), 286.

[67] C. Madanes, *Sex, Love and Violence* (New York: W.W. Norton & Co, Inc, 1990), 5. See also, V. Goldner, P. Penn, M. Sheinberg and G. Walker, 'Love and Violence: Gender Paradoxes in Volatile Attachments', *Family Process* 29(4) (1990), 343–364.

[68] N. Naffine, 'Possession: Erotic Love in the Law of Rape', *Modern Law Review* 57 (1994), 18. Naffine discusses how such discourses have been normalised and reinforced in the laws of sexual assault. Possessiveness is also central to Nagle's examination of love and hate as opposing forces within the emotional dimensions of human personality: E. Nagle, 'Love and Hate', *Family Therapy* XVI(2) (1989), 185–191.

preferred objects of love and preferred ways *to* love. For example, Towns and Adams show how narratives of perfect heterosexual love (a kind of fairytale love) can bind women into violent relationships by encouraging them to dichotomise men's subjectivity so that the violent man (the beast) can be separated from the good man (the prince) who is, in turn, the 'real' man.[69] As an attachment or a way of relating to others, heterosexual love is thus culturally constituted in part through the various narratives that dominate discourses of sexuality: narratives of possessive and perfect love are examples that have particular pertinence to violence.

Even if an act of violence can never express the emotion of love – which is far from certain – much sexual assault and domestic violence is still rooted in narratives of heterosexual love (and sex). Such narratives suggest that possessive forms of sexual love are perfect forms of sexual love. In so doing, they provide a crude discursive context for the enactment and rationalisation of the kinds of violence that heterosexual men tend to commit against heterosexual women.[70] If narratives of love have this level of explanatory force in relation to gendered violence it follows that they may also have explanatory force in relation to the violence that heterosexual men commit against lesbian women; as I have suggested above, such violence is also gendered. Yet, this is not an unproblematic line of analysis to pursue. One obvious objection is that to conceptualise violence as a 'love crime' is to preclude it from being conceptualised as hate crime; or vice versa. I wish to suggest, however, that this is only a problem if we assume love and hate to be mutually exclusive of each other.[71] Like most oppositions, love and hate can also be understood as contradictory emotions that interact with, and are dependent upon, each

---

[69] A. Towns and P. Adams, ' 'If I Really Loved Him Enough, He Would Be Okay': Women's Accounts of Male Partner Violence', *Violence Against Women* 6(6) (2000), 566.

[70] This is not to say that these are the only narratives that provide a social climate conducive to the commission of violence by men towards women. Moreover, these narratives must compete with other narratives that encourage non-possessive and non-violent forms of heterosexuality. In the context of violence, however, it is probably fair to say that narratives that encourage violence are highly influential, even if only momentarily.

[71] In Freud's early work love and hate were said to be non-identical twins: love was a pleasure-seeking instinct while hate was a counter-instinct, a drive to expel the unpleasurable into the outside world. In later Freud, love was said to be part of the life instinct, whilst hate became the death instinct or an expulsive-destructive function: C. Bollas, 'Loving Hate', *Annual of Psychoanalysis* 12–13 (1994/5), 211. According to Suttie, in Freud's theory of infantile development the self is the object of love. It is defended from the death-instinct, which is projected onto others in the form of an instinct of destruction. That is, hate is related to death, the urge from destruction, and functions to compliment love for the self. In his radical critique of Freudian theory – which has been said to be a precursor to object relations theory – Suttie suggested that love is the basis of life. For Suttie, love,

other. This means that we do not have to reject the explanatory power of hate in order to recognise that love may also help us to understand certain types of violence. Let me explain.

Social psychologist, Gordon Allport made much of the relationship between hate and love in his examination of the nature of prejudice. Writing in the United States in the 1950's, against the background of World War II and within a climate of McCarthyism, his work has been highly influential in the analysis of racism, homophobia and other forms of group hate.[72] What is significant about Allport's account of prejudice is his assertion that hate is actually the product of love. To make this argument he draws an initial distinction between prejudice that is grounded in love and prejudice that is grounded in hate.[73] In a general sense, we experience love for the things that we value and to which we are attached; this may be a group of people, an individual or a way of life. These affiliations are not necessarily a problem. They are only experienced as love-prejudice when we 'overgeneralize our categories of attachment and affection':[74] that is, when we care about something more than we can really afford to. In such instances we will hate (hate-prejudice) those who we believe are responsible for threatening, violating or thwarting the attachments that we value. Bollas' psychoanalytic account of 'loving hate' throws particular light on how this might operate in relation to sexual love.[75] For Bollas, hate is also a substitute for love. The variable that turns love to hate is the absence of reciprocity. That is, the person who hates with 'loving passion' lives in fear of the other's indifference to their love: 'inspired hate or passionate hate is generated as an alternative to love which is assumed to be unavailable'.[76]

---

which is social rather than sexual, comes before hate. Hate is a thwarted form of love (a point which I will pick up on shortly): Suttie, *supra* n. 60, at 30.

[72] G. Allport, *The Nature of Prejudice* (Boston: The Beacon Press, 1954). From a contemporary position, there are many aspects of Allport's theory that call for criticism, for example: his understanding of difference is somewhat deterministic; he excludes homosexuality from the vast array of differences that he canvasses; and at times his definition of prejudice is so all-encompassing that it loses utility.

[73] *Ibid.*, 25–26. Allport draws upon the work of the philosopher Spinoza to make this distinction: *Ibid.*, 363.

[74] *Ibid.*, 25

[75] Bollas, *supra* n. 71, at 224. Other examples of the interrelation between love and hate can be found in D. Mertz, 'The Racial Other in Nationalist Subjectivations: A Lacanian Analysis', *Rethinking Marxism* 8(2) (1995), 77–88. Mertz disputes the suggestion that racism is about hate and nationalism is about love. The transformation of love into hate as a context for violence has also been emphasised in research on stalking: A. Burgess and others, 'Stalking Behaviors within Domestic Violence', *Journal of Family Violence* 12(4) (1997), 389–403.

[76] Bollas, *supra* n. 71, at 222. Bollas questions the assumption that hate is always about the desire to destroy suggesting instead that it has a positive function, which is to conserve

This kind of hate may be less a case of disliking particular groups of people and more a case of defending our 'privileges', 'position' and 'cosy way of live' because we love the 'status quo'.[77] Thus, Allport suggests that the genesis of hate is 'a matter of frustrated affiliative desire and the attendant humiliation to one's self-esteem or to one's values'.[78] Indeed, hate cannot exist 'unless something one values has been violated.'[79] Simply put, '[l]ove is a precondition of hate.'[80]

Whilst Allport and Bollas write about love and hate through different theoretical frameworks, there is a rough compatibility in the way that they articulate the relationship between the two.[81] In suggesting that love is a precondition of hate, Allport is not simply talking about the attachments that we feel for a particular individual. We may also be deeply attached to the status quo of a particular lifestyle or social system. This is a love for the sense of comfort that comes with knowing that things are as they should be, that everything and everyone is in its rightful place and, to borrow from Sartre, that one's place in that order is assured. For example, a heterosexual man may experience love not just for a particular woman but also for the gendered system of heterosexuality itself and the privileges it affords him: a love for a certain kind of sexual love. The point that Bollas makes is that this sense of love may be substituted by hate if it is not reciprocated. That is, those groups of people that have the potential to be objects of love, may well become objects of hate if they threaten to deny or thwart the pleasure that this love promises.[82] It is the fear of indifference – an indifference that lesbianism embodies – that turns such love to hate.

---

the object of hate. His view is antipathetic to the Freudian view of hatred as instinct. Instead, he draws upon the work of Winnicott, Balint, and Searles: at 222–224. There are also interesting echoes of Sartre's philosophy in Bollas' account of love and hate. Sartre suggested that hate is driven by passion, rather than reason. The anti-Semite chooses the emotional state of hate because he or she gains pleasure from the hate itself: Sartre, *supra* n. 39, at 168.

[77] Allport, *supra* n. 72, at 26.

[78] *Ibid.*, 365, 364. In rejecting the idea that hate precedes love Allport follows Suttie and, hence, is at odds with Freud.

[79] *Ibid.*, 364.

[80] *Ibid.*, 364.

[81] For example, Allport emphasises group hate, whilst Bollas does not. Bollas emphasises the fear that undergirds love whilst Allport pays less attention to fear. Allport is more attuned to the social conditions that produce love, whilst Bollas focuses upon its psychic conditions of existence.

[82] In this context it is also interesting to consider Zizek's observations in relation to racial conflict, nationalism and the theft of enjoyment. Zizek suggests that racial hatred emerges from a fear that the other will steal our forms of enjoyment, at the same time that they enjoy themselves in ways that we cannot comprehend. Hence, when we characterise

The scenarios of violence that I mapped out earlier exemplify instances of possessive narratives of heterosexual love. In both the men appear to assume that the women's choices in sexual love – their choice of lovers – are fundamentally misdirected. For example, Barbara appears to be unpalatable to Bruce and Bazza because she does not choose men as her lovers. Jenny, too, refuses to reciprocate the sexual love that John is offering. This is a gender specific kind of love. It is both a love for the pleasures of heterosexuality and a love for the feminine other that enables those pleasures.[83] The fear that lesbianism engenders in the hearts of Bruce, Bazza and John cannot be solely encapsulated by the logic of 'I fear myself, therefore I fear you, therefore I hate you.' Instead, or in addition, it follows a logic that says 'I love the pleasures that you embody for me, I fear that you do not reciprocate, therefore I hate you.' Hence, the fear that prompts such violence must be as much a fear of *in*difference as a fear *of* difference; a fear of *being rejected* by the other as much as a fear of *becoming* the other. In this sense, violence towards lesbians may be conceptualised as the product of a love for the other – the difference that gender embodies in the context of heterosexuality – just as readily as it may be conceptualised as a hate for the other – the difference that homosexuality embodies. To look at violence in this way enables us to recognise that violence by heterosexual men towards homosexual women may involve a kind of fear we are unlikely to find in the violence that heterosexual men direct towards homosexual men. This fear, in turn, may engender a particular kind of hate.

Caution is needed here. To say that there are different kinds of fear and different kinds of hate is not to say that these differences eclipse the similarities between anti-gay and anti-lesbian violence (one might say that it is at this point that I depart company with the woman who saw difference as an insurmountable obstacle to her participation in the Hate Crime Conference). To look at violence through the lens of love, as I

---

the other as a menace to our 'way of life' the thing that is usually at stake is the way in which a community *'organizes its enjoyment'*: S. Zizek, *Tarrying with the Negative: Kant, Hegel and the Critique of Ideology* (Durham: Duke University Press, 1993), 206. Whilst Zizek's particular mode of Lacanian analysis is not necessary to the point that I wish to make, it is worth noting that the idea that we hate the other because we imagine that they have the capacity to erode the ways in which we organise our forms of enjoyment might be relevant to an interpretation of anti-homosexual sentiment amongst heterosexual men by tying it to the fear that lesbians 'steal' the pleasures of heterosexuality because they refuse to participate in or reciprocate this mode of enjoyment.

[83] This love of difference is, of course, entwined with a fear of the difference that femininity represents for masculinity. Grosz discusses this paradox in relation to the way in which heterosexual men are simultaneously attracted to and repelled by the female body: E. Grosz, *Volatile Bodies: Toward a Corporeal Feminism* (Sydney: Allen & Unwin, 1994).

have articulated it here, is to simultaneously look through the lens of hate: unreciprocated love engenders hate, it does not surpass it.[84] Moreover, the possibility that one mode of fear may well dominate a given incident at a given time does not mean that other modes of fear are automatically excluded. Violence towards lesbians may well embody a fear of the homosexual other (the difference that sexuality represents) at the same time that it embodies a fear of not having access to the feminine other (the difference that gender represents). Thus, my purpose in highlighting the kind of fear that love shows us, is not to deny that violence towards lesbians may also be grounded in the kind of fear that hate shows us. Rather, my purpose is to open up a means for thinking about such violence as an interaction of the two (to move beyond the impasse of asking whether such violence is about gender or about sexuality). This way of looking at violence towards lesbians allows us to remain attuned to the intimate connection that it shares with violence towards gay men. In addition, it may open up another avenue for thinking about the ways in which violence towards gay men is also tied to narratives and emotions of love. Consider, for example, the fear that some men are said to experience in the face of homosexuality. It is not difficult to characterise this as a fear of the sexual love between men that homosexuality embodies and a fear of losing the security and comfort of an unambiguous heterosexual and masculine identity. This is the kind of fear – of having and losing certain types of sexual love – which breeds hate. Further, it is interesting to speculate about the explanatory significance of love beyond the question of homosexuality. In one way or another, the violent expression of all kinds of group hate can probably be tied to the sense of love and attachment that individuals feel for other groups of people, for a way of life, or for a mode of pleasure.[85] Quite simply, at that very moment when we may feel the need to emphasise the differences between various kinds of hate crime, the possibility arises that,

---

[84] Although Allport, Bollas and Suttie argue that love precedes hate (in contrast to Freud), my argument is not dependent upon establishing that one is more fundamental than the other or that one necessarily precipitates the other. The point that I take from their work is that the two are deeply entwined with each other; to understand hate we need to understand love.

[85] The connections between love, hate and racist violence have been made in a number of contexts: Allport, *supra* n. 72; Mertz, *supra* n. 75; B. Dobratz and S. Shanks-Meile, 'Ideology and the Framing Process in the White Separatist/Supremacist Movement in the United States', *Quarterly Journal of Ideology* 19(1–2) (1996), 3–29. Love has also been connected to hate crimes against people with disabilities, see M. Sherry, 'Hate Crimes Against People with Disabilities', Paper presented at *Hate Crime: Politics Practice Power* Conference, Department of Gender Studies and the Institute of Criminology, The University of Sydney, Australia, 9–10 December 1999.

in another sense, these same behaviours continue to be loosely linked as particular kinds of 'love crimes'.

The idea that certain forms of violence are just as likely to be grounded in a love for difference as they are in a rejection of difference does not preclude them from being conceptualised as hate crimes: this is the importance of the interrelation between love and hate. However, it does raise a broader question about the types of explanations that we privilege when we look at violence through the concept of hate. Crudely put, if violence towards lesbians and gay men can be articulated, explained or categorised through the concept of hate, then why not through the concept of love?[86] I am not advocating that we do this. But I am advocating that we remain alert to the kinds of explanations that are encouraged and prioritised when violence is characterised as a material expression of hate. Just as this has implications for our engagements with the concept of hate crime in general, so too does it have implications for the kinds of concepts that we choose to introduce into the law. Terms such as hate crime, hate speech, or incitement to hate are not mere descriptions. They contain assumptions about the nature and origins of the social wrongs that are outlawed. They suggest, even if unintentionally, that hate is a prime determining factor in the commission of certain unacceptable acts. My concern is not that this is a false or incorrect claim to make at law but rather that it tends to privilege a chain of causation that, in light of the above discussion, leaves a little to be desired. As we have seen, explanations of homosexual hate tend to follow well-worn paths. When the law looks for signs of hate in the act of violence itself – which is assumed to provide access to the psychological disposition of the perpetrator – it is likely to recognise those dynamics that follow these same paths. In the context of violence towards lesbians and gay men, this means that it is more likely to recognise the signs of hate that emerge from a fear of difference, from a fear of the homosexual other, than those that emerge from a fear of indifference, from a love of the feminine other. Quite simply, in the quest to identify violent expressions of hate such legal categories make it easy for law to fail to deal with the full diversities of mischief it is designed to address.

CONCLUSION

My intention in this article has been to raise some questions about hate as a means of understanding and explaining certain types of violence.

---

[86] In fact, phrases such as 'love crime' or 'fear crime' make just as much sense as 'hate crime'.

In a broad sense, this exploration of the nexus between hate and anti-homosexual violence has been prompted by an encounter with an indi-vidual – the woman who chose not to speak at the Hate Crime Conference – who drew definite lines between different kinds of hate. I can never know why she chose to do this and perhaps this is not really important. What is important is that she brought home to me the reality that differences between modalities of hate do matter. For me, this significance lies in the fact that different kinds of hate demand different explanations.

In explanatory accounts of violence towards lesbians and gay men, hate has primarily been traced to the perpetrator's fear of homosexuality and particularly of his own homosexual desires. I have no wish to dispute this interpretation. It provides us with one avenue for understanding such violence. I am, however, concerned that we miss other important issues when we predominantly characterise this violence as a fear of difference; that is, I doubt very much that this way of looking at violence tells us the whole story. For example, my research into the violence that heterosexual men direct towards lesbian women suggests that such violence can also be understood as a product of the perpetrator's fear that homosexuality in women renders his own heterosexuality redundant. I have not arrived at this position by following existing analyses of the relationship between hate, fear and homosexuality. Instead, it has been my engagement with the concept of love – specifically the ways in which dominant narratives of heterosexuality mark out appropriate objects of love – which has high-lighted this modality of fear. In short, looking at violence through love has opened up the space for interpretations that I might otherwise not see.

Examining violence through the concept of love does not, however, call for a rejection of the concept of hate. This is because the kind of love (the love of heterosexuality and gender conformity) that prompts anti-lesbian violence is likely, in turn, to engender a form of hate (the hate of homosexuality and gender ambiguity). Whilst different kinds of hate will involve different modalities of love, the overall idea that all hate is tied to some form of love may thus assist us to understand violence towards gay men and, possibly, other kinds of hate crime. In short, there are very real differences between 'my' kind of hate crime and 'your' kind of hate crime but this does not preclude us from speaking of them in the same breath.

Department of Gender Studies
The University of Sydney
NSW 2006
Australia
E-mail: gail.mason@genderstudies.usyd.edu.au

[17]

UNDERSTANDING SYSTEMIC VIOLENCE: HOMOPHOBIC ATTACKS IN JOHANNESBURG AND ITS SURROUNDS

GRAEME REID AND TERESA DIRSUWEIT

1. INTRODUCTION

Urban citizenship entails freedom to move, use and express identity in the city. Violence is an extreme instance of the curtailment of these rights. It impairs a sense of safety and restricts choice. In gay mythology, the city embodies an accepting cosmopolitan lifestyle. Young gay men and lesbians are drawn to Johannesburg from smaller towns within South Africa and from other African cities as far afield as Harare, Windhoek, Gabarone, Kampala, Accra and Dar-es-Salaam. They are attracted to the promise of a more tolerant society. South Africa stands alone in Africa in terms of its constitution, which expressly protects the rights of lesbian and gay citizens. Johannesburg offers well-developed social networks and a number of gay public spaces. And yet there is an undercurrent of extreme violence and trauma in the city.

In a climate of pervasive crime and profound fear, hate crimes are hidden within broad statistics. The South African government does not keep specific statistics on xenophobic, racist and homophobic crime. This has the effect of increasing the invisibility of gay men and lesbians. Homophobic victimisation is endemic in violent, masculine cultures and has extensive implications for gay men and lesbians. It profoundly affects the way in which the city is used in terms of movement and the use of social spaces. However, few research efforts exist around these issues in South Africa and those that do deal primarily with gay white men. The scope of this research is thus wide-ranging providing an overview of existing work on violence and broadening this body of literature to include the experiences of those who have not been acknowledged in research efforts in the past. This paper places homophobic violence on the agenda of urban policy makers as well as informing future research around violence, fear and safety.

Theorising Homophobic Violence in an Urban Context

Valentine (1993) points out that while most people feel that sexuality belongs to the private space of the home, most public spaces are coded to be heterosexual. Furthermore, she points out that most feel that they have "no objection to homosexuals as long as they did not flaunt their sexuality in public" (Valentine, 1993: 396). She draws on Foucault (1988) and Butler (1990) to argue the opacity of heterosexual codification of public space. The power of this codification is to normalize a heterosexual hegemonic order to the extent that lesbians often feel the need to"pass"as heterosexual by conforming to a feminine identity (ibid.). The essence of Valentine's position is whereas"heterosexuals take for granted their freedom to express their sexuality publicly and therefore transcend the so-called public-private dichotomy", the onus is on lesbians and gay men to maintain the separation. The separation is subverted through the attendance of a publicly codified gay space (such as a gay and/or lesbian night club or a gay cruising ground) or through the overt assumption of signifiers of gay identity.

> To be gay, therefore, is not only to violate norms about sexual behaviour and family structure but also to deviate from the norms of'natural'masculine or feminine behaviour. These norms change over space and time, and hence sexuality is not defined merely by sexual acts but exists as a process of power relations. (Ibid.: 396)

Gay-bashing is an instance where gays and lesbians are punished for subverting the taken-for-granted heterosexuality of the public. The majority of gay-bashing incidents occur in the public realm. Of the forty women Valentine interviewed, 75 percent had been verbally assaulted at least once and three had been chased, threatened and/or physically assaulted. In most cases women reported that the incidents had been triggered by a display of affection or by a lack of response to male sexual overtures. Homophobic violence is, hence, formulated in relation to the subversion of norms, particularly norms around masculinity. Namaste (1996) further explores the relationship between gender subversion and gay-bashing. Her research finds that men and women who assume signifiers of the opposite gender, for example through dress and speech, are at increased risk of gay-bashing.

Skelton (1995: 267) locates her work on homophobic elements in Jamaican ragga"within wider discourses that debate race, sexuality and masculinity". Drawing on hooks (1992), Collins (1991) and Harper (1993), she (p.

277) refers to the"...subject of black masculinity and its linkage with a lack of power within racist/sexist societies". In this formulation, Skelton (ibid.) argues that homophobia is related to the need to assert power through the trajectory of masculinity. Homophobia, in this case calls for the 'crucifixion' of homosexuals, acts as "proof positive of their masculinity". This hypothesis relates closely to Vogelman's (*The Star*, 23 February 1995) formulation of violence in post-Apartheid South Africa (see Dirsuweit, this issue). He argues that the previous lack of full citizenship under apartheid left people with a deep sense of disempowerment. Coupled with an increasingly strained economy and high levels of unemployment, this sense of disempowerment has reached new depths. The desire to gain control and recognition motivates violence. In addition, South Africa is a sexist society and so violence is used to strengthen the one area in which men feel they have more power, their masculinity. This is exacerbated by the perceived threat of women's increased empowerment in contemporary South Africa.

Hate crimes directed at socially excluded groups are endemic to most societies. Statistics from governmental agencies such as the police are subject to some inaccuracy due to underreporting and the classification of hate crimes under headings such as grievous bodily harm and rape. In 1995, the Federal Bureau of Investigation reported 1 019 incidences of crime directed towards homosexual people with 1 266 offenses, 1 347 victims and 1 273 known offenders. The majority of these crimes were against gay men. Canadian statistics (Multiculturalism, 1998) report a total of 60 000 hate crimes for the year 1998. Eleven percent of these were committed against gay men and lesbians. The most staggering statistics are reported in the *London Free Press* (4 March 2000). In this report, 83 percent of respondents (aged 14-25 years) reported that they had been gay bashed. Interestingly, many of the perpetrators were not strangers, but family members and others known to the victim. In terms of perpetration, Franklin found that 25 percent of students surveyed reported that they had harassed people considered gay or lesbian. Of the men surveyed, 18 percent admitted to assaulting or threatening gays or lesbians and 32 percent had verbally abused gays and lesbians.

Valentine and other urban commentators insert the question of gay identity politics as part of a "New Urban Politics" (Brown, 1995). In this formulation, the politics of the body dominate discussions of sexuality. Young (1990a) contextualises homophobic violence within urban politics. She classifies homophobic crime as systemic violence and argues that it disallows gay men and lesbians full participation in the city. Ingram et al. (1999: 92) expand the point:

How are denied access and limited freedom of expression enforced?...One of the most effective means of control is the threat of violence. For example, the threat of dyke and gay-bashing has had a tremendous impact on where we choose to live and to socialise...

Young (1990b: 320) proceeds to call for the development of "discourse and institutions for bringing differently identified groups together without suppressing or subsuming the difference". This call is particularly pertinent to understanding the different experiences of homophobic violence along the axes of race, ethnicity, age and gender in Johannesburg. To speak of the aetiology and the effects of hate crime on "the gay community" is to bury the experiences of those who do not fit into the more vocal white and male grouping in Johannesburg's gay culture.

2. HOMOPHOBIC VIOLENCE IN SOUTH AFRICA

Historical Context

The Second World War saw a proliferation of bars frequented by gay men in the city centre. It also provided new cruising opportunities. With this proliferation of gay spaces came homophobic violence. In 1941 an important case received considerable publicity: Two soldiers accompanied a gay man to his flat. He was later found severely beaten and strangled. He had also been robbed. This was one of the first cases in which the "homosexual panic" defence was used successfully and the assailants were given a suspended sentence. The judgement was clearly indicative of gross homophobia and serves as an early marker of the antagonistic relationship between law and security services and the gay community in Johannesburg which was to continue through the apartheid years.

There was a dramatic turnaround in 1996 when South Africa adopted a constitution that outlawed discrimination on the basis of sexual orientation. Political transformation extended to the police force and a draft policy document compiled by the minister of safety and security in 1994, highlighted the need for the police to "assist in fostering a human rights culture and in providing the climate within which development and reconstruction can take place" (Minister of Safety and Security, September 1994: 28). In a ground-breaking speech, the Gauteng Member of the Executive Council for Safety and Security, Jesse Duarte, called for better relationships between the police and the gay community. She announced that instead of harassing gay men, the police would patrol and protect well-known cruising areas in Johannesburg. In the mid-1990s, the South African Police Services career-planning department introduced a diversity training programme that included sexual orientation as well as racism and sexism.

The promise of political transformation was accompanied by an unprecedented growth of gay and lesbian political activism and social organisation. Never before had gay people been so visible in South Africa. In 1990, a few months after the release of Nelson Mandela, the first Gay and Lesbian Pride March took place through the streets of Johannesburg, accompanied by extensive media coverage. By 1995 the national umbrella body formed to lobby for the retention of sexual orientation in final constitution, the National Coalition for Gay and Lesbian Equality (NCGLE), boasted some 78 affiliated organisations, many of these based in Johannesburg and its surrounds. In the 1990s there was a proliferation of diverse community groups such as gay netball clubs, lesbian soccer teams, gay church communities, catering groups and lesbian social clubs. There was also a growth in public visibility through political activism and public events such as the annual gay and lesbian film festival, clubs, parties and gay beauty pageants. The media paid considerable attention through radio and television talk shows, documentaries and news items. Print media ran stories in magazines and newspapers on a regular basis. Books on gay and lesbian issues in South Africa started to be published, and for a few years there were three main gay publications produced in Johannesburg and distributed country-wide. Increased visibility, the political climate of the time and the promise of equality enshrined in the constitution, created an environment conducive to "coming out" and many people did so, sometimes in the full glare of the public eye.

It appears that increased visibility may have had another consequence, in the form of growing levels of gay bashing. It is difficult to gauge the exact extent of this violence as, despite fundamental changes in the law, underreporting of gay-bashing continues and it is estimated that in 1996, 91 percent of lesbians and gay victims of hate crimes did not report them to the police (Bonham et al., 1996). Reasons for underreporting were given as being in the closet; police indifference and hostility; and fear of sensational public disclosure. In 1994, a memorandum signed by twenty organizations was presented to the regional minister of safety and security, Sydney Mufamadi. The memorandum included the recommendation to institute an "anti-hate crimes" Act that included gay-bashing and to establish a formal police liaison to the gay community. In 2000, the "Promotion of Equality and Prevention of Unfair Discrimination Act" was promulgated. This Act is read in conjunction with the Constitution and precludes hate speech and the harassment based on "prohibited grounds," which includes sexual orientation.

Research on Homophobic Violence in South Africa

In 1995, the AIDS Law Project, University of the Witwatersrand, commissioned the Human Science Research Council to complete an investigative report on South African public attitudes on issues concerning gays, lesbians, and AIDS. The survey took place at a time when the inclusion of 'sexual orientation' in the constitution was a hotly contested issue, serving as a rallying point for the South African lesbian and gay community and galvanising the small but vociferous Christian right under the banner of the African Christian Democratic Party. The report was based on a national survey (n = 2163). The study was the first national poll of its kind. The results were both predictable and surprising; predictable in that the public were opposed to granting equal rights to gays and lesbians, surprising in that a majority of South Africans wanted homosexuality decriminalised. Surprising too, in the narrow margins between those in favour and those opposed to a number of issues concerning homosexuality in South Africa. Public opinion was more evenly split than was perhaps to be expected in a country where homosexuality had been seen both as a threat to white civilization by the National Party government and as "un-African" by many in the post-apartheid order. In the survey 41 percent of Africans thought that homosexuality was un-African. The public were split on giving homosexuals equal rights in the constitution, with 44 percent against and 38 percent in favour. However, some 46 percent of the public opposed criminalizing consensual gay sex between adults, while 38 percent wanted it illegal. On an attitude index over all 8 questions, 48 percent of the public was rated 'anti-gay', 34 percent 'pro-gay', and 18 percent in the middle. The differences between the anti- and pro-gay groups were found to be socio-economic and religious, more than racial or political.

The study also provided rare insight into public perceptions of gay-bashing. Among the general public 5 percent had seen homosexuals assaulted, and 10 percent verbally insulted. According to the report, those likeliest to have witnessed abuse were tertiary educated, city dwellers, and whites. The proportion who had seen gays abused were substantially greater among those who actually knew homosexuals. In this group, 11 percent had seen gays or lesbians physically assaulted and some 28 percent (or over one in four) had seen them verbally insulted. Roughly half of the sample (49%) thought that if a gay or lesbian is beaten up, police will give them the same help as others, however just over one fourth (28%) thought that homosexuals would receive less help, while one fifth (20%) were not sure.

Other quantitative research shows a disturbing relationship between gay-bashing and sexual assault in South Africa. Theron (1994) reports that 22 percent of gay hate crimes involved the rape of the victim (see Table 1). Theron's sample is predominantly white. Theuninck (2000) presents the results of his surveys of white gay men under the rubric of post-traumatic stress disorder. Part of his argument is that gay men through various forms of gay bashing, ranging from verbal to physical, experience a fairly constant state of trauma. This has implications in terms of the literature on

Table 1

Two South African surveys compared to the average of seven surveys conducted in the United States between 1988-1991

Study	Average of seven surveys conducted in United States 1988-1991	South African survey (Theron, 1992)	South African survey (Theuninck, 2000)
N	397	611	329
Men	333	565	329
Women	230	45	0
Type of victimisation			
Verbal Abuse	85%	67%	75%
Threats of Violence	44%	39%	33%
Property Violence	19%	15%	16%
Objects thrown	25%	12%	18%
Followed or chased	32%	32%	31%
Spat on	12%	4%	8%
Punched, hit and/ or kicked	19%	22%	22%
Weapon assault	8%	8%	9%
Sexual assault	7%	22%	17%
Victimised by police	-	-	4%

fear of crime. Pain (2000) argues that lower level forms of violence such as harassment promote a higher degree of fear with debilitating effects on the manner in which people use the city.

No quantitative surveys have been completed within black, coloured and Asian communities. Qualitative evidence, however, suggests that gay bashing and the prominence of rape is not uncommon (Shelver, interview, 2002; Vimbela, 1994).

Phumi Mtetwa, an interim executive committee member of the National Coalition for Gay and Lesbian Equality who grew up in Kwa-Thema, reflected on gay and lesbian experiences of violence in former townships:

> Rape is quite common in the townships. ...The law might be promising us equality, but you're dealing with grassroots level radicals who don't know or care about the law. It is very hard for black lesbians to come out openly because of African culture. Once a group of boys suspects so-and-so is a lesbian she be-

comes a target, often for gang-rape. ...If you are afraid to tell you mother you're a lesbian, how can you tell your story to a male policeman. (*Exit*, 70, 1995)

In Soweto, Beverley Ditsie, the first lesbian to publicly acknowledge her sexual orientation, recounts her experiences of coming out in her documentary 'Simon and I'.

That first [Gay] Pride [March] was one of the best days of my life, but I was on TV that night. It was a religious show and the priest was saying, "these people should be killed". All of a sudden I was getting funny looks from people in the street. Oh oh...What have I done...two days later I was sitting in my room when I heard voices outside calling my name. I ran into the lounge and my granny opened the door and told me to hide. About twenty angry men were surrounding our house, demanding that I come with them so they could teach me a lesson. The worst thing was that they threatened to take my grandma if I didn't go with them...I was angry but mostly at myself, I shouldn't have made that speech. Now I put my whole family in danger. I was so terrified I couldn't leave the house for weeks...In terms of sexual violence and violence against women and the way women are treated here. As soon as you're anywhere, you got a dangerous element right there. You're always looking out for yourself, because anything could happen anytime. You know, rape, being beat up, just being treated like shit, you know things. But coming out as a lesbian is even harder because you are putting yourself in the firing line. ...Any angry man will use his machismo to try and prove to you that you are straight although he's proving absolutely nothing...I felt that the gay men, especially within GLOW were not really caring very much about what became big lesbian issues like lesbian rape which increased at a point, you know. Where lesbians would be targeted for rape...I was living that life of being afraid to be in the streets, to go anywhere.

Similarly, Mamaki (1993: 1) recounts a teenage experience of fear and humiliation at the hands of a gang of young men in Soweto:

Being a girl in Soweto you play safe, find safe streets to use, and I had mine just like most girls. On my way to school and from school I turned a corner where most gangs hanged out, but for me it was still safe 'cause I knew some of the guys and it was near my place...But a time came when it was the most dangerous corner for me to turn and that was after one of the guys proposed to me, and after a long argument I told him I was gay. I knew I shouldn't have said it, but the whole thing was getting scary. The following day my lover and myself turned that corner just to hear our names and immediately they laid eyes on us it sounded as if a cassette of insults was being played. Some were promising to rape us and others were promising to beat us up...It was not very long afterwards that I was on my way home from school and I saw six boys I knew holding sticks. And somehow I knew they were coming for both of us. But I was alone, my lover was still at school playing chess. They came and made a ring around me and started using the sticks they were holding, and they were swearing. I didn't cry for help 'cause I knew that nobody was there for a 'sinner' and an

'Aids-bringer', as we were called. I didn't even try to fight or run. I just stood in the circle with tears running down from my eyes.

Bongie (Chan Sam, 1994) a member of the lesbian forum of the Gay and Lesbian Organisation of the Witwatersrand (GLOW) describes some of the trauma of coming out of the closet in Soweto.

> I do wish for lesbians to come out and say, 'Yes, we are here!' I'm scared to do it for myself, but I see many young girls being confused and I want to help. But how? Sometimes these *tsotsis* (gangsters) and these Jackrollers (a notorious Soweto gang) go out in gangs and rape women. The Jackrollers go particularly for lesbians, and when they catch one they say, 'We'll put you right.' So it's really dangerous for a young woman living in the townships to be open as a lesbian.

3. TOWARDS AN UNDERSTANDING OF HOMOPHOBIC VIOLENCE IN JOHANNESBURG AND ITS SURROUNDS

Methodology

It is exceedingly difficult to do research on homophobic violence particularly in the context of a culture of violence. Black gays and lesbians are under-represented in violence research. In interviews with staff from the Lesbian and Gay Equality Project, this reluctance to report was ascribed to the belief that police officials are often complicit with the perpetrators, if not perpetrators themselves. This was born out in a workshop on gay-bashing in Kwa-Thema where discussions around secondary victimisation indicated that hospital and policing staff often ridiculed gay-bashing victims and made derisive comments about their sexuality. Interviews were held with key informants from the Equality Project and with the former co-ordinator of the Equality Project, (who was also the convener of the Pink Panthers community policing group). Cases reported to the Equality Project were reviewed by Equality Project staff. Generalised survey questionnaires were used to maintain the anonymity of the complainants. Newspaper reports in the gay and mainstream press were reviewed. Finally, workshops around homophobic violence in Kwa-Thema were attended and follow up interviews were completed with 11 attendees. Ten more interviews were completed in Soweto. Both sets of interviews were completed in isiZulu, seSotho, and English with the help of two research assistants who were part of the lesbian and gay communities in each area. Where required, interviews were translated into English. The interviews were then grouped into themes.

The Statistics

The South African Police Service does not collect statistics within the categories of homophobic, xenophobic or racially motivated hate crimes (Ina du Plessis, Crime Information and Analysis Centre, e-mail communication). Survey questionnaires (see table 2) completed by the Equality Project for the years 2001 and 2002 indicate a higher level of sexual assault as an element of homophobic violence. An analysis of these statistics must come with two caveats attached. Firstly, many of the communities most affected by violence do not report to the Equality Project because they are afraid of making any formal complaint, hence the interviews in township areas. Second, the sample size is small and therefore cannot be generalized. The statistics do open up an agenda for ongoing research of homophobic violence in South Africa.

There were a total of 25 incidents with 42 victims (see table 2a). Most of these were perpetrated against a single victim, but a substantial proportion (44%) involved two or more victims (table 2b). The number of perpetrators and victims in the incidents were evenly distributed between the categories of one perpetrator to one victim; and multiple perpetrators to multiple victims. Slightly more cases were reported with more than one perpetrator and 40 percent of the incidents involved four or more perpetrators. This would suggest that gay bashing often occurs in the context of gang violence. The bulk of victims were women (table 2f). The perpetrators of these incidents are predominantly men (table 2h). The following most dominant category is women on women violence (20%). The interviewees did not mention violence between women. This requires further research attention. Contrary to trends in other countries, violence between men accounts for only 12 percent of the sample. Violence against transgendered people makes up 20 percent of the incidents.

The majority of cases took place in the central business district of Johannesburg (table 2j) and in suburban areas (all areas outside of Johannesburg not located in townships). While many (28.6%) of the incidents took place at gay bars (table 2k) or in a space which was overtly identified as having gay people in it, a significant number (35.7%) of the cases occurred in spaces familiar to the victim; their own home or their family's home. The next important locational category is public space. Interestingly, none of the incidents were reported in the traditional cruising areas of Delta, Emmarentia, Zoo Lake and Rhodes Park. The statistic of 7.1 percent of the incidents taking place in the perpetrator's home reflects a flagrant disregard for any legal consequence.

In most cases there were multiple forms of violence perpetrated against the victim (table 2l). The form of violence in most cases was verbal abuse (92%). Scuffles, including the pulling of clothes, slapping and the pulling of hair made up 40 percent of the cases. Objects were thrown in 20 percent of the cases and serious physical assault took place in 20 percent of the cases. Disturbingly, 32 percent of the cases involved sexual assault. One of these cases was perpetrated against a man.

Table 2

Analysis of Survey of Cases Reported to the Equality Project 2001/2002

Table 2a: Number of incidents and victims	
Total number of incidents	25
Total number of victims	42

Table 2b: Number of victims				
1	2	3	4	5
14	7	3	0	1

Table 2c: Gender of victim						
Male	%	Female	%	Transgendered	%	TOTAL
5	11.9	31	73.8	6	14.3	42

Table 2d: Race of victim								
Black	%	White	%	Asian	%	Coloured	%	TOTAL
20	47.6	10	23.8	3	7.1	9	21.4	42

Table 2e: Number of perpetrators					
1	2	3	4	>4<10	Unknown
11	2	1	5	5	1

Table 2f: Gender of perpetrator				
Male	%	Female	%	TOTAL
50	78.1	14	21.9	64

Table 2g: Race of perpetrator								
Black	%	White	%	Asian	%	Coloured	%	TOTAL
23	35.9	24	37.5	0	0.0	17	26.6	64

Table 2h: Gendered composition of violence

Female victim - male perpetrator	12	48.0%
Female victim - female perpetrator	5	20.0%
Male victim - male perpetrator	3	12.0%
Transgendered victim – male perpetrator	4	16.0%
Transgendered victim – female perpetrator	1	4.0%
Total number of incidents	25	100.00%

Table 2i: Number of victims and perpetrators

Single victim - single perpetrator	10	40.0%
Single victim - multiple perpetrators	4	16.0%
Multiple victims – multiple perpetrators	9	36.0%
Multiple victims - single perpetrator	1	4.0%
Multiple victims – unknown number of perpetrators	1	4.0%
Total number of incidents	25	100.0%

Table 2j: Location

Johannesburg CBD	11	44.0%
Former township	4	16.0%
Suburb	10	40.0%
TOTAL	25	100.0%

Table 2k: Type of location

A gay bar	7	25.0%
Delta/Emmarentia/Zoo Lake/Rhodes Park	0	0.0%
Another park	1	3.6%
A place frequented by gay people other than a bar?	1	3.6%
Another public space	7	25.0%
At victim's home	6	21.4%
At perpetrator's home	2	7.1%
At family home	4	14.3%
TOTAL (2 cases multiple location)	28	100.0%

Table 2l: Type of attack

Type of violence	No. of incidents	Percentage of overall number of incidents of violence (n = 55)	Percentage of total number of cases (n = 25)
Verbal abuse	23	41.8%	92%
Throwing objects at victim	5	9.1%	20%
Scuffle (pulling clothing and/or hair)	10	18.2%	40%
Robbery	3	5.5%	12%
Physical assault	5	9.1%	20%
Rape	8	14.5%	32%
Murder	1	1.8%	5%
TOTAL	55	100.0%	

Cruising for a Bruising: Gay Bashing in the Press

The relationship between cruising in certain parks and gay-bashing is well-documented in popular gay publications and the general press. The combination of casual sex and violence provides the material for sensational stories. For example, the gay publication, *Exit* (2001) noted that about ten cases of gay-bashing a month were reported to the Parkview Police Station, a figure that is seen to be grossly inaccurate. According to the head of community policing in the precinct:"They are easy prey and 99.9 percent of cases are not reported" (*Exit*, 70, 1995: 8).

Two well-known cruising sites, the Zoo Lake and Emmarentia Dam fall within the jurisdiction of the Parkview Police Station. Many men who frequent these areas are married or otherwise identify themselves not as gay, but as 'men who have sex with men'. These men are the 'soft targets' who are most susceptible to extortion and least likely to report an assault for fear of being 'exposed'. Three themes emerge in these articles: firstly, gay men are vulnerable to crime. Criminals view gay men as easy targets because they are regarded as weaker and are less likely to report the crime as it will publicly out them. Secondly, there are very few affluent people in Johannesburg who would frequent isolated areas after dark—gay men thus become lucrative targets for robbery. While these kinds of attacks are specifically directed at gay men, they are not necessarily predicated by homophobia. Thirdly, it shows the commitment of certain police stations to the gay community. There have, however, been vicious gay-bashing incidents in these areas, including the murder of gay men.

Cruising, Cottaging and Renting

Articles in the gay press in the last decade serve as warnings and, in some instances, morality tales about the risks of engaging in sex in public with strangers. Simultaneously they glamorise and eroticise danger "...the elements of danger and discovery seem to incite such risqué sexual behaviour" (*Exit*, 132: 5)."With the crime rate at the level it is, frequenting dark and unsafe areas is putting not only your health at risk, but also your life. However, boys will be boys" (*Exit*, 131: 1).

Articles are often accompanied by erotic pictures or illustrated with stories that have a salacious edge. As journalist Karen Lotter admits about her own article entitled "Boys of the Night":

> This story may sound like some sensationalistic piece of garbage dished up for a gay porn magazine. (*Gay SA*, 3: 3).

Photographs of men in provocative poses are juxtaposed with grim headlines such as "Gay Murders are You Next?", "Death Rap: Cruising Turns to Bruising" and "When is 'Rent' Safe?"

In addition, implicit in the articles is a judgement about the closeted nature of many men who frequent public spaces in search of sex. "What these men will have to live with, however, is the idea of having abandoned someone who may very well have suffered greatly because of their neglect" (*Exit*, 132: 5).

The gay press in South Africa has a predominantly white, male readership. The emphasis on cruising precludes a detailed analysis of the problem from different perspectives. Firstly, the focus on the relationship between public spaces and violent attacks by strangers denies the frequency of attacks by family and acquaintances. Furthermore, the problem of domestic violence is concealed. According to the Equality Project domestic violence is increasingly reported to them. Second, gay men cruise in Johannesburg and so the targeting of lesbians remains under-reported in the press. The emphasis on a particular readership reinforces the culture of silence in lesbian circles and in black gay communities.

Bashings in Kwa-Thema

Kwa-Thema, a township on the outskirts of Springs, east of Johannesburg has an established anti-apartheid and gay activist history. According to Paddy Nhlapo (Archival Source AM2894; Gay and Lesbian Archives of South Africa; Historical Papers; UWL), a gay man and youth activist during the height of apartheid,

Some of the guys from the liberation movement wanted to start some kind of gay bashing campaign and I had to go through a harsh time of convincing people and lobbying people.

Paddy and other gay and lesbian activists who worked in political structures were able to convince the 'comrades' in the area that this would be counter productive. By the early 1990s the local gay community had organised itself into the strongest and most active branch of the Gay and Lesbian Organisation of the Witwatersrand (GLOW). The organisation aligned itself with the anti-apartheid movement. However, subsequently an elder of the local gay community, British Sgxabai, was killed by a family member in a homophobic attack. Violence against lesbians and gay men in the area escalated until, in 2001, a public meeting was called by local gay and lesbian activists to address the problem. The local branch of the African National Congress, the South African Communist Party, the local gay and lesbian organisation, parents, representatives of community structures and social organisations met in the Kwa-Thema community hall to discuss the problem and seek solutions. Concerns raised at the meeting dealt with

Understanding Systemic Violence 113

lack of community support, inadequate social services and health care, police complicity and problems experienced by the parents and families of gay men. Ten attendees of the meeting were subsequently interviewed in depth.

Sexual Assault

A high number of the interviewees described their experiences of rape and attempted rape. When leaving a tavern, A (a gay man) was followed by three men who, armed with knives, accosted him. They noticed that he was wearing unusual shoes,"...unfortunately my shoes were ladies shoes."They made him strip to check whether he was a *stabane*. He was subsequently beaten and raped by all three perpetrators. As a survival strategy, the victim convinced two of the perpetrators to engage in thigh sex. The third rapist insisted on anal sex, but chased the others away.

In South Africa, the majority of sexual violence is perpetrated by someone known to the victim (*Rape Crisis*, 10 April 2002). This statistic was reflected in the interview with B (a gay man) who was raped by a childhood acquaintance during the day. As in the first case, the victim was leaving a tavern. The perpetrator offered to walk home with him and severely assaulted and raped him. Despite knowledge of the perpetrators identity, B's case was not taken seriously."...I took further steps because I knew where he was staying. I knew his parents, I knew everything. Then it happened that when I took further steps it was like I am playing or I am joking...the police...took it very light, very light."C (a gay man) was also assaulted and raped by someone known to him. While visiting the perpetrator at his home, he was locked in, beaten with an iron rod and raped in the bedroom. The victim only reported the incident to the police after he had been raped several times and the same man had raped his friend. The victim explains his reluctance to report,"...after he finished to rape me, I went to my place. I was scared to tell them what happened. I saw myself. I don't belong to the boy's life. What he did, it was nice that time."The victim experienced confusion around the perpetrator's culpability as he felt a degree of physical pleasure in the rape and subsequently came out to himself as being gay. F met a man at a party and went home with him. The man tried to rape him, 'but he was not that successful'. The next day he escaped and went to the police.

Gang Violence

Lesbians are often victimised by gangs. D (a lesbian) had also been drinking alcohol at a shebeen (tavern). She was walking home with a friend when they were attacked by a group of thirteen men. Her friend was hit on the head and she was raped by twelve of the men. The thirteenth took her to his house, but did not rape her. As in A's experience there is an element of gender subversion involved in the motivation for the attack. D stated that the perpetrators had called her a"soccer player"which has the connotation of a "masculine-looking" woman. E (a lesbian) reported that she had intervened in an incident where another woman was being sexually harassed. The harasser returned with a group of men who called them *stabane*, hit her over the head with a brick, beat her friend with a gun and physically assaulted both of them.

Police and Health Services Responses

Police responses in most of the cases were unsympathetic and are best described as secondary victimisation. Some respondents do not report incidents to the police because, based on what they have heard about other people's experiences, they did not expect to be taken seriously:

> Interviewer: Why didn't you tell the police?
> A: Who was going to believe that?
> G [a gay man]: We didn't think of going to the police. It's just that the police don't take us seriously, they think that we are playing or that we look stupid.
> H [a lesbian]: When you tell the police that you are gay, they don't help us, they just laugh at us.

The interviewees also reported that they feared reprisal from the perpetrators if they reported the crime to the police. In the case of E, she felt that the assailants would accost her at school if she spoke about the incident.

B describes a typical case of secondary victimisation. In the wake of a violent rape, the police in the charge office subjected the complainant to public ridicule:

> B: The other one say to another one; hey come this side, come listen to this. 'Oh! This is funny, repeat again what you have just said to me.' And that one went to fetch other police to come listen to this...Ja, you know when I left that police station, it was like I didn't know whether I had been raped or not...it was fun to them...

C had a similar experience after reporting his experience of repeated rape to the police:

> C: I just blamed myself. Why did I go there in the first place? After I left the place, they were laughing at me and making jokes about me.

In the case of F, who reported an attempted rape, the police thought that he was lying and the case was not followed up. At the public meeting an activist summarised the difficulties of reporting:

We have four cases of rape at the moment. At the police station they just take your case and if you ask for privacy to report your case, they do not grant it to you. The way they assess your statement is that they ask if you are gay. If you say you are lesbian they ask you, 'why do you want to be a man?'

In one case a young man who had been raped had initially had a similar experience with male police officers. He subsequently sought out a woman inspector who took his case seriously and supported him.

Health service responses to rape associated with gay-bashing are disturbing. There is a high HIV risk with victims reporting that neither lubricants nor condoms were used. At the Kwa-Thema public meeting it was reported that anti-retroviral medication was not made available to victims at hospitals. Many of the victims show a lack of awareness of the psychological effects of the trauma they have experienced. In interviews, however, these effects were apparent. Many of the victims were reluctance to tell anyone, "It was like I didn't even tell anybody, I was so ashamed". E still feels the physical effects of her assault, "…as soon as I got injured, maybe I am mad. Because it's like I'm crazy. So that's why sometimes I get pains."

Responses

B characterises the resilience of many of the victims of violence. After being scorned by the police, B reconstructs himself as a stronger person. "No instead I was strong. I became a real woman in a certain way". A more positive experience of the police was reported when one of the victims was accompanied by a veteran gay activist. Lesbians have formed support groups and in some cases have formed defensive teams (*Exit* 70, 1995). In several cases of attempted assault, gays and lesbians have fought back physically. In one case, a woman beat her tormentor on the head with a brick after being called a *stabane*. Two lesbians who ran a gay friendly shebeen thwarted an attack by three men who had hidden in their house by beating and fining them five hundred rand in exchange for not reporting them to the police. When asked why they didn't report the case to the police, they replied, "…we better fight for ourselves".

Bashings in Soweto

In the late 1980s the first discussions around the formation of an inclusive gay and lesbian organisation were held at 'Mhlanga Rocks', a gay-friendly shebeen in Soweto. Today Soweto has become home to a number of gay and lesbian groups and social spaces such as lesbian soccer clubs and gay netball teams; shebeens; catering groups and lesbian political organisations such as Nkateko. Soweto also has a level of violent crime manifested in high rates of violence against women. As no research has been completed on the effect of domestic and stranger violence against women on fear of crime, it is difficult to situate the results of this research. However, homophobic violence against women, cannot be separated from other violence against women. The intense and pervasive fear of violence that most women experience is compounded by sexual identity:

When you are a lesbian you fear as both a woman and a gay woman (Q).

Rape

Bev Ditsie comments that at one time lesbians were specifically targeted for sexual assault. As in the Kwa-Thema interviews, lesbians in Soweto indicated that there was a high level of threats of rape, attempted rape and rape in incidents of homophobic violence.

> M: ...I met three men. They greeted and I responded. They offered to take me halfway, but I refused. One said I was being cheeky. One walked faster to overtake me. The other two were behind me. One burnt me with a cigarette on my arm while the other two were holding my hands tightly. They closed my mouth and started raping me. They all took turns. When they were finished, they walked away... Two weeks before my rape, I was on TV on the Take 5 talk-show. So many people in the location saw me and many people know that I am lesbian. So I believe these boys knew about me because they don't stray far away from home.

While travelling on a train from Johannesburg to Soweto, three lesbians and a gay man were confronted by a knife-wielding gang. K narrates the story:

> K: Here in the township, mostly boys have a problem. They test us, by proposing love to us. They want to see our reaction. ...He called me a bitch. I was hurt, I asked him, who's a bitch? He said we annoy him because we think we are boys. They said they were going to kill the gay man and rape us. ...These boys saw us by our dress code that we are lesbians and the gay man had a hairstyle...
> J: ...I visited my girlfriend. In the streets she wanted to kiss me and I stopped her. I knew that people were probably looking at us. Two guys approached us. I told my girlfriend to go back to her home. One of the guys said he was going to punish me because I think I am a boy. ...I escaped. I ran back to my girlfriend's home. I fought because I promised myself that if I ever get raped again, I will kill myself.
> H: He was drunk and determined to prove a point. We started fighting. When things got hotter, I realised that I was being overpowered by the boys. I was hopeless because they are boys and they were may. Fortunately 10111 (police rescue) showed up and I ran away.

Lesbians as a Threat to Masculinity

A central theme emerges from the interviews, boys and men perceive lesbians as threatening to their masculinity. This manifested in two ways: (1) sexual rivalry and (2) punishment [lesbians were punished because they are more masculine-looking and because they are sexually unavailable].

H: In my location, a group of boys call themselves the 'top bouncers'. They have a problem about me dating girls. They propose any girl they think I'm dating. They are always after my case, but I ignore them.

N: When I was at school I was punched by a boy who thought I was going out with his girlfriend

J: One of the guys said that he was going to punish me because I think I am a boy.

L: ...they say I have two sexual organs

Q: Then he found out that I was a lesbian. And then he started, you know how men are, when they find out that you are a lesbian, especially straight men, when they find out that you are a lesbian, then they'll start saying things that, um, they can show you how you should be treated and then if you want the real thing and all that. Those are insulting statements. And they say you don't know what you are missing. Which they don't understand that you really don't need that.

R: This guy walks in he's a gangster he's a car thief, right. He comes directly to me and says to me and I don't even know him, okay. He says, "No I must speak to you right now, come." We go outside, we sit in front of the door, he says to me. "Why don't you leave my girlfriend the fuck alone? Because my girlfriend is the one you are with right now". ...[Later] I walked to the balcony [on the eleventh floor]...and he comes out onto the balcony and he says that this is going to be very painless. I am not going to shoot you, I am just going to ask you to jump.

Public Reaction

Sexual violence is so pervasive, in many communities it is normalised. Many of the interviewees commented on public apathy and complicity with the attackers.

J: I tried to run away to the taxis but one woman told the driver to leave me because I knew the guy [the attacker]. He tore my sweater and hit me with a fist.

K: They said they were going to kill the gay man and rape us. They left the coach. When they came back they were six. They took knives out, people left to the next coach. Nobody interfered or stopped them.

At times, however, the victims were assisted by the public. J managed to escape temporarily when a passerby distracted her attacker. K's experience was interrupted when an armed civilian boarded the train and intervened.

Police Responses

Police were viewed by all of the women interviewed in Soweto with deep mistrust and were generally thought to be inefficient, uncaring and homophobic:

> H: Police are the last people we think of in the location. They do not do their job. Even if you report a case, nothing will be done about it.

M had a mixed response with security services. She called emergency services after being raped by three men, but they failed to respond. Her pastor took her to a specialised rape unit in the inner-city the next day and they attended to the case. However, they were unable to provide her with anti-retroviral medication and she was advised to purchase it from the pharmacy. The state does not provide anti-retrovirals to women who have been raped and has actively discouraged non-governmental organisations from distributing anti-retrovirals to rape victims in state hospitals. She was unable to afford the medication.

Perhaps the most telling response was Q's:

> [*Incredulous silence; raucous laughter throughout*] Of course not! I go to the police and the police are going to make a joke about me. And they would just see that we are two woman, and they will say that we are wasting their time [*more laughter*]. So I never. You see with the system *and still* if you go to report the case you'll find two [police]men probably they'll be homophobic too, they'll be like lots of people are very homophobic, so they will not take your case.

Responses

The women reported four responses to the high incidence of gay-bashing in Soweto. Many took refuge in their family. Others suggested coping strategies such as walking in groups at night. In keeping with the responses of Kwa-Thema gays and lesbians, many called for public education. Lastly, since the police were viewed as weak and inefficient, a few of the women carried or wanted to carry weapons. We focus on two of these coping strategies in more detail:

Family

Many of the women reported that their families were very supportive. An unknown gunman shot at L and she was lucky to escape with her life when the gun jammed. She believed that the motivation for the unprovoked attack was her sexuality. Her grandfather is a traditional healer and she believes that he protected her.

> L: My grandfather said he is the one who made the gun jam and I was saved...I did get support from my family, because I am the only child my mother has. She loves, protects and treasures me.

H mentioned that her "family supported me as always. They never blame it on me". J's family had a mixed response. On the one hand they said that the incident was a result of going out at night. On the other hand, she reports that "they were hurt that it happened. They never thought of counselling or talking to me about it". While there was some support for victims, there was also blaming. Q reports that her sister responded by saying that she should be extra careful and that she should know better than to flaunt her sexuality in public.

Public Education

Public education was seen by the majority of the interviewees from Soweto and Kwa-Thema as a panacea.

> H: People must be taught about gay and lesbian lifestyles and issues.
> K: People should not discriminate against us, we are human too...They need to learn acceptance and know that we are here to stay.
> M: The community must be taught about lesbians. We have a right to live. Constitutional rights are just in papers, people do not know anything about them. There should be more education on TV and radio.
> L: The community should be taught about gay and lesbian lifestyles and they should know that we are created by God.
> O: The hate crimes piss me off. People need to be educated.

There has been an unprecedented proliferation of media coverage of sexuality in general and gay and lesbian issues in particular. While a number of gay people are positive in their response to television and radio talk shows, whether these have the effect of further stigmatising gay men and lesbians through a sensationalised othering or whether they are beneficial public education forums is debatable. While talk shows are often cited as a catalyst for coming out to family members, one of the respondents was gang raped shortly after appearing on a magazine programme on gay and lesbian youth.

Policing Hate Crimes in South Africa

In 1993, Glen Retief painted a bleak picture of gay-bashing in relation to gay men. Until 1998, a host of legislation concerning same-sex activity was on the South African statute books. The most extensive powers vested in the police were in their dealings with the crime of sodomy. Sodomy was included as a Schedule 1 offence in terms of the Criminal Procedures Act (51 of 1977), along with murder, rape and fraud. In terms of Schedule 1 offences police were permitted to arrest, without a warrant, any person suspected of committing sodomy. Most chillingly, it also authorised the killing of a person reasonably suspected of having committed sodomy when that person could not be arrested or prevented from fleeing.

Gays and lesbians not only had to contend with a police force that would charge them if they reported a gay-related incident, but they were often subjected to police raids. Police were also known to frequent well-known cruising areas and to make arrests if propositioned. Gay men were often told that if they did not admit guilt, they would be exposed in the media. In the eighties, the South African media served to create a particularly homophobic climate with a number of homosexual paedophile stories. Finally, the use of the "homosexual panic" defence in several cases of murder of gay men and the subsequent leniency of judges serves as an indicator of the degree to which homophobic discourses were normalised at the time.

In 1998 the Constitutional Court declared all laws that criminalized sex between men unconstitutional. In this post-apartheid period, three distinct narratives about the police emerge in the media and interviews with gay activists and people who have been gay-bashed.

The Police as Heroes

"Join gay policing structures" urged GAY SA in 1997, announcing the formation of two formal gay and lesbian structures within the South African Police Services. When a delegation of lesbians and gay police officers from the South African Gay and Lesbian Police Network participated in the annual gay and lesbian Pride Parade in 1996, *Priscilla* (gay lingo for police) seemed to be finally redeemed in the eyes of the gay and lesbian community. No longer monitoring the march from the sidelines, they were participating in the parade, in uniform, as openly lesbian and gay police officers. In 2000 *Exit* newspaper proclaimed that "In one of the most positive examples of the spirit and freedom of the new South Africa, the SAPS and the lesbian and gay community are taking definite steps to tackle increasing numbers of crimes committed in well known cruising spots" (Issue 124, 2000: 1).

Hero status was accorded to the hardworking police officers of the Parkview Police Station under the headline "Straight Cop—Gay Hero" and there was much press interest in the launch of Pink Panthers. In a front page advertisement in *Exit*, cruisers were urged to join this initiative, "And if you are into Ornithology while at the same time doing you bit for the community, join the Pink Panthers..." Another police station stepped up patrols in Rhodes Park in the eastern suburbs of Johannesburg and under the photograph of a handsome blonde and a uniformed police officer was the caption: "Sgt. Dennis Adriao stressed in a comment to *Exit* that men cruising should not be wary of the police patrols which were meant only to ensure their safety" (Issue 86, 1997: 1).

Recently, the Sunday papers carried the story of a police superintendent who had gone under-cover to apprehend a serial hi-jacker, 'the car-jack queen' who had targeted gay men at Emmarentia and Zoo Lake (both well-known cruising sites). The investigating officer enlisted his wife's expertise and emerged with "skin-tight clothes, big buckle rubber shoes and coy come-on lines to attract the gunman" (*Sunday Times*, 18 February 2001). While the story was sensationalised by the media, it showed that at a station level, an in particular the Parkview police station, extensive effort is being made to intervene in gay-related crime. In one of the interviews it was deeply ironic that the unconstitutional sodomy legislation was used to prosecute the rapists of a male victim who had been raped before 1998.

The Police as Victimisers

At the workshop held in Kwa-Thema, the issue of secondary victimisation was raised on several occasions. In many of the interviews discussed previously, police response to homophobic violence was extremely humiliating for the victim and amounted to secondary victimisation, which was often equally or more traumatic than the initial incident. Moreover, serious problems have been identified within the police services regarding the reporting of rape. A report completed by Human Rights Watch (1995) summarises the situation:

> Widespread reports of police mistreatment of rape survivors contributes to the low percentage of reported rapes. Raped women frequently have to relate their experience over the counter to busy, indifferent and often judgmental police officers in a crowded charge office...beliefs about rape victims include the assumption that rape is a "natural" masculine response...and that women must have done something to provoke such an attack.

In many cases police incompetence and corruption has led to low offender convictions. Under these circumstances it is not surprising that many of the victims felt that they would not report the incident because it involved both rape and sexual identity. Headlines such as "Police shield gay's assailants" (*Exit*, 1997) and "Wipe out the lesbians!" (*Exit*, 1997) pointed to a more sinister undercurrent within the police force. When lesbian mother Mrs Smith was assaulted by three men in her home, she went to the local police station in Carltonville (a mining town west of Johannesburg) to report the incident. She was told "If I ever see you lesbians in this police station, I will kick you so hard under your arses that you will not find your way back to Carltonville. You are sick people and you disgust us" (Issue 84, 1997: 1). "Is this the 'transformed' SAPS?" asked the writer of the article, activist Zackie Achmat.

The Police as Perpetrators

With exceptions, police have traditionally viewed homosexuality with deep contempt. Despite diversity training, an acrimonious culture towards gay men and lesbians persists. The Equality Project reports a recent incident in a Johannesburg community where gays and lesbians requested an intervention from the Equality Project with the local police who had been victimising them for some time. S (a white gay man), reported an incident where he had been beaten in the parking lot of an inner-city gay club by a group of men who drove away in a police vehicle (identified by the registration number). He reported the case to the police services with the registration number, but was told that the investigation had dead-ended. The victim felt that not enough had been done to apprehend the perpetrators (interview, 2002).

Policy Issues

Several policy issues emerged in the research. The most primary and urgent is the free provision of anti-retroviral medication in cases of homophobic rape. This medication also needs to be administered promptly and efficiently. Police are not adequately trained to handle homophobic violence and rape is not receiving enough attention. Measures to alleviate the trauma of reporting, such a private space for statement-taking, are being ignored. There is clearly a need for further diversity training. In a similar vein to the specialised rape reporting centres, specific police stations should be identified as gay-friendly particularly in former townships. While attempts have been made to attend to these issues, many of these efforts are profoundly misdirected. While post-apartheid South Africa has sophisticated policy and legislation around sexual choice, these are not implemented with any consistency. For example, the lack of specific categories for hate crime reporting in national statistical surveys is disturbing. Furthermore, it is the task of government and gay and lesbian organisations to actively educate the public around issues of masculinity, rape and sexuality. Currently, there are no gay counselling services in Johannesburg. There are, however, a number of organisations that offer support services. Gay and lesbian groups should co-ordinate with these structures to ensure that they are widely utilised.

4. CONCLUSION

This research has much in common with the work of Valentine (1993) and Namaste (1996). A more public homosexual landscape has been enabled through the post-apartheid constitution, which subverts the heterosexual landscape of Johannesburg. Gay men and lesbians are victimised in response to this subversion. Lesbians who adopt masculine signifiers in dress and manner are actively targeted and punished for this subversion through sexual violence. This violence is intended to "teach" them what it is to be a woman and is a reassertion of masculine power. This is in keeping with Namaste's (ibid.) comments on the element of gender subversion in her analysis of gay-bashing patterns.

There are also important differences from the work of Valentine and Namaste. Firstly, interviews indicate that hate crimes committed in Johannesburg are exceptionally violent. In comparison to international figures, incidence of homophobic rape is much higher. This points to a difference in spatial context. Without essentialising or generalising masculine identities, the results of interviews suggest linkage to Skelton (1995) and Vogelman's (ibid.) work relating a lack of social and economic power to the need to assert masculine identity. Drawing on comments made in interviews, we hypothesise that the reason rape is more frequent in homophobic hate crime in Johannesburg is that rape is the reinforcement of masculine dominance. Lesbians are seen as threats to masculine power, which in the context of poverty, transition and structural inequality is the only power that many men feel they have at their disposal. It is clear, however, that configurations of masculinity require further investigation in a South African context. Johannesburg faces the challenge of turning around an endemic culture of violence. This requires further reflection on masculinity and its relationship to sexual violence.

Furthermore, men who are effeminate in dress and speech are viewed as women and are thereby relegated to an inferior position. Ironically, in evidence emerging in research on South African sexual identity (Reid, 2000), gay men with a strong feminine identity are often more integrated within local communities. However, this status does not protect them from violent attacks experienced by many women. Indeed their gendered identity as women relegates them to an inferior position and they are thus equally vulnerable to male violence. Future research on perceptions of the relationship between gender identity and sexuality in Africa will serve to explicate these findings.

M, a young Sowetan captured the complex irony of the public space that has opened up for lesbians and gay men in the wake of political transition: "Constitutional rights are just in papers, people do not know anything about them. There should be more education on TV and radio". On the one hand there is a high level of legal protection and public visibility, on the other there remains a high level of violence. M reflects on the failure of the constitution to protect citizens, particularly in terms of the Bill of Rights. Yet she retains a belief in education, despite being gang raped shortly after appearing in a television talk show on gay and lesbian youth.

Despite the enormous legislative and social gains made by lesbians and gay men in South Africa, Johannesburg remains a homophobic landscape. This is evident in existing research and in the gay media. However, within this landscape of exclusion lie the further peripheralised experiences of less vocal communities. Extensive research which actively embraces difference is required for a detailed analysis of the many forms of homophobic violence in Johannesburg without drawing on "clichéd notions of victim and hero" (Ingram, 1999: 30). Rather these investigations need to be embedded in discussions of the complexity and suppleness (ibid.) of gay urban politics in Johannesburg.

ACKNOWLEDGEMENTS

We would like to thank the following people for their assistance: Nhanhla Zwane, Busi Kheswa, Phineas Riba, Carrie Shelver, Anthony Manion [archivist, Gay and Lesbian Archives], Jonathan Berger, Evert Knoessen and Wendy Isaacs from the Lesbian and Gay Equality Project, Ruth Morgan [director, Gay and Lesbian Archives], and Bev Ditsie for permission to use excerpts from her documentary.

REFERENCES

Bonham, S., A. Hassett, J. Caulfield, V. Kapentenakis, and P. Stobbs. 1994. *Diversity Workshop: Sexual Orientation.* Equality Project Training Module in Diversity Training Programme, Technikon South Africa, Johannesburg.

Brown, M. 1995. Sex, scale and the 'new urban politics': HIV-prevention strategies from Yaletown, Vancouver. In D. Bell and G. Valentine (eds.), *Mapping Desire.* Routledge, London.

Butler, J. 1990. *Gender Trouble: Feminism and the Subversion of Identity.* Routledge, London

Chan Sam, T. 1994. Five women: Black lesbian life on the reef. In M. Gevisser and E. Cameron (eds.), *Defiant Desire: Gay and Lesbian Lives in South Africa.* Ravan Press, Johannesburg.

Charney, C. 1995. Between Ignorance and Tolerance: South African Public Attitudes on Issues Concerning Gays, Lesbians, and AIDS. Unpublished Report, AIDS Law Project, University of the Witwatersrand, Johannesburg. Archival source: AM2784 Kevan Botha Collection; Gay and Lesbian Archives of South Africa; Historical Papers; UWL.

Collins, P. 1991. *Black Feminist Thought*. Routledge, London.

Ditsie, P. D. and N. Newman. 2002. *Simon and I*. Documentary. Johannesburg.

Exit, Monthly Newspaper. Archival source: AM2723; Gay and Lesbian Archives of South Africa; Historical Papers; UWL.

Foucault. 1988. Technologies of the Self. In L. Martin, H. Gutman, and P. Hutton (eds.), *Technologies of the Self: A Seminar with Michel Foucault*. Tavistock, Andover, Hants.

Gay SA, Monthly Newspaper. Archival source: AM2907; Gay and Lesbian Archives of South Africa; Historical Papers; UWL.

Harper, P. 1993. Eloquence and epitaph: Black nationalism and the homophobic impulse in responses to the death of Max Robinson. In T. Murphey and Poirier (eds.), *Writing AIDS: Gay Literature, Language and Analysis*. Columbia University Press, New York.

Hooks, B. 1992. *Black Looks: Race and Representation*. Turnaround, London.

Human Rights Watch. 1995. *Violence Against Women in South Africa: State Response to Domestic Violence and Rape*. Human Rights Watch, New York.

Ingram, G. B., A. Bouthillette, and Y. Retter. 1997. *Queers in Space*. Bay Press, Seattle.

London Free Press. 2000. 4 March. http://www.canoe.ca/LondonFreePress/home.html

Department of Safety and Security. 1994. Draft Policy Document Change. Archival source: AM2910 Paul Stobbs Collection; Gay and Lesbian Archives of South Africa; Historical Papers; UWL.

Mamaki. 1993. Two episodes: Corner of insults. In M. Krouse and K. Berman (eds.), *Invisible Ghetto*. Cosaw Publishing, Johannesburg.

Multiculturalism. 1998. Web-based magazine.

Namaste. 1996. Genderbashing: Sexuality, gender, and the regulation of public space. *Environment and Planning D: Society and Space*, 14: 221-240.

Rape Crisis. 2002. (accessed 10 April) http://www.rapecrisis.org.za/.

Reid, G. and P. Alberton. 2000. *Dark and Lovely, Soft and Free*. Documentary. Johannesburg.

Retief, G. 1993. 'Policing the Perverts': An Exploratory Investigation of the Nature and Social Impacts of Police Action towards Gay and Bisexual Men in South Africa. Institute of Criminology, Research Report Series, Cape Town.

Skelton. 1995. 'BOOM, BYE, BYE': Jamaican ragga and gay resistance. In D. Bell and G. Valentine (eds.), *Mapping Desire*. Routledge, London.

Sunday Times. Weekly Newspaper.

The Star. Daily Paper.

Theron, A. 1994. Anti-gay violence and discrimination: The need for legislation against anti-gay hate crimes in the socio-politically changing South Africa. *Occasional Paper*. University of Pretoria, Pretoria.

Theuninck, A. 2000. The Traumatic Impact of Minority Stressors on Males Self- Identified as Homosexual or Bisexual. Unpublished Masters Thesis, University of the Witwatersrand.

Valentine, G. 1993. (Hetero)sexing space: Lesbian perceptions and experiences of everyday spaces. *Environment and Planning D: Society and Space*, 11: 395-413.

Vimbela, V. 1994. Climbing on her shoulders: An interview with Umtata's 'first lesbian'. In M. Gevisser and E. Cameron (eds.), *Defiant Desire: Gay and Lesbian Lives in South Africa*. Ravan Press, Johannesburg.

Young, I. M. 1990a. *Justice and the Politics of Difference*. Princeton University Press, Princeton.

Young, I. M. 1990b. The ideal of community and the politics of difference. In L. Nicholson (ed.), *Feminism/Postmodernism*. Routledge, New York.

Kinship

[18]

FAMILY, LAW AND SEXUALITY: FEMINIST ENGAGEMENTS

SUSAN B. BOYD

University of British Columbia, Canada

ABSTRACT

The author explores feminist frameworks within which questions of family, law and sexuality can best be explored, drawing on recent efforts to (re)establish materialist feminist theory. She suggests that in order to make the important link between questions of gender, sexuality, difference, desire, identity and subjectivity on the one hand, and problems of production and exploitation on the other, a materialist feminist theory must incorporate the strengths of Marxist feminism with those of postmodernist feminism. As a way of exploring the politics of current struggles for legal recognition of lesbian and gay relationships as 'spousal', she engages with the debate between Nancy Fraser and Judith Butler on the 'recognition/redistribution' dichotomy. She argues that neither theorist takes seriously enough the role of the family in the privatisation of the costs of social reproduction within capitalism. She concludes that the important lesbian/gay struggles for legal recognition of 'spousal' relationships, such as in the *M* v *H* lesbian spousal support case in Canada, should not be seen as sufficient to achieve social equality. Such legal struggles must be accompanied by trenchant critiques of the limits of such recognition in redistributing wealth and well-being.

One of the questions I ask in this book is why the dominant feminist theory in the postmodern moment – ludic feminism – has largely abandoned the problems of labor and exploitation and ignored their relation to gender, sexuality, difference, desire, and subjectivity. (Ebert, 1996: ix)

I am irritated now by certainties and also by the belief in progress. (Smart, 1995: 126)

THE 1998 Keele Conference on Law, Gender and Sexuality gave me a welcome opportunity to explore some questions that had been vexing me over the past few years; these questions relate to feminist frameworks within which to explore questions of family, law and sexuality. My key concern has been the way in which many contemporary feminist theorists have failed to link questions of gender, sexuality, difference, desire, identity

and subjectivity, on the one hand, with problems of production and exploitation on the other. In this article, I argue that in order to make this link, a
materialist feminist theory must incorporate the strengths of Marxist feminism and the strengths of postmodernist feminism.

My personal journey towards this argument involves the fact that it was
socialist feminist analysis of law, ideology and legal struggle that first generated my intellectual excitement about what feminism might offer to legal
studies (e.g. Gavigan, 1988; Smart, 1984). A great deal of my early work, on
child custody law especially, related to a critique of the nuclear family form,
the institution of marriage, the sexual division of labour, and their relationship to women's oppression within capitalism (e.g. Boyd, 1989). As I moved
on to look at lesbian family law claims, it seemed to me that lesbian oppression was explicated at least in part by this critique, since the nuclear family
form was quintessentially heterosexual (see Boyd, 1994). It also made a lot of
sense to me that a feminist who had developed a critique of the nuclear family
norm in law would have some interest in, and an understanding of, lesbian
oppression, regardless of her own sexual identity. I have found that I resist
the notion that lesbian oppression is completely distinct analytically from
women's oppression generally, or that one needs to be a lesbian to understand
the dynamics of lesbian oppression; rather, both forms of oppression are connected to other forms of oppression related to the material and ideological
supports for the heterosexual nuclear family. There is therefore a need to
develop a lesbian feminist analysis that traces the connections between heteronormativity,[1] gendered power relations between men and women (including the sexual division of labour) and capitalist social relations. From this
position, I am disturbed by analyses that focus on the discourses of gender
or sexuality without examining how such discourses relate to wider trends of
globalisation, privatisation and economic privation, and the role of 'family'
in these trends. In short, I hold the view that it is crucial to bring the political economy of sexuality and gender more firmly into our analyses of law's
contradictory role in emancipatory politics. However, it is admittedly very
often difficult to do so, especially when engaging in progressive struggle
through litigation, as I shall later explore in a discussion of the Canadian
lesbian spousal support case *M* v *H*.

I acknowledge the important ways in which poststructuralist work has
enhanced recognition of the complex nature of the constitution of the subject,
the lack of certainty in this postmodern world and the need to take nothing
for granted, and the problems with universalising and essentialising discourses about women. But I often feel that something is missing in analyses
of social movements or of legal identities. I want to argue that there is still
some way – perhaps especially in these times of 'regress and of the undoing
of things once thought of as immutable' (Smart, 1995: 126) – to think about
emancipatory politics and law's place in it, without falling right back into the
problematic assumptions of orthodox Marxism or orthodox feminism. I
share Nancy Fraser's desire to challenge 'the current "postsocialist" de-
coupling of cultural politics from social politics' (although she has recently

been criticised for doing just that (see Butler, 1997/1998; Iris Marion Young, 1997), and to find a critical approach that is 'bivalent', one that integrates 'the social and the cultural, the economic and the discursive' (Fraser, 1997a: 5).

(RE)READING MATERIALIST FEMINISM

In the early months of 1998, I revisited the question of materialist feminism with two graduate students in a reading course. Together we read some of the classic texts of socialist and materialist feminism (for example, Barrett, 1988; Delphy, 1981/1997; Young, 1980/1997) and explored more recent contributions as well (for example, Ebert, 1996; Hennessy, 1993; Seccombe, 1992; Smith, 1993/1997). We discovered some American authors who are attempting to re-establish a tradition of materialist feminism in part in order to resist the hegemony of postmodernist, or as Teresa Ebert (1996) would say, 'ludic' feminism in academia.[2] 'Ludic' means 'playful' and is related to the word 'ludicrous'.[3] Ebert argues that ludic theory displaces one notion of theory (as explanatory critique) for another: 'theory as play and as a playful (vigilant) reading of the play of immanent differences in the text/system' (1996: 14).

The new materialist feminist literature emerging from the United States is particularly interesting given the relative lack of attention to class relations historically in academia in the United States (in contrast to the UK and to Canada, where somewhat more attention has been paid to the Marxist tradition) and given general moves everywhere towards 'postsocialist' politics. In 1993, Hennessy described materialist feminism in the United States as 'just beginning to address these issues and to formulate a strongly materialist and feminist resistance postmodernism' and building on 'a critical articulation of postmodernism and marxism by British socialist feminists' (1993: 3). Nevertheless, together with Chrys Ingraham, Hennessy has produced a reader, or archive, on materialist feminism (Hennessy and Ingraham, 1997) and their introduction provides a useful brief review of the relationship between Marxist, socialist, cultural, postmodernist and materialist feminisms. Although they very clearly locate the relationship between Marxist and materialist feminism, they argue that materialist feminism was the conjuncture of several discourses, including postmodern and psychoanalytic theories of meaning and subjectivity: '[i]n drawing on postmodern critiques of the humanist subject and neo-marxist theories of ideology, materialist feminism constituted a significant shift from the feminist debates of the early '70s, both radical and socialist alike' (Hennessy and Ingraham, 1997: 7). This body of work therefore is important to scholars working from both Marxian and poststructuralist frameworks.

It was refreshing for me to revisit materialist feminist literature and explore the newer efforts to re-establish the tradition of materialist analysis while also taking into account the postmodern turn. Ebert calls this oppositional space within the postmodern from which she speaks 'resistance postmodernism'

(1996: 16). She argues that postmodernism itself is 'a contradictory historical condition, and its contradictions are those of the material base' (1996: 130). Because both postmodernism and the theories that try to explain it are divided by the social contradictions of capitalism, there are in turn different ways of theorising postmodernism, depending on how they account for these contradictions and resulting changes (Ebert, 1996: 130). This insight that there is a choice of approaches under postmodernism was inspiring, but I was also rather startled to realise that I have been so influenced by the dominance of ludic feminism in the academy that I rarely expose my students to the materialist feminist tradition in any systematic way. This failure on my part has occurred despite my published efforts (e.g. Boyd, 1991, 1994) to argue that the two traditions are more compatible than is often thought and that socialist feminist work on law offered at least some of the insights now claimed by poststructuralism. It seems I am not alone in failing to expose my students to the materialist feminist tradition: my graduate student from Australia observed that until this reading course, she had rarely been exposed to the tradition of materialist feminism; in her academic career, postmodernist work had been presented as *the* answer to the problems of second wave feminism.[4]

So, what are the questions that have been dropped off the intellectual agenda in feminist work over the past decade? If historical materialists take as a starting point 'real living individuals and what they need in order to produce their means of subsistence' (Hennessy and Ingraham, 1997: 4), then arguably these issues of survival and the emancipatory critical knowledge needed to understand social life under capitalism and transform it have been diminished in favour of more local or contingent knowledges. Ebert argues that in its effort to move away from essentialising concepts of experience, ludic feminism has moved towards a focus on 'linguistic play, difference, and the priority of discourse' and that it 'substitutes a politics of representation for radical social transformation' (1996: 3). Paradoxically, in this latter respect of the politics of representation, postmodernist feminism bears some resemblance to liberal feminist arguments of the 1970s for the benefits of increasing the voice of women in politics, the legal system and other institutions.[5] Of course poststructuralists are much more critical of the notion that an authentic voice of women can be identified, let alone expressed. Nonetheless, in (rightly) moving away from the excessive economic determinism of much Marxian analysis, poststructuralists have redefined the social as discourse or textuality, and have posited desire or pleasure as the dynamics of the social, thereby displacing questions of economics, labour and class struggle (Ebert, 1996: ix). In other words, in exploring what one of my graduate students calls the 'trite truth' (Pearlston, 1998) of ludic theory – that we understand the world around us only through systems of signification – ludic feminists have lost a way of understanding the complex interactions between discourses and lived actuality, or social relations. Ebert also argues that ludic theory aims to affirm what exists rather than to transform it (1996: 14).

As a result, ludic feminism arguably has generated a rather pessimistic analysis that often focuses excessively on how we are constructed and less on how we resist or challenge dominant structures and ideologies. In its own way, this approach has essentialising tendencies. As Shelley Gavigan (2000) has argued, even Carol Smart's influential 'woman of legal discourse' (Smart, 1992) can be seen as 'discursively unidimensional': 'Constituted as she is by (legal) discourse, she has neither experience nor agency: she has neither breath nor breadth.' Similarly, Dany Lacombe (1998) has suggested that Smart goes too far in her argument that law necessarily outlaws women, reinforcing a notion that 'law is a tool which eternally reinforces the prison walls of the patriarchy'. Lacombe identifies the problem with this position as follows: 'it reduces the complexity of social practices and struggles to a unitary logic that works mainly through law to reproduce a unified social body' (1998: 158). Carol Smart herself included a short, but important, cautionary note in her 'Postscript' to *Law, Crime and Sexuality* that 'we must never forget that women discursively construct themselves. . . . If we do forget this, we risk disempowering "women" and overinflating the power of more organized discourses' (1995: 231). Focusing mainly on the discursive construction of the legal subject at the expense of other material practices that constitute the subject thus reinforces the centrality of 'the power of law' identified so effectively by Smart (1989).

Another characteristic of postmodernist feminist work is a focus on the body (see, for example, Butler, 1993; Grosz, 1994; Smart, 1995: ch.13). While clearly analysis of how women's bodies are constituted by law and other discourses is crucial to feminist analyses – indeed such analyses have opened important research avenues in relation to women with disabilities (Wendell, 1996), women of colour (Roberts, 1997) and lesbians (Zetlein, 1995) – it is crucial not to stop with the insight that the body is always discursively constructed. This type of analysis too often excludes other issues such as how women are constructed as workers both in the home and in the labour force, and it has a tendency to veer towards an essentialist notion of the body. In the words of Rosemary Hennessy, we also need 'to explain how the discursive construction of the body is related to nondiscursive practices in ways that vary widely from one social formation to another' (1993: 46). Ebert also points to the dangers in over-emphasising the body as a site of resistance, arguing that this approach inscribes a 'bourgeois ludic materialism (of pleasure) in place of historical materialism' (1996: 31).

Although the work of the new materialist feminist American authors can be criticised on many grounds (including in Ebert's case a tendency towards economic determinism and a narrow definition of the production paradigm, and in Hennessy's case a blurring of the realms of production, ideology and politics[6]), they reassert a form of dialectical analysis of the ways in which discursive constructions relate to resources and power struggles, without reducing everything to discourse. These authors also reassert the importance of the concept of ideology in thinking about how women and other marginalised groups come to understand their lives, and resist oppressive forces, including discourses. Ebert puts it this way, in explaining the strength of what she calls 'resistance postmodernist feminism':

> Resistance postmodern feminism moves beyond the limitations of ludic femin-
> ism to explain and theorize the way diverse and *seemingly* autonomous social
> institutions, cultural practices, meanings, desires, and subjectivities in post-
> modernism (the superstructure) are dialectically related to the relations of pro-
> duction and expropriation of labor (the base) in global late capitalism. As part
> of this undertaking and its intervention in the patriarchal capitalist knowledge
> industry, resistance postmodern feminism returns to the problem of ideology
> and develops a materialist critique. (Ebert, 1996: 148–9)[7]

Thus, Ebert argues for a mode of analysis that links cultural issues with questions of material exploitation.

BACK TO THE FAMILY, LAW AND SEXUALITY: THE FRASER/BUTLER DEBATE

What has all of this to do with family, law and sexuality? I want now to consider ways of linking materialist feminist critiques of 'the family' in its normative sense with questions of lesbian/gay struggles in relation to the legal
regulation of family. I shall make my starting point Nancy Fraser's article on
the recognition/redistribution dichotomy (Fraser, 1995/1997) which has
given rise to a very interesting debate in *New Left Review* and *Social Text*, in
particular between Fraser and Judith Butler. The debate concerns the larger
question of the relationship between Marxism, including socialist feminism,
and more recently developed paradigms such as discourse analysis, cultural
studies and poststructuralism. One specific question is whether the cultural
focus of recent left political theories has problematically diminished the
materialist project of Marxism. The debate thus relates to the concerns of the
'new materialist feminism' discussed above. For the purposes of this article,
I shall focus on the ways in which Fraser and Butler engage with the question of oppression of lesbians and gay men, and how this oppression relates
to women's oppression and capitalism. After reviewing the stances of Butler
and Fraser, I shall (with all due respect!) explain my ultimate concerns with
the arguments of both authors and go on to develop the theme of the privatisation of the costs of social reproduction that is underplayed in their
work.

In her work on the recognition/redistribution dichotomy, Fraser articulates a distinction – which she stresses is a heuristic one only – between
groups that are subject mainly to economic injustice (such as the working
class) and those that are subject mainly to cultural injustice (such as lesbians
and gays). In addition, some groups are subject to both cultural injustice and
economic injustice (such as women and people of colour).[8] As a remedy for
their oppression, the first group requires economic restructuring, the second
requires cultural recognition, and the third requires both. Gays and lesbians
are the only example that Fraser provides of the second group that needs only
cultural recognition; she states that any attendant economic injustices would
be redressed as a consequence of recognition because they result from an

unjust cultural valuation structure, not the economic structure per se. Fraser thus argues that '[o]vercoming homophobia and heterosexism requires changing the cultural valuations (as well as their legal and practical expressions) that privilege heterosexuality, deny equal respect to gays and lesbians, and refuse to recognise homosexuality as a legitimate way of being sexual' (1997a: 18–19). Presumably, then, recognition of lesbian relationships through redefining the definition of 'spouse' in family law statutes, as was requested in *M* v *H*, the case I mentioned earlier, would be a significant step in overcoming the oppression of lesbians.

Fraser's dichotomy bothered me from the start, in that she seemed to sever issues of sexuality (which she argued could be dealt with through 'recognition') from issues related to political economy (redistribution). Since I believe that heterosexuality and heteronormativity are intrinsically connected to gender and the sexual division of labour, I found Fraser's singling out of lesbian oppression as grounded mainly in cultural injustice to be problematic. I was therefore quite excited to discover the conversation that had emerged in *New Left Review* and *Social Text* about Fraser's model, with responses from Iris Marion Young (1997), Anne Phillips (1997) and Judith Butler (1997/1998) as well as two rejoinders from Nancy Fraser (1997b; 1997c).[9] In the *New Left Review* conversations, Judith Butler and Iris Marion Young, for different reasons, both argue that Fraser's dichotomy between cultural recognition and economic redistribution is overdrawn.[10] I will focus on Judith Butler's response to Fraser's argument,[11] in particular Butler's points about 'queer politics and the disparagement of the cultural' (1997/1998: 38 et seq.).

I must confess to being surprised and excited when I first read Butler's response. She asks how the lesbian/gay move to criticise and transform the ways in which sexuality is socially regulated can *possibly* be understood as separate from the functioning of political economy. She then refers to the trenchant critique of the family made by socialist feminists in the 1970s and 1980s, who drew on the work of Marx and Engels to show that the production and reproduction of life in the family is a crucial component of the mode of production. These feminists showed not only that the family was part of the mode of production, but also that 'the very production of gender had to be understood as part of the "production of human beings themselves", according to norms that reproduced the heterosexually normative family' (Butler, 1997/1998: 40). Socialist feminists regarded the family not as a natural given, but rather as a specific social arrangement of kin functions that was 'historically contingent and, in principle, transformable'. The reproduction of gendered persons – of 'men' and 'women' – depended on 'the social regulation of the family and, indeed, on the reproduction of the heterosexual family as a site for the reproduction of heterosexual persons, fit for entry into the family as social form' (Butler, 1997/1998: 40).

Thus, Butler points out, 'the regulation of sexuality was systematically tied to *the mode of production* proper to the functioning of political economy' (Butler, 1997/1998: 40). In other words, Butler sees sexuality and gender as intrinsically connected, and so it makes no sense to argue, as Fraser does, that oppression of lesbians/gays is a question of cultural recognition, whereas gender is a question of both cultural recognition and economic redistribution. Butler points out that gender and sexuality are part of material life not only because of the way in which they serve the sexual division of labour, but 'also because normative gender serves the reproduction of the normative family':

> The point here is that, contra Fraser, struggles to transform the social field of sexuality do not become central to political economy to the extent that they can be directly tied to questions of unpaid and exploited labour, but also because they cannot be understood without an expansion of the 'economic' sphere itself to include both the reproduction of goods as well as the social reproduction of persons (Butler, 1997/1998: 40).

She then questions how it can be that the 'queer question' of how normative sexuality is 'confounded by the non-normative sexualities it harbours within its own terms – as well as the sexualities that thrive and suffer outside those terms' – can be viewed as 'only a matter of cultural recognition' and not a question of the mode of production (Butler, 1997/1998: 41).

Because, in Butler's view, the production of normative heterosexuality is related to the mode of production, struggles over the recognition of non-normative sexualities (for example, in the legal realm) must of necessity be relevant to challenges to the mode of production (Butler, 1997/1998: 41). In support of this argument, she cites the relationship between poverty rates among lesbians and the normative heterosexuality of the economy. She seems to consider legal struggles for recognition of lesbian relationships as 'family' as important because they confound normative sexuality, which is in turn a part of the mode of production.

At this point, I find myself parting ways with Butler's analysis. Although the production of normative heterosexuality is undoubtedly related to the mode of production, it does not follow that legal recognition of non-normative sexualities (for example, same-sex relationships) will necessarily, of itself, constitute a fundamental challenge to the capitalist mode of production. Reaffirming 'the family', even by including same-sex spouses within it, will not necessarily stop the ways in which the 'holy family' (Butler, 1997/1998: 41) constrains the routes by which property interests are regulated and distributed.

Ironically, I find myself agreeing with aspects of Fraser's own response to Butler, in *Social Text*, although her response is geared towards the defense of her own argument (with which I disagree) that lesbian and gay oppression is primarily cultural. I agree with her that it is implausible that gay/lesbian struggles, at least for familial recognition, will challenge capitalism in its actually existing historical form (Fraser, 1997c: 285).[12] It is the role of the family, no matter whether lesbians and gays are included in it or not, in the privatisation of the social costs of reproduction (Picchio, 1992) that prevents me from going all the way with Butler's argument that struggles for cultural recognition necessarily implicate the political economy. Having done a beautiful summary of socialist feminist thought on family, and having articulated an appropriately enlarged concept of the mode of production that includes the production of human beings and thus of gender and the heterosexually normative family, Butler returns to her tactic of confounding normative sexuality 'by the non-normative sexualities it harbours within its own terms' (Butler, 1997/1998: 41).[13] But spousal recognition may not in fact confound the material place of the family in capitalist relations, and this material place may exist regardless of whether same-sex cohabitants or opposite-sex cohabitants people it. To understand the material role of the family in capitalism, we must examine the sexual division of labour and its relationship to the privatisation of the costs of social reproduction.

PRIVATISATION OF THE COSTS OF SOCIAL REPRODUCTION

The ideology of the heterosexual nuclear family as the base of society remains strong and has a clear material underpinning in that it is allocated primary responsibility for the costs of producing and raising children, and caring for dependent family members (Iyer, 1997; Teghtsoonian, 1997; Young, 1997). Women continue to assume greater responsibility than men for these caring roles and the sexual division of labour prevails both within the family and in the labour force (Armstrong and Armstrong, 1994; Picchio, 1992: ch. 5). This gendered and privatised role of the family continues *despite* the fact that the Canadian legal system, among others, has begun to recognise lesbian and gay relationships as well as to recognise women's rights and thereby has created significant cracks in the edifice of heteronormativity. The family has grown more 'public' in the course of the 20th century, as more women work outside the home, as state/legal regulation increases, and as more relationships are 'caught' within family law. However, family work remains privatised and largely in women's hands; the material underpinnings of the family are simultaneously changing *and* remaining amazingly the same (Boyd, 1997).

Thus we currently live within a contradiction. Heterosexism does not seem to be essential to contemporary capitalism, which permits 'significant numbers of individuals to live through wage labor outside of heterosexual families' (Fraser, 1997c: 285; see also Matthaei, 1997).[14] Yet, 'while the privatised family is not essential to the survival of capitalism, its abolition is not at all likely while capitalism exists' (German, 1989/1997: 152). Such a change would require massive investment in the socialisation of the family by each capitalist state; any one state trying to do this would be at a competitive disadvantage, for example if it were to increase spending on child care. In the meantime, even if men can be convinced to assume a share of housework, in other words to assume a greater share of social reproductive labour, the costs of social reproduction are merely redistributed as between women and men, while still privatised within 'the family'. Moreover, Jacobs has argued that 'the fight for alternative families does not confront the structures of women's economic oppression that have become increasingly significant with the development of public patriarchy, and thus it does not threaten gay men's economic privilege with respect to women' (1997: 173). In other words, real transformation of the mode of production would require massive redistribution of resources away from production toward the reproduction (living standards) of those without access to the means of subsistence (see, for example, Picchio, 1992).[15]

Ultimately, I think that neither Butler nor Fraser develops an adequate dialectical analysis of the ways in which discursive challenges (for example, to the heteronormativity of the family) relate to resource distribution in late capitalist societies. If my argument about privatisation and the role of the family is at all accurate, then the incorporation of lesbians and gay men within family law may be as much about the domestication of deviant sexualities within a safe, useful and recognisable framework than about the transformatory confounding of normative sexualities (for analogous arguments in different contexts, see Hennessy, 1994–5; Stychin, 1995). A redistributive politics is therefore crucial to lesbian and gay liberation.

Now let me be clear that, despite my reservations, I am not arguing against recognition of lesbian/gay relationships per se. The symbolism and thrill of moments of legal recognition is real,[16] as is the vitriolic resistance to such legal recognition,[17] which makes one reluctant to raise questions about such strategies. Moreover, recognition of spousal status will undoubtedly bring beneficial changes to at least some lesbians and gay men at a practical level and it may redistribute resources, at least *within* private relationships, in a meaningful way. For lesbians living on a modest income, even minimal property settlements or spousal support payments can make a significant difference in living standards. Furthermore, where public moneys are involved (for example, income tax benefits), an appropriate redistribution of resources between heterosexual and gay/lesbian taxpayers may result from the recognition of same-sex spouses. It must, however, be kept in mind that the benefits of inclusion are always matched by disadvantages. In family law, obligations will ensue as well as rights; in tax law, Claire Young (1994) has shown that depending on the economic status of a couple, recognition as 'spouses' may result in disadvantages overall, especially for those couples where both partners are at a low income level.

My key concern is that lesbian/gay struggles for legal recognition of relationships, while clearly necessary, ought not to be seen as *sufficient* to achieve social equality across class, race and gender differences as they intersect with sexuality (see generally Smith, 1993/1997, 1997). Fraser's heuristic separation of recognition and redistribution strategies may diminish our attention to the intersectionality of indices of oppression. Poverty is as much a lesbian/gay issue as sexuality in many contexts, and the two are intertwined, as are racism and other conditions of oppression such as disability (Allen, 1993). In a society whose sense of social justice appears to be eroding, these intersections must be kept ever present in analysing new developments and developing strategies. As Fraser herself has pointed out, anyone who is both gay and working class will, in some way, find himself within the recognition/redistribution dilemma (1997a: 32). However Fraser's analysis does not necessarily generate an understanding of how legal recognition strategies may distract us from an appreciation of how social inequalities are structured within capitalism and class relations (see Bakan, 1997, especially ch. 3).

The latest case on sexual orientation discrimination to be argued before Canada's highest court provides a good example. *M* v *H* was argued at the Supreme Court of Canada in March 1998 and, almost one year later, as I complete final revisions to this article, a decision has not yet been handed down. This case is a constitutional challenge based on the section 15 equality guarantee of the Canadian Charter of Rights and Freedoms, which reads as follows: 'Every individual is equal before and under the law and has the right to the equal protection and equal benefit of the law without discrimination and, in particular, without discrimination based on race, national or ethnic origin, colour, religion, sex, age or mental or physical disability'. Although sexual orientation is not listed as a prohibited ground of discrimination in this constitutional document, the Supreme Court of Canada has acknowledged that it is an analogous ground of discrimination in section 15 in *Egan* v *Canada* (1995) (see also *Vriend* v *Alberta* 1998). In *M* v *H*, the plaintiff, M, challenged the exclusion of same-sex cohabitants from a definition of 'spouse' in Part III of the Ontario Family Law Act, arguing that the statutory definition was unconstitutional because it infringed her section 15 equality rights. This particular definition of spouse enables only married spouses and opposite-sex cohabitants to make claims for spousal support from their spouses.[18] When M's 10-year lesbian relationship terminated, leaving her in a vulnerable economic position, she was thus unable to claim financial support from her ex-partner H due to this definition of spouse.

I worked with the intervenor,[19] the Women's Legal Education and Action Fund (LEAF), on its argument at the Supreme Court (LEAF, 1998). LEAF's submission challenged the heterosexist bias of the family law system, and argued for expansion of the definition of spouse to include same-sex cohabitants. During my involvement in the case, I experienced several dilemmas. I was troubled by the respondent H's argument that she and M had been 'best friends' rather than spouses and that she should therefore not have to pay spousal support despite a 10-year period of cohabitation (Boyd, 1996). Yet I was also disturbed by the difficulty we had in avoiding 'assimilationist' arguments – that lesbian relationships were just the same as heterosexual ones – despite our concerted efforts to emphasise that similarity of situation is not the measure of entitlement to equality rights. My next, more profound, dilemma was our inability to avoid – indeed our reinforcement of – the privatisation argument: that part of the objective of support law is to reduce the burden on the public purse (the wider community) by creating private (familial) obligations to provide spousal support. It was frustrating not to be able to present more radical arguments than these although we did make efforts to avoid an 'assimilationist' argument and to provide cautionary notes about privatisation. Overall, I was concerned about an argument to include lesbian relationships in a family law system that is flawed, limited in its ability to redistribute resources, and class based. These dilemmas reveal the limits of seeking cultural recognition through law as well as the disciplining effects of engaging with law as a tool of social change – limits that have been pointed out eloquently by Canadian authors who have written about the politics of using the Charter of Rights and Freedoms in progressive struggles (e.g. Bakan, 1997; Fudge, 1987, 1989; Fudge and Glasbeek, 1992; Gotell, 1995). Yet I could not resist becoming involved in this very interesting case.

The arguments in *M* v *H* in favour of including lesbian relationships in Ontario's Family Law Act for the purposes of support claims can be read as adopting the problematic dichotomy between recognition and redistribution that Nancy Fraser constructs. Both the plaintiff M and the intervenor LEAF argued in their submissions for recognition of lesbian relationships and described the harms that flow from lack of recognition. For instance, M argued in her submission before the Supreme Court of Canada that the Act's failure to include same-sex couples 'leaves same-sex couples standing outside of the law, both metaphorically and literally' (M, 1998: para. 55(e)). M then made a recognition argument reminiscent of Nancy Fraser: 'Since the law articulates community standards, lesbian and gay people may internalize such an exclusion as a denial of worth. This internalization eats away at the place that love starts: self-love and the recognition of oneself as a valuable human being' (see also LEAF, 1998: paras 17, 18).

But both M and LEAF also emphasised that one legislative goal of the support provisions was the private nature of the remedy (M, 1998: paras 62–4; LEAF, 1998: paras 22, 27), which would alleviate demands on public funds, as part of their argument in favour of recognition. The LEAF submission did note concerns about the privatising effects of inclusion with the Family Law Act: 'the more that private remedies for economic disadvantage are created for some, the less responsibility the government may accept for the economic well-being of all individuals' (1998: para. 49). But it then avoided the issue by going on to state that 'in the current era of economic retrenchment by government, these concerns may be somewhat moot' (1998: para. 49). LEAF also stated, realistically, that leaving lesbians with poor remedies was 'particularly problematic in an era when state economic support for individuals – including lesbians – is being eroded' (1998: para. 45). Moreover, there was little sense in attempting to reduce the strain on the public assistance system by creating a private right for support that was only available to the segment of the population of potential welfare claimants who are heterosexual' (1998: para. 37).[20]

So those who argued in favour of expansion of the definition of 'spouse' in order to recognise gay/lesbian relationships in *M* v *H* were, at least implicitly, endorsing family law's purpose as being (at least in part) the privatisation of economic responsibility. The connections between heteronormativity, gender and the family, and the allocation of the costs of social reproduction were therefore elided. It was suggested, at least implicitly, that the oppression of lesbians and gay men can be significantly addressed through recognition of the spousal nature of their relationships, without acknowledging the complex intersections between family, sexuality, poverty and capitalism. I do not know whether the Supreme Court of Canada will accept the argument in *M* v *H* that same-sex cohabitants should be defined as 'spouses' for the purposes of making spousal support claims; but if it does, I would wager that the Court relies in part on the fact that this statute deals with obligations between individuals who were once intimate partners, as opposed to economic obligations that the state might owe to individuals. Canadian courts have demonstrated a recent tendency to find it easier to uphold private obligations because there is no perceived cost to the state (Claire Young, 1997, 1998). In other words, the Court may reinforce the assumption that private economic obligations are preferable to public ones (for discussion of this trend in an Australian context, see Millbank, 1998). Although courts cannot be expected to entirely transform the means through which resources are distributed, the difficulty is that an apparent victory in a lesbian/gay struggle will occlude remaining problems of inequality.

Thus, when cases are brought forward that challenge heteronormativity by arguing that the term 'spouse' should be redefined, I suggest that more attention needs to be paid to whether the 'heterosexual economy' is challenged or whether the lesbian or gay subject is naturalised into it. For instance, in *M* v *H*, although heteronormativity *was* of course challenged, the ways that the legal arguments had to be formulated meant that the potentially disruptive lesbian subject was absorbed back into familiar roles and, to a large extent, her disruptive potential was displaced. In many ways the dominant relations of production and ruling were reproduced by our equality arguments: the role of the family in absorbing social costs of dependency and social reproduction was explicitly reinforced, including through the intervention of a feminist organisation, LEAF. As others have pointed out, the more that legal arguments deploy conventional (and often essentialist) tenets, the more influential they may be (Gotell, 1997; Smart, 1994: 25), and it is not surprising that this should occur in the family law context.

It is not clear to me that M or LEAF could have done much that was different in formulating their equality arguments, due to the power of the legal form. However, it seems to me that unless lesbian and gay efforts to achieve symbolic recognition of their families are accompanied by trenchant critiques of the limits of such recognition in delivering a redistribution of economic well-being, they will remain incomplete as political strategies, while they may simultaneously be the only *legal* strategies available. Although the limitations of family law remedies for heterosexual women have begun to be identified (see, for example, Boyd, 1994; Eichler, 1990; Mossman, 1994), it may be some time until lesbians and gay men, or even most heterosexual women, make the same discovery. The ideology of the family remains compellingly strong in most of our societies despite, or perhaps because of, the fact that there are so many radical changes all around the family (Smart, 1997), and there seems to be a widespread and compelling belief that keeping it (whatever 'the family' actually is!) strong will solve our social problems (see, for example, Kline,

1997). This political difficulty cuts across the strategic claims of both feminism and the lesbian/gay movement, and it is an important connection to keep in mind when looking towards strategic decisions and coalition politics in the future.

CONCLUSION

My sense is that it is now quite inevitable that, at least in Canada, slowly but surely lesbian/gay relationships will be made analogous to those of unmarried opposite-sex cohabitants, *if* we fall within the normative model of 'spouses': showing that a conjugal relationship existed, complete with joint bank accounts and so forth. In other words, as Gavigan (1998) has argued, the legal form of 'spouse' is flexible enough to accommodate this change. However, I remain unconvinced of the potential for such recognition to disrupt heteronormativity sufficiently to result in fundamental social change, particularly redistributive change, unless the gay/lesbian communities find a way to offer a simultaneous critique of current familial structures as they relate to structured economic inequalities. We must not be so eager for recognition that we settle for too little when we receive it (see Gluckman and Reed, 1997: xviii).

For example, in addition to participating in litigation such as lesbian claims for recognition of intimate relationship as in the *M* v *H* case, we must lobby strenuously for measures that enhance the redistribution of economic well-being that are not contingent on whether we have had a wealthy spouse at some point in our lives or whether we conform to the model of 'good' lesbians and gays. As Ruthann Robson (1994) suggests, only if recognition of lesbians and gay men as 'family' eventually destroys or displaces the centrality of 'family' in how society organises redistribution of economic well-being would such recognition lead to more fundamental social change. The difficulty is how to formulate a legal argument that would even come close to such a radical displacement of 'the way things are'.

In concluding, I will draw on Charlotte Bunch's early article: 'Not for lesbians only' (1975/1997). She argues that lesbianism is not just cultural, or a question of civil rights, but rather political: 'Lesbian-feminist politics is a political critique of the institution and ideology of heterosexuality as a cornerstone of male supremacy' (1975/1997: 55). 'It is not okay to be queer under patriarchy – and the last thing we should be aiming to do is make it okay' (1975/1997: 58). I think that being defined as a 'spouse' may make it okay for some lesbians and gay men to be at least somewhat queer under patriarchy and does not in itself sustain a political critique of heterosexuality or the political economy of the heterosexual family. This issue needs far more serious treatment in academic and political analyses of oppressions related to family, law and sexuality, even if we find it difficult to avoid assimilationist arguments in legal struggles in the courts, and even if we find it difficult to resist the call of the power of law in progressive struggle.

CASE AND STATUTES CITED

Egan v *Canada* (1995), 124 DLR (4th) 609 (Supreme Court of Canada).
M v *H* (1996), 27 OR (3d) 593 (Ontario Court, General Division); (1996), 31 OR (3d)
    417 (Ontario Court of Appeal); (1999) S. C. J. No 23 (Q. L.) (Supreme Court
    of Canada).
Rosenberg v *Canada* (1998), 158 DLR (4th) 664 (Ontario Court of Appeal).
Vriend v *Alberta* (1998), 156 DLR (4th) 385 (Supreme Court of Canada).
Canadian Charter of Rights and Freedoms, Part I of the *Constitution Act, 1982*, being
    Schedule B of the *Canada Act 1982 (UK)*, c.11.
Family Law Act, RSO 1990, c. F3.

NOTES

Keynote Talk, Conference on Law, Gender and Sexuality, Keele University, UK, 21
June 1998. Some of the analysis in this article will appear in a different form in *Constellations*.

I would like to thank Judy Fudge, Reg Graycar, Jenny Morgan, Karen Pearlston, Lisa
Philipps, Elizabeth Pickett, Mehera San Roque, Claire Young, the Keele group, and
the anonymous reviewers for comments on earlier drafts. I would also like to acknowledge the financial support of the Social Sciences and Humanities Research Council
of Canada through a strategic grant under the 'Women and Change' theme. Mehera
San Roque also provided excellent research and editing assistance.

1.   Chrys Ingraham defines 'heteronormativity' as 'the view that institutionalised
    heterosexuality constitutes the standard for legitimate and prescriptive socio-
    sexual arrangements' (1994/1997: 275).
2.   Carol A. Stabile (1997: 395) also notes the hegemony of postmodernist femin-
    ism in the academy.
3.   *Chambers English Dictionary* (Cambridge: W & R Chambers and Cambridge
    University Press, 1988).
4.   Another graduate student mentioned to me some time ago that ludic theory was
    'more fun' and if we cannot have fun in academia, why are we here? She might
    be right, but many activists struggling to make change outside academia would
    argue that we have been having too much fun deconstructing and playing word
    games in academia, and that it is time for a return to engagement with emanci-
    patory politics in the intellectual work that we do. A similar call can be found
    in many places (see, for example, Grossberg, 1997).
5.   Thanks to Elizabeth Pickett and an anonymous member of the Keele group for
    making this point after reading an earlier draft.
6.   This reflects Hennessy's greater affinity with the postmodernist trend to define
    discourse as material, and sets her apart from Ebert in this regard.
7.   Hennessy (1993) elaborates the role of ideology critique in developing a col-
    lective politic. Importantly, she notes that:

> Women's lives are shaped by ideology in the sense that their lived experi-
> ence is never served up raw but is always made sense of from a host of
> vantage points, including those of the woman experiencing the events and
> those of the feminist critic, scholar, or theorist who appeals to women's
> lives as the basis for her knowledge . . . Understood as always ideologically

constructed, women's lives can be read in terms of woman's contradictory position under capitalist and patriarchal arrangements where the symbolic economy of an opposition between man and woman comprises only one of the preconstructed anchors and articulating principles of the prevailing truths. (Hennessey, 1993: 78–9)

Drawing on Gramsci, she emphasises that far from being a monolithic determining force, ideology is 'an articulated ensemble of contesting discourses which produce what comes to count as "the way it is" ... In any historical moment there are only ideologies; but their circulation is bound to the (re)production of "reality" through the process of hegemonic articulation' (1993: 76). Thus, the 'dominating ideology never dominates without contradiction' and 'cannot exhaust all social experience'. The dominating ideology therefore contains space for alternative discourses and there are never hegemonic ideologies without cracks in their coherence. Hennessy notes that 'it is the potentially subversive force of these slips that constitutes the epistemological basis or the authority of ideology critique' emanating from, for example, feminism as a counter-hegemonic discourse.

8.   Fraser does acknowledge that the redistribution/recognition distinction is a heuristic device and that 'we may question whether there exist any pure collectivities of this sort' (1995/1997: 18). Nonetheless she defends (1995/1997: 35, note 18) her decision to treat sexuality as importantly different from gender, which is grounded in the sexual division of labour.

9.   My thanks to Judy Fudge for drawing my attention to this conversation.

10. Iris Marion Young (1997) argues, in response to what she calls Fraser's 'dual systems theory', that lesbians and gay men conceive cultural recognition as a means to economic and political justice.

11. Butler (1997/1998) characterises Fraser's argument as follows: that the study of culture and cultural/identity politics have detracted from Marxism's materialist project and from the task of addressing questions of economic equity and redistribution.

12. Fraser's answer to Butler is to say that Butler conflates the material and the economic (1997c: 286); Fraser agrees that cultural struggles are 'material' and of equal material importance to economic struggles; but argues that the 'economic' is something separate from the cultural.

13. See Ebert, who argues that Butler 'confines "the regime of heterosexuality" entirely to the superstructure, to a discursive order' (1996: 216–17), which is exactly what Butler complains that Fraser does. Ebert points out that approaches such as Butler's do not break 'the logic of the dominant ideology of capitalism' (1996: 217). Note also that Smart (1994: 26) has pointed out that Butler's insights may not translate well to the legal forum.

14. Ebert (1996) agrees with Fraser (from a more Marxian materialist perspective) that the emergence of the 'homosexual' is characteristic of 'a historical moment in which the forces of production have reached such a level of sophistication in their productivity that heterosexuality (as a means of maintaining the reserve army of labor at a relatively high level) is no longer necessary' (1996: 65–6). Ebert adds:

The fact that homophobia is an obstacle to full legal and social integration of lesbians and gays is more a matter of the contradictions between the social relations of production and forces of production, contradictions that are now the substance of what conservatives call 'culture wars' ... (1996: 66).

15. My thanks to Lisa Phillips for drawing Picchio's book to my attention and assisting with this analysis.

16. I found the decisions of both Epstein J and Charron J A in the lesbian support case *M v H* to be great reads and important challenges to traditional definitions of 'family'. Epstein J eloquently rebutted assumptions that our relationships do not manifest the interdependence found in heterosexual relationships and she showed how the objectives of family law would be advanced by reading same-sex cohabitants into the definition of 'spouse' (see Boyd, 1996). The problem is that there are serious difficulties with some of the objectives of family law, such as the privatisation of economic responsibilities.

17. See Edward Greenspon, 'Reform seeks curbs on judicial activism' *The Globe and Mail* 11 June 1998, A4, on the Reform Party's motion in parliament declaring that courts should not be able to alter federal legislation, and offering as its sole complaint the recent ruling of the Ontario Court of Appeal in *Rosenberg v Canada* (1998), 158 DLR (4th) 664 (which extended the definition of 'spouse' in the Income Tax Act for certain purposes related to survivor benefits from pension plans to include same-sex cohabitants). The motion also called on the government to appeal the ruling (which the government has not done). Reform is the opposition party in the federal parliament. A notable example of the resistance to decisions extending the protection of anti-discrimination legislation was the full-page advertisement published in Canada's national newspaper, following the *Vriend* decision, by a group calling themselves 'Canada's Civilised Majority', which headed, 'Canada's Supreme Court has No Business Imposing "Bathhouse Morality" on the Churches and in the Nation's Living Rooms', *The Globe and Mail*, 18 April 1998, A9.

18. The definition of 'spouse' varies in the Family Law Act, RSO 1990, c. F3, depending on the issue at hand (for example, matrimonial property division versus spousal property). Only married spouses can invoke the matrimonial support provisions.

19. An intervenor is a third party that is permitted to make arguments in order to assist a court in its deliberations. It must obtain leave of the court to participate by showing that it has special knowledge related to an aspect of the case.

20. The privatisation argument was made in part to counter the pseudo-feminist argument of the Ontario government – which resisted inclusion of same-sex couples in the definition of 'spouse' – that the Family Law Act was aimed at protecting dependent women and children, and that this objective was pressing and substantial. In rebutting this argument, but at the same time trying not to undermine the issue of the economic inequality of heterosexual women, LEAF argued there were three objectives of the legislation: reducing the burden on the public purse; imposing legal duties on spouses to treat one another in an economically fair fashion upon relationship breakdown; and assisting heterosexual women (LEAF 1998: para. 22).

REFERENCES

Allen, Carol (1993) 'Who Gets to be Family: Some Thoughts on the Lesbian and Gay Fight for Equality', pp. 101–7 in Linda Carty (ed.) *And Still We Rise: Feminist Political Mobilizing in Contemporary Canada*. Toronto: Women's Press.

Armstrong, Pat and Hugh Armstrong (1994) *The Double Ghetto: Canadian Women and Their Segregated Work* (3rd edn). Toronto: McClelland & Stewart.

Bakan, Joel (1997) *Just Words: Constitutional Rights and Social Wrongs.* Toronto: University of Toronto Press.

Barrett, Michèle (1988) *Women's Oppression Today: The Marxist Feminist Encounter* (revised edn). London: Verso.

Boyd, Susan B. (1989) 'From Gender-Specificity to Gender-Neutrality? Ideologies in Canadian Child Custody Law', pp. 126–57 in Carol Smart (ed.) *Child Custody and the Politics of Gender.* London: Routledge.

Boyd, Susan B. (1991) 'Some Postmodernist Challenges to Feminist Analyses of Law, Family and State: Ideology and Discourse in Child Custody Law', *Canadian Journal of Family Law* 10: 79–113.

Boyd, Susan B. (1994) '(Re)Placing the State: Family, Law and Oppression', *Canadian Journal of Law and Society* 9(1): 39–73.

Boyd, Susan B. (1996) 'Best Friends or Spouses? Privatization and the Recognition of Lesbian Relationships in *M. v. H.*', *Canadian Journal of Family Law* 13: 321–41.

Boyd, Susan B. (ed.) (1997) *Challenging the Public/Private Divide: Feminism, Law, and Public Policy.* Toronto: University of Toronto Press.

Bunch, Charlotte (1975/1997) 'Not for Lesbians Only', pp. 54–8 in Rosemary Hennessy and Chrys Ingraham (eds) *Materialist Feminism: A Reader in Class Difference and Women's Lives.* New York: Routledge.

Butler, Judith (1993) *Bodies that Matter: On the Discursive Limits of 'Sex'.* London: Routledge.

Butler, Judith (1997/1998) 'Merely Cultural', *New Left Review* 227: 33–44. Previously published in (1997) *Social Text 52/53* 15(3, 4): 265–77. Fall/Winter.

Delphy, Christine (1981/1997) 'For a materialist feminism', pp. 59–64 in Rosemary Hennessy and Chrys Ingraham (eds) *Materialist Feminism: A Reader in Class Difference and Women's Lives.* New York: Routledge.

Ebert, Teresa L. (1996) *Ludic Feminism and After.* Ann Arbour: The University of Michigan Press.

Eichler, Margrit (1990) 'The Limits of Family Law Reform or, The Privatisation of Female and Child Poverty', *Canadian Family Law Quarterly* 7(1): 59–84.

Fraser, Nancy (1995/1997) 'From Redistribution to Recognition? Dilemmas of Justice in a "Postsocialist" Age', pp. 11–39 in Nancy Fraser *Justice Interruptus: Critical Reflections on the 'Postsocialist' Condition.* New York: Routledge. Originally published in (1995) *New Left Review* 212: 68–93. July/Aug.

Fraser, Nancy (1997a) *Justice Interruptus: Critical Reflections on the "Postsocialist" Condition.* New York: Routledge.

Fraser, Nancy (1997b) 'A Rejoinder to Iris Young', *New Left Review* 223: 126–9. May/June.

Fraser, Nancy (1997c) 'Heterosexism, Misrecognition, and Capitalism', *Social Text 52/53* 15(3 and 4): 279–89. Fall/Winter.

Fudge, Judy (1987) 'The Public/Private Distinction: The Possibilities of and the Limits to the Use of Charter Litigation to Further Feminist Struggles', *Osgoode Hall Law Journal* 25: 485–554.

Fudge, Judy (1989) 'The Effect of Entrenching a Bill of Rights upon Political Discourse: Feminist Demands and Sexual Violence in Canada', *International Journal of the Sociology of Law* 17: 445–63.

Fudge, Judy and Harry Glasbeek (1992) 'The Politics of Rights: A Politics with Little Class', *Social and Legal Studies* 1: 45–70.

Gavigan, Shelley A. M. (1988) 'Law, Gender and Ideology', pp. 283–95 in Anne Bayefsky (ed.) *Legal Theory Meets Legal Practice.* Edmonton: Academic Printing and Publishing.

Gavigan, Shelley A. M. (1998) 'Legal Forms, Family Forms, Gender Norms: What is a Spouse?', paper delivered at the International Conference on Gender, Sexuality and Law, Keele University, UK, June 20, 1998.

Gavigan, Shelley A. M. (2000) 'Mothers, Other Mothers, and Others: The Challenges and Contradictions of Lesbian Parents', in Dany Lacombe and Dorothy Chunn (eds) *Law as a Gendering Discourse.* Toronto: Oxford University Press, forthcoming.

German, Lindsey (1989/1997) 'Theories of the Family', pp. 147–59 in Rosemary Hennessy and Chrys Ingraham (eds) *Materialist Feminism: A Reader in Class Difference and Women's Lives.* New York: Routledge.

Gluckman, Amy and Betsy Reed (eds) (1997) *Homo Economics: Capitalism, Community, and Lesbian and Gay Life.* New York: Routledge.

Gotell, Lise (1995) 'Litigating Feminist "Truth": An Antifoundational Critique', *Social and Legal Studies* 4: 99–131.

Gotell, Lise (1997) 'Shaping *Butler*: The New Politics of Anti-Pornography', pp. 48–106 in Brenda Cossman, Shannon Bell, Lise Gotell and Becki Ross (eds) *Bad Attitude/s on Trial: Pornography, Feminism, and the Butler Decision.* Toronto: University of Toronto Press.

Grossberg, Lawrence (1997) 'Re-placing Popular Culture', pp. 217–37 in Steve Redhead (ed.) *The Clubcultures Reader.* Oxford: Blackwell.

Grosz, Elizabeth (1994) *Volatile Bodies: Towards a Corporeal Feminism.* Sydney: Allen and Unwin.

Hennessy, Rosemary (1993) *Materialist Feminism and the Politics of Discourse.* New York: Routledge.

Hennessy, Rosemary (1994–5) 'Queer Visibility in Commodity Culture', *Cultural Critique* 29: 31–76. Winter.

Hennessy, Rosemary and Chrys Ingraham (eds) (1997) *Materialist Feminism: A Reader in Class, Difference, and Women's Lives.* New York: Routledge.

Ingraham, Chrys (1994/1997) 'The Heterosexual Imaginary: Feminist Sociology and Theories of Gender', pp. 275–90 in Rosemary Hennessy and Chrys Ingraham (eds) *Materialist Feminism: A Reader in Class Difference and Women's Lives.* New York: Routledge.

Iyer, Nitya (1997) 'Some Mothers are Better Than Others: A Re-examination of Maternity Benefits', pp. 168–94 in Susan B. Boyd (ed.) *Challenging the Public/Private Divide: Feminism, Law, and Public Policy.* Toronto: University of Toronto Press.

Jacobs, Michael P. (1997) 'Do Gay Men Have a Stake in Male Privilege? The Political Economy of Gay Men's Contradictory Relationship to Feminism', pp. 165–84 in Amy Gluckman and Betsy Reed (eds) *Homo Economics: Capitalism, Community, and Lesbian and Gay Life.* New York: Routledge.

Kline, Marlee (1997) 'Blue Meanies in Alberta: Tory Tactics and the Privatization of Child Welfare', pp. 330–59 in Susan B. Boyd (ed.) *Challenging the Public/Private Divide: Feminism, Law, and Public Policy.* Toronto: University of Toronto Press.

Lacombe, Dany (1998) 'Does Law Outlaw Women?', pp. 155–62 in Kevin D. Bonnycastle and George S. Rigakos (eds) *Unsettling Truths: Battered Women, Policy, Politics, and Contemporary Research in Canada.* Vancouver: Collective Press.

LEAF (1998) *Factum of the Women's Legal Education and Action Fund,* Intervenor, *M* v. *H* in the Supreme Court of Canada (Appeal from the Court of Appeal for the Province of Ontario), Court File No. 25838.

M (1998) *Factum of the Respondent M on Appeal and Cross-Appeal, M* v. *H,* in the Supreme Court of Canada (Appeal from the Court of Appeal for the Province of Ontario), Court File No. 25838.

Matthaei, Julie (1997) 'The Sexual Division of Labor, Sexuality, and Lesbian/Gay
    Liberation: Toward a Marxist-Feminist Analysis of Sexuality in US Capitalism',
    pp. 135–64 in Amy Gluckman and Betsy Reed (eds) *Homo Economics: Capital-
    ism, Community, and Lesbian and Gay Life*. New York: Routledge.
Millbank, Jenni (1998) 'If Australian Law Opened Its Eyes to Lesbian and Gay
    Families, What Would It See?' *Australian Journal of Family Law* 12: 99–139.
Mossman, Mary Jane (1994) 'Running Hard to Stand Still: The Paradox of Family
    Law Reform', *Dalhousie Law Journal* 17(1): 5–34.
Pearlston, Karen (1998) 'Mode of Production, Ideology and Feminist Legal Theory',
    unpublished paper, on file with author.
Phillips, Anne (July/August 1997) 'From Inequality to Difference: A Severe Case of
    Displacement', *New Left Review* 224: 143–53.
Picchio, Antonella (1992) *Social reproduction: the political economy of the labour
    market*. Cambridge: Cambridge University Press.
Roberts, Dorothy (1997) *Killing the Black Body: Race, Reproduction, and the
    Meaning of Liberty*. New York: Pantheon.
Robson, Ruthann (1994) 'Resisting the Family: Repositioning Lesbians in Legal
    Theory', *Signs* 19(4): 975–96.
Seccombe, Wally (1992) *A Millennium of Family Change: Federalism to Capitalism
    in Northwestern Europe*. London: Verso.
Smart, Carol (1984) *The Ties That Bind*. London: Routledge.
Smart, Carol (1989) *Feminism and the Power of Law*. London: Routledge.
Smart, Carol (1992) 'The Woman of Legal Discourse', *Social and Legal Studies* 1(1):
    29–44.
Smart, Carol (1994) 'Law, Feminism and Sexuality: From Essence to Ethics?' *Can-
    adian Journal of Law and Society* 9(1): 15–38.
Smart, Carol (1995) *Law, Crime and Sexuality: Essays in Feminism*. London: Sage
    Publications.
Smart, Carol (1997) 'Wishful Thinking and Harmful Tinkering? Sociological Reflec-
    tions on Family Policy', *Journal of Social Policy* 26(3): 301–21.
Smith, Barbara (1993/1997) 'Where's the revolution', pp. 248–52 in Rosemary
    Hennessy and Chrys Ingraham (eds) *Materialist Feminism: A Reader in Class
    Difference and Women's Lives*. New York: Routledge.
Smith, Barbara (1997) 'Where has Gay Liberation Gone? An Interview with Barbara
    Smith', pp. 195–207 in Amy Gluckman and Betsy Reed (eds) *Homo Economics:
    Capitalism, Community, and Lesbian and Gay Life*. New York: Routledge.
Stabile, Carol A. (1997) 'Feminism and the Ends of Postmodernism', pp. 395–408 in
    Rosemary Hennessy and Chrys Ingraham (eds) *Materialist Feminism: A
    Reader in Class Difference and Women's Lives*. New York: Routledge.
Stychin, Carl (1995) 'Essential Rights and Contested Identities: Sexual Orientation
    and Equality Rights Jurisprudence in Canada', *Canadian Journal of Law &
    Jurisprudence* 8: 49–66.
Teghtsoonian, Katherine (1997) 'Who Pays for Caring for Children? Public Policy
    and the Devaluation of Women's Work', pp. 113–43 in Susan B. Boyd (ed.)
    Challenging the Public/Private Divide: Feminism, Law, and Public Policy.
    Toronto: University of Toronto Press.
Wendell, Susan (1996) *The Rejected Body: Feminist Philosophical Reflections on Dis-
    ability*. New York: Routledge.
Young, Claire F. L. (1994) 'Taxing Times for Lesbians and Gay Men: Equality at What
    Cost?', *Dalhousie Law Journal* 17: 534–59.
Young, Claire F. L. (1997) 'Public Taxes, Privatizing Effects and Gender Inequality',
    pp. 307–29 in Susan B. Boyd (ed.) *Challenging the Public/Private Divide:
    Feminism, Law, and Public Policy*. Toronto: University of Toronto Press.

Young, Claire F. L. (1998) 'Spousal Status, Pension Benefits and Tax: Rosenberg v. Canada', *Canadian Labour and Employment Law Journal* 6: 435–453.
Young, Iris Marion (1980/1997) 'Socialist Feminism and the Limits of Dual Systems Theory', pp. 95–106 in Rosemary Hennessy and Chrys Ingraham (eds) *Materialist Feminism: A Reader in Class Difference and Women's Lives*. New York: Routledge.
Young, Iris Marion (1997) 'Unruly Categories: A Critique of Nancy Fraser's Dual Systems Theory', *New Left Review* 222: 147–60. (March/April)
Zetlein, Sarah (1995) 'Lesbian Bodies Before the Law: Chicks in White Satin', *Australian Feminist Law Journal* 5: 49–63.

ADDENDUM

On May 20, 1999, by an 8 to 1 majority, the Supreme Court of Canada handed down a positive decision in terms of legal recognition of same-sex relationships in *M v H*. The appeal by the Government of Ontario from the decision of the Ontario Court of Appeal was dismissed, with only one dissent by Gonthier J. The majority found that the failure to accord individual members of cohabiting same-sex couples the right to apply for spousal support was discriminatory under section 15 of the Charter of Rights and Freedoms, and was not saved by section 1. The offending section of the Ontario Family Law Act that defined 'spouse' for the purposes of spousal support was declared to be of no force or effect. However, the effect of that declaration was suspended for a period of 6 months to allow the Ontario government to amend its legislation (in particular to allow same-sex cohabitants to opt out of the statutory provisions by contract). Cory and Iacobucci JJ., writing for 6 justices of the majority, agreed that same-sex relationships are capable of being both conjugal and lengthy. They urged the Ontario Government to consider the implications of the decision for the numerous other statutes that rely upon a similar definition of 'spouse'. At the same time, they noted that there was no need to consider whether same-sex couples must, for all purposes, be treated in the same manner as unmarried opposite-sex couples (para. 55).

As I predicted, the Justices emphasized several times that alleviating the burden on the public purse was an important objective of the spousal support provisions. The welfare system was portrayed as a negative last resort: 'the impugned legislation has the deleterious effect of driving a member of a same-sex couple who is in need of maintenance to the welfare system and it thereby imposes additional costs on the general taxpaying public' (para. 115). The Justices also stressed that the case had nothing to do with marriage per se, as the definition of 'spouse' in question dealt only with unmarried cohabitants. They therefore distanced the decision from the same sex marriage debates. They also noted that the case did not predetermine questions such as whether financially interdependent individuals who live together in non-conjugal relationships, e.g. friends or siblings, ought to be constitutionally entitled to apply for support on the breakdown of their relationships (para. 135).

Reaction to the decision has been mixed. Many lesbian and gay groups, including the Foundation for Equal Families were enthusiastic. The applicant M said that the decision would bring us one step further to the long overdue goal that lesbian and gay people be recognized and included as full, valuable, participating members of Canadian society, rather than just being tolerated. The Westboro Baptist Church planned to picket at the Supreme Court of Canada building on June 28, 1999, to protest against the (inaccurate) fact that the Court had approved same-sex marriage. A spokeswoman for the right-wing group REAL Women of Canada said that this was not something that the average Canadian had been clamouring for. The Premier of Ontario stated that Ontario would have to conform with the law and that the Government's lawyers would have to look at how to comply with the Constitution. However, the Premier of Alberta suggested that his province might use the Constitution's notwithstanding clause to override any similar decision affecting Alberta. The federal government stated that although the decision affects support obligations entirely within provincial jurisdiction, it might also have implications for federal legislation which extends benefits to non-married couples. It undertook to examine the decision closely, but cautioned that this did not mean that same-sex couples were legally recognised as 'married'. It added that it was not necessary to redefine concepts like marriage in order to ensure access to benefits and obligations for people in committed relationships in a way that is fair to all Canadians. It will be important to study how both provincial and federal governments deal with the implications of *M* v *H* over the next few years and to examine the practical consequences of the decision in the lives of lesbians and gay men.

[19]

OUR CHILDREN: KIDS OF QUEER PARENTS & KIDS WHO ARE QUEER: LOOKING AT SEXUAL MINORITY RIGHTS FROM A DIFFERENT PERSPECTIVE

Ruthann Robson[*]

I. INTRODUCTION

Much of the conservative right's rhetoric in the realm of minority sexualities has focused on children.[1] Drawing on themes of disease and seduction, Christian fundamentalists have portrayed gay men and lesbians as predators who target children, hoping to "seduce them into a life of depravity and disease."[2] As Jeffrey Weeks noted many years ago, it was no accident that Anita Bryant called her anti-homosexual campaign "Save Our Children, Inc."[3] The United

---

[*] Professor of Law, City University of New York School of Law. The author's books include *Sappho Goes to Law School* and *Lesbian (Out)Law*, and she has published numerous articles on lesbian legal theory. The author expresses her appreciation to CUNY School of Law Professional Development Fund for subsidizing the work of research assistants Donna Canfield and Pavita Krishnaswamy and to S.E. Valentine for her comments.

[1] *See* Herma Hill Kay, *Symposium on Law in the Twentieth Century: From the Second Sex to the Joint Venture: An Overview of Women's Rights and Family Law in the United States During the Twentieth Century*, 88 CAL. L. REV. 2017, 2091 (2000) (stating that "children and the traditional family are the focal point around which conservatives rally to implement their call for a return to 'family values,'" and that "the religious conservative critique of twentieth-century family life seems to suggest that . . . homosexuals in search of social approval of alternative lifestyles . . . threaten to destroy the sanctuary once provided by the father-dominated, home-centered, mother-dependent, traditional family").

[2] DIDI HERMAN, THE ANTIGAY AGENDA: ORTHODOX VISION AND THE CHRISTIAN RIGHT 78-79 (1997). Professor Herman notes the similarity of this disease and seduction discourse to anti-Semitic discourses associating Jews with disease, filth, urban degeneration, and child-stealing. *Id.* at 79; *see also* MICHAEL BRONSKI, THE PLEASURE PRINCIPLE: SEX, BACKLASH, AND THE STRUGGLE FOR GAY FREEDOM 112 (1998) ("While all studies show that physical and sexual abuse of children is far more likely to occur within the heterosexual biological family, the fear of the homosexual molester is persistent and powerful.").

[3] *See* JEFFREY WEEKS, SEXUALITY AND ITS DISCONTENTS: MEANINGS, MYTHS AND MODERN SEXUALITIES 224 (1985) (observing that the "guardians of morality may have given up hope of changing adult behavior, but they have made a sustained effort to protect our young, whether from promiscuous gays, lesbian parents or perverse pornographers").

States Supreme Court implicitly considered the issue of whether gay men should have contact with children with its recent decision in a case involving the Boy Scouts of America.[4] In the family law arena, adoption and custody of children remain concerns of conservative legal writers, and one conservative law professor has recently argued that "homosexual parenting" is dangerous to children.[5]

In composing their anti-gay rhetoric in terms of child protection, conservatives have inaccurately grouped children into a monolithic category, often excluding the real interests of two specific classes of children: children of sexual minority parents and minors who are themselves lesbian, gay, transgendered, or bisexual.[6] First, the conservative right's rhetoric has monolithically constructed the children of sexual minority parents as victims in need of rescue.[7]

---

[4] *See* Boy Scouts of Am. v. Dale, 120 S. Ct. 2446, 2449 (2000) (noting the Boy Scouts organization maintains that "homosexual conduct is inconsistent with the values it seeks to instill"). In considering whether forcing the Boy Scouts to include a gay scoutmaster "would significantly affect the Boy Scouts' ability to advocate public or private viewpoints" that are protected by the First Amendment, the Supreme Court concluded that the "application of New Jersey's public accommodations law to require that the Boy Scouts accept [a gay man] as an assistant scoutmaster runs afoul of the Scouts' freedom of expressive association." *Id.* at 2452, 2455. This decision reversed a decision of the New Jersey Supreme Court, where a concurring justice noted that the case raised the "pernicious stereotype" of homosexuals as child molesters, but that the "myth that a homosexual male is more likely than a heterosexual male to molest children has been demolished." Dale v. Boy Scouts of Am., 734 A.2d 1196, 1243 (N.J. 1999) (Handler, J., concurring), *rev'd*, 120 S. Ct. 2446 (2000).

[5] *See* Lynn D. Wardle, *The Potential Impact of Homosexual Parenting on Children*, 1997 U. ILL. L. REV. 833, 837-38 & n.12 (expressing concern that "the extension of parental rights to nonbiologically related homosexuals who wish to assume parental status (custody, visitation, adoption, foster care, etc.)" would result in "the elimination of consideration of homosexual behavior by a parent or prospective parent as a factor in parenting cases (disputes over custody, visitation, etc.) and legal endorsement of the equivalence of homosexual parents to heterosexual parents"); *see also id.* at 852-67 (discussing potential dangers arising from homosexual parenting, such as children living with homosexual people developing homosexual interests and lacking the "strengths and attributes" that are contributed by parents of different genders).

[6] I prefer the term "sexual minorities" because it is both inclusive of lesbians, gay men, transgendered persons, and bisexuals and because it emphasizes their minority status in a world of heterosexuality and gender conformity. At times, however, this term becomes unwieldy, and I resort to the term "queer," which is inclusive, even if suffering from faults ranging from being offensive to being trendy. When terms such as "gay," "lesbian," or "gay and lesbian" are used, they are meant specifically.

[7] *See* Stephen Macedo, *Homosexuality and the Conservative Mind*, 84 GEO. L.J. 261, 285 (1995) (quoting a conservative group's view of the homosexual movement as "'aggressively propos[ing] radical changes in social behavior, religion, morality and law'" and marriage and the family as "'the most effective institutions for the rearing of children,'" leading to the group's conclusion that "'homosexuality is preeminently a concern about the vulnerabilities of the young'" (quoting Colloquy, *The Homosexual Movement: A Response by the Ramsey Colloquium*, 41 FIRST THINGS 15-21 (1994), *available at* http://www.firstthings.com/ftissues/ft9403/articles/homo.html)); Micah R. Onixt, Note, *Romer v. Evans: A Positive Portent of the Future*, 28 Loy. U. Chi. L.J. 593, 617 n.190 (1997) (noting a

These children are presumably akin to abused children who will suffer more from contact with their parents than from a deprivation of their parents; any love such children have for their parents is presumptively overwhelmed by the assumed disapproval such children would have of their parents' sexuality.[8]

Second, the conservative right's rhetoric has excluded minors who are themselves sexual minorities, even while conservatives fear that children will become sexual minorities by exposure to gay, lesbian, bisexual, or transgendered adults.[9] Regardless of what causes people to become sexual minorities, the conservatives' tactic of hostility towards such people harms children and adolescents who are—or who may become—sexual minorities.

At its most basic level, my argument is that we—those of us who are members of a sexual minority—must continue to take

---

conservative group, Colorado for Family Values (CFV), asserts that children would be unhappy victims of homosexual marriages if these unions were allowed).

[8] *Cf.* Wardle, *supra* note 5, at 864-66 (observing that "homosexual-parenting-affirming studies," which emphasize homosexual parents' ability to love, care for, and raise children while de-emphasizing those parents' homosexuality, "pose[] a comparison between incomparable considerations—between a potentially positive parenting quality on one hand and a potentially negative parenting quality on the other—and speculates in the abstract that having the positive is more important than avoiding the negative"). The author further points out that the "'sexuality of the parent includes some serious risk factors that are just as important to child welfare as positive factors such as nurturing." *Id.* at 866.

[9] *See* Carlos A. Ball & Janice Farrell Pea, *Warring with Wardle: Morality, Social Science, and Gay and Lesbian Parents*, 1998 U. ILL. L. REV. 253, 287 (1998) (noting that Wardle espouses a social constructionist theory that sexual orientation is not innate, but, rather, determined by one's social environment, under which the "possibility [exists] that parents' sexual orientation plays an important role in determining the sexual orientation of their children"); Macedo, *supra* note 7, at 291-92 (exploring the possibility that "political equality for homosexuals will . . . harm the young" by discussing E.L. Pattullo's argument that public censure of homosexual practices will turn "'young waverers'" away from sexual minority lifestyles and back towards heterosexuality); Wardle, *supra* note 5, at 855-57 (noting that "social science research . . . does suggest that there are some particular and unique potential risks to children raised by active homosexual parents"); David S. Dooley, Comment, *Immoral Because They're Bad, Bad Because They're Wrong: Sexual Orientation and Presumptions of Parental Unfitness in Custody Disputes*, 26 CAL. W. L. REV. 395, 396 (1989-1990) (observing that "courts fear that exposing [a] child to the gay parent's homosexuality might cause the child to be sexually disoriented"). *But see* S.N.E. v. R.L.B., 699 P.2d 875, 879 (Alaska 1985) (finding no evidence that an infant boy's exposure to his lesbian mother would increase the likelihood of his becoming homosexual); Conkel v. Conkel, 509 N.E.2d 983, 986 (Ohio Ct. App. 1987) (rejecting the appellant's argument that exposing her two boys to their homosexual father may cause them to become homosexual, and taking judicial notice that, while the causes of homosexuality are elusive, most experts agree that it is not caused by contact with a homosexual parent); Wardle, *supra* note 5, at 852-56 (conceding that the "sympathetic orientation and methodological bias" of social scientific studies tending to demonstrate that children of homosexual parents are more likely to become homosexual renders such studies unreliable); David P. Russman, Note, *Alternative Families: In Whose Best Interests?*, 27 SUFFOLK U. L. REV. 31, 58 (1993) (stating that "[a]lthough some courts fear that children of gay parents will become gay themselves, little evidence suggests that a parent's sexual orientation influences that of the child").

responsibility for our children. Part II of this article considers the children to whom we are biologically related, the children we would adopt, and the children with whom we live.[10] Part III of this article addresses the minors who are presently sexual minorities or who may be in the future.[11] In both cases, we must ensure that our children are not damaged by the law.

II. THE BEST INTEREST OF OUR CHILDREN

Depriving a child of the continued care of his or her sexual minority parent, based on parental sexuality, harms children, despite any court's findings that such a deprivation is in the "best interest of the child." The established standard in custody disputes between parents, the "best interest of the child" test,[12] has devolved into several different approaches regarding parental sexuality.[13]

---

[10] *See infra* Part II (discussing the "best interest of the child" standard, and arguing that the standard is often a ruse for discrimination against homosexuals, that such decisions violate constitutionally protected family relationships, and that society has entered a watershed period with respect to our perception of children).

[11] *See infra* Part III (discussing difficulties facing homosexual adolescents, particularly in academic environments, and how different jurisdictions have responded to teenagers' attempts to bring homosexual awareness to their respective schools and curricula).

[12] *See, e.g.*, Peters v. Peters, 433 N.Y.S.2d 693, 693 (App. Div. 1980) (mem.) ("The best interest of the child involved must govern in the adjudication of custody." (citation omitted)); Berard v. Berard, 749 A.2d 577, 579 (R.I. 2000) ("It is well-settled that the best interests of the child remain the 'lode-star principle' for determining child custody awards."); Price v. Price, 541 A.2d 79, 81 (Vt. 1987) (stating that both Vermont common law and state legislation used the best interest of the child standard to determine custody); *see also* David M. Rosenblum, Comment, *Custody Rights of Gay and Lesbian Parents*, 36 VILL. L. REV. 1665, 1665 (1991) (asserting that courts "overwhelmingly apply" this standard when making custody determinations). Rosenblum also notes that the "best interest of the child" test is "highly problematic" because "judges often inject their biases and prejudices about societal norms and morality under the guise of the 'best interest' of the child." *Id.* at 1666.

[13] As Rosenblum notes,

Courts making custody determinations differ with respect to the standards and tests applicable when one parent is homosexual. Several courts have held that a parent's homosexuality may be an absolute bar to his or her custody rights. Other courts apply a conclusive presumption of unfitness, and find that a person's status as a gay man or lesbian woman directly contradicts his or her status as a parent. Some courts, rather than applying a conclusive presumption, nevertheless require gay and lesbian parents to rebut the presumption that homosexuality renders them unfit to raise their children.

Rosenblum, *supra* note 12, at 1669-70 (citations omitted); *see also* Russman, *supra* note 9, at 42-55 (discussing the various approaches to homosexual parental fitness in custody disputes between homosexual parents and heterosexual parents, heterosexual non-parents, or the state). While I have noted elsewhere that there were three approaches, (*see* RUTHANN ROBSON, LESBIAN (OUT)LAW: SURVIVAL UNDER THE RULE OF LAW 130-31 (1992) (noting there are three approaches to ascertaining the parental fitness of a homosexual: first, treating homosexuality as a per se disqualification; second, the "middle ground" approach, which presumes that exposure to a gay lifestyle will harm children even though parental homosexuality is not inherently harmful; and, third, the "nexus approach," by which living with a homosexual parent is considered to be in a child's best interest unless the parent's

Spanning the continuum, a court may decide that a parent's sexual minority status is a per se disqualification of custody or that parental sexuality is irrelevant.[14] Between these two poles is the nexus approach, which requires the court to find a relationship between parental sexuality and harm to the child.[15] Under the

---

homosexuality is shown to actually harm the child)), in accordance with the accepted views, (*see, e.g.*, D. KELLY WEISBERG & SUSAN FRELICH APPLETON, MODERN FAMILY LAW: CASES AND MATERIALS 830-31 (1998) (noting that the "emerging consensus" of courts use the nexus approach)), I believe it is important to add a fourth—and, I would argue, the only acceptable—approach: that of irrelevance.

[14] *See In re* J. S. & C., 324 A.2d 90, 94-97 (N.J. Super. Ct. Ch. Div. 1974) (noting that, although depriving a parent of visitation rights solely on the basis of parental homosexuality would constitute "unjustified discrimination," the court restricted parental visitation rights on the basis of the father's homosexual conduct, purportedly in the child's "best interest"). *Compare*, G.A. v. D.A., 745 S.W.2d 726, 727-28 (Mo. Ct. App. 1987) (awarding custody of a preschool-age boy to his heterosexual father instead of his homosexual mother, even though the mother's household was superior with respect to physical comfort), *and* L. v. D., 630 S.W.2d 240, 243-44 (Mo. Ct. App. 1982) (holding that a Missouri trial court did not err in observing that homosexuality was not entitled to constitutional protection, and that homosexuality was a crime of "[d]eviate sexual intercourse"), *with* Bezio v. Patenaude, 410 N.E.2d 1207, 1215-16 (Mass. 1980) (accepting expert testimony that parental sexual orientation was "irrelevant" to parental capability, and finding a "total absence of evidence suggesting a correlation between the mother's homosexuality and her fitness as a parent"), *and* Doe v. Doe, 452 N.E.2d 293, 296 (Mass. App. Ct. 1983) (reaffirming that "a parent's life-style, standing alone, is insufficient ground for severing the natural bond between a parent and a child"), *and In re* Marriage of Cabalquinto, 669 P.2d 886, 888 (Wash. 1983) (en banc) (noting that homosexuality is not a per se bar to visitation rights), *modified* 718 P.2d 7, 8 (Wash. Ct. App. 1986).

[15] *See* Dooley, *supra* note 9, at 396 ("[U]nder the nexus approach, the court requires proof that the parent's homosexuality has or will adversely affect the child before custody can be denied. Only in this approach does the court rely on the evidence, rather than on presumption, to determine the parental capabilities of each parent." (citation omitted)). *See also, e.g.*, S.N.E. v. R.L.B., 699 P.2d 875, 879 (Alaska 1985) (holding that a lesbian mother's sexual orientation bore no negative impact upon an infant child's development, which would have justified awarding custody to a heterosexual father); *In re* Marriage of Birdsall, 243 Cal. Rptr. 287, 289-91 (Cal. Ct. App. 1988) (stating "a parent is not unfit, as a matter of law, merely because he or she is homosexual," and finding no connection between a gay father's lifestyle and religious practices and undesirable behavior in his child); M.P. v. S.P., 404 A.2d 1256, 1263 (N.J. Super. Ct. App. Div. 1979) (noting a lack of evidence suggesting that a lesbian mother's homosexuality will adversely affect her daughters, as well as the strong likelihood that exposure to their lesbian mother will benefit the children by making them more tolerant and accepting of the differences of others); Conkel v. Conkel, 509 N.E.2d 983, 986-87 (Ohio Ct. App. 1987) (rejecting three arguments—that exposure to homosexual father would trigger homosexuality in two young boys, the likelihood of the boys contracting AIDS from their father, and a desire to shield the boys from the "'slings and arrows of a disapproving society'"—in sustaining the trial court's decision to award visitation rights to the father); Vicki Parrott, Note, *The Effect on the Child of a Custodial Parent's Involvement in an Intimate Same-Sex Relationship—North Carolina Adopts the "Nexus Test" in* Pulliam v. Smith, 19 CAMPBELL L. REV. 131, 132 (1996) (stating that after the *Pulliam* decision, North Carolina courts could not find adverse effects on a child based solely on "the judge's opinion, speculation and conjecture"). *But see* T.C.H. v. K.M.H., 784 S.W.2d 281, 284-85 (Mo. Ct. App. 1989) (rejecting the per se approach to determining parental unfitness, but nevertheless finding a nexus between a lesbian mother's homosexual conduct and adverse effects on the "morality" and "well-being" of her children).

"true" nexus approach, the burden of persuasion is allocated so that there must be proof that parental sexuality will have an adverse impact on the child.[16] Nonetheless, some courts presume adverse impact, demanding that the sexual minority parent prove an absence of harm to the children.[17]

In all of these approaches, except for the irrelevance approach, the courts construe the sexual minority parent as a potential cause of harm to the child.[18] In fact, much greater harm is caused by judicial decisions that deprive a child of the care and companionship of his or her parent. In the notorious situation of Sharon Bottoms and her son Tyler, the Virginia Supreme Court deprived Sharon Bottoms of custody because of her lesbianism.[19] In doing so, the

---

[16] *See, e.g., S.N.E.,* 699 P.2d at 879 (holding that there was no presumption of parental unfitness based on sexual conduct, and that "[c]onsideration of a parent's conduct is appropriate only when the evidence supports a finding that a parent's conduct has or reasonably will have an adverse impact on the child and his best interests"); *M.P.,* 404 A.2d at 1259 (noting that, in custody disputes, the party seeking modification of custody orders "bears the burden of showing sufficient changed circumstances so as to require modification," and, thus, a heterosexual father bears the burden of demonstrating that a lesbian mother's homosexual conduct constitutes "changed circumstances" sufficient to warrant change of custody orders); *see also Conkel,* 509 N.E.2d at 985 (noting that "an irrebuttable presumption [of parental unfitness based on sexual activity] offends . . . constitutional standards"); Parrott, *supra* note 15, at 132 (noting the court in *Pulliam* determined that "a court cannot conclude that a child is adversely affected by a parent's involvement in an intimate same-sex relationship, unless the moving party produces evidence that 'the conduct has or will likely have a deleterious effect on the children'").

[17] *See, e.g.,* Thigpen v. Carpenter, 730 S.W.2d 510, 513-14 (Ark. Ct. App. 1987) (noting that Arkansas courts entertained a presumption that "illicit sexual conduct on the part of the custodial parent is detrimental to the children" and that the trial court determined that "homosexuality is generally socially unacceptable"). Professor Julie Shapiro calls this a standard of "permissible determinative inference." Julie Shapiro, *Custody and Conduct: How the Law Fails Lesbian and Gay Parents and Their Children,* 71 IND. L.J. 623, 639-41 (1996).

[18] *See* Roe v. Roe, 324 S.E.2d 691, 694 (Va. 1985) (finding that a burden will be placed on a child due to the social "condemnation" of her father's homosexual relationship); *see also* Shapiro, *supra* note 17, at 644-45 (noting that a finding of harm is often justified by an assumption of societal bias against homosexuality). This bias, and the resulting stigmatization of the child, is itself seen as "harm" to the child. *Id.* at 645.

[19] *See* Bottoms v. Bottoms, 457 S.E.2d 102, 108 (Va. 1995) [hereinafter *Bottoms II*] (stating that "living daily under conditions stemming from active lesbianism practiced in the home may impose a burden upon a child"). The trial court decision and subsequent appeals attracted national media attention and inspired several periodical articles. *See, e.g.,* Amy D. Ronner, Bottoms v. Bottoms: *The Lesbian Mother and the Judicial Perpetuation of Damaging Stereotypes,* 7 YALE J.L. & FEMINISM 341 (1995); Peter Nash Swisher & Nancy Douglas Cook, Bottoms v. Bottoms: *In Whose Best Interest? Analysis of a Lesbian Mother Child Custody Dispute,* 34 U. LOUISVILLE J. FAM. L. 843 (1995-96); Joseph R. Price, Comment, Bottoms III: *Visitation Restrictions and Sexual Orientation,* 5 WM. & MARY BILL RTS. J. 643 (1997); B. Drummond Ayres, Jr., *Judge's Decision in Custody Case Raises Concerns,* N.Y. TIMES, Sept. 9, 1993, at A16; Debbie Howlett, *Judge Rules Lesbian "unfit" mother,* USA TODAY, Sept. 8, 1993, at 1A; Elizabeth Kastor, *The Battle for the Boy in the Middle; Little Tyler's Mom is a Lesbian, so Grandma Got to Take Him Away,* WASH. POST, Oct. 1, 1993, at C1, *available at* 1993 WL 2096263.

court had to overcome the constitutional doctrine of parental autonomy recognized by the Supreme Court for almost a century, because the person seeking custody was not Tyler's father—a man who had abdicated any responsibility for the child—but Tyler's grandmother.[20] As a grandparent, Sharon Bottoms' mother, Pamela Kay Bottoms, was a classic third party without any recognized claim to custody absent unusual circumstances.[21] In a third party custody challenge the court would not even reach the best interest of the child test without first overcoming an initial hurdle, such as parental unfitness or abandonment.[22] The trial judge predicated the finding of unfitness on Sharon Bottom's lesbianism, stating that,

> The mother, Sharon Bottoms, has openly admitted in this court that she is living in an active homosexual relationship.

The amount of attention devoted to *Bottoms* might lead one to believe it was an aberration. However, the courts of Mississippi confronted a similar situation. In *White v. Thompson*, 569 So.2d 1181 (Miss. 1990), paternal grandparents sought custody of their grandchildren on the grounds that the mother was an unfit parent. *Id.* at 1182. The bulk of the testimony concerned the mother's lesbian relationship, which prompted the trial court to find the mother "unfit, morally and otherwise, to have custody of her children." *Id.* at 1183. On appeal to the Mississippi Supreme Court, the mother argued the trial court's finding was impermissibly predicated solely on her lesbianism. *Id.* The Mississippi Supreme Court finessed the issue of her sexuality, deciding not to reach the issue of whether lesbianism alone was sufficient to render a parent unfit, stating that, although

> the predominant issue in this case seems to have been Mrs. White's lesbian relationship, and the chancellor may have relied almost entirely on this, we find that a review of the entire record and the circumstances present . . . shows that the chancellor's decision that Mrs. White was an unfit mother, morally and otherwise, was not against the overwhelming weight of the evidence.

Id. at 1184. The circumstances included some testimony that the "children had not been properly supervised," clothed or fed. *Id.* The mother testified that conditions at the trailer in which she lived with her children "were a lot better" than when her husband, the grandparents' son, had lived there. *Id.* at 1183. The dissenting justice in *White* began his opinion by observing that any neglect of the children was "no more than one would expect to find in any case where a twenty-four year old mother with but a high school diploma and no independent means" was attempting to support her children. *Id.* at 1185 (Roberston, J., dissenting). However, such neglect was sufficient to satisfy the state standard for rebutting the presumption of custody accorded to a legal parent. *Id.* at 1184 (stating that "[a] parent's chosen manner of living may not take precedence over the well-being of the children involved").

[20] *See Bottoms II*, 457 S.E.2d at 103, 105.

[21] *See, e.g.*, Bennett v. Jeffreys, 356 N.E.2d 277, 280 (N.Y. 1976) (holding "[t]he State may not deprive a parent of the custody of a child absent surrender, abandonment, persisting neglect, unfitness or other like extraordinary circumstances"); Bailes v. Sours, 340 S.E.2d 824, 827 (Va. 1986) (affirming an award of custody to a child's stepmother instead of his mother that was based upon "extraordinary" circumstances); *see also* Ruthann Robson, *Third Parties and the Third Sex: Child Custody and Lesbian Legal Theory*, 26 CONN. L. REV. 1377, 1385 (1994) (exploring the court's traditional view of the family unit of one mother and one father, and the relegation of those not meeting this criteria to the lesser status of "third parties").

[22] *See Bottoms II*, 457 S.E.2d at 104 (recognizing the presumption of parental custody, but stating that "it is rebutted when certain factors, such as parental unfitness, are established by clear and convincing evidence").

She admitted she is sharing a bedroom and her bed with another, her female lover, whom she identified by name as April Wade. Sharon Bottoms in this courtroom admitted a commitment to April Wade, which as she contemplates will be permanent, and as I understand her testimony, long lasting if not forever.

She readily admits her behavior in open affection shown to April Wade in front of the child. Examples given were kissing, patting, all of this in the presence of the child. She further admits consenting that the child referred to April Wade, her lover, as to quote the words "Da Da."[23]

The trial judge found that the "mother's conduct [was] illegal," rendering her "an unfit parent," and that, while he was cognizant of the "presumption in the law in favor of the custody being with the natural parent," "Sharon Bottoms' circumstances of unfitness" were "of such an extraordinary nature" as to rebut the presumption of parental custody.[24] The trial court granted visitation to Sharon Bottoms on Mondays and Tuesdays, provided that it not "be in the home shared with April Wade or in April Wade's presence."[25] Although this decision was reversed by the intermediate court of appeals,[26] the trial court's decision was affirmed by the Virginia Supreme Court, which stated it would "not overlook" Sharon Bottoms' lesbian relationship: "living daily under conditions stemming from active lesbianism practiced in the home may impose a burden upon a child by reason of the 'social condemnation'

[23] Transcript of Hearing at 195-96, Bottoms v. Bottoms (Va. Cir. Ct. Henrico Co. 1993) (No. CH93JA0517-00) (on file on with *Albany Law Review*).

[24] Bottoms v. Bottoms, 444 S.E.2d 276, 279-80 (Va. Ct. App. 1994) [hereinafter *Bottoms I*]; see VA. CODE ANN. § 18.2-361[A] (Michie 1996) ("If any person carnally knows in any manner any brute animal, or carnally knows any male or female person by the anus or by or with the mouth, or voluntarily submits to such carnal knowledge, he or she shall be guilty of a Class 6 felony . . . .").

[25] *Bottoms I*, 444 S.E.2d at 280. After the Virginia Supreme Court affirmed the denial of custody, Sharon Bottoms petitioned for a modification of visitation. See Bottoms v. Bottoms, No. 0589-98-2, 1999 WL 1129720, at *1 (Va. App. June 29, 1999). The trial court denied the petition except to the extent that it extended the summer visitation from one week to two weeks. *Id.* Sharon Bottoms appealed, contending that the trial judge's order that visitation with her child shall occur outside the presence of her lover, April Wade, violated state law and her constitutional rights under the Equal Protection and Due Process clauses of the United States Constitution. *Id.* The appellate court refused to consider the constitutional issues, finding that they were not properly raised in the trial court, and affirmed the trial judge's restrictive visitation as being within the judge's broad discretion. See id. at *2 (stating that the standard to be used in determining visitation is the best interest of the child).

[26] See *Bottoms I*, 444 S.E.2d at 283-84 (Va. App. 1994) (noting that the trial court erred in adopting "a *per se* approach in finding Sharon Bottoms to be an unfit parent without finding that she engaged in conduct or exposed her son to conduct that would be harmful to him").

attached to such an arrangement, which will inevitably afflict the child's relationships with its 'peers and with the community at large.'"[27]

The harm of social condemnation in the context of race has been declared an unconstitutional consideration in custody determinations. In *Palmore v. Sidoti*,[28] the United States Supreme Court declared that, although "[p]rivate biases may be outside the reach of the law, . . . the law cannot, directly or indirectly, give them effect."[29] Furthermore, judicial concern with social condemnation of homosexuality is questionable, since it does not attach any societal or peer disapproval to being raised by one's grandmother rather than one's mother.[30] Presumably, an argument that the child might be teased for living with his grandmother would not be taken seriously. The real basis of the decision is not societal disapproval of lesbianism, but judicial disapproval of lesbianism, which is buttressed by the court's reference to the illegality of lesbian sexual practices under Virginia's sodomy law.[31]

The emphasis that both the trial court and the Virginia Supreme Court placed on the family's private interactions, including the displays of affection between Sharon Bottoms and her lover, the integration of the lover into the household, and Sharon Bottoms' lack of shame about her relationship,[32] suggests that the real harm

---

[27] *Bottoms II*, 457 S.E.2d at 108 (quoting Roe v. Roe, 324 S.E.2d 691, 694 (Va. 1985)).

[28] 466 U.S. 429 (1984).

[29] *Id.* at 433. In *Palmore*, a father sought to modify a prior judgment awarding custody of his daughter to his former wife. *Id.* at 430. The father argued that the mother's cohabitation with and marriage to a man of a different race constituted changed circumstances. *Id.* The trial court awarded custody to the father based in part on the court's belief that the child would face "'social stigmatization'" as a result of living in a mixed race home. *Id.* at 431. The Supreme Court rejected this argument, and awarded custody back to the mother. *Id.* at 434. *See also* City of Cleburne v. Cleburne Living Ctr., Inc., 473 U.S. 432, 448, 450 (1985) (applying the *Palmore* rule to reject an "irrational prejudice against the mentally retarded" in an exclusionary zoning context).

[30] This proposition is supported by the fact that the Supreme Court of Virginia affirmed the decision of the trial court, finding that awarding custody of Tyler to the senior Mrs. Bottoms would be in the child's best interest. *See Bottoms II*, 457 S.E.2d at 103-04, 108.

[31] *See id.* at 108 (noting that the court had previously held that homosexuals are not per se unfit parents, but that "[c]onduct inherent in lesbianism" is a felony in Virginia and, "thus, that conduct is another important consideration in determining custody").

[32] The attorney representing the grandmother, Pamela Kay Bottoms, called as his first witness Sharon Bottoms and, after establishing her identity as the child's legal mother and the identity of his client as the child's grandmother, immediately focused his questions on lesbianism:

Q: Now, in the juvenile court you stated that you are in a lesbian relationship with whom?

A: April Wade.

Q: Now, for the record, would you tell me your definition of a lesbian relationship. What does it mean?

924   Albany Law Review   [Vol. 64]

the courts envisioned for the toddler was not social condemnation, but exposure to homosexuality, with the increased chance that the child "will develop homosexual interests and behaviors."[33]   While any link would be the result of the normalization of homosexuality in the child's perspective and, thus, the removal of some of the socially imposed terrors, some legal thinkers argue that the increase in homosexuality is the consequence of a lack of "cross-gender parenting."[34]   In Tyler's case, however, this lack of dual-gender parenting is equally applicable to the household of Tyler's grandmother. The senior Ms. Bottoms had excluded her current boyfriend from her household on the advice of her attorney, given Sharon Bottoms' history of complaints concerning sexual abuse perpetrated by him.[35]

The belief that exposure to homosexuality breeds homosexuality provokes several responses. The first, and, I believe, the correct response, is a resounding "so what?" As a lesbian myself, I am unwilling to engage in an argument that assumes that my sexual desires are pathological. Others have argued, however, that social science research does not support a correlation between being raised by a lesbian or gay parent and becoming a sexual minority.[36]

A: It means two people of the same sex are together.
Q: In what way are they together?
A: In a relationship.
Q: Now, you say a "relationship," does that entail sex?
A: Yes.
Q: Hugging and kissing?
A: Yes.
Q: Sleeping in the same bed?
A: Yes.
Q: Now then, you're not at all ashamed of that relationship, is that correct?
A: No, sir.

Transcript of Hearing at 9-10, Bottoms v. Bottoms (Va. Cir. Ct. Henrico Co.) (No. CH93JA0517-00) (on file with *Albany Law Review*).

[33] Wardle, *supra* note 5, at 852 (asserting that "[t]he most obvious risk to children from their parents' homosexual behavior suggested by the current studies relates to the sexual development of the child").

[34] *Id.* at 860-61 (arguing that a lack of heterosexual parenting can cause emotional damage to children, "[f]or example, the absence of a father in the home may result in a daughter having trouble relating to men throughout her adult life").

[35] *See Bottoms I*, 444 S.E.2d 276, 278-79 (Va. Ct. App. 1994) (noting that this history of sexual abuse against Sharon Bottoms was her motivating factor in deciding to remove her son from her mother's home). The Virginia Supreme Court more simply noted that the grandmother's "boyfriend ceased living with her shortly before the juvenile court hearing, and has not returned." *Bottoms II*, 457 S.E.2d at 105.

[36] For an excellent rehearsal of the social science research from a legal perspective, see Ball & Pea, *supra* note 10, at 280-285, discussing studies used by Wardle to argue that children raised by gays and lesbians risk becoming homosexual. For Wardle's response, see Lynn D. Wardle, *Fighting with Phantoms: A Reply to* Warring with Wardle, 1998 U. ILL. L. REV. 629, 629-31, concluding that courts should apply a rebuttable presumption in child

Furthermore, a correlation would not prove causation; other factors could explain any discrepancy.[37]

In the context of the *Bottoms* litigation, any underlying belief that the harm to the toddler in being raised by his mother would be his eventual homosexuality is especially ironic: he is now in the custody of the one person in the litigation with the proven track record of raising a sexual minority, Sharon Bottoms' mother, Kay Bottoms.

Bottoms is illustrative rather than unique. Countless children have been removed from their sexual minority parents.[38] In many cases, sexual minority adults fought such removal in court, and the reporters are filled with our defeats, as well as our more recent successes.[39] In many other situations, lesbians and gay men did not bring their cases to court, believing that to do so would be a fruitless endeavor that would injure their children.[40] Yet, whether we fought

---

support cases that a parent's homosexuality is not in the best interests of the child. *See also* Susan Golombok & Fiona Tasker, *Do Parents Influence the Sexual Orientation of Their Children? Findings from a Longitudinal Study of Lesbian Families*, 32 DEV. PSYCHOL. 3, 8 (1996) (reporting that "the commonly held assumption that children brought up by lesbian mothers will themselves grow up to be lesbian or gay is not supported" by a study of lesbian and heterosexual families, and "there was no statistically significant difference between young adults from lesbian and heterosexual family backgrounds with respect to sexual orientation"); Charlotte J. Patterson & Richard E. Redding, *Lesbian and Gay Families with Children: Implications of Social Science Research for Policy*, 52 J. SOCIAL ISSUES 29, 30 (1996) (concluding, from an overview of social science literature, that gay and lesbian parents are as likely as heterosexual parents to provide a positive home environment).

[37] *See, e.g.,* Ball & Pea, *supra* note 10, at 286-288 (discussing heredity and a contemporary atmosphere of tolerance as other factors influencing sexuality).

[38] It seems the most frequent manifestation of this "removal" occurs when courts deny custody or visitation based on sexual orientation. *See, e.g.,* Marlow v. Marlow, 702 N.E.2d 733, 736-38 (Ind. Ct. App. 1998) (holding that visitations restrictions were appropriate where a sexual minority parent took a child to a "lesbian choir" and other gay-oriented activities); Alison D. v. Virginia M., 572 N.E.2d 27, 29 (N.Y. 1991) (denying visitation rights to a sexual minority partner who had raised a child from infancy because she was not the biological or adoptive mother and, therefore, "not a parent" for the purposes of the state's statute).

[39] *See, e.g., In re* Adoption of Evan, 583 N.Y.S.2d 997, 1001 (Sur. Ct. N.Y. County 1992) (granting adoption to sexual minority parents, noting that "a child's best interest is not predicated or controlled by parental sexual orientation"). *But see Marlow*, 702 N.E.2d at 737-38 (Ind. Ct. App. 1998) (holding that a restriction on a gay father's visitation rights by prohibiting the father from taking his child to "'gay activist social gatherings'" was appropriate).

[40] As one lesbian poet has written:
Women ask: *Why didn't you—*?
like they do of women who've been raped.
And I ask myself: Why didn't I? Why
didn't I run away with them? Or face
him in court? Or—
                    Ten years ago I
answered myself: No way for children to live.
Minnie Bruce Pratt, *The Child Taken from the Mother, in* CRIME AGAINST NATURE 24 (1990).

or not, when our children were deprived of their parents—us—they were seriously harmed.

In most cases, we assume that it is wrong to remove children from their parents.[41] For example, one conservative legal writer decries the cruel persecution of the Amish, whose children were "declared wards of the state, removed from their homes, and placed in institutions" because the parents refused to be assimilated into the common culture.[42] The writer is referring to the Amish in support of his argument against compulsory assimilation,[43] although his argument is equally applicable to other persecuted groups, such as Native Americans.[44] For example, the United States Congress and Supreme Court have recently admitted that the former removal of Native American children from their parents in order to civilize the children was a brutal mistake.[45] Native American lesbian theorist Beth Brant has explicitly made the connection between the forced removal of indigenous children by the United States government in the nineteenth century and a custody battle involving a lesbian parent.[46] The dominant regime removes the children of minorities

---

[41] The exception to this general rule is for parental abuse and neglect, which is variously phrased in different jurisdictions, and which allows the state to remove a child for his or her protection. As in other areas of family law, however, definitions and applications of abuse and neglect are culturally conditioned and historically contingent, as is evident in an examination of cases involving corporeal punishment of children.

[42] *See* Richard F. Duncan, *Public Schools and the Inevitability of Religious Inequality*, 1996 BYU L. REV. 569, 575-76 (noting ways the state carries out "religious persecution under the authority of education").

[43] *Id.*

[44] *See* Miss. Band of Choctaw Indians v. Holyfield, 490 U.S. 30, 32 (1989) (noting that "[s]tudies undertaken by the Association on American Indian Affairs in 1969 and 1974, and presented [at] Senate hearings, showed that 25 to 35% of all Indian children had been separated from their families and placed in adoptive families, foster care, or institutions"). For a discussion of the multiple paradoxes posed by fundamentalist objections to a liberal education that exposes children to a variety of ideas, see Nomi Maya Stolzenberg, *"He Drew a Circle that Shut Me Out": Assimilation, Indoctrination, and the Paradox of a Liberal Education*, 106 HARV. L. REV. 581, 584-87 (1993), noting that "liberalism condemns indoctrination but refuses to acknowledge its own reliance upon it."

[45] *See* 25 U.S.C. §§ 1901-1902 (1994) (stating that "the States, exercising their recognized jurisdiction over Indian child custody proceedings through administrative and judicial bodies, have often failed to recognize the essential tribal relations of Indian people and the cultural and social standards prevailing in Indian communities and families"); *Choctaw Indians*, 490 U.S. at 32-37 (noting that the enactment of the Indian Child Welfare Act of 1978 was in response to concerns "over the consequences to Indian children, Indian families, and Indian tribes of abusive child welfare practices that resulted in the separation of large numbers of Indian children from their families and tribes through adoption or foster care placement, usually in non-Indian homes").

[46] *See* BETH BRANT, *A Long Story, in* MOHAWK TRAIL 77, 77-79 (1985) (telling the parallel stories of a Native American woman and a lesbian woman who had custody of their children taken away and who were told "[i]t [was] good for [the children]" and "it was in [the child's] best interests").

so that the children do not become like their parents: the Amish children were removed so they would not be Amish adults, the native children were removed so they would become unfamiliar with native culture, and the children of sexual minorities are removed so they will not become homosexuals.

In all of the above-mentioned situations, the constitutional rights of the parents and of the children were violated. The Amish emerged victorious from the fight for control of their children, the results of which can be found in the United States Supreme Court decision in *Wisconsin v. Yoder*.[47] Native American parents did not have a similar constitutional victory in the courts.[48] However, the practice of removing Native American children was finally addressed by Congress, resulting in the Indian Child Welfare Act of 1978.[49] Meanwhile, the persecution of sexual minority parents by

---

[47] 406 U.S. 205, 234 (1972) (holding that compulsory education beyond the eighth grade violated the First and Fourth Amendment rights of the Old Order Amish).

[48] *See, e.g., In re* Cantrell, 495 P.2d 179, 181-82 (Mont. 1972) (affirming a district court order removing a Native American child and awarding custody to the Department of Public Welfare of Valley County, Montana); *In re* Adoption of Doe, 555 P.2d 906, 921-22 (N.M. Ct. App. 1976) (finding that a Native American father had abandoned his child and granting custody of the child to non-Native American adoptive parents, instead of the child's Native grandfather, against the father's wishes). The court in *Doe* disregarded the argument asserted by the father that he could not have abandoned his child under Navajo custom because maternal grandparents traditionally assumed the responsibilities of raising children if a Navajo father did not carry out parental duties. *Id.* at 920.

[49] 25 U.S.C. §§ 1901-1963 (1994) (setting forth legislation intended "to protect the best interests of Indian children and to promote the stability and security of Indian tribes and families by the establishment of minimum Federal standards for the removal of Indian children from their families"). For discussions of the history of forced child removal as the genesis of the Act, see Patrice H. Kunesh, *Transcending Frontiers: Indian Child Welfare in the United States*, 16 B.C. THIRD WORLD L.J. 17, 22-24 (1996). The Act was described as "one of the singular most important pieces of federal legislation recognizing tribes' sovereign rights to protect the interests of their communities and their children." *Id.* at 33-34. *See generally* Jose Monsivais, *A Glimmer of Hope: A Proposal to Keep the Indian Child Welfare Act of 1978 Intact*, 22 AM. INDIAN L. REV. 1 (1997) (detailing the Act, analyzing the state courts' application of the Act, and illustrating political pressures limiting implementation of the Act). The removal of Native American children from their parents occurred by two different methods. The earlier plan, administered by the Bureau of Indian Affairs, resulted in the wholesale removal of children from their families and tribes and in their "education" in boarding schools for eight years, during which time the children were not permitted to speak their native language, wear native clothes, or keep their hair long. *See* B.J. Jones, *In Their Native Lands: The Legal Status of American Indian Children in North Dakota*, 75 N.D. L. REV. 241, 247-48 & n.44 (1999) (noting that "federal policymakers targeted Indian children as the agents of change in an era when Indian people were perceived as 'savages' who needed to be rehabilitated and Christianized"); Kunesh, *supra*, at 21 (describing the federal government's policy of attacking Native American familial bonds with education as "one of the most pernicious Indian child removal methods"). The later removal policy was based on the presumption that Native American children were abused and neglected. The claims were often based on poverty or on cultural practices, such as extended kinship systems that viewed parental responsibility differently from the dominant white culture. *See id.* at 23-24 (maintaining the reservation system itself created the dependence and poverty that was then

child-removal is lessening in some states through judicial decisions, usually based on judicial interpretations of state substantive law rather than on constitutional grounds.[50]

While parental constitutional rights are important, the constitutional rights of the children, which are implicated when children are removed from their parents, are important as well. Discrimination against the children of sexual minority parents is analogous to discrimination against the children of unwed parents. The Supreme Court has decided more than thirty cases dealing with illegitimate children.[51] Most of these cases proceed from the premise that it is constitutionally problematic to discriminate against children based on conditions they cannot control.[52] The Court has measured various state provisions regarding illegitimate children against the Equal Protection Clause of the Constitution, relying on the notion that the provisions make a quasi-suspect classification.[53] When considering what government interests are

---

used against the Native Americans to take their children). The extent to which the state welfare practices have been ameliorated is doubtful; as one recent commentator noted, "[a]n Indian child in North Dakota is over eight times more likely to be placed in foster care than a non-Indian child." Jones, *supra*, at 246 (explaining that this disproportionate foster care placement prompted Congress to enact the Indian Child Welfare Act).

[50] *See, e.g.*, Pryor v. Pryor, 709 N.E.2d 374, 378 (Ind. Ct. App. 1999) (relying on precedent to hold that "sexual orientation as a single parental characteristic is not sufficient to render that parent unfit to retain physical custody of a child"); Hodson v. Moore, 464 N.W.2d 699, 701 (Iowa Ct. App. 1991) (finding that a "discreet homosexual relationship" is not a per se bar to custody of a child); Paul C. v. Tracy C., 622 N.Y.S.2d 159, 160 (App. Div. 1994) (citing state case law to hold that "[w]here a parent's sexual preference does not adversely affect the children, such preference is not determinative in a child custody dispute").

[51] *See* Laurence C. Nolan, *"Unwed Children" and Their Parents Before the United States Supreme Court From Levy to Michael H.: Unlikely Participants in Constitutional Jurisprudence*, 28 CAP. U. L. REV. 1, 1 n.1 (1999) (citing all of the United States Supreme Court cases decided between 1968 and 1989 involving unwed parents and their children).

[52] The *Weber* Court expressed this view most eloquently:

The status of illegitimacy has expressed through the ages society's condemnation of irresponsible liaisons beyond the bonds of marriage. But visiting this condemnation on the head of an infant is illogical and unjust. Moreover, imposing disabilities on the illegitimate child is contrary to the basic concept of our system that legal burdens should bear some relationship to individual responsibility or wrongdoing. Obviously, no child is responsible for his birth and penalizing the illegitimate child is an ineffectual—as well as an unjust—way of deterring the parent.

Weber v. Aetna Cas. & Sur. Co., 406 U.S. 164, 175 (1972) (citation omitted). A few years earlier, the Court noted that no action of the children was relevant to the case, and quoted William Shakespeare's, *King Lear*, act 1, scene 2: "Why bastard, wherefore base?" Levy v. Louisiana, 391 U.S. 68, 72 n.6 (1968).

[53] *See* Jill Dinneen, Comment, Equality Foundation of Greater Cincinnati, Inc. v. City of Cincinnati: *The Sixth Circuit Narrowly Construes* Romer v. Evans, 73 ST. JOHN'S L. REV. 951, 962 (1999) (stating that "[o]ver the years, the Supreme Court found that classifications . . . based on illegitimacy and gender are quasi-suspect, and has applied the developed levels of review to uphold or strike down challenged laws" (citations omitted)). Dinneen notes that homosexuals have not obtained any level of protected status. *Id.* at 963.

sufficient within the context of illegitimacy, the Court has rejected the asserted interests of encouraging and strengthening marriage or supporting traditional family life.[54] However, illegitimacy classifications have been upheld when the government interest supporting the provisions' constitutionality has been related to the proof of paternity.[55]

The Court's Equal Protection jurisprudence regarding the children of unwed parents is applicable to the children of sexual minority parents, children who likewise had no control over the conditions of their birth. Neither the children of sexual minority parents nor the children of heterosexual parents make a proper category for Equal Protection classification because both interfere with the fundamental right of intimate familial relationships between children and their parents. The asserted state interests of encouraging marriage and traditional family life are no more valid when applied to discrimination against the children of sexual minority parents than when applied to the children of unwed parents. Furthermore, there is no other valid state interest—such as problems relating to the proof of paternity—that could support the governmental interest in discrimination. Thus, state laws and practices that impose a higher burden on a child's right to maintain an intimate familial relationship with a sexual minority parent should be deemed an unconstitutional violation of the child's rights.

Shifting the focus to the child's interests, such as to the toddler Tyler, instead of his mother, Sharon Bottoms, is consonant with the orientation of family law toward the best interest of the child[56] and

---

[54] See e.g., N.J. Welfare Rights Org. v. Cahill, 411 U.S. 619, 619-20 (1973) (quoting Weber for the proposition that a statutory scheme intended to preserve family life cannot constitutionally deny benefits to illegitimate children while granting them to legitimate children); see also Weber, 406 U.S. at 175, (acknowledging a state's interest in protecting "legitimate family relationships," but rejecting it as a compelling reason to discriminate against illegitimate children).

[55] The problems regarding proof of paternity became dispositive in Lalli v. Lalli, 439 U.S. 259 (1978), in which the Court found the state's interest in the "just and orderly disposition of property at death" was served by the statutory requirement that the father's paternity be determined prior to his death in a judicial proceeding. Id. at 268, 275-76. Earlier, the Court, in Fiallo v. Bell, 430 U.S. 787 (1977), deferred to Congressional judgment regarding the exclusion of illegitimate children of men (but not women) from an immigration statutory preference, citing the "serious problems of proof that usually lurk in paternity determinations." Id. at 797, 799. Proof of paternity concerns may not be enough in some circumstances. For example, the Court declared unconstitutional a Texas common law practice denying illegitimate children the right to legal support from their fathers, despite the Court's recognition of the "lurking problems with respect to proof of paternity." Gomez v. Perez, 409 U.S. 535, 538 (1973).

[56] See, e.g., Troxel v. Granville, 120 S. Ct. 2054, 2073 (2000) (calling the best interest of the child rule an "entirely well-known" standard). In Troxel, the Court explained that there is a strong presumption that parents act in the best interest of their child, but that "there may be

is apparent in such practices as unlinking visitation and child support.[57] Admittedly, asserting the constitutional interests of children can be problematic. For example, although the child is central in constitutional illegitimacy jurisprudence, the decisions also balance the child's interests with parental rights, or allow the child's rights to be encompassed by parental rights.[58] Moreover, although the Supreme Court has famously stated that the Bill of Rights, in general, and the Fourteenth Amendment, in particular, are not "'for adults alone,'"[59] juveniles are generally relegated to the position of having lesser constitutional rights than adults, as the constitutional developments in a minor's right to abortion amply illustrate.[60] The ambivalence of the United States towards the

---

circumstances in which a child has a stronger interest at stake" that may be more important than an isolated right of the parents, at least where the parents act arbitrarily. *Id.*

[57] *See, e.g.*, Hodge v. Hodge, 507 F.2d 87, 92 (3d Cir. 1975) (holding the denial of visitation rights is not justified if this is done only to punish the father for failure to pay child support); Stewart v. Soda, 642 N.Y.S.2d 105, 106 (App. Div. 1996) (holding that failure to pay child support was not a proper reason to terminate visitation).

[58] *See* Lehr v. Robertson, 463 U.S. 248, 266-67 (1983) (noting that, in evaluating the rights of a parent and the best interest of a child, a relevant criterion is "the existence or nonexistence of a substantial relationship between parent and child"); Caban v. Mohammed, 441 U.S. 380, 383-84, 392-93 (1979) (finding the father of illegitimate children had an equal protection interest in blocking the adoption of his natural children by the children's stepfather).

[59] *See In re* Gault, 387 U.S. 1, 13, 42 (1967) (holding that due process requires the state to appoint an attorney for indigent minors in juvenile delinquency proceedings that might result in commitment to an institution in which the juvenile's freedom is impaired); *see also Troxel*, 120 S. Ct. at 2072 n.8 (citing precedent acknowledging "that children are in many circumstances possessed of constitutionally protected rights and liberties").

[60] The Court has decided numerous cases regarding a minor's restricted constitutional right to abortion, and instituting the compromise of a judicial bypass procedure to guarantee a minor's rights are not overborne by her parents. *See, e.g.*, Lambert v. Wicklund, 520 U.S. 292 293-94 (1997) (reversing the Ninth Circuit's holding that a judicial bypass procedure was too narrow to protect the minor's rights because bypass was limited to situations where notification was not in the best interest of the child, but did not extend to scenarios where the abortion itself was in the child's interest); Planned Parenthood v. Casey, 505 U.S. 833, 899 (1992) (rejecting a challenge to the requirement of the informed consent of one parent where an adequate judicial bypass procedure was provided); Ohio v. Akron Ctr. for Reprod. Health, 497 U.S. 502, 510 (1990) (finding that the state's bypass procedure met the requirements the Court had previously established for parental consent statutes, but leaving open the question of whether parental notification statutes required bypass procedures); Hodgson v. Minnesota, 497 U.S. 417, 448-49 (1990) (upholding a forty-eight hour waiting period and a two-parent notice requirement with a sufficient bypass procedure); H.L. v. Matheson, 450 U.S. 398, 411, 413 (1981) (upholding a parental notice statute because, unlike consent, requiring notice did not give the parent veto power over the minor's decision and, thus, no bypass was required); Bellotti v. Baird, 443 U.S. 622, 647 (1979) (holding that a minor should be able to utilize a mechanism for judicial bypass without first giving notice to her parents); Planned Parenthood v. Danforth, 428 U.S. 52, 74 (1976) (rejecting a blanket provision requiring parental consent because the state had no constitutional authority to give any third party, even a parent, absolute veto power over a decision made by a patient and her doctor).
Relying on their state constitutions, supreme courts in California and Florida have held that minors' rights to an abortion are co-extensive with adults. *See, e.g.*, Am. Acad. of

rights of children is demonstrated by this nation's unique failure to ratify the United Nations Convention on the Rights of the Child.[61] Conservatives argue that recognition of constitutional rights for children is antithetical to family values.[62] However, a more liberal perspective advances the credible argument that children have a constitutional right to maintain a relationship with "parent-like" individuals[63] and further, that the Constitution should be amended to include children, just as it was amended to protect the rights of former slaves and to grant suffrage to women.[64] Certainly, we are in

Pediatricians v. Lungren, 940 P.2d 797, 816 (Cal. 1997) (concluding that the abortion decision is a protected privacy interest "so central to the preservation of her ability to define and adhere to her ultimate values regarding the meaning of human existence and life, and . . . *is a decision that cannot be postponed until adulthood*"); *In re* T.W., 551 So. 2d 1186, 1193 (Fla. 1989) (explaining the Florida Constitution extends to "every natural person"). For an argument that the Montana statute regulating a minor's access to abortion, held to be constitutional by the United States Supreme Court in *Lambert*, violates the Montana state constitution's explicit privacy provision, see Matthew B. Hayhurst, Comment, *Parental Notification of Abortion and Minors' Rights Under the Montana Constitution*, 58 MONT. L. REV. 565, 574, 586 (1997).

Interestingly, there has been no discernable litigation or scholarship concerning a minor's right to have HIV-testing without parental notification or consent as a constitutional matter. Perhaps this is because a large number of states statutorily authorize testing and treatment for HIV and/or sexually transmitted diseases. *See* Roger J.R. Levesque, *The Peculiar Place of Adolescents in the HIV-AIDS Epidemic: Unusual Progress & Usual Inadequacies in "Adolescent Jurisprudence,"* 27 LOY. U. CHI. L.J. 237, 261-62, nn.97-99 (1996) (noting that the general requirement that children have parental consent prior to receiving health care has some exceptions and that states are increasingly listing HIV testing among those exceptions); *cf.* William Adams, *"But Do You Have to Tell My Parents?" The Dilemma for Minors Seeking HIV-Testing and Treatment*, 27 J. MARSHALL L. REV. 493, 495 (1994) (noting that, as of 1994, only eleven states, by statute, allowed minors to consent for HIV testing). For a comprehensive summary of state legislation related to HIV and AIDS as of 1998, see Staff of Volume 8, *State Statutes Dealing with HIV and AIDS: A Comprehensive State-by-State Summary (1999 Edition)*, 8 LAW & SEXUALITY 1 (1998).

[61] *See* Barbara Bennett Woodhouse, *The Constitutionalization of Children's Rights: Incorporating Emerging Human Rights into Constitutional Doctrine*, 2 U. PA. J. CONST. L. 1, 1 (1999) (noting this "U.N. Convention has been adopted by every nation in the world community except the United States").

[62] *See id.* at 2 ("[M]any conservatives reject the concept of rights for children as a threat to family values."); *see also* Lynn D. Wardle, *The Use and Abuse of Rights Rhetoric: The Constitutional Rights of Children*, 27 LOY. U. CHI. L. J. 321, 322-23, 348 (1996) (arguing that, although the recognition of the constitutional rights of children is important for children and society, the "'cult of rights'" is misplaced in the context of family law and that "[p]arents—a mother and a father—who are committed to their marriage can best protect children's rights").

[63] *See, e.g.*, Gilbert A. Holmes, *The Tie that Binds: The Constitutional Right of Children to Maintain Relationships with Parent-Like Individuals*, 53 MD. L. REV. 358, 410 (1994) (encouraging courts to recognize a "child's liberty interest in a child-parent relationship" which would promote stable relationships that are beneficial to the child).

[64] *See* Charles D. Gill, *A Constitutional Amendment for Children*, 5 GEO. J. ON FIGHTING POVERTY 273, 273 (1998) (suggesting that "using children's rights as a vehicle, as a political strategy, may well be a double-barreled shotgun that can help children and alleviate poverty with one pull of the trigger").

the midst of a cultural and legal disagreement regarding our understandings of children.[65]

Nevertheless, even if our notion of children's right to the companionship of their parents, regardless of sexual orientation or gender identification, is not grounded in the Constitution, we should not allow the "best interest of the child" standard to function as a hollow sentiment, deployed to validate discrimination against sexual minority parents and their children. Such discrimination is predicated on the fear that children of sexual minorities will become sexual minorities. From a legal reform standpoint, the appropriate strategy is to remove legal barriers and install legal safeguards that will assist young people in surviving a "queer adolescence."

III. SURVIVING A QUEER ADOLESCENCE

"It's always open season on gay kids."[66] Whether conservatives proceed from an essentialist (biological and immutable) basis for sexuality, a constructionist (psychological and environmental) basis for sexuality, or some combination of the two,[67] the message is one of exclusion and hostility. Theorist and judge Richard Posner, for example, discusses the different theories on the cause of homosexuality, but argues that regardless of its cause, homosexuality should be discouraged.[68] Regarding the theory that the basis of homosexuality is biological, Posner states,

> Maybe we should just be patient; science, which has worked so many wonders, may someday, perhaps someday soon, discover a "cure" for homosexuality. . . . [I]f the hypothetical cure for homosexuality were something that could be administered—costlessly, risklessly, without side effects—

---

[65] See Janet L. Dolgin, The Fate of Childhood: Legal Models of Children and the Parent-Child Relationship, 61 ALB. L. REV. 345, 347-50 (1997) (explaining how the law relies on two different and simultaneously existing models with regard to children: a nineteenth-century model of children within families and a late twentieth-century model of children as autonomous individuals).

[66] Eve Kosofsky Sedgwick, How to Bring Your Kids Up Gay, in FEAR OF A QUEER PLANET: QUEER POLITICS AND SOCIAL THEORY 69, 69 (Michael Warner ed., 1993).

[67] See RICHARD A. POSNER, SEX AND REASON 295 (1992) (noting that three theories as to the cause of homosexuality are: 1) that homosexuality is biologically determined, 2) that it is a choice of lifestyle, and, 3) that it is influenced by developmental factors, such as a child's relationship with his parents).

[68] See id. at 295-97 ("The more that homosexuality can be persuasively depicted as a biologically determined condition like sickle-cell anemia or male pattern baldness, the less sense it makes to place it under restrictions designed to protect children from succumbing to its allures. If, however, it is merely a vicious choice of life-styles, it ought to be repressed as firmly as possible.").

before a child had become aware of his homosexual propensity, you can be sure that the child's parents would administer it to him, believing, probably correctly, that he would be better off, not yet having assumed a homosexual identity.[69]

Yet, as is made clear by the passage's continuation, Posner does not fully subscribe to an immutable preference. According to Posner, there is a possibility parents can prevent the "formation of homosexual preference ... by discouraging gender-nonconforming behavior *at its outset* (later is too late)," by not "condoning 'sissyish' behavior in infancy."[70]

Whatever the genesis, the fact remains that many adolescents are sexual minorities. When I was a teenager, we existed in a far less "gay-friendly" (though perhaps less conservative) era, and, long before I was a teenager, there were sexual minority adolescents. For one conservative law professor, however, preventing sexual minority youth from existing (by preventing sexual minority parents from parenting) is important because "[h]omosexual behavior ... is associated with suicidal behavior, prostitution, running away from home, substance abuse, HIV infection, highly promiscuous behavior with multiple sex partners, and premature sexual activity."[71] This logic argues for a stigmatizing regime and then concludes that the results from the stigmatization prove the inadequacy of those being stigmatized. Such circular reasoning would support an annihilation of Native youth based on a finding that "Native Americans have the highest suicide rate of any adolescent group in the country."[72] This logic also fails to address the legal and social conditions that make alternatives such as suicide and other self-destructive behaviors attractive. Nor can it account for the reality that the chances of suicide, homelessness, or substance abuse, for a sexual minority or sexually questioning adolescent, vary with the tolerance for sexual variation within the home.[73] The overwhelming majority of youths

---

[69] *Id.* at 308.

[70] *Id.* at 309. Supporting his advice that parents discipline an infant for displaying "sissyish behavior" is Posner's underlying thesis: while a person's sexual preference is given, not chosen, the decision to engage in a particular act is a rational choice made in light of pertinent costs and benefits. *Id.* at 308-09.

[71] Wardle, *supra* note 5, at 854 (citation omitted).

[72] Kunesh, *supra* note 49, at 30.

[73] *See, e.g.*, Elvia R. Arriola, *The Penalties for Puppy Love: Institutionalized Violence Against Lesbian, Gay, Bisexual, and Transgendered Youth*, 1 J. GENDER, RACE & JUST. 429, 439-440 (1998) (relating both anecdotal and statistical evidence of the propensity for these misunderstood youths to attempt suicide or be kicked out of their homes); Scott Hershberger, et al., *Predictors of Suicide Attempts Among Gay, Lesbian, and Bisexual Youth*, 12 J.

who leave their homes do not go because they are ready to have adult lives of independence and adventure; they are evicted or constructively evicted by their parents or guardians because of the adults' intolerance.[74]

Some parents have forced psychiatric treatment on their children because of the minors' sexual variance. As Daphne Scholinski relates, she spent four years institutionalized in a psychiatric hospital, "sentenced to an adolescence spent surrounded by white walls and lab coats—quite a punishment for a 14-year-old who was showing the typical signs of growing up gay in a heterosexist society."[75] Her situation is not unique.[76] It is imperative that parents not be legally permitted to institutionalize youth because of sexual or gender identity.[77] Moreover, "therapists" who engage in "conversion therapy," which attempts to change a person's sexual

---

ADOLESCENT RES. 477, 479 (1997) (discussing studies suggesting that sexual minority youth who attempt suicide are less likely to have supportive friends and parents).

[74] *See* Ritch C. Savin-Williams & Eric M. Dubé, *Parental Reactions to Their Child's Disclosure of Gay/Lesbian Identity*, 47 FAM. REL. 7, 9 (1998) (noting some parents react to a child's disclosure of sexual minority identity with rage, physical abuse, or ejection from the home). As the Gay, Lesbian & Straight Teachers Network (GLSTN) reports, "19% of gay men and 25% of lesbians report suffering physical violence at the hands of a family member[] . . . 11.5% of gay youth report being physically attacked by family members," and "26% of adolescent gay males report having to leave home as a result of conflicts with their family over their sexual orientation." *Just the Facts: On Gay, Lesbian, and Bisexual Students and Schools, at* http://www.uncg.edu/edu/ericcass/diverse/docs/gayfacts.htm (last updated May 6, 1997) (reporting statistics on self-realization, school climate, the family, and anti-gay violence and harassment). This is not to imply, however, that the majority of parents reject their children upon disclosure of sexual minority status or behaviors. "Although parents often react in a less than ideal fashion after learning of their child's same-sex attractions, limited research indicates that most eventually arrive at tolerance or acceptance of their son's or daughter's sexual orientation." Savin-Williams & Dubé, *supra*, at 7.

[75] Daphne Scholinski, *After-Wards*, 48 HASTINGS L.J. 1195, 1197 (1997).

[76] *See id.* at 1196 (stating that "the United State's mental health system remains an extremely hostile environment for [lesbian, gay, bisexual and transgendered] youth, who are routinely viewed by child and adolescent psychiatrists as being 'emotionally disturbed' and in need of aggressive psychiatric treatment 'to prevent adult homosexuality'" in spite of the fact that the "American Psychiatric Association removed homosexuality from its official list of mental disorders in 1973").

[77] For further discussion, see generally Miye A. Goishi, *Unlocking the Closet Door: Protecting Children from Involuntary Civil Commitment Because of Their Sexual Orientation*, 48 HASTINGS L.J. 1137 (1997), discussing the institutionalization of sexual minority youth and proposing a reform of the psychiatric admissions process for sexual minority youth. *Cf.* Samuel M. Leaf, Note, *How Voluntary is the Voluntary Commitment of Minors? Disparities in the Treatment of Children and Adults Under New York's Civil Commitment Law*, 62 BROOK. L. REV. 1687 (1996) (discussing New York's procedures and proposing a revised voluntary commitment statute that would afford due process protections for the growing number of adolescents placed in psychiatric institutions by their parents for troublesome adolescent behavior rather than for serious mental illness).

identity, should be held legally liable and the practice should be condemned by respectable psychological organizations.[78]

Some parents who object to their children's sexuality turn to the courts rather than to psychiatry for assistance, often with equally destructive results. A parent can seek court intervention if a teenager is sexually active. For example, in *In re Lori M.,*[79] a mother sought to have her child declared a "person in need of supervision" under a New York statute.[80] The fifteen-year-old child, Lori, was associating with a twenty-one-year old lesbian.[81] Lori was fortunate in that the judge found her mature enough to express her sexuality and denied the petition, even while admonishing Lori that, because she was a minor, any sexual actions with an adult could violate New York law.[82] One could hope that Lori M. is not an anomaly,[83] but although there are few reported cases in this area, minority sexuality is certainly an area that can lead a parent to juvenile court, resulting in a judgment adjudicating the sexual minority adolescent as delinquent. As one commentator on female

[78] For further discussion, see Laura A. Gans, *Inverts, Perverts and Converts: Sexual Orientation Conversion Therapy and Liability,* 8 B.U. PUB. INT. L.J. 219, 245, 249 (1999), arguing that the tort of intentional infliction of emotional distress should be applicable to the outrageous conduct involved when a conversion therapist's "sole aim . . . is to eradicate homosexuality," and that the American Psychiatric and Psychological Associations should issue an unconditional ban on the practice. *Cf.* David B. Cruz, *Controlling Desires: Sexual Orientation Conversion and the Limits of Knowledge and Law,* 72 S. CAL. L. REV. 1297, 1345-48, 1361-63 (1999) (discussing conversion therapy in epistemological terms and concluding that at a minimum, informed consent is necessary).

[79] 496 N.Y.S.2d 940 (Fam. Ct. 1985).

[80] *Id.* at 940; *see* N.Y. Fam. Ct. Act § 712(a) (McKinney 1999), *amended by* 2000 N.Y. Laws 596 (McKinney) (effective Nov. 1, 2001) (defining a person in need of supervisions as one who is "incorrigible, ungovernable or habitually disobedient and beyond the lawful control of parent or other lawful authority"); *see also* Jonathan C. Juliano, *Detention of Persons in Need of Supervision: The Dilemma in Grounding the Flight of the Fleet-footed Status Offender,* 13 J. SUFFOLK ACAD. L. 95, 106-116 (1999) (discussing the legality of detention for persons in need of supervision under section 720 of the Family Court Act).

[81] *Lori M.,* 496 N.Y.S.2d at 940.

[82] *See id.* at 942-43 (noting that the child had "given a great deal of thought to her decision and its possible ramifications," although she should be aware that because she is a minor "she is not free to act entirely as she wishes"). The court also found that Lori's rights fell "within the constitutionally protected zone of privacy." *Id.* at 942. *See also* N.Y. Penal Law § 130.40 (McKinney 1997), *amended by* 2000 N.Y. Laws 1 (providing that it is a Class E felony for a person over twenty-one years of age to engage in "deviate" sex with someone younger than seventeen).

[83] As Colleen Sullivan notes in her discussion of this case, if Lori had been younger than fifteen years of age, had expressed hostility to her mother for bringing the case, had stated conclusively that she was a lesbian, or if there had been a different judge exercising his or her broad discretion in a different manner, Lori could have been declared as a "person in need of supervision" and remanded to state custody. *See* Colleen A. Sullivan, *Kids, Courts, and Queers: Lesbian and Gay Youth in the Juvenile Justice and Foster Care Systems,* 6 LAW & SEXUALITY 31, 42-43 & nn.70-71 (1996).

juvenile delinquency notes, "[w]hen young women 'get caught' exploring lesbian desire, the social stigma and marginalization arising from homophobia" may lead them to "troubles with the juvenile justice system."[84]

Parents can also trigger child welfare laws unintentionally. In another New York case, a family court judge adjudicated a fourteen year old boy as abused by both his parents based upon his father's "unrelenting torrent of verbal abuse" directed at the child's "sexual identity," specifically the father's taunts of "'fag,'" "'faggot,'" and "'queer,'" despite the boy's denial of his homosexuality.[85] The family court judge rejected the father's justification of a right to discipline his child for the boy's "'girlie' behavior" and noted that the courts must intervene in the parent child relationship, despite the parents' constitutional rights, because "children have constitutional rights which must be respected by all, including their parents."[86] As a result of the court's finding, Shane was removed from his parents and placed in foster care.[87]

It is arguable whether the foster care system would be more hospitable to Shane T. than his homophobic father. As one juvenile rights attorney has commented, there are two things a young person in the foster care system does not want to be: "'gay and an arsonist.'"[88] There are very few placements that are specifically designed for sexual minority youth, although in recent years there have been some programs in larger cities such as Los Angeles, Washington, D.C., Boston, and New York.[89] Sexual minority youth

---

[84] Laurie Schaffner, *Female Juvenile Delinquency: Sexual Solutions, Gender Bias, and Juvenile Justice*, 9 HASTINGS WOMEN'S L.J. 1, 18 (1998). On the other hand, Schaffner also suggests that many young women come into contact with the juvenile justice system for criminal acts because of involvement with an older boyfriend. *Id.* at 17-18.

[85] *In re* Shane T., 453 N.Y.S.2d 590, 591 (Fam. Ct. 1982).

[86] *Id.* at 593 (noting the comments of Shane's father, who stated he would be embarrassed if his son were homosexual).

[87] *See id.* at 594 (detailing the court order, including the remanding of the child to the Commissioner of Social Services). The court found that Shane's mother was culpable because she had "failed to protect her son from an ongoing, serious abuse." *Id.*

[88] *See* Sullivan, *supra* note 83, at 46 & n.93-94 (quoting Samuel Dulberg, Deputy Attorney in Charge at the Juvenile Rights Division of the Legal Aid Society in Bronx, New York). Mr. Dulberg noted that placing sexual minority youth is difficult, because he knew of no placements in New York providing programming specifically for gay or lesbian youths in the family court system. *Id.* at 47.

[89] *See* Nancy D. Polikoff, *Resisting "Don't Ask, Don't Tell" in the Licensing of Lesbian and Gay Foster Parents: Why Openness Will Benefit Lesbian and Gay Youth*, 48 HASTINGS L.J. 1183, 1189-90 (1997) (stating that cities are places where one would expect to find such programs); Sullivan, *supra* note 83, at 58-61 (explaining that California, New York, and Massachusetts have programs that are "beginning to serve the needs of gay and lesbian youth" and that these programs should be used as models for other states).

in foster care have recently become more visible,[90] and their struggle to be heard remains ongoing.[91]   Often, sexual minority youth struggle for a safe environment not only in their homes, whether familial or state, but also in their schools. Many young people have endured from teachers and classmates treatment similar to the judicially declared abuse that Shane T. suffered from his father. Sexual minority students are now attempting to hold educators legally responsible for the violence perpetrated against them.

In the ground-breaking case of *Nabozny v. Podlesny*,[92] the Seventh Circuit held that Jamie Nabozny stated a claim under the Equal Protection Clause of the Fourteenth Amendment for discrimination based upon sex and sexual orientation because of the school district's failure to enforce its anti-harassment policies.[93] Beginning in the seventh grade, Nabozny's "classmates regularly referred to him as 'faggot,' and subjected him to various forms of physical abuse, including striking and spitting on him."[94] Despite Nabozny's complaints to school officials and a temporary reprieve, the violence continued and intensified, escalating to an incident in a classroom where Nabozny was pushed to the floor by two students and subjected to a "mock rape" while twenty other students looked on and laughed.[95] When Nabozny went to the office of Principal Mary Podlesny, she told him "that if he was 'going to be so openly gay,' he should 'expect' such behavior" from other students.[96]   Nabozny's years in the eighth, ninth, and tenth grades were no better, although his parents repeatedly sought the cooperation of school

---

[90] For example, a recent issue of Foster Care Youth United, a publication of Youth Communication/New York Center, ran a cover feature entitled *Out on the Inside: Gay Teens Struggle to Survive in Foster Care*, with pieces by transgendered, lesbian, and gay youth. FOSTER CARE YOUTH UNITED, Jan/Feb. 2000 (on file with *Albany Law Review*).

[91] For instance, sexual minority youth in foster care in New York City were plaintiffs in a motion to intervene in the lawsuit *Marisol v. Giuliani*, 929 F. Supp. 662, 669, 693 (S.D.N.Y. 1996), *aff'd*, 218 F.3d 132 (2d Cir. 2000), which alleged "systemic deficiencies of gross proportions" in the New York City Administration for Children's Services. *Id.* at 669. The court granted class certification to the plaintiffs, defining the class represented as "children who are or will be in the custody of the New York City Administration for Children's Services ('ACS'), and those children who, while not in the custody of ACS, are or will be at risk of neglect or abuse and whose status is known or should be known to ACS." *Id.* at 693.

[92] 92 F.3d 446 (7th Cir. 1996).

[93] *Id.* at 460-61 (concluding a reasonable finder of fact could find the defendants violated Nabaozny's equal protection rights through sexual orientation or gender discrimination). Additionally, the court held "the law . . . was sufficiently clear to inform the defendants . . . that their conduct was unconstitutional." *Id.*

[94] *Id.* at 451 (noting that the guidance counselor to whom the student first went for help took action, but was subsequently replaced).

[95] *Id.* (noting the offending students exclaimed that Nabozny should enjoy the mock rape).

[96] *Id.*

officials.[97] Nabozny attempted suicide, ran away, and refused to go to school until ordered to do so by the State Department of Social Services.[98] After a particularly vicious beating, a school official again told Nabozny that he deserved such treatment because of his sexuality.[99] Finally, in the eleventh grade, school administrators told Nabozny and his parents that they were "unwilling to help him" and that their son should "seek educational opportunities elsewhere."[100]

Reversing the trial court's granting of summary judgment for the school district and officials, the Seventh Circuit stated that it was "impossible to believe that a female lodging a similar complaint [to a mock rape] would have received the same response."[101] The court further held that the officials were not entitled to qualified immunity.[102] On remand, a jury found the school district and officials liable and the case was settled for almost a million dollars.[103]

In addition to constitutional claims, sexual minority students who are harassed by peers with the tacit approval of school officials can seek redress under a federal statute known as Title IX.[104] The Supreme Court has recently interpreted Title IX as allowing a private claim for damages against a school district[105] for peer harassment if the harassment is "so severe, pervasive, and objectively offensive that it effectively bars the [student's] access" to educational opportunities and if the school district has acted with "deliberate indifference" to known harassment.[106] Although the Court was considering a situation of sexual harassment perpetrated by a male student against a female student, the same standard should be operative in a situation of same-sex harassment, based on

---

[97] *Id.* at 451-52 (noting that after each incident the perpetrators were reported to the principal who promised to take action but failed to do so).

[98] *Id.* at 452.

[99] *Id.* (noting that Nabozny's beating resulted in internal bleeding, from which he collapsed several weeks later).

[100] *Id.*

[101] *Id.* at 454-55 (noting the court's belief that Nabozny was treated unfairly and differently because of his gender).

[102] *Id.* at 455-56 (holding that the defendants were not eligible for qualified immunity because the law requiring equal protection of the genders is clearly established).

[103] *See Gay Man Wins $900,000 in School-District Case*, WALL ST. J., Nov. 21, 1996, at B14 (noting the suit was the first federal case against a school district for not protecting sexual minority students, and was settled for $900,000 prior to the jury reaching a verdict on damages).

[104] 20 U.S.C. §§ 1681-85 (1994).

[105] Title IX only applies to school districts that receive federal funds. *Id.* § 1681.

[106] Davis v. Monroe County Bd. of Educ., 526 U.S. 629, 633 (1999).

the Court's unanimous decision in *Oncale v. Sundowner Offshore Services, Inc.*,[107] which held that same-sex harassment was within the purview of Title VII.[108] Nevertheless, the substantial obstacle of the deliberate indifference and severe harassment requirements for students seeking protection from their school districts for peer violence[109] limits the efficacy of Title IX.[110]

Furthermore, remedies for past acts of violence are an unsatisfying solution. The focus should be on preventing such acts from occurring. Suggestions for preventing the harassment of sexual minority students include creating student groups that support sexual minorities and instituting official diversity, tolerance, or curricular programs that include sexual minority issues. However, these solutions have created their own legal controversies. For example, tremendous contention erupted in the school system in Salt Lake City, Utah, when students tried to form a student interest group on sexual minority issues. In 1995, high

---

[107] 523 U.S. 75 (1998).

[108] *Id.* at 79. The Court stated,

[M]ale-on-male sexual harassment in the workplace was assuredly not the principal evil Congress was concerned with when it enacted Title VII. But statutory prohibitions often go beyond the principal evil to cover reasonably comparable evils, and it is ultimately the provisions of our laws rather than the principal concerns of our legislators by which we are governed. Title VII prohibits "discriminat[ion] . . . because of . . . sex" in the "terms" or "conditions" of employment. Our holding that this includes sexual harassment must extend to sexual harassment of any kind that meets the statutory requirements.

Id. at 79-80 (second alteration in original). For a discussion of *Oncale* in the context of peer sexual harassment, pre-*Davis v. Monroe County Board of Education*, see Joan E. Schaffner, *Approaching the New Millennium with Mixed Blessings for Harassed Gay Students*, 22 HARV. WOMEN'S L.J. 159 (1999).

[109] One commentator has proposed a model statute that not only addresses the problems with the "because of sex" language in federal sexual harassment statutes, but also requires the school district "to take reasonable steps to remedy the harassment" if it "knows or reasonably should know" of the harassment or abuse. *See* Amy Lovell, *"Other Students Always Used to Say, 'Look at the Dykes'": Protecting Students from Peer Sexual Orientation Harassment*, 86 CAL. L. REV. 617, 643-44 (1998) (providing the text of the model statute, which lists examples of harassment, including "name-calling, references to sexual activity or practices, 'joke'-telling, and physical assault").

[110] A recent lawsuit instituted by Derek Henkle, a student in the Reno, Nevada school system, who faced a situation similar to that of Jamie Nabozny, does not make any Title IX claims, but instead argues on the basis of Equal Protection (as in *Nabozny*), the First Amendment (based on school officials requiring Henkle to conceal his sexual identity and failing to protect him when he revealed it), and state law claims of negligence and intentional infliction of emotional distress. *See* Complaint Henkle v. Gregory, at 2-3,8, *available at* http://www.lambdalegal.org (last visited January 28, 2001) (alleging the plaintiff was continually harassed, beaten, and humiliated for several years by his peers, while school administrators failed to provide him with aid or protection).

school senior Kelli Peterson met with official disapproval when she decided to form a gay/straight alliance at East High.[111]

School officials' desire to ban or otherwise discriminate against a particular student group can run afoul of the First Amendment.[112] Interpreting the First Amendment in a suit by a conservative Christian student group, the Supreme Court held that a university could not deny funding to a student group because it was "'religious.'"[113] Likewise, the Court disapproved of a public school's denial of access to its facilities by a Christian organization that wanted to show a family values program.[114] Most recently, a unanimous Court rejected a First Amendment challenge to a university's mandatory student activity fee because the university allocation was viewpoint neutral.[115] Thus, it is clear that a public educational institution cannot engage in content or viewpoint-based restrictions of expression.

In addition to the First Amendment, the Equal Access Act[116] may thwart a school district's inclination to ban a particular club. Congress passed the Equal Access Act in 1984 in response to disputes regarding religious organizations' access to public school facilities.[117] The Act provides that

> [i]t shall be unlawful for any public secondary school which receives federal financial assistance and which has a limited open forum to deny equal access or a fair opportunity to, or discriminate against, any students who wish to conduct a meeting within that limited open forum on the basis of the

---

[111] *See* Doni Gewirtzman, *"Make Your Own Kind of Music": Queer Student Groups and the First Amendment*, 86 CAL. L. REV. 1131, 1132 (1998) (stating that Ms. Peterson's efforts were met with hostility and the school attempted to minimize her chances of implementing the group by effectively banning all student groups on campus that were non-curricular in nature).

[112] *See* John A. Russ IV, *Creating a Safe Space for Gay Youth: How the Supreme Court's Religious Access Cases Can Help Young Gay People Organize at Public Schools*, 4 VA. J. SOC. POL'Y & L. 545, 552 (1997) (noting that beginning in the 1970s, "gay students at the college level consistently won First Amendment victories against efforts to deny their organizations funding, benefits, and recognition").

[113] Rosenberger v. Rector and Visitors of the Univ. of Va., 515 U.S. 819, 825, 837 (1995).

[114] *See* Lamb's Chapel v. Ctr. Moriches Union Free Sch. Dist., 508 U.S. 384, 393-94 (1993) (finding that the school's denial of access to the organization violated the First Amendment because the school's reasoning for the denial was based solely upon the organization's religious perspective).

[115] *See* Bd. of Regents v. Southworth, 529 U.S. 217, 233 (2000). ("When a university requires its students to pay fees to support the extracurricular speech of other students, all in the interest of open discussion, it may not prefer some viewpoints to others.").

[116] 20 U.S.C. §§ 4071-74 (1994).

[117] *See* S. REP. NO. 98-357, at 3 (1984), *reprinted in* 1984 U.S.C.C.A.N. 2348, 2349 (stating that the purpose of the Equal Access Act was to "clarify and confirm the First Amendment right[] of . . . free exercise of religion").

religious, political, philosophical, or other content of the speech at such meetings.[118]

While the initial intent and usage of the Act benefited religious groups, it is also applicable to sexual minority student groups.[119]

Constrained by the First Amendment and the Equal Access Act, the Salt Lake City school board prohibited all extra-curricular clubs rather than allow the Gay/Straight Alliance.[120] In reaction to the situation at East High, the Utah legislature passed a statute requiring school boards to deny access to any organization whose program or activities involved human sexuality.[121] Somewhat inconsistently, the Utah Administrative Code provides that educators shall not exclude any student from participating in any program on the basis of sexual orientation and may not encourage a student to develop prejudice on this ground.[122]

---

[118] 20 U.S.C. §4071(a). *See id.* § 4071(b) (defining a "limited open forum" as being any public secondary school that grants an opportunity "for one or more noncurriculum related student groups to meet on school premises during noninstructional time").

[119] For arguments about the efficacy of the Equal Access Act for sexual minority student groups, see Susan Broberg, Note, *Gay/Straight Alliances and Other Controversial Student Groups: A New Test for the Equal Access Act*, 1999 BYU EDUC. & L.J. 87, 116 (discussing evolving uses of the Equal Access Act for sexual minority students in educational settings, and stating that, although religious and gay rights groups disagree ideologically, they may need to work together to protect the constitutional rights of all high school students); Regina M. Grattan, Note, *It's Not Just for Religion Anymore: Expanding the Protections of the Equal Access Act to Gay, Lesbian, and Bisexual High School Students*, 67 GEO. WASH. L. REV. 577, 578-79 n.8 (1999) (explaining that, although envisioned for the protection of religiously based student groups, the Act also protects sexual minorities, and noting that Senator Hatfield, one of the Act's sponsors, conceded during floor debates that sexual minority students would be protected under the Act).

[120] E. High Gay/Straight Alliance v. Bd. of Educ., 81 F. Supp. 2d 1166, 1168 (D. Utah 1999). The school board also denied the Rainbow Club, a student group "whose subject matter was to include the 'impact, contribution and importance of gay, lesbian, bi-sexual and transgender individuals,'" approval as a "'curriculum-related'" student group. *Id.* at 1196.

[121] The statute states,

The Legislature finds that certain activities, programs, and conduct are so detrimental to the physical, emotional, psychological, and moral well being of students and faculty, the maintenance of order and discipline on school premises, and the prevention of any material and substantial interference with the orderly conduct of a school's educational activities, that local school boards shall deny access to any student organization or club whose program or activities would materially and substantially:

(i) encourage criminal or delinquent conduct;

(ii) promote bigotry; or

(iii) involve human sexuality.

UTAH CODE ANN. § 53A-3-419(2)(a) (Supp. 2000). *See also* Adrianne Goldsmith, *Recent Legislative Developments in Utah Law: Education: Limitations Regarding Student Clubs and Responsibilities of School Employees*, 1996 UTAH L. REV. 1374, 1377-78 (noting the Utah legislature reasoned that since Utah laws prohibited all sexual activity outside of marriage, a student club for gays would be encouraging criminal conduct).

[122] The Utah Administrative Code, R686-103-6, entitled "Competent Practice Related to Students," provides:

An educator shall:

In the ensuing litigation, the district judge hearing the case initially denied the motion for a preliminary injunction filed by the Gay/Straight Alliance.[123] The judge later granted a partial cross-summary judgment motion on the Equal Access Act claims finding the school district did violate the Act during one school year,[124] and in the final judgment, found there was insufficient proof that an unwritten policy prohibiting "'gay-positive'" viewpoints existed.[125] Unsuccessful in their quest to be recognized by the school district, the students formed two additional clubs, the Rainbow Club, and the PRISM club.[126] PRISM ("People Recognizing Important Social Movements") sought to be recognized as an extracurricular club, linking the club's purpose to East High courses in American government, history, and sociology.[127] As such, it would be within the new policy recognizing only clubs related to the curriculum.[128] When the school district denied PRISM's application, the students sued again.[129] On April 26, 2000, District Judge Tena Campbell issued a ruling that imposed a preliminary injunction in favor of the students, holding that the plaintiffs had a substantial likelihood of succeeding on the merits of the case.[130] The student group can now

---

(E) not exclude a student from participating in any program, deny or grant any benefit to any student on the basis of race, color, creed, sex, national origin, marital status, political or religious beliefs, physical or mental conditions, family, social, or cultural background, or sexual orientation, and may not engage in a course of conduct that would encourage a student to develop a prejudice on these grounds or any others.

UTAH ADMIN. CODE R686-103-6(E) (2000), *available at* LEXIS U.A.C. R686-103-6.

[123] East High Gay/Straight Alliance v. Bd. of Educ., 30 F. Supp. 2d 1356, 1364 (D. Utah 1998).

[124] *See* East High Gay/Straight Alliance v. Bd. of Educ., 81 F. Supp. 2d 1166, 1197-98 (D. Utah 1999) (concluding that the school district did maintain a limited open forum under the Equal Access Act during the 1997-1998 school year and that the Gay/Straight Alliance was excluded from that forum). The judge further found that the school district subsequently maintained a closed forum policy and that the Equal Access Act was thus inapplicable after the 1997-98 school year. *Id.* at 1197-98.

[125] East High Gay/Straight Alliance v. Bd. of Educ., No. 2:98-CV-193J, 1999 U.S. Dist. LEXIS 20254, at *6 (D. Utah Nov. 30, 1999).

[126] *See id.* at *3 (discussing whether the denial of the Rainbow club reflected the existence of an unwritten school policy); *see also* East High Sch. PRISM Club v. Seidel, 95 F. Supp. 2d 1239, 1243 (D. Utah 2000) (citing the denial of the club's application by the defendant, who objected to the perceived focus of the club on gay and lesbian issues).

[127] *See East High Sch. PRISM Club*, 95 F. Supp. 2d at 1242 (expressly stating that the club did not advocate a certain sexual ideology but "that all students should have an equal voice and be treated with equal respect").

[128] *See id.* at 1243.

[129] *Id.* at 1240 (stating that the issue before the court was whether the school district applied the appropriate standard in its review of the application).

[130] *Id.* at 1251.

meet, and the school board is reportedly reassessing its denials to other student groups, including a Women's Studies Club.[131]

Tolerance and diversity programs have also engendered legal controversies for students, teachers, and school districts. For example, *Solmitz v. Maine School Administrative District No. 59*[132] resulted from a "Tolerance Day" at a high school and from a history teacher's invitation to a local lesbian activist to speak about gay and lesbian issues during the program.[133] The principal and school superintendent rejected the lesbian speaker as too controversial; some parents protested the plan for a lesbian speaker, and there were bomb threats.[134] As a result, the school board cancelled the entire "Tolerance Day" program,[135] a move reminiscent of that of the Salt Lake City School Board. The history teacher and a student brought an action in state court, arguing that their First Amendment rights had been violated.[136] The Supreme Judicial Court of Maine held that the school board had discretion to cancel the program as a safety measure, carefully noting that the school board had not simply excluded the lesbian speaker but had jettisoned the entire "Tolerance Day."[137]

More difficult First Amendment issues arise when "tolerance" of sexual minority issues are not relegated to an easily cancelled separate program, but are instead part of the school's curriculum. These situations are usually conceptualized as implicating the First Amendment rights of teachers rather than those of students.[138] For

---

[131] *See* Heather May, *School District to Review Veto of 2 Clubs*, SALT LAKE TRIB., April 28, 2000, at B5, *available at* 2000 WL 3760244 (reporting that the Salt Lake City superintendent would review at least two other club decisions).

[132] 495 A.2d 812 (Me. 1985).

[133] *See id.* at 815 (emphasizing the speaker's role as a group representative who would, in keeping with the purpose of "Tolerance Day," discuss with students the issue of tolerance as it extended to her particular minority). The school principal instructed the teacher that "he should not invite a homosexual to speak at Tolerance Day." *Id.*

[134] *See id.* at 815-16 (noting that callers threatened to picket the school, to "sabotag[e] . . . the school['s] furnace," and some parents considered keeping their children home from school that day or attending the symposium as chaperones).

[135] *Id.* at 816, 820 (citing the "'safety, order, and security'" of the school as justification for cancellation of "Tolerance Day").

[136] *Id.* at 815-16.

[137] *See id.* at 818 (clarifying that the school board may choose, even "where first amendment rights are *directly implicated*," to take actions that "restrict protected speech" for the purpose of maintaining order and stability in the classroom). Because the board acted to "suppress" all of the viewpoints that would have been presented, it could not have targeted any specific idea. *See id.* at 820.

[138] For a discussion of the First Amendment rights of public school teachers to "teach tolerance," see Theresa J. Bryant, *May We Teach Tolerance? Establishing the Parameters of Academic Freedom in Public Schools*, 60 U. PITT. L. REV. 579 (1999).

example, in *Boring v. Buncombe County Board of Education*,[139] the Fourth Circuit narrowly split in a lawsuit spawned by an advanced drama class teacher's selection of a play that featured both a lesbian and an unwed mother-to-be.[140] Despite the fact that the drama students won numerous awards for their production of the play, the teacher's attempt to comply with school board policies by obtaining parental permission slips,[141] the deletion of certain sections of the play at the state competition, and the teacher's performance evaluation after the play as "'superior,'"[142] the teacher was transferred from her assignment teaching advanced drama in high school to teaching introductory drama in middle school due to "'personal conflicts.'"[143] The teacher sued in state court alleging a violation of her First Amendment rights, and the defendant school officials removed the action to federal court.[144] The majority of the closely divided court decided that the drama production was a curricular decision in which a teacher possesses no First Amendment rights.[145] The court further held that even if a teacher does have a First Amendment right of expression, school officials have a "legitimate pedagogical interest" in restricting the teacher's speech.[146] The United States Supreme Court denied certiorari,[147]

---

[139] 136 F.3d 364 (4th Cir. 1998) (7-6 decision).

[140] *Id.* at 366.

[141] The student whose parent complained to school officials about the content of the play had viewed a scene of the play without his parents' authorization. Boring v. Buncombe County Bd. of Educ., 98 F.3d 1474, 1476 (4th Cir. 1996).

[142] *Id.*

[143] *Boring*, 136 F.3d at 366-67 (noting the principal attributed those personal conflicts to "'actions [Boring] initiated during the course of this school year'").

[144] *Boring*, 98 F.3d at 1476-77. Boring alleged that the school's transfer of her was done with "'malice toward [her]' over the ideas expressed in the play'" and as a result of such oppression, she suffered damages to her reputation that resulted in lost job opportunities. *Id.* at 1477.

[145] *Boring*, 136 F.3d at 369-70 (noting that the doctrine of academic freedom has never been recognized to give teachers control of the public school curricula). The court concluded that because Boring's dispute with the school was related to the employment relationship, it did not qualify to receive First Amendment protection. *Id.* at 369.

[146] *Id.* at 369-70. The "legitimate pedagogical interest" test is derived from *Hazelwood School District v. Kuhlmeier*, 484 U.S. 260, 273 (1988). For an excellent analysis of the various opinions in *Boring*, as well as the split between the analyses in *Hazelwood* and *Pickering v. Board of Education*, 391 U.S. 563 (1968), see Kara Lynn Grice, Note, *Striking an Unequal Balance: The Fourth Circuit Holds that Public School Teachers Do Not Have First Amendment Rights to Set Curricula in* Boring v. Buncombe County Board of Education, 77 N.C. L. REV. 1960 (1999). *See also* Recent Case, *Constitutional Law—First Amendment— Fourth Circuit Rules That a Teacher's Selection of School Curriculum Is Not Protected Speech.—*Boring v. Buncombe County Board of Education, *136 F.3d 364 (4th Cir.) (en banc),* cert. denied, *119 S. Ct. 47 (1998),* 112 HARV. L. REV. 982, 985-87 (1998) (critiquing the *Boring* decision as overly restrictive of speech).

[147] Boring v. Buncombe County Bd. of Educ., 525 U.S. 813 (1998).

and thus the precise scope of a public school teacher's First Amendment right to introduce sexual minority material into the curriculum remains uncertain.

However, more is at issue than the content of the curriculum alone. Although First Amendment jurisprudence disfavors viewpoint restrictions on expression, controversial subjects often engender attempts to mandate the expression of particular messages. For example, statutes in Arizona and Alabama both require that discussions about sexual education or sexually transmitted diseases include the view that "homosexuality" is unacceptable.[148] Such statutes arguably violate teachers' First Amendment rights. Moreover, students should have a First Amendment right not to be subjected to such viewpoints.[149] It seems contradictory to deem school officials responsible for peer violence against sexual minority students while permitting the schools to promulgate an official message of disapproval of sexual minority youth. Moreover, the ostracism of sexual minority adolescents has an adverse affect on students, regardless of their ultimate sexual choices.

IV. THE IMPORTANCE OF ADULTS IN THE LIVES OF OUR CHILDREN

The conservative rhetoric concerning children fails to consider "our" children: the children of sexual minority parents and the children who may become lesbian, gay, bisexual, or transgendered themselves. However, an even broader statement must be made: that conservative rhetoric and actions against sexual minority adults harms children. In this brief final section, I would like to shift the focus away from conservative adults, and towards what

---

[148] The Alabama statute requires that sex education include "[a]n emphasis, in a factual manner and from a public health perspective, that homosexuality is not a lifestyle acceptable to the general public and that homosexual conduct is a criminal offense under the laws of the state." ALA. CODE § 16-40A-2 (8) (1995). The Arizona statute is more prohibitive, stating that:
> no [school] district shall include in its course of study [about AIDS any] instruction which:
> 1. Promotes a homosexual life-style.
> 2. Portrays homosexuality as a positive alternative life-style.
> 3. Suggests that some methods of sex are safe methods of homosexual sex.

ARIZ. REV. STAT. ANN. § 15-7169(c) (2000).

[149] For an extended argument of a student's right to be free from certain viewpoints, see Nancy Tenney, Note, *The Constitutional Imperative of Reality in Public School Curricula: Untruths about Homosexuality as a Violation of the First Amendment*, 60 BROOK. L. REV. 1599, 1629-33 (1995), dividing a student's freedom of viewpoint into two categories; specifically, the right to not be compelled to embrace a certain belief and the right to receive accurate and useful knowledge.

liberal, progressive adults might do to disclaim the rhetoric and promote the reality of children and youth today.

Acts of discrimination, intolerance, and violence caused by sexual minority status, conduct, or beliefs harm children, even when those acts are not directed at them. In the context of schoolteachers, that connection is easily perceived. Although apparently not sexual minorities themselves,[150] high school teachers such as Mr. Solmitz, the social studies teacher from Maine and Ms. Boring, the drama teacher from North Carolina, asserted their own First Amendment rights to academic freedom in the context of educating young people about sexual minority issues.[151] Additionally, schoolteachers and other adults, who are visible sexual minorities, are role models for younger people.[152] Students will know if a schoolteacher is terminated for his or her sexuality, and that knowledge will influence them. Students will also be affected when their teachers are harassed for their sexual orientations or gender preferences.[153] This role model rationale applies with equal force to foster

---

[150] *See* Solmitz v. Me. Sch. Admin. Dist. No. 59, 495 A.2d 812, 815 (Me. 1985) (noting Mr. Solmitz planned Tolerance Day "in reaction to the tragic drowning of a Bangor homosexual by three Bangor high school students"); *Boring*, 136 F.3d at 366 (noting Ms. Boring chose the play because it "'powerfully depicts the dynamics within a dysfunctional, single-parent family'").

[151] *Solmitz*, 495 A.2d at 815; *Boring*, 136 F.3d at 366.

[152] The role model quality of schoolteachers is, in fact, a reason that conservatives often give when arguing that sexual minority teachers should be excluded from their profession. Consider the statement of Senator Ashcroft, a Republican senator from Missouri, in which he objected to the proposed Employment Nondiscrimination Act (ENDA), which would prohibit discrimination on the basis of sexuality:

in hiring schoolteachers, or camp counselors, or those who deal with young people, you never just hire a teacher. You are always hiring more than a teacher. You are hiring a role model. I cannot think of a single teacher in my past who was simply a teacher to me. Whether he or she liked it or not, that teacher was a role model.

142 CONG. REC. S9986, 9999-10,000 (daily ed. Sept. 6, 1996) (statement of Sen. Ashcroft). For an analysis of ENDA's potential effect on public school teachers and further discussion of the debates, see Anthony E. Varona, *Setting the Record Straight: The Effects of the Employment Non-Discrimination Act of 1997 on the First and Fourteenth Amendment Rights of Gay and Lesbian Public Schoolteachers*, 6 COMMLAW CONSPECTUS J. COMM. L. & POL'Y 25, 29 (1998), rejecting the suggestion "that gay and lesbian people are a bad influence on youth and thus should be excluded categorically from teaching positions" and emphasizing that this stance "belies the nature of homosexuality and the . . . longstanding presence of lesbian and gay teachers in the nation's schools.

[153] For example, in *Murray v. Oceanside Unified School District*, 95 Cal. Rptr. 2d 28 (Cal. Ct. App. 2000), the court considered the allegation by high school biology teacher Dawn Murray that she was subjected to "harassing and obscene graffiti" painted outside her classroom on several different occasions. *Id.* at 30-31. The court reversed and remanded the case back to the trial court to determine whether she stated a claim under the state labor code using the standards they set out. *Id.* at 44-45. However, the court declined to state whether a claim under state labor law was made out at that point of litigation, noting that Murray's complaint was sufficient under common law as it pertained to the intentional infliction of emotional distress allegation. *Id.* at 44.

parents,[154] social workers,[155] Boy Scouts,[156] coaches,[157] and all adults who interact daily with young people. For many sexual minority youths, the knowledge that sexual minority adults exist and survive can be life-saving,[158] but adults who form relationships with young people risk being branded as child molesters.

Discrimination against adult sexual minorities harms the children for which they care, whatever the sexual or gender identity

---

[154] *See* Polikoff, *supra* note 89, at 1184 (explaining that licensing gay foster parents by state agencies not only provides homes for gay teenagers, but, also, sends "a powerful message to those youth that it's okay to be gay").

[155] One of the few cases involving sexual minority discrimination against social workers is *Brass v. Hoberman*, 295 F. Supp. 358 (S.D.N.Y. 1968), in which two men instituted suit after they had both passed the caseworker exam. *Id.* at 359-60. The two were refused employment because the department maintained a policy of disqualifying "homosexuals" from caseworker positions, although both men denied being homosexuals. *See id.* at 360, 364 (noting that the two men maintained there was no evidence to prove they were presently homosexuals or had ever been in the past). The City of New York had recently repealed its blanket policy against hiring homosexuals in civil service jobs, but the city retained that policy for positions involving contact with children. *See id.* at 361 (noting the defendants "d[id] not contest the proposition that a blanket policy excluding homosexuals as a class from city employment would be arbitrary, capricious and hence unconstitutional"); *see also* Rhonda R. Rivera, *Our Strait-Laced Judges: The Legal Position of Homosexual Persons in the United States*, 50 HASTINGS L.J. 1015, 1044 n.152 (1998-99) (noting that the "New York Civil Service Commission has also been relatively progressive in recognizing the rights of homosexual employees"). The Rivera article also mentions that, in *Brass*, the city eventually entered into a settlement agreement in which it stated that its policy was not a blanket disqualification for homosexuals, and that the city would consider each case individually to determine whether the position fell within a disqualifying category, such as requiring contact with children or others who may "easily be influenced." *Id.*

[156] As Senator Nickles, a senator from Oklahoma, stated during congressional debate over ENDA, "I think if some organizations said they did not want to have openly gay or homosexual people as role models or mentors for young people—Boy Scouts come to mind ... then they should not have to hire them." 142 CONG. REC. S9986-9997 (daily ed. Sept. 6, 1996) (statement of Sen. Nickles). Then-Senator Ashcroft (who was recently appointed to the position of Attorney General) agreed, stating that boyhood and adolescence "are critical times when role models are very important. I think Senator Nickles was on target when he said that we have to be careful of who we have in the Boy Scouts. I commend the sponsors of this legislation for exempting the Boy Scouts." *Id.* at S10,000.

[157] *See, e.g.*, Holt v. Rapides Parish Sch. Bd., 685 So.2d 501, 504 (La. Ct. App. 1996) (reversing termination of a female basketball coach and teacher where charges of an improper relationship with a female student were not supported by substantial evidence); Weaver v. Nebo Sch. Dist., 29 F. Supp. 2d 1279, 1281 (D. Utah 1998) (holding that termination of a volleyball coach who replied "[y]es" when a student asked her if she was "gay" violated the coach's First Amendment rights).

[158] The historian John D'Emilio writes movingly of his research on homosexual activists Harry Hay, Chuck Rowland, and the Mattachine Society of the 1950s:

love .... barely touches the depth and variety of feeling that I have for them. I was three years old when they wrote the Mattachine initiation ceremony: "No boy or girl, approaching the maelstrom of deviation, need make that crossing alone, afraid, and in the dark ever again." They were talking about me.

JOHN D'EMILIO, *Dreams Deferred: The Birth and Betrayal of America's First Gay Liberation Movement, in* MAKING TROUBLE: ESSAYS ON GAY HISTORY, POLITICS, AND THE UNIVERSITY 17, 54-55 (1992).

of those children. This occurs not only in the child custody context, but also in less obvious areas, such as hate crimes and employment discrimination. Issues of violence and discrimination are usually theorized as affecting only the victim as an isolated individual, but many of these people are parents or caretakers of children. If a sexual minority is a victim of violence, for example, and is also a parent, that violence affects the child. Likewise, a sexual minority parent who loses a job because of discrimination has not suffered a purely individual loss; his or her children have been deprived of economic support.

Our attempts at legal reform for sexual minority adults thus affect our children. This includes both the children of sexual minority parents and the youth who are members of a sexual minority themselves. Therefore, it is imperative that our legal reforms not be narrowly directed at a select group of sexual minority members—what I have elsewhere called the whitest and brightest among us. Our children are neither predominantly white nor rich, they may be disabled, and they may not practice their sexualities as long-term, monogamous, and "traditional" in the ways our legal reform movements have often presented us. While there are some sexual minority members who have opined that "gay" politics and legal reforms should be limited to specific sexual minority issues, our children cannot afford such a constrained perspective. Instead, our legal reforms must flow from a broad conceptualization of justice, including economic and environmental justice, with attention to those who are marginalized in society. Perhaps, there is even a bit of self-interest in this: when children now are powerful adults, adults now who are still alive will be elderly and perhaps dependent. We can only hope that "our children" will afford us the justice we have fought for and earned.

[20]

Same-sex Marriage Revived: Feminist Critique and Legal Strategy

Rosemary AUCHMUTY

In June 2003 the UK government published proposals for a civil partnership registration scheme for same-sex couples that would confer almost all the legal rights and responsibilities of marriage. The paper discusses its provisions in the context of the debates on same-sex marriage over the past decade and argues that they hardly represent any advance on existing rights and that same-sex marriage will inevitably be won in the UK. The author herself is unenthusiastic about marriage, and concludes that lesbians and gay men should not let themselves be assimilated into a heterosexual model, but should draw attention to the potential for our relationships to act as better models for all relationships, inside or outside marriage.

Key Words: *civil partnerships, equality, family law, heterosexuality, homosexuality, lesbian feminism, rights*

In June 2003 the UK's Women and Equality Unit published its long-awaited paper on *Civil Partnership: A Framework for the Legal Recognition of Same-Sex Couples.*[1] It set out the government's proposals for a registration process that would confer on lesbian and gay partners a package of rights and responsibilities and provide a procedure for dissolution of the relationship. Prior to the publication of this document, two bills had already been before Parliament, Jane Griffiths MP's Relationships (Civil Registration) Bill (House of Commons, October 2001) and Lord Lester's Civil Partnership Bill (House of Lords, January 2002).[2] These both extended a range of spousal benefits to registered civil partners, including unmarried heterosexual partners. Lord Lester's bill was withdrawn after the second reading following assurances from the government that it was carrying out its own review. *Civil Partnership* is the result.

The government's proposals are considerably less radical than those of the earlier bills. A new legal status of 'registered partner' is to be created and references to 'spouses' across a range of legislation amended to include registered civil partners. In legal terms, civil partnership will *almost* amount to same-sex civil marriage in all but name. But name is important, and the government was at pains to deny any intention to introduce same-sex marriage. 'This consultation is about a civil partnership registration scheme,' it insisted (Women and Equality Unit, 2003: 13).

My article, however, is about same-sex marriage. The terms 'same-sex marriage', 'registered partnership', 'civil union' and 'commitment ceremony' are often used interchangeably, as though they all amount to the same thing. In one sense, of course, they *do*: they all represent recognition, in one form or another, of same-sex relationships. In this article, however, I wish to distinguish legal regimes for registered partnerships (known as civil unions in some countries) from the institution of marriage, and both from commitment ceremonies and religious blessings of same-sex relationships. Even though the expressed aim of the British government's proposals was to offer lesbian and gay couples a form of legal protection equivalent to marriage, it is clear to me that marriage is more than simply a set of legal rules. It has a symbolic significance that exists beyond, and sometimes in spite of, the legal and material reality. Marriage confers upon individuals the highest social status and approval. That is what makes the concept of registered partnerships or civil unions qualitatively different from marriage, even if, legally speaking, they guarantee the same rights.

It must be remembered, too, that registered partnerships/civil unions mean different things in different places. Some are closer to legal marriage than others. Some, for example, are open to heterosexual couples;[3] some allow adoption, others do not.[4] Even within one country there may be a range of different arrangements nationally and/or locally. In this paper, I shall be focusing on the UK, but even here there is room for confusion. A local partnership registration has been available since 2001 in a number of cities. This offers same-sex and heterosexual unmarried couples formal acknowledgment of their relationship, but confers no legal status, rights or responsibilities. It is quite separate from the new scheme and will not be transferable to it.

Different again, though often chosen to accompany the registration procedure, is the 'commitment ceremony' or religious blessing of the union. This public statement of a couple's private vows bears much the same relationship to a legal registered partnership as a wedding bears to legal marriage and is, indeed, often referred to as a 'wedding'. Such ceremonies are less common in the UK than they appear to be in the USA, presumably (and ironically in a country with an established church) because religion plays a much less important role in public life here. Nevertheless, it is said that the reason the British government stopped short of proposing same-sex marriage was because of pressure from the churches, which not unnaturally regard the institution as primarily a *religious* one.

Marriage therefore encompasses the public statement, the religious sacrament, the social status and the legal state. The registered partnership scheme outlined in the government's consultation paper concerns itself only with the first and last of these: the public acknowledgment of same-sex relationships as valid and socially valued, and the conferment of legal rights and responsibilities similar to those enjoyed by married people. Whether same-sex registered partners will enjoy the same *social* status as married couples is, to my mind, doubtful, and not just because of homophobia and heterosexism. Simply because they are different, registered partnerships are unlikely to be seen as truly 'equal' to marriage. This means that the pursuit of same-sex marriage will remain on the legal agenda even if and after the registered partnership proposals become law.

Such a goal has been immeasurably strengthened by the attainment of same-sex marriage in The Netherlands, Belgium and (since the government's paper was published) certain Canadian provinces. Indeed, I would go so far as to suggest that the question is no longer whether same-sex marriage is a possible or desirable goal for lesbians and gays in the UK, but *when* and *how* it will arrive here. To my complete surprise, for this is not the article I meant to write, I have come to the conclusion that same-sex marriage is inevitable. The question for lesbians and gays, therefore, is not whether we want this (it is too late for that), but how far we can influence the process, what we intend to do with the product, and how far we can predict and prepare for the consequences.

The article begins with an outline of the debates on same-sex marriage since the British lesbian and gay legal lobby, Stonewall, first addressed the issue in the mid-1990s. I then examine the legal implications of marriage in England and Wales and compare these with the existing rights available to gay and lesbian couples and those proposed in the UK government's civil registration scheme. My view is that enormous misconceptions exist among the general public (and that includes educated lesbians and gay men) as to the legal rights conferred by marriage. Hand in hand with these misconceptions goes a surprising degree of ignorance as to the rights already available to same-sex couples with respect to matters such as property division and inheritance, as well as the *disadvantages* of the legally married state with respect to, for example, access to state benefits and the potential financial impact of divorce.

The article goes on to consider the reasons why, in spite of the civil registration proposals, same-sex marriage remains a goal and, indeed, an inevitability. It concludes with a discussion of how lesbians and gays might influence the institution of marriage, whether or not they themselves choose to marry.

BACKGROUND

I come to the subject of same-sex marriage with a particular set of personal and ideological baggage which should be declared at the outset. *I am opposed to marriage.* My views were formed, not by my observation of my parents' marriage, which was happy, nor by any personal experience of the institution, but by the ideas of second-wave feminism which was just emerging when I was an undergraduate in Australia in the early 1970s. I well remember the impact of my first reading of Germaine Greer's *Female Eunuch* and the subsequent radical and socialist feminist critiques of marriage. I chose to write my (history) PhD on the subject of 'Victorian Spinsters'. After immersing myself for three years in the conditions of 19th-century marriage, and inspired by the courageous efforts of unmarried women to transcend the stigma attached to their single state and live often more fulfilled lives than most wives of the era (many were involved directly or indirectly in first-wave feminism), I vowed that I could never marry. The legal situation of married women in the late 20th century was obviously quite different from that of married women a century before, but some things had not changed. Marriage, it seemed to me, demanded a surrender of individual personality that I was not prepared to make.

I was heterosexual in those days. I have not changed my view of the institution since coming to Britain and becoming a lesbian, even after 15 years in a relationship in my mind as 'committed' as a marriage.

The other major factor that has influenced me against marriage has been my legal training and current teaching and research in the field of law. Knowledge of the law and its workings has clarified for me the nature and extent of the legal 'privileges' attaching to marriage, as well as the availability to those who want to make their own arrangements of equal or possibly better protections in some areas. It has also made me suspicious of allowing the legal system too much say in my life. I am frequently astonished at how the very feminists who warn of the dangers of increased legal regulation of pornography or prostitution will yet willingly embrace the legal regulation of marriage.

This article is thus in part a personal exploration. When Stonewall ran a debate on same-sex marriage in the pages of its newsletter in March 1996, I found myself in sympathy with the approach of lesbian solicitor Gill Butler, who declared: 'Call me old fashioned, but I find it very difficult to summon up any enthusiasm for the idea of lesbian and gay marriage' (Butler, 1996: 9). Butler recognized the importance for lesbians and gays of obtaining formal equality with heterosexuals but felt that marriage, well recognized as a site of women's oppression, was hardly the arena in which to pursue it. She drew a parallel with the then current campaign to remove the ban on homosexuals in the military: 'I support the right of lesbians and gays to join the armed forces but this does not stop me believing that armies are repressive institutions and the sooner they are abolished the better.' She left unsaid the implicit sequitur that marriage, too, is oppressive and the sooner *it* is abolished, the better.

Butler herself supported the idea of a partnership law, which lacked the oppressive history of marriage and could be used by both same-sex and heterosexual couples for the recognition and legal protection of their relationships (Butler, 1996: 9). So too did Peter Tatchell, speaking in a 'People's Parliament' debate aired on British television on 5 October 1996. Ironically, in that programme the majority of the studio audience came out in favour of the idea of same-sex marriage, though some concern was expressed at the dangers of allowing gays to adopt children. In a double irony, lesbian and gay couples now have that right under the Adoption and Children Act 2002, while still being denied the right to marry.

There was a contradiction in Butler's approach that I found difficult to resolve. The contradiction lies in the fact that, as long as heterosexuals are permitted to marry and gays and lesbians are not, gays and lesbians cannot be said to enjoy equal rights with heterosexuals. If marriage is regarded as a desirable and privileged institution, as it appears to be in our society, then exclusion from it constitutes a significant penalty. A civil partnership may be a 'better' device, objectively speaking, but it will always be seen as second-best if marriage is unattainable.

The problem for feminists like myself is that marriage is such an unattractive goal. Despite significant legal and social changes to the institution over the past 200 years, the radical critiques of marriage have remained remarkably consistent in their portrayal of the effects of its socially approved unequal dynamics of power on men and women. Marriage has been shown to endow men with a better lifestyle, greater freedom and more power, while it has the opposite effect on women, limiting, impoverishing, and rendering them vulnerable to abuses of power by their husbands (Bernard, 1973). From Mary Wollstonecraft in 1792 (1929[1792]), who refused to marry because she would have had to surrender to her husband all her rights to her money, her children and her body, to Germaine Greer's exposure of 'The Middle-Class Myth of Love and Marriage' in *The Female Eunuch* (1970); from John Stuart Mill in the mid-19th-century (Mill, 1869), who publicly renounced his rights as a husband when he married Harriet Taylor, to Lee Comer's bitter revelations in *Wedlocked Women* (1974); from Mona Caird's edited collection of a 10,000-strong correspondence to *The Times* on 'The Morality of Marriage' (Caird, 1897) at the end of the 19th century, to the second-wave feminists' analyses of the gendered exploitation and abuse of late 20th-century marriage (Wandor, 1974): 200 years of feminist agreement that marriage permits, even encourages, oppression makes the institution untouchable and irredeemable in the eyes of many women, including myself. For many feminists today, revulsion against it is so engrained it feels instinctive. Others who have chosen to marry do so with an awareness that the gesture is in part a compromise and that they will have to struggle against a set of normative assumptions they themselves reject.

Gay men may argue that, as men, these dynamics do not affect (or actually *benefit*) them. They rarely do argue this: they just ignore the ignoble history of marriage, as men routinely ignore women's oppression. Lesbians may (and do) argue, on the other hand, that the heterosexual dynamics of marriage are irrelevant to *same*-sex marriage. The gendered power difference is absent from the more egalitarian lesbian and gay relationship. My view, however, is that marriage *means* something different to lesbians and gays who favour same-sex marriage from what it means to those opposed to it. For advocates, marriage represents an accepted and, indeed, privileged status. This makes it desirable whatever its terms or associations. Across the last two centuries, the superior social status of marriage has rendered acceptable to many aspirants the actual undesirability of its conditions. How else, for example, could women who had experienced the freedom of war-time work be persuaded to exchange their independence, purpose and the companionship of workmates for the dependence and isolation of post-war marriage? Women rushed to marry in the late 1940s and 1950s not just because they 'fell in love' but because society ascribed to the single state a distinctly second-class status and represented marriage as a prize in a competition in which wives were the winners and the losers those who 'missed out'. No matter that you often gave up more than you 'won'. What mattered was that you had gained acceptance by entering the noble company of married women, from which the poor spinster was excluded.

Linked to this rationale was another, more principled, one. 'I don't think couples should have privileges single people don't have,' admitted a gay man interviewed by Suzanne Sherman in her *Lesbian and Gay Marriage*. ' . . . But as long as there is this institution of marriage and heterosexuals are getting that privilege, then gay people should be able to do it too' (Sherman, 1992: 57). If the thought of marriage sticks in our throats, the fact that lesbians and gays are prevented by law from doing what heterosexuals can do almost without even thinking about it prompts equally strong feelings. Gill Butler conceded the contradiction: 'As a matter of legal equality of course lesbians and gay men should have the right to marry if they choose to do so' (Butler, 1996: 9). Since she despised marriage, however, she did not confront the pain of exclusion.

I think this is probably true for most lesbian feminists. Certainly I am rarely troubled by my exclusion from marriage. But every so often, when a friend or relative 'chooses' to get married, I am forced to think about it, and then – I have to admit – *I get angry*. Ruth Colker has explained how it felt to her as a lesbian:

> I really hated the institution of marriage. I would refuse to go to weddings of my straight friends, because I felt that their marriages contributed to my own subordination . . . I was quite baffled as to why so many of my straight friends got married when they knew that marriage was an exclusive private club that didn't want me as a member. (Colker, 1991: 322–3)

But then Colker got involved with a man and (for a perfectly reasonable practical reason) got married. If and when same-sex marriage becomes available in this country, I wonder how many lesbian-feminists will (for perfectly reasonable practical reasons) avail themselves of the opportunity?

FEMINISM AND THE SAME-SEX MARRIAGE DEBATE

Arguments in favour of same-sex marriage can be divided into two categories: the practical (mainly legal and financial) and the symbolic. The practical arguments emphasize the benefits, less so the obligations, enjoyed by married couples, from which lesbian and gay couples are unfairly excluded. These are often linked to notions of *equality* and *justice*, as in the observations of gay solicitor, Mark Harper, representing the pro-marriage view in the Stonewall debate:

> The right to marry, for me, is about the right to equality before law. As a solicitor specializing in family law, it is clear to me that marriage of some sort would wipe out the injustice faced by many lesbians and gay men on the death of a partner or breakdown of the relationship. It would also be a gateway to a whole host of legal rights, whether housing or immigration. (Harper, 1996: 9)

Advocates of same-sex marriage pointed out the contingent nature of justice for lesbian and gay households, who might be treated as 'family' for some purposes but not for others. Legal academic Stephen Whittle, a leader in the transgender movement in Britain, wrote:

> Marriage in the 1990s is no longer inextricably linked to the right to procreate and bear children. Same sex and transsexual marriages are increasingly being placed on the political agenda, as we see an expanding diversity in the ways in which families are formed. It would seem illogical to recognise same-sex couples as constituting a family for some purposes, such as parental rights and obligations, whilst failing to recognise their relationship as a marriage. Denying same-sex couples the right to marry is a denial of the fundamental right to enjoy the numerous benefits and privileges that marriage brings. (Whittle, 1996: 358)

The assumption that marriage is the sole measure of commitment in a relationship, evident in statements like an Immigration Minister's 'The only objective test for the strength of a relationship in an immigration context is marriage' (Stonewall, May 1996: 4), plainly discriminates against lesbian and gay couples. Comments of this sort feed into public perceptions of same-sex relationships as uncommitted and, until challenged, place the claims of gay and lesbian partners beyond consideration. Stonewall did challenge them, causing the immigration rules to be altered in 2000 to permit same-sex partners to enter the country under the same test as that applied to unmarried heterosexual couples.

The immigration example illustrates how the practical claims of the same-sex marriage campaigners can often be met by relatively minor changes in individual legal provisions – in the application of rules, as here, or by the extension of legal principles in court judgments (as with succession by same-sex partners to residential tenancies) or by Parliament (as with adoption rights).[5] They could also be met by a registered partnership scheme of the kind proposed by the government. But with the *symbolic* arguments for same-sex marriage we are in rather different territory. In this area the US led the way, largely because its written constitution facilitated a rights-based legal reasoning historically alien to England and Wales. But once the UK incorporated the European Convention on Human Rights into domestic law in the Human Rights Act 1998, which came into force in October 2000, the rights culture flourished here too, transforming the legal terrain. Stonewall's agenda is testimony to this, and the government's registered partnership proposals but one product of the new climate.

In the USA, gay men dominate the same-sex marriage debate (Mohr, 1994 and 1997; Sullivan, 1995 and 1997; Strasser, 1997; Eskridge, 1999 and 2002). In general, their stance is liberal; they argue on an equal rights basis; they emphasize the similarities between heterosexual marriage and lesbian and gay relationships (as in the title of Andrew Sullivan's book, *Virtually Normal* [1995]); and they have no real problems with the institution of marriage, save that it excludes them.

Lesbian pro-marriage commentators tend to focus more on the personal benefits than the public ones. Suzanne Sherman's *Lesbian and Gay Marriage* (1992) is a collection of interviews underpinned by insights into the meaning and actual dynamics of lesbian and gay relationships. In many ways these real-life testimonies contradict the argument that same-sex relationships are just like marriages, not least in the more considered approach of most gays and lesbians to the legal and financial arrangements of their relationships and their greater commitment to an egalitarian balance of power. Some of Sherman's interviewees emphasized marriage as a means of making public what society had forcibly confined to the private sphere: knowledge of how we live. 'I think that by marrying, gays and lesbians help establish what our community is about', 'Juan' told Sherman. 'It shows that we have those kinds of relationships and we like to celebrate them, too' (p. 67). A lesbian ('Robin') took the critique further, mindful of the usual absence of any acknowledgment of the specifically lesbian experience in public perceptions of homosexuality. 'Lesbians are pretty much invisible', she declared. 'Women's sexuality is invisible. To recognize us through legalized marriage would shake a lot of people in the heterosexual world up' (p. 83).

Social acceptance and status were perceived as bringing psychological benefits. On the one hand, there is the public reinforcement of the private commitment through both the 'wedding' or commitment ceremony and the daily acknowledgment of the union. Opponents of same-sex marriage may and do argue that feelings expressed and acted out in private are no less binding and sincere than those proclaimed in public, but clearly for many couples the public avowal of their feelings is important. On the other hand, there is the public support for the couple at difficult times in the relationship. 'Marriage gives a certain stability to the relationship', explained 'Juan'. ' . . . Publicly committing yourself means that you don't go back in the closet' (p. 68). 'Legalized marriage would also lend some social support for same-sex relationships to stay together', added 'John'. 'That support is almost non-existent now' (p. 64).

Most of the edited volumes on same-sex marriage (and there are quite a few) are collections of published articles 'for and against' the idea. These are almost all edited by men. Though purporting to give equal attention to both sides of the argument, they are invariably biased towards the 'for' camp. They give a measure of attention to religious and conservative opposition to same-sex marriage. They give very little to the *feminist* critique, which is represented in almost every case by one short article, as if to emphasize the marginality of the position. That the editors have put very little effort into the search for lesbian-feminist viewpoints on same-sex marriage is evidenced by the fact that very often the *same* article is called upon to do service: Paula Ettelbrick's 'Since When Is Marriage a Path to Liberation?' of 1989 (see, for example, Baird and Rosenblum, 1997; Sullivan, 1997).

Ettelbrick's article fairly captured the horror and disbelief so many of us felt that anyone should consider marriage an institution worth saving, let alone joining, as well as our alarm at the potential closing off of lesbian-feminist and radical gay alternatives. She pointed out that those who stood to gain most from joining the institution were those who had jobs offering spousal health benefits and property and incomes where tax liability made a difference – that is, middle-class white men. The idea of emphasizing our likeness to heterosexuals by claim-ing the right to marry was abhorrent to Ettelbrick: 'It rips away the very heart and soul of what I believe it is to be a lesbian in this world. *It robs me of the opportunity to make a difference*' (Ettelbrick, 1989:166, my emphasis).

Yet some lesbian voices *have* been raised in support of same-sex marriage, and feminist rationales found for doing so. Barbara J. Cox sought to counter Ettelbrick's last point by claiming that her decision to have a commitment ceremony with her partner *did* make a difference:

> The impact was so wide-ranging, not just on my partner and myself, but on our families, our friends, and even the clerks in the jewelry stores when we explained we were looking for wedding rings for both of us. Or on the two hundred people who received my mother's annual xeroxed Christmas letter with a paragraph describing the ceremony . . . (Cox, 1997: 29)

Cox also repudiated the idea that by 'marrying' she and her partner were allow-ing themselves to be assimilated into a patriarchal institution. 'How can anyone view these small victories in coming out and acceptance as part of flocking to imitate, or worse join, an oppressive heterosexual institution?' she demanded. '. . . What is more anti-patriarchal and rejecting of an institution that carries the patriarchal power imbalance into most households than clearly stating that women can commit to one another with no man in sight?' (p. 29).

New York law professor Nan Hunter argued that lesbian and gay marriages had the potential 'to disrupt both the gendered definition of marriage and the assumption that marriage is a form of socially, if not legally, prescribed hier-archy' (Hunter, 1994: 112). Heterosexual marriage purported to be a union of equals but, however 'equal' husbands and wives were in the eyes of the law, they were far from being so politically, socially or economically. Same-sex marriage would make possible a conception of marriage as a *genuine* relationship between equals. This, Hunter argued, must have a knock-on effect on heterosexual married couples, with consequent benefits for women in particular:

> Legalizing lesbian and gay marriage is often thought of as the next frontier for gay rights law. It could also be the next frontier in democratizing marriage. I do not claim that gay marriage alone would necessarily reshape marriage law, out

of the context of other feminist reforms. *But it is difficult to imagine any other change in the law of marriage that feminists could achieve today that would have even remotely as significant an effect.* (p. 114, my emphasis)

Such an approach has been rejected by another New York law professor, Ruthann Robson, who argues that we must resist 'domestication'. For Robson, social and legal justice for lesbians and gays involves recognition of what is different, not what is *similar* to heterosexuality, about our relationships and lifestyles. This goal would be better served, not by marriage, but by *the abolition of marriage.* If such a goal seems breathtakingly radical, Robson points out how easily, legally speaking, it could be achieved. A single legislative act or a judicial decision that marriage was unconstitutional or in contravention of the rights of a named group (for example, homosexuals) would suffice (Robson, 1998: 149–50). Politically speaking, though, the idea seems unimaginable in a country that passed the Defense of Marriage Act in1996.

Robson's suspicion of incorporation is shared by many lesbian feminist legal academics inside and outside the USA. Didi Herman, for example, notes that 'the extension of existing liberal categories to "new identities" [as in same-sex marriage] not only "recognises", but regulates, contains, and constitutes them' (Herman, 1993: 250). We run the risk of losing the distinctive identities that lesbians and gays have been able to evolve out of pejorative discourses and exclusionary treatment, such as affirmative cultures, egalitarian practices and supportive community structures.

More recently, Cheshire Calhoun has argued that same-sex marriage is central to lesbian and gay liberation as the best means of overcoming their exclusion from both the public sphere and the protected private sphere (Calhoun, 2000: 15). In the public sphere, she explains, the assumption that everyone is heterosexual unless proved otherwise means that lesbians and gays are forced to present themselves as heterosexual or risk opprobrium for drawing attention to their sexuality. The fact that heterosexuals can remain happily unaware of a lesbian or gay presence renders overtly discriminatory practices unnecessary (p. 77). In the private sphere, society reduces homosexuality to mere sex, thereby excluding any conception of marriage, parenting or family life. People can and do believe that children brought up in same-sex households will not learn appropriate gender roles, or that lesbian and gay relationships are inherently unstable, because, thanks to our exclusion from the public sphere, we have not been able to tell the world what it is really like to be a lesbian or gay man. 'The culturally authorized conception has instead emerged largely from within medical, psychiatric, and scientific work' (p. 20):

> One particularly striking feature of psychoanalytic constructions of homosexuality was the insistence that, because of their multiple psychological defects, neither homosexuals nor lesbians were emotionally competent to experience genuine romantic love or sustain stable intimate relationships (p. 146).

The stumbling-block for same-sex marriage is not, therefore, our choice of same-sex partner but the fact that we are *the kinds of people* who are not fit for marriage.

Calhoun understands that many lesbians and gays have no wish to join an institution they see as oppressive and limiting. Nevertheless it is a challenge we must accept. 'What is at stake is not the right to participate in a traditional form of family life', she concludes, 'but the right to *define* what counts as a family' (p. 132). Accepting the challenge as, perhaps, an inevitability, other lesbian-feminists continue to warn of the dangers ahead. Unless our efforts to have our relationships recognized 'are accompanied by trenchant criticisms of the limits of such recognition in delivering a redistribution of economic well-being', Canadian Susan Boyd points out, 'they will remain incomplete as political strategies, while they may simultaneously be the only *legal* strategies available' (Boyd, 1999: 381). The shortcomings of legal remedies for heterosexual women in marriage are already apparent. Lesbians and gays should not, therefore, expect too much from legal reform. As one of Sherman's male interviewees observed:

> Passing the domestic-partners bill in San Francisco didn't stop this city from being the main capital of hate crimes in the nation in 1990. What it does in some ways is create a complacent atmosphere where gay people may feel everything's better here. (Sherman, 1992: 56–7)

Perhaps lesbians and gays will only fully realize the limitations of marriage, like wives, *after* they get married – and then it may be too late.

In the UK, as in the USA, those principally interested in same-sex marriage have been gay men. This is certainly true of the academic debate (for example, Wintermute and Andenaes, 2001). Feminist writing in support of same-sex marriage has been conspicuous by its absence. Two factors present themselves as explanations for the general lack of concern: the particular legal regime that governs marriage here (I can only speak for England and Wales; Scotland and Northern Ireland have their own legal systems), and the ambiguous (and I would argue declining) status of marriage.

THE LEGAL IMPLICATIONS OF MARRIAGE

Recent research into the reasons why heterosexual couples choose to marry reveals that, apart from the small proportion who do so to acquire a specific legal benefit (to bring themselves within the immigration rules of their partner's country, for instance), most people see marriage as a statement about love, commitment and the permanence of the relationship. The legal details are secondary and, indeed, often unknown. Researchers from the Centre for the Study of the Family, Law and Social Policy at Staffordshire University, UK, found that, of 172 respondents, only *one* (a woman) said she was marrying for legal reasons; the most popular explanations were 'love' (30 percent) and 'commitment' (13 percent). Only 17 percent of those marrying for the first time even considered the legal implications (Hibbs et al., 2001: 200, 205).

What is clear is that the emotional importance of marriage renders the legal aspects incidental to a more fundamental impulse which may be so strong as to make marriage inevitable, whatever the conditions. For such people, the benefits of marriage (for example, tax or pension breaks) are largely taken for granted and sometimes exaggerated (for example the common belief that a wife automatically receives a half-share in the matrimonial property). Indeed, Hibbs and her colleagues found a marked resistance among couples preparing to marry to giving any thought at all to the legal issues: 'we don't want legal advice', declared one, ' – we trust each other' (p. 205).

There is certainly an assumption that the legal regime for marriage will be favourable. After all, governments up to the present have never lost an opportunity to reinforce its primacy, especially as a site for raising children. Section 1 of the Family Law Act 1996, for example, makes support for marriage a primary goal of the courts. So one would naturally assume adequate legal protection and, indeed, preferential treatment in most areas of law. Running in curious parallel to this view, however, is the oft-held assumption that marriage makes *no* legal difference – that it is simply a public statement, and lies outside the legal realm altogether. Hibbs and her colleagues found that 41 percent of their interviewees genuinely believed that marriage would not change the legal nature of their relationship with their partner (Hibbs et al., 2001: 201).

The truth is that most people have only the vaguest idea of the legal implications of marriage. There are several reasons for this. First, practical legal information of this sort forms no part of our educational curriculum. There is no practical reason why teenagers could not be taught aspects of family law and other useful subjects like housing law and consumer law at school, but I suspect the omission is not accidental. A failure to dispel misconceptions about the law is an efficient mechanism for social control, and history shows that women, in particular, have frequently entered into marriage in total ignorance of legal effects more far-reaching than those attaching to the institution today.[6] Second, where in the 19th century the rights and obligations of marriage were set out in weighty tomes devoted solely to that subject, today marriage occupies only a section of a legal training in family law, a subject which is not even compulsory on a law degree in England and Wales. Thus, even legal professionals may not know much about marriage, legally speaking, particularly about the *practical* application of the rules about marriage. These are not confined to family law but straddle a range of legal specialisms such as tax law, property law, housing law and immigration law. Trying to keep on top of all the provisions in these areas is a difficult task, especially as they are changing so rapidly. Third, many people still believe there is a status called 'common law marriage' which, after a certain period of cohabitation, confers on an unmarried heterosexual couple the rights (or some of them) of marriage (Hibbs et al., 2001: 202). But common law marriage is not recognized in England and Wales (Dyer, 2002).

However, much of Family Law these days *is* concerned with the intimate relationships of people outside marriage – for example, the relation of parents' new or former partners to their children and remedies against domestic violence by cohabitants. The law's recognition of increased unmarried cohabitation over the past 30 years has resulted in the gradual extension of rights formerly held only by married people to heterosexual cohabitees and then, sometimes, to lesbian and gay cohabitees. These changes may emanate from legislation but quite often, these days, from the courts. For instance, in the landmark case of *Barclay's Bank v. O'Brien* [1993] 4 All ER 417, the House of Lords extended the court's equitable protection against undue influence in mortgage transactions from married couples to unmarried couples, both heterosexual and homosexual. Even then, distinctions remain in the *application* of the rules to the different groups. People's confusion over the legal effect of marriage is therefore not surprising.

The government and the courts continue to avow the primacy of the institution yet, in marked contrast to 20 years ago, strive not to penalize or even criticize those who remain outside it. What is clear today is that the differences between the way the law treats married couples and the way it treats unmarried couples, either heterosexual or same-sex, are less than they used to be; they are uneven in practical application (for instance, some pension schemes provide 'spousal' survivor rights to unmarried heterosexual and even homosexual partners), and appear to be diminishing. But some important marital privileges remain which, paradoxically, the campaigns for same-sex marriage and registered partnerships have probably done more to publicize than any deliberate policy of education.

The government's proposals on registered partnerships offer a partial survey of the legal areas where marriage makes a difference. The imposition of a formal legal procedure for the dissolution of the relationship is probably the most important one, though the least publicized among lesbians and gays. Apart from this, the government has recommended that same-sex partners be treated as 'spouses' for the purposes of immigration, elections, testifying in court against a partner, making financial decisions on behalf of adults with mental incapacity, visiting a partner in prison and protection from domestic violence. It further proposes to amend the adoption rules to 'take account of the new status of registered civil partnership' (Women and Equality Unit, 2003: 37) and to allow registered partners to apply to the court to gain parental responsibility for their partner's child/ren in the same way as step-parents. For the purposes of income-related benefits, registered partners would under the proposals be treated as a single family unit, and partners will be liable to maintain each other as spouses currently are. State pensions would also come into line with those of married couples. Registered partners would be assumed to have an unlimited insurable interest in each other's lives.

Another set of provisions relates to the death of a partner. For most people, this is the most emotive part of the package; we have all read the dreadful stories in the press and on Stonewall's website about gays and lesbians left impoverished or homeless or excluded from their partner's deathbed or funeral, and it all plays into our own fears for ourselves. Under the proposed changes to the law, registered partners will be able to register a death and be treated as 'properly interested persons' at an inquest. They will be eligible for bereavement benefits, survivor pensions, injury benefits, fatal accidents compensation and criminal injuries compensation. They will be able to inherit under the intestacy rules in the same way as spouses and to challenge a will as if they were spouses. They will have an automatic right to tenancy succession on the death of a partner.

A number of observations can be made about this (at first sight impressive) list. First, there are some conspicuous gaps. I cannot see any reference to the spousal exemption from inheritance tax. Transfers between non-spouses attract a tax of 40 percent on property over the nil-rate band currently set at £250,000. That means that if a lesbian or gay couple's jointly owned property were worth more than £500,000, not an unusual situation in the increasingly wealthy gay community today, then on the death of one partner the other would be liable to tax on the surplus, which may oblige him or her to sell the family home. I find it hard to get too upset about this omission from the government's plans, since lesbians and gay men in this position must obviously be comfortably off, but anecdotal evidence suggests that it would be an important factor for same-sex couples of my class and generation in deciding whether or not to register their partnership.[7]

My second and more significant observation is that a number of the rights offered by the government are already enjoyed by lesbian and gay couples, independent of registration – for example, the right to tenancy succession and the ability to be considered as joint adopters of children. It is highly unlikely that the government intends to *withdraw* these concessions from lesbian and gay couples who do not register their relationship, since they are also available to unmarried heterosexual couples who cannot register theirs. Moreover, some of the rights proposed by the government are also intended to apply 'to all partners, whether married, registered or neither' (Women and Equality Unit, 2003: 34) – for instance, the right to make financial decisions on behalf of adults with mental incapacity. Others could as easily be extended piecemeal to lesbian and gay couples without any need for registration.

On the issue of 'next-of-kin' status and hospital visiting or consenting to medical treatment the government has little useful to offer. 'Next-of-kin' has no legal significance in England and Wales: anyone can be nominated to that role. As the paper points out, there is no law governing who can visit a person in hospital and no one has the right to consent to medical treatment on behalf of another adult. The problem is not a legal but a social one: ignorance and sometimes homophobia on the part of hospital staff leading to the exclusion of partners from patient care. 'The Government believes that the creation of the status of "registered partner" will help to bring about a culture change and to remove the difficulties currently faced by same-sex couples when one partner becomes ill', the paper asserts hopefully (p. 39).

Finally, in the areas of access to state benefits and dissolution of the relationship there is potential in the government's proposals for individual gays and lesbians to fare worse than at present. A married couple's state pension is less than two single people's aggregated, and same-sex partners will now be financially responsible for their partners. The dissolution procedures, which are similar to divorce (except that adultery is not a ground), do offer a safeguard for estranged same-sex partners who have not protected themselves financially. But for those who *have* made clear arrangements, the dissolution procedure could result in a nasty shock for the person ordered by a court to hand over some of their assets to an estranged partner.

It has always been perfectly possible (and desirable) for home owners in any sort of relationship to make formal arrangements to own their property in equal or any other shares, and thus to acquire it automatically on the death of one, either by right of survivorship (if they have elected to be joint tenants) or by will. The advantage of organizing your own legal affairs concerning property and *not* marrying (or registering your partnership) is that no one is likely to interfere with the arrangements you have made, whereas a divorce court has an unlimited discretion to redistribute property as it thinks fit. For me, this is a powerful argument against partnership registration.

Set against these potential losses, of course, is the certainty of succeeding to a partner's pension benefits (assuming s/he has any) under the new proposals. But is this always justified? The principle behind survivor benefits was always to look after dependent wives who had given up the possibility of an adequate pension of their own to run a home and raise a family. How many lesbian and gay partners are in this position today? For my part, I would rather abolish survivor pensions and make sure that every individual has his or her own pension arrangements.

The official response of the legal lobby Stonewall to the government's *Civil Partnership* paper has been positive and largely uncritical. But comments from members posted on the Stonewall website have been more robust. 'It is a step in the right direction . . . but is it a step far enough?' demanded Adam Bartram in September 2003. He, and others, wanted nothing short of marriage. Yet other contributors to the debate were equally clear they did not want this. 'I will be pleased to sidestep marriage,' wrote Richard Coates. 'I'm content to celebrate my difference'. Their comments illustrate the diversity of attitudes to marriage within the lesbian and gay community.

THE AMBIGUOUS STATUS OF MARRIAGE

Marriage has an ambiguous status in the UK. In principle it is privileged. In practice it is increasingly irrelevant. Out of this paradoxical dichotomy (the fact that it matters so much, yet so little) I draw the perhaps startling conclusion that the right to same-sex marriage must eventually be won.

In a society where a benefit is relatively inconsequential, it matters little if it is extended to a previously excluded group. The truth is that most British people could not care less whether gays and lesbians have the right to marry or not. They would certainly not object to any such extension. For them, marriage has been stripped of so much of its religious, legal or social status as to be immaterial – a mere lifestyle choice. Marriage in the UK is emphatically not as it has been described in the USA, 'the one institution that touches on everything that Americans really care about' (Alan Wolfe, quoted by Gary Younge in *The Guardian*, 27 August 2003) – quite the contrary.

What is my evidence for its relative unimportance? 'Marriage is now so unfashionable that the number of people getting wed has fallen to its lowest since 1897,' ran an article in *The Guardian* on 21 March 2003 (Carter, 2003). Only 250,000 marriages took place in England and Wales in 2001, the lowest number for more than a century. The past 30 years in particular have seen a rapid decrease (40 percent) in the national rate. By 2005, it is predicted, fewer than half the country's adults will be married (Law Commission, 2002: 5). The government's *Civil Partnership* paper assumes 33 percent (Women and Equality Unit, 2003: 76). Cohabitation has become so common as to seem completely normal, and two out of every five children are born out of wedlock.

Yet despite the fact that marriage appears to be in terminal decline – or perhaps because of this – successive governments right up to the present have openly promoted it. In a recent discussion paper on unmarried home-sharers, the Law Commission declared:

> We accept that there is a very strong case for singling marriage out as a status deserving of special treatment. Not only does the government consider that marriage provides the surest foundation for the raising of children, Parliament has itself recognized that the institution of marriage is deserving of protection and respect by the courts (FLA 1996 s1[a]). The European Court of Human Rights also accords to marriage special privileges. (Law Commission, 2002: 83–4)

Yet there is something half-hearted about the Law Commission's remarks about the importance of marriage. By starting with the qualifying 'We accept that . . . ', the statement lacks the authority of a simple assertion that marriage *is* a status deserving of special treatment. There is only 'a very strong case', not an open-and-shut one.

Perhaps this lack of conviction is inevitable in a document whose goal is, after all, the consideration of legal provisions for *unmarried* home-sharers. But it mirrors a very clear movement in the law towards the recognition of the needs, now designated as *rights,* of people in other relationships besides the married one. This does not quite amount to a de-privileging of marriage. But in increasing areas of the law (for instance, domestic violence and parental rights), the law offers protection to unmarried couples very similar to that given to married couples. In family law, the issues attracting attention at the moment are those arising from the needs of individuals, especially children, in family arrangements of increasing complexity and informality. Children today may grow up with one parental figure or half a dozen, as parents split up, form new relationships, and split up again, in a process which produces a multiplicity of step-parents, step-grandparents, and more distantly linked or even unlinked carers. Breaking the connexion between biological and social parenting has resulted in the possibility of a range of legally enforceable relationships, a process in which lesbian and gay parents have played an important part. Where illegitimacy was once a stigma and divorce shameful, now the nuclear family is but one of a number of perfectly normal family forms.

In this context, then, the lack of a strong movement for same-sex marriage here is readily explicable. Why should anyone wish to join an institution of so little relevance to our lives?

On the other hand, some people *do* have strong feelings about it. Conservative and religious voices are often raised in defence of marriage in the British press. The owners of these voices are usually opposed to the idea of same-sex marriage. But there is a powerful conservative argument for extending the right to marry to gays and lesbians. History shows that when ideologically significant institutions find themselves under threat, the solution that often presents itself is to strengthen them by opening their ranks to new blood. Clearly, the extension of the franchise to propertied men stabilized government in nervous nations at risk of revolution in the 19th century; likewise, the spread of land ownership in the 20th century bought off many members of potentially disaffected property-less classes. It is arguable that marriage itself is under threat of extinction at the start of the 21st century and that the response of those anxious to preserve the institution might be to extend it to deserving candidates – that is, lesbians and gays in 'stable' relationships. If marriage conferred on gays and lesbians the legal rights presently enjoyed by heterosexual spouses, there can be little doubt that many more couples would consider marrying. In short, Britain's marriage rate would rise.

Since marriage is identified with a whole range of conservative social norms (settling down, investing in a home, raising a family, getting involved in the community and so on), this development could be welcomed, even by those who might have to overcome a homophobic distaste for sharing the institution with couples who challenge gendered domestic arrangements and do unimaginable things in bed. Most of the new applicants would be 'deserving' in the sense that they would be living in long-term, monogamous relationships and espouse traditional values. For the others, marriage would be anticipated to have a domesticating effect.

There is, therefore, a strong conservative rationale for allowing gays and lesbians to marry. And there is a historical precedent for relaxing the conditions of marriage in order to boost its popularity. In the second half of the 19th century, too, Britain suffered a steady decline in the marriage rate, to the extent that, by the end of the century, a good quarter of the population would never marry. In a society premised on the centrality of marriage, especially for women, this was a calamity and sparked a volume of agonized debate in the journals of the day. The reasons for the decline were many and various, but one undoubted factor was the legal and social framework in which marriage took place, according to which a husband was completely responsible for his wife, children and household, while the wife was virtually without legal protection against any abuse of his power. If middle-class men baulked at the weight of duty and expense (for Victorian families were large and households expensive, while one could lead a comfortable bachelor life with only a housekeeper and a mistress), more and more women of the same class began to feel little inclination to enter an institution which enforced total dependence, especially as alternatives in the form of fulfilling careers were opening up in the second half of the century (Auchmuty, 1975). The liberalization of the marriage laws in the same period was likewise due to many factors, but one was certainly a panic response to the marriage crisis. The divorce law of 1857, the Married Women's Property Acts of 1870 and 1882, the right granted to women in the Matrimonial Causes Act 1878 to separate from violent husbands and receive maintenance, custody of children and access provisions for divorced and separated mothers in the Infant Custody Acts of 1839 and 1873 – these changes were all in part motivated by Parliament's recognition that, without them, marriage was becoming an increasingly unattractive option for the educated classes. As a result of them, marriage received a huge boost in numbers and enjoyed increased popularity and prestige in the first half of the 20th century.

The extension of marriage to same-sex couples would almost certainly have the same effect now. The very fact that more and more people who already have the right to marry are refusing to exercise that right may make lesbian and gay inclusion more welcome and easier to obtain. We may yet be called into service to save an endangered species.

THE RISE OF A RIGHTS CULTURE

The main criticism that has greeted the UK government's paper on *Civil Partnership* has been that, unlike the two earlier Parliamentary bills, it excludes unmarried heterosexual couples. The government was, however, clear that it meant to confine civil registration to same-sex couples, since opposite-sex couples had the option (which the government was trying to encourage) of getting married. Lawyers pointed to the hardships faced by heterosexual cohabitants on the breakdown of relationships they had believed to be safe or safeguarded, and the need for a protective regime for these women. I suspect that if such a regime is ever introduced, it will vastly strengthen the case for same-sex marriage. Under the government's proposals as they stand, there will be marriage for heterosexuals and civil registration for lesbians and gays. But if unmarried heterosexual couples are brought into the civil registration scheme (which may well happen when the subject is debated in Parliament) or if a separate regime is provided for them, then heterosexuals will have two options – marriage or registered partnership – and lesbians and gays only one. This unequal treatment will immediately give rise to an argument for parity in a legal system which has now (at last) outlawed discrimination against gays and lesbians – and thus the opening of marriage to same-sex couples.

It would be difficult to exaggerate the impact of the equality provisions of European law and most recently the Human Rights Act 1998 in this area. Only a decade ago in her ground-breaking book, *Family Law Matters*, British legal academic Katherine O'Donovan doubted that same-sex marriage stood much chance of acceptance in the UK. The entry of gays, lesbians and transsexuals into marriage 'would not only alter the sacred character of the institution but the very definition, the constitution, the understanding from time immemorial' (O'Donovan, 1993: 48). But the legal world of the 21st century is a very different one from that of the 20th century. As part of my research for this article, I looked through the last couple of years of issues of *Family Law*, the English practitioners' journal in the area. References to same-sex partnerships, unmarried cohabitation, and gay and transsexual marriage were scattered throughout its pages. For a lesbian feminist, it was a sobering experience to realize that *our* issues are now the public property of the law-making community, that legal academics, family lawyers, judges and MPs (mostly straight and mostly male) are expressing opinions, making pronouncements and recommending policy in every area of our lives that carries legal implications, including same-sex marriage. Indeed, I sometimes wondered if the subject was of more interest to them than it was to most lesbians and gay men.

But reading the legal literature further persuaded me that, whether we want it or not, the eventual legalization of same-sex marriage is pretty much inevitable. It is a paradox that, just at the moment that British lesbians and gays seem prepared to settle for civil partnership recognition, same-sex marriage is actually much more likely to be attainable than anyone could have imagined when the issue was debated in the mid-1990s.

In English law, marriage is defined as 'the voluntary union . . . of one man and one woman, to the exclusion of all others' (*Hyde v. Hyde and Woodmansee* [1866] LR1 P & D 130). Under section 11 of the Matrimonial Causes Act 1973 a marriage may be declared void if the parties are not respectively male and female. In *Corbett v. Corbett* [1971] P 83 the marriage of transsexual April Ashley was annulled, the English courts insisting (as they still insist) that for the purposes of marriage transsexual people remain the gender they were assigned at birth. Until 2002 the European Court of Human Rights accepted, in response to a number of subsequent cases brought by transsexuals wishing to marry, the UK government's power to determine its own conception of marriage. Then, in *Goodwin v. UK* [2002] 2 FLR 487, it ruled that the UK government's refusal to amend the claimant's birth certificate and to allow her to marry violated both Article 8 of the Convention, which guarantees respect for private life, and Article 12, which guarantees the 'right to marry and found a family' to 'men and women of marriageable age' according to 'the national laws governing the exercise of this right'.

This is not the place to rehearse the issues surrounding the rights of transsexual people, but the Goodwin case has important implications for lesbians and gays. On the face of it, the acceptance of transsexual people's right to marry merely accommodates existing notions of marriage as the union of one man and one woman. Even if the parties were the same sex at birth, they will no longer be considered so (or consider themselves so) at the point of marrying. Ironically, however, it has always been and remains possible for a transsexual to marry someone of his or her opposite *birth* sex, but same *assigned* sex: indeed, this has already happened. In March 2000, Diane Maddox, born male and about to embark on male-to-female gender reassignment surgery, married Clare Ward-Jackson, a biological female. The couple now identify as lesbian – and they are married.

As solicitor Charlotte McCafferty comments:

> If public policy in the UK deems that such marriages are unacceptable, it has only one option. Legislation would have to be introduced so that not only are transsexuals entitled to obtain a new birth certificate showing their post-operative gender, but, indeed, that they are obliged to do so. Any marriage that took place after gender reassignment would, therefore, record that a male was marrying a female, and appearances would be satisfied. This option, however, does not prevent a pre-operative transsexual who intends to identify as gay once his gender has been altered, from entering into an apparently gay but valid marriage. Yet more legislation would have to be passed to prevent this. (McCafferty, 2002: 366)

Noting that the Dutch have already introduced same-sex marriage, without troublesome consequences, McCafferty queries: 'Is it necessary for public policy to so restrict the right to marry? *How adverse would be the effect of granting equal access to marriage, so that not only transsexuals, but also gays, can marry?*' (p. 366, my emphasis)

The rights culture has brought material possibility to claims of equality and justice made by pro-marriage gays and lesbians in the mid-1990s. At the same time, with equality as an overt social goal, European Union law has established that discrimination against people on the ground of their sexuality is no longer acceptable.[8] As a result, English judges are often in advance of Parliament in their acceptance of the right of lesbians and gays to legal protection. It has even been suggested that the judges are ahead of public opinion (Duckworth, 2002: 369). All that is needed now is an enterprising and self-evidently 'deserving' lesbian or gay couple and a gender-free equality reading of Article 12 of the European Convention on Human Rights – one, that is, that sees the right to marry as one available to 'men and women of marriageable age' read disjunctively not conjunctively. Should the claimants succeed, the UK government would be obliged to amend its national marriage law to accommodate same-sex unions.

There is one further avenue through which same-sex marriage could become law in the UK. Marriages contracted abroad are recognized under British law. With three countries now allowing same-sex marriage, and with British citizens choosing to marry within these jurisdictions, it is only a matter of time before a couple seeks to have their marriage recognized in their home country. The very fact that two of our European neighbours and one of Britain's former dominions now permit same-sex marriage must provide a powerful incentive for the UK to follow suit. I look forward to legal developments in this area!

RESPONDING TO THE CHALLENGE

In the mid-1990s, many feminists feared that the possibility of same-sex marriage would drive a wedge between those who qualified for social and legal recognition and those who remained outside the protection of legal marriage, possibly even forcing people to marry in order to get respect and equal treatment. My view now is that this will not happen. Social disapproval of unmarried intimacy has all but disappeared, marriage has become a personal choice conferring few substantive legal or financial advantages, and the law has gone too far down the road of extending marital privileges to unmarried heterosexual couples, and now to homosexual couples, to be able to turn back. There is general agreement that, even if a civil partnership scheme were introduced, legal mechanisms would have to be in place to serve those outside the formal regimes. The Law Society of England and Wales, for example, has proposed a set of fall-back provisions to come into operation on the ending of a relationship, to give legal protection to heterosexual couples who were not married and same-sex couples who did not register their partnership (Thorpe, 2002: 893–4).

At the same time as the primacy of the married couple is being challenged, other legal and political forces are weakening the status of the couple itself. The Law Commission's discussion paper on *Sharing Homes* (2002) refused to confine itself to co-owners in intimate relationships but, adopting English property law's formal indifference to marital status, tried (and unfortunately failed) to come up with a workable scheme for the resolution of home ownership disputes between unmarried couples, family members and/or friends. Property lawyers argue that there is no justification for offering legal remedies to couples that are not available to other individuals. This is, of course, a moot point (the Law Commission was roundly criticized by a Court of Appeal judge for even suggesting it [Thorpe, 2002: 894]), for couple relationships may arguably induce greater trust and self-sacrifice, and therefore provide opportunities for greater exploitation and loss, than relationships conducted at arm's length. But the difference is only one of degree, for few of us conduct our relationships with our co-owners, whether family or friends, at arm's length either.

A stronger argument can be made against the privileging of couples in the provision of benefits like spousal pensions or company perks. Benefits introduced to compensate wives for giving up their careers to care for husband, home and children are increasingly inappropriate in a world where families no longer take this form and this kind of compensation is no longer seen as adequate. Single people form the fastest growing sector in the housing market – a quarter of all households in London alone – and one-parent families are also on the increase. Many adults live with and care for elderly parents. Next-of-kin recognition, inheritance tax liability, pensions all affect them as much as they do the members of a couple. Why claim rights for the latter, while ignoring the former?

Couples, after all, are already privileged: happily coupled people enjoy love, company, mutual support, extra money and higher status than single people. They have someone to share the housework and childcare, someone to go on holiday with, someone to care for them when ill; they can afford nicer homes, indeed, they can afford to buy a home when many single people cannot. Most of all, they live each day in the comfortable assurance that they have succeeded in finding love and *being chosen* – in contrast to the undesirable uncoupled or unfortunate de-coupled. Do they deserve extra privileges when they are already so richly served?

One of the shortcomings of the campaigns for same-sex marriage and civil partnerships is that they do not address this issue. There is after all no particular reason why people should live in twos, except in so far as this arrangement has served patriarchy by ensuring that each woman is kept under the personal control of a man. As a form of social organization, the couple is convenient and relatively easy to manage, but limited, and risky, too, as too great a dependence on one person involves putting all one's eggs (emotional, financial, sexual) in one basket. The couple model is normative because of our society's long history of family formation based on heterosexual marriage, but the form of marriage most current today – the one that originates in romance and proceeds to companionship in a nuclear setting – is a relatively modern construction. In the past marriage was based on matters like dynastic alliance, property succession, and the economic need for children to contribute to the family income. Romance did not come into it; sex might take place outside of it; companionship was not an issue, as the sexes socialized separately; and families were larger and extended.

Many people live contentedly in couples. But the existence of other (equally, possibly more, satisfactory) forms of household organization and relationships of mutual dependency must be recognized, for the people in these households and relationships also deserve recognition and rights. Some companies now allow employees to nominate the recipient of any work-related benefits: spouses, lovers, relatives or friends are equally eligible. Others have abolished them altogether or made them optional by payment of additional contributions. Such schemes seem fairer and more transparent than the current subsidising of the married by the unmarried. Given the inability of many British financial institutions to meet their pension and insurance obligations today, one might expect political support for this latter development. It is probable that *all* the practical equality measures claimed by the same-sex marriage and civil partnerships lobbies could be achieved by these sorts of means and need not be confined to couples. The inheritance tax exemption, for example, could be extended to all co-owners of the family home. Such developments would go a long way towards meeting the lesbian-feminists' critique of the marriage privilege. If the institution is unlikely to abolished, as Ruthann Robson and some of the rest of us would like, it could at least be made a mere 'first among equals'.

CONCLUSION

Homosexual relationships get a very bad press. They are said to be less stable, less faithful, and shorter-lived than those of heterosexuals (Duckworth, 2002). In so far as this is true, it is hardly surprising, given society's condemnation and silencing of homosexual relationships and the absence of social and legal support to contain and mediate their strains and tensions. Equally, it could be argued that the shorter-lived relationships of lesbians and gay men reflect our unwillingness or lack of compulsion to settle for the inferior sorts of relationships many married women endure; or that fidelity is a relatively modern and over-hyped requirement of a domestic relationship. In fact, of course, our relationships may *not* be shorter and less stable than those of heterosexuals. We have all come across long-lasting ones. But so little research has been undertaken into the subject that no one knows the real statistics.

A recent article in *Family Law* stated that homosexual practices are 'at best unsatisfactory and at worst life threatening . . . The highest exposure to AIDS in the USA occurs in the practising gay community.' The same writer, a male barrister, claimed that children brought up in same-sex households risked 'bullying at school, confused identity and a decreased sense of self-worth' (Duckworth, 2002: 371). One could point out, in response, that the highest exposure to AIDS in Africa occurs in the heterosexual community. Or that heterosexual practices are often unsatisfactory and sometimes life-threatening for women. Or that the incidence of AIDS among *lesbians* is much less than the incidence among heterosexuals. Or that research has shown that children brought up in lesbian households score *higher* in the standard tests of social adjustment than many other children (Tasker and Golombok, 1997). Or, as Cheshire Calhoun observed, that heterosexual men pose 'the biggest threat to marriage through divorce, abandonment, spouse abuse, promiscuity, alcohol abuse, lack of marital commitment, watching Sunday football, and having children out of wedlock' (Calhoun, 2000: 146).

Important as it is to make these points, lesbians and gay men need to move beyond defensiveness. We need to tell the heterosexual world how we live. We could start by drawing attention to the fact that same-sex relationships demonstrate the possibility of more egalitarian relationships. This is not because the parties are innately egalitarian but because an unequal division of labour is not arbitrarily imposed on them by virtue of gender difference. Having no traditional (gendered) roles, the same-sex couple must negotiate its own. Couples who cannot marry also have more reason to think about the nature and terms of their relationships. Without the bonds of the non-negotiable marriage contract, same-sex couples have the freedom to order their financial and legal arrangements through joint home ownership, mutual wills and so on, as far as is available to them. It was noteworthy how carefully the couples interviewed by Suzanne Sherman had ordered their financial and legal affairs. The volume of case law on unmarried women left high and dry by male partners for want of sensible legal arrangements suggests that this is not the case for many heterosexuals.

The public appropriation of lesbian and gay rights campaigns has many positive aspects. It means we are now well and truly out of the closet. But it also means that the future may be out of our hands. This must give us pause. The liberal agenda may, indeed, grant us rights to hitherto heterosexual privileges. But unless we are careful, it will do so on its terms, naturally assuming that heterosexual values are the norm, if not the best. In so doing, it may lose the opportunity presented by the recognition of lesbian and gay existence to gain two important insights. One is that the ways heterosexuals live may not be the best. The second is that the ways lesbians and gays live might be better. In sum, rather than assimilate us to their preferred relationship models, heterosexuals might do well to look at how gays and lesbians conduct their relationships, necessarily still (in the UK) outside marriage.

NOTES

1. http://www.dti.gov.uk/publications
2. For a discussion of the two bills, see Cooke, 2002.
3. For example, The Netherlands, Belgium, France, Portugal, Hungary, Hawaii and some Australian states.
4. For example, The Netherlands, Denmark and Vermont in the USA do; most countries do not. See Women and Equality Unit, 2003: 15–16.
5. *Fitzpatrick v. Sterling Housing Association Ltd* [1993] 3 WLR 1113, *Antonio Mendoza v. Ahmed Raja Ghaidan* [2002] EWCA Civ. 1533; the Adoption and Children Act 2002.
6. For example, Caroline Norton's discovery that she had no rights at all to her children led her to campaign for rights of access and custody for mothers under the Infant Custody Act 1839. See Acland, 1948.
7. The inheritance tax exemption was part of both the earlier bills for Civil Partnerships, and Stonewall believes that the government proposals meant to include it ('This is implied . . . but not made explicit'). I think this is disingenuous. See http://www.stonewall.org.uk, accessed 11 September 2003.
8. The Equal Treatment Directive should be implemented by the end of 2003.

REFERENCES

Acland, A. (1948) *Caroline Norton*. London: Constable.
Auchmuty, R. (1975) 'Victorian Spinsters', unpublished PhD thesis, Australian National University.
Baird, R.M.and Rosenblum, S.E., eds (1997) *Same-Sex Marriage: The Moral and Legal Debate*. Amherst, NY: Prometheus Books.
Bernard, J. (1973) *The Future of Marriage*. New York: Bantam.
Boyd, S.B. (1999) 'Family, Law and Sexuality: Feminist Engagements', *Social and Legal Studies* 8: 369–90.
Butler, G. (1996) 'Why Be a Wife?' *Stonewall Newsletter* 4: 9.
Caird, M. (1897) *The Morality of Marriage*. London: Redway.

Calhoun, C. (2000) *Feminism, the Family, and the Politics of the Closet: Lesbian and Gay Displacement.* Oxford and New York: Oxford University Press.

Carter, H. (2003) 'Marriage Falls Out of Fashion . . . Or Does It?', *The Guardian*, 21 March: 3.

Colker, R. (1991) 'Marriage', *Yale Journal of Law and Feminism* 3: 321–6.

Comer, L. (1974) *Wedlocked Women.* Leeds: Feminist Books.

Cooke, E. (2002) 'Registered Partnerships – Coming Soon?', *Family Law* March: 232–3.

Cox, B. (1997) 'A (Personal) Essay on Same-Sex Marriage', in R.M. Baird and S.E. Rosenblum (eds) *Same-Sex Marriage: the Moral and Legal Debate*, pp.27–9. Amherst, NY: Prometheus Books.

Duckworth, P. (2002) 'What is a Family? – A Personal View', *Family Law*, May: 367–71.

Dyer, C. (2002) 'The Common-Law Wife Myth', *The Guardian* 23 August: 16.

Eskridge, W.N., Jr (1999) *Gaylaw: Challenging the Apartheid of the Closet.* Cambridge, MA: Harvard University Press.

Eskridge, W.N., Jr (2002) *Equality Practice: Civil Unions and the Future of Gay Rights.* New York and London: Routledge.

Ettelbrick, P. (1989) 'Since When is Marriage a Path to Liberation?', in R.M. Baird and S.E. Rosenblum (eds) *Same-Sex Marriage: The Moral and Legal Debate*, pp.164–8. Amherst, NY: Prometheus Books.

Greer, G. (1970) *The Female Eunuch.* London: Granada.

Harper, M. (1996) 'It's About Equality', *Stonewall Newsletter* 4: 9.

Herman, D. (1993) 'The Politics of Law Reform: Lesbian and Gay Rights into the 1990s', in J. Bristow and A.R. Wilson (eds) *Activiating Theory: Lesbian, Gay, Bisexual Politics*, pp.246–63. London: Lawrence and Wishart.

Hibbs, M., Barton, C., and Beswick, J. (2001) 'Why Marry? – Perceptions of the Affianced', *Family Law*, March: 197–207.

Hunter, N.D. (1995) 'Marriage, Law and Gender: a Feminist Inquiry', in L. Duggan and N.D. Hunter (eds) *Sex Wars: Sexual Dissent and Political Culture*, pp.107–22. New York and London: Routledge.

Law Commission (2002) 'Sharing Homes: A Discussion Paper', *Law Com. No. 278.* Available: http://www.lawcom.gov.uk

McCafferty, C. (2002) 'Gays, Transsexuals and the Right to Marry', *Family Law*, May: 362–6.

Mill, J.S. (1869) *The Subjection of Women.* London: Longmans, Green, Reader and Dyer.

Mohr, R.D. (1994) *A More Perfect Union: Why Straight Americans Must Stand Up for Gay Rights.* Boston: Beacon Press.

Mohr, R.D. (1997) 'The Case for Gay Marriage', in R.M. Baird and S.E. Rosenblum (eds) *Same-Sex Marriage: the Moral and Legal Debate*, pp.84–104. Amherst, NY: Prometheus Books.

O'Donovan, K. (1993) *Family Law Matters.* London: Pluto.

Robson, R. (1998) *Sappho Goes to Law School.* New York: Columbia University Press.

Sherman, S., ed. (1992) *Lesbian and Gay Marriage: Private Commitments, Public Ceremonies.* Philadelphia, PA: Temple University Press.

Stonewall, UK (1996) ' Government Deny Immigration Rights', newsletter, May: 4.

Strasser, M. (1997) *Legally Wed: Same-Sex Marriage and the Constitution.* Ithaca, NY, and London: Cornell University Press.

Sullivan, A. (1995) *Virtually Normal: An Argument about Homosexuality.* London: Macmillan.

Sullivan, A., ed. (1997) *Same-Sex Marriage: Pro and Con.* NewYork: Vintage Books.

Tasker, F.L. and Golombok, S. (1997) *Growing Up in a Lesbian Family: Effects on Child Development.* New York: The Guildford Press.

Thorpe, Rt Hon L.J. (2002) 'Property Rights on Family Breakdown', *Family Law*, December: 891–99.

Wandor, M. (1974) 'The Conditions of Illusion', in S. Allen, L. Sanders and J. Wallis (eds) *Conditions of Illusion: Papers from the Women's Movements*, pp. 186–207. Leeds: Feminist Books.

Whittle, S. (1996) 'An Association for as Noble a Purpose as Any', *New Law Journal* 15 March: 366–8.

Wintermute, R. and Andenaes, M. (2001) *Legal Recognition of Same-Sex Partnerships.* Oxford: Hart.

Wollstonecraft, M. (1929[1792]) *A Vindication of the Rights of Woman.* London: Dent.

Women and Equality Unit (2003) *Civil Partnership: A Framework for the Legal Recognition of Same-Sex Couples.* London: DTI Publications.

Younge, G. (2003) 'Gay Americans Go North to Take the Plunge', *The Guardian* 27 August: 13.

Rosemary AUCHMUTY is a Principal Lecturer at the School of Law, University of Westminster. She writes about feminism, sexuality and law as well as lesbian history and children's literature. Her publications include *Australia's Daughters* (Methuen, 1978), *A World of Girls* (The Women's Press, 1992), *A World of Women* (The Women's Press, 1999), chapters in the Lesbian History Group's book *Not a Passing Phase* (The Women's Press,1989), and articles in *Feminist Legal Studies* and the Cavendish series *Feminist Perspectives on Law*. ADDRESS: Rosemary AUCHMUTY, School of Law, University of Westminster, 4 Little Titchfield Street, London W1W 7UW, UK.
[email: auchmur@wmin.ac.uk]

The Cultural Turn

[21]

From Butch to Butcher's Knife

Film, Crime and Lesbian Sexuality

JENNI MILLBANK*

1. *Introduction: Why Cinema is Jurisprudence*

Lesbians and gay men in Australia have been subjected to a vast array of discrimination and oppression at the hands of majority culture, including legal culture. Expressions of hatred, such as discrimination and violence against lesbians and gay men, remain endemic despite relatively recent reforms such as State-based anti-discrimination legislation.[1] Measures of widespread abuse are always difficult, but homicide statistics provide a chillingly "clean" figure: lesbians and gays were victims in at least 25 per cent of the homicides perpetrated by a stranger from 1988 to 1994 in New South Wales.[2] A more

---

* Lecturer in Law, University of Sydney. Thanks to Hilary Astor, Suzanne Christie, Karen O'Connell, Mehera San Roque, Catherine Zimdahl.

1 Sexual orientation discrimination remains lawful in Western Australia, Tasmania and at a federal level. New South Wales led the way in 1982 when it included "bisexuality" and "homosexuality" in its *Anti-Discrimination Act* 1977 (NSW). "Sexuality" is the prohibited ground of discrimination in South Australia under the *Equal Opportunity Act* 1984 (SA), the ACT under the *Discrimination Act* 1991 (ACT) and the Northern Territory under the *Anti-Discrimination Act* 1992 (NT). "Lawful sexual activity" is the ground in Queensland under the *Anti-Discrimination Act* 1991 (Qld) and in Victoria under the *Equal Opportunity Act* 1995 (VIC). Notably, in addition to the huge range of general exceptions in all such legislation (eg, religious schools etc), Queensland (s28), the Northern Territory (s37) and Victoria (s25) all include specific exemptions which apply only to lesbians and gays. The above three States specify that sexual orientation discrimination is lawful when it concerns "work with children" (including the "care, supervision or instruction of minors") if it is "reasonably necessary to protect the physical, psychological or emotional well being of minors". Thus some of the very statutes which are meant to assist in overcoming discrimination are actually busy entrenching it.

2 The percentage may in fact be higher, as these figures reflect recorded hate crimes where the victim's sexuality was apparently the basis for killing. It excludes cases where the motive was not apparent, or where surviving friends and relatives either didn't know the victim was lesbian/gay or did not impart this to the police. See Steve .Tomsen, "Hatred, Murder and Male Honour: Gay Homicides and the 'Homosexual Panic Defence'" (1994) 6(2) *Criminology Aust* 2. Also see *Final Report of the Streetwatch Implementation Committee*, ADB, Sydney, 1994. Cases involving the murder or attempted murder of women who were, or were thought to be, lesbian by a man known to them include: *Radford v R* (1985) 42 SASR 266 (Full Court); *McGhee v R* (1995) 183 CLR 82; *R v McGhee* (1994) Unreported, Tas CCA, Green CJ, Wright and Zeeman JJ, 17 March 1994; *Lovec v R* (1987) 27 A Crim R 40 (SA CCA). Also see: *R v Cook* (1995) Unreported, Qld Full Court, Fitzgerald P, Pincus and Davies JJA, 23 March 1995 (stalking by known accused); *Tamayo v Department of Immigration* (1994) AAT, Sydney, 23 December 1994, noted (1994) 37 ALD 786 (malicious wounding of lesbian couple by stranger); and *Question of Law Reserved on Acquittal* (1993) 59 SASR 214 (Full Court) (rape and battery by husband). Cases involving the murder of a gay man by a gang of several unknown boys or men include: *R v Howard and Ors* (1992) 29 NSWLR 242 (CCA); *R v Grmusa and Ors* [1991] 2 VR 153 (Full Court); *Giakas v R* [1988] VR 973 (Full Court). Cases involving the murder of a gay man by a sole male assailant include: *R v Green* (1995) Unreported,

subtle but widespread denial of lesbian and gay personhood occurs in the failure to see lesbian and gay relationships as familial; both statute and common law have generally refused to recognise lesbians and gays as parents or partners.[3]

Richard Dyer says, "How we are seen determines in part how we are treated; how we treat others is based on how we see them; such seeing comes from representation."[4] Cinematic images of lesbian characters (or, more usually, caricatures) have a profound impact on how others view lesbians, which in turn influences perceptions of lesbians within the law. In Tania Modleski's words, "... we exist inside ideology ... we are all victims, down to the very depths of our psyches, of political and cultural domination (although we are never only victims)."[5] This is not to say that images in popular culture simply form what the public and the judiciary think about lesbians and lesbian relationships. Just as judges are influenced by cultural representations (appearing most obviously as "common sense" ideas in case law),[6] judgments are also texts that represent, and are themselves often translated back into popular culture in the form of news reports and, sometimes, movies. The film *Heavenly Creatures*, to be discussed later, was based heavily on court transcripts. Those transcripts in turn reveal the extent to which the law and legal actors were influenced by popular representation of lesbianism at the time.[7]

NSW CCA, Preistley JA, Smart and Ireland JJ, 8 November 1995; *R v Pritchard* [1991] 1 VR 84, *R v Craggs* (1995) Qld Full Court, McPherson JA, Moynihan and Fryberg JJ, 1 September 1995. (In the above three cases the accused all unsuccessfully argued versions of "homosexual panic" — provocation and/or self defence in repulsing a sexual advance by the victim.) In every case noted above, whether the accused was known or unknown, the sexual orientation of the victim was the substantial or whole motive for the attack.

3   For a discussion of exclusions in NSW and federal legislation on issues such as intestacy, guardianship, superannuation and worker's compensation see: Gay and Lesbian Rights Lobby, *The Bride Wore Pink* (2nd edn, 1994). *Brown v Commissioner of Superannuation* (1995) 21 AAR 378, confirms the exclusion of lesbians and gays from legislation which passes superannuation benefits to a spouse or spouse-like relationship on the death of a contributor. See also the child custody cases, *L and L* (1983) FLC 91-353, and *A and J* (1995) 19 Fam LR 260 for stunning invalidations of lesbian relationships. Legislation which does recognise same-sex partnerships tends to do so on other grounds, such as financial dependence: see *Family Provision Act 1982* (NSW), *Domestic Relationships Act 1994* (ACT), *Migration Regulations 1992* (Cth). The ACT provides a recent and notable exception. In 1996 it passed the *Administration and Probate (Amendment) Act* no 15 of 1996 (ACT) and *Family Provision (Amendment) Act* no 16 of 1996 (ACT). In both Acts "spouse" includes same-sex and opposite sex live-in partners on an equal footing, entitled to inherit under intestacy rules, and to contest wills. In the *Family Provision (Amendment) Act* the spouse provision is in *addition* to a section which gives recognition to "domestic relationships", thereby recognising the broadest possible range of relationships of interdependence.

4   Richard Dyer, *The Matter of Images: Essays on Representation* (1993) at 1.

5   *Feminism Without Women: Culture and Criticism in a 'Postfeminist' Age* (1991) at 45.

6   For a discussion of "common sense" in family law judgments concerning lesbian mothers see my article, "Lesbians, Child Custody and the Long Lingering Gaze of the Law" in Susan Boyd (ed), *Challenging the Public/Private Divide: Feminism and Socio-Legal Policy*, University of Toronto Press, forthcoming. For a discussion of "common sense" as a form of judicial notice see Regina Graycar, "The Gender of Judgments: An Introduction" in Margaret Thornton (ed), *Public/Private: Feminist Legal Debates* (1995).

7   The prosecution argued that the girls' relationship evinced their evil natures, while the defence argued that the girls' relationship evinced their insanity, see below n74 and accompanying text.

This article will discuss the cultural fantasies/distortions/reconstructions of lesbians who have killed. First, I will look at Tracey Wigginton and Aileen Wuornos, both of whom were self-identified lesbians who were tried in the early 1990s for killing men to whom they were strangers, in Australia and America respectively. I will then go on to focus on two historical murders involving alleged (assumed?) lesbian couples who jointly killed women they were closely connected to. Christine and Lea Papin were sisters who killed their employer and her daughter in France in 1933. Pauline Parker and Juliet Hulme killed Pauline's mother in New Zealand in 1955. What links all four of these crimes is the manner in which sexuality, specifically lesbian sexuality, was posited as causal in contemporaneous media accounts, as well as later "true crime" and fictional representations. A further point linking the Papin sisters with Parker and Hulme across continents and decades is that both were thought to have acted as sexual/criminal couples and both were the subject of films in the 1990s — being *Sister my Sister* and *Heavenly Creatures* respectively. They thus provide an interesting counterpoint to each other in both contemporaneous and subsequent discourse, and will be the focus of the latter part of this paper.

In discussing these representations this article makes no pretence at knowing what "really" happened. Indeed, whether all of the accused were "really" lesbians is open to some doubt. The Papin sisters appear to have been largely silent throughout the trial process and their imprisonment, with popular belief in their sexual relationship arising from the publicly expressed opinion of others at the time (including their jailer and also a psychiatrist who had not met either of them). When Christine was asked by the judge if the relationship was sexual, she denied it.[8] Juliet Hulme as an adult (now known as Anne Perry) denied that her relationship with Pauline Parker was sexual, and Aileen Wuornos latterly stressed that her relationship with her partner was "spiritual" rather than sexual. (However both Hulme and Wuornos had undergone "born again" religious conversions at the time they made these claims.[9]) Ruthann Robson makes the point that such denials may be prompted by fear of lack of

---

8   See Lynda Hart, "'They Don't Even Look Like Maids Anymore': Wendy Kesselman's My Sister in This House" in Hart (ed), *Making a Spectacle: Feminist Essays on Contemporary Women's Theatre* (1989).

9   It was Pauline's diary entires, including descriptions of the girls bathing and sleeping together and discovering "sin" and "bliss" in the process, which led to a general belief that their relationship was lesbian (although many of the expert opinions at the time added the coda that it was not sexual). Julie Glamuzlina and Alison Laurie extract and discuss in some detail the various diary entires suggesting a romantic and sexual relationship; see *Parker and Hulme: A Lesbian View* (1991) ch4. As an adult, Juliet/Anne claimed that such diary entries were taken out of context. However, two journalists observing the trial at the time noted that when a witness was questioned about how many times Pauline had sex with a man, Juliet, who had been still and silent throughout the trial, flushed and lent across a wardress to hiss something at Pauline and motioned as though to hit her: see Tom Gurr and H H Cox, "Pauline Parker and Juliet Hulme: 'Let's Kill Mother'" originally published in *Famous Australian Crimes* (1958) reprinted in Richard Glyn Jones (ed), *The Giant Book of Killer Women* (1995). The journalists interpreted this action as motherly, but I am more inclined to see it as loverly. Moreover, in the very interview in which Anne/Juliet denied her relationship with Pauline was sexual, she also went to some lengths to deny that Pauline had the heterosexual relationship noted above: see Barbara Wickens, "Haunted by Homicide" (27 March 1995) *Macleans* 61.

public support and harsh sentences as a result of homophobia.[10] I agree with Robson that the women were seen to be, and treated as, lesbians; thus lesbianism is an issue even if the women were not actually lesbian or did not see themselves as such.

Deb Verhoeven, writing about Tracey Wigginton says, "Without clear information ... it was difficult to make a convincing case against the media that was not already reliant on its — albeit contradictory and ambivalent — presentation of the trials."[11] Of all the women discussed, only Wuornos gave her own version of events as evidence in court.[12] As legal and cultural subjects, they were thus overwhelmingly spoken *for* and spoken *about*, whilst remaining silent themselves. I am uncomfortably aware that academic inquiry, such as this article, in some ways continues such a process of appropriation.[13] For this reason I stress that my focus is not on the women themselves, nor the crimes of which they were convicted, but on the manner in which mass culture took their experiences and reproduced them as "lesbian criminality". For this reason, I open with a discussion of cultural representations of lesbians more broadly, before examining the cases specifically.

2. *Seeing is Believing*

"In many minds the leap from the butch to the butcher's knife is but a tiny one."[14]

In mainstream cinema, "[t]he representation of women and other oppressed groups was, and by and large still is, a relentless parade of insults".[15] Lesbians have appeared in film in a series of derogatory "types".[16] Typically, lesbians

---

10 In the USA this fear seems to be borne out; for example in 1992 some 40% of the women on death row were "implicated" as lesbian. See Ruthann Robson, "Convictions: Theorizing Lesbians and Criminal Justice" in Didi Herman and Carl Strychin (eds), *Legal Inversions: Lesbians, Gay Men and the Politics of Law* (1995).

11 Deb Verhoeven, "Biting the Hand that Breeds: The Trials of Tracey Wigginton" in Helen Birch (ed), *Moving Targets: Women, Murder and Representation* (1993) at 102.

12 The Papin sisters gave a factual outline of events to the magistrate upon arrest but were largely silent during their trial (which lasted 14 hours, continuously from 1pm until 3am). Nor did either of them appear to speak thereafter, and both have since died. Tracey Wigginton pleaded guilty and did not speak during her (9 minute) trial. She is currently in jail and has not shed any light on the incident. Parker and Hulme were juveniles and under New Zealand law of the time were not permitted to testify, although their statements to police were in evidence. The case rested almost entirely on Pauline's diaries. After release they both took new identities; Pauline's is still unknown but when Juliet was "uncovered" by the press in 1994 she gave interviews in which her account of events differed slightly to Pauline's: see Wickens, above n9 and Pam Lambert and Ellen Stein, "Blood Memory" (26 September 1994) *People* 57. Aileen Wuornos gave evidence in one trial only (she faced seven charges), although she has since spoken in numerous press interviews.

13 Ruthann Robson thoughtfully discusses this issue, above n10.

14 Lindsay Van Gelder, "Attack of the Killer Lesbians" (1992) 2 *Ms Magazine* 80 at 82.

15 Dyer, above n4 at 1. Vito Russo examined stereotypes of gays and, to a lesser extent lesbians, in mostly Hollywood film in *The Celluloid Closet* (rev edn, 1987). The death of a lesbian or gay character was so common that Russo appended a morbidly funny necrology to his book, listing the manner in which they met their end. With a knowledge of such history, when a nice gay man appeared recently in the English film *Four Weddings and a Funeral* (1994) it wasn't hard to guess who was going to get the funeral.

16 For a discussion of how the representations of lesbians in literature interact with the law see Anne Goldstein, "Representing the Lesbian in Law and Literature" in Susan Heinzelman and Zipporah Wiseman (eds), *Representing Women: Law, Literature and Feminism* (1994).

were, and are, depicted as masculine or "butch" and/or manhating, and lesbian relationships as immature/a schoolgirl phase, as narcissistic, as involving a mother/daughter pairing or as a sadistic/vampiric dynamic.[17] Through representation, lesbian sexuality is inexorably tied to aggression and carnality, with murderous and vampiric lesbians the supreme, and most common, embodiment of these traits.[18] The film *Basic Instinct* (1992) is a succinct case in point, as it contains virtually every pathological lesbian type ever depicted in cinema, often disjunctively.[19] The protagonist of *Basic Instinct*, Catherine (the notoriously knickerless Sharon Stone) is a rich, blond, murder mystery writer; a vampish "femme fatale" with an insatiable (bi)sexual appetite, suspected of murdering a male lover. Importantly, murderousness and lesbianism are deliberately conflated in *Basic Instinct* as all four female characters are bisexual or lesbian and all of them are revealed as suspected or convicted killers.[20] When the male detective, Curren (Michael Douglas) confronts Beth and shoots her, his remark, "Do you still like girls?" stands as a simultaneous accusation of murder — as her lesbianism is her undoubted motive for killing her husband.

---

17 I proceed from the assumption that none of these types are "true", in the sense that while some lesbians may be accurately described by them, it would be no more true of lesbians than women in any other section of the population. Such typologies pathologise lesbians qua lesbians and ignore much clinical research showing that lesbian and non-lesbian women are similar in their placement along the entire spectrum of mental health and self identity. See, eg, Noreen O'Connor and Joanna Ryan, *Wild Desires and Mistaken Identities: Lesbianism and Psychoanalysis* (1993).

18 For an analysis of lesbians as vampires/killers, see, eg, Andrea Weiss, *Vampires and Violets: Lesbians in the Cinema* (1992); Barbara Creed, *The Monstrous-Feminine: Film, Psychoanalysis, Feminism* (1993); and Shameem Kabir, "Lesbian Desire on the Screen: The Hunger" in Liz Gibbs (ed), *Daring to Dissent: Lesbian Culture from Margin to Mainstream* (1994). A number of commentators also argue that fear of lesbianism underlies portrayals of ostensibly heterosexual female killers/criminals, eg, in *Black Widow* (1986) and *Thelma and Louise* (1991), see: Christine Holmlund, "A Decade of Deadly Dolls: Hollywood and the Woman Killer" in Birch, above n11; Lynda Hart, *Fatal Women: Lesbian Sexuality and the Mark of Aggression* (1994) at 67–80; Valerie Traub, "The Ambiguities of 'Lesbian' Viewing Pleasure: The (Dis)articulations of Black Widow" in Corey Creekmur and Alexander Doty (eds), *Out in Culture: Gay, Lesbian and Queer Essays on Popular Culture* (1995).

19 Lesbianism as a form of *carnality or animality* is established through Catherine. She uses base language, and in her first encounter with the police asserts her pleasure in impersonal sex (which she calls, to their horror, "fucking"), she rakes her male sexual partners with her fingernails and draws blood, and is shown in riding boots, surrounded by animal trophies after the first killing. Catherine also establishes lesbianism as intended for the explicit *voyeuristic* pleasure of heterosexual men in that she offers up her lesbian relationship visually, and also engineers displays of herself naked on numerous occasions. *Butch/femme* lesbianism is established by the character of Roxanne, Catherine's girlfriend, who is known as Roxy, dresses frequently in black leather, and is called "Rocky" by the male detective Curren (who also addresses her "man to man" and kills her in a driving duel, no less). Lesbianism as a type of *narcissism* is recurrent, both in the visual pairing of Catherine and Roxy in some scenes, and in the story of Beth/Lisa mirroring Catherine in appearance and mannerisms after they had a sexual encounter years earlier. *Mother/ daughter* lesbianism is suggested by a sexualised shot of Catherine and a middle aged woman, Beryl, who was earlier shown as a "mother figure" to her. For other recent films in which lesbian desire is semi-repressed, pathological and leads to murder, see *Single White Female* (1992) and *Poison Ivy* (1992). Both also involve metaphorical vampirism.

20 Lesbians are frequently shown as criminals on television also; see Rosie Collis, "Screened Out: Lesbians and Television" in Gibbs, above n18.

Basic Instinct was an enormous hit, and grossed US $385 million at the box office alone. It also drew enormous protest from lesbians and gays. In the USA a copy of the script was leaked during production and protests disrupted both the shooting and various premiere screenings of the film.[21] "I don't know any lesbian ice-pick killers" said Ellen Carlton of GLAAD, "Do you?"[22]

The crux of much criticism of the film (which is, despite all this, kind of fun)[23] was that it was unrealistic, and a cruel reversal of the truth. In *Basic Instinct* all the victims are men, and most are husbands and lovers of the killer women (there are also two brothers killed). Women who desire other women are portrayed as *vagina dentata*, luring men in through sexual means for the purpose of devouring/killing them. In *Basic Instinct*, lesbians court male desire, lesbians kill men. The converse is actually true, in that lesbians are consumed by men through heterosexual pornography (and films like *Basic Instinct*), lesbians are at risk of violence by men, and women who leave men for a lesbian relationship are at particular risk. In the Australian criminal cases, *Radford*, *McGhee* and *Lovec*, the killer/attempted killer was a male ex-partner of a woman in a lesbian couple.[24] Child custody cases where the mother is now lesbian are replete with violence by the father towards her and her lover.[25]

Fictional representations of murderous lesbians are thus a form of cultural attack. By placing lesbians always as anti-social, as a threat to men and "the family", who must be cast out or destroyed for order and safety to be returned, fictional representations encourage hostility and rights denials to lesbians. For instance, in both *Single White Female* and *Poison Ivy*, the pseudonymous interloper is a young woman, admired and desired by the heroine. The interloper is jealous of the heroine's familial relationships (fiance and parents, respectively)

---

21 John Gallagher, "Hollywood Under Fire" (1991) 578 *The Advocate* 46; L A Kauffman, "Queer Guerillas in Tinseltown" (1992) 56 (7) *The Progressive* 36; Janice Simpson, "Out of the Celluloid Closet" (1992) 139 (14) *Time Magazine* 65. Interestingly, there did not appear to be any protest at the much nastier English film *Butterfly Kiss* (1995) in which Amanda Plummer plays a psychotic, babbling, ugly, sadomasochistic bisexual who bloodily kills a number of people in her travels along the motorways and drags poor adoring Saskia Reeves along with her. However one reviewer drolly noted that, "Psycho lezzie nutters on the lam" may have been a more appropriate title than *Butterfly Kiss*.

22 Gay and Lesbian Alliance Against Defamation. Quoted in "The Power and the Pride" (June 21 1993) *Newsweek* at 59. Similar protest was focused on the earlier film *Silence of the Lambs* (1991) because the cross dressing male serial killer was portrayed as bisexual or gay and his social/sexual dysfunction was explicitly posited as his motive.

23 Within the film's slick implausibility, Catherine as the metaphorical vampire is the most interesting character. The story is unusual in that it does not close with the typical killed or cured lesbian erasure. Catherine is neither slain by Curren's gun nor tamed by his penis, and there is more than a hint that he is about to cop it in the closing sex scene. Andrea Weiss discusses the camp attraction of lesbian vampires in her book, above n18. Richard Dyer discusses reasons why lesbians and gays may identify with fictional depictions of vampires even if they are negative in "Children of the Night: Vampirism as Homosexuality, Homosexuality as Vampirism" in Susannah Radstone (ed), *Sweet Dreams: Sexuality, Gender and Popular Fiction* (1988). For a truly intriguing lesbian vampire tale, see *The Hunger* (1983).

24 See above n2.

25 Some of these cases are discussed in my article, "Lesbian Mothers, Gay Fathers: Sameness and Difference" (1992) 2 *Australian Gay and Lesbian LJ* 21. In addition see the Canadian case, *N v N* [1992] BC J No 1507 (Unreported, QUICKLAW, BC SC, Warren J, 2 July 1992), and American cases, *Diehl* 582 NE 2d 281 (Ill App 2 Dist 1991) and *Williams* 563 NE 2d 1195 (Ill App 3 Dist 1990).

and she sleeps with and kills members of the family in an attempt to destroy it — as well as making a sexual play for the heroine herself. The climax of both films is the heroine's realisation that murder has taken place, and her killing the interloper.[26] In the fictional world such destruction may be an extreme fantasy, but it is thematically consistent with conservative rhetoric that lesbians and gay men "threaten the fabric of society" or are a "threat to the family". When lesbians are characterised as a threat in this manner an implicit social and legal agenda is operative — a defence of family and society is necessary by continuing (or stepping up) oppression of lesbians and gays.[27] This theme is often implicit in "family values" discourse, but is occasionally made explicit. "You are fifteen times more likely to be murdered by a homosexual than a heterosexual" was one of the catchcries of a Tasmanian group opposing the decriminalisation of gay sex in that State.[28]

3. *"Real" Killers, "True" Crime*

When a non-fictional lesbian is accused of killing, the basis of fact gives cultural representation an added measure of authority. Films, books and magazine articles representing the murderous lesbian are justified as "true". The established fact of "real" death, coupled with generally scant information on anything else surrounding it, permits outlandish reconstructions which simultaneously lay claim to authenticity. Sensationalism, often with a salacious tone, is a stock in trade of the "true crime" genre and, to a slightly lesser degree, of news reports. Misrepresentation (including simple factual errors) and a certain lip-smacking enjoyment is not something particular to representation of crimes involving lesbians, but there are elements which are specific. As with fictional representations of murderous lesbians "true crime" accounts posit lesbianism as pathological, violent and necessarily causal — in contrast to cases where a heterosexual man murders and neither masculinity nor heterosexuality are queried or viewed as causal.[29] Guy Kerr provides a consummate

---

26 Lynda Hart argues that the heroine in *Single White Female* is explicitly punished for her desire to live independently of men and her narcissism/lesbianism in seeking "same": above n18 at 113–7. Another, less explicit, example is Alfred Hitchcock's 1940 version of Daphne Du Maurier's *Rebecca*. For discussion of lesbianism as depravity and anti-marriage in the film and book (embodied by both Rebecca and Mrs Danvers), see Mary Wings, "Rebecca Redux: Tears on a Lesbian Pillow" in Gibbs, above n18. Also see Rhonda Berenstein, "'I'm not the sort of person men marry': Monsters, Queers and Hitchcock's *Rebecca*" in Creekmur, above n18. In the book Rebecca's husband murdered her, in the film the killing was accidental, and in both Mrs Danvers burns to death.

27 Didi Herman discusses the ideology and legal interventions of the "New Christian Right" in Canada in *Rights of Passage: Struggles for Lesbian and Gay Equality* (1994). A recent example in the USA is the Right's response to interim sucesses in lesbian and gay marriage claims in Hawaii — a federal Act defining marriage as exclusively opposite sex. It is called the *Defence of Marriage Act*.

28 Quoted in *Toonen* reported in (1995) 69 *ALJ* 600. Notably this very quote was reprinted with no further comment on the cover of that same issue of the journal. Didi Herman also notes the claim in an American publication of the New Christian Right that "out of all the mass murders in the US over the past 17 years, homosexuals killed at least 68% of the victims": id at 88.

29 Of course many feminists have pointed out this silence in mainstream approaches and vigorously interrogated it, see, eg, Jane Caputi, *The Age of Sex Crime* (1988).

458   SYDNEY LAW REVIEW   [VOL18: 451

example, blending wild reconstruction with equally wild assumptions of causation, when he writes for a Queensland tabloid newspaper,

> Quick to spot the nascent depravity that was to later turn her into a killer, [a private school] expelled her for molesting other girls, thereby saving its pupils from the reign of terror Tracey initiated at the nearby Range Catholic School where she was sent instead.

> In the quiet cloisters and under the massive old trees of this haven of learning, Tracey Avril Wigginton was honing the aggressive lesbianism that climaxed eight years later when she plunged a knife into the neck of her male victim and drank his blood from the gaping hole.[30]

Leonard Gribble's florid "true crime" reconstruction of the Papin sisters' crime goes even further. Gribble puts words into the mouths of the Papin sisters, their victims, the investigators, and at times quotes the thoughts of various key people for the reader. Gribble has the policeman exclaiming, "Sacre Bleu!" on discovering the bodies, the Magistrate staring at Christine "in horror, seeing a twenty-eight years-old woman who was a bitter lesbian butch-type female who revolted him" and subsequently wishing for some cognac.[31] A remarkable feat, indeed, especially writing some 50 years after the event. The plethora of unlikely quotations and lack of any sourcing casts some doubt on his extensive "quotes" of the women from statements of interview, where he has them, among other things, telling the police that they had sex by candle-light after the murders.[32] Gribble lingers on descriptions of aggressive animalistic sexuality, returning numerous times to the idea that the sisters had sex after the murder, and using metaphors such as "animal-like", "panthers" and "mongrel bitch in heat" when discussing Christine's well documented distress when separated from her sister in prison. Animal imagery and connections of lesbian sexuality with bestiality are extremely common, both within this genre and without it.[33] (Although in his use of metaphor, at least, Gribble is in accord with the historical record: the prosecution refuted the insanity defence with the remark, "they are not enraged dogs, they are snarling dogs."[34])

Claims to authenticity combined with unbridled reconstruction are also a feature of fictionalised accounts. The Production notes of *Sister my Sister*, distributed by Palace Films to reviewers include the following:

> [In the production of the play My Sister in This House, on which the film was closely based] [w]e added some slides of the real murders at the beginning, which worked extremely well ...

> [The writer of the play and film] came to England for the last week or so of shooting, bringing with her photographs of the real scene of the crime, position

---

30 Guy Kerr, "Cradle of a Demon: Hate-Filled Home Bred a Vampire" (17 February 1991) *Sunday Mail* at 5, cited in Deb Verhoeven, above n11.

31 Leonard Gribble, *Such Lethal Ladies* (1985), esp at 44–7.

32 Gribble also liberally peppers the sisters' speech with swear words, whereas other accounts note their compulsive manners, such that they would even address their jailers in the polite French third person; see Janet Flanner, "The Papin Sisters: The Housemaids Revenge", originally published in 1934 *Vanity Fair*, reprinted in Richard Glyn Jones, above n9.

33 See, eg, Rupert Furneaux, "like wild animals" in "The New Zealand Girl Murderers" in Allan Wingate, *Famous Criminal Cases 2* (1955) at 47. Richard Dyer makes this point about filmic representations also: see Richard Dyer (ed), *Gays and Film* (1984) at 31.

34 Nicole Ward Jouve, "An Eye for an Eye: The Case of the Papin Sisters" in Birch, above n11 at 27.

of the bodies, and some haunting portraits of the two sisters. She found that the production had got all the main details exactly right.

This was a production which erased a husband and a fiance, changed the ages of characters, added an incestuous relationship, and had all four French women played by English actresses. And it's always "a true story".

4. Killing the Father

In 1991 the Australian print media named Tracey Wigginton "the lesbian vampire killer". In 1989 Wigginton had stabbed an unknown man to death, assisted by her lover (of one week), Lisa Ptaschinski, and accompanied by her friends (of two weeks), Kim Jervis and Tracey Waugh (themselves a couple). Although the murder was arranged by all four women jointly two days before it occurred, media attention came to be almost exclusively focused on Wigginton. Unsubstantiated claims by her co-accused that Wigginton was a vampire came to be blithely reproduced in both tabloid and broadsheet newspapers without even so much as the query a pair of inverted commas might offer to the term "vampire".[35] The prosecutor himself proffered the view in court that Wigginton could not eat food and survived on blood.[36] Lisa Ptaschinski claimed that she was so dominated by her lover that she slit her own wrists on a number of occasions to feed her. All three co-accused expressed the belief that Wigginton had drunk the victim's blood.

The co-accused were arrested after Wigginton, and all three effectively claimed to be "victims" of her vampiric powers, afraid of or mesmerised by her. Much of their joint trial was spent on the issue of Wigginton and her satanic powers, as they attempted to exculpate themselves.[37] Wigginton herself never publicly claimed anything to do with vampirism, however by the time of the co-accused trial, her own trial was already over. The Queensland Mental Health Tribunal had refused to accept that Multiple Personality Disorder (with which Tracey had been diagnosed) was an "abnormality of the mind" under the Criminal Code, and held therefore that she was sane and fit to plead.[38] At that point, Tracey pleaded guilty and received a nine minute trial. Officially guilty and silent by choice, the path was clear for the version of Wigginton's co-accused to enter popular folklore. Domination and sadism were the central elements of the co-accused claims; allegations of "Hitler-like" influence, marriage to the devil, hypnotic eyes and garden variety sexual dominance were reproduced in loving hyperbole by the press,[39] without any

---

35 See, eg, "Woman Gets Life Term for Vampire Murder" (16 February 1991) *SMH* 3; "My Daughter, The Vampire" (17 February 1991) *Sunday Herald* 1 and other examples below n39.
36 Stewart MacArthur, "Three 'Helped Killer Who Drank Blood'" (1 February 1991) *The Australian*.
37 Tracey Waugh, who claimed that she believed herself to be the "reserve victim" was the only one found not guilty.
38 See Ron Hicks, *The Vampire Killer: A Journey Into The Mind of Tracey Wigginton* (1992). Apart from a rather turgid reconstruction of Wigginton's childhood, Hicks argues strongly for the MPD diagnosis.
39 See, eg, Stewart MacArthur, "Accused 'fed lover her blood'" (7 February 1991) *The Australian*; Stewart MacArthur, "Killer was 'devil's wife with power to control minds'" (5 February 1991) *The Australian* at 5; "Vampire controlled my mind, court told" (5 February

question about how three adult women (of lengthy acquaintance with each other) came to be so utterly under the power of someone they had met only one to two weeks earlier. Thank god for the occult, or none of it would have made sense.[40] Wigginton was characterised as vampirising not only her male victim but her female co-accused. "Lesbian vampire killer" was a claim easily made and gladly accepted according, as it did, with a cultural frame of reference which views lesbianism as carnal, contagious and sadomasochistic.[41]

Likewise, claims that Aileen Wuornos was America's "first female serial killer" slipped seamlessly into populist discourse. Wuornos' alleged motive for shooting seven men in Florida was that she was a (lesbian therefore) "man-hater", luring men into the woods to kill them. "There may be an intrinsic hatred of males here, as well as an identification with male violence …" says an FBI investigator. "You might not expect a woman of clear sexual identity to do this … If this woman's makeup is such that she takes pride in being masculine, her motivation would be a psychological challenge to the male — 'I'm more masculine than you'," says a psychiatrist.[42]

Wuornos was a highway prostitute, whose own version of events was that in each case the victim had raped, or attempted to rape, and threatened to kill her in the course of her work. Investigators were so devoted to the "man-hater" theory of events that they believed Wuornos had posed as a hitchhiker or motorist in distress to "lure" men (in their own cars) into secluded areas. The prosecution in the first case successfully argued this version of events and obtained the death penalty as a result of "aggravating factors" such as "cold, calculating premeditation".[43]

Wuornos was inscribed and re-inscribed as a prostitute in the media, but somehow the victims were not engaged in that prostitution when they picked her up by the roadside. At one stage investigators claimed that condom packets found in the cars were left by Wuornos to "sully" her victim's reputations.[44] (The victims, as it happens, included two former police and an evangelical missionary.) In popular understandings, Wuornos' prostitution precluded her claims of sexual assault[45] and therefore self defence, while her lesbianism

---

1991) *SMH* at 2; "Vampire killer set out to scare" (2 February 1991) *SMH* at 4; "Vampire murderer feared sun and mirrors, court told" (7 February 1991) *Courier Mail* at 3; "Vampire killer had Hitler-like influence, court told" (13 February 1991) *Courier Mail* at 3.

40 Deb Verhoeven notes that a few articles sought explanation in Wigginton's abuse by her grandparents: Birch, above n11. However no explanations, other than Wigginton's influence, were sought for the actions of the other three.

41 It hasn't escaped me that these particular homophobic claims were originated by lesbians themselves. For a discussion of lesbian-instigated homophobia in civil cases see my article, "An Implied Promise to Parent: Lesbian Families, Litigation and *W v G*" (1996) 10 *Aust J Fam L* 112.

42 In "The First Woman Serial Killer?" (September 1991) *Glamour*, quoted in Lynda Hart, above n18 at 184–5. Candice Skrapec also characterises Wuornos as masculine and man-hating in her piece, "The Female Serial Killer: An Evolving Criminality" in a feminist collection, Birch, above n11.

43 The first conviction and sentence were upheld in *Wuornos v Florida* 644 So 2d 1000 (Fla App, 1994).

44 See Carys Bowen-Jones, "Diggin up Bones" originally published in *Marie Claire* (August 1991), reprinted in Richard Glyn Jones, above n9.

45 Lynda Hart notes the incredulity of interviewers regarding the idea that prostitutes can be raped: above n18 at 141.

provided the motive for premeditated murder. A lesbian serial killer story was too immediately accessible, too eminently sellable to resist: several investigators and the central prosecution witness had signed movie deals before the arrest was even made, and two of Wuornos' own defence lawyers simultaneously negotiated with film companies on her behalf.[46] Thus far some 15 different production companies have involved themselves in the case, two films and two books have already appeared and more are on the way.[47] A critical evaluation of this media frenzy, and its perversion of the course of justice inspires a sense of outrage but surprisingly little to say. Lynda Hart, in her eloquent piece, says that Wuornos' story is "banal" and the coverage of it "an all-too-ordinary repetition in a culture of paranoid male fantasies that eroticize their worst nightmares".[48]

What links Wigginton and Wuornos, and goes some way to explaining their vilification in the media, is that they both killed in "male" ways, attacking strangers in public places. They also both killed male victims 20 to 30 years older than themselves. Lesbianism thus provided popular and readily accessible explanations for their behaviour. They were lesbian, so were "like" men and killed like men. They were lesbian, so they hated men and killed men. They were lesbian, so they hated society and the family — represented by "the father" — so they killed men who were father figures. Notably the victims were often represented in the press as "fathers" and "family" men and the relationship between both accused and their own fathers and (father figure) grandfathers[49] was the subject of much reporting. The Papin sisters and Parker and Hulme, in contrast, killed women with whom they were intimately connected in the domestic realm. They also killed jointly, and may have killed to protect their relationship. The coverage of these two crimes, and subsequent fictionalised representations are far more complex, nuanced, and have varied over time.

5. Killing the Mother

Christine and Lea Papin were sisters in their 20s, who worked as live-in maids in provincial France. In 1933, they spontaneously bashed their employer and her adult daughter to death and mutilated their bodies.[50] Upon discovery, they confessed their actions but never apparently offered any explanation beyond the fact that they had blown a fuse in the house which had angered their employers. Pauline Parker and Juliet Hulme were friends, and possibly lovers, who had met at school in New Zealand. In 1954 (aged 16 and 15 respectively) they planned to, and did, bash Pauline's mother to death.

---

46 Details of these and numerous other examples of spectacular injustices in the investigation and prosecution of Wuornos, including failures to call crucial defence witnesses, are discussed in Phyllis Chestler, "A Woman's Right to Self Defence: The Case of Aileen Carol Wuornos" (1993) 66 *St John's LR* 933.

47 Including: *Overkill: The Aileen Wuornos Story* (1992, US TV-movie); *Aileen Wuornos: The Selling of A Serial Killer* (UK documentary actually about media and legal exploitation); Dolores Kennedy, *A Killing Day* (1994).

48 Hart, above n18 at 141.

49 Both women lived for large parts of their childhoods with their grandparents.

50 I have omitted details of the violence in all cases as much as possible, not from a desire to exculpate the perpetrators, but in an attempt to avoid becoming a salacious "true crime" writer myself.

Both girls claimed the death was accidental; when this was clearly disbelieved Pauline at first took the blame for the murder. Under subsequent questioning, Juliet confessed to also taking part.

The coverage of the two joint trials, some 20 years apart, provides some contrasts and also some fascinating comparisons in terms of how the crimes were linked to sexuality both within and without the court room. Such connections are apparently unconscious ones, as at no stage in Parker and Hulme's trial or the available coverage does it appear the Papin sisters were ever mentioned (instead all parallels were drawn with Leopold and Loeb, two young gay men who as a couple had committed a kidnapping and murder of a young boy in America in the 1920s).[51] The omission of any mention of the Papins is particularly startling when it is noted that both trials heard an identical insanity defence. The defence was *delire a deux* or *folie a deux* — a largely unsupported theory of communicated or joint madness, such that each party is individually sane if separate but acts insanely when together. This theory, and the insanity defence generally, were rejected in both cases — but nevertheless deeply influenced popular understandings of the crimes as an expression of, or result of, a lesbian relationship. It also influenced the state's decisions about incarceration and punishment; the Papin sisters were separated in prison and Christine starved herself to death as a result. Pauline and Juliet were sent to separate prisons, permitted no contact whilst there and subsequently released on the condition that they never have contact again in their lives. Indeed, Pauline's release was specifically delayed so that Juliet had left the country by the time they were both free. New Zealand authorities actually considered revoking Pauline's parole when it was discovered, some years after her release, that she was socialising with lesbians.[52] The parole revocation, although ultimately not carried out, belies an implicitly homophobic reading of the *folie a deux* theory, that it is not a relationship which makes one murderously insane, but a lesbian (or gay) relationship, possibly *any* lesbian relationship.

In the case of the Papin sisters, the fact of their crime was held sufficient evidence in itself that their relationship must be sexual. Their crime — double murder — was explained as an outcome of their already extant double criminality; incestuous and lesbian sexuality. What is amazing is how quickly this idea arose from many separate sources, and how universally it was accepted. In the trial itself, the sisters' defence psychiatrist made a "delicate allusion to the girls [sic] as a 'psychological couple'" and the chief of the insane asylum where they were held made reference to Sappho.[53] The psychiatrist had never

---

51 The major defence expert, Dr Medlicott drew this comparison. The press adopted the parallel with vigour: see, eg, Rupert Furneaux' opening gambit, "We have to go back to Chicago in the early nineteen-twenties to find a murder case as shocking", above n33 at 33. Leopold and Loeb differ from Parker and Hulme in that they killed a relative stranger to them, apparently for pleasure. Both prosecution and defence agreed that Parker and Hulme killed because they were going to be separated and could think of no other way to prevent it. The only connection between the crimes is that they acted as a (probably homosexual) couple. Hitchcock based *Rope* (1948) on Leopold and Loeb. *Swoon* (1991) is based far more closely on the incident and differs from the other films under discussion in that it is made by a gay film maker.

52 Glamuzlina and Laurie, above n9 at 107–8.

53 Flanner, above n32 at 311–2.

met them, and based his opinion on the fact of their crime alone. The asylum chief appears to have based his opinion on Christine's excessive grief at being separated from Lea, Christine's reference to being her sister's husband in a former life (other sources say a clairvoyant had told Christine this) and Christine's cry when she was briefly permitted to see Lea after six months of incarceration, "Say yes, Lea, say yes to me."[54] Additional speculation seems to have arisen from the fact that the sisters shared a bed, and spent much of their scarce leisure time together in their room[55] — although bed sharing among the working classes was surely common in that era, and leaving the house rarely could be explained by the fact that the sisters had no money of their own (as for much of their working lives their wages had been paid to their mother and not to them).[56] Jaques Lacan, like the defence psychiatrist, did not require any of this slight evidence to come to his conclusion — he knew at once the cause of their evil. How did he know? Why, because it fitted in so nicely with a thesis he had just finished on another female criminal where he first posited the "mirror stage".[57] Lacan's thesis was that female violence was a manifestation of suppressed homosexual urges arising from narcissism and the failure to separate self from other. Lacan's version of the *delire a deux* was that the sisters wanted (but did not have) each other sexually, and displaced their anxiety and aggression (necessarily generated by such improper closeness and involving sadistic/masochistic urges) to attack the "other" couple, the mother and daughter.[58]

The circularity of Lacan's argument — that female crime is caused by suppressed lesbianism, the existence of which is proven by the crime — does not end there, however. Because the other couple were a mother and daughter, Lacan supposed that Christine and Lea were too; Christine as the oldest was placed by him as the "dominant" one, or mother.[59] Lacan was pleased to announce a correlation of abnormality in homosexuality and sado-masochism, and the Papin sisters were the proof of it.[60] Thus the way was firmly paved for later psychoanalytic theory, subsequent pop-psychology, and mass media representation, to (re)present lesbianism as inherently narcissistic, immature, likely to involve power imbalances such as dominant/submissive or mother-daughter role play, and likely to lead to violence and criminality. If all of this sounds dreadfully familiar, it is. It is *Basic Instinct, Poison Ivy, Single White Female* etc & etc. It is the history of lesbianism in mainstream cinema.[61] In a final, dazzling moment of circularity, these themes — arising from the speculation around the kernel of the Papin sisters, to become so common in post-1940s filmic representation of lesbians — are pervasive in *Sister my Sister*, the 1996 film of the Papin sisters' crime.

Lynda Hart contends that there were two reasons why contemporary coverage of the Papins, both within and without the court room came to be so focused on

---

54 Ibid. See also Jouve in Birch, above n11.
55 Lynda Hart, above n8.
56 See Jouve in Birch, above n11.
57 See Hart, above n18 at 144–8; also Jouve in Birch, above n11.
58 Ibid.
59 Ibid. See also Hart, above n8 at 135.
60 Hart, above n8 at 135.
61 See introduction; also Russo, above n15; Weiss, above n18; Dyer, above n4.

their sexuality. As alluded to above, the crime coincided with the bloom of modern psychoanalysis; indeed Hart stresses that the crime occurred in the very year that Freud wrote "Femininity".[62] They were thus timely fodder for a new industry. Hart also eloquently argues that there was a powerful class motive for viewing the crime as a product of sexuality:

> The issue of the sisters' guilt was resolved by their mutual confession. But the apparent absence of a motive (they had said the murder was prompted by Madame's unexpected return and reprimand for blowing the fuse) led to extensive exploration of the sisters' sanity, which in turn depended on affirmation of their sexual 'normality.' In the provincial town of Le Mans, there were powerful incentives for proving the maids insane. Virtually every family employed domestic servants. The right-wing newspapers were full of warnings about the 'Red Terror.' ... The courts were eager to suppress any analysis of the Papin murders as a class insurrection. If the 'pearls of Le Mans,' as Christine and Lea were called, could revolt, then all bourgeois employers were in grave danger.[63]

In light of all circumstances discussed thus far, it is hard to imagine the sisters getting any positive press at all, but intriguingly, it was this class element which gave the sisters a number of vigorous public defenders, particularly among the Parisian intelligentsia. Simone de Beauvoir, among others, wrote sympathetically of the sisters.[64] Prominent leftists and anarchists argued that the maids had killed in response to their life of slavery and oppression at the hands of their mistresses, and some went so far as to argue that, "[t]his trial should not have been only that of the sisters, but also that of the sacrosanct bourgeois family".[65] Even among the mainstream press of the day, more than passing comment was made about the petty tyrannies of domestic service generally and in the Lancelin house in particular.[66] The Surrealists took a somewhat different bent, and championed the maids as launching a poetic, symbolic emancipation from "the mother".[67] A huge volume of descriptive, critical, analytical and creative material grew from the Papin sisters' crime. In subsequent years there appeared, among others,[68] a short story by Jean-Paul Sartre, a play by Jean Genet, *Les Bonnes/The Maids* (also produced as an opera and later filmed),[69] a film inspired by the play,[70] a novel,[71] and then the play that led to the film *Sister my Sister*.[72]

---

62 Hart, above n8 at 131 and Hart, above n18 at 147.
63 Hart, above n8 at 133–4.
64 Discussed by Jouve, in Birch, above n11.
65 Hart, above n8 at 132.
66 Particularly in *Paris-Soir*. The Tharaud brothers wrote, "God knows the Madame Lancelins exist on earth. ... As good servants, the girls had been highly contraried." These views are reproduced and gently parodied but not altogether departed from in Janet Flanner's 1934 piece, above n32.
67 Jouve in Birch, above n11.
68 Much of this material is analysed by Jouve, ibid.
69 Originally Genet denied the connection with the Papins, as his play is quite a symbolic reading of events — and, for example, there are two maids but only one mistress. Later Genet recanted and acknowledged the inspiration: see Edmund White, *Genet* (1993) at 349–52.
70 *Les Abysses* (1962), was originally to be based on Genet's play, but Genet withdrew the rights. The director therefore returned to the original event. When released the film was attacked for its violence, and was defended, as the sisters were, by de Beauvoir, Sartre and co: see White, id at 528–9.
71 Paulette Houdyer, *Le Diable dans la paeu*. There appears to be no English edition.
72 See n81. Furthermore, the Ruth Rendell novel, *Judgment in Stone* (and subsequent West End play and 1996 film by Claude Chabrol) also concern a french maid who kills her employers.

Parker and Hulme were received very differently. Their relationship was also universally presumed to be lesbian, although this was based on Pauline's diaries and so was not without substantial foundation.[73] Opinion was only divided as to whether the relationship had been consummated. The defence experts proffered that it was not, because of course repressed homosexuality was an integral part of the insanely paranoid *folie a deux* defence which they were running.[74] The prosecution expert countered that, "... there was nothing repressed about the homosexuality",[75] so there was no paranoia, no insanity, just depravity. This was a view put most forcefully in the Crown's opening address, when it was argued that they were "highly intelligent and perfectly sane but precocious and dirty-minded girls".[76] There appears to have been little reflection, then or later, on the irony of this particular medico-legal construct: that the girls were mad if they didn't have sex with each other, but sane if they did.

Unlike the Papin sisters, whose double murder had been significantly more brutal, Parker and Hulme do not appear to have had any sympathy in the extensive press coverage at the time. But then New Zealand in the 1950s didn't have Simone, Jean Paul and an avant guard intelligentsia prepared to read the crime as an interesting anti-bourgeois statement or as a revolt against the symbolic mother.[77] In fact New Zealand at the time was so firmly bourgeois that Juliet's disbelief in god and the girls' decision not to go to see the Queen when she visited the country were used *as evidence* in Court that they had no idea of right and wrong and must be insane.[78]

Moreover, whereas the Papin sisters had killed a metaphorical mother and their crime could be celebrated as a symbolic act, Parker and Hulme had killed a real mother who was by no means tyrannical. There was frankly no one prepared to see their act as anything other than evil or insane. Defence and prosecution claims were jumbled in together in the press, combining "dirty minds" with insanity, to give the most salacious account possible. Some articles went so far as to connect the illnesses which both girls had suffered as children with their sexuality, to give an overall picture of disease.[79]

In the context of the post-war concern over the "breakdown of the family" and juvenile delinquency, Parker and Hulme were to be viewed as a salutary lesson indeed. Many press and "true crime" reports noted the fact that Pauline's parents had never married (though no one had known of this until

---

73 See above n9.
74 See the evidence of defence psychiatrist Dr Medlicott, discussed in Glamuzina and Laurie, above n9 at 88–91, substantially agreed with by Dr Bennett, 92–4. Dr Medlicott based much of his later work on Parker and Hulme, continuing to argue *folie a deux* and a connection between repressed homosexuality and violent paranoia, see Glamuzina and Laurie, id at 110, 120–33.
75 Glamuzina and Laurie, id at 95.
76 Id at 84. This remark is ubiquitous in all subsequent newspaper and true crime coverage.
77 And, obviously, there was no gay liberation movement yet, in NZ or elsewhere, prepared to sympathise with the stress which the girls must have faced at the level of parental and medical intervention in their relationship.
78 I'm not kidding. See Glamuzina and Laurie, above n9 at 92–3.
79 See, eg, Gurr and Cox, "Juliet Hulme's tuberculosis (a disease often found in cases of sexual divergence)", above n9 at 335.

the arrest), and that Juliet's mother was in the process of leaving her husband for another man. A committee into degeneracy among teenagers, focusing upon "sexual delinquency", was set up a month after the murder, partially as a response to it.[80]

Subsequent re-presentations of the two crimes in 1990s film versions provide further reinterpretations, revisions and contrasts.

6. Back to the Scene of the Crime: Sister my Sister *and* Heavenly Creatures

> [The play on which *Sister my Sister* was based][81] would make a good film, bursting at the seams as it was with good cinematic ingredients: suspense, incest and violent murder ...
>
> > From the Production notes of *Sister my Sister*, distributed by Palace Films to reviewers
>
> I thought, 'After 40 years, who cares?' The Berlin Wall has come down, Communism has fallen, the whole world has changed since then.
>
> > Anne Perry/Juliet Hulme, on the release of *Heavenly Creatures*[82]

All of the publicity for *Heavenly Creatures*, the 1994 film about Parker and Hulme, foregrounded the "true-crime" element, with the large print subtitle, "The true story of a crime that shocked a nation."[83] The lesbian part of the story was more subtle but equally present: several of the advertisements contained the surtitle "Not all angels are innocent", and almost all of them displayed one of the many frames from the film of the girls in smiling embraces, or with faces close together. (Although the video jacket went further: "Two teenage schoolgirls whose obsessive friendship leads to an unspeakable crime.") Interestingly, this choice of foregrounding and backgrounding was reversed in the publicity for the 1996 film *Sister my Sister*. The poster and advertisements for *Sister* did not make direct mention of the crime, although the surtitle reads, "Bound by love ... and blood."[84] Lesbian sexuality and incest are highlighted by the picture, which shows the sisters in a passionate embrace behind a cupboard. Lea has her head back, mouth open, and Christine is kneeling, with her face pressed, at crotch level, against Lea. This photo still is from the conclusion of a sex scene in the film, and there is no way it could be mistaken for a friendly cuddle in the way the *Heavenly Creatures* pictures could.

Within the films themselves the visual and textual claims to authenticity and truth are established by strikingly similar devices. Both films open and close with the "scene of the crime". The opening sequences allude to the murder without showing how it came about — *Sister* shows a bloody banister and

---

80 Id at 58–60.
81 Wendy Kesselman, "My Sister in This House" in Gillian Hanna (ed), *Monstrous Regiment: A Collective Collaboration* (1991).
82 Quoted in Barbara Wickens, above n9.
83 This was uniform across posters, print media advertisements and also the video jacket.
84 The review on the reverse side of the publicity flier mentions that a crime "inspired" the film, but immediately leaps to the film's "potent mix of intrigue and incest".

stairwell, panning across the feet of two dead women, *Heavenly Creatures* has a blood spattered Pauline and Juliet screaming and running up a hill, at the summit of which Pauline cries out, "It's Mummy, she's terribly hurt."[85] The films thus set out to solve, or perhaps, explain, how the murders came about. Both then close with the actual sequential conduct of the murders missing from the opening scenes. Both films also frame their narrative within opening and closing text windows, the opening one stating that the story is "true"[86] and the closing one noting the sentences passed and what subsequently "became" of the women.[87]

Sister my Sister is based on an American play which was in turn based on contemporaneous media accounts and trial transcripts.[88] *Heavenly Creatures* was not based on prior theatrical renditions, nor on press reports, but almost entirely upon the trial transcripts (which reproduced large sections of Pauline's diary) supplemented by interviews with former schoolmates of Pauline and Juliet.[89]

While *Sister my Sister* was meticulous as to the details of the murders themselves (location, method, time of day), it altered two crucial aspects of events.[90] Notably, the writer Wendy Kesselman entirely removed Mme and Mlle Lancelin's husband and fiance, in order to make it a story about women, and to enhance a mirroring of Christine and Lea as a pair with their mother and daughter employers. She also included an explicit sexual relationship between the sisters, although much contemporary opinion regarded the relationship as unconsummated, and she herself admitted that she didn't know whether they had been lovers.[91] Nevertheless the film was received by reviewers as factual.[92]

Factual material was neatly fitted into the story to support its own hypothesis; for instance, the suspicious shared bedroom of history becomes even more pointedly evidence of a sexual relationship in the film. Madame tells her daughter that she offered the maids two rooms (how likely? she was a noted miser) and they wanted only one. So viewers are told that the sisters *chose* to share a bed. Likewise the handmade lingerie found in the maids' room is

---

85 This is intercut with brief black and white shots of the girls running, laughing, along the deck of a ship, calling out "Mummy" to a woman we later learn is Mrs Hulme.

86 *Heavenly Creatures* makes a more direct claim to truth, reading, "During 1953 and 1954 Pauline Yvonne Parker kept diaries recording her friendship with Juliet Marion Hulme/ This is their story/ All diary entires are in Pauline's own words." While *Sister my Sister* reads, "A small town in Provincial France 1932/ Based on true events", *Heavenly Creatures* also includes, towards the end of the film, clocks in numerous of the frames of scenes depicting the day of the murder, emphasising the exact time of events (as recorded by Police).

87 *Heavenly Creatures* also noted the time of arrest and pleas entered.

88 See Hart, above n8.

89 See Howard Feinstein, "Death and the Maidens" (15 November 1994) *Village Voice* 60.

90 A third, more minor but still pointed, alteration was that while the Papin sisters retained their names, their victims were given pseudonyms: the surname Lancelin became Danzard.

91 Hart, above n8 at 142.

92 For example, "When the sisters' security is threatened hot incestuous passion busts into maniacal frenzy. ... The film is ... a case history, not a drama, with nothing ultimately to offer other than a chronicle of breakdown, the fracturing of two minds under psychosexual pressures," Stanley Kauffmann, "Cry Havoc" (17–24 July 1995) *New Republic* 34 at 35.

made, in the film, by Christine for Lea alone (rather than to sell or for herself), and becomes a means by which she seduces her.[93]

Christine and Lea's conflict with their mother is subtly reconfigured in the film such that it is Christine who wants to separate from her, and not Lea (where in fact they both wanted to). Christine is thus firmly placed as a mother to Lea from the very outset of the film. Christine is shown feeding and dressing Lea when they were children (in flashback), she competes with her own mother for Lea's devotion, tries to prevent Lea from seeing their mother, and calls Lea a "baby", infantilising her both in anger and in love. The scene in which Christine finally convinces Lea not to see their mother any longer is, not coincidentally, the very scene in which they realise their sexual desire for each other. Only with the rejection of the "real" mother can Christine finally take her place as mother in their role-play.

The relationship of Christine and Lea (who in fact were only six years apart in age) is also explicitly depicted as mirroring that of their mistresses in intercut scenes.[94] There are numerous parallels of the mother berating, manipulating or dominating her daughter and Christine doing likewise to Lea. One scene cuts back and forth between the two "couples" several times, stressing both their sameness and their difference. As the Lancelins are shown to be unhealthily sexually repressed, fighting it out in a frenzied card game downstairs, Christine and Lea are shown to be unhealthily sexually expressed, tearing each other's clothes off upstairs. Although Kesselman gives the Papins a sexual relationship in a way Lacan never did, she seems to have been highly influenced by his theory, as the film chooses to stress an interpretation of Christine and Lea's relationship as mother/daughter, "like" the Lancelins, and as emotionally sado-masochistic.

It is notable that the sisters' sexual relationship is not completely gratuitous in that it provides the basis for the other major addition in the film; which is to actually give the sisters a rational motive for their crime. When the fuse blows, the film has Lea react hysterically and Christine calm her — the sisters then leave their work undone for the first time in their years of service and go to their room. The murders occurred on a landing in the house, and the film portrays the Lancelins advancing up the stairs, towards the maids room, an unprecedented invasion of the only private space the sisters had. Christine is shown to intercept the advance and Madame taunts her viciously at this point, telling her that she will never get another job, that they smell of sex, are not children of God, are filth, are "scum sisters". Madame is particularly degrading in her references to Lea. It is at this point that Christine is shown to lose her temper and attack, closely followed by Lea.

---

93 Long hair and lingerie being staples of titillating film representations of lesbian sex. This is a marked contrast to the white singlets and no-nonsense Bonds cottontails the girls wear in *Heavenly Creatures*.

94 For example, the famous and rather glamorous photo which the sisters had taken of themselves in life is made into a mimicry of the mistresses. In the film Madame gives her daughter such a photo of themselves for her birthday, and Christine is shown being inspired by this to go and get one of her own. There is no evidence the Lancelins ever had such a photo.

Sister my Sister resists, through this penultimate scene, the contemporaneous "lesbian therefore insane" presumption. It serves to reconfigure the widespread assumption of a sexual relationship into something which provides a rational motive, rather than an irrational basis. Within the film logic if the sisters had not killed Madame (and her daughter, a more of less passive witness to the scene), they would have had to face exposure of their doubly taboo relationship, the loss of their livelihoods and most likely the ruination of their lives. The sisters' choices are constrained, within this scenario, and they choose to go down fighting.

However, Christine and Lea's relationship is so frankly pathologised so early in the film that it belies the proffered rationality of their actions. The sisters quiver with hysteria almost from the first; they simply must kill someone.[95] The film offers the view that they were forced to protect themselves and their relationship — but it portrays the relationship as so extremely dysfunctional and destructive that it can hardly be seen as worth protecting. Moreover, by pathologising the sisters' relationship to such an extent it is easy to overlook Madame's provocation and to return to the historical view that saw the murders as a simple and inevitable result of the sisters' twisted and aggressive sexuality. It is in this aspect that *Sister my Sister* and *Heavenly Creatures* differ so markedly.

The attention to detail and efforts at factual correctness are stunning in *Heavenly Creatures*, as is the use of perspective.[96] The film soundtrack is in fact peppered with the girls' favourite music; "the world's greatest tenor" Mario Lanza. Although filled with period detail, the film is in no way wedded to realism or to a documentary stance, as it mixes in surreally filmed fantasy sequences depicting the inner world of Pauline, and to a lesser extent, Juliet. The girls wrote several novels and plays together, and invented between them a fantasy world called "Borovnia", peopled with a lineage of royal characters whom they acted out (even writing letters to each other in character). The film brings this world to life in numerous vividly filmed sequences where life sized plasticine figures appear and Borovnia becomes real. Various occurrences in Borovnia parallel the action and as time goes on and the fantasy world becomes more important, the two worlds overlap increasingly.

The soundtrack, made up of music that the girls themselves loved and listened to, becomes itself an important part of the film's subtext. Early in the film as the girls' friendship is established there are a series of sequences of them playing together (over an unclear period of time) with Mario Lanza singing, such that the action is largely unheard.[97] This series includes scenes of the

---

95 To be fair, the play on which the film was based was received as very thoughtful, complex and feminist: see Hart, above n8.

96 Down to where the girls spent their holidays, the childhood illnesses both had suffered, how Mrs Hulme's extra marital affair began, the length of the Hulmes's absences from their daughter, the films the girls saw and the stars they admired, and the doctor Pauline was sent to when the parents felt that the girls' attachment was becoming "unwholesome".

97 This device in itself suggests romance to me, being commonly used as a cinematic shorthand for falling in love. Moreover, the sequence begins when Pauline sees Juliet standing in golden light on a bridge in her garden, dressed as a princess. Pauline's face is shown, awed, even lovestruck, and cuts to a shot which rushes toward the radiant Juliet. (One is at first unsure whether this vision of Juliet is Pauline's fantasy or reality, until Juliet's brother appears and it is clear they are playing dress-ups.)

girls laughing, singing along to the song and taking off their clothes as they run hand in hand through woods. They eventually collapse in their underwear on the ground, whereupon they hug and quickly kiss, still laughing all the while. Viewers may read this as platonic if they care to, but the scene closes with Mario Lanza singing the last line of the accompanying song — "You're the one for me!" Likewise, much later in the film when the girls dance together in a playful high spirited waltz, Mario Lanza sings, "When you're in love". Lastly, in an ironic or sympathetic postscript, "You'll never walk alone" is sung over closing credits which tell the viewer that the girls were never to see each other again.[98] The use of this music highlights a sense that the film is in many ways more a romance than a murder mystery.

In focusing largely upon the developing relationship between the girls, *Heavenly Creatures* appears at first to accord with conventional wisdom of *folie a deux*, in that the explanation for the crime is the relationship. However, I believe that the film radically departs from this tenet by presenting the relationship as a positive thing in itself. Sequence after sequence depict the girls' delight in each other, and the scene which shows the girls kissing in bed together is both tender and humorous. Mr Hulme, and Dr Bennet, in interrogating the sexual nature of the relationship, are depicted as prurient, even lip smacking, and voyeuristic. The film suggests that the murder is a result, not of the relationship, but of the girls' distress at their imminent forced separation (the Hulmes were to leave the country and in any case both sets of parents were eager to separate the girls upon Dr Bennet's "diagnosis" of Pauline as homosexual).

A dream/fantasy sequence on the night before the murder adopts an internal perspective, wrenchingly romantic and naive. In this sequence, Juliet is singing on the balcony of her home, drenched in a rosy light. This cuts away to a black and white shot of Pauline and Juliet laughing and running towards the Hulmes on the deck of a large ship. Mrs and Mr Hulme embrace both girls, and, importantly, look proudly on as the girls kiss each other. The next scene shows the girls waking, pale, miserable and frightened as their alarm clocks ring in the morning. It is this dream, of their joyful union, overseen by approving parents, which appeared, almost subliminally intercut in the opening shots of the murder. The closing scene of the murder is also intercut with a black and white scene on the ship, but this time Juliet is on board and Pauline is left behind on the docks. The girls' sobbing and screams of distress from the boat scene blend seamlessly in with those of Pauline's mother as she is killed. The murder is in no way excused (and in fact is portrayed bloodily with matter of fact brutality), but it is established, with all the short sightedness of teenage logic, as an "us or them" scenario.[99]

---

98 "Keep your chin up high and don't be afraid of the dark. At the end of the storm is a sweet sun … walk on through the wind, walk on through the rain, though your dreams be tossed and blown, walk on, walk on, with love in your heart, and you'll never walk alone."

99 Pauline and Juliet had sold belongings, stolen money and goods and discussed prostitution as a method of raising sufficient funds to be able to go overseas together. These plans were thwarted when Pauline applied for a passport and was refused, as she was a juvenile. Pauline appears to have believed she would carry the entire blame for the murder, be declared insane and be released into the care of the Hulme family: See Glamuzina and Laurie, above n9.

The film thus steers an entirely different course from the stories which appeared at the time. While the prosecution argued the girls were evil, the defence claimed they were insane, and the media produced a loving hybrid, *Heavenly Creatures* depicts them as immature, inflated, tragically misguided but also misunderstood and desperately in love. Mandy Merck has written, in the context of English film and television, that lesbian and gay romance is more likely to be presented positively in "white flannel" drama: historical narratives of young, upper class characters.[100] She argues that the youth and the historical distance in such narratives are of crucial importance,

> making homosexuality a sort of phylogenetic phase on the way to a more
> mature culture. This, together with the remote class location of its characters
> and ... museum mise en scene, puts its homosexual romance at what is often
> seen to be a safe distance from contemporary appropriation.[101]

The largely positive and empathetic tone of *Heavenly Creatures* could be a result of some of these factors. However, this is not to say that it embodies all of these traits, or that they are sufficient explanation for its approach. While the film is firmly historical,[102] with the youth of the characters and school setting playing firmly into an established genre of lesbianism-as-a-schoolgirl-phase,[103] class is not used as a distancing marker. Rather, class is pervasively explored within the film, as Juliet's upper middle class professional family is valorised by lower middle class Pauline.

By the time of the murder in the film, as in life (at least in her diary), Pauline was referring to the Hulmes as "Mother" and "Father". Pauline's mother is shown in their small house, often in the kitchen or cleaning, careworn and catering to the needs of the boarders they took in for income. Pauline's family are low, and she is mortified when a new boarder arrives while Juliet is over for tea. Juliet's family live in a grand house on large grounds provided by the university where her father works. They are elegant, give garden parties, and travel overseas. The Hulmes' emotional neglect of Juliet — for instance going on a trip overseas for several months while Juliet had tuberculosis and was hospitalised — is countered by Juliet's, and thus Pauline's, fervent idolisation of them. It was Dr Hulme's idea to separate the girls, it was Mrs Hulme who was the "neglectful" mother, yet it was Pauline's mother who was killed. The film suggests that class had no small part to play in this, not only in the symbolic manner in which Pauline and Juliet transferred aggression to the less powerful mother, but in a very concrete sense. The film shows that

---

100 Mandy Merck, *Perversions: Deviant Readings* (1993) at 112.
101 Id at 113. I see this point as particularly true concerning historical narratives and applicable to films from various countries. For instance, see the generally positive portrayal of a romantic relationship between women in the US film *Fried Green Tomatoes at the Whistle Stop Cafe* (1992 — set in the 1930s). Also see the 1970s Australian films *Picnic at Hanging Rock* and *The Getting of Wisdom*, both set in turn-of-the-century girls' schools.
102 Down to an ironic establishing sequence of 1950s file footage promoting Christchurch as a tourist destination, including the contemporary voiceover, "Christchurch gardens are gay and colourful".
103 This view arose from the work of Havelock Ellis, Freud and Lacan positing lesbianism as a form of arrested development (see Noreen O'Connor and Joanna Ryan, *Wild Desires and Mistaken Identities: Lesbianism and Psychoanalysis* (1993)) and has ensured the place of lesbianism as an immature, titillating and ultimately passing phase in popular film.

it was Pauline who was taken off to the doctor to be diagnosed, at Dr Hulme's suggestion; implicitly it was she who was viewed as the contaminating agent. It was Pauline's mother who took her. Class privilege thus made it easy for the Hulmes to blame Pauline, prevail upon Pauline's parents to believe it so, and produce a situation where Pauline in turn blamed her own mother for it. This layering of meaning, and failure to posit either a sole cause or an insane irrationality, makes *Heavenly Creatures* very much an anomaly in the filmic representation of both lesbians and "true crime", although it does at times veer into more usual conventions.[104]

7.   Conclusion: *Unhappy Endings Are Not All Alike*

Both *Heavenly Creatures* and *Sister my Sister* offer interpretations of real crimes which differ significantly from those which appeared contemporane-ously. As such, they are examples of the ways in which popular cultural forms re-present, reinterpret and recreate commonplace understandings of crime and sexuality. Against a cultural backdrop in which lesbian sexuality has been, and often still is, used to signify aggression, irrationality and carnality, these two films both defy and comply with such popular reductionism.

In terms of defiance and complexity, *Heavenly Creatures* is by far the more successful film. It displays an unprecedented empathy for the difficulties of being a teenager in a lesbian relationship in the repressive 1950s, and per-vasively interrogates issues of class as well as sexuality. In doing so it offers a series of paradoxes; the girls' relationship is lovely, but they kill as a couple; they are powerless as children whom their parents are determined to separate, yet they are powerful as murderers. Their imaginative world is vivid, gorgeous, filmed in a technicolour whirl, but also full of make believe violence which seems inestimably more sinister in retrospect. In contrast *Sister my Sister* shifts away from the contemporary focus on class to fully embrace sexuality as the central motif. Paradoxically it offers a motive to an apparently wildly irrational crime, but undermines it through the pathology of the motive itself.

However, despite their complexities, *Heavenly Creatures* and *Sister my Sister* still comply to some extent with the cultural context of film as a "re-lentless parade of insults". This is because the very choice of stories which are told in a mass medium such as film is indicative of a society which views lesbians as anti-social, aggressive and dangerous. True stories of jolly nice, non-murdering, or even heroic lesbians don't tend to appear in film and, if they do appear, the character's lesbianism is almost always muted or erased.[105] Whereas when lesbians are killers, or killers are presumed to be

---

104   Notably the extreme gruesomeness of the murder, and the fact that the girls both get paler in the latter part of the film, with dark rings around their eyes and lank hair, adopting a distinctly sinister and vampiric appearance. This could well be justified by the fact that Juliet was recovering from TB and Pauline was not eating properly but nevertheless sug-gests a vampiric aesthetic. This is mirrored in the depiction of Christine and Lea as pale and bloodless with dark sunken eyes on the day of murder in *Sister my Sister*.

105   For examples of "true non-crime" stories re-written for the screen see: Gertrude Stein and Alice B Toklas stilted and asexual in *Waiting for the Moon* (1987), bisexual George Sand as straight in *Impromptu* (1990), likewise Dora Carrington in *Carrington* (1995), likewise Janis Joplin in *The Rose* (1979), Vita Sackville West appearing to "get over" her life long

lesbian, the story is told and retold and their sexuality is always central to the tale. In the context of filmic representation of lesbian characters generally, and of lesbian killers in particular, *Sister my Sister* is standard fare despite its efforts at originality and *Heavenly Creatures* is unusually positive. But as "true stories" they speak volumes about the kind of story which is spoken and heard about lesbian lives; moreover their authenticity validates by extension an entire genre of fictional lesbian killers which continues to flourish.

---

lesbianism at the conclusion of *Portrait of a Marriage* (1990), Margarethe Cammemeyer looking like she had to be subpoenaed to hug her live-in lover in *Serving in Silence* (1994), and anything at all representing the life of Florence Nightingale.

[22]

HEROS AND BROTHERS IN LOVE:
THE MALE HOMOSEXUAL AS LAWYER
IN POPULAR CULTURE.

Leslie J. Moran

INTRODUCTION

Images of law and lawyers abound in popular culture (Post 1987). Legal scholarship in popular culture has begun to document and reflect upon the significance of these images.[1] Its agendas and objectives are diverse, ranging from a desire for a legal theory of popular culture to a popular cultural theory of law (Redhead 1995, p. 30). The following analysis examines a neglected aspect of the interface between law and popular culture: the representation of homosexuality and law. More specifically, by reference to two mainstream films, Basil Dearden's *Victim* (Dearden 1961) and Jonathan Demme's *Philadelphia* (Demme 1993), the analysis focuses upon the representation of the male homosexual as a lawyer. The two films show still rare instances of male homosexuals as agents of the law in the cinema.[2]

The characterization of the lawyer in these films is important in various ways. The lawyer is not merely a representation of an agent of the law. Throughout, the character of the lawyer is the very embodiment of the law. The staging of the corporeality (Collier 1998) of the lawyer provides an opportunity to investigate the valorization of the body of law. When considering the body as an image of law, corporeality functions at the level of metaphor. Recent feminist scholarship has begun to explore the ways in which the staging of this body is produced by way of distinctions—between sex (male and female) and gender (masculinity and femininity—Glass 1990; Naffine 1997; Shapiro 1995; Spelman and Minow 1996; Young 1988, 1995) and, to a lesser extent female sexuality (lesbianism—Alcock and Robson 1990; Heller 1994; Kennedy 1994; Whitlock 1994; Wilson 1996).[3] This work has drawn attention to sex, gender, and sexuality as violent hierarchies of values through which corporeality stages the law. The following analysis seeks to draw upon that scholarship but to deploy it in the context of a different corporeality: the male homosexual as lawyer.

In analyzing the corporeality of the male homosexual as a metaphor of law in the context of popular culture, this study is a departure from the small but rapidly growing body of lesbian, gay, and more recently "queer" legal scholarship. A major characteristic of most of this new legal scholarship has been its inability to challenge or escape the confines of conservative or dominant progressive parameters of legal scholarship that limit its practice, albeit in different ways, to the arcane and esoteric peculiarities of legal discourse (Herman 1994; Stychin 1995; Wintermute 1995; Bamforth 1997; cf. Moran et al. 1998). By way of an engagement with the representations of law in popular culture, this paper seeks to examine law "from the outside" (Chase 1986, p. 527). Through an analysis of the terms of the gendered and sexualized corporeality of law in popular culture produced in the characterization of the male homosexual lawyer, this paper seeks to open up a new domain within the law and popular culture scholarship and to challenge the limits of lesbian, gay, and "queer" legal scholarship.

FROM *VICTIM* TO *PHILADELPHIA*

Victim, premiered in the United Kingdom[4] in 1961, is of interest in various ways. It was produced by Michael Relph and Basil Dearden from an original screenplay by Janet Green and John McCormick.[5] *Variety* described the film as "a detective yarn with the taboo theme secondary but tastefully handled" ("Ralph and Dearden" 1961). The film utilizes the genre[6] of detective/police procedure thriller to address a "social problem"—most immediately, the blackmail of male homosexuals, and more generally, the criminalization of all genital relations between men. It uses the detective/police procedure thriller genre to present the arguments for law reform found in the Wolfenden Report, a report commissioned by the U.K. government to investigate and report on the law and practice applicable to homosexuality and prostitution (Wolfenden 1957). In contrast to earlier and other contemporary films that included representations of homosexuality and law (particularly, two films about Oscar Wilde: Hughes 1960 and Ratoff 1960), *Victim* has been singled out as a path-breaking departure in the representation of homosexuality (Russo 1981; Medhurst 1984; Dyer 1993). It is also a departure in another respect. Melville Farr is the first portrait of a male homosexual as an agent of law, a "successful barrister," in mainstream popular cinema. Rather than the male homosexual being represented as an object of law's attention by way of the character of Melville Farr, the film examines the possiblity of the male homosexual as a subject of law.

The contemporary context of the second film, *Philadelphia,* is not a formal review of the law but the HIV/AIDS pandemic and the discrimination generated in responses to this health crisis. In contrast to *Victim, Philadelphia* is a courtroom drama. Tom Hanks, as Andrew Beckett, a gay lawyer, is engaged in a legal battle against his former employers, a prestigious firm of corporate lawyers, for unfair dismissal on the grounds that they discriminated against him due to their knowledge of his HIV status and, as the film suggests, his homosexuality. By way of a courtroom drama, the film examines the terms of the attitudes that inform these practices of discrimination and puts forward an argument for a change in attitudes and a plea for tolerance.

Formally, much separates *Victim* from *Philadelphia*: time (1961 and 1993, respectively); jurisdictions (England and America); jurisprudence (a liberties-based legal system to a rights-based one); criminal law (blackmail) in contrast to civil law (an employment dispute); the first steps toward the decriminalization of male homosexual acts in contrast to employment rights protection and the HIV/AIDS pandemic; English in contrast to Hollywood cinema. *Victim* has been celebrated as a radical departure in terms of representation of the male homosexual (Dyer 1993; Metcalfe 1984; Russo 1981) whereas *Philadelphia* was criticized for its treatment of gay men (Cox 1994; Errigo 1994). At the same time, much connects them. Both might be characterized as social problem films that seek to promote change; *Victim* by way of advocating law reform, and *Philadelphia* primarily by way of changing attitudes. Both are rare instances where the role of the lawyer and, more specifically, a litigator has been made a male homosexual/gay man. The following analysis examines the terms of the representations of the male homosexual as the embodiment of law in *Victim* and *Philadelphia*.

VICTIM: THE MALE HOMOSEXUAL LAWYER AS HERO

The central character in *Victim*, Melville Farr, is a successful barrister. He is married. His homosexuality is revealed by way of a story of blackmail. The blackmail and suicide of "Boy Barrett," Farr's most recent male liaison, sets in motion the investigation that is the main focus of the story. Within the parameters of the detective/police procedure thriller genre, Farr as the agent of law is the character who takes up the role of investigator. In order to analyze the gendered and sexualized terms of the personification of Farr as an agent of the law, it is necessary not only to focus on the characterization of Farr but also to place that character in the context of other agents of the law who personify the law: two policemen, Det. Inspector Harris and Sergeant Bridie, and Miss Benham.

Farr appears early in the film. His first appearance is in the barristers' chambers in conversation with his clerk, Patterson. The conversation is about a client, Major Humphries, who is described as "a giant killer." He is engaged in an heroic struggle over a land dispute. The villain is the state more specifically, a branch of the local state, the Rural District Council (R.D.C.). The R.D.C. want to compel the Major to sell his land for the development of state housing. However, this is a "giant killer" with a problem. He is relatively poor and is in need of help as he is caught up in red tape. Farr, having dismissed the problem of limited resources as a problem for the solicitors to resolve, expresses his enthusiasm for the major's noble cause and declares his determination to take up that cause in order to make the villain squirm.

This exchange sets out some key characteristics of Melville Farr as a male agent of the law. In general, it presents the lawyer in terms of the male hero (Greenfield and Osborn 1995). The lawyer as hero is staged in many ways. As a barrister, Farr's character is already the lawyer as litigator, which is the most widely produced image of the lawyer as hero

(Greenfield and Osborn 1995). In that sense, the characterization of the lawyer as hero in *Victim* draws upon a well-established tradition.[7] As a specialist litigator who is sufficiently eminent in his profession to be considered for the position of Queen's Counsel, Farr personifies the lawyer as a hero with established credentials. The litigator as "heroic" in contrast to the litigator as villain is represented in Farr's dismissal of Patterson's concerns about the funding of litigation. As Post has commented, the lawyer's fee is a sign of the lawyer's corruption, representing the lawyer's (and the law's) partiality (Post 1987, p. 380). This distance from money presents Farr as someone more closely associated with law as justice.

The "heroic" is also represented in terms of the struggle that is referred to in this exchange—a David and Goliath struggle between the (little) individual and the (oppressive) state, represented by the R.D.C. The latter is particularly significant as it gives a very specific class dimension to the struggle. As a struggle over the compulsory purchase of (rural) land for the purpose of building state housing, it is a battle of the (petty) bourgeois against the welfare state which stands as a tool of the working class. Here, the hero is the big man who takes up the battle for the little man who struggles against the leviathan of the state. The terms of the struggle are symbolized by way of a modern metaphor of the labyrinth: red tape. The hero, as the representative of the Major (the giant killer), is the persona who will give voice to one silenced in the formal arena of the battle of good and evil, the law. In this instance, as a lawyer, the heroic takes on a particular persona. Here, the heroic is rule and reason (the 1957 Housing Act) in contrast to the violent and arbitrary nature of the state beyond the law.

The lawyer as hero has a particular significance. The litigator takes up the position of the intextual agent of a narrative (re)ordering. In *Victim*, it is important to note that the litigator as hero occupies a distinctive position with respect to the traditional site of legal heroics, the courtroom. In courtroom dramas, the heroic practice of narrative (re)ordering takes the form of an adversarial battle, of examination and cross-examination, whereby the truth is produced. The decision of the jury and/or judge merely provide the formal closure to the law and to the generation of truth which has always already been secured by way of the heroic litigator. In contrast to this, *Victim* tells a story of law by way of different themes. While the courtroom, as a sign of law, is an ever-present absence in *Victim*, the law is represented by way of the agents of the law operating in another context: detection and police procedure. As a detective/police procedure thriller, the courtroom as the stage upon which the truth is told is displaced onto the process of investigation and detection. Here, the trial might be said to be "inscribed in the truth revealed" in this process (Hurd 1980, p. 57). Rather than closure being secured in the determination of the jury or judge, where the emphasis is upon detection as the process of truth, closure/conviction is secured by way of the moment of capture, which ends the film. In *Victim*, the litigator as hero performs the role of agent of narrative (re)ordering always outside the courtroom in the process of detection.

With respect to the detail of the representation of the heroic, the first exchange in the film between Farr and Patterson is significant in generating a complex portrait of the hero. It is an exchange informed by gender and sexuality. It is an exchange between two men. As such, it rehearses the absence of women from the world of law as represented in legal processes of investigation and detection and the courtroom in the remainder of the film. Here, the world of law in general and the heroic in particular is staged in terms of the homosocial (Lipman-Bluman 1976; Sedgwick 1985). The exchange is informed by gender displayed by way of particular sartorial codes of masculinity (Bird 1996; Collier 1998) inflected by social hierarchies of class and profession; of stiff, formal (archaic) petty bourgeois and haute bourgeois masculinity.[8]

In the first instance, the sexual dimension of the homosocial is the unmarked exchange between Farr and Paterson. However, at the same time, the sexuality of the homosocial is marked in the moment that it is problematized in this exchange. This occurs in various ways. First, it is problematized by way of the narrative structure and the editing of the film. This is achieved through the juxtaposition of the enigma of "Boy Barrett's" hasty departure from his place of work, the presence of the police who are searching for Barrett, and the barristerial exchange. Second, it is problematized in the closure of the exchange between Farr and Patterson. This exchange closes with a telephone call from Barrett. Central to the success of this closure is the use of the camera. At the start of the exchange between Barrett and Farr, the camera is placed immediately behind Farr. It focuses upon the intercom, the telephone, and a framed photograph of a woman (his wife) between the two. During the brief telephone conversation with Barrett, the camera swings around to focus upon Farr's anxious face. As the conversation draws to a close, the camera swings back to focus upon the telephone and the photograph of his wife, ending in a close-up of the photograph. The image of Farr's wife locates the homosocial within the heterosexual at the moment that it conjoins Farr's heterosexuality with the enigma of "Boy Barrett's" hasty departure.

HOMOSEXUALIZING THE HERO

In resorting to the format of detective/police procedure thriller, *Victim* tells a story by way of a genre that has traditionally depended upon the hetero-male detective as central character, that has cast the homo-male in the role of sexual monster or sexual victim. Almost by definition, detective/crime fiction has entailed this relation of male sexualities: the strong hetero and the weak or corrupt homo. Action and authority in the conventional detective/investigative thriller belong to hetero men (Naffine 1997, p. 127; Krutnick 1991) *Victim* is a radical departure from this genre's requirements, putting the male homosexual in the role of knowing and inquiring subject (cf. Thornton 1996), both as writer and as the subject of the story written.[9]

A distinctive feature of the film lies in the fact that Farr's homosexualization does not automatically disqualify him from being the hero. This is achieved in various ways. His position as hero is represented in the homosexual context in an exchange with Henry (a homosexual hairdresser), one of the "victims" of the blackmail ring. Henry explains the heroic role of Farr as an agent of the law in the following terms:

> HENRY: Yes. I'm weak and I'm selfish. You're different. You've got a big position—they'd listen to you, a lawyer—you ought to be able to state our case. Tell the public how we walk in fear and loneliness. Tell them there's no magic cure for how we are (Green and McCormick 1961, p. 100).

It is important to note that this exchange suggests that it is not Farr's homosexuality per se that is the corporeality of the heroic but his position as a lawyer that generates this possibility; it separates him out from the other homosexuals. All the other homosexuals in *Victim*, no matter what their socioeconomic status, are represented as victims. The homosexual as lawyer/hero is the voice that will be heard when all others are silenced.

While the sexual economy of detective/police procedure thrillers would suggest that Farr's relationship with "Boy Barrett" might threaten to destroy Farr's heroic condition, this does not occur for much of the film. Various factors seem to sustain his position as hero in this context. First, we are informed in an exchange between Patterson and Farr that there is no evidence that Farr has ever violated the law in his relations with other men. Furthermore there is no representation of an (erotic) encounter between Farr and Barrett; the closest the film gets to this is in the final sequence of the film, where the photograph that is the vehicle for Farr's blackmail burns in the fire. All we see is the distressed face of Barrett framed by a car window. Finally, Barrett's suicide early in the film sustains the heroic as it renders Farr incapable of a homoerotic encounter.

At the same time, this death is crucial to the heroic in a different way. It is at this point in that narrative that Farr takes up the position of male homosexual as intextual agent of narrative ordering, willing to sacrifice his reputation in order to "challenge the existing law" against homosexuals. He sets out to avenge the death of his friend by bringing the blackmailers to justice.

These dimensions of the homosexualization of the hero are significant in various ways. First, it would be a mistake to suggest that the absence of an erotic encounter between Farr and the male object of desire is peculiar to the homosexualized hero within the genre of detective/police procedure narratives. As others have noted, the detective as loner is a requirement of this genre, particularly where it is informed by classical detective themes (Cawelti 1976; Whitlock 1994). Furthermore, with respect to the juxtaposition of the death of the object of desire and Farr's elevation to the position of the agent of narrative (re)ordering, Decure notes that female detectives draw attention to the proximity of the work of detection and desire. The work of detection is a labor of love; here, the love of someone who has come to grief. The death of "Boy Barrett" places Farr's position within this tradition of the detective genre (Decure 1992). While this may be a requirement of the genre, it might produce different effects in different contexts. Thus, the requirements of the genre work to make the homosexual Farr an acceptable hero to some liberal audiences. This is captured in Russo's observation that in Farr, *Victim* creates a gay hero "with credentials enough to get into heaven, let alone society" (Russo 1981, p. 130). His acceptability to liberal audiences lies in the fact that he admits that homosexual acts are wrong and refrains from acting on his urges. But this does not exhaust the effects of the homosexualization of the heroic litigator.

There is also another reading of Farr as hero which is captured in Russo's observation that Farr is "heroic enough to be a genuine menace" (Russo 1981, p. 128). Here, Farr becomes a hero from another perspective—the gay perspective. He is willing to lend a little dignity to his homosexual relationship by fighting to legitimize its existence. Here, the conjunction of the heroic and homosexual seem to reconfigure the homosexual. As Russo commented, the heroic is now to be found in the fact that Farr is not the homosexual as "a sad-eyed queen"(Russo 1981, p. 129).

In order to further understand the personification of law in the character of Farr, it is necessary to contrast that character with the two other male agents of law, Detective Inspector Harris and Sergeant Bridie. Their characters are displayed through a series of exchanges in which the terms of the Wolfenden reform debates are explored.

The Harris/Bridie relationship is a binary relationship of good cop/bad cop. Harris, as good cop, as reason, is contrasted to Bridie as bad cop, who is emotion. Harris is justice, in contrast to Bridie as rulebound formality. Harris is the Hart libertarian in contrast to Bridie, the Devlin communitarian. In gendering these characters, Harris is the soft, caring, and avuncular male in contrast to the clipped, stiff, formality of the harsh, tyrannical father of Bridie. This exchange represents the world of policing is a world of men, a homosocial world. In the context of a homosocial world, the sexualization of these men is again the unmarked, the heterosexual.

The character of Detective Inspector Harris is also important in another context. Harris is intimately connected with Farr. This connection has particular significance in an exchange which comes toward the end of the film. It takes place immediately after the blackmailer and her assistant have been arrested. It takes the following form:

HARRIS: They're going to be very vicious when they get into court, sir.

MEL:(ironically) Don't worry, Harris, I won't let you down.

HARRIS: No, sir.

MEL: What will they get?

HARRIS: With your evidence—the limit....

HARRIS: I'm glad we've got them. But it seems tragic that your career has to go west in the getting. [Thoughtfully] Somebody once called this law the blackmailer's charter.

MEL: Is that how *you* feel about it?

HARRIS: (ironically) I'm a policeman, sir. I don't have feelings.

> His expression gives the lie to his words. He hesitates, then turns away and is
> brisk again (Green and McCormick 1961, pp. 149-150).

This exchange is of interest in various ways. Prior to this, the police officers have played a limited role in the film as intextual agents of narrative ordering. The exchanges between the police officers tend to take the form of set pieces where the arguments for and against law reform are staged. As such, they are outside the narrative drive for truth associated with the process of investigation and detection providing a critical commentary on that truth. In the exchange between Farr and Harris, a significant change occurs in this relationship. In this exchange Farr is denied the role of agent of law. Henceforth, Farr will become a victim in/of law not its hero. Harris takes up the place of the knowing legal subject in his place.

This exchange is also a moment in staging the sexualization of the knowing legal subject. What in the first instance takes the form of a homosocial encounter between the hetero and the homo where the homo is hero, ends in the displacement of the homosexual as hero and in the substitution of the hetero as the future agent of narrative ordering. Furthermore, in this exchange, we are informed that the homo as hero who has been the agent of law for most of the film, will now be destroyed by the law. It is at this point that he must face the reality of his position as the law's sacrificial victim (Moran 1995), and this is despite the fact that Farr represents the "good homosexual." Both good and bad homosexuals are victims according to the law. For the law, homosexuality is death (cf. Loizidou 1998).

Before leaving the matter of the gender and sexuality of the agents of law, it is important to refer to the fourth personification of law in *Victim*, Miss Benham. Miss Benham is perhaps the most interesting character in this respect; she brings femininity into the frame of the personification of law. First, it is necessary to examine her role as agent of law. This is most clearly revealed in the moment when her role as the blackmailer is revealed. The scene is the living room of an Edwardian flat. Miss Benham returns and the conversation relates to the imminent cessation of the blackmail, pending Farr's arrival with the money with which a collection of negatives will be purchased. Miss Benham's assistant, the Sandy Youth, begins the dialogue thus:

> Sandy Youth: As usual, beautifully timed. A week's notice and no attention
> drawn. Are we going to let our friend off the hook?

Miss Benham: We'll give him that impression. I told him to come over; should be here soon. [Pause] Of course when we start up business again, we'll jerk the line a bit—remind him the hook's still there. Show him the photostats.

The Sandy Youth looks at her with something between admiration and disgust.

Sandy Youth: You really are a bit off, aren't you?
Miss Benham: (immediately defensive)   What d'you mean?
Sandy Youth: I don't know—a sort of cross between an avenging angel and a peeping Tom.

Miss Benham turns away, caught on the raw.

Miss Benham: It just disgusts me to see people behaving like animals, that's all.

On being arrested, as she accompanies the police officer to the door, she comments:

I never thought I'd live to see the ungodly in great power. And flourishing like the green bay tree (Green and McCormick 1961, pp. 149-150).

The proximity between blackmail and law and between the black-mailer and the lawyer as agent of law is captured in the description of the relevant law as "the blackmailer's charter." Here, law and blackmail are one and the same. Blackmail, is the enforcement of the law by way of a threat to enforce the law. As such this instance of blackmail is not simply an act against the law it is a usurpation of the law (Moran 1996, ch. 3). As the blackmailer, Miss Benham seeks to take up the position of the law. She deploys the law by way of naming the act a wrongful act and using that prohibition to impose a penalty, and extract a charge. At the same time, she substitutes herself as the agent of law in part in order to deal with the failure of law (which has allowed the ungodly into positions of great power) and, thereby, to reestablish the law.[10]

While rarely mentioned by the film critics, those who do describe Miss Benham's character describe her in a particular way, as "grotesque" (Whitebait 1961) and "embittered" (Anon 1968). She is in sharp contrast to the only other substantial female character, the wife of Farr, played by Sylvia Syms, who is hyperfeminine (Dyer 1993). In the representation of Miss Benham as an agent of the law, she is placed outside the boundaries of femininity. In part, this is achieved in the way her body is coded masculine (lesbian?) by way of her glasses, and her dress code. It is reinforced by the fact that she works in the world of books (a world of men and, more specifically, a world of homosexual men). She is also placed outside the feminine in the contrast of the Mrs./Miss distinction—between Mrs. Farr and Miss Benham. The former is not only a wife but more generally the maternal, both in her work at a school and in her relationship with her husband. Miss Benham's domestic world remains outside the frame of the film. Her corruption is signified by the fact that in both her work and her "domestic" relations, she is in close proximity to the world of homosexual men. She works for a homosexual and works with a homosexual. In the character of Miss Benham as agent of law, woman is not the intextual agent of narrative order so much as villain, as sexual monster and sexual victim. In her arrest and prosecution, a particular order of femininity is made as the legal order.

In *Victim*, we find the first representation of the male homosexual as lawyer as hero. Through the medium of a well-established genre, the film deploys gender and sexuality in particular ways to portray this new hero. Far from giving rise to other films which exploited and explored the terms of this new departure, there appears to have been no attempt to portray a male homosexual as a heroic lawyer until 1994 in the film *Philadelphia*. It is to the specifics of that film that I now turn.

PHILADELPHIA: MALE LITIGATORS AND BROTHERLY LOVE

There are important points of connection and contrast between the character of Farr as the homosexual lawyer in *Victim* and Andrew Beckett (Tom Hanks) as the gay lawyer in *Philadelphia*. Farr and Beckett are both litigation lawyers. Both are rising stars in the most prestigious aspect of the legal profession. Both are involved in a David and Goliath struggle. In *Philadelphia*, it takes the form of a struggle between the David of the outcast lawyer and the Goliath of the corporate law firm (Green 1994). By way of the deployment of a particular genre in *Victim*, Farr, the homosexual as the heroic litigator, plays the predominant role as the intextual agent of a narrative (re)ordering outwith the court room. *Philadelphia* is of a different genre, a courtroom drama. This might generate expectations that in *Philadelphia*, the male homosexual/gay man as heroic litigator would be firmly located within the quintessential space of the law, the courtroom. However, this is not the case. While the character of the gay lawyer Beckett is, as a litigator, always already connected to the courtroom as the site of the heroic, he is also distant from it as he does not perform the role of litigator in the courtroom scenes but appears in those scenes only in the role of the plaintiff/victim. In *Philadelphia*, the position of the gay lawyer as the agent of narrative (re)ordering is staged through the gay lawyer's relation with another lawyer. Joe Miller (Denzel Washington). While formally Hanks/Beckett was presented as the lead actor/character, commentators and critics have drawn attention to the central significance of the Miller/Washington character (Green 1994; Taubin 1994).

It is in this respect that the portrait of a gay lawyer in *Philadelphia* departs dramatically from that of the homosexual lawyer in *Victim*. In *Philadelphia*, the portrait of the gay man as a litigator is produced through the conventions of a buddy movie between the gay and the straight litigator. Furthermore, this is a biracial buddy relationship (Fuchs 1993; Tasker 1995; Guerrero 1995). It is the terms of this relationship and, in particular, the characterization of the gay white lawyer in relation to the straight black lawyer that I now want to turn.

The opening sequence of the film foregrounds the relationship between Beckett and Miller. We first meet them in a litigation context: a judge's chambers. Both appear in the role of masculine litigator. Not only are they in opposition to each other by virtue of the litigation, but they are also constituted as very different litigators. Beckett works for a prestigious firm of commercial lawyers and represents corporate clients, in this instance, a construction company. Beckett is at the top of his profession. In sharp contrast to this, Miller is a "low life ambulance chaser ... a sleazebag ... [at] the bottom of his profession" (Davis 1993, pp. 1-2, 5). During the course of their exchanges before the (female) judge, Beckett is portrayed as reason and morality. In this context, corporate power (which is usually portrayed as greed and violence) is presented as the power to create jobs and rebuild communities. In contrast, Miller, representing those affected by corporate urban redevelopment, is presented as lawyer as partial, as emotional, driven by greed, both his own and the greed of his clients, exploiting a legal system that promotes vexatious litigation, and an ambulance chaser whose income is entirely dependent upon the success of litigation, driven by his own greed.

These distinctions are further developed by way of consecutive scenes in their respective offices. Beckett is caring, hardworking, and incisive when it comes to legal matters. He is portrayed as a defender of justice, as represented by his support for the outsider in a civil litigation conflict (a small innovative software company which is being threatened by a large predatory business organization). As a lawyer, Miller is represented as a corrupt lawyer. This is portrayed by way of an exchange with a potential accident litigation client. Hopeless though the case may be, Miller takes it, driven by a desire for money. His greed is represented by reference to his T.V. adverts touting for business. The reference to the T.V. commercial is an image of law not as justice but as just another commodity to be bought and sold for profit. In terms of the earlier analysis of Farr, the film would appear to assign the professional, cultural, racial, and class credentials for the role of male lawyer as hero to Beckett in contrast to Miller, who is coded as the lawyer as male villain.

At the same time, their personas in this public world are also represented as a point of commonality, a point of similarity. For example, in the scene in the judge's chambers, the closure of the exchange between the lawyers brings Miller in line with Beckett as litigator (as a proto-hero). The judge comments that while Beckett fails on behalf of his clients, he has demonstrated that he is an articulate and compelling litigator. Another point of similarity is the staging of the gender of the litigators. Both are coded masculine. This aspect is elaborated by way of sartorial codes, gestures, and verbal exchanges.

Particular attention is paid to this aspect of Beckett's characterization by way of a series of exchanges with the senior partners of his employer, the firm Wyant, Wheeler, Hellerman, Tetlow and Brown. In this representation of the working world of the litigator, women appear in a supporting role, as receptionists, secretaries, paralegals, or largely absent/silent partners. This is predominantly a world of men, a homosocial world. The masculine is portrayed by way of the sombre (dark wood) interiors, banter between men, firm handshakes, brief hugging, back slapping, and the smoking of fat cigars in a world at times populated only by men. While Miller's wider work context is less well developed, like Beckett's world, men play the leading role.

The theme of the difference between the two litigators returns by way of their representation within the private realm. It is this context in which they are formally sexualized. Beckett's character is defined by reference to his (compromised) health, HIV positive/living with AIDS which also marks his sexuality: gay male. Miller, on the other hand, is marked by way of domesticity, the birth of his first child, his wife, and his heterosexuality.

It is in the interface between the public world of work and the private world of sexuality that we discover more about the gender and sexualization of the public and homosocial world of the litigator. A recognition of Beckett's compromised health and, hence, his sexuality transforms Beckett's professional, cultural, and social position as insider, litigator, and hero to that of outsider, unemployed villain. As such, his health/sexual persona (gay) is radically other to the world of the litigator. The sexual/gender dynamics of this state of affairs are explored at various points in the film.

The courtroom provides an important forum for the display and consideration of gender and sexuality in the homosociality of law. For example, the masculinity of the homosocial world of lawyers is represented by way of the metaphors deployed by the senior partner in his description of the firm and Beckett's recruitment. The firm is described as "a major league ball club;" new recruits are referred to as "hot rookies." The sexuality of the homosocial world is portrayed by way of Beckett's examination in chief. In response to questions about his failure to inform his employers of his sexuality, he explains his silence by reference to the public/private distinction. No only is the private associated with the sexual, but in the public (masculine) world of the legal professional, the two realms of the private and the public are to be formally separated. However, this formal separation of the private (sexual) and the public (nonsexual) is problematic. Beckett explains that he decided to withold information about his sexual orientation after he discovered, while in the all-male sauna with the firm's senior partners, that homophobia was a key component of the homosocial culture within which he worked and socialized. In this instance, the proximity of the public and the sexual is made apparent. Rather than the sexual being remote from the public, the sexual is intimately connected with the public but figured in a particular way, as heterosexual, and more specifically, as a heterosexual that demands the homosexual as the excluded other.

This erotic dynamic of the homosocial of law is represented in its recognition and simultaneous denial in an encounter between the partners of Beckett's old firm Wyant, Wheeler, Hellerman, Tetlow and Brown. This takes place in the wake of the service of the summons initiating the dismissal proceedings. When Seidman, another partner, suggests that the firm offer to settle the case, Wheeler, the senior partner who recruited Beckett, responds by way of a catalogue of the "damage" Beckett's presence in the firm represents: "Andy brought AIDS into our offices, into our men's room's, he brought it into our goddamn family picnic." Here, the homoerotic is an unruly contagion that will corrupt the homosocial in its individual and institutional settings.

His exclusion is further represented in his failure to find a litigator to take up his case of unfair dismissal. It is by way of this particular metaphor of the homosociality of law that the film explores Miller's position within that homosociality. Miller is placed within that scheme of things. When Beckett comes to seek Miller's aid, he again comes up against the homosocial/heterosexual of the world of law. The character of Miller reenacts the terms of Beckett's threat to individual and social order: a threat to the self, to the family, a threat to masculinity. Here, Miller is portrayed as an insider, both masculine and heterosexual, hostile to Beckett's pleas for assistance.

It is at this point that the character of the male homosexual/gay litigator in *Victim* and *Philadelphia* begins to diverge. In contrast to Farr in *Victim*, where the sign of his violent exclusion (the death of the object of his desire) turns him into the hero, in *Philadelphia*, while this rejection creates the possiblity for the gay litigator to become the intextual agent of narrative (re)ordering, Beckett does not take up this role. In *Philadelphia,* the heroic is staged not through an individual but through the biracial buddy relationship: between the gay litigator, Beckett, and the straight litigator, Miller.

Within this buddy relationship, the focus is on the straight lawyer. This is particularly important. In *Victim,* Farr's battle for understanding and tolerance as a struggle within the law is also a struggle within himself, over his own identity as a struggle over the law of homosexuality. While in *Philadelphia,* the struggle within the law is also represented as a struggle over identity, in that film the struggle of the hero is a struggle with the law of heterosexuality.[11] It is to the terms of that struggle as played out through the biracial buddy relationship that I now turn.

THE LAW OF BROTHERLY LOVE

The tension between the characters of Beckett and Miller, portrayed by reference to social, cultural, professional, racial, and sexual differences, fits within the cinematic conventions of buddy relations. While the initial relation between buddies might be hostile, in part, the buddy relation is about the transformation of this hostility and tension into a consensus, a camaraderie, a common sociality. In *Philadelphia* in the first instance, Beckett's function is to persuade, cajole, and seduce the straight lawyer to take up the role of the hero. In part, this is presented as a process of transformation from difference to sameness. An important moment in this process of seduction occurs in a scene in the law library. Miller is witness to what is presented as an act of discrimination against Beckett. It is a moment of recognition for Miller. It gives rise to an exchange between Beckett and Miller. Beckett outlines the terms of a decision of the U.S. Supreme Court, the Arline decision, in which the Court decided that discrimination based on a person's health condition was unlawful. In this moment, they share the common experience of discrimination, "civil death." It is a moment of exchange, of the text of law given literal form as Beckett pushes the law report toward Miller.

However, while the buddy relation requires this commonality, it also renders it problematic. This was captured in the review of the film by a journalist writing for a U.K. tabloid daily newspaper, *The Sun*, who commented that the relationship between Beckett and Miller was a "bent buddy" relationship (Cox 1994).

The phrase "bent buddy" draws attention to one dynamic within this relationship of sameness, the erotics of the buddy relationship. While the homoerotics of buddy relations is not a matter unique to *Philadelphia* (Fuchs 1993), this film is a rare instance where the buddy relationship is between a gay man and a straight man. This foregrounds the sexualizing dynamic of buddy relations: the transformation from difference to sameness as a movement from gay/straight to gay/gay. Through the buddy relation, there is a danger that the hetero character of Joe Miller will be homosexualized in his homosocial relation with Andrew Beckett.

As in other buddy films, both biracial and uniracial, at various points in the film the homoerotic of the buddy relation is both recognized and negated through the character's expression of overt hostility to homosexuality. This occurs in the context of encounters between Miller and his wife, encounters between Miller and his male drinking companions in a bar, and in an exchange between Miller and a black gay law student in a local store. Also, it is in this context that the biracial aspect of the buddy relation in *Philadelphia* has a particular symbolic significance. The racial signifies difference and, thereby, helps to keep the homoerotic always already elsewhere.

However, in *Philadelphia*, the denial of the homoerotic dynamic of the homosocial as a matter that has to be denied and repressed is problematic. A central theme of the film is the place of homophobic/homoerotic dynamic within a homosocial/heterosexual economy. In this context, an important distinction then becomes the division between those instances where it is formally addressed and those instances in which it appears but is passed over.

BROTHERLY LOVE OF LAW

In the relationship between Beckett and the law, another aspect of the homosocial/homoerotic emerges. It appears in the context of Beckett's declaration that he "loves the law." His love is explained in various ways. First, it is located within the homosocial context of the law firm. Beckett's love of the law is his love of the male senior partner, Wheeler: his encyclopedic knowledge, his performance as a razor-sharp litigator, his leadership qualities, his ability to bring the best out in others, his capacity to illuminate complex legal concepts, his elegance, and his adventurous spirit. Within the wider context of the film, this love of the senior partner is a part of the homosocial. As a homosocial love, this is a love between men where the homoerotic is always already elsewhere. That this has a potential erotic component that has to be denied is marked by the violence of Wheeler's response to Beckett's sexuality: "Andy brought AIDS into our offices, into our men's room's, he brought it into our goddamn family picnic."

This love of the law also takes another form in the context of the buddy relation. In the "Production Information" pamphlet that accompanied the release of the film, Denzel Washington explains, "What brings us [Miller and Beckett] together is our love of the law." He continues, "These are two very good lawyers, and once I start getting into the case with him, I can't turn back." Here, it is the love of the law that would appear to create the bond between gay and straight male.

Again, this joint love of the law has a homoerotic dynamic. This is most apparent in the sequence in the film where Beckett and Miller come together for a final question and answer rehearsal. The intimacy of their common love of the law is produced by way of lighting, camera angles, music, editing, and dialogue. With respect to the latter, Beckett translates an aria being performed by Maria Callas from Andrea Chenier by Giordiano. Madeleina tells how, during the French Revolution, a mob set fire to her house and her mother died saving her:

I look. The place that cradles me was burning. It was during that sorrow that love came to me. A voice filled with harmony said, Live still! I am life! Thy heaven is in my eyes! Thou art not alone! I gather thy tears, I walk along thy path and sustain thee. Smile and hope for I am love.... I am Love! Love! Love! (Davis 1993).

Together these produce a disorientating moment for the two men. The disturbance is marked by Miller's speedy departure and in his turn to return. He never returns to Beckett's apartment but returns to his wife and child. We next see him with his newborn child and wife, both of whom are asleep. The aria is repeated. This closure both connects Miller to Beckett (by way of the music) and spearates him placing him in the world of heterosexuality in contrast to the gay world.

The scene that follows reenacts this closure in the courtroom itself—the impossibility of an erotic relationship between Miller and Beckett. It is in this scene that the final destruction of Tom Hank's character begins. He collapses and the proceedings continue in his absence, marked by the empty plaintiff's chair. Death swiftly follows, rendering all possibility of the homoerotic impossible. At the same time, it is important to recognize that through the repetition of the aria, Miller connects to Beckett's pain, which is the vehicle that informs Miller's struggle with his heterosexual identity. As such, the buddy relation both joins the homo and hetero and works to separate them. It is both the means of translation of the effects of the HIV pandemic from the homosexual body to the heterosexual body and a way of securing the heterosexual as the intextual agent of narrative (re)ordering.[12]

This brotherly love also has another form in the film. Here, it is represented by way of law as a disembodied phenomenon. Beckett loves the complexity of the law but, most of all, he loves being "part of justice." While this love of the law might formally appear in a disembodied form, it is not remote from the other corporeal representations of that love where corporeality is a metaphor of law. What *Philadelphia* raises in this instance is another location of the homosocial/homoerotic encounter in the abstract idea of law as a site of brotherly love.

Before leaving the buddy relation, it is important to return to the biracial structure of that relationship. As Guerrero notes, the biracial buddy movie which emerged in the 1980s was developed in part in order to attract the demographically broadest audience.[13] At the same time, the biracial buddy relationship is also concerned with "negotiating, containing and fantastically resolving the tangled and socially charged issue of race relations on the screen" (Guerrero 1995, p. 240). It is to the terms of that biracial relation in the generation of the intextual agent of narrative (re)ordering that I now turn.

In the narrative, Miller takes up the case in order to give Beckett a voice; both in his place and as his voice in the court room. While the narrative sets the struggle with the homoerotic/homophobia in the context of Miller's heterosexuality that struggle is also one that is relevant to Beckett. It might also be understood as a representation of the struggle to come to terms with the place of homoerotic/homophobia within the institutional practices of homosociality and heterosexuality; a homosociality and heterosexuality that Beckett has aspired to within the firm. Within this scheme of things Miller as the black buddy is in danger of being reduced to a passive object. There is a danger that the buddy relation volunteers the racial other to solve the problems of the dominant, white, social order. The film does make some effort to address this in various ways. For example some effort is made to locate Miller within a wider world of black culture. This occurs in those domestic scenes where an examination of homophobia in black hetero-masculinity is explored and in the exchange between a black masculine (sports loving) gay law student and Miller who is engaged in the purchase of nappies for his new child.

In *Philadelphia,* the character of the gay male litigator raises very different issues from those addressed by way of the character of the homosexual barrister in *Victim.* Set within the context of a biracial buddy relationship *Philadelphia* provides an opportunity to examine the place of the homoerotic/homophobic dynamic in the homosociality of the law.

CONCLUSION

Victim and *Philadelphia* remain exceptions within mainstream portrayals of the lawyer in popular culture. While the context of each separates these rare representations of the male homosexual as the embodiment of law there are significant points of contact between them. In different ways in their representation of the male homosexual as the knowing legal subjects both deploy a spacial metaphor which represents the paradoxical position of this knowing subject; both inside and outside. As such on the one hand the male homosexual/gay male is never the authentic place of the law. At best he is passing as the agent of law in the place of law. On the other hand, passing as the agent of law draws attention to a different way of understanding that law; law as masquerade. As a metaphor of law the male homosexual/gay male stands as that which is outwith the law; a metaphor of civil death. In *Philadelphia* that corporeal metaphor of civil death is shown in the withering of Beckett's body in the courtroom. As portraits of lawyers both films are distinctive and important. *Victim* remains important not only as the first representation of the male homosexual as litigator but in the detail of that representation of the homosexual as hero. It is also distinctive as an example of the use and transformation of genre in order to generate new narratives. *Philadelphia* is significant not so much in the representation of the male homosexual as litigator but in its deployment of the buddy relation. It is significant, perhaps dispite itself, as an examination and exploration of the homoerotics of law as a homosocial institution. While this exploration has its limits it raises questions about the relationship between desire, erotics, gender, sexuality and law. A heady combination. In that sense, it pioneered and opened up an agenda that legal scholarship has only now begun to examine.

NOTES

1.   Within the context of legal scholarship, the study of law in popular culture is an emerging body of work that comes out of a range of recent traditions of left/progressive legal scholarship: the sociology of deviance and critical criminology; jurisprudence and the sociology of law—more specifically, law in context, and the law and society movements; the Marxist tradition; and most recently, critical legal scholarship. There is a growing body of work in this field (e.g., Bergman 1996; Chase 1986; Denvir 1996; Joseph and Carton 1992; Freedman 1989; Harris 1992; Redhead, 1995; Rosen 1989; Scharf and Robert 1994; Stark 1987).

2.   There are also few images of male homosexuals/gay men as lawyers (or policemen) in either television or literary form. In the United Kingdom, a T.V. serial about a group of young legal professionals, *This Life*, included a gay male as a (trainee) lawyer. This character, "Warren," was written out in the second series. The character left to undertake a trip to Australia after being involved in a sexual offense of "gross indecency." In the second season, a lesbian lawyer appeared as a peripheral character. A lesbian lawyer appeared in the T.V. show *L.A.Law*. The character appeared in the fifth season of the show and disappeared in the sixth season (Kennedy 1994). In literary works, detective fiction has provided a vehicle for the representation of lesbians as agents of law, including police and private detectives (see Decure 1992; Wilson 1996; Whitlock 1994). For examples of gay men as police officers or private investigators, see, for example, Kavanagh (1991), Ricardo (1992), and Seabrook (1991).

3.   The choice of references here focuses upon lesbians as agents of law. Other work on law and popular culture has looked at lesbianism in the context of criminality (see, e.g., Hart 1994). It would be wrong to conclude that such works do not focus upon

24   LESLIE J. MORAN

the interface between legality and the body, but my intention here is to focus specifically upon those images of law produced by way of the lawyer.

4.   Its distribution in the United States was more problematic as it was refused a production code Seal. The explanation for the refusal of the Seal was that the film dealt too clinically with homosexuality. Explicit references to homosexuality violated the code's requirement that "sexual aberration could only be suggested and not referred to directly" (*Variety* 1961; Russo 1980). On the reception of the film in the United Kingdom, see Bourne (1996).

5.   It is part of a series of "social problem" realist films produced by Relph and Dearden in the 1950's and is similar in some respects to the film *Sapphire* scripted by Green (also a writer of detective fiction) and her husband McCormick, which dealt with race discrimination.

6.   The seminal critical text on genre and cinema is Neale (1980).

7.   It is also important to remember that the lawyer as litigator might also personify another character, the villain (Post 1987).

8.   Haute bourgeois masculinity might also be read as a sign of perversion.

9.   It turns the male homosexual reader himself into an investigator and generator of truth as he is required to solve the problem along with the male investigator. The reader engages in an act of creation while reading and is not the passive recipient of the text on the screen (Naffine 1997, p. 125)

10.   The reference to "the green bay tree" is a reference to a successful play which explicitly dealt with homosexuality that ran in the West End of London.

11.   There are other differences between the respective heroes in *Victim* and *Philadelphia*. In the former, the hero is an insider, as represented by his position as a member of the Bar, which is still thought of as the superior branch of the legal profession, and by his class position, as a member of the upper middle class. In contrast, Joe Miller is the hero as outsider: outside by reference to his professional status as an ambulance chaser, by his class (his favorite bar is a working-class bar) and by reference to his color. But it is in the context of the hetero/homo divide that the respective positions of Farr/ Beckett and Miller shift; Farr's (and Beckett's) homosexuality will in the final instance make them outsiders in contrast to Miller's heterosexuality, which will secure his position as the narrative agent of (re)ordering, which brings him inside.

12.   The importance of the heterosexual to the homosocial is explored in another context, an exchange in cross-examination. In part, Beckett's exclusion from the firm is due to his disruption of the homosociality of the law firm. In part, Beckett's situation is also explained as an effect of the necessary exclusion or repression of the homosexual that is a necessary part of that homosociality.

13.   This point is referred to in some of the articles written at the time of the film's release (see Taubin 1994).

REFERENCES

Alcock, B., and J. Robson. 1990. "Cagney and Lacey Revisited." *Feminist Review* 35(Summer): 42-53.

Anon. 1968. *Human Rights Season, Programme Notes.* London: National Film Theatre.

Bamforth N. 1997. *Sexuality, Morals and Justice: A Theory of Lesbian and Gay Rights Law.* London: Cassell.

Bergman, P., and M. Asimow. 1996. *Reel Justice: The Courtroom Goes to the Movies.* Kansas City, KS: Andrews and McMeel.

Bourne, S. 1996. *Brief Encounters: Lesbians and Gays in British Cinema 1930-1971.* London: Cassell.

Cawelti, J.G. 1976. *Adventure, Mystery, and Romance: Formula Stories as Art in Popular Culture.* Chicago, IL: University of Chicago Press.

Chase, A. 1986. "Toward a Legal Theory of Popular Culture." *Wisconsin Law Review* 527-569.

Collier R. 1998. "'Nutty Professors', 'Men in Suits' and 'New Entrepreneurs': Corporeality, Subjectivity and Change in the Law School and Legal Practice. *Social and Legal Studies* 7(1): 27-53.

Cox, P. 1994. "The Sun's Peter Cox says...." *The Sun* (February 25): 27.

Decure, N. 1992. "From Closet to the Bleachers. Kate Delafield: Portrait of a Lesbian as a 'Lady Cop'." *Women's Studies Forum* 15(2): 267-279.

Davis, C. 1993. *Phildelphia.* London: Penguin.

Dearden, B. 1961. *Victim.* London: Rank.

Demme, J. 1993. *Philadelphia.* Los Angeles, CA: Tristar Pictures Inc.

Denvir, J., ed. 1996. *Legal Reelism: Movies as Legal Texts.* Urbana, IL: University of Illinois Press.

Dyer, R. 1993. "*Victim*: Hegemonic Project." Pp. 93-111 in *The Matter of Images: Essays on Representations*, edited by R. Dyer. London: Routledge.

Errigo, A. 1994. "Philadelphia." *Empire* 57(March): 25.

Freedman, L.M. 1989. "Law, Lawyers and Popular Culture." *Yale Law Review* 98: 1579-1601.

Fuchs, C.J. 1993. "The Buddy Politic." Pp. 53-70 in *Screening the Male*, edited by S. Cohan and I.R. Hark. London: Routledge.

Fuss, D. 1991. *Inside/Out.* London: Routledge.

Glass, D. 1990. "Portia in Primetime: Women, Lawyers Television, and L.A. Law." *Yale Journal of Law and Feminism* 2: 371-417.

Green J. 1994. "The Philadelphia Experiment." *Premier* (January): 54.

Green J., and J. McCormick. 1961. *Victim* [Final Shooting Script].

Greenfield, S., and G. Osborn. 1995. "Where Cultures Collide: The Characterisation of Law and Lawyers in Film." *International Journal of the Sociology of Law* 23: 107-130.

Guerrero, E. 1995. "The Black Image in Protective Custody: Hollywood's Biracial Buddy Films. Pp. 93-115 in *Black American Cinema*, edited by M. Diawara. New York: Routledge.

Harris D.A. 1993. "The Appearance of Justice: Court TV, Conventional Television and Public Understandings of the Criminal Justice System." *Arizona Law Review* 35: 785.

Hart, L. 1994. *Fatal Women: Lesbian Sexuality and the Mark of Agression.* Princeton, NJ: Princeton University Press.

Heller, D.A. 1994. "Almost Blue: Policing Lesbian Desire." Pp. 171-188 in *Internal Affairs*. In *The Lesbian Postmodern*, edited by L. Doan. New York: Columbia University Press.

Herman, D. 1994. *Rights of Passage: Struggles for Lesbian and Gay Legal Equality.* Toronto, Canada: University of Toronto Press.

Hughes, K. 1960. The Trials of Oscar Wilde. London: Warwick [pub. in U.S. as *The Man with the Green Carnation*].

Hurd, G. 1980. "The Television Presentation of the Police." Pp. 53-70 in *Popular Television and Film*, edited by T. Bennett et al. London: BFI Publishing and The Open University Press.

Joseph, P., and S. Carton. 1992. "The Law of the Federation: Images of Law, Lawyers and the Legal System in 'Star Treck: The Next Generation'." *University of Toledo Law Review* 24: 43-85.

Kavanagh, D. 1991. *The Duffy Omnibus.* London: Penguin.

Kennedy R. 1994. "The Gorgeous Lesbian in *L.A. Law*: The Present Absence?" Pp. 132-141 in *The Good, the Bad and the Gorgeous: Popular Culture's Romance with the Lesbian*, edited by D Hamer and B. Budge. London: Pandora.

Krutnik, F. 1991. *In a Lonely Street: Film Noir, Genre and Masculinity.* London: Routledge.

Lipman-Blumen, J. 1976. "Toward a Homosocial Theory of Sex Roles: An Explanation of the Sex Segregation of Social Institutions." Pp. 5-23 in *Women and the Workplace*, edited by M. Blaxall and B. Reagan. Chicago, IL: University of Chicago Press.

Loizidou, E. 1998. "Intimate Queer Celluloid: Heavenly Creatures." In *Legal Queeries*, edited by L.J. Moran, D. Monk, and S. Beresford. London: Cassell.

Medhurst, A. 1984. "*Victim*: Text as Context." *Screen* 25(4/5): 22-35.

Moran, L.J. 1995. "Violence and the Law: The Case of Sado-masochism." *Social and Legal Studies* 4(2): 225-251.

Moran, L.J. 1996. *The Homosexual(ity) of Law.* London: Routledge.

Moran, L.J., D. Monk, and S. Beresford. 1998. *Legal Queeries.* London: Cassell.

Naffine, N. 1997. *Feminism and Criminology.* Cambridge, UK: Polity Press.

Neale, S. 1980. *Genre.* London: British Film Institute.

Post, R. 1987. "The Popular Image of the Lawyer." *California Law Review* 75: 379-389.

"Ralph and Dearden No Savez Hollywood Seal Nix Their 'Victim'." 1961. *Variety* (December 20).

Ratoff, G. 1960. *Oscar Wilde.* London: Vantage.

Redhead, S. 1995. *Unpopular Culture: The Birth of Law and Popular Culture.* Manchester, UK: Manchester University Press.

Ricardo, J. 1992. *The Night G.A.A. Died.* London: St. Martin's Press.

Rosen, R.E. 1989. "Ethical Soap: *L.A.Law* and the Privileging of Character." *University of Miami Law Review* 43: 1229-1261.

Russo, V. 1981. *The Celluloid Closet.* New York, Harper and Rowe.

Scharf, M.P., and L.D. Robert. 1994. "The Interstellar Relations of the Federation: International Law and 'Star Trek: The Next Generation'." *University of Toledo Law Review* 25(3): 577-665.

Shapiro, C. 1995. "Women Lawyers in Celluloid: Why Hollywood Skirts the Truth." *Toledo Law Review* 25(4): 955-1011.

Seabrook, M. 1991. *Conduct Unbecoming.* London: Gay Men's Press.

Sedgwick, E.K. 1985. *Between Men: English Literature and Male Homosocial Desire.* New York: Columbia University Press.

Spelman, E.V., and M. Minow. 1996. *"Outlaw Women."* Pp. 137-153 in *Legal Reelism: Movies as Legal Texts*, edited by J. Denvir. Urbana, IL: University of Illinois Press.

Stark S.D. 1987. "Perry Mason Meets Sonny Crockett: The History of Lawyers and the Police as Television Heroes." *University of Miami Law Review* 42: 229-283.

Stychin, C. 1995. *Law's Desire*. London: Routledge.

Tasker, Y. 1995. *Sepactacular Bodies: Gender, Genre and the Action Cinema*. London: Routledge.

Taubin, A. 1994. "The Odd Couple." *Sight and Sound* 4(3, March): 24.

Thornton, M. 1996. *Dissonance and Distrust: Women and the Legal Profession*. Oxford, UK: Oxford University Press.

Victim. 1960. *Programme Notes for the Venice Film Festival*. Rome: Rank.

Victim. 1960a. [Pressbook.] London: Rank.

Young, A. 1988. *Femininity in Dissent*. London: Routledge.

Young, A. 1995. *Imagining Crime*. London: Sage.

Whitebait, W. 1961. "Silken Miseries." *New Statesman* (September 8) 15.

Whitlock, G. 1994. "'Cop It Sweet': Lesbian Crime Fiction." Pp. 96-118 in *The Good, the Bad and the Gorgeous: Popular Culture's Romance with the Lesbian*, edited by D. Hamer and B. Budge. London: Pandora.

Wilson, A. 1996. "Death and the Mainstream: Lesbian Detective Fiction and the Story of Killing the Coming-Out Story." *Feminist Studies* 22(2, Summer), 251-278.

Wolfenden, Sir J. 1957. *Report of the Departmental Committee on Homosexual Offences and Prostitution*. Cmnd. 247. London: Her Majesty's Stationary Office.

Wintermute, R. 1995, *Sexual Orientation and Human Rights*. Oxford, UK: Oxford University Press.

Name Index

Acker, J. 321, 338
Ackermann, Justice 218–19
Adams, P. 408
Adkins, L. 322, 324, 338
Adriao, Dennis 437
Alcock, B. 554
Aldrich, Donald 185, 189
Allan, Maud 137, 138, 140, 141, 143, 144,
      145–6 *passim*, 149, 152, 153–5 *passim*,
      158, 159
Allen, Carol 454
Allport, Gordon 409
Ames, M.A. 281
Andenaes, M. 511
Armitage, William 123, 124
Armstrong, Hugh 453
Armstrong, K. 334
Armstrong, Pat 453
Ashiagbor, D. 327
Ashley, April 87–90 *passim*, 91, 92, 94, 519
Asquith, Herbert 146
Asquith, Margot 138, 146
Aubin, Justice 94–5 *passim*
Auchmuty, Rosemary xvii, xix, xx, 501–26

Backer, L.K. xvii
Backhouse, Constance 37
Bagilhole, B. 322
Bailey, Robert W. 373–88
Baird, R.M. 509
Bakan, Joel 455, 456
Balzac, Honoré de 142
Bamforth, N. 269, 330, 554
Barnard, C. 334
Barney, Nathalie 142
Barrett, Michèle 448
Barthes, Roland 257
Bartram, Adam 515
Batts, Deborah 367
Baudelaire, Charles 142
Bayley, D. 297, 299, 306
Bays, J. 282
Beadle, Chief Justice 71

Beaman, Lori 219, 220
Beardsley, Aubrey 138
Beck, E.M. 380
Beauvoir, Simone de 542, 543
Bell, Derrick 7, 298, 326
Bell, M. 334
Beresford, S. 327
Berk, Richard A. 374
Bernard, J. 505
Bhabha, Homi 65
Billing, Noel Pemberton 138–40 *passim*, 141,
      142–4 *passim*, 147, 148, 150, 151, 152–5
      passim, 157–8 *passim*, 159
Binnie, Jon 202, 205, 220, 221, 326
Bird 558
Blalock, Hubert M. 380
Bleys, Rudi C. 105
Bolas, C. 409
Bonham, S. 419
Boothby, Police Chief 308
Boring, Margaret 498
Bottoms, Sharon 472–7 *passim*, 481
Bottoms, Pamela Kay 473, 477
Bottoms, Tyler 472, 473, 474, 481
Bourke, Joanna 152
Boyd, Elizabeth A. 374
Bowers, Lisa xvi
Boyd, Susan B. xvii, xviii, xx, 445–66, 511
Braidotti, Rosi 9, 203
Brant, Beth 478
Bray, Micelle B. 15
Brewis, J. 321
Britton, Paul 237–8
Brodsky, J.I. 261
Brown, M. 417
Brown, Wendy xvii, 192–4 *passim*, 195, 196
Bryant, Anita 467
Bryant, Michael 227
Bryson, Laurie 308
Bulger, James 230, 241, 243
Bunch, Charlotte 458
Burke, M. 323, 324
Burke, T. 67

Burrell, G. 322
Burton, Justice 332
Butler, Gill 504, 505, 506
Butler, Judith xiii, 5, 8, 9, 10, 21–2 *passim*, 24,
    25 85, 321, 447, 449, 451–3 *passim*,
    454
Buxton, Jean 66
Byre, A. 327

Caird, Mona 505
Calhoun, Cheshire 510, 523
Callas, Maria 570
Campbell, C.S. 290
Campbell, D.T. 374
Campbell, Tena 494
Carlton, Ellen 534
Carter, H. 516
Castells, Manuel 212
Cave, Justice 255
Cavior, H.E. 282
Cawelti, J.G. 560
Chadwick, Charles 144
Chanock, M. 68
Chan Sam, T. 423
Chapin, Jessica 207
Chapman, A. 327
Chase, A. 554
Chauncey, G. 301
Chavanduka, Gordon 68
Chesney-Lind, M. 283
Chigwedere, Anias 63
Cirak, Miomir xix, 297–316
Coates, Richard 515
Cohen, Ed 145
Cohen, R. 399
Colker, Ruth 506
Collier, Richard xiv, xix, xx, 227–48, 321, 327,
    554, 558
Collins, H. 328
Collins, P. 416
Colson, E. 68
Comer, Lee 505
Comings, D.E. 290
Comstock, Gary D. 374, 380
Conaghan, J. 326
Connell, R.W. 322
Cooke, Serrell 153, 155–6 *passim*, 158
Cooper, D. 298
Corbett, Arthur 87, 90, 91, 92
Covington, J. 282

Cox, Barbara 509
Cox, P. 556, 569
Crawford, A. 297
Crenshaw, Kimberley xviii
Cross, S. 322
Cullen, Lord 239, 240, 244
Curry, P. xvii

Dabs, J.M. 281
Dale, Catherine 9
Dangelo, Kathleen 11, 15
Darian-Smith, Eve 206
Darrah, Roy 116
Davies, Margaret 5–30
Davis, E. 301
Davis, M. xvi, xvii, 298
Deakin, S. 328
Dearden, Basil xxi, 553, 554
Decure, N. 560
Delphy, Christine 447
Deleuze, G. 258, 265
Delgado, Richard 177
Demme, Jonathan xxi, 553
De Rachewiltz, B. 66
Derrida, Jacques 14, 24, 258
Devlin, Lord Patrick xvii, 259
Dickson, Shadreck 69
Diefenbaker, John 126
Dirsuweit, Teresa xx, 415–42
Ditsie, Beverley 422
Dornfield, M. 282
Douglas, Lord Alfred 143, 145, 147, 156–8
    passim
Douglas, Michael 533
Drahos, Peter 22
Duarte, Jesse 418
Dubi, Beli Enock 71
Duckitt, J. 399
Duckworth, P. 520, 523
Duncan, Nancy 323
Duncan, S. 266
Dunne, G. 323, 324, 325
Dunton, C. 63
Dyer, C. 512
Dyer, Richard 530, 555, 563

Eaton, Mary xviii, 38–41 *passim*, 48, 64
Ebert, Teresa L. 445, 447, 448, 449–50 *passim*
Edward VI, King 145
Edgeworth, Brendan 7, 20

Ehrhardt, A.A. 280
Eichler, Margrit 457
Eleftheriadis, Pavlos 6, 19, 23
Ellis, Justice 97–9 *passim*
Ellis, L. 281
Engels, Friedrich 451
Epprecht, M. 69, 70
Epstein, R. 328
Errigo, A. 556
Eskridge, W.N. Jr 508
Espín, Olivia 202
Ettelbrick, Paula 509
Evans, D. 327
Evans-Pritchard, E.E. 66

Farshae, K. 249
Favell, Adrian 206
Feinman, C. 283
Feltoe, G. 69
Field, Michael 142
Fishbein, Diana H. xviii, xx, 277–94, 281
Fiske, D.W. 374
Fitzjames Stephen, Sir James 254
Flynn, L. 333
Folbre, N. 72
Foucault, Michel xiii, xv, xvi, 67, 68, 75, 260, 261, 416
Fox, A. 327, 328
Fraser, Nancy 447, 450–51 *passim*, 452, 453, 454, 455, 456
Frazier, C.E. 282, 290
Fredman, S. 326, 328, 329
Freedman, E.S. 280, 282, 289
Freud, Sifmund 542
Frow, John 15
Frye, Marilyn 49–50 *passim*
Fuchs, C.J. 565, 569
Fudge, Judy 456
Fuhrman, Mark 182
Fuss, D. xiii, xiv

Gagnier, Regenia 145
Galaburda, A.M. 290
Gautier, Théophile 142
Gavigan, Shelley A. 446, 449, 458
Genet, Jean 542
German, Lindsey 453
Geschwind, N. 290
Girard, R. 258, 259–60 *passim*, 264, 265, 266
Gladue, B.A. 291

Glasbeek, Harry 456
Glass, D. 554
Glick, Paul C. 374, 376
Gluckman, Amy 458
Goldberg, D.T. 393
Golombok, S. 523
Gooding, C. 326
Gotell, Lise 457
Gray, Kevin 6, 10, 20, 26
Green, Donald P. xx, 373–88
Green, Janet 554, 559, 563, 564, 565
Greenberg, D.F. 66
Greenfield, S. 556, 557
Greer, Germaine 504
Grein, J.T. 137, 138, 155, 156, 158
Grey, Thomas 6, 20
Gribble, Leonard 536
Griffiths, Jane 501
Grossman, A.H. 291
Grosz, Elizabeth 449
Guerrero, E. 565, 571

Hale, Lady Justice 332
Halford, S. 322
Hall, J.M. 291
Hall, M. 323
Hall, Stuart 171, 192
Halley, Janet E. xv, xvi
Hamilton, Thomas 227, 228, 229–31 *passim*, 233–4 *passim*, 235, 236–44 *passim*
Hamner, Karl M. 374
Handler, Justice 92, 93, 94
Hanks, Tom xxi, 555, 564, 565, 571
Harper, Mark 507
Harper, P. 416
Harris, Cheryl 7
Harris, J.W. 11, 15
Harrison, A.E. 291
Harrison, V. 327
Hart, H.L.A. xviii
Hart, Lynda 539, 541, 542
Hassard, J. 321
Hearn, J. 322
Hegel, Georg W.F. 12, 13
Heller, D.A. 554
Hennessy, Rosemary 8, 10, 447, 448, 449, 454
Herbert, Alan 127, 128
Herek, Gregory M. 374
Herman, Didi 510, 554
Herrera, Jessica 20

Heun, S. 333
Hibbs, M. 512
Hoare, Philip 140
Hobbes, Thomas 313
Hogan, D. 305
Hoygenga, D.B. 281
Hoygenga, K.T. 281
Hughes, G. 255
Hughes, K. 555
Hulme, Henry R. 548, 549, 550
Hulme, Hilda 548, 549, 550
Hulme, Juliet 531, 539–40 *passim*, 543, 544–5
    passim, 547–50 *passim*
Humphrey, J. 321, 324
Humphreys, Sir Travers 148–50 *passim*, 151
Hunt, P.M.A. 69
Hunter, Nan 509–10
Hurd, G. 558
Hutchinson, D.L. xviii

Ibsen, Henrik 138
Ihlenfeld, Dr 93, 94
Ingraham, Chrys 447, 448
Ingram, Gordon B. xviii, xix, xx, 103–36, 417–18
Irigaray, Luce 7, 9, 16, 21
Isaacs, D. 322
Iyer, Nitya 453

Jackson, D. 241
Jackson, L.A. 73
Jackson, Peter xxi
Jackson, S. 321
Jacobs, Michael P. 453–4
Jacobs, S.M. 72
Jagose, Annamarie xvi, 9
Jauncey, Lord 253, 254, 258
Jefferson, T.R. xviii
Jervis, Kim 537
Johnston, L. 298

Kahn-Freund, O. 329
Kapur, R. xviii
Kassebaum, G. 280
Katz, J.N. xiii, xiv
Kearns, T. 251, 252, 258, 259
Kempa, M. 298
Kennedy, M. 301
Kennedy, R. 554
Kerner, M.S. 291
Kerr, Guy 535–6

Kershaw, A. 249
Kesselman, Wendy 545, 546, 547
Kettle, Michael 141
Kilpatrick, C. 329
King, Rodney 180
Kinsman, Gary 49, 300
Kitzinger, C. xiv
Kline, Marlee 457
Knapper, Rob 302
Knightly, Philip 141
Knoll, C. 324, 325
Koon, Stacey 182
Kötz, H. 329
Krafft-Ebing, Ricard von 155
Krate, R. 283
Krutnick, F. 559
Kruttschnitt, C. 282
Kwan, P. xviii

Lacan, Jacques 21, 22, 541
Lacey, Nicola xvi, 328
Laclau, Ernesto 23
Lacombe, Dany 449
Lancelin, Madame 545, 546, 547
Lancelin, Madamoiselle 545, 546
Lane, Lord 252–6 *passim*
Lanza, Mario 547, 548
Laplanche, J. 262
Laumann, Edward O. 375
Lauristen, J. xv, xviii
Laut, Agnes C. 106, 107
Leap, W. 298
Lee, J.A. 261
Leigh, L.H. 255
Leopold, Nathan 540
Le Roux 71
Lester, Lord 501
Leventhal, G. 283
Levi, R. 305
Levine, Martin 380
Levi-Strauss, Claude 7, 16
Lipman-Bluman, J. 558
Locke, John 11, 13
Loeb, Richard 540
Loizidou, E. 562
Lousy, Pierre 142
Lowry, Lord 255
Lushington, Dr 87

M., Lori 487

Maas, J. 323, 336
McCafferty, Charlotte 520
McColgan, A. 328
McCormick, John 554, 559, 563
McDowell, L. 322, 326
McGhee, D. 327
Mackie 71
MacKinnon, Catharine 11, 321
Macpherson, C.B. 6
Maddox, Diane 520
Magnusson, Roger 11
Mahan, S. 283
Majury, Diana xvii, xviii, xix, 31–62
Maher, Aidan 310
Mallarmé, Stéphane 144
Malt, M. 331
Mamaki 422–3
Mandela, Nelson 419
Mantha, Leo A. 125–6 *passim*
Marhold, F. 334
Marschner, A. 334
Martin, Biddy 9
Marx, Karl 451
Mason, Gail xvi, xviii, xx, 389–414
Mata Hari 146, 147
Matthaei, Julie 453
Mayor, Gwen 237
Medd, Jodie 137–65
Medhurst, A. 555
Merck, Mandy 549
Metcalfe 555
Meyer-Bahlburg, H.F.L. 280
Mill, John Stuart 505
Millbank, Jenni xviii, xix, xxi, 457, 529–51
Miller, Chris 184
Minow, Martha 554
Modleski, Tania 530
Mohr, R.D. 508
Monk, D. 327
Moore, Clive 105
Moran, Leslie J. xiv, xv, xvi, xvii, xviii, xix, xxi, 249–75, 326, 327, 338, 553–77
Morris, G. 328
Moss, Donald 403, 404
Mossman, Mary J. 457
Moyer, I.L. 283, 290
Mtetwa, Phumi 421
Mückenberger, U. 328
Mudariki, Tirivanhu 66
Mufamadi, Sydney 419

Mugabe, Robert 63–5 *passim*
Mustill, Lord 256
Myslik, W. 326

Nabozny, Jamie 489–90 *passim*
Naffine, Ngaire 11, 14, 18, 554, 559
Namaste, Ki 416, 439
Nedelsky, Jennifer xix, 7, 11, 13, 14, 17, 18, 25
Nhlapo, Paddy 428
Nowell, Charle J. 115
Noyes, C. Reinold 12
Nyborg, H. 281

O'Brien, Michael 215
O'Donnell, T. 328
O'Donovan, K. 327, 519
O'Malley, P. 306
Omerjee, Yunus 69
Ormrod, Justice 88, 89, 90–92 *passim*, 94
Osborn, G. 556, 557
Otis, M.D. 291
Owens, R. 326

Pain 421
Palmberg, M. 63
Palmer, A. 324, 325
Papin, Christine 531, 536, 539, 540–41 *passim*, 542, 543, 544–7 *passim*
Papin, Lea 531, 536, 539, 540–41 *passim*, 542, 543, 544–7 *passim*
Parker, Honoré 539, 548, 549, 550
Parker, Pauline 531, 539–40 *passim*, 543, 544–5 *passim*, 547–50 *passim*
Parker, M. 321
Parkin, James 308
Pateman, Carol 7, 16
Pearlston, Karen 448
Penelope, J. xiv
Penner, James E. 6, 17
Penzance, Lord 86
Perry, Adele 111
Perry, Anne 531 *see also* Hulme, Juliet
Peterson, Kelli 492
Phelan, Shane xvi, xvii, xx
Phillips, Anne 451
Phillips, Oliver xiii, xviii, xix, xx, 63–83
Picchio, Antonella 452, 453, 454
Pittin, R. 66
Podlesny, Mary 489

Pollack-Byrne, J.M. 279, 283
Pontales, J.B. 262
Poole, M. 322
Posner, Richard A. 484–5
Post, R. 553, 557
Pringle, R. 321
Prosser, Lord 332
Ptaschinski, Lisa 537

Radin, Margaret 11, 12–13, 15, 17, 20
Rae, Kyle 301, 309, 310
Ransome, Arthur 145
Ratoff, G. 555
Rauhofer, J. 333
Rechy, James 301
Redhead, S. xxi, 553
Reed, Betsy 458
Reich, Charles A. 13, 305
Reid, Graeme xx, 415–42, 439
Reinhardt, Stephen 346, 368
Relph, Michael 554
Resnik, Judith 353
Retief, Glen 435
Rich, A. 324
Richardson, D. xiv
Ristow, M. 289
Rizzi, Detective 118–21 *passim*
Roberts, Dorothy 449
Robertson, R.G. 282
Robson, J. xvii, 554
Robson, Ruthann 10, 60, 61, 458, 467–500, 510,
    522, 531
Rose, Carol 14, 18
Rose, G. 258
Rose, Jacqueline 142
Rose, N. 314
Rosenaum, J.L. 283
Rosenblum, S.E. 509
Rosga, AnnJanette xvii, xx, 171–97
Ross, Robert 145, 155
Rubenstein, William B. xix, xx, 345–69
Rubin, G. 261
Runcie, Robert 227
Russo, V. 555, 560, 561
Ryan, Mary P. 113
Ryan, Michael 228, 232

Sade, Marquis de 265
Sarat, Austin 251, 252, 258
Sartre, Jean-Paul 400, 410, 542, 543

Schimmel, R. 333
Scholinski, Daphne 486
Schroeder, Jeanne 16, 20, 21, 2
Schuklenk, U. 289
Schultz, V. 333
Scott, Joan 178
Seccombe, Wally 447
Sedgwick, Eve K. xiii, xviii, 142, 558
Seidman, G. 73
Seligman, B.Z. 66
Seligman, C.G. 66
Shapiro, C. 554
Sharpe, Andrew xiv, xvi, xviii, xix, xx, 85–99
Shaw, George Bernard 138
Shearing, Clifford 297, 298, 299, 306
Sheldon, S. 320
Shelver, Carrie 421
Sherman, Suzanne 506, 508, 511, 523
Sherwin, R.K. xxi
Shiva, Vandana 11, 15
Simon, N.G. 281
Sinclair, J. 321
Singer, Barbara 7, 15
Singh, Bela 118, 120
Skeggs, B. xvii
Skelton, T.L. 416, 417, 439
Skidmore, Paul xix, xx, 319–43
Skinner, W.F. 291
Smart, Carol 449, 455, 457
Smith, Anna Marie 207, 208, 210, 216
Smith, Barbara 447, 454
Smith, I. 331
Snape, D. 324
Snell, T. 279, 282, 290
Solmitz, Mr 498
Spelman, E.V. 554
Stanko, E. xvii
Staves, Susan 11
Stenning, P. 297, 298
Stephen, Justice 253, 254
Stone, Sharon 533
Strasser, M. 508
Strolovitch, Dara Z. 373–88
Stychin, Carl F. xvi, xix, xx, 9, 10, 199–223,
    264, 268, 269, 327, 454, 554
Sullivan, A. 508, 509
Sumner, C. 77
Swinburne, Richard 142
Swinford, Jeffrey 184
Symons, Arthur 144

T., Shane 488, 489
Talbot, P.A. 66
Tasker, F.L. 523
Tasker, Y. 565
Tatchell, Peter 504
Taubin, A. 565
Taussaud, Madame 138
Taylor, Harriet 505
Taylor, S. 324
Tebbitt, Lord Norman 216
Teghtsoonian, Katherine 453
Templeman, Lord 251
Terraine, John 147
Testa, M. 282
Teubner, G. 338
Thatcher, Margaret 210
Theuninck, A. 420
Thomas, G. 331
Thompson, Robert 230, 241
Thomson, M. 320
Thornton, M. 559
Thorpe, L.J. 521
Thorstad, D. xv, xviii
Toigo, R. 280
Tolnay, Steart E. 380
Towns, A. 408
Trudeau, Pierre 127
Tucker, S. 261
Tyler, Carole-Anne 5, 19
Tyler, M. 324

Valdes, F. xviii
Valentine, Gill 205, 298, 326, 416, 439
Valverde, Mariana xix, 297–316
Venables, Jon 230, 241
Verhoeven, Deborah 532
Vibela, V. 421
Vivien, Renée 142
Vogelman, L. 417, 439

Waaldijk, K. 327
Wade, April 474
Waldron, Jeremy 6
Walkowitz, Judith R. 113
Walters, Suzanne 8,10
Wandor, M. 505
Wang, L. 376
Ward, D. 280
Ward-Jackson, Clare 520

Warner, M. xv, 327
Washington, Denzel xxi, 565, 570
Watson, Irene 7
Waugh, Tracey 537
Weber, Max 313
Wedderburn, B. 327, 329
Weeks, Jeffrey xiii, xiv, xv, 338, 467
Weingourt, R. 282
Weisheit, R. 283
Wendell, Susan 449
West, Nicholas 185, 186
West, Robin 177
Weston, Kath 201
Whalen, R.E. 281
Whitebait, W. 563
Whitlock, G. 554, 560
Whittle, Stephen 507
Widdecombe, Ann 216
Widom, C.S. 282
Wigginton, Tracey 531, 532, 537, 538
Wigman, Joe 123
Wilde, Oscar 105, 111, 137, 138, 140–41
    passim, 143, 144, 145, 146, 148, 149,
    155, 156, 157, 158, 159, 555
Wilkinson, S. xiv
Williams, Ellis Hume 150–51 *passim*, 157
Williams, G. 255
Williams, Patricia 23
Willmer, Lord Justice 88
Wilson, A. 554
Wilson, Elizabeth 113
Wilson, M. 68
Wilson, Trevor 147
Winburne, W. 399
Wintemute, R. 332, 511, 554
Winterbottom, Michael xxi
Wittig, Monique 7, 10, 16
Wolfe, Alan 516
Wolfenden, Sir J. 555
Wollstonecraft, Mary 505
Wong, Janelle S. 373–88
Wood, J. 304
Woolf, Virginia 137
Wuornos, Aileen 531, 532, 538–9 *passim*

Young, Alison 554
Young, Claire 454, 457
Young, Iris M. 403, 417, 418, 447, 451, 453
Younge, Gary 516

Zelle, Margeretha Geetruida 146 *see also* Mata Hari

Zetlein, Sarah 449

Zillich, N. 323

Zola, Emile 142

Zucker, Ross 24

Zweigert, K. 329